The Byzantine Hellene

This book tells the extraordinary story of Theodore II Laskaris, an emperor who ruled over the Byzantine state of Nicaea established in Asia Minor after the fall of Constantinople to the crusaders in 1204. Theodore Laskaris was a man of literary talent and keen intellect. His action-filled life, youthful mentality, anxiety about communal identity (Anatolian, Roman, and Hellenic), ambitious reforms cut short by an early death, and thoughts and feelings are all reconstructed on the basis of his rich and varied writings. His original philosophy, also explored here, led him to a critique of scholasticism in the West, a mathematically inspired theology, and a political vision of Hellenism. A personal biography, a ruler's biography, and an intellectual biography, this highly illustrated book opens a vista onto the eastern Mediterranean, Anatolia, and the Balkans in the thirteenth century, as seen from the vantage point of a key political actor and commentator.

DIMITER ANGELOV is Dumbarton Oaks Professor of Byzantine History at Harvard University. His publications include *Imperial Ideology and Political Thought in Byzantium, 1204–1330* (Cambridge, 2007) and *Church and Society in Late Byzantium* (edited, 2009).

The Byzantine Hellene

The Life of Emperor Theodore Laskaris and Byzantium in the Thirteenth Century

DIMITER ANGELOV

Harvard University, Massachusetts

CAMBRIDGE
UNIVERSITY PRESS

CAMBRIDGE
UNIVERSITY PRESS

University Printing House, Cambridge CB2 8BS, United Kingdom

One Liberty Plaza, 20th Floor, New York, NY 10006, USA

477 Williamstown Road, Port Melbourne, VIC 3207, Australia

314–321, 3rd Floor, Plot 3, Splendor Forum, Jasola District Centre, New Delhi – 110025, India

79 Anson Road, #06–04/06, Singapore 079906

Cambridge University Press is part of the University of Cambridge.

It furthers the University's mission by disseminating knowledge in the pursuit of
education, learning, and research at the highest international levels of excellence.

www.cambridge.org
Information on this title: www.cambridge.org/9781108480710
DOI: 10.1017/9781108690874

© Dimiter Angelov 2019

First published 2019

Printed in the United Kingdom by TJ International Ltd. Padstow Cornwall

A catalogue record for this publication is available from the British Library.

Library of Congress Cataloging-in-Publication Data
Names: Angelov, Dimiter, 1972- author.
Title: The Byzantine Hellene : the life of Emperor Theodore Laskaris and Byzantium in the
    thirteenth century / Dimiter Angelov.
Description: Cambridge, United Kingdom ; New York, NY : Cambridge University Press, 2019. |
    Includes bibliographical references and index.
Identifiers: LCCN 2018057973 | ISBN 9781108480710 (hardback : alk. paper) |
    ISBN 9781108727952 (pbk. : alk. paper)
Subjects: LCSH: Theodore II Lascaris, Emperor of Nicaea, 1222-1258. | Theodore II Lascaris,
    Emperor of Nicaea, 1222-1258-Political and social views. | Theodore II Lascaris, Emperor of
    Nicaea, 1222-1258-Criticism and interpretation. | Nicaea (Turkey)-Kings and
    rulers-Biography. | Byzantine Empire-Kings and rulers-Biography. | Philosophers-Byzantine
    Empire-Biography. | Intellectuals-Byzantine Empire-Biography. | Hellenism-History-To 1500.
    | Byzantine Empire-History-1081-1453.
Classification: LCC DF626.5 .A54 2019 | DDC 956.2/014092 [B] –dc23
LC record available at https://lccn.loc.gov/2018057973

ISBN 978-1-108-48071-0 Hardback

φιλτάτῃ Εὐρυδίκῃ

Contents

Illustrations

Note: All figures appear between pages 108 and 109, with the exception of
Figure 28, which appears on page 211.

Maps

Tables

Acknowledgments

The idea of writing this biography was first conceived over fifteen years ago in the vibrant academic environment of Cambridge, Massachusetts, where, by fortuitous coincidence, the book is now seeing its completion. Many scholars have contributed to its genesis in the meantime. I am grateful to Angeliki Laiou for encouraging me to pursue my interests in an extraordinary historical figure and embark on the difficult project of reconstructing his life and thought world. I have greatly benefited from intellectual exchanges with my former Birmingham colleagues Joseph Munitiz and Ruth Macrides. I owe a special debt of gratitude to the erudition and generosity of Panagiotis Agapitos, with whom I have had many illuminating discussions over the past year about the literary output of Theodore Laskaris. Colleagues from around the world who have contributed to this book with insightful suggestions and in many other invaluable ways include Jean-Claude Cheynet, Christian Förstel, Antonia Giannouli, Timothy Greenwood, Martin Hinterberger, Mark Jackson, Joni Joseph, Cemal Kafadar, Tsvetana Kyoseva, Linda Lott, Michael McCormick, Marijana Mišević, Margaret Mullett, Pagona Papadopoulou, Jake Ransohoff, Marcus Rautman, Jonathan Shea, Jo Van Steenbergen, Elena Stepanova, Alexandra Wassiliou-Seibt, and Bahadır Yıldırım. Henry Buglass and Louise Parrott helped me to devise the three maps. My amazing mother Doreta and my father Georgi have been a continual source of wisdom, each in a unique way. I learned a lot from Eurydice during our memorable and inspiring visits to historical sites in Turkey, Greece, Bulgaria, and the Republic of North Macedonia as we retraced some of the travels and campaigns of Theodore Laskaris. Lastly, I must thank the History Department of Harvard University for providing me with a publication grant and my patient editor, Dr. Michael Sharp, at Cambridge University Press.

List of Historical Figures

Alexios Strategopoulos: a general blood-related to the imperial Komnenos family; a small expeditionary force led by him resulted in the surprise recapture of Constantinople on July 25, 1261

Anna, Nicaean empress: daughter of the emperor Alexios III Angelos; wife of the first Nicaean emperor Theodore I Laskaris; mother of the Nicaean empress Irene; see Table 1, p. 36

Basil Vatatzes: putative father of the Nicaean emperor John III Vatatzes and grandfather of Theodore; provincial official in Asia Minor and high general (d. 1194); married to an anonymous lady who was a great-granddaughter of Alexios I Komnenos and a first cousin of Isaac II Angelos and Alexios III Angelos

Constantine: chamberlain (*koubouklarios*) of Theodore and addressee of a theological work

Constantine Strategopoulos: son of Alexios Strategopoulos; married to a niece of John III Vatatzes

Constantine (Komnenos) Tornikes: son of Demetrios Komnenos Tornikes; general and high court official

Constanza-Anna of Hohenstaufen, Nicaean empress: daughter born out of wedlock to the Western Roman emperor Frederick II Hohenstaufen and Bianca Lancia; second wife of John III Vatatzes; stepmother of Theodore; sister of Manfred, King of Sicily

Demetrios Komnenos Tornikes: long-term chief minister in the empire of Nicaea from at least 1216 until his death between 1248 and 1252

Eirenikos family: a prominent family before and after 1204; Theodore Eirenikos was head of the imperial chancery in Constantinople before 1204, "consul of the philosophers" in Nicaea, and patriarch of Constantinople in exile (1214–16); Nicholas Eirenikos was a court poet in Nicaea; Theodore's head tutor at the court may have belonged to this family

Elena Asenina: Nicaean empress and wife of Theodore from 1235 until her death in 1252; daughter of Tsar Ivan Asen II of Bulgaria

Germanos II: patriarch of Constantinople in exile (1223–40); born in a village on the Bosporus; deacon of the patriarchal clergy before 1204; influential orator and homilist

George Akropolites: born in Latin-held Constantinople (1217) and educated under Nikephoros Blemmydes, he was one of Theodore's influential tutors and correspondents; imperial secretary, teacher, and civil servant in the empire of Nicaea; Theodore promoted him to the office of grand logothete (*megas logothethes*), which he held until his death (1282)

George Mouzalon: one of three brother pages who were sons of a palace functionary and were raised at the court; talented musician and faithful courtier; addressee of many of Theodore's letters and works; he held a number of offices during Theodore's rule and served as his chief minister

Irene, Nicaean empress: eldest daughter of the Nicaean emperor Theodore I Laskaris and the empress Anna; first wife of John III Vatatzes; mother of Theodore; see Table 1, p. 36

John III Vatatzes, emperor of Nicaea (John Doukas Vatatzes): father of Theodore; see Table 1, p. 36

John Phaix: imperial secretary; addressee of letters and a theological work

Joseph Mesopotamites: imperial secretary and close friend and correspondent of Theodore; his influential family included Constantine Mesopotamites, head of the imperial chancery before 1204 and later metropolitan bishop of Thessalonica

Hagiotheodorites: private secretary of Theodore and a descendant of a powerful twelfth-century family of imperial ministers

Laskaris family: the family rose in prominence in the twelfth century and intermarried with the ruling dynasty of the Komnenoi; the Laskaris were quite possibly descendants of a foreign grandee naturalized in Byzantium in the eleventh century from the Shaddadid family, which ruled Dvin and Gandzak in Armenia

Michael of Epiros: Michael II Komnenos Doukas, ruler of Epiros; illegitimate son of Michael I Komnenos Doukas, the founder of the state of Epiros; nephew of Theodore Komnenos Doukas (Theodore of Epiros); see Table 1, p. 36

Michael Palaiologos: son of Theodora Palaiologina and the general and *megas domestikos* Andronikos Palaiologos, who served the Nicaean emperors for more than twenty-five years; grandson of Despot Alexios Palaiologos who was married to a daughter of Alexios III Angelos; hence a second cousin of Theodore by matrilineal descent (see Table 1,

p. 36); political rival of Theodore; the high aristocratic family of the Palaiologoi had intermarried with the imperial dynasties of the Komnenos and the Doukai in the twelfth century

Nikephoros Blemmydes: the leading philosopher and teacher in the empire of Nicaea

Nikephoros Pamphilos: archdeacon in the imperial clergy; later metropolitan bishop of Ephesos (1243/1244–60) and patriarch of Constantinople in exile (1260)

Theodore (Theodore Laskaris, Theodore Doukas Laskaris, Theodore II Laskaris, the younger Theodore): crown prince and emperor of Nicaea

Theodore the elder (Theodore Komnenos Laskaris, Theodore I Laskaris): founder and first emperor of Nicaea; father of the empress Irene and grandfather of Theodore II Laskaris

Theodore of Epiros: Theodore Komnenos Doukas, ruler and briefly emperor of the state of Epiros; see Table 1, p. 36

Theodore (Komnenos) Philes: Nicaean governor of Thessalonica and the surrounding region; he had a bitter conflict with Theodore, whom he accused of sexual misconduct

Zabareiotes: a teacher who may have been Theodore's head tutor at the court

List of Rulers in Byzantium and Beyond

Byzantine Emperors before 1204

Alexios I Komnenos (1081–1118)
John II Komnenos (1118–43)
Manuel I Komnenos (1143–80)
Alexios II Komnenos (1180–83)
Andronikos I Komnenos (1183–85)
Isaac II Angelos (1185–95)
Alexios III Angelos (1195–1203)
Alexios IV Angelos (1203–04)
Nicholas Kanavos (1204)
Alexios V Doukas Mourtzouphlos (1204)

Byzantine Emperors and Rulers after 1204

Nicaea
Theodore I (Komnenos) Laskaris (1204–21)
John III (Doukas) Vatatzes (1221–54)
Theodore II (Doukas) Laskaris (1254–58)
John IV Laskaris (1258–61)
Michael VIII Palaiologos (1259–82), ruling in Constantinople after 1261
Epiros
Michael I Komnenos Doukas (1204–c. 1215)
Theodore Komnenos Doukas (1215–30, c. 1237–53)
Manuel Komnenos Doukas (1230–c. 1237)
John Komnenos Doukas (c. 1237–44)
Demetrios Komnenos Doukas (1244–46)
Michael II Komnenos Doukas (c. 1231–c. 1267)
Trebizond (the Grand Komnenoi)
Alexios I (1204–22)
David (1204–12)
Manuel I (1238–63)

Latin emperors of Constantinople
  Baldwin I (1204–05)
  Henry (1206–16)
  Peter of Courtenay (1217–18)
  Yolanda (1217–19), regent
  Robert of Courtenay (1221–27)
  John of Brienne (1229–37)
  Baldwin II (1240–61)
Sicily and Italy
  Frederick II Hohenstaufen, King of Sicily (1198–1250) and Western
      Roman emperor (1220–50)
  Conrad IV, King of Sicily (1250–54)
  Conradin (1254–58), underage King of Sicily (in absentia)
  Manfred, Prince of Taranto (after 1250) and King of Sicily (1258–66)
Seljuk sultans of Rum
  Ghiyāth al-Dīn Kaykhusraw I (1192–96, 1205–11)
  Rukn al-Dīn Süleyman II (1196–1204)
  ʿIzz al-Dīn Kılıç Arslān III (1204–05)
  ʿIzz al-Dīn Kaykāwūs I (1211–19)
  ʿAlāʾ al-Dīn Kayqubād I (1219–37)
  Ghiyāth al-Dīn Kaykhusraw II (1237–45/46)
  ʿIzz al-Dīn Kaykāwūs II (1246–56, 1257–61)
  Rukn al-Dīn Kılıç Arslān IV (1248–54, 1256–65)
  ʿAlāʾ al-Dīn Kayqubād II (1249–57)
Tsars of Bulgaria
  Peter and Asen (1185–97)
  Kaloyan (1197–1207)
  Boril (1207–18)
  Ivan Asen II (1218–41)
  Koloman (Kaliman I) (1241–46)
  Michael Asen (1246–56)
  Kaliman Asen II (1256)
  Mitso (Micho) Asen (1256–57)
  Constantine Tikh (1257–77)
Kings of Cilician Armenia
  Leo I (1187–1219), king after 1199
  Hetoum I (1226–69)

Author's Note

I have used a mixed approach in rendering Byzantine names into English. Whenever possible, the English equivalent of personal names has been preferred: thus, Theodore, not Theodoros; John, not Ioannes. I have adhered to the practice of transcribing Byzantine family names and not Latinizing them: thus Palaiologos, not Palaeologus; Kantakouzenos, not Cantacuzenus. In the case of Byzantine court titles and offices, I have again attempted to strike a balance. I have provided the standard translation of many titles, with the Greek term left in parenthesis: thus, grand logothete (*megas logothetes*) and consul of the philosophers (*hypatos ton philosophon*). Court titles whose translation is especially problematic or impossible, such as *mesazon* and *sebastokrator,* have been given in transcription. The discussion of the sources as well as various supplementary and technical matters has been confined to the notes and the appendices, which lay out the evidentiary basis of this book in great detail. All references to the Old Testament follow the nomenclature and numeration of the Greek Septuagint. References to classical Greek texts are based on the standard editions.

Introduction

One year before he passed away at the age of thirty-six, the subject of this biography sent a polemical letter to his teacher and spiritual father. The letter ended on a note of hope that his arguments "would be judged by future generations."[1] The author called for the judgment of history because he was conscious of criticism of him as a public personality. Throughout his life, he had observed with rising concern the vilification of rulers before and after their deaths. The inevitable lot of the individual vested with royal authority, he reasoned, was "to be the target of reproach."[2] He had a good reason to fear that he would suffer the same fate, for his policies had upset many among the ruling elite and had troubled his former teacher, the addressee of the letter. He wished his lone voice to be heard through the ages and intended his writings to become a lasting monument. "I know," he wrote over a decade earlier, "that in this way I will gain an icon of remembrance before the eyes of the future generations and a clearing of my name."[3]

The author of these poignant words was the Byzantine ruler and philosopher Theodore Laskaris (1221/22–58). He is known as Theodore II Laskaris and his full official name is Theodore Doukas Laskaris, but we will be referring to him in the following pages with the shorter version of his name that was already circulating while he was alive.[4] Theodore Laskaris ruled over the "empire of Nicaea" (1204–61), a polity established in exile in Asia Minor after the dramatic fall of Constantinople, the imperial capital of the Byzantine (Eastern Roman) Empire, to the Latin armies of the Fourth Crusade in April 1204. *Nicaea*, like *Byzantium*, is a Western calque and a misnomer for a state that always named itself "the empire of the Romans." Attested already in a contemporary thirteenth-century Latin text, the designation originates from the main city of the Byzantine successor state: Nicaea, today's Iznik, in northwestern Asia Minor.[5] This biography takes up the challenging task that Theodore Laskaris prepared for us seven and a half centuries ago through his own writings. It tells the story of a single person that is also the story of the transformation of his native culture, Byzantium.

Why should we, as moderns, respond to a cry for attention by an individual who lived long ago and had experiences different not only from

our own but also from those of the common people in his time? The first
and simplest reason is the extraordinary opportunity it provides for
empathy with a real human being from the distant past. Thanks to his
vivid and self-revealing prose, Theodore Laskaris emerges before our eyes
as a man of flesh and blood – with attachments to family and friends, with
emotions and mood changes, with anxieties about the direction of his life,
and with an interest in the principles of the universe and God's role in it.
His impulsive self-confidence and his curiosity that bordered on naïvité are
easily recognizable and timeless features of youth. "Let me say something
most unusual," he loved to exclaim.[6] He readily invoked his young age and
commented, not always with due reverence and respect, on the seniority of
people around him.[7] His writings reveal details of his daily life and create a
fully human portrait.

All this is hardly insignificant. Medieval history suffers from a shortage
of private lives due to the inadequacy of our sources.[8] Biographies of men
and women of the Middle Ages tend to present us with their deeds and
actions rather than their thoughts, ideas, and emotions. Only rarely do
utterances of medieval people, including royalty, survive in sufficient
quantity to enable the reconstruction of their evolving thoughts and
characters in a coherent biography. One historian concluded with uncon-
cealed frustration his meticulous study of the reign of the seventh-century
Byzantine emperor Heraclius: "We can never know what was inside
Heraclius' head."[9] Theodore Laskaris belongs to a very small number of
premodern individuals who have left an autobiographical record of their
life, such as Augustine of Hippo in late antiquity or the fifteenth-century
merchant of Prato, Francesco Datini. His literary confessions reveal the
unique personal voice of an emperor in Byzantium, a voice whose scope
and depth is unmatched until a century and a half later when we encounter
the scholar-emperor Manuel II Palaiologos (1350–1425). We see Theodore
torn between politics, philosophy, and artistic angst. We see him feeling
anguish on account of a demanding life and grappling to reconcile old
theories with lived experience and practices.

The gripping historical setting, of which Theodore Laskaris was a part, is
another attractive aspect of the life of this little-known figure of the past. The
Fourth Crusade was a turning point in Mediterranean and world history,
when the relations between the medieval East and West entered a new phase.
Latins settled on the territory of a wounded Byzantine Empire by right of
conquest. Their arrival brought about the emergence of new polities, colonial
as well as irredentist, and a territorial fragmentation that would terminate
only under Mehmed the Conqueror in the fifteenth century. Byzantium

ended its traditional political and economic dominance in the Christian northern Mediterranean. The personal story of a key contemporary opens up a vista on these phenomena. Tracing the events of his life means retelling some of the well-known episodes of the political history of the eastern Mediterranean, Asia Minor, and the Balkans from the unique vantage point of a contemporary leader and eyewitness. Theodore Laskaris held distinctive opinions on many aspects of this political transformation. Indeed, it is the eloquent and engaged voice of the historical character that makes this biography so special. His writings cover a variety of genres and consist of epistles, orations, essays, polemics, theological works, discourses addressed to saints and holy figures, hymns, philosophical tracts, political treatises, and a newsletter – a written output of more than 960 pages of printed editions and, if these are still lacking, manuscript folios. These works form a rich and substantial body of evidence. They are the basis for reconstructing his life and penetrating his thought world. They enrich our knowledge of the historical setting. They reveal new forms of identity construction, which cannot be adequately understood without a focus on the individual himself.

The oeuvre of Theodore Laskaris generates methodological insights into the opportunities and challenges of basing a historical biography on letters and other texts written in the living tradition of Byzantine rhetoric and literature. Starting most prominently in the eleventh century, with Michael Psellos being the foremost example, Byzantine authors embedded their own personae and I-voice in letters, orations, histories, and other kinds of works. Much attention has recently been paid to the construction of the self in these texts. This productive discussion, which has understandably been driven and dominated by literary scholars, has advanced our knowledge of the themes, models, and ploys of authorial self-fashioning.[10] We are approaching a better understanding of the Byzantine author, yet we still lack coherent portraits of the individuals behind the words. Two questions naturally arise. What are the main methods of extracting biographical information from the letters, orations, and hymns written by a learned Byzantine author? Can the themes and devices of self-presentation contribute to our understanding of the historical self?

Theodore Laskaris did not write a narrative autobiography, yet many of his works are markedly self-referential and autobiographic, in the sense that he wrote, in the first person, about his experiences, feelings, and thoughts – that is, about himself.[11] The most important type of self-descriptive texts, as well as the largest single body of his writings, are his more than 200 letters. His letters do not form a continuous narrative. They represent capsules of information in a developing story and pieces of a puzzle that need to be assembled to tell the story. Considered in their totality, the letters form a rich and variegated canvas. They vary widely in theme and content: narrative, confession, polemic, satire, consolation, and ordinance. They allow us to learn about his studies, travels, daily routine, diet, friendships, campaigns, and the reception he granted to distinguished foreign visitors.[12] Some of the letters are long and informative. For example, a series of letters to his childhood friend, confidant, and chief minister George Mouzalon dating from a campaign in the Balkans (1255) relate the movements of the army. Other letters are shorter and deal with trifles, such as "keep in touch" and "missing you" notes accompanied by philosophical musings. Theodore's twenty-seven correspondents represent the political and intellectual elite of the empire of Nicaea: officials, secretaries, teachers, and churchmen, including the patriarch and leading bishops, as well as a Roman pope and his cardinals. Letters give us insights into affairs of church and state and into Theodore's duties and activities as a coemperor and a ruling emperor.[13]

The letters enable us to trace Theodore's relationship with three individuals in particular. Mouzalon tops the list of his correspondents with sixty-five letters. He was also the dedicatee of a treatise on friendship and politics, and the philosophical treatise *Explanation of the World*. He is followed by Theodore's teachers Nikephoros Blemmydes (1197–c. 1271), the addressee of the polemical epistle quoted at the outset, with about forty-eight letters and George Akropolites (1217–82) with about forty-two letters.[14] The reading audience of Theodore's literary and philosophical works intersected with the circle of his correspondents. The author often announced by letter that he was sending a composition to Mouzalon, Blemmydes, Akropolites, a metropolitan bishop, and secretaries.[15] He himself received and read works written by his correspondents. An urban official from Philadelphia, thus, shared with Theodore a church hymn and an abbot dispatched a prayer of blessing for the food on his table. Blemmydes sent Theodore Laskaris his mirror of princes (instructive book on kingship), *The Imperial Statue*, and addressed to him theological treatises.[16] The correspondents formed an active, critical, and interconnected group of readers and writers.

The letters are marked by the features of the genre of the epistle in Byzantium.[17] One of these features is the phenomenon of the edited collection. Authors in Byzantium kept copies of their letters and valued them as literary products. At a certain stage of their lives, they made a selection of letters with the aim of preserving the texts, advertising their relations with specific individuals, and presenting an authorial self-portrait. The creation of a collection is the equivalent of publication today.

Theodore Laskaris followed this practice. His main epistolary collection was prepared in early 1254 when he was thirty-two years of age.[18] It has come down to us in a single fourteenth-century manuscript in the Biblioteca Medicea Laurenziana in Florence (Cod. Laur. plut. 59, 35). The "Laurentian collection," as it is called hereafter, arranges the 133 letters in batches by correspondent. One of Theodore's agendas was to display his closeness with and intellectual lineage from his two main teachers, because the collection opens with his letters to them. Epistles addressed to the same correspondent form thematic clusters – clusters in which they usually follow chronological sequence and form a quasi-narrative. As was the common practice, his edited letters lack any indication of the time of their composition.

The process of editing the letters into a collection meant the introduction of revisions that we, as historical detectives, must attempt to identify and interpret.[19] One sign of editorial intervention was the removal of unnecessary factual detail, a phenomenon known as "de-concretization." Thus, the name of a Latin individual was replaced in a letter to the pope with the phrase "so-and-so" in order to conceal his identity.[20] Another sign of revision was the removal of diplomatic components from letters that originally served an official purpose. Two of his letters are orders issued by him as a coemperor (he refers to himself as "my imperial majesty") to metropolitan bishops, but they still bear the hallmarks of his writing style. He was clearly the author rather than secretaries in the imperial chancery. One is a letter of command addressed to the metropolitan of Ephesos and refers to itself as "an order" (*prostagma*), a specific kind of imperial charter. This epistolary ordinance is unusual from a diplomatic point of view because it lacks the standard closure (eschatocol) that includes the date of issue.[21] The ordinance must have featured this ending, but at the time of the production of the epistolary collection the author – with the help of his editor – removed the eschatocol.[22] Interestingly, two letters dating to the period of his sole rule (and incorporated into a collection produced after the Laurentian one) retain signs of their diplomatic origins. The first letter has his signature at the end.[23] The second one, addressed to the pope, contains a standard diplomatic component at the beginning: the name and title of the recipient, the sender's name and title, and a salutation.[24] The presence of these features in only two surviving letters confirms the impression that Theodore made an effort to fashion his edited letters as pieces of personal correspondence in accordance with the Byzantine literary tradition, even though some letters had served earlier as "official" communications. In this regard, his letters differ greatly from the charters and epistles of the contemporary Western emperor Frederick II Hohenstaufen (1194–1250), with whom Theodore Laskaris has been compared.[25]

The letters of Theodore Laskaris are not easy texts to read and understand. Couched in a learned language with many rare words and composed in an idiosyncratic style, they abound in quotations, circumlocutions, allegories, learned allusions, and philosophical digressions. The text of the letter was only one part of the message in the interpersonal interaction based on epistolary exchange. The letter-bearer delivered an oral report, which could be the gist of the communication. The messenger will "tell you precisely all matters pertaining to me," Theodore wrote on one occasion, and on another urged his correspondent to "accept as if from me what the (letter bearer's) mouth says to you."[26] The letter-bearer served as an explicator of opaque letters.[27] The epistolary communication was accompanied by the dispatch of gifts – hunting trophies, cheese, butter, and sour milk, for example – and the exchange of manuscripts and works composed by Theodore Laskaris and his addressees.[28] Frustratingly, the author often resorted to using code names. He chose wittily, using nicknames from among ancient heroes such as Nestor or Guneas the Arab. Animal species stood for specific people and human types.[29] The anonymity of ridiculed individuals was justified through the authority of Hermogenes (second century AD), the chief theoretician of rhetoric for the Byzantines.[30] Comic neologisms served as code names for specific individuals – "a scion of goats" (*tragophylon*) and "a ram-bearer" (*kriophoros*), for example. Today it is regrettably impossible to identify the people Theodore had in mind, except for cases when he made puns on personal and family names. The "scion of goats" was a playful reference to the surname of Theodore Komnenos Philes, the governor of Thessalonica. The "ram-bearer" appears to have been his attendant and companion Christopher, a play both on his name and the individual's physical characteristics.[31]

These features of the Byzantine epistle explain why historians have traditionally refrained from using them as sources for biography. We have been warned that "the mist of rhetoric is the besetting sin of Byzantine epistolography."[32] This book takes a different view. The rhetorical features of the letters, if approached with due consideration of genre and authorship, are an opportunity rather than obstacle for historical biography. Theodore Laskaris skillfully manipulated the conventions of self-fashioning. In Byzantium, the epistle was understood as an "image" (*eikon*) of one's soul – hence, letters focused on feelings and impressions rather than recordkeeping.[33] The same is true of Theodore's letters, which tend to convey emotional reactions to events and situations. He aestheticized the literary expression of youthful feelings – love and hatred, attraction and repulsion. He poured out his feelings without inhibition. He writes in grief, for example: "My hand is numbed, the flesh shivers and my soul is overcome by great commotion."[34]

Friendship is a common trope in Byzantine letter writing.[35] A brief guide to epistolography dating to the last two decades of the twelfth or the first half of the thirteenth century defines the letter as "a report and communication from a friend to a friend."[36] Accordingly, Theodore portrayed many of his correspondents as his friends and called them his equals, alter egos, and soul mates.[37] But he also became deeply interested in the sociology and psychology of friendship. Another characteristic of the Byzantine letter is the ample use of quotations from admired ancient Greek and Christian texts. The guide to epistolography recommends the inclusion of "maxims of wise men, the so-called apothegms, proverbial sayings," as well as verses from Homer and other poets. Theodore judiciously selected the quotations and textual allusions so as to convey his thoughts and emotions. When he begged for pardon after being unjustly accused, he wrote in contrition: "I was given a thorn in my flesh (2 Corinthians 12:7), so that Satan can torment me in an abusive way and I cannot rise toward the first fruits of the intellect. Heaven, lament for me! Earth, cry! Sun, weep!"[38] Grief drove him to elaborate on a phrase from the Book of Proverbs (14:30): "A sensitive heart is a moth in the bones."[39]

As in his letters, so in many of his other writings Theodore adopted an autobiographical approach and brought a personal touch to old themes and traditional rhetorical strategies. Genres and generic expectations supplied loose templates for recounting past experiences. He wrote and structured his *Satire of the Tutor* as an invective (*psogos*), a reversed encomium, in accordance with the recommendations of Aphthonios (fourth century AD), another influential late Roman theoretician of Greek rhetoric.[40] He drew themes from the religious poetry of compunction (*katanyxis*) in order to channel feelings and thoughts of the moment. There is no doubt that the self in his eminently literary works, such as orations and many of his epistles, reflected his individuality. Outspokenness and a sense of immediacy are two hallmarks of his writing. As an heir to the throne and emperor, he felt no need to dissimulate and boasted of "the imperial character of my free spirit."[41] The only limit was his own sense of literariness and the boundaries of literary convention.

The impression of immediacy emerges not only from Theodore's vivid language and developed sense of the dramatic, but also from the free and seemingly improvised flow of his prose. Theodore Laskaris had a rare authorial gift. The historian George Pachymeres, born in Nicaea in 1242, tells us that he had "a writing talent by nature rather than education, so that he could compose a lot with great fluency should he start."[42] While the cantors were singing the introductory psalms before matins, he improvised church hymns suitable for the feast day. He was able to compose the poetic works so speedily that the cantors, joined by his chamberlains and body-guards, performed the new piece during the same service. The manner in which Theodore wrote "with great fluency" corresponds to a characteristic stream-of-consciousness style that he cultivated and cherished. Its features are loose syntax, floating rhythmical clauses, figurative language, wordplay, idiosyncratic expression, and a marked fondness for neologisms that seem to have been coined during the creative process of composition. A work replete with new usages is his theological treatise *On the Divine Names* (the sixth book of his *Christian Theology*), which consists of more than 700 designa-tions for God. Words derived from the spoken register served a literary function and occasionally contributed to a comic effect.[43] One critic has judged this style to be clumsy due to the disregard for the rules of classical grammar and syntax, but this view is unduly harsh.[44]

The massive textual production of Theodore Laskaris is explainable also in light of other aspects of the writing process. He often devoted himself to creative work at night, in spite of the warning of court physicians, because public responsibilities occupied him already in his twenties.[45] He had no qualms in admitting that he practiced composition by dictation. Both as a coemperor and a sole emperor, he was surrounded by secretaries and scribes. His trusted companion Hagiotheodorites served as his recording secretary. Theodore describes him as "the expert connoisseur of my tongue, of my heart and of the thoughts of my mind, and an admirable secretary."[46] His teacher Akropolites helped him to prepare for publication his main epistolary collection (the Laurentian collection) and wrote a versified preface introducing the author. The particularly loose structure of some of Theodore's works, especially the treatise *Representation of the World, or Life*, can be explained as the result of dictation. Nonetheless, he kept tight authorial control and oversight, as is seen in a brief essay on the difficult and unhealthy life of rulers. The piece concludes with a comment suggesting composition by dictation: "He (the author) presented the maxim after having examined these things with a far-seeing eye."[47] The phrase "with a far-seeing eye" is a quotation from Aristophanes' *Clouds* featured in the influential mirror of princes by Blemmydes and could have come only from the pen or mouth of Theodore Laskaris. The remarkable consistency in style and vocabulary of his works precludes the possibility that he used the professional ghostwriters who assisted emperors between the eleventh and the early thirteenth century in the composition of speeches and newsletters.[48]

Theodore Laskaris cared deeply about his written word reaching future generations. Five known editions of collected works were produced under his auspices. Characteristic manuscript headings point to the approximate chronology of composition of individual works included in the collections. Narrower timeframes of composition can be suggested in a number of cases.[49] The Laurentian epistolary collection and another collection of nine religious and theosophical *Sacred Orations* were prepared in early 1254. His letters to Mouzalon are conspicuously missing from the Laurentian collection, which suggests that Theodore was somewhat apprehensive at the time about advertising the close relations with his confidant. A collection of ten secular works dates to the later months of the same year, 1254, but before his accession as sole emperor in November. Another collection, titled *Christian Theology*, consists of eight religious works that were mostly composed during the period of his sole rule (1254–58). To the year of his death (1258) belongs another collection that includes letters, the philosophical treatise *Explanation of the World*, essays, and other works.[50] The deluxe manuscript of the philosophical treatise *Natural Communion* – BnF, Parisinus Suppl. gr. 460 (Fig. 26), with its gilded headings, initials, and elaborate drawings executed also in gold – was part of the same editorial project.[51] None of the original codices of the five collections has come down to us, with the possible exception of BnF, Parisinus Suppl. Gr. 472, an expensive and carefully made parchment codex of his ten secular works. There are good reasons to suspect, however, that there were other costly productions prepared in scriptoria close to the court.[52] No working copies are attested, in contrast to the manuscripts of the works of Manuel II Palaiologos, the other famous late Byzantine scholar-emperor.[53] The absence of revisions and additions is partly a reflection of Theodore's confidence as an author, but is also due to his early death, which deprived him of the opportunity to revisit the composed texts.

Writing a biography of Theodore Laskaris would have been impossible without other sources that fill in gaps and complement – while often challenging – his own voice. First and foremost, they include narrative accounts written by his teachers Blemmydes and Akropolites. Blemmydes' autobiography borders on self-hagiography and consists of two accounts completed in 1264 and 1265.[54] Akropolites was the author of the main historical work on the period of the empire in exile.[55] The two authors tend to have different opinions about events and characters from those held by their royal tutee, immersing us directly in the controversies of his reign.

Blemmydes and Akropolites had frictions with Theodore and, for reasons
that will become clear at the end, they painted a negative portrait of him.
The exact opposite – highly positive – view of Theodore is found in
Synopsis chronike, a world chronicle that relies faithfully on Akropolites
for the period after 1204, but occasionally makes precious additions. The
anonymous author, a clergyman in Theodore's entourage who followed
him on military campaigns, removed all of Akropolites' criticisms. He has
traditionally been identified as Theodore Skoutariotes, metropolitan
bishop of Kyzikos during the second half of the thirteenth century, but
this remains uncertain.[56]

George Pachymeres wrote a history of the period from 1258 to 1309, with
flashbacks into the empire in exile. Pachymeres grew up in Nicaea and
derived some of his information from people who knew Theodore personally, such as Gregory, the archbishop of Mytilene, who administered the last
rites and received the confession of the dying emperor.[57] The masterfully
written work of Pachymeres has to be treated with caution. The historian
idealized the emperors in exile as a foil to their less competent successors,
whom he blamed for weakening the defenses of western Asia Minor in the
later thirteenth century and facilitating its conquest by the Turks. A similar
critical agenda informs the account by the fourteenth-century historian
Nikephoros Gregoras, who provides details missing from other sources.[58]
Relevant information on prosopography, land-ownership, and social relations can be derived from documentary evidence preserved in the cartularies
of the monasteries of Lembos near Smyrna, St. Paul on Mount Latros, and
Hiera-Xerochoraphion on Mount Mykale, and in a collection of forty
formularies for notarial documents used in the empire of Nicaea.[59] Few
charters of Theodore Laskaris have survived in the monastic archives – acts
issued by his chancery rather than "epistolary ordinances" and foreign
correspondence included in his letter collections. Two ordinances (*prostag-
mata*) of 1256 have been copied in the cartulary of the Lembos monastery.[60]
Latin, Seljuk, Armenian, Bulgarian, and Mamluk sources add valuable details
of the historical context of Theodore's life from the dynamic world of
international affairs in Europe, Asia Minor, and the Mediterranean.

The intriguing personality and writings of Theodore Laskaris have long
made scholars aware of the potential for a biography. In 1897, Karl
Krumbacher, the founder of Byzantine studies as an academic discipline,
recommended in the second expanded edition of his *History of Byzantine
Literature* the "highly enticing task of producing an overall literary and
psychological portrait in finest detail."[61] August Heisenberg, his professor-
ial successor at the University of Munich, remarked three years later that

"the presentation of the life and writings of the emperor Theodore Doukas Laskaris is one of the most fascinating tasks of Byzantine cultural history."[62] In Krumbacher's view, the Nicaean ruler was a larger-than-life individual and a mirror image, even if a distorted one, of Frederick II Hohenstaufen, the *stupor mundi* ("wonder of the world").

> As a statesman, author, and a human being, Theodore Laskaris is one of the most interesting phenomena in Byzantium, a sort of oriental counterpart to his great contemporary Frederick II, yet doubtlessly a type of degenerate: spiritually highly endowed, bodily weak, without power of the will and with a corruptive predominance of the nervous system.[63]

Following the medical explanation of Theodore's gifted mind given by the historian Pachymeres, Krumbacher and others after him have inaccurately viewed the Nicaean emperor as a man affected by chronic epilepsy.[64] Theodore Laskaris seemed a neurotic to Krumbacher, yet this is a trap set by the medieval author's intensely emotional style. There is no evidence whatsoever that Theodore Laskaris suffered from a chronic disease or a psychological disorder.[65] Otherwise, Krumbacher's comparison between the two thirteenth-century emperors is fully justified, even though Theodore Laskaris never benefited from the massive modern interest in the figure of Frederick Hohenstaufen.[66] Both were eccentrics, with distinctive personalities. Both were patrons of scholars and education. Both left a legacy of social division, such as a politically tinted church schism in thirteenth-century Byzantium and the conflict between Guelfs and Ghibbelines: the factions supporting, respectively, the pope and the Western Roman emperor in the Italian city-states. Furthermore, their courts were connected through a strategic alliance. Theodore felt solidarity with Frederick, whose daughter was his stepmother, and responded to his death with a thought-provoking memorial speech.[67]

The project recommended by Krumbacher was postponed for several reasons. For one, it began with a false start. In 1908 Ioannes Papadopoulos published *Théodore II Lascaris, empereur de Nicée*, a short biography that painted a glowing and crudely reconstructed portrait of its subject.[68] The book scratched the surface of Theodore's writings, most of which were unpublished at the time. Only relatively recently did key works by Theodore Laskaris become available in critical editions by Luigi Tartaglia. Another hindrance – the difficulty of understanding the author's idiosyncratic vocabulary – has largely been overcome thanks to the advances in the study of medieval Greek lexicography and the completion of the monumental *Lexikon zur byzantinischen Gräzität* (Vienna, 1994–2017). But the main cause of the delay has been the tendency of modern historians of Byzantium to direct their energies toward the study of aggregate groups formed by class, economic status, or gender, leaving little room in the process for biography. Only aspects of Theodore Laskaris' thought that fit into diachronic frameworks, such as his Hellenism and his political philosophy, have consistently received attention.[69] The relative lack of scholarly interest in the fate of Byzantium and its elite in the aftermath of 1204 has also helped to push Theodore Laskaris to the margins of history. The period of exile has often appeared unattractive in comparison with the achievements of late antiquity and the cultural vibrancy of the twelfth century.

The structure of this book is chronological, with the voice of the main character continually helping us to tell key historical episodes. Chapters 1 and 2 introduce the context of his life and times: his family, the world of living memory before his birth, and the physical and human geography of Byzantine Asia Minor, especially as he saw and interpreted them. Chapters 3 and 4 reconstruct his childhood and upbringing, his early education, and the kindling of his love for philosophy. Chapter 5 pieces together the evidence of his duties in governance as a coruler in his twenties. Chapter 6 examines his circle of companions, his views on friendship, and his ideas on reforming the aristocracy. Chapter 7 discusses seminal episodes in life that led him to reflections on the meaning of love, human existence, and relations with the Western world. Chapter 8 focuses on his four-year reign as a sole emperor, when he led a long military campaign and launched political reforms that were cut short by his untimely death. The concluding chapters 9 and 10 focus on his contributions to the intellectual life of his time, in particular his involvement in philosophical debates and his passionate Hellenism. The book weaves together strands of personal, political, and intellectual biography in the hope that the resulting multifaceted portrait would do justice to a complex and gifted individual who appealed to the judgment of the "future generations."

1 | Byzantium in Exile

In 1204 the political elite of the Byzantine Empire faced for the first time in its centuries-long history the prospect of a forced relocation from Constantinople, the city of New Rome, to the former provinces. This move led to ruptures with the past and shaped the world in which Theodore Laskaris was born. The fall of Constantinople to the crusaders on the night of April 12, 1204, was traumatic and unexpected. Medieval Christians and Muslims were in rare agreement that Constantinople was a city of wonders. Its concentration of power and wealth was unparalleled: a population of as many as 400,000 inhabitants in the twelfth century, splendid palaces, spectacular public squares adorned with monuments of antiquity, and churches packed with holy relics.[1] For centuries the Byzantines knew Constantinople as "the queen of cities," "the eye of the inhabited world," and "the navel of the earth" – just a few of the expressions of admiration for the metropolis of New Rome.

The capture of Constantinople was marked by violence and destruction. Two fires started by the foreign army and the native mob raged in July and August 1203, and together with a third one in April 1204, ruined as much as one-sixth of the built environment of the city.[2] The acts of pillage and plunder belong to the darkest annals of history. One rank-and-file crusader reckoned that the wealth of Constantinople surpassed the forty richest cities in the world taken together and estimated the captured booty as three large towers filled with silver. Another complained that poor knights were allowed to keep only the silver chamber pots of the Constantinopolitan ladies.[3] The looting did not spare ancient statues on open display, especially at the Hippodrome, a large public venue where the populace gathered to attend ceremonies, chariot races, and hunts with exotic wild animals. The crusaders melted down into coins the colossal bronze statue of Hercules at the Hippodrome, the work of the great ancient sculptor Lysippus.[4] Byzantine contemporaries, including Theodore's father, who was a mere child in 1204, noted the irony that the Muslims had treated crusader-held Jerusalem less brutally when it fell into Saladin's hands in 1187.[5] The outbursts of Constantinopolitans added to the damage. In January 1204 a crowd shattered the large bronze statue of Athena

Promachos, a famous work of the ancient sculptor Phidias displayed on a pedestal at the Forum of Constantine, because they interpreted the figure's beckoning gesture toward the west as welcoming the crusaders.[6]

The Westerners saw themselves as masters by the right of conquest. Before the sack of Constantinople, they struck agreements on the division of territory. The large island of Crete, for example, had been promised by the Byzantine prince Alexios – a key player in the diversion of the crusade to Constantinople – to Boniface, the marquis of Montferrat. Several months after the fall of Constantinople, on August 12, 1204, Boniface ceded his rights to Venice, which in the following decades established its grip on the large island and ruled it until its conquest by the Ottomans in the seventeenth century. In March 1204, before the final assault, the leaders of the crusade agreed on the principles of division and the manner of election of a Latin emperor of Constantinople. Soon after the conquest, most probably between April 12 and May 9, they issued a detailed partition document, the *Partitio terrarum imperii Romaniae*, which was based, as it has been argued, on the proceeds from taxation for the fiscal year ending on August 31, 1203.[7] Even though most of the *Partitio* could not be put into effect, it showed the far-reaching conquering ambitions of the Latins in the Balkans, Asia Minor, and the Aegean. Soon after its capture Constantinople became the seat of a Latin emperor and patriarch. The first emperor, Baldwin of Flanders, was anointed and crowned in the church of St. Sophia on May 16, 1204. The patriarch Thomas Morosini, a Venetian, arrived in Constantinople in midsummer 1205, and a hierarchy of Latin bishops was introduced. A Venetian plenipotentiary (*podestà*) became resident in the city and defended the interests of the republic of St. Mark.

The events of 1204 confronted the Byzantines with the almost unthinkable. Eschatological imagination and the scriptures provided some, but not all, of the answers. The fall of New Rome was considered in certain twelfth-century circles to be one of the possible cataclysms presaging the end of the world.[8] The Second Coming was slow to arrive, however, and the disaster was soon attributed to communal sin and compared to the well-known biblical example of the Babylonian captivity of the Jews. Exile, after all, had a scriptural precedent with an eventual happy ending. Born seventeen years after 1204, Theodore Laskaris felt seething anger about the loss of Constantinople – "the city of Constantine," "the queen of cities" and "Byzantis," as he called it in a way traditional for medieval Greek authors.[9] Like other contemporaries, he referred to the event simply as "the capture" (*halosis*).[10] Like them, he grappled with understanding its long-term significance. Reports of the violence that accompanied the crusader capture of

Constantinople stirred his emotions. In 1256 he described ongoing warfare with the Latins as entirely motivated by vengeance. He declared with pride: "Now the sword of the Hellenes has taken a double revenge for the massacre of the Hellenes in Constantinople by shedding the blood of the perpetrators."[11]

A flood of refugees, both common folk and aristocrats, streamed out of the densely populated metropolis in 1204. They included Niketas Choniates, a high civil minister and judge, who was the author of the main historical account of events in Byzantium between 1118 and 1207.[12] He provides us with the human side of the story. After witnessing five days of looting, he decided to leave and joined a large party of people, including courtiers and judges, who were swarming "like ants" as they made their way out of Constantinople. As he walked out through the Golden Gate, the parade entrance for Byzantine emperors returning from campaign, he was struck by the contrast between the impregnable fortifications and the captivity of the city. He writes that he knelt on the ground and cried out in desperation: "Queen of the queen of cities, song of songs and splendor of splendors, and the rarest vision of the rarest visions of the world, who is it that has torn us from thee like darling children from their adoring mother? What shall become of us? Whither shall we go?"[13] An answer to the last question was already forthcoming. Those who left the city in the search of protection and shelter were already setting up centers of resistance against the Latins.

The Elder Theodore Laskaris

Ambitious commanders in the former provinces established lordships, three of which developed into irredentist kingdoms claiming to be the legitimate heirs to the twelfth-century empire: the kingdoms of Epiros, Trebizond, and Nicaea. One successor state was centered on Arta in the Epiros region in western Greece. It owed its swift rise to the enterprising rebel Michael Komnenos Doukas, who was a bastard son of the *sebastokrator* John Doukas (a high court title second only to that of despot), a brother of the emperors Isaac II Angelos (r. 1185–95) and Alexios III Angelos (r. 1195–1203).[14] The Pindos Mountains separated Epiros from the main route of crusader campaigns and settlement. The principality grew into an imperial polity ruled by self-styled "emperors of the Romans" in the years 1224–46, when Thessalonica, Byzantium's second city, became its capital. Epiros was to have a long political history. Traditionally known as the "despotate of Epiros," because many of its rulers titled themselves despots, it submitted to Constantinople only temporarily in the fourteenth century and was incorporated into the Ottoman Empire in 1449.[15]

Another splinter state with Byzantine political identity, which was even longer-lived (it did not fall to the Ottomans until 1461) arose at Trebizond, on the southeastern shore of the Black Sea. Its founders, Alexios and David Komnenos, the Grand Komnenoi, were sons of a Georgian princess and grandsons of the emperor-usurper Andronikos I Komnenos (r. 1183–85). Scholars have debated whether the rulers of Trebizond assumed the Byzantine imperial title in April 1204, or later, by the middle of the thirteenth century. What is certain is that in 1282 John II Grand Komnenos consented to exchange the title of emperor for that of despot and married into the governing dynasty in Constantinople. In the fourteenth century the ruler of Trebizond titled himself "Emperor and Autokrator of the Entire East, the Iberians and Perateia (that is, the overseas territory in the Crimea) Grand Komnenos."[16]

The third principality was closest to the Bosporus and was established in western Asia Minor. The walled city of Nicaea, around 56 miles (90 kilometers) away from Constantinople as the crow flies, became a center of anti-Latin resistance and attracted politically powerful refugees. Nicaea had excellent natural defenses thanks to its location on the eastern shore of Askania, a large freshwater lake, and lay at the intersection of major routes leading into inner Asia Minor.[17] The founder of the state of Nicaea was Theodore Komnenos Laskaris, a.k.a. Theodore I Laskaris, the grandfather and namesake of the subject of this biography. He is designated here as "the elder Theodore Laskaris" so as to distinguish him from his homonymous grandson, who will be called "the younger Theodore Laskaris" or simply Theodore. The younger Theodore Laskaris admired the elder's spectacular achievements, even though he never knew him as he was born a few months after his death. He lauded his grandfather as a dynamic man and a founding figure who turned the city of Nicaea into the beating heart of the revived Byzantine state: "the great-hearted, eagle-swift, great emperor."[18]

The elder Theodore Laskaris was born between 1171 and 1176.[19] Very little is known about his family. He had at least six brothers: Constantine, George, Alexios, Isaac, Manuel, and Michael. The names of his parents, grandparents, sisters, or any twelfth-century members of his family are not recorded.[20] The silence of the sources confirms the impression that his ancestors climbed the social hierarchy from the provincial "second-tier" aristocratic elite through intermarriage. His mother belonged to an unknown side branch of the Komnenos family, for the elder Theodore advertised his royal surname. His father may have been called Nicholas, a name that he gave his firstborn son following the common Byzantine practice of papponymy, the naming of a child after the grandparent. His father may have remarried, for two of the elder Theodore's brothers, Manuel and Michael, had the additional surname or nickname Tzamantouros and long outlived him.[21] By the late twelfth century, the Laskaris were connected with western Asia Minor and Constantinople. An early seal of the elder Theodore, which identifies him as the *sebastos protovestiarites* Theodore Komnenos Laskaris (Fig. 4a), and a similar seal of his brother Constantine (designated on it as Constantine Komnenos Laskaris) give clues as to the family's local ties. Both seals represent on their obverse St. George described by the accompanying inscription as "Diasorites." The monastery of St. George Diasorites was located in the town of Pyrgion (Birge) in the Kaistros valley. The Laskaris family, thus, advertised its association with the region.[22] The monastery makes an appearance in a letter of the younger Theodore Laskaris, who mentions its abbot-elect as a messenger between him and the patriarch.[23] The Laskaris brothers were close to the Phokas family, which around the year 1200 resided in the region of Palatia (Miletos) in the lower Maeander valley. In 1209 a certain Theodotos Phokas who bore the high honorific title of *panhypersebastos* is called an "uncle" of the elder Theodore Laskaris – he may have been married to his aunt – and served as his *megas doux*, a title given to the commander of the fleet in the twelfth century.[24]

The origins of the Laskaris family in the eastern provinces is confirmed by the etymology of the name. The root is most probably Persian (from *lashkarī*, "warrior"), but a derivation from Arabic (from *alašqar*, "the blond one") has also been suggested.[25] The name is first attested in Byzantine sources during the eleventh century. In 1059 the magnate Eustathios Boilas, who was exiled to the theme (province) of Iberia, manumitted a slave named Laskaris and bequeathed him a small plot of land.[26] The frontier theme of Iberia – a melting pot of Armenians, Georgians, and Greek-speakers – was formed after the death c. 1000 of the local Georgian client ruler, the *kouropalates* David, and grew after the annexation of the Armenian Bagratid kingdom in 1045. The other Laskaris known from the eleventh century was a naturalized foreign grandee and a descendant of the Kurdish noble family of the Shaddadids, who ruled Dvin and Gandzak in Armenia from the second half of the tenth century onward. The Persian name Lashkari was common among the Shaddadids and was rendered into Greek as Laskaris. The introduction of the name in Byzantium is illustrated by an important representative of the family who was incorporated into the empire's elite. A certain Lashkari ibn Musa, the governor of Gandzak between 1034 and 1049, had a son by the name of Artasir who was sent as a hostage to Constantinople. Artasir's lead seal demonstrates his acculturation and cooption into the Byzantine military administration. Found at Kličevac on the Danube near Braničevo, the seal identifies him as "Artasir, the son of Laskaris," *patrikios anthypatos* ("patrician and proconsul"), and *strategos* ("general"). The "son of Laskaris" held a high title and was transferred from the empire's eastern to its western frontier with Hungary.[27] He must have been a Christian, a precondition for holding an office, and seems never to have returned to his homeland, because the invading Seljuk Turks annexed the last independent Shaddadid territories in 1075 and put an end to the theme of Iberia. Artasir's identification as the son of Laskaris was the first step in the emergence of a family name, because aristocratic surnames were formed from a foreign first name. The aristocracy of the empire of Nicaea provides plenty of examples: the Tornikes (Tornikios) family descended from Tornik, an Armenian integrated into Byzantium during the tenth century; the Nestongoi were the issue of Nestong, a Slav who entered Byzantine service in the early eleventh century; the Raoul family stemmed from Rudolfus, a Norman of the later eleventh century.[28] Even though the evidence is inconclusive, it is quite possible that the Shaddadid governor of Gandzak whose son settled in Byzantium was the eponymous ancestor of the elder Theodore.

The Laskaris family gained importance during the twelfth century through its marriage into the Komnenian dynasty established by the emperor Alexios I (r. 1081–1118). Documents, letters, inscriptions, and seals consistently render the surname of the elder Theodore as "Komnenos Laskaris."[29] His parents had sufficient connections with the imperial court in Constantinople to secure him a job in the palace guard of the emperor Alexios III Angelos, which was the platform for his meteoric rise to power. The inscription on the elder Theodore's early seal featuring St. George Diasorites (Fig. 4a) mentions his holding the title of *sebastos* and the office of *protovestiarites*. *Sebastos* was introduced as a court rank in the late eleventh century as a mark of special distinction for the emperor's relatives. The title was greatly devalued by the late twelfth century. Choniates writes sarcastically that Alexios III offered the rank of *sebastos* for sale to foreigners and baseborn people, such as moneychangers and linen merchants.[30] But taken together with the family name Komnenos, the title offers supporting evidence that the elder Theodore Laskaris belonged at the time to the social and political elite. As *protovestiarites*, the elder Theodore headed a cadet regiment of palace guards which had been set up in the eleventh century and was known as the *vestiaritai* (literally "attendants of the *vestiarion*," the imperial wardrobe and treasury).[31] Contemporaries referred to the military career of the elder Theodore by describing him as "an officer and a commander" and "a daring youth and fierce in military matters."[32] Both *protovestiaritai* and *vestiaritai* could perform the function of imperial agents and tax officials in the provinces during the twelfth and the thirteenth centuries.[33] The elder Theodore was probably not charged with such responsibilities given his military duties in the capital, but *vestiaritai* subordinate to him would have traveled to provincial areas for ad hoc tasks and kept him abreast of news from outside Constantinople.

Shortly before the fall of Constantinople, the praetorian Theodore became involved in the politics of succession and usurpation. The imperial office in Byzantium was based on the Roman model, which meant there were no laws of succession. Emperors made arrangements for their sons or other coopted individuals to become their heirs (for example, by proclaiming them as coemperors), but nonetheless gaining the throne often resulted from power struggles among leading generals, with the occasional involvement of civil officials, churchmen, and the populace of Constantinople. In 1195 Alexios III Angelos deposed his brother Isaac II Angelos, the ruling emperor for the past ten years, who was blinded and kept in comfortable confinement in a suburban palace. Alexios III had no male offspring. By 1200 his two eldest daughters, Irene and Anna, were widowed, and the third, Eudokia, resided at the Serbian court. The lack of a designated heir fired the ambitions of Alexios III's relatives. The elderly *sebastokrator* John Doukas, the brother of Isaac II and Alexios III, saw himself as a potential heir. Nephews of the two emperors borne by their sisters also had designs on the imperial crown.[34]

The young widows Irene and Anna were tools for solving the problem of the succession, and in the late winter of 1200 were married in a double wedding to Alexios Palaiologos and the elder Theodore Laskaris.[35] Alexios Palaiologos, who wed Irene, the firstborn daughter, received the title of despot (literally, "lord"), the highest court rank after the emperor. Since its introduction into the court hierarchy in 1163, this title was granted to the emperor's son-in-law and heir to the throne.[36] Anna became the wife of the elder Theodore. The impressive genealogical credentials of Alexios Palaiologos and the former, deceased sons-in-law of Alexios III suggest indirectly that the Komnenos Laskaris family was considered aristocratic and worthy of special honors. Anna's first husband had been the *sebastokrator* Isaac Komnenos Vatatzes, a grandson of the general Theodore

Vatatzes and Eudokia Komnene who was a daughter of the emperor John
II Komnenos (r. 1118–43).[37] Despot Alexios Palaiologos was the great-
grandson of George Palaiologos, Alexios I's loyal general married to his
wife's sister, and the son of the *megas hetaireiarches* George Palaiologos, a
prominent diplomat.[38] As the designated heir, Despot Alexios Palaiologos
was the second man in command after the emperor. Soon after the
wedding he was charged with calming the unrest of the artisans of Constantinople and crushing the sedition of a certain John Spyridonakis, the
rogue governor of the theme of Smolena in Macedonia.[39] Alexios' seal
flaunts his marriage, identifying him as "an in-law of the ruler of all the
Roman land" married to "the firstborn imperial princess." The couple had
vast economic resources at their disposal. The *Partitio* refers to "the estates
of the Lady Irene, daughter of the emperor Lord Alexios" in the western
Peloponnese.[40]

The elder Theodore Laskaris did not remain long in the shadow, because
Despot Alexios Palaiologos passed away before 1204 in unknown
circumstances. Theodore was elevated to the first position in the line of
succession and assumed the vacant title of despot. This important twist of
events is evidenced by a fragmentary seal that features the warrior saint
Theodore and the inscription "Despot Theodore Komnenos Laskaris,
husband of the emperor's daughter Anna." The choice of the saint on
the seal matched both the name and the military vocation of the elder
Theodore. The same saint would appear on his imperial seal (Fig. 4b). His
grandson would follow in his footsteps by placing an image of St. Theodore
on seals and coins (Figs. 17a, 17b, 21c).[41] The arrival of the armies of the
Fourth Crusade transformed the political landscape and made it possible
for the elder Theodore to embark on a risky adventure that made him the
celebrated rebuilder of the Byzantine state. The young prince Alexios, Isaac
II Angelos' son who had fled to the West in 1201, joined the crusader army
in May 1203 at Corfu as it sailed to the Levant aboard Venetian ships. The
strategic goal of the expedition was an attack on Egypt, the heartland of the
Ayyubid kingdom, but the leaders of the crusade owed massive debts to
Venice and had welcomed the proposition of the fugitive prince Alexios to
provide them with the required funds if they helped him to gain the throne
and redress the injustice suffered by his father. Around twelve thousand of
the thirty-one thousand seaborne crusaders, both Franks and Venetians,
were fully equipped for battle.[42] On July 6, 1203, the army captured the
fortress of Pera (Galata) and the ships entered the bay of the Golden Horn.

From the upper apartments of the Blachernae Palace, Alexios III and his
family observed the alarming sight of the Latin army positioned before the

city walls. The elder Theodore led harassing sallies from Constantinople and had his first taste of battle with the crusaders. His brother Constantine Laskaris (Constantine Komnenos Laskaris), also a commander stationed in Constantinople, followed his example but was captured by the Burgundian knight Gautier de Neuilly during a skirmish opposite the Blachernae Palace; he was soon released. The situation took a turn for the worse on July 17, 1203, when the Venetians scaled the seawalls and set fire to the adjacent neighborhoods, while the emperor Alexios III, with the elder Theodore Laskaris by his side, brought the Byzantine army outside the land walls seemingly in order to attack the crusaders. At this crucial moment Alexios III made the fateful decision to avoid pitched battle. Fearing that his grip on power was slipping away, he left the city during the night of July 17–18, with a few trusted men and the entire imperial treasury. Choniates remarks that the emperor shared his plans only with his daughter Irene, but kept them secret from his wife, Euphrosyne, his daughter Anna, and her husband, Theodore. The fleeing emperor sought to consolidate his authority outside Constantinople. He moved first to the fortress of Develtos in northeastern Thrace and later to Adrianople and Mosynopolis in Thrace.[43]

His desertion meant the surrender of the city. A peaceful transfer of power took place on the morning of July 18, 1203, and Alexios III's blinded brother Isaac Angelos was released. The young prince Alexios received the imperial crown, reigning as Alexios IV, and took revenge on those responsible for his father's dethronement. Organizers of the coup of 1195 were summarily hanged. Alexios III's son-in-law, Despot Theodore Laskaris, was thrown into prison.[44] Alexios IV was unable to keep his promise to pay the crusaders who raised him to the throne, because his fugitive uncle (Alexios III) had appropriated the treasury. His reliance on the Latin army encamped around the city roused ever-growing public discontent. Constantinopolitans of every walk of life gathered in the church of St. Sophia between January 25 and 28, 1204, and refused to be governed by the Angelos family any longer. A young man, Nicholas Kannavos, was acclaimed emperor, but lacked the backing of the army. Alexios Mourtzouphlos ("the bushy-eyebrowed") – a former rebel against Alexios III and now a general and confidant of Alexios IV – benefited from the turmoil and the anti-Latin sentiment. He usurped the throne, had Alexios IV and Isaac II cruelly murdered, and speedily dispensed with Kannavos.[45] The crusaders found a convenient justification to take Constantinople by force.

The younger Theodore Laskaris heard stories told by eyewitnesses about the rapid turnover of emperors before the fall of Constantinople. His elderly tutor frequented the court of the Angeloi and was close to an emperor who was imprisoned and murdered with poison. This was none other than Isaac II Angelos who assisted his son Alexios IV during their ill-fated and brief joint rule (1203–04). The usurper Mourtzouphlos is known to have offered a poisoned drink to the imprisoned Alexios IV, whom he in the end ordered to be strangled. Evidently, Isaac died of poisoning.[46] Such stories of palace intrigue and betrayal taught lessons to the younger Theodore. One was the value of unflinching loyalty. Another was the heavy burden of his royal responsibilities and the consequences following from the poor judgments made by those in power. The Angelos emperors were held accountable for the events of 1204. An instructive book on kingship composed by Theodore's main teacher in the late 1240s places the blame for the fall of Constantinople – "our shrine, the city exceeding over all others" – on the "infamous conduct of its protectors."[47]

The crusaders made their final assault on the city between April 9 and 12, 1204, once again breaching the seawalls facing the Golden Horn. Mourtzouphlos fled in panic to Mosynopolis, to join Alexios III, but the latter showed no mercy – punishing him with blinding and banishment from his camp. Ultimately Mourtzouphlos was taken captive by the Latins and brought back to Constantinople as a prisoner. As the crusaders were pouring into the city on the night of April 12, another emergency assembly gathered in the church of St. Sophia to choose an emperor. There were two candidates: Constantine Laskaris, the brother of the elder Theodore, and Constantine Doukas.[48] The choice was not obvious, and the dilemma was resolved by lot, in favor of Constantine Laskaris. The latter declined to accept the imperial insignia under such extraordinary circumstances and urged resistance against the crusaders. Only the Varangian Guard, consisting mostly of Englishmen and Danes, took his call to heart, but gave up the fight once they realized that they were alone and surrounded by fellow Latins. Constantine Laskaris had no option but to board a boat bound for the coast of Asia Minor. A crusader of the rank and file wrote: "When the Greeks saw that their emperor (Mourtzouphlos) had fled, they took a high man of the city, Laskaris was his name, straightaway that very night and made him emperor. When this man was made emperor, he dared not remain there, but he got on a galley before it was day and passed over the Arm of St. George (the straits) and went off to Nicaea the great, which is a fine city. There he stayed and he was lord and emperor of it."[49] What the Latin knight did not realize was that the Laskaris who reigned in Nicaea was not the man chosen to be emperor in Constantinople, but his brother, Theodore Laskaris, who had already begun consolidating anti-Latin resistance before the fall of the city.

From Constantinople to Nicaea

The elder Theodore did not see the fall of Constantinople. Before September 1203 he slipped away from prison, helped by acquaintances from the imperial guard or by another means. Several years later, at the beginning of Lent in 1208, he would tout his providential deliverance in a speech ghostwritten by Choniates that addressed soldiers, clerics, and others who had flocked to Asia Minor to support him: "God miraculously 'removed me from prison and the hands of another Herod' (Acts 12:11) as He did with the ancient disciple (St. Peter) 'who walked on the waves' (Matthew 14:29) and guided me toward the areas here."[50] The prison escape appeared in hindsight to be a heroic and divinely ordained act. Another glorified account of the same event, of which a fragment survives, refers to the elder Theodore finding safety in a church dedicated to St. Michael.[51] In the words of yet another author, he fled Constantinople without any military backing and "armed only with practical wisdom and a brave spirit."[52]

The choices the elder Theodore made in the summer months of 1203 bear witness to his independent-mindedness and ancestral connections with Asia Minor. He felt bitterly disappointed with Alexios III, who had left him and his family in the lurch during his disgraceful escape, and decided not to take refuge with him in Thrace – preferring to set out for his native Anatolia. He must have boarded a ship bound for Bithynia, if we take the expression "he walked on the waves" to allude to a brief sea journey. From now on he played a double game with his father-in-law Alexios III. His public image was that of a legitimate heir.[53] But his actions were those of a lord in his own right, for in the eyes of many imperial subjects Alexios III had forfeited the title of emperor by abandoning Constantinople to the foreign army. The fleeing party included his wife, his three daughters Irene, Maria, and Eudokia (all under the age of four), and possibly a handful of trusted servants and soldiers from his guard regiment.[54] Travelers normally disembarked at a Bithynian port on the Sea of Marmara, such as Pylai (near Yalova), a day's horse ride from Nicaea.[55] As the elder Theodore arrived before the imposing gates of Nicaea, he must have looked at the fortifications with the hope of finding safety and using the city as a base for challenging the crusader-supported regime in Constantinople.

Byzantine Asia Minor had been a region rife with revolt in the years leading up to 1204 – "the breeding ground of eager champions of resistance," in Choniates' words.[56] The urban elite of Nicaea anxiously followed the news of the recent coup in Constantinople and made the decision to admit Anna and her three daughters, but refused entry to her husband.[57] The citizens followed the least hazardous choice in a volatile situation; less than twenty years earlier they had been punished with death and exile for supporting an insurrection against the emperor Andronikos I who usurped the throne between 1183 and 1185.[58] If Alexios IV solidified his rule in Constantinople, the refusal to receive the elder Theodore could be cited as an act of loyalty. But if Alexios III regained the throne, he was likely to thank the Nicaeans for helping his daughter and granddaughters, and for turning a deaf ear to the request of his son-in-law who had avoided joining forces with him in Thrace.

In fact, most of the Anatolian insurrections in the late twelfth century broke out not in Bithynia, but in the valleys of the Maeander and Hermos rivers. The rebels were both defectors from the Komnenian family and local grandees. During the brief reign of Andronikos I, for example, the governor (*doux*) of the Thrakesion theme, John Komnenos Vatatzes, who had been a leading general of his maternal uncle Manuel I Komnenos (r. 1143–80), raised the flag of rebellion in the city of Philadelphia. He passed away peacefully from illness and the Philadelphians surrendered their city to the government in Constantinople.[59] In 1188–89 a certain Theodore Mangaphas, a native of Philadelphia, proclaimed himself emperor and even minted silver-copper (billon) coins in his name. This rarest of acts for a provincial rebel may suggest an agenda of establishing a local territorial state and anticipates the fragmentation of the Byzantine empire in the thirteenth century. Mangaphas was compelled by a display of military force to lay down the imperial title and took refuge among the Seljuks, but the sultan arrested him and sent him to Constantinople as a prisoner.[60] In about 1200 Michael Komnenos Doukas, the illegitimate son of the *sebastokrator* John Doukas and the governor (*doux*) of the theme of Mylassa, south of the Maeander River, rebelled. The emperor Alexios III, his cousin, forced him to flee to Seljuk territory, from where he led forays across the frontier.[61] Michael would regain prominence shortly after the fall of Constantinople; he joined forces with Boniface, marquis of Montferrat, and eventually carved out his own lordship in the Balkans, founding the principality of Epiros.[62]

In late 1203 and early 1204, many cities and regions in Asia Minor were already under the authority of local lords. Conspicuously missing from the *Partitio* are Smyrna, Nymphaion, Magnesia, and Philadelphia, which apparently fell again under Theodore Mangaphas.[63] The document omits the Kaystros valley and the town of Pyrgion connected with the Laskaris family, as well as Nicaea and the neighboring Bithynian cities of

Prousa and Lopadion. The island of Rhodes, also absent from the *Partitio*, was already under the authority of Leo Gavalas, its real or nominal ruler for most of the first half of the thirteenth century.[64] There were nevertheless areas still loyal to Constantinople: cities, such as Nikomedeia, Achyraous, Atramyttion, Chliara, Pergamon, and Laodikeia; islands, such as Lesbos, Samos, and Chios; and entire themes, such as Optimatoi, Paphlagonia and Boukellarion, Mylassa and Melanoudion, and Neokastra.[65]

This fluid situation was riddled with risks and filled with opportunities for a charismatic adventurer. In his Lenten speech of 1208, ghostwritten by Choniates, the elder Theodore remembered the difficulties of trying to restore Byzantine imperial rule in Asia Minor: "You all know my travails, my sleepless nights, my moves from one region to another, the traps and evil designs by some people, my frequent journeys to the neighboring peoples, and the help I got from there."[66] The "moves" and "frequent journeys" took him to the Seljuk sultan, a traditional ally of Anatolian rebels. The elder Theodore already had financial resources at his disposal (possibly including tax revenues from areas unregistered in the *Partitio*) and reportedly offered a large amount of money to Sultan Rukn al-Dīn Süleyman II (r. 1196–1204) before the latter's death in the summer of 1204. A treaty with Rukn al-Dīn's underage son, the sultan ʿIzz al-Dīn Kılıç Arslān III (r. 1204–05), followed. After the fall of Constantinople, Seljuk soldiers assisted him in repulsing the invading Latin knights.[67]

The need for protection from the crusaders tipped the balance in western Asia Minor decisively in favor of the elder Theodore Laskaris. In the autumn of 1204 the Latin emperor Baldwin I enfeoffed Count Louis of Blois with the "duchy of Nicaea" and Stephen of Perche with the "duchy of Philadelphia." The knight Peter of Bracieux received Pegai on the Asiatic coast of the Sea of Marmara and immediately began to strengthen its defenses.[68] Key ports on the European side of the Hellespont, such as Herakleia, Rhaidestos, and Kallipolis (Gallipoli), were granted to Venice, which also acquired Lampsakos facing Kallipolis across the Hellespont.[69] The elder Theodore Laskaris is said to have crisscrossed western Asia Minor in an attempt to win the hearts and minds of the local population. He spoke at assemblies and dinner parties, raising the "fallen Roman spirit" and encouraging resistance. In an encomium written in 1206, Choniates remarked in the present tense: "You journey around the eastern cities, converse with their inhabitants, and make them realize the horrible things they will suffer if they do not speedily obey you."[70] His efforts paid off as Nicaea and other cities recognized him to be their overlord, even though he failed in his first battles with the invading Latin knights. On December 6, 1204, Peter of Bracieux defeated him on the plain near Poimanenon and took control of Bithynian fortresses.[71] On March 19, 1205, Henry, the brother of the emperor Baldwin, dealt a crushing blow to the army commanded by Constantine Laskaris and Theodore Mangaphas before the walls of Atramyttion.[72] An unexpected respite occurred due to the forays of the Bulgarian ruler Kaloyan (r. 1197–1207) into Thrace, which necessitated the withdrawal of Latin knights.[73] Years later the younger Theodore would stress the importance of right timing for the success of a ruler by remarking that "in the right moment inaction is also action."[74] On April 14, 1205, near Adrianople, Kaloyan and his formidable Cuman cavalry won a resounding victory in a pitched battle, in which the flower of the crusader nobility perished, including Louis of Blois and Stephen of Perche, the dukes of Nicaea and Philadelphia. The Latin emperor Baldwin was captured and died in the Bulgarian royal capital of Turnovo.[75] His brother Henry assumed the regency. When news of Baldwin's death reached him, he was crowned on August 20, 1206, in the church of St. Sophia as the second Latin emperor of Constantinople.

The withdrawal of Latin troops to the Balkans and the demise of internal rivals motivated the elder Theodore Laskaris to claim the imperial title. In the autumn of 1204 the blinded ex-emperor Mourtzouphlos escaped from his detention in Constantinople and tried to cross into Asia Minor, but the Latins apprehended him and sentenced him to death by public execution.[76] In early 1205 the crusaders captured the wandering emperor Alexios III at Halmyros in Thessaly and forced him to give up his imperial insignia.[77] Not long afterward David Komnenos, one of the two Grand Komnenos brothers who had established themselves in Trebizond before the fall of Constantinople, invaded the Bithynian lordship of the elder Theodore, but his troops were defeated.[78] In the following year the forces of David, based in Amastris and Pontic Herakleia on the Black Sea shore of Paphlagonia, now allied with the Latins, suffered another military setback near Nikomedeia.[79] Also in 1205, the ambitions of yet another powerful adversary, Manuel Mavrozomes, were thwarted. A grandson of the emperor Manuel I through an illegitimate daughter, Mavrozomes left Constantinople after its capture in the company of his son-in-law, the Seljuk sultan Ghiyāth al-Dīn Kaykhusraw I (r. 1192–96, 1205–11).[80] The elder Theodore Laskaris detained both of them in Nicaea temporarily in late 1204 or early 1205. Once reinstalled in Konya, Kaykhusraw gave full support to his ambitious ally Mavrozomes, who plundered the Maeander valley with the help of Turkish warrior bands. Mavrozomes was swiftly defeated and had to content himself with the status of Seljuk governor of the frontier fortresses of Chonai and Laodikeia. On his victory over the blue-blooded Mavrozomes, in the spring of 1205, the elder Theodore Laskaris put on the imperial purple buskins and had himself acclaimed emperor in all cities under his control. From now he was not merely a local lord: he was an emperor of the Romans.[81]

The transformation of the elder Theodore from an Anatolian lord to a rebuilder of the Byzantine state was a piecemeal and multifaceted process. He gained allies from among local urban and landed elites, whom he coopted by the recognition of their rights and the bestowal of titles. He is said to have "skillfully pursued" Theodore Mangaphas of Philadelphia and Sabbas Asidenos, a lord over the lower Maeander valley who controlled Sampson (ancient Priene) and Palatia (Miletos).[82] Mangaphas surrendered his lordship over Philadelphia peacefully, while his family remained well-off proprietors in the city and its environs.[83] Asidenos' lordship was absorbed before April 1214 through a marriage alliance that made him an in-law of the elder Theodore Laskaris. Asidenos was granted the court title of *sebastokrator*. Nikephoros Kontostephanos who belonged to a landowning family in the Maeander valley was enticed in a similar fashion. We find him decorated with title of *sebastokrator* in a document dated March 24, 1216.[84] The elder Theodore kept inviting prominent members of the twelfth-century elite to help him in the reestablishment of the imperial government. In return he promised political and religious freedom from the Latins. The fugitive metropolitan bishop of Athens compared the emperor's call to settle in Nicaea to Christ's words, "Come to me all … and I will give you rest" (Matthew 11:28).[85] The accommodation of refugees was to become one of the missions of the empire in exile. The younger Theodore Laskaris would consider the welcoming of "newcomers from among the brethren" to be one of his duties as a ruler and would personally take care of displaced individuals.[86] The families of twelfth-century officials, including those with ancestral Balkan connections such as Raoul, Vranas, Kantakouzenos, and Palaiologos, were incorporated into the Anatolian Byzantine state.[87]

The generals and civil officials who relocated to Asia Minor brought with them much needed expertise, as is seen in the case of four individuals who entered the service of the elder Theodore soon after 1204: John Steiriones, Basil Kamateros, Andronikos Palaiologos, and Demetrios Komnenos Tornikes. The admiral John Steiriones was a former Calabrian pirate who had been Alexios III's commander of the fleet. In 1207 we find him operating along the Aegean coast of Asia Minor and assisting Nicaean military operations in the Sea of Marmara.[88] A brother of Alexios III's wife, Euphrosyne, Basil Kamateros was the son of Andronikos Kamateros, a high judge and a diplomat, and had served in the twelfth century as logothete of the drome, a minister responsible for foreign relations.[89] In the trying times of Andronikos' reign he was blinded and exiled among the Rus, but he returned to Constantinople after the death of the "tyrant." Kamateros remained an influential figure in Nicaea. He was credited with the reestablishment of the imperial government and the patriarchate, and led an embassy to Cilician Armenia in 1213.[90] Toward the end of his reign, the elder Theodore appointed as chief commander of the field army (*megas domestikos*) Andronikos Palaiologos. The son of a twelfth-century head of the navy (*megas doux*), Andronikos Palaiologos would serve as Nicaean *megas domestikos* for more than twenty years. He married his distant cousin Theodora, the orphaned daughter of Despot Alexios Palaiologos, thus uniting two branches of the powerful Palaiologos family.[91]

Another appointee, Demetrios Komnenos Tornikes, served as the chief minister and head of the imperial chancery (a position known as *mesazon*) from at least 1216 until his death between 1248 and 1252. He was a third-generation civil servant. His grandfather, Demetrios Tornikes from Thebes, held the chancery office of keeper of the inkstand (*epi tou kanikleiou*) and was logothete of the drome for ten years, until about 1200. His father, Constantine Tornikes, married to a Komnene, had served as master of petitions, eparch (mayor) of Constantinople, and logothete of the drome. Constantine Tornikes preferred to remain in Constantinople and join the administration of the Latin emperor Baldwin, but had the misfortune to fall into Bulgarian captivity at the Battle of Adrianople in April 1205 and did not come back alive.[92] Constantine's brother Euthymios Tornikes settled on the island of Euboea and maintained close contacts with bishops in the state of Epiros.[93] The fate of the Tornikes family exemplifies the dispersal of the twelfth-century Byzantine elite and the split loyalties of its members – a challenge that the younger Theodore Laskaris kept facing in the 1250s.

Key Byzantine institutions were revived with remarkable rapidity. The patriarchate of Constantinople found its new home in Nicaea. In June 1206 the last patriarch of Constantinople ordained before the fall of the city passed away in Didymoteichon in Thrace and in March 1208 the elder Theodore Laskaris selected as his successor Michael Autoreianos, a former patriarchal official. The latter immediately performed Theodore's coronation and anointing.[94] The empire in exile came to resemble a legitimately constituted Byzantine polity, ruled by an emperor of the Romans and with a patriarch of Constantinople at the helm of the church. It was a tax-gathering state following the Byzantine model. Taxes were periodically assessed and flowed into the central imperial treasury first attested in 1216.[95] The main land tax and supplementary levies were collected in coin. The elder Theodore issued electrum and billon coins, and his successor restored the full pre-1204 range by adding gold (*hyperpera*) and copper (*tetartera*) coins.[96] Writing in the 1250s, the younger Theodore Laskaris observed that tax-collectors came to the countryside as early as the spring season, many months before the harvest, to demand payment and discovered that the peasants lacked sufficient liquid wealth and needed to borrow money.[97] Royal authority maintained tight control over taxation. Extortion and violence by tax-collectors were punishable offences at the imperial tribunal.[98] The first Nicaean emperor followed the twelfth-century policy of rewarding elite families with distributions of landed resources and grants of tax-collecting rights over lands. Documentary evidence shows that the Vranas, Gavalas, Philes, and Zagarommates families benefited economically from the move of the government to Asia Minor, often at the expense of previous landowners, such as Constantinopolitan churches and monasteries.[99]

The elder Theodore relied heavily on his family, following in the footsteps of the emperor Alexios I Komnenos, who had made the degree of kinship with the emperor the organizing principle of the court hierarchy. A patriarchal document dating to between 1208 and 1210 describes his polity as consisting of "the blood relatives of the mighty and holy emperor of ours, then the grandees and other officials, and after them the entire civil and military order, and the inhabitants of the cities and lands in this Roman state."[100] His brothers received the highest titles. Constantine settled for the rank of despot, the most exalted at the court, after refusing to become the emperor just before the fall of Constantinople. Constantine appears to have settled down in Nicaea, for he donated manuscripts containing saints' lives, a catena to the psalms and orations by Gregory of Nazianzus to the little-known monastery of Christ Savior "of the Deaf Man" (*tou Kophou*) in the city. The bestowal of the title of despot on him as well as on local lords marks a departure from its original function in the twelfth century as a designation of the son-in-law and heir.[101] Three other brothers of the elder Theodore – George, Alexios, and Isaac – held the title of *sebastokrator*. George was the governor (*doux*) of the large and wealthy theme of Thrakesion.[102] The brothers were powerful military men with their own retinues. An attack on Latin-held Nikomedeia in 1207 was reportedly carried out by "Theodore Laskaris and his brothers." An ordinance of 1207 mentions a certain Alexios Komnenos, a "dearest brother of my imperial majesty," holding command over *vestiaritai* of the emperor. This individual may have been none other than his biological brother before he assumed the title of *sebastokrator*, referred to here with his prestigious surname "Komnenos" rather than "Laskaris."[103] Continuity with the twelfth century is only one aspect of the restored government, however. A smaller territory and fewer resources inevitably led to changes. The administration was simplified. Offices connected to the imperial household gained prominence and court titles borrowed from the Latins and the Seljuks are first attested in the empire in exile.[104] The fate of the high imperial minister (*logothetes ton sekreton*) Choniates exemplifies the diminished opportunities available for former Constantinopolitan civil officials. In 1206 Choniates made his way to Nicaea, where he joined the staff of an anonymous keeper of the imperial chest (*protovestiarios*), a high household official of the emperor, but could not obtain honors matching his pre-1204 career. Barely able to feed his servants and residing in an uncomfortable wooden house, he felt embittered and complained of "dwelling like a captive" on the shores of Lake Askania.[105]

The political success of the elder Theodore Laskaris was due, in no small part, to his sanguine and pragmatic approach. He conducted business on the move rather than residing in a capital city, communicating face to face with local elites and commanding the troops in person. Patriarchal elections held in Nicaea in 1213 and 1216 were delayed due to his prolonged residence in the Thrakesion theme, in the southern part of his realm, which became a center of governance alongside Nicaea.[106] Significantly, in 1211–12 the Latin emperor Henry occupied Nymphaion in the same theme.[107] Although the wound of 1204 was still fresh, the elder Theodore Laskaris reached out across the divide by recruiting Latin mercenaries and draining manpower from his enemies. On December 7, 1210, Pope Innocent III urged the Latin patriarch of Constantinople to excommunicate crusaders who were swarming to Nicaea for better pay.[108] Realizing that he could not recapture Constantinople by military means alone, the elder Theodore relied increasingly on diplomacy. In the late spring or early summer of 1207 he came to a two-year truce with the Latins, who agreed to dismantle the recently strengthened fortress of Kyzikos and the fortified church of St. Sophia in Nikomedeia.[109] Peace was difficult to maintain, however. Sometime before March 17, 1208, the elder Theodore complained in a letter to Pope Innocent III that the Latins did not keep their word. He requested negotiations for a "permanent and stable peace" and the establishment of "the sea" (of Marmara) as the frontier between the two powers.[110]

A totally new international order was in the making in the eastern Mediterranean, an order marked by extreme territorial fragmentation and shifting alliances that ran across religious boundaries and political rivalries. After years of peregrinations that included time spent in Lombardy as a hostage, the fugitive ex-emperor Alexios III Angelos moved to the court of the Seljuk sultan Kaykhusraw, whom he had once baptized and adopted in Constantinople, and convinced the Latin emperor Henry to join an anti-Nicaean coalition. In the early summer of 1211, a bloody battle between the Seljuk sultan and the Nicaean emperor was fought at Antioch on the Maeander, in which nearly all the 800 Latin mercenaries in Nicaean service fell. The sultan himself was killed.[111] Alexios III Angelos was captured and imprisoned in the monastery of Hyakinthos in Nicaea, where he ended his days. Newsletters announcing the elder Theodore's victory were disseminated throughout the former Byzantine provinces, urging the population to assist him in the struggle against "the Latin dogs."[112] Soon, however, his fortunes turned. The Latin emperor Henry landed at Pegai and crushed the weakened Nicaean army in a battle fought on October 15, 1211, on the banks of the Rhyndakos River. Henry seized Nymphaion and Pergamon, from where on January 13, 1212, he reported sweeping victories in a circular letter to the courts in western Europe. His letter ended on a note of confidence: "From this day onward (October 15, 1211), Laskaris has fully been deprived of troops . . . All the population as far as the frontier with Turkey has submitted to our empire, except for some fortresses that we strongly believe we shall compel next summer to surrender with God's help."[113]

The peace treaty that Theodore concluded with Henry sometime between 1212 and 1214 recognized the Latins as masters of a large portion of western Asia Minor. They controlled the Troad region and many towns and fortresses, such as Atramyttion, Achyraous, Lentiana (near Tophisar), Poimanenon, and Pegai. The newly drawn frontier drove a wedge into the Nicaean state and impeded communications between its northern and southern parts. One of the border points, Kalamos, which lay on the main road between Nicaea and Nymphaion, was left an uninhabited no-man's land. The Latins held Achyraous, farther north on the same arterial route.[114] The swift success of their invasion demonstrated to the elder Theodore the importance of diplomacy and the continual need for improving defensive fortifications. Inscriptions on the city walls of Nicaea, Prousa, and Pontic Herakleia attest to a flurry of building activity, praising the emperor as a "tower maker." The construction and maintenance of fortresses was to become a systematically pursued policy, as both archaeological evidence and documents show. The emperors charged local governors to settle population in fortresses and allocate grants of agricultural lands in their vicinity.[115]

One Big Family

By 1214 the elder Theodore was enmeshed in a web of diplomatic dealings with the Latin emperor of Constantinople, the Armenian king of Cilicia, the Seljuk sultan, the tsar of Bulgaria, and the ruler of Epiros. The question of the succession continually preoccupied him. At different times he designated a son, disinherited another son, and designated a son-in-law as his heir.

The birth of his three daughters, Irene, Maria, and Eudokia, in Constantinople was followed by that of two sons, Nicholas and John, in Asia Minor. The elder son, Nicholas, had been proclaimed emperor by his sixth birthday. He is called "an emperor and heir" in a document issued between 1208 and 1210.[116] However, by 1213 the empress Anna had died, and nothing more is heard of the two sons, who also seem to have passed away. In the late 1213 or 1214 the elder Theodore married Philippa, a niece of the ruler of Cilician Armenia, Leo I (1187–1219), but he repudiated her for an unknown reason after she had given birth to a son. The son himself was disinherited.[117] Later in his reign, the elder Theodore remarried for a third time in an attempt to take advantage of a vacancy on the throne of Latin Constantinople. The emperor Henry died in 1216, and in the following year his successor, Peter of Courtenay (husband of Henry's sister Yolanda), was killed in Albania during his journey to Constantinople after his coronation in Rome on April 9, 1217. Later in 1217, Peter's wife Yolanda gave birth in the purple-decorated room (*porphyra*) of the Great Palace of Constantinople to Baldwin, the future Baldwin II of Constantinople (r. 1240–61). An elder son of Peter and Yolanda, Robert of Courtenay, was selected as the next emperor, but he did not arrive in Constantinople until March 1221. In the meantime, before September 1219, the elder Theodore sought to acquire rights to Constantinople by diplomatic means and married Maria, a daughter of Peter and Yolanda.[118] Although the attempt failed, it shows how much he had come to rely on dynastic marriage policy.

The marriages of his three daughters were connected with foreign alliances and succession politics. In 1218 the Hungarian king Andrew II (r. 1205–35) was returning overland from the Fifth Crusade and made stops in Cilician Armenia and the empire of Nicaea, where he arranged for the marriage of his firstborn son, Béla, the future King Béla IV of Hungary (r. 1235–70), to the emperor's second daughter, Maria.[119] When Robert of Courtenay at last came to Constantinople to reign as the Latin emperor (1221–27), Theodore offered him the hand of his youngest daughter, Eudokia. This marriage, vigorously opposed by the patriarch, fell through because of the death of the Nicaean emperor in the autumn of 1221.[120] The eldest daughter, Irene, was married to a certain Andronikos Palaiologos, a man different from the *megas domestikos* of the same name. Designated as a despot, her husband served as a general during the Latin invasion in 1211–12 and died soon thereafter without fathering children.[121] The widowed Irene seems then to have been given in marriage to Constantine Doukas Palaiologos, whose relation to other members of the Palaiologos family is not known. The metropolitan bishop of Ephesos celebrated the wedding in Nicaea in February 1216.[122] Nothing more is heard of Constantine or of any offspring from this marriage. It is clear, however, that members of the Palaiologos family continued to be deemed suitable candidates for imperial office after 1204.

Toward the end of his reign, the emperor selected as Irene's next husband the *protovestiarites* John Doukas Vatatzes, known simply as John Vatatzes, who was the head of his guard regiment of the *vesitaritai* – the position the elder Theodore held at the beginning of his career.[123] It was out of the union of Irene and John Vatatzes that the younger Theodore Laskaris was born. Contemporaries kept silent about the nomination of John Vatatzes as the heir and treated his rights to the succession with conspicuous defensiveness. Orators wrote that he received the imperial office "as a just inheritance" from his father-in-law, but also asserted that he was no usurper and that his accession resembled the Old Testament story of the shepherd David who dethroned Saul.[124] After marrying his third wife, the Latin princess Maria of Courtenay, the elder Theodore may well have left the question of the succession open in case another son was born. John Vatatzes' imperial elevation did not go unchallenged, as we will soon see.

Who was John Vatatzes? The history of the Vatatzes family is better known than that of the Laskaris. The putative father of John Vatatzes – namely, Basil Vatatzes – is said to have come from an "undistinguished family," but this comment by Choniates should be interpreted as a comparison between his status and that of the aristocracy that descended from the Komnenoi and the Doukai.[125] After all, the same historian described Constantine Angelos from Philadelphia, from whom the Angeloi emperors originated, as lacking illustrious origin before he married a daughter of the emperor Alexios I Komnenos.[126] The Vatatzes family had gained prominence in the early eleventh century and had its power and wealth concentrated in Thrace. Their endowments of almshouses, guesthouses, and monasteries in the city of Adrianople left a lasting memory.[127] The provincial family of the Vatatzes, just like the Laskaris and Angelos families, benefited from marriages into the imperial Komnenian dynasty and clawed their way into the governing elite. The general Theodore Vatatzes was deemed worthy of marrying a daughter of the emperor John II Komnenos.[128]

John Vatatzes was born in 1192 in Didymoteichon in Thrace.[129] It is unknown how much time he spent in Constantinople in his childhood, but it is not unlikely that he knew the imperial metropolis firsthand. No contemporary source mentions his parents. Of the three hypotheses that have been raised, the most plausible is that he was the son of Basil Vatatzes, a general and high-ranking provincial official in Asia Minor active in the late 1180s and early 1190s.[130] In August 1189 Basil Vatatzes was the governor (*doux*) of the theme of Mylassa and Melanoudion. He was married to a paternal first cousin of the emperor Isaac II Angelos, and styled himself as an in-law (*gambros*) of the emperor in a document.[131] His wife was a great-granddaughter of the emperor Alexios I Komnenos through the Angelos line (see Table 1).[132] John Vatatzes, his son, would assume the double surname "Doukas Vatatzes" and would boast in a letter to the pope about his descent – a matrilineal one – from the families of Doukas and Komnenos.[133] The younger Theodore Laskaris imitated his father in using the surname Doukas alongside that of Laskaris in his official signature and thus linked himself with the ruling dynasty of the past.[134] In the early 1190s, Basil Vatatzes served as *domestikos* of the East, that is, commander of the mobile armies in Asia Minor. In this capacity he forced the rebel Mangaphas to abandon his stronghold of Philadelphia. Subsequently Basil Vatatzes was posted in the Balkans as *domestikos* of the West and was killed in 1194 in a battle fought in Thrace against the Bulgarians.[135] John Vatatzes' date of birth in 1192 fits with Basil's Thracian assignment and accounts for the fact that he was the youngest brother in his family.[136]

The parents of the younger Theodore Laskaris were related through their common descent from Alexios I Komnenos. John Vatatzes was the uncle of his wife Irene, who was about nine years his junior, and was a second cousin of his wife's mother Anna (see Table 1). This marriage was consanguineous to the seventh degree and prohibited by church legislation, but was tolerated in the late eleventh and the twelfth centuries in cases when the husband and wife belonged to the ruling Doukas and Komnenos families. Indeed, elite marriages with the same degree of incestuous relationship continued to be practiced in the empire of Nicaea, whose rulers claimed a customary right to break the laws on marriage for reasons of state.[137] Politics of the fragmented Byzantine world looked to the younger Theodore Laskaris like a family affair: one extended family, cooperative as well as quarrelsome. The uppermost layer of the governing elite in the Nicaean state consisted of families ennobled by twelfth-century royal blood flowing in their veins. A man of Komnenian extraction among the imperial officials was addressed as "a most noble Komnenos and *oikeios*" of the emperor (literally, a member of the emperor's household) in contrast to other grandees (*archontes*) who lacked this illustrious pedigree.[138] The heads of the three successor states – Nicaea, Trebizond, and Epiros – were related. Michael Komnenos Doukas of Epiros and his half-brother and successor, Theodore Komnenos Doukas (Theodore of Epiros), were uncles of John Vatatzes (see Table 1). Theodore of Epiros was a key political player. He resided initially in Asia Minor, where he assisted the elder Theodore Laskaris in reestablishing the imperial government and swore an oath of allegiance to him.[139] But when he took over the expanding lordship in Epiros after the assassination of his half-brother in 1215, he adopted highly confrontational policies toward Nicaea. The younger Theodore Laskaris would face a powerful aristocracy of twelfth-century descent driven in its social behavior by a sense of entitlement to court titles and landholding. This reality was born in the aftermath of 1204, when former generals and rebels became stateless lords and were in a strong position to negotiate their reincorporation into the revived imperial state.

Table 1 *One big family: The relatives and imperial ancestors of Theodore Laskaris*

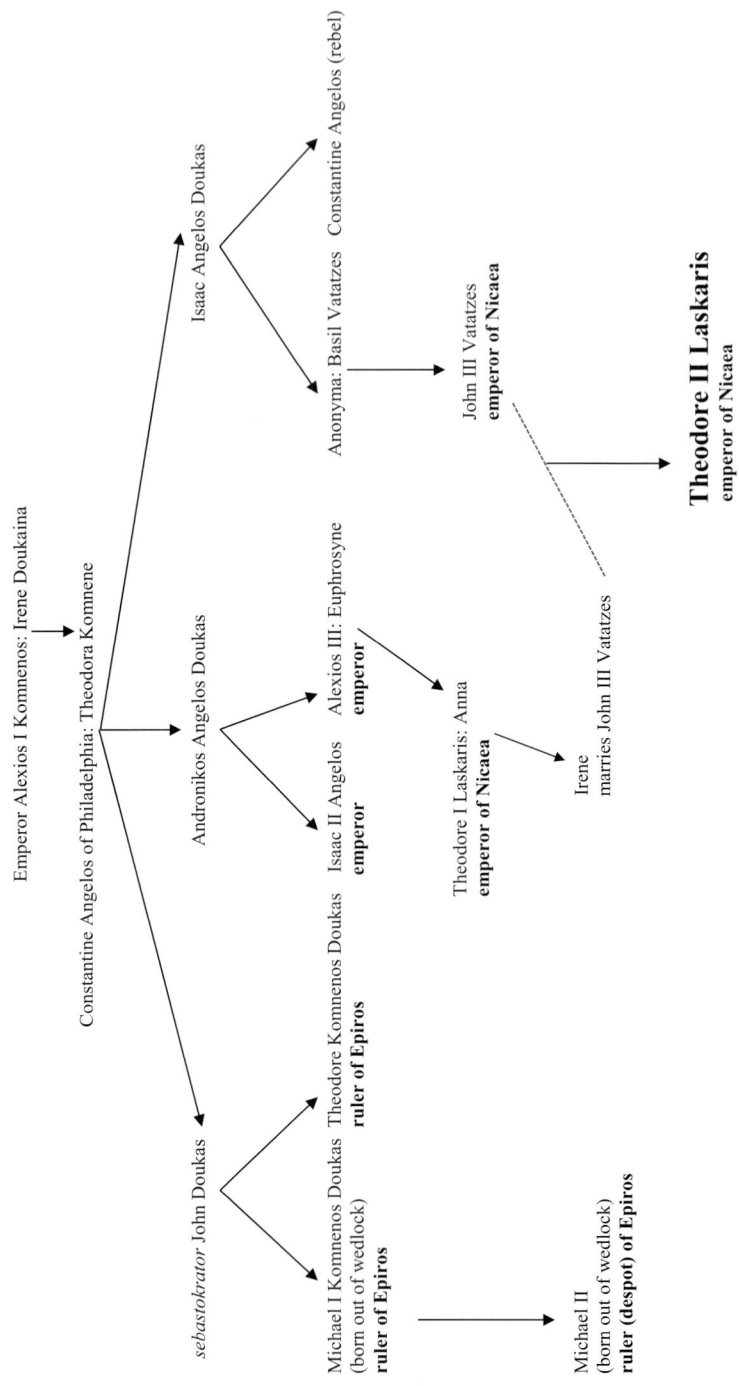

Emperor Alexios I Komnenos: Irene Doukaina

Constantine Angelos of Philadelphia: Theodora Komnene

Isaac Angelos Doukas

Constantine Angelos (rebel)

Anonyma: Basil Vatatzes

John III Vatatzes
emperor of Nicaea

sebastokrator John Doukas

Andronikos Angelos Doukas

Alexios III: Euphrosyne
emperor

Isaac II Angelos
emperor

Theodore I Laskaris: Anna
emperor of Nicaea

Irene
marries John III Vatatzes

Michael I Komnenos Doukas
(born out of wedlock)
ruler of Epiros

Theodore Komnenos Doukas
ruler of Epiros

Michael II
(born out of wedlock)
ruler (despot) of Epiros

Theodore II Laskaris
emperor of Nicaea

2 | "The Holy Land, My Mother Anatolia"

The younger Theodore Laskaris grew up in the cities, coastal plains, and mountainous river valleys of western Asia Minor, a most unusual spatial setting for the life of a Byzantine prince and emperor. Only at the age of thirty-two (1255) is he first attested to have crossed the boundary between Asia and Europe and set foot in the Balkans. His life was embedded in the physical and human geography of Asia Minor. His native land seeped into his sense of identity and entered his psyche. He was attached to it and gave it endearing names, such as "beloved ground," "fatherland (*patris*)," and "the holy land, my mother Anatolia."[1] In what ways did he perceive and imagine his native land? What was Byzantine Asia Minor like in the first half of the thirteenth century?

Asia Minor had been Byzantium's heartland since the foundation of Constantine's Christian Roman empire – embattled but never lost during the Persian and Arab invasions of the seventh century, and the home of powerful armies and the foremost aristocratic families that rose to prominence from the ninth century onward. By 1250 the section of Asia Minor controlled by the empire of Nicaea consisted of about one-third of the peninsula (see Maps 1 and 3). The largest part lay under the authority, whether real or nominal, of the Seljuk sultanate of Rum, with which Nicaea had an extensive land frontier. Other areas of Asia Minor belonged to lesser powers. After the late 1220s, the few remaining territories of the Latin empire were restricted to a section of Bithynia near Constantinople. The Pontos area along the Black Sea and the region of Cilicia in southeastern Asia Minor were controlled, respectively, by the empire of Trebizond and the kingdom of Armenia. The Seljuk Turks cut off the land connection between Nicaea and Trebizond in 1214, when they wrested the fortress of Sinope on the Black Sea from the state of Trebizond. In the same fateful year the elder Theodore captured (possibly for the second time) the towns of Pontic Herakleia and Amastris on the Black Sea coast from Trebizond.[2] The kingdom of Cilician Armenia, lying beyond the sultanate of Rum, also lacked a contiguous frontier with Nicaea. Located not too far away, Trebizond and Cilician Armenia were familiar to Theodore through the reports of visitors, ambassadors, and travelers. His knowledge is

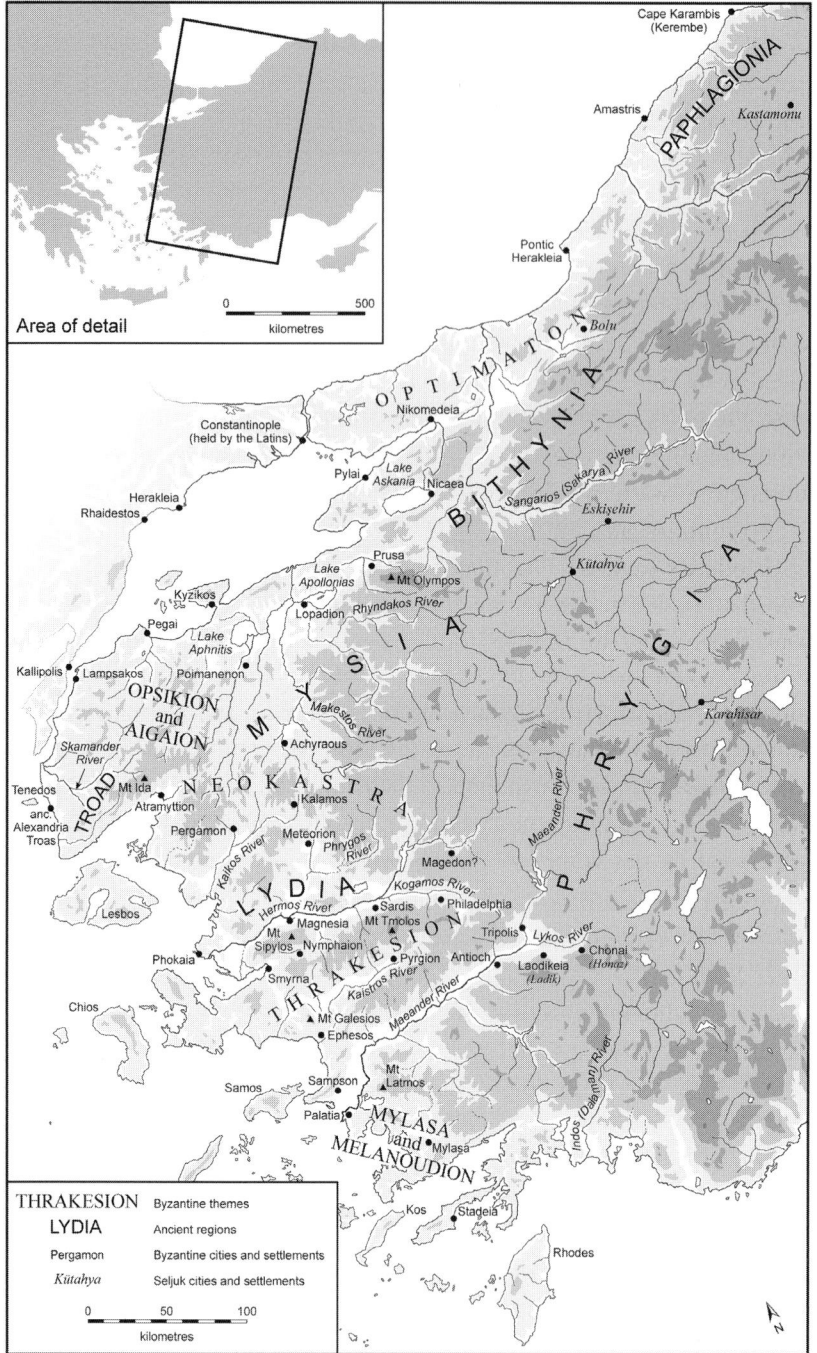

Map 1 Western Asia Minor in the lifetime of Theodore Laskaris

reflected, for example, in his passing comment that ten or more days were needed for someone to journey across Asia Minor from Trebizond on the Black Sea to Tarsus in the kingdom of Cilician Armenia on the Mediterranean coast.[3] Theodore called his native land Anatolia (*Anatole* in Greek). The word signified first and foremost *east*, but had also other meanings: the land mass to the east of Constantinople, namely Asia Minor; the entire continent of Asia; and the East generally.[4] The empire of Nicaea was identified as Anatolian both by its inhabitants and by outsiders. Venetian documents of the early thirteenth century called people from the empire of Nicaea *anatolici*, and a metropolitan bishop of Athens greeted the elder Theodore as the "Emperor of *Anatole*."[5] The younger Theodore considered himself to be a proud resident of Anatolia and described the Balkans as the West: crossing the Hellespont (the Dardanelles) into Europe meant entering the "western fields," namely, the lowlands of Thrace.[6]

Two contrary, almost incompatible discourses about Anatolia resonated in Theodore's ears from his childhood onward. One was the rhetoric of exile that he heard from refugees, a rhetoric bursting with feelings of displacement and longing for return to Constantinople. Religious and secular oratory – and even an inscription on a defensive tower constructed during the reign of the elder Theodore (Fig. 6) – modeled Nicaea after Babylon, the place of exile of the Jews after the fall of Jerusalem.[7] Images of exile are notably rare and muted in Theodore's writings. He seems, for instance, to be alluding to the Babylonian captivity of his political community when he presents himself as weeping "by the rivers of Babylon" (Psalm 136:1) in a personal polemic against enemies.[8] To be sure, Constantinople was hardly forgotten either by him or by individuals close to him. His father John Vatatzes kept trying to regain the "queen of cities" through military and diplomatic means. His iron resolve to fight for Constantinople was articulated clearly in his letter to the Roman pope dating to 1237. The "laws of nature, the traditions of the fatherland, the graves of the ancestors, and the holy and divine churches in the Constantinople" justified his mission of reconquest.[9] Vatatzes provided generous maintenance to religious buildings in or around the Latin-held city. He endowed Constantinopolitan churches, such as the Blachernae and the earthquake-damaged Holy Apostles, and nearby monasteries, such as Rouphinianai near Chalcedon and St. Michael in Anaplous on the Bosporus. Patriarchs residing in Nicaea addressed letters of pastoral care to the orthodox Constantinopolitans living under Latin rule.[10] In a religious oration Theodore recalled how the Virgin had once miraculously assisted the city during the naval attack carried out by the Rus in 860. Revealingly, he switched to the present tense, writing that the Mother of God is "the guardian" of "the pious people (of Constantinople)." A note of hope for renewed divine protection of Constantinople can perhaps be read between the lines.[11]

A different kind of public discourse, opposite in spirit and closer to Theodore's heart, presented Anatolia as paradise rediscovered. The East had special significance in the holy scriptures. The Garden of Eden lay in the East, according to the Book of Genesis (2:8–14). The Resurrection was expected to come from the East – "the rising sun (*anatole*) from on high" in the prophecy of Zacharias (Luke 1:78). Byzantine church buildings and private prayers were directed toward the east. A thirteenth-century author explained that "in this way we look towards Paradise and are reminded of our former native land."[12] The sacredness of the East nourished Anatolian patriotism. The move to Asia Minor was compared rhetorically to a homecoming to God's promised land and the terrestrial paradise. A few years after 1204, the former deacon of the church of St. Sophia, Nicholas Mesarites, described his arrival at the port of Pylai on the Asiatic shore of the Sea of Marmara as an entry into God's promised land, "our paradise planted in the East (*kat' anatolas*)," where he could practice religion freely.[13] "I know," a patriarch of Constantinople residing in Nicaea declared proudly in a sermon, "that I am a citizen of paradise," humankind's "ancient fatherland." He contrasted the paradisiacal East with the dark land of Hades, the Byzantine word for hell, lying in the West. It was to the West that God had exiled the sinful humans after the fall of Adam and Eve. In this interpretation, which the patriarch conveyed to the Constantinopolitans, the Latin-held former imperial capital was relegated to being the "second" paradise, while Anatolia was Eden rediscovered.[14] In his writings Theodore Laskaris exploited the East's sacred associations and the light-versus-darkness antithesis of the East and the West.[15] He reminded Pope Alexander IV (1254–61) in a letter that Christ, "the true sun," came from the East, which was both the cradle of Christianity and his own homeland. In another work he remarked that God resided in the East.[16] These powerful images are implicit in his expression "the holy land, my mother Anatolia."

The physical features of Asia Minor were closely tied to its political geography in the early thirteenth century. Its western part, with fertile coastal plains and river valleys, contrasts to the rest of Asia Minor, which consists of an elevated plateau marked by dry climate and cold winters.[17] Nomadic Turkmen from the Asian steppes settled on the plateau and its pastures during the late eleventh century in the wake of the Battle of Manzikert (1071) and proceeded to conquer most of Asia Minor. The restoration of Byzantine authority was most successful along the Anatolian littoral and in western Anatolia. Agriculture flourished in the region of Bithynia, where the city of Nicaea lay, and especially in the valleys of the Hermos (Gediz), Kaistros (Küçük Menderes), and Maeander (Büyük Menderes) rivers in the southern part of the empire of Nicaea. No city – not even Nicaea itself – lay far from agricultural land. A twelfth-century Byzantine traveler saw "seas of fertile fields" after leaving Nicaea on his way to Konia and the Holy Land.[18] Theodore speaks of a "multitude of crops cultivated all around and abundantly inside the city."[19] "Good and fertile land" was for him a metaphor as well as an economic reality.[20] He lived close to the agrarian countryside and was well informed about farming practices. The most cultivated crops were cereals, fruits, grapes, pulses, and olives. The leaves of olive trees in coastal areas, he observed, were more numerous than grains of sand.[21]

Theodore was captivated by the diversity of the natural landscapes. Some of his contemporaries, he wrote to his secretary Joseph Mesopotamites, admired the fecund soil of Asia Minor, its fruit-bearing trees, and the abundance of vineyards. For this reason, "the Poet" (namely, Homer) had once called the valley of the Kaistros River "a blooming field." Other contemporaries, he continued, celebrated different features of Anatolia: its thick mountain forests, its rivers and streams, the proximity of the sea, and its lush greenery.[22] Mountains were constantly in Theodore's view: Sipylos (Spil Dağı), Tmolos (Bozdağ), Latros (Beşparmak Dağı), Ida (Kaz Dağı), and Bithynian Olympus (Uludağ near Prousa), to name just a few (see Map 1). Theodore mentions climbing mountains while hunting and frequently invokes the mountain as a metaphor, speaking of "mountains of sorrow," a "mountain of prayers," "mountains of arrogance," and "impassable Bulgarian mountains of folly."[23] He never uses the mountain as a synonym for the frontier with the Turks, as the historian Pachymeres does.[24] The mountains as well as the plains were suitable for raising livestock, an important economic pursuit of the peasantry. Contemporary and later historians note the extensive crown lands that served as agricultural estates and as animal farms, breeding horses, sheep, cows, camels, pigs, and chickens.[25] In 1247 a monastery near Philadelphia possessed pastures with sheep, cows, buffaloes, and pigs.[26] "The One who grows pasturage for the flocks" is among Theodore's designations of God in *On the Divine Names*.[27] He was never far from the sea and visited a number of locations along the Aegean Sea and on the Asiatic side of the Hellespont. Occasionally, in a way traditional for Byzantine authors, he resorted to powerful sea metaphors, such as "the many-waved sea of the lives of mortals" and "the surging wave" of sins and worldly concern.[28] The imperial fleet was revived soon after 1204, and Smyrna on the Aegean and the area of Holkos near Lampsakos on the Hellespont served as its bases of operation. The capacities of the fleet are witnessed by John Vatatzes' naval expeditions in support of anti-Venetian rebels in Crete and in his offer in April 1234 to transport the visiting Latin friars back to Apulia.[29]

Theodore speaks of four distinct seasons in western Asia Minor, which ranged from cold winters to hot summers. He structured one of his philosophical works, *Representation of the World, or Life* (the third book of his *Explanation of the World*), around the change of the seasons – using them as an example of variety in the world and in human life. The winters were harsh and marked by heavy precipitation and snow. Once the spring came, he observed with delight how sunlight became stronger and natural aromas filled the air. Green became the dominant color as vegetation grew and foliage covered the trees. He makes a rhetorical comparison between the company of a charming courtier and the exhilarating arrival of the spring after a disheartening and gloomy winter.[30] Tax collection and preparations for war took place in springtime, whereas summer was the season for the harvest, military campaigns, trade, and embassies. Leading the troops in the scorching heat of summer made him dream of drinking ice-cold spring water. Autumn was a season when his subjects prepared for the winter by storing grain and olive oil.[31]

Cities and Regions

The historical trajectory of the cities of the empire of Nicaea reflected the overall trends of medieval urbanism in Asia Minor. The seventh century had seen the survival, but also the profound transformation and even disappearance of renowned ancient poleis. Nicaea itself was a Hellenistic foundation named after the wife of the Macedonian king Lysimachus and had flourished in the Roman period. It was famous in medieval Christendom as the venue of the First Ecumenical Council in 325 convened by the emperor Constantine I. Nicaea was also loaded with symbolism in another way. The name derived from the root of the Greek word for "victory" (*nike*): Theodore engaged in wordplays that represented Nicaea as the city of victory.[32] For him, Nicaea was "the queen of cities" and "the city of cities, the queen of queens, ruler of rulers," mirroring the common description of Constantinople as the "queen of cities."[33]

By the thirteenth century, Nicaea had survived foreign invasions and natural disasters, such as a destructive earthquake that hit the city in 1065. In the late eleventh century, the warrior bands of the Seljuk Turks swept into Asia Minor. Nicaea fell in 1081 into the hands of Sultan Süleyman from a side branch of the family of the Grand Seljuks, the conquerors of Baghdad (1055), and became his main residence. In 1097 Alexios I - Komnenos recovered the city peacefully after a dramatic siege by the army of the First Crusade (1096–99) and regained control over much of western Asia Minor in the following years. In the meantime, a new polity, the sultanate of Rum, arose under Süleyman's son Kılıç Arslān I (r. 1092–1107) centered on Konya (Ikonion) in the central Anatolian plateau.[34] The Byzantine reconquest in the twelfth century was accompanied by the systematic construction and enlargement of defensive fortifications, including those of Nicaea, which continued to be improved after 1204.[35] Nicaea's twelfth-century urban defenses featured battlements, towers, and a moat. The fortifications were the city's most distinctive feature.[36] A lakeside gate allowed the inhabitants of the city to receive supplies during times of siege and flee by boat. In 1097 the besieged Turks were fully isolated only when Byzantine ships were transported overland for 10 miles (16 kilometers) from Kios (Gemza) on the Sea of Marmara and entered Lake Askania. The fish and crayfish in the lake were considered to be a delicacy and were reputed to relieve fevers and coughs.[37]

The elder Theodore further strengthened Nicaea's walls. Dedicatory inscriptions on towers attest to additions and repairs carried out during his reign.[38] His successor, John Vatatzes, constructed an outer circuit of walls, and the city's defenses thus came to resemble those of Constantinople: a triple system with inner walls, a moat, and outer walls.[39] In an encomium on the city Theodore Laskaris lauded its fortifications, which he likened to an "unbreakable rock," and spoke of splendid homes and churches, aqueducts supplying water to every house, and fine vineyards and groves within and outside the walls.[40] The demography and urban landscape of Nicaea changed after 1204. Refugees from Constantinople streamed into the city, and its population swelled. A cemetery for strangers is attested in the area of Agalmates, around 2 miles (just over 3 kilometers) from the city.[41] Nicaea's inhabitable space (understood here as that enclosed by the city walls) was about nine times smaller than that of Constantinople, and overcrowding understandably became a problem. The historian Choniates complained about his living conditions, and decades later Theodore mentioned newcomers to Nicaea who were "without a shelter and roof."[42] New buildings were constructed, and old ones acquired different functions. Archaeologists are yet to identify the imperial palace.[43] John Vatatzes founded a monastery dedicated to St. Anthony in the city. His son Theodore renovated the church of St. Tryphon, an early Christian saint reputed to have been martyred in Nicaea. Aristocratic families, such as the Tornikes, were patrons of ecclesiastical buildings.[44]

The patriarchate in exile and its administration were accommodated in preexisting churches. In 1209 the urban monastery of Hyakinthos and its main church dedicated to the Dormition of the Virgin functioned as the patriarchal cathedral (Fig. 7).[45] The captive emperor Alexios III Angelos, his daughter Anna, and the elder Theodore himself were buried in the monastery. The seat of the patriarchate may have been transferred to the church of St. Sophia, the episcopal cathedral, during the reign of John Vatatzes (Fig. 8).[46] Alternatively, the church of the Holy Fathers of the First Ecumenical Council, which has not survived – a domed rotunda where the patriarchal synod occasionally met – may have become the patriarchal headquarters.[47] In 1223 the new patriarch, Germanos II, delivered his inaugural sermon in the church of the Holy Fathers.[48] According to medieval legend, the First Ecumenical Council had convened in this church, which was part of a large monastery and attracted visitors and pilgrims from throughout the Christian world. Four Franciscan and Dominican friars who came in 1234 for a disputation initially held in Nicaea prayed there and were impressed by the depictions of the Holy Fathers.[49]

Nicaea was not a fixed capital like Constantinople and the emperors in exile were continually on the move. At least five cities in Anatolia – Nicaea, Nymphaion, Magnesia, Smyrna, and Philadelphia – had royal residences. With the prominent exception of Nymphaion, these palaces are known so far solely from textual sources.[50] Theodore speaks revealingly of "residences (*oikoi*) of the emperor." He also talks about "the palace" in the singular without, unfortunately, specifying the location he had in mind.[51] The patriarchal synod followed the traveling emperor and his court, and held sessions in Nicaea, Nymphaion, and Magnesia.[52] Royal itinerancy was seasonal. The favorite summer and winter residences of the imperial family were, respectively, Nicaea and Nymphaion. John Vatatzes is reported to have "had the habit" of spending the winter in Nymphaion, which had a milder climate than Nicaea. His custom was to leave Nymphaion at the end of the winter and pitch the royal tents in the nearby plain of Klyzomene, identified as the valley of the Kryos River (Nif Çayı), a tributary to the Hermos. The imperial horses regained strength after the long winter by grazing in the lush pastures.[53]

Nymphaion (Kemalpaşa) is located in the immediate vicinity of Mount Nif about 180 miles (290 kilometers) southwest of Nicaea and 15 miles (25 kilometers) east of the coastal town of Smyrna.[54] In letters Theodore mentions Nymphaion as a place of residence and destination of travel almost as frequently as Nicaea.[55] Like Nicaea, Nymphaion had an abundance of drinkable water. Its very name means a "fountain." A fortified acropolis surrounded with two rings of walls towered over the lower town, where the palace of the emperors was located. The surviving remains of the royal residence consist of a three-story, single-block building 84 feet 6 inches (25.75 meters) long and 37 feet 9 inches (11.5 meters) wide (Fig. 9).[56] A bath complex has been identified on the ground level. This aspect of palace life, or life in this palace in particular, makes understandable Theodore's enthusiasm about bath-construction in Anatolian cities and his penchant for bathing metaphors.[57] The palace probably had other adjacent structures, such as pavilions and gardens, resembling those found in contemporary Seljuk palaces.[58] Comparing its dimensions with those of other royal residences outside of the empire of Nicaea is revealing. The foundations of the Seljuk palace in Kubadabad constructed for ʿAlāʾ al-Dīn Kayqubād I (r. 1219–37) are more than twice as large (165 by 98 feet/50 by 30 meters). The main building of the thirteenth-century palace of the Bulgarian kings in Turnovo (95 by 55 feet/29 by 17 meters) and that of the fifteenth-century palace of the despots in Mystras (121 by 54 feet/37 by 16.5 meters) also occupy more space.[59] The relatively small size of the palace in Nymphaion is symptomatic of the downsizing of the court in exile. Another important building in Nymphaion, one known solely from documentary evidence, was an urban monastery dedicated to "the holy great martyrs Theodore," Theodore Stratelates and Theodore Tyron, the namesakes of two Nicaean emperors. The monastery must have been a large enough structure, because it accommodated the patriarch and his synod in March 1256.[60]

Another imperial residence lay in Magnesia (Manisa), a city about 14 miles (22 kilometers) north of Nymphaion along the valley of the Hermos River at the foot of Mount Sipylos (Fig. 10). Protected by two circuits of fortified walls, Magnesia was an international center of commerce and the location of the royal treasury and mint. Theodore calls the city "the golden Magnesia" and spent extended periods of time there in the later years of his life.[61] The importance of the city is echoed in the statement of a Byzantine historian who wrote two centuries later that John Vatatzes had once "ruled in Magnesia."[62] Magnesia would indeed continue to serve as a residence of the Ottoman sultans. On Mount Sipylos, in the close vicinity of

Magnesia, Vatatzes built and endowed the imperial Sosandra monastery dedicated to the Virgin Gorgoepekoos ("the One Quick to Listen"), which he intended to use as a royal burial shrine. Its location has been identified at the Şehzāde Plateau (Sultān Yaylasi) southwest of Magnesia.[63]

Smyrna (Izmir) on the Aegean coast was a flourishing city. John Vatatzes strengthened the fortifications on Mount Pagus, the ancient acropolis of Smyrna, and constructed a new fortress, the *neon kastron,* next to the imperial navy yard. The palace was built at the natural springs of Periklystra. The toponym refers to abundance of water, which seems to have been the reason why this location was chosen as a royal residence.[64] The Nicaean emperors often paid visits to the well-fortified frontier town of Philadelphia (Alaşehir) situated about 60 miles (100 kilometers) eastward from Magnesia along the valley of the Kogamos River, a tributary of the Hermos, close to the Seljuk frontier. Philadelphia was famous for its able soldiers and in particular its archers.[65] The twelfth-century Angelos dynasty descended from Constantine Angelos of Philadelphia and Theodore had genealogical connections to the city, because both of his grandmothers belonged to the Angelos family.[66]

Theodore frequently traveled the length of the main road between Nicaea and Nymphaion, a distance of about 180 miles (290 kilometers) as the crow flies. On leaving Nicaea (see Map 1), he would have traveled westward toward Prousa (Bursa) on the slopes of Bithynian Olympus. Famous for its hot springs and baths, Prousa had been visited by emperors in the past, and its fortifications had been strengthened by the elder Theodore.[67] The road continued farther west to Lopadion (Ulubat) on the shores of Lake Apollonias (Apolyont), which was heavily fortified in the twelfth century. It then curved south along the Makestos River (Simav Çayı) and followed it as far as the fortress of Achyraous (south of Balıkesir). The journey continued south, passing through Kalamos (Gelembe) and by the fortress of Meteorion (Gördük Kale near Selcikli).[68] From here the road led toward Magnesia on the plain of the Hermos River and onward around Mount Sipylos toward Nymphaion. Traveling from Nicaea to Nymphaion was a routine matter, even though it was risky for those without an escort, as the report of the travels of the four above-mentioned friars demonstrates. They left Nymphaion for Kalamos on May 6, 1234, in the company of local guides and covered the distance of about 55 miles (90 kilometers) in two days. A traveler well supplied with horses and provisions would therefore have needed six or seven days to reach Nicaea from Nymphaion. In Kalamos, the friars quarreled with the patriarchal envoys and left, on foot and without guides, in the hope of reaching "the sea of Constantinople" (the Sea of Marmara) in six days.[69] However, after

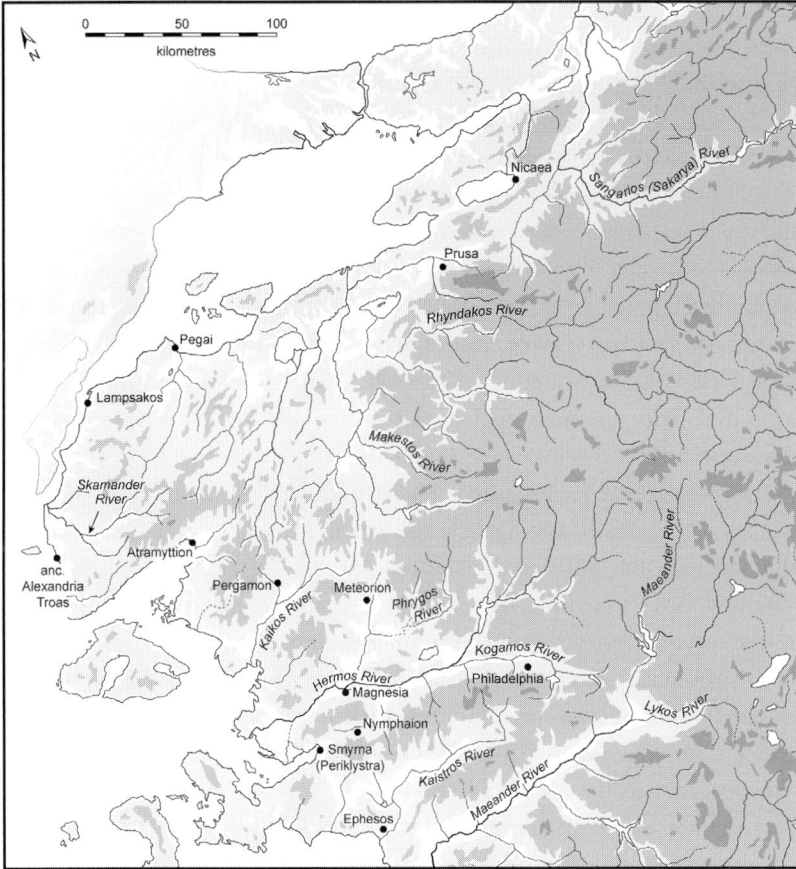

Map 2 Locations in which Theodore Laskaris is attested to have been before 1254

walking only 6 or 7 miles (10–11 kilometers) they were overtaken by the envoys, who told them that unaccompanied travel was hazardous because of the danger of being attacked by bandits. The envoys convinced them to accept the emperor's safe conduct.

Some cities and locations in Byzantine Asia Minor were more important for Theodore than others. The map of the places in which he is attested to have been (see Map 2) is based mainly on undated letters of the 1240s and early 1250s, so his movements cannot be traced over time in a systematic way. Nonetheless an overall pattern does emerge. His travels were concentrated in an area framed in the east by the Nicaea-Magnesia-Nymphaion corridor and in the west and north by the coasts of the Aegean Sea and the Sea of Marmara. This core area encompassed rich agricultural lands and included strategic centers of administration, communications, and trade. Theodore frequently visited Ephesos (Selçuk), south of Smyrna near the delta of the Kaistros River. A fortified hilltop town overlooking the remains of the once-flourishing antique city, thirteenth-century Ephesos seems to have retained its role as the main city of the theme of Thrakesion. Ephesos was famous for the church and relics of St. John the Theologian, whose feast day (May 8) was accompanied by a great trade fair.[70] Its role as a center of governance is reflected in the statement of an Armenian historian that the Nicaean emperor "rules in Ephesos."[71] Theodore mentions that it was the custom of the grandees or officials (*archontes*) of Ephesos to come to pay their respects to him in his capacity as junior coemperor.[72] His servants (*hyperetai*) passed through Ephesos, probably on official business.[73] He speaks of money changers, tavern owners, leatherworkers, fishermen, and butchers, which shows that the city was an important economic center.[74]

Theodore visited Pergamon (Bergama), a famous Hellenistic and Roman city south of the Troad, and wrote a moving description of the imposing ancient ruins in the lower part of the city, a description to which we will turn in the last chapter. Pergamon had nearly disappeared in the seventh century and grew into an important fortified settlement during the restoration of Byzantine control over the area in the twelfth century.[75] The Troad region, known also as the Scamander, rose in strategic importance in 1204 because of its closeness to the Hellespont. Theodore visited the remains of ancient Troy – not the famous Homeric Troy, which had lain buried since antiquity, but Alexandrian Troas, a Hellenistic city, whose ruins were still visible in the Middle Ages. He had his treasury deposited in the fortress of Astritzion in the Troad.[76] On the southern side of the Troad, at the foot of Mount Ida, lay the coastal city of Atramyttion (Edremit), to which Theodore referred by the Homeric name Thebe under Plakos.[77] In the early twelfth century Alexios I had restored and resettled Atramyttion after its destruction during the Turkish invasions. The twelfth-century Arab geographer al-Idrisi describes Atramyttion as a fortified settlement, and the crusaders found it "well supplied with corn, meat, and other provisions."[78] North of the Troad along the Hellespont lay Lampsakos (Lapseki), which faced Kallipolis, known as Gallipoli (Gelibolu), on the European side of the straits. Lampsakos was the preferred place for crossing by boat into the Balkans (Fig. 11).[79] Farther east along the Sea of Marmara was the fortress of Pegai (Karabiga), which had strategic importance as an assembly point of troops about to embark on campaign in the Balkans (Fig. 12). Merchants from Monemvasia in the Peloponnese were resettled in Pegai during John Vatatzes' reign after the Latin conquest of their native city.[80] Theodore visited Lampsakos and Pegai in order to welcome back his father and prepare himself to cross the Hellespont.

The pattern reflected on Map 2 does not mean that Theodore ignored other areas in Byzantine Asia Minor, such as Paphlagonia and the lower Maeander valley, although he appears to have been there less frequently. He speaks exceedingly rarely of territories east of Nicaea: the valley of the Sangarios River, Paphlagonia, and the Black Sea coast. His silence does not indicate lack of knowledge or interest. After 1214 the empire in exile controlled a narrow strip along the Black Sea that included Pontic Herakleia (Ereğli) and Amastris (Amasra). Soldiers from Paphlagonia formed an essential part of his army. In 1257, Theodore referred specifically to Cape Karambis (Kerembe) about 45 miles (75 kilometers) east of Amastris as the easternmost limit of the empire of Nicaea in the Black Sea area.[81] Curiously, he never mentions the valley of the lower Maeander, even though in 1257 he noted that the fortress on Tripolis along the upper course of the river marked the border with the Seljuks.[82] Near the alluvial estuary of the Maeander lay Sampson (ancient Priene), a city controlled by Sabbas Asidenos in the early thirteenth century before its incorporation into the empire of Nicaea. South of the estuary was Palatia (Miletos), which had long ceased to be a seaport due to sedimentation brought by the river. Theodore never referred to the settlement by its contemporary name, but he knew that the philosopher Thales, the "inventor of geometry," had been a Milesian and described the Milesians, presumably the inhabitants of the city in antiquity, as experts in naval warfare.[83] Further south, Stadeia (Datça) on the Knidian peninsula was a key port used for Nicaean naval operations. The nearby island of Rhodes marked for Theodore the limits of the empire of Nicaea in the Aegean area.[84]

The cities and fortified settlements were part of a tight administrative and ecclesiastical structure. The theme (*thema*) was the main unit of local governance, which had been remilitarized during the twelfth century in the wake of the reconquest of western Asia Minor from the Turks. Each theme was under the jurisdiction of a governor (*doux*), who was simultaneously the chief military and civil official. He headed a staff of tax collectors and assessors responsible for the management of smaller districts, known as *katepanikia*.[85] At least some of the Nicaean themes – including Thrakesion, the largest and most prosperous – grew out of smaller provincial districts, sometimes also called themes, in the late twelfth century. Ephesos, Smyrna, Nymphaion, and Philadelphia were all part of the Thrakesion theme.[86] The Maeander region was also under the jurisdiction of the governor (*doux*) of Thrakesion in 1213 and in the 1240s.[87]

Regrettably little is known about other themes on account of the sparsity of documentary evidence. To the south of the Maeander River lay the theme of Mylassa and Melanoudion.[88] To the north of Thrakesion was the theme of Neokastra, meaning "new fortresses," whose formation marked the consolidation of the Byzantine defenses against the Turks in western Asia Minor in the twelfth century. Neokastra included Atramyttion, Pergamon, and Chliara.[89] In the first half of the thirteenth century, Kalamos and possibly Meteorion further south were parts of Neokastra. The mountainous frontier area east of Meteorion, in the area of Magedon or Magidia (ancient Saittai), provided the army with skilled archers in the second half of the thirteenth century.[90] Scholars have debated whether Magnesia was under the jurisdiction of the theme of Neokastra or of Thrakesion.[91] North of Neokastra was the theme of Opsikion and Aigaion.[92] Another theme, Optimatoi, stretched to the north and east of Nicaea toward the Black Sea.[93] Remarkably, Theodore referred only once to a contemporary theme – Thrakesion – and preferred to identify regions in Anatolia by their ancient names: Bithynia, Mysia, mountainous Phrygia, and Lydia stretching along the Hermos and Maeander valleys. He spoke of himself residing "somewhere in Mysia," invited his correspondents to cross Mysia and Phrygia in order to see him in Bithynia's main town (Nicaea), and fondly used the classical proverb "apart are the boundaries of the Mysians and Phrygians," meaning things do not fit together.[94] His use of ancient geographical names feeds naturally into his interest in classical sites, an aspect of his thought discussed in the last chapter.

Bishoprics, both metropolitan and suffragan, were more numerous than themes. The move of the center of government to Asia Minor led to the elevation of certain bishoprics to metropolitan status: Philadelphia, Prousa, Pontic Herakleia, Achyraous, Antioch on the Maeander, Pegai, Pergamon and Lopadion became archbishoprics.[95] The bishops were important figures in the urban communities. They presided over ecclesiastical courts and funded charitable institutions through the income derived from ecclesiastical tax (kanonikon), notarial fees (nearly all notaries in the empire of Nicaea were clerics), and country estates.[96] Ephesos was a particularly large and wealthy see, whose metropolitan bishop (called also archbishop) held the exalted title of "exarch of all Asia." In 1229 John, the metropolitan of Ephesos, lists as his suffragans the bishops of urban centers, such as Atramyttion, Magnesia, Pyrgion, Priene, and Trallis.[97]

Ethnicity and the Frontier

The Nicaean state is traditionally considered to have been more ethnically and linguistically homogeneous – more Greek-speaking – than the twelfth-century Byzantine empire. This impression arises from the loss of Slav-inhabited territories in the Balkans, such as Bulgaria, which became an independent kingdom in 1185, and from the fall of Constantinople itself. The imperial metropolis was remembered as a melting pot – "a mixture of the seeds of the nations," wrote a patriarch of Constantinople residing in Nicaea.[98] Even so, Theodore encountered a mosaic of languages and peoples: Latins, Armenians, Jews, Cumans, and Turks. Individuals mentioned in his correspondence include a certain Tzys (a name of non-Greek origin) and a Cuman general who was baptized as Cleopas.[99] The royal household included foreigners. His wife was born in Bulgaria and his stepmother was a Latin.

Latin mercenaries already played a prominent role in the Nicaean army under the elder Theodore Laskaris.[100] The friars who came for a religious disputation in 1234 found to their surprise that Latins lived peacefully among the enemy. When praying in a church in Nicaea, they were joined by "Italians, French, and English."[101] The English were probably members of the axe-bearing Varangian Guard, who were known as "English Varangians." One of the responsibilities of the Varangians was to guard the imperial treasury, as they did in 1258 in the palace in Magnesia.[102] The Armenians formed a sizable community in western Anatolia. In the first half of the thirteenth century they are attested near Smyrna and in the Troad. Relations between the Greek-speaking orthodox majority and the Armenians were close, yet ridden with confessional tension leading back to the Fourth Ecumenical Council of Chalcedon (451). A thirteenth-century bishop from near Thessalonica viewed the non-Chalcedonian Armenians as "the other," listing them alongside Jews and Muslims, and recommended that they live in separate urban neighborhoods.[103] In 1205 many of the Armenians of the Troad, allegedly 20,000 in number, allied themselves with the invading crusaders. They followed the Latins on their retreat to Thrace and fell victim to revenge at the hands of the locals.[104]

Jews were another ethnic and religious minority. In the twelfth century Jewish communities are attested in cities in the Maeander valley, such as Chonai and Mastaura, and on the islands of Chios, Samos, and Rhodes along the Aegean coast of Asia Minor. There is epigraphic evidence of the presence of Jews in Nicaea after 1204. The dossier of letters of an anonymous bishop of a city identified as Pyrgion mentions Jews in his diocese in the 1250s; their occupation was dyeing fabrics, a traditional specialization of Byzantine Jewry. Most Jews resided in cities, although there were exceptions, such as the village of Bare near Smyrna in 1258.[105] There were efforts to convert the Jews during the reign of John Vatatzes. A eulogy of the emperor mentions preaching, gifts, and the alleviation of heavy "annual taxes" as enticements for the Jews to adopt the Christian religion.[106] Theodore writes that the Jews who had once been numerous were "now only a vestige of impiety" and praises the patriarchal officials Xiphilinos and Argyropoulos for preaching among the Hypsistarians, by whom he evidently meant the Jews. Notably, the Jewish fabric dyers mentioned by the anonymous bishop in the 1250s were converts to Christianity.[107]

Another ethnic group were the Turkic-speaking Cumans who migrated from the Black Sea steppe under Mongol pressure and crossed the Danube in about 1237. The nomads poured into eastern Thrace, part of which was under Nicaean control at the time. After subjugating them by force, John Vatatzes resorted to the traditional imperial policy of the transfer of population and settled the newly baptized Cumans in Thrace, Macedonia, and Asia Minor. His son Theodore saw various groups of Cumans whom he always designated as "Scythians": noblemen, soldiers, and slaves. Cumans lived in border areas along the Maeander valley and in Phrygia, the mountainous frontier region with the sultanate of Rum. There were Cuman peasants, too. A community near Smyrna had a reputation for heavy wine drinking.[108] A Cuman military commander by the name of Cleopas, who served Theodore in 1256, must have been a recent convert to Christianity, because he was named after Christ's disciple (Luke 24:13–27). The Cumans brought with them their own steppe culture. Those settled in Thrace are reported to have concluded a treaty with the Latin emperor by sacrificing a dog and drinking from a chalice full of wine and water mixed with drops of blood, both their own blood and that of their Latin partners.[109] The ancestral ritual of dog sacrifice was probably known to Theodore. He likened "my dearest Scythian," Cleopas, to a trusted speedy dog, and Akropolites compared the Cumans to faithful dogs who "bark against" the offenders of God.[110] The Turkic Cumans must be distinguished from the Turks who began to settle en masse in Asia Minor from the late eleventh century onward. Their presence can be inferred through personal names. A testament drawn up in 1247 mentions landowners with names of Arabic Islamic origin, such as Amourasanes and Amiras, in the region of Philadelphia in proximity to the Seljuk frontier.[111] Turks served in the Nicaean army and attained the rank of high officers.[112]

Nicaea's long and fluid frontier – or rather frontier zone – with the Seljuk sultanate of Rum ran across Asia Minor for more than 430 miles (700 kilometers) from north to south. Starting east of Amastris on the Black Sea, a city controlled by the empire of Nicaea in Theodore's lifetime, the frontier terminated in the south near the mouth of the Indos (Dalaman) River, which flows into the Aegean.[113] The allegiance of key cities and fortresses can give us an approximate sense of the political division of Asia Minor. The frontier generally followed that established in the twelfth century, but there were some losses for the Byzantines in the years leading up to 1204. In the aftermath of the Seljuk victory at Myriokephalon (1176), the strategic and newly refortified fortresses of Dorylaion (2 miles/3 kilometers from today's Eskişehir) and Kotyaion (Kütahya) fell into the hands of the Turks. Neither was recovered.[114] Two urban centers along the Lykos River, a major tributary of the Maeander, also submitted to the Turks: Laodikeia (Ladik, near modern Denizli) and Chonai (Honaz, near ancient Kolossai), the birthplace of the historian Choniates and the location of a famous church at the site of a miracle believed to have been wrought by Archangel Michael.[115] Around 1204 a certain Aldebrandinos, a man of Italian (probably Pisan) origin who was brought up in Byzantium, established himself as the master of the Aegean port city of Attaleia. In 1207 the sultanate of Rum gained authority over Attaleia, marking the end of direct Byzantine control of the Pamphylian coast.[116]

The Greek-speakers in the Seljuk sultanate of Rum felt affiliated with the political and ecclesiastical authorities of the empire of Nicaea. Inscriptions in Cappadocia dating to the early thirteenth century mention the elder Theodore Laskaris, not the current sultan of Rum.[117] The younger Theodore received information regarding these "expatriate" communities. He called Cappadocia the "eye of Asia" and attributed to Cappadocia the birth of the martyr Tryphon, which runs contrary to other versions of the hagiographical story and may have been a local legend.[118] The patriarchate in Nicaea communicated regularly with bishops of cities in the sultanate and ruled on matters pertaining to religious practice across the frontier. The metropolitan bishops of Caesarea (Kayseri), Melitene (Malatya), Ancyra (Ankara), and Pisidia took part in meetings of the patriarchal synod.[119] On three different occasions, in 1239–40, 1241, and 1248, the synod sent the metropolitan bishop of Melitene, John, on embassies to King Hetoum I (r. 1226–69) of Cilician Armenia and to the chief bishop (*katholikos*) of the Armenians.[120] He was once joined (1248) by the metropolitan bishop of Philadelphia, Phokas.[121] The sultans of Rum themselves employed local Greeks in their service. The descendants of Manuel

Mavrozomes, who had been appointed in 1205 to govern Laodikeia and Chonai in the sultan's name, took pride in their Christian identity and Komnenian lineage.[122] The sultans maintained a Greek chancery and employed Greeks in their service. For example, a certain *kyr* (meaning "lord") Alexios was ʿIzz al-Dīn Kaykāwūs I's ambassador to the Latin king of Cyprus in 1216. On this occasion the two rulers communicated in Greek, which served as a diplomatic *lingua franca*.[123]

The Byzantine emperor and the Seljuk sultan had established a relatively stable, if not fully peaceful, mode of coexistence in the course of the twelfth century. They struck alliances and shared a common interest in preventing the nomadic Turkmen from raiding cities and agricultural areas.[124] One prominent aspect of peaceful cohabitation across the frontier was trade.[125] The frontier zone continued to be porous and permeable after 1204. Asylum-seekers, adventurers, and merchants crossed with ease to the other side, whether temporarily or permanently. In the twelfth and the first half of the thirteenth century, powerful Byzantine defectors sought refuge among the Seljuks. The elder Theodore Laskaris himself benefited from the assistance of the sultans when he was still a rebellious local lord (1203–04) opposed to the crusader-supported regime in Constantinople.[126] There were powerful defectors and fugitives from the Seljuk side, too. The sultans traditionally divided the realm among their sons and appointed them as governors of different regions, an arrangement that led to succession struggles and involved the powers on the other side of the frontier. The sultan Kaykhusraw I, for instance, sought refuge in Constantinople before 1204 during a contested succession. After he perished in the Battle of Antioch on the Maeander, the sultan's sons established themselves in different cities: ʿIzz al-Dīn Kaykāwūs in Malatya, ʿAlāʾ al-Dīn Kayqubād in Tokat, and Kay-Faridun Ibrāhim in Antalya. ʿIzz al-Dīn Kaykāwūs I (r. 1211–19) prevailed over his siblings and restored peaceful relations with Nicaea that persisted, with brief interruptions, throughout the younger Theodore's lifetime.

The Seljuk realm expanded eastward and southward during the reign of ʿIzz al-Dīn's brother, the famous ʿAlāʾ al-Dīn Kayqubād I. Kayqubad took control of Alanya (Kalonoros) on the Aegean Sea, which became his preferred summer residence, and annexed Erzurum (Theodosioupolis, Karin) and Erzincan (Keltzene) from local Turkish dynasties. Commercial competition with Trebizond over the lucrative slave trade in the Crimea led to a naval expedition across the Black Sea, during which a Seljuk force briefly occupied Sogdaia (Sudak) before the Mongols conquered the city.[127] Relations with the empire of Nicaea soured between 1225 and 1231, but this confrontation over border fortresses ended with a lasting agreement in 1232.[128] The emergence of a Eurasian superpower – the Mongols under Genghis Khan (d. 1227) – drove the Nicaeans and Seljuks back into their older strategic partnership. The first alarming signs of the westward Mongol advance occurred in the reign of Kayqubād. In about 1230 a horde under the command of Chormaghun set up their tents in the fertile Mughan plain southwest of the Caspian Sea.[129] Crushed by the Mongols, Turkish Khorezmian warriors from Cenral Asia threatened the eastern frontier of the sultanate, but were defeated by Kayqubād at Yassı Çimen near Erzincan.[130] But the Mongols continued to pose a threat. Chormaghun is reported to have devastated the region of Sebasteia (Sivas) in 1231–32.[131] The Georgian kingdom and the principalities of Greater Armenia were reduced to tributary status between 1236 and 1239.[132] Kayqubād's son, Ghiyāth al-Dīn Kaykhusraw II (r. 1237–45/46), was to face a mighty Mongol invasion of Asia Minor that would seal the fate of the sultanate of Rum.

The Nicaean emperors took special care of the Anatolian borderlands. Their policies toward the frontier population, the *akritai*, were considered in the early fourteenth century to be the chief reason for the successful equilibrium they maintained in their relations with the Turks.[133] The *akritai* were local warriors exempt from paying taxes to the emperor, who augmented their lands and flocks through forays across the border. Their wealth grew apace with their fighting spirit, but their heavy taxation after 1261 is alleged to have demotivated them to serve as guardians of the border. The neighbors of the *akritai*, the nomadic Turkmen, had a similar lifestyle and dislike for central authority. An Arab author of the middle of the thirteenth century, Ibn Saʾid, writes that the Turkmen of the mountains – he refers in particular to the 200,000 or so households of Turkmen who lived near the mountains of Denizli – attacked the *akritai* living on the coast and sold the plunder to other Muslims. Akropolites, who was well aware of this type of border skirmish, speaks of "the Persian who is quick to attack, plunder and escape."[134]

Theodore Laskaris heard firsthand reports about the situation in the sultanate of Rum, yet left no record of what he knew. His silence is disappointing yet understandable. The world on the other side of the frontier did not fit as a subject into the topics traditionally treated by Byzantine letter-writing, rhetoric, and philosophy. His attitude to Islam, the religion of "the descendants of Hagar," is marked by a religious cliché. His head tutor is mocked for resembling "a son of Mohammed, due to the exceeding roundness of the figure." The comparison could be based on a real person whose father was a Muslim or could reflect a contemporary stereotype.[135] He made only brief mentions of areas in the Islamic world and the Far East. Syria had a notoriously bad climate. Egypt had massive agricultural wealth in contrast to the Aegean island of Kos. India was a land filled with exotic animals.[136] In the encomium on his father (1250–52), Theodore makes clear that the sultanate of Rum was no longer the dominant power in Anatolia, because it was hard-pressed by the Mongols, its overlords. He regarded the stability of the frontier as divinely ordained. "God is at the center, God is at the frontiers," he remarked confidently and optimistically in 1256, toward the end of his life.[137] Theodore Laskaris grew up training for war and preparing to face a devastating Mongol invasion, yet the turn of events was different. His mature years coincided with a rare period of tranquility in western Anatolia, which gave him the necessary peace of mind to develop into an insatiable reader and prolific writer.

3 | "I Was Raised as Usual for a Royal Child"

The autumn of 1221 was a season of change in the Anatolian Byzantine state, which was well into the second decade of its existence. The elder Theodore passed away in November. His son-in-law John Vatatzes acceded to the throne in November or December, though possibly as late as early January 1222, amid a brewing dynastic conflict (Fig. 13).[1] John Vatatzes stayed in Nicaea at the onset of the winter. The royal couple paid their last respects to the elder Theodore by attending the customary memorial service on the fortieth day after his death at the burial site, the monastery of Hiakynthos. His wife Irene was in an advanced stage of pregnancy. In the last two months of 1221 or early in 1222, their son, the younger Theodore Laskaris, was born in the imperial palace in Nicaea.[2] "Nicaea loved by me," he called it, "where I dropped to the earth from my mother." His words echo the Book of Wisdom, one of his favorite texts: "I myself, when I was born, drew in the common air and fell upon the kindred earth" (Wisdom 7:3).[3]

The public mood was changing, seventeen years after Constantinople's fall. The disaster of the Fourth Crusade was beginning to seem like a beginning of an era rather than an easily reversible setback. A new sense of chronology was in the making. In his inaugural sermon of 1223, the exiled patriarch of Constantinople spoke of himself as the "fifth judge Gideon," because he was the fifth patriarch ordained in Nicaea since the move of the government to Anatolia.[4] The dream of recapturing Constantinople remained alive, but the political elite was preparing itself for a period of retrenchment in Asia Minor with an unpredictable end date. The firstborn son was understandably named after the recently deceased emperor, something that attracted the notice of Byzantine and Western historians.[5] The choice of name followed onomastic tradition and honored the ruler who had revived the state after the fall of Constantinople, conveying a much-needed sense of political continuity. At the very onset of his rule, John Vatatzes confronted the elder Theodore's surviving brothers, who felt sidelined and threatened by the accession of an emperor outside of the Laskaris bloodline. They had all acted in solidarity in the reestablishment of the Byzantine government in the wake of 1204. The late

Constantine had even been selected to be the emperor on the day of Constantinople's fall. Two of the brothers, the *sebastokratores* Alexios and Isaac Laskaris, connived with the widowed wife of the elder Theodore, Maria of Courtenay, and all three defected to the court of Maria's brother, the emperor of Constantinople, Robert. The Laskaris brothers planned to seize the throne with Western help. They led an invading army of Latins as well as Greeks into Asia Minor and outnumbered the Nicaean troops, but misjudged the military acumen of the new emperor. John Vatatzes made a surprise foray into Latin-held territory rather than waiting passively in the Thrakesion theme and engaged the enemy in the winter of 1223–24 in a pitched battle fought near Poimanenon (Eski Manyas).[6]

The Nicaean victory was complete and resulted in numerous casualties and captives. The prisoners included the ringleaders Alexios and Isaac Laskaris, who were punished with blinding and disqualified from claiming the throne. Two other brothers of the elder Theodore Laskaris – Manuel and Michael, known as "Tzamantouroi" – lost Vatatzes' favor and were exiled for most of his reign.[7] The bloody internecine conflict between John Vatatzes and the leading members of the Laskaris family was well remembered. Nearly thirty years later a panegyrist remarked that his accession resembled the rise of David and the fall of Saul, a common comparison justifying the accession of usurping emperors in Byzantine court rhetoric.[8] Yet the close blood relatives of the new emperor never attained such a commanding position as the Laskaris brothers. He is said to have mistrusted his kin, especially after the discovery in 1225, just one year after the Battle of Poimanenon, of a dangerous conspiracy organized by his cousins on his mother's side, the brothers Andronikos and Isaac Nestongos. (His mother, who came from the Angelos family, evidently had a sister married into the Nestongos family.) While John Vatatzes was staying at Lampsakos, which he had just retaken from the Latins, he learned of a planned attempt on his life. A trial held in Achyraous implicated leading members of his entourage. Isaac Nestongos, the failed assassin, and a certain Makrenos were sentenced to blinding and hand amputation. Andronikos Nestongos was imprisoned in Magnesia, from where he managed to escape and settled permanently among the Seljuks of Rum.[9]

John Vatatzes would fill in the vacuum left by the Laskaris brothers and his disgraced maternal cousins by cultivating alliances with select aristocratic families in the empire of Nicaea through the marriages of his nieces and nephews. He designated as *sebastokrator* his trusted brother Isaac Doukas, whose son John married Eudokia, the daughter of John Angelos, a man in all likelihood identical with the governor (*doux*) of the

Thrakesion theme in 1235–36.[10] A daughter of the *sebastokrator* married Constantine Strategopoulos, who belonged to a little-known but influential family that was blood-related to the Komnenoi. Constantine's father, the general Alexios Strategopoulos, boasted of his Komnenian descent on his seal without mentioning holding any office (Fig. 14). A certain John Strategopoulos, whose relationship to Alexios is unclear, had been grand logothete (*megas logothetes*) in 1216 during the reign of the elder Theodore.[11] Another niece of John Vatatzes, the daughter of an unknown brother, married the general Alexios Raoul, who had held the office of *protovestiarios* since at least 1242.[12]

John Vatatzes capitalized speedily on his victory at Poimanenon by conducting a highly successful winter campaign, a practice he followed throughout his reign. The Latin knights and the Venetians were poorly prepared for battle in the coldest months of the year. The pact they concluded in 1205 had specified the campaign season as lasting from June 1 to September 29.[13] The flurry of John Vatatzes' reconquests included the fortified towns of Achyraous, Pergamon, Atramyttion, Verveniakon, Lentiana, Charioros, Poimanenon, and Lampsakos. Lampsakos' port of Holkos became a base for the Nicaean navy, which harassed lucrative maritime traffic through the Hellespont and endangered vital supply lines to Constantinople. Vatatzes' soldiers penetrated into areas on the European side of the straits.[14] Islands adjacent to the Aegean coast – Lesbos, Chios, Samos, Ikaria, Kos, and Rhodes – also submitted to the empire of Nicaea.[15] A patriarchal sermon delivered in 1224 makes the telling comment that the newly conquered lands were far-reaching and "in need of many days to cross."[16] The Latin emperor recognized in a peace treaty the Nicaean acquisitions in Asia Minor and surrendered to John Vatatzes the fortress of Pegai on the Sea of Marmara.[17] Confidence grew in Nicaea that a fatal blow had been dealt to the Latin empire of Constantinople. A patriarchal ruling issued in September 1229 called rhetorically on the Latins to "throw down their weapons" and "forget about resistance."[18] Theodore Laskaris would himself take pride in the removal of their lordships in Anatolia and the humiliation of the people who had once been "strong-armed like lions."[19] The Western individuals whom he saw in Asia Minor during his mature years were mercenaries, diplomats, and merchants rather than invading armies.

Much of Theodore's early childhood was spent in the city of his birth, Nicaea, which he compared to a parent who "brought him up in maternal fashion."[20] Reading between the lines of his writings suggests that he grew up in a loving and nurturing family. It was in the nature of things, he remarked, that parents easily forgot anger at their children and gave them a comforting embrace. Parental love, he remembered at around the age of twenty, made Irene and John turn a deaf ear to his head tutor when he accused the teenage Theodore of misdemeanors. Paraphrasing Christ's saying (Luke 11:11–12), he wrote that a father would not give his son a snake instead of a fish or a scorpion instead of an egg.[21] He recalled in his mature years that he "often received greatest solace" from his father and called his encomium on him "a tribute of pure love."[22]

Theodore was particularly precious to his parents, for he turned out to be their only child. Not long after his birth, his mother Irene had a hunting accident in which she fell from her horse and suffered an injury that left her unable to bear more children. The young prince became a key figure of political and dynastic continuity.[23] Curiously, he never mentions that his mother played an important role in the way he was raised, partly because this was so common that it was not worthy of notice and partly because she was already deceased by the time his literary voice developed. Mother-empresses were expected to take care of royal children.[24] Irene was still involved in his upbringing when he was thirteen despite the recent assignment of a head tutor. At that time (1235) she is reported to have arranged for his further education and care and that of his newly arrived child bride.[25]

The palace in Nicaea, and probably also the other palaces, had women's quarters (*gynaikonitis*), which provided special living space for the empress and her entourage in accordance with Constantinopolitan tradition. Theodore sometimes mentioned the women's quarters in which he grew up. This microcommunity in the palace bustled with different kinds of activities related to child-rearing, religious life, and the empress' public role. Ladies-in-waiting and eunuch servants attended to the needs of the royal child and his mother. Omnipresent guards maintained security.[26] The empress had her own clergy servicing her female entourage. A future patriarch of Constantinople, Joseph I Galesiotes (1266–75, 1282–83), is known to have started his career as Irene's lector.[27] The child Theodore would have encountered chancery officials and stewards who came to report to the empress. Like other Byzantine empresses born into an imperial family rather than inducted from the outside as spouses, Irene contributed to the legitimation of her husband's rule. Her imperial lineage – she preferred the name Komnenos and occasionally Doukas – and her birth in the palace in Constantinople before 1204 were important political assets. A work of occasional rhetoric refers to her as a child of the "holy *porphyra*" and "beloved offspring of the palace." A letter composed in the chancery of the Latin king of Cyprus between 1234 and 1239 heaps praises on her as "the all-pious *augousta,* surpassing all women, and *autokratorissa* of the Romans, Irene Komnene, who was nourished and brought up from her swaddling clothes in the imperial palace and who assumed imperial rule (*basileia*) as paternal inheritance."[28] Irene enjoyed a powerful public position and had the authority to issue official acts, such as an ordinance granting tax exemptions to the monastery of St. John on the island of Patmos. Her official lead seal, which bears her image, was attached to such documents (Fig. 15).[29] She had great wealth at her disposal, possibly from revenues from landed estates, which enabled her to be a patron in her own right. Her endowments included the monastic church of St. John the Baptist in Prousa and the monastery dedicated to the Virgin *tou Kouzena* on Mount Sipylos near the Sosandra monastery erected by her husband.[30] The monastery of the Virgin *tou Kouzena* remained an imperial foundation after her death and her son Theodore favored a certain monk Antony for the post of abbot, contrary to the wishes of leading metropolitan bishops.[31]

The relationship of the young prince with his parents was shaped by his royal birth. Passing comments reveal public expectations of him from an early age. In the early 1240s, he described his upbringing as the customary one for imperial princes: "I was raised as usual for a royal child."[32] A decade later, he recalled that it had been his destiny to be the center of attention from birth: "I was born in the light of day and in a worldly valley."[33] Contemporary evidence proves beyond any doubt that he was proclaimed a junior coemperor. Orators praised him as an emperor who reigned alongside his father and called him as "an emperor from birth."[34] If the usual practice in Byzantium during the twelfth and the early thirteenth centuries was observed, he would have been officially made coemperor in his early childhood. The elder Theodore had his son Nicholas designated as coemperor during his infant or toddler years.[35] By his twentieth birthday the younger Theodore Laskaris acted in the capacity of coruler, for in the summer of 1241 he is mentioned as an official party in a treaty with the Latins.[36] He referred to himself as "my imperial majesty" in letters dating to his twenties, which demonstrate his coemperorship and the role that he played in governance, as will emerge in Chapter 5.[37] Curiously, subsequent Byzantine historians contradicted historical truth when they declared that Theodore never obtained the imperial title during his father's reign.[38] This misinterpretation may be due to the fact that he was an uncrowned emperor (*basileus*), in contrast to the crowned junior coemperors of the later thirteenth century, following the restoration of Constantinople.

Theodore was already taking part in ceremonies in his adolescent years. Later in life he would refer to performing obeisance (*proskynesis*) to his father and would call him the "lord and emperor" or simply his "lord," conveying a sense of filial obedience and a respect for hierarchy cultivated at the court.[39] Echoes of official pronouncements and rhetoric in praise of the emperor are regularly heard in his written works. He would describe his father as the sun and himself as an orbiting planet, and would compare the earthly with the divine kingdom, thus likening the emperor to God.[40] His self-comparison with King David followed the spirit of court oratory as well as the rhetorical representation of the empire in exile as the Babylonian captivity of God's Chosen People. He wrote during his coemperorship on the basis of Psalm 2, one of the royal psalms: "God anointed me, honoring me with independent power, and made me his son by the Holy Spirit, as David sings in the psalms."[41] A sense of monarchical self-righteousness and a belief in a divinely ordained mission were impressed on him from childhood.

What did Theodore mean by saying that he was "raised as usual for a royal child"? One aspect of tradition was that he grew up in the women's quarters of the palace. Another was the opulence of his surroundings, something that never ceased to amaze him. In writings dating to his coemperorship, he commented on the omnipresence of luxury goods and symbols of status around him: gold, silver, precious stones, the protective company of servants (*hyperetai*), glamorous clothing, handsome horses, cold drinks, and delicacies.[42] He commented on his carefree and richly provided existence with the following words: "I was brought up in pleasure like 'an innocent lamb'" (Leviticus 1:10; Jeremiah 11:19).[43] Surrounded by a retinue of people willing to serve, he was accustomed from childhood to observe the sharp differences in social status. One of his letters opens with the saying "great is the distance between lordship and servitude," which for him was a truism reflecting the natural and unchallenged state of affairs.[44]

Servants who were part of the royal household included various palace personnel, ranging from chamberlains, attendants and physicians to food suppliers and managers of imperial estates.[45] Armed guards provided what Theodore calls a "protective company."[46] The empress Irene insisted on very tight security in the palace after the discovery of the conspiracy of Andronikos and Isaac Nestongos.[47] The guards included the axe-bearing Varangians and the whip-carrying Vardariots. In the fourteenth century the Vardariots were recruited from among the Turks and wore distinctive cucumber-shaped hats and red uniforms made from the same canvas as the imperial tent, but in Theodore's lifetime at least some of them were native soldiers.[48] There was also the corps of the *vestiaritai* headed by a trusted man, the *protovestiarites* George Zagarommates, who held this position for more than twenty years from at least 1235 onward.[49] Pages close in age to the prince assisted the royal family on ceremonial and private occasions. They are known to have had the duty of holding candles on feast days and fetching the emperor's staff and shoes from the imperial chest during the fourteenth century.[50] Theodore, who encountered pages during his daily routine, played games with them, such as throwing knucklebones and collecting fruits.[51] Lasting lifelong relationships bound him with several of his pages who became his closest companions and confidants.

He referred to his servants both as *hyperetai* and as *douloi,* a word that can signify "slaves," "servants," and imperial subjects generally.[52] Whether there were slave servants around him is not known, but Theodore was certainly familiar with the social phenomenon of slavery. Formularies for slave sale and manumission demonstrate that household slavery was common in the empire of Nicaea and that the enslaved individuals were usually foreign-born: Scythians (Cumans), Russians, and Muslims.[53] A mass enslavement and sale of Cuman captives occurred during Theodore's late teenage years. Cumans defeated by his father in Thrace in around 1237 were sold as slaves at markets in Adrianople, Didymoteichon, Vizye, Kallipolis, and elsewhere.[54] The Mongol conquests of the northern Black Sea area led to a booming long-distance slave trade, in which Italians were heavily involved. In 1246 Pisan, Genoese, and Venetian merchants are reported to have transported Bulgarian, Wallachian, Greek, and Ruthenian slaves – that is, enslaved Christians from the Black Sea area – to the Latin kingdom of Jerusalem and to have sold them to the Muslims.[55]

By the time of Theodore's first childhood memories, his father was poised to recover twelfth-century Byzantine territories in the Balkans, where his ambitions clashed with those of a dangerous competitor, the ruler of the state of Epiros, Theodore Komnenos Doukas (Theodore of Epiros). In the autumn of 1224, the latter took control of Thessalonica, which became the capital of his expanding kingdom. He soon proclaimed himself emperor, and between April and August 1227 was crowned and anointed by the autocephalous and powerful archbishop of Ohrid, Demetrios Chomatenos ("archbishop of Justiniana Prima and all Bulgaria").[56] His soldiers reached Adrianople in Thrace, where they encountered John Vatatzes' troops who were quartered in the city.[57] Theodore of Epiros won the allegiance of the Adrianopolitans with generous promises, entered the city, and the urban population was required to recognize him as the legitimate Byzantine emperor.[58] From there he devastated eastern Thrace and set his eyes on Constantinople. The one-year treaty he concluded in September 1228 with the bailiff of the Latin empire, Narjot de Toucy, allowed the Thracian population to return to their homes and authorized merchants to cross the frontier unimpeded.[59] The Epirote advance threatened to derail Nicaea's mission of imperial restoration. Relations deteriorated further during the bitter schism between the churches of Nicaea and Epiros that lasted from 1228 until 1233.[60]

The power of the Epirote ruler crumbled as speedily as it had risen after a sudden and heavy military defeat, which bore out Theodore's maxim that "in the right moment inaction is also action." The Bulgarian ruler Ivan Asen II (r. 1218–41) inherited the independent policies of his father, the elder Asen – one of the three brothers from Turnovo who restored the Bulgarian kingdom in 1185. In the 1220s Ivan Asen II played an increasingly important diplomatic and military role in the Balkans. Always on the lookout for an advantageous alliance, he had plans to intervene in the succession problems in the Latin empire of Constantinople. His diplomatic relations with the Latin West were close at the time. The Bulgarian church had been in ecclesiastical union with Rome since 1204 and he was married to a sister of the Hungarian king, Béla IV.[61] The Latin emperor, Robert of Courtenay, who was forced by his barons to leave Constantinople and sailed to Rome to ask for the pope's support, passed away in Greece during his return journey in late 1227.[62] Baldwin, his brother and successor, was only eleven years old. In an agreement struck with the Latins in 1228, Ivan Asen proposed his daughter Elena as a fiancée for Baldwin.[63] A powerful faction in Constantinople quickly foiled the planned dynastic alliance and offered the crown of Constantinople to the elderly John of Brienne (Jean de Brienne), a one-time king of Jerusalem and a leader of the Fifth Crusade, who belonged to the celebrated generation of the founders of the Latin empire. The pact concluded in Perugia on April 9, 1229, stipulated that John of Brienne was to be emperor of Constantinople for life and that his successor Baldwin be betrothed to Jean's daughter Marie of Brienne. The Latin claims to Asia Minor were not forgotten. On reaching the age of twenty (in 1237), Baldwin was to be invested with all domains in the "Nicaean realm" and other Anatolian lands once held by the Latins.[64] Before he could sail from Venice and take up his duties in Constantinople, John of Brienne needed to collect money and troops. He arrived on the Bosporus only in the late summer of 1231 and was crowned emperor in the church of St. Sophia. At that time, or somewhat later, Marie of Brienne was united in marriage with Baldwin (Fig. 16).[65]

In the meantime Theodore of Epiros planned to eliminate the power of Ivan Asen II and led a large army into northern Thrace in the spring of 1230. Ambushed at Klokotnitsa in the valley of the Maritsa (Hebros) River, he was heavily defeated and taken captive. The Epirote realm was split and fatally weakened. Theodore of Epiros' brother, the despot Manuel, came to rule in Thessalonica with the support of Ivan Asen, whose daughter he married. In around 1231 Michael II, an illegitimate son of Michael Komnenos Doukas (the founder of the Epirote principality), established himself as an independent lord in Arta.[66] Extensive areas in Thrace and Macedonia accepted Ivan Asen's direct or indirect rule. An inscription on a column in the church of the Forty Martyrs in Turnovo boasts that after the Battle of Klokotnitsa, Ivan Asen controlled all territory from Dyrrachion on the Adriatic to Adrianople in Thrace.[67] Theodore of Epiros was held prisoner in Turnovo and was eventually punished with blinding on the charge of plotting against the tsar. Thus, John Vatatzes seemed to have rid himself of a serious rival for the Byzantine political inheritance and eyed a dynastic alliance with Ivan Asen.

At the time of all these political tremors in the Balkans, Theodore Laskaris was making progress with his elementary education, the so-called holy letters (*hiera grammata*). Urban and elite children in Byzantium were normally assigned to an elementary teacher around the age of six, so Theodore would have started his education in 1228.[68] He was introduced to the shape of the letters of the Greek alphabet and memorized scriptural texts, such as psalms and parables from the New Testament, which became indelibly ingrained on his mind. He listened to Aesopian fables, from which he would draw ample references to animals in letters and other writings. Later in life he would write boastfully about skills and abilities he had derived from his childhood education. His comments evoke the image of a precociously developed adult-like child, which is common in medieval literature, yet they also represent retrospective, even if exaggerated, interpretations of real experiences. He writes that he was accustomed to Ares, the ancient god of warfare, from his infancy. He notes also that he was "nourished from infancy in the church with its intellectual and spiritual food" and that he absorbed philosophy "from a tender age."[69] The reference to warfare is explainable by the fact that news of the outcome of battles kept reaching him at the court as a child. His "nourishment" in the church refers to a pious religious upbringing and his early immersion in philosophy reflects his elementary and secondary education.

Theodore was raised as a devout Christian who had the habit, as he writes, of praying three times during the day: in the morning, at noon, and in the evening. He claimed in a letter to the patriarch that he was ready to follow in the footsteps of the martyrs and give his own life for the church of Christ, his true mother.[70] Listening to the singing and services of the liturgical cycle was an enthralling experience, for he felt inspired in his later years to write hymns in praise of holy figures and other devotional texts. He was particularly fond of St. Tryphon, a third-century Christian martyr, whose cult was centered on the city of Nicaea. His laudatory *vita* of the saint is partly a record of his observations of the annual festival on February 1. Many people of every walk of life gathered in the church of St. Tryphon in Nicaea for the morning service: children and the elderly, soldiers and peasants from surrounding villages, monks and priests, the patriarch and the emperor. Afterward the multitude went to the lakeshore to watch with amazement the annual "miracle" of the blooming of the winter lilies on Lake Askania.[71]

The young Theodore would have attended some of the sermons of Germanos II, Patriarch of Constantinople residing in Nicaea from January 1223 until the middle of 1240.[72] The ecclesiastical orator had a strong influence on his mind. Born in Anaplous on the Bosporus, Germanos had served as a deacon of the cathedral clergy of St. Sophia in Constantinople. His pre-1204 career resembled that of previous patriarchs ordained in exile, but he had the added advantage of deep familiarity with the spiritual needs of the population in Anatolia living under Latin rule. The emperor's accession in late 1221 found him the abbot of the monastery of St. George the All-Beautiful (*paneumorphos*) in Achyraous in Latin-held Asia Minor. In his inaugural address, given in 1223 in the church of the Holy Fathers of the First Ecumenical Council in Nicaea, Germanos boasted how he had instructed the people of Achyraous to stand by their ancestral faith and to prefer it to life itself.[73] His pastoral care for his congregation is also seen in the compilation of a standardized collection of sermons for the annual cycle of church feasts (*kyriakodromion*), a valuable aid to priests, whose authorship has been attributed to him.[74] He composed as patriarch a series of fiery sermons to his flock in Nicaea on subjects of lay and clerical discipline, heresy, and social issues.

The language and imagery deployed in the sermons suggests that Germanos designed them for delivery before officials of the emperor and people familiar with life at the court. The patriarch compared parishioners not paying attention to the liturgy to courtiers turning their back to the emperor during a reception. If the latter were punished with lashes for their disloyalty, the patriarch asked, what would God do to careless churchgoers on Judgment Day?[75] And would not the lack of proper order at the emperor's table be punished with lashes?[76] God's response to sincere prayer resembled the way in which the emperor granted pardon to prisoners who rattled their chains to capture his attention.[77] Plotting against the emperor provided Germanos with similes that he considered suitable for his congregation. A loyal retainer who somehow found himself in the middle of a coup against the emperor would never accept the offer of imperial insignia, Germanos observed. On the Day of Judgment, he wrote elsewhere, God will hold accountable the relatives of the emperor who committed the bloodiest crimes in order to seize the throne – an allusion to the plotting Laskaris and Nestongos brothers.[78]

Which sermons Theodore heard and when is a mystery, but he makes clear his knowledge of the patriarch's works when he expresses delight that his oration on the Virgin had been compared to the style of Germanos.[79] The patriarch's and the prince's views on nobility and identity converge, and this can hardly be a coincidence. One of Germanos' sermons is a riposte to criticisms of his humble birth levied by certain Mouzalon, an imperial official holding the title of personal secretary (*mystikos*) and keeper of the inkstand (*epi tou kanikleiou*).[80] Were not the Constantinopolitan émigrés who ridiculed him at marketplaces and in dinner parties, Germanos asked in the polemical sermon, like mules born from intermarriages with Russian and Muslim servant girls? Was not Constantinople filled with every ethnicity like a Noah's ark? The standard by which nobility should be judged was not family origin but good Christian conduct, including a sense of social responsibility of the rich toward the poor.[81] Paragons of nobility were Zerubbabel who was born in Babylon, Moses, the shepherd David, the goatherd Amos, and Jesus himself, who was raised in the family of a carpenter.[82] This non-genealogical view of nobility – derived from the writings of the Greek fathers – deeply influenced Theodore, who would use it as a social commentary in his writings.[83]

The patriarch's patriotic praise of Anatolia resembled sentiments later aired by Theodore Laskaris. In the sermon addressed to his detractors, Germanos reminded his parishioners of the expulsion of Adam and Eve from the Garden of Eden in the East (*anatole*) and Christ's redemption of humankind from its dark, Western abode. Was not his flock living again in the East, he asked?[84] Elsewhere the patriarch formulated the political mission of the empire of Nicaea. He called for an incessant war with the Latins, in spite of temptations to strike agreements with them, and for the speedy recovery of Constantinople – the frontier between Nicaea and Constantinople, he pointed out, was the Sea of Marmara. Were not the Latins like the Gibeonites of the Old Testament who tricked Joshua into making peace?[85] The view of the Latins as the archenemy foreshadows Theodore's intransigent attitudes. The patriarch also anticipates Theodore's views in another way. In his letters Germanos referred to the orthodox Christians within and beyond the empire of Nicaea as *Graikoi*, usually in contexts distinguishing the latter from the Latins.[86] In July 1229, for example, he urged the *Graikoi* in the Latin kingdom of Cyprus to pray at home rather than attend church services conducted by Catholic priests.[87] Theodore would adopt and elaborate the same nexus between Hellenism and anti-Latin orthodoxy, yet he preferred the word "Hellene," which was more problematic than *Graikos* for Byzantine churchmen on account of its pagan connotations.

Sometime between the ages of eight and ten (in 1230–32), Theodore proceeded from his elementary schooling to grammar, the first subject of the general education (*enkyklios paideia*), the Byzantine term for secondary education.[88] He describes the sequence of subjects that he studied in his "general education" as follows: grammar, poetry, rhetoric, logic, and more advanced disciplines that consisted of the *tetraktys* (elementary mathematics, astronomy, geometry, and music: known in Latin as the *quadrivium*). This progression is consistent with the usual educational practice.[89] The study of grammar had the goal of teaching the student correct reading and writing. Its focus was on the parts of speech, orthography, the correct inflection of verbs, and the morphology of Attic Greek, a language that differed grammatically and sometimes lexically from the spoken tongue. Grammatical drills included exercises on etymology and lexicography.[90]

The introduction to the learned register of the Greek language not only set Theodore on the course of amassing the rich vocabulary characteristic of his literary language, but it stimulated a lifelong interest in etymological wordplay and the multiple meanings of words. He often commented on the polysemy of words. He noted, for example, that the Greek *kosmos* had various meanings: "universe," "adornment," and the human being as a microcosm. The word shrewdness (*panourgia*) signified "deceit," but also "cleverness."[91] Grammatical and rhetorical drills known as schedography had evolved and had become a popular school practice in the twelfth century. The *schedos*, literally "a riddle," was a brief composition. It could feature a commentary on a text through which the teacher illustrated grammatical and lexicographical problems, or it could contain mistakes in orthography of the vowels, which was discussed and corrected in the classroom. The twelfth-century schedographic compositions of Theodore

Prodromos – a foremost example of the "new" schedography of the period – captured the attention of students with their humor and mixture of high-register Greek with the vernacular. Schedography continued to be taught after 1204.[92] The peculiar vocabulary, loose syntax, and even the humor of the writings of Theodore Laskaris and other thirteenth-century authors were influenced by this playful school practice. The occasional variation between the learned and spoken registers in some of Theodore's letters brings him particularly close to the spirit of the schedography of his twelfth-century namesake, Theodore Prodromos.[93]

Theodore studied poetry alongside grammar and practiced memorizing passages from Homer – "the Poet," as he called him.[94] Homer was an essential component of the Byzantine literary canon and was introduced at the early stage of general education (*enkyklios paideia*). Michael Senachereim, who taught grammar and poetry during Theodore's lifetime at the school of St. Tryphon in Nicaea, wrote scholia on Homer.[95] Theodore's references to Homer tend to be to the first books of the *Iliad*, with which he was most familiar. He used Homeric lines and phrases proverbially. Some of his quotations are widely attested among Byzantine authors.[96] Other quotations appear exclusively in his writings as part of the literary jargon of his circle of pen-friends. In one of his letters, for example, he comments on a famous episode in the first book of the *Iliad*, which itself was the subject of a Byzantine school *schedos:* the plague at the camp of the Achaeans caused by the Trojan priest Chryses. He writes that Agamemnon should have accepted the gifts of Chryses and freed his daughter Chryseis from Achaean captivity in order to forestall the anger of the gods. The phrase "rejection of the girl" used in this letter means, as the context suggests, the rejection of unacceptable gifts and the preservation of honor. The very same expression recurs in another epistle, where it is used proverbially without any reference to Homer.[97] The Psalms and the *Iliad* became foundational texts for Theodore's literary language and provided him with ample material for playful allusions. Their impact on his vocabulary and his literary imagination can be traced back to the formative and impressionable years of his early education.

4 | Pursuit of Learning

On the verge of his adolescence, two events steered Theodore's life in new directions: the appointment of a court tutor and his betrothal to a foreign princess who likewise was an early adolescent. Theodore writes that he had just "come of age" and was "running the course of his twelfth year" (1233) when his parents made the decision to select his tutor.[1] He refers to him as his "pedagogue" without ever describing his duties or giving us his name. The manuscript heading of his devastating *Satire of the Tutor* ascribes to him the title of *baioulos* or "preceptor," and this is significant. The position of *baioulos,* or grand (*megas*) *baioulos,* was given from at least the fifth century to a court educator in charge of the upbringing of an imperial prince. According to the *Satire,* the "pedagogue" wore a tall, red hat made of wool when he entered the palace on a feast day, which made him resemble a crocodile and a mouse emerging from its hole. The spoof shows that he held a ranked court position, because hats had become an attribute of holding an imperial title in Byzantium by the twelfth century. In the fourteenth century, the *megas baioulos* ranked seventeenth or eighteenth among more than sixty court titles. In other words, the tutor belonged to the middle-to-upper segment of the court hierarchy.[2]

Theodore portrays the tutor as an abominable individual in every respect, so one needs to read between the lines of his *Satire* in order to understand the functions that the "pedagogue" performed. Written when Theodore was around twenty, the work is one of abuse and mockery. The tutor is voiceless like a fish, shameless as a dog, bad-tempered as a camel, nimble as an elephant, musical as a pack-ass, sociable as a bear, dignified as a boar.[3] Theodore describes his duty succinctly as that of a "guardian" and "teacher of what will be beneficial."[4] The tutor is not said to have taught him in the classroom and is reported to have never seen a book of rhetoric in his life.[5] The latter comment is an exaggeration, because he had been educated in a school in Constantinople before 1204. Theodore blames him for teaching him "ability" rather than philosophy, a comment suggesting that he instructed him in practical matters suitable for his future royal duties.[6] In fact, the tutor directed a team of teachers and educators. Theodore remembers that he "attended to the gates" – meaning the lips – of wise people for a long time while being under the supervision of the "peda-gogue."[7] The position of the "pedagogue" can therefore be described as that of a head tutor who oversaw the education and training of the teenage prince.

The head tutor was chosen to fulfill the important intergenerational role of being a living link with the Komnenian court. A few hard facts of his biography can be drawn from the *Satire*. He was at least in his sixties, for he had had a career before 1204 and Theodore repeatedly referred to his "old" age.[8] He belonged to a well-connected Constantinopolitan family. His surname may have been Zabareiotes, as traditionally assumed, or Eirenikos.[9] Both names are well attested in the twelfth-century civil service. A certain Gregorios Zabareiotes, for example, was a tax official and had the honorific court title of *kouropalates*. Theodore Eirenikos was keeper of the inkstand (*epi tou kanikleiou*) under the emperor Alexios III Angelos in the years leading up to 1204. In Nicaea, he pursued a career in the patriarchate, assuming the offices of consul of the philosophers (*hypatos ton philosophon*), head of the patriarchal chancery (*chartophylax*), and eventually patriarch (1214–16). Another Eirenikos, Nicholas, wrote occa-sional poetry at the Nicaean court during the reign of John Vatatzes.[10] The mother of the head tutor had enjoyed a high enough position to introduce him to "the emperors," that is, the Angeloi emperors, who arranged for his education in the capital. His life was eventful before 1204 and he was close to powerful people. After finishing his studies he spent time in the prov-inces, at the Haimos (Balkan) Mountains near Byzantium's frontier with the newly independent Bulgarian kingdom, where he may have held an administrative or military posting. Theodore made the acerbic comment that the only thing his tutor accomplished there was to learn magic.[11] An adulterous affair led to his trial at the imperial tribunal and punishment with mutilation of the nose.[12] As the *Satire* reveals, he was an eyewitness to the dramatic turnover of emperors on the eve of Constantinople's fall and moved secretly afterward to Anatolia, where his career prior to his appointment as *baioulos* is not known. Familiarity with the twelfth-century court qualified him to assume this position. He told the adolescent prince stories about his experiences in Constantinople, and Theodore described him pejoratively as a "great babbler" in his old age.[13] Indeed, the very act of his recruitment exemplifies the effort of the Nicaean emperors to preserve twelfth-century traditions.

The curriculum of general education (*enkyklios paideia*) mandated that Theodore proceed from grammar to rhetoric – a progression he himself mentions – at around the age of twelve.[14] His study of rhetoric involved writing school compositions, familiarizing himself with the exercises, figures, and styles described by the late-antique theoretician of rhetoric Hermogenes (and his Byzantine commentators), and reading select examples of ancient rhetoric. Theodore read about myth and allegory, which he thought had great persuasive power in the hands of a skillful rhetorician.[15] He mentions on several occasions Hermogenes and his rhetorical terminology – attributing to him, for example, the "law" of the anonymity of ridiculed individuals in a lampoon and satire (*komodia*).[16] It is hardly surprising that he viewed Demosthenes as a model of rhetoric, but it is significant that he was familiar with lesser known rhetorical texts of antiquity, such as the funerary oration on Cynaegirus and Callimachus, two great heroes of the Battle of Marathon, by the second-century sophist Polemon of Laodicea.[17] He continued his studies of rhetoric after his secondary schooling, so it cannot be known at what stage of his education he read this work. Nor is it known when he was first introduced to the writing of Christian authors as examples of rhetoric. He came to admire Gregory of Nazianzus, the "trumpet of theology" in his words, for his literary style and would treasure a codex containing his works.[18]

As Theodore advanced with his "general education," preparations for his marriage were well underway. His chosen bride, Elena, born in 1224, was the daughter of the powerful Bulgarian tsar Ivan Asen II and his Hungarian wife, Maria.[19] Vatatzes sought closer links with the Bulgarians, the dominant power in the Balkans after the Battle of Klokotnitsa in 1230, in the hope that this anti-Latin alliance would facilitate the reconquest of Constantinople and boost the status of the patriarchate in Nicaea. The Bulgarian church, which had seceded from Constantinople in November 1204, was still in union with Rome without having adopted Latin theological doctrines.[20] In the second half of 1232, probably in response to Ivan Asen II's overtures, Vatatzes sent an embassy to Turnovo and proposed a military alliance cemented by the engagement of the ten-year-old Theodore with the eight-year-old Elena. The tsar gave his oath to pursue the rapprochement with Nicaea, ousted the unionist archbishop of Turnovo, who entered monastic life on Mount Athos, and selected the monk Ioakim, a former Athonite, as the new leader of the Bulgarian church.[21] In 1232 Patriarch Germanos wrote exultantly to the Roman cardinals: "Many peoples agree and associate themselves with us, the *Graikoi*." He pointed to the Ethiopians, the Syrians, the "bravest Georgians," the Abasgians, the Laz, the Alans, the Goths, the Khazars, the "countless offspring of the Russians," and the "victorious kingdom of the Bulgarians." All these people, he wrote, obey "our church as their mother" and abide steadily by "ancient orthodoxy."[22] In around 1234 Ioakim traveled to "the great Nicaea" to be ordained by the patriarch.[23] His visit was an occasion for further discussion of the marriage alliance. An echo of the planned military assault on the Latin empire is found in the diary entry for March 26, 1234, made by the friars who came to the empire of Nicaea as papal envoys. They noted that Constantinople was menaced from each direction: Vatatzes to the south and east, Asen to the north, and Manuel of Epiros to the west.[24]

The marriage and the siege of Constantinople were set for 1235. In the spring of that year Vatatzes mustered a fleet of as many as 100 warships, including Rhodian reinforcements led by Leo Gavalas. He captured Kallipolis from the Venetians, and was joined there by Ivan Asen II and his army of Bulgarians, Vlachs, and Cumans. Elena, her Hungarian mother and a delegation of Bulgarian ecclesiastics – all accompanied by Vatatzes – crossed into Lampsakos on the Anatolian shore of the Hellespont. Acting with the approval of the orthodox patriarchs of Alexandria, Antioch and Jerusalem, Patriarch Germanos formally proclaimed the promotion of Ioakim, archbishop of Turnovo, to the rank of autocephalous patriarch. The marriage of Theodore and Elena was solemnly conducted in Lampsakos.[25] The world of politics, both domestic and international, came to look even more like a family affair to Theodore, for the couple's families were already linked by matrimony. Elena's maternal uncle, the Hungarian king, Béla IV, was married to Theodore's maternal aunt, Maria Laskarina. Theodore well remembered the independent status that the Bulgarian church received at his marriage. In his mature years he would observe that the Bulgarians were "autonomous and autocephalous": politically and ecclesiastically independent from the empire of Nicaea. But he also stressed that until relatively recently (that is, until 1185), the Bulgarians had been subjects of the Byzantine empire and had maintained "Roman loyalty."[26]

The bridegroom was thirteen and the bride eleven at their marriage, slightly below the minimum legal age of fourteen for boys and twelve for girls. This experience was not uncommon in Byzantium. Thirteenth-century aristocrats and peasants often arranged the marriages of their sons and daughters earlier than the legal age.[27] In his sermons Patriarch Germanos treated holy matrimony as a childhood event. He observed that when parents brought their children to the church to be married, they put crowns on the heads of the newlyweds that symbolized victory over the uncontrollable passions of the soul. The empress Irene effectively acquired another child in the imperial household and took care of the upbringing of the foreign girl.[28] The eleven-year-old Elena was expected to adopt the customs of her new homeland. Neither her proficiency in Greek nor the composition of her entourage can be judged from the sources. If we consider the experience of twelfth-century foreign princesses married into the Byzantine royal family, we can determine that Elena would have been taught Greek in order to communicate with her new family. Bertha-Irene, the German wife of the emperor Manuel I Komnenos, was the dedicatee of an allegorical paraphrase of Homer, which she was expected to appreciate. A twelfth-century princess who came from France as an eight-year-old girl – Agnes, the wife of Manuel's son – was able to converse with the crusaders twenty years later only through a translator, because she could no longer speak French.[29] In an oration on the healing saints Cosmas and Damian, Theodore mentioned that Elena prayed in a church dedicated to the two saints, which suggests that she was able to immerse herself in the Greek liturgy. Here she is called "an icon of virtue and my soul partner by the law of human nature."[30] As the teenage Theodore and Elena grew up together, a genuine affection between the two was kindled. The husband wrote about his marriage as "a bond of incomparable love" that made the couple "happier than all people." Elena was "the flower of my youth," "the beehive of the words and wishes of my heart," and the "springtime of my soul."[31] This is the language of romantic love, one rarely heard in nonfictional texts in Byzantium. The couple would in due course acquire six children. Five daughters were born in the 1240s – Irene, Maria, Theodora, Eudokia, and an anonymous fifth – and a son named John was born around Christmas 1250.

In the summer of 1235 the troops of Vatatzes and Ivan Asen II carried out a joint attack on Constantinople. The Nicaeans occupied the European coast of the Hellespont and territories in Thrace that included Kissos (Keşan) and stretched as far as the Maritsa River. The two armies laid siege to Constantinople and outnumbered its defenders, who were in dire need of reinforcements. The doge of Venice, Giacomo Tiepolo, a onetime Venetian *podestà* in Constantinople, was informed early of the grave danger and speedily dispatched twenty-five armed galleys, which defeated the Nicaean navy at Abydos (near Çanakkale) on the Hellespont. The blockade of the city continued, however. In a letter of December 16, 1235, Pope Gregory IX urged the Hungarian king, Béla, to lead a relief expedition. It was the prince of Achaia, Geoffrey II of Villehardouin – a vassal to the Latin emperor under the obligation to send annual subsidies – who saved the day. At the head of a substantial force of allegedly 120 Venetian, Genoese, and Pisan ships and 900 warriors (knights, crossbowmen, and archers), he broke the siege in the spring of 1236 and brought security to Latin Constantinople.[32] The Latin empire survived a severe military crisis, but the problem of the viability of its defenses remained. In the second half of 1236, Baldwin left Constantinople on a tour of Western courts aimed at raising funds and soliciting a crusade, a tour that lasted for more than three years and took him to Paris, London, and Flanders.[33] In the meantime, the financial problems in Constantinople deepened and the Latin barons took the desperate step of mortgaging to the Venetians the Crown of Thorns, a famous relic kept in Constantinople, for a loan of 13,134 gold coins (*hyperpyra*).[34]

The military cooperation between John Vatatzes and Ivan Asen II was not to last in the dynamic world of balance-of-power politics in the thirteenth-century eastern Mediterranean. Fearful of the rising power of Nicaea, Ivan Asen made a volte-face and struck a deal with Constantinople. In 1237 Bulgarians and Latins jointly attacked Tzouroulos (Çorlu), a fortress in Thrace recently taken by Nicaea. Ivan Asen forced his recently married daughter, whom he requested to see in Adrianople, to follow him back to Turnovo. He had been using Elena as a pawn of international diplomacy ever since his planned rapprochement (1228) with the Latin empire of Constantinople. The affinity to the sixth degree between the newlyweds on account of the marriage of Theodore's aunt (Maria Laskarina) to Elena's uncle (Béla IV) may have given him a pretext to seek a divorce.[35] In the same year, however, the shifty tsar changed his mind, lifted the siege of Tzouroulos, and sent Elena back to her husband in Nicaea. Elena's separation from Theodore, thus, did not last long. "Perjury" was a word Theodore used readily in the 1250s when he described the actions of another tsar of the Bulgarians. The events surrounding his marriage instilled doubts in him about the trustworthiness of his northern Balkan neighbors in diplomatic dealings.[36] As we will see in Chapter 5, soon after 1237 Vatatzes began to distance himself from Ivan Asen and sought another strategic ally – the Western emperor Frederick II Hohenstaufen.

In the meantime, the teenage Theodore was getting ready for his future tasks as a general, diplomat, and administrator under the watchful eyes of his head tutor, a man he increasingly came to dislike. The head tutor gave priority to preparing the prince for a life dedicated to warfare and action. Theodore is revealingly defensive when he writes that his zest for learning did not divert him from studying "the laws of warfare, lest the listener slanders my speech."[37] His apologetic tone tacitly acknowledges the existence of a contrary view embraced by his head tutor, according to whom too much time spent with books was not good for a future emperor. In Theodore's words, the tutor went so far as to accuse him of philosophizing.[38] Advanced philosophical study met with his stern disapproval.

Theodore's military education included combat training and exercises aimed at developing physical stamina. He was praised in a speech in 1254 for having mastered "a long time ago" the skills of horseback riding, wielding the quiver, shooting arrows, handling a spear and a shield, and other martial skills. Toward the end of his life he would speak of his proficiency in horseback riding, arrow-shooting, jumping, and running, which he especially enjoyed.[39] Horsemanship was a particularly important aspect of physical and military training. Hunting helped to develop skills in horseback riding. Around the age of twenty, Theodore reveals in a letter an almost maddening passion for the hunt.[40] "The scream of the cranes," he wrote, made "us crazily chase the creatures making these sounds ... We breathe one thing, the capture of winged creatures."[41] He repeatedly speaks of hunting trophies, such as deer, cranes, herons, bears, wild boars, and wild cats.[42] Polo, a traditional royal pastime in Byzantium, contributed to the improvement of horseback riding abilities, even though it was criticized in some circles as a useless addiction that added little to the development of warrior skills.[43] The game had been fashionable in Constantinople – there was a polo ground (*tzykanisterion*) on the premises of the Great Palace – and continued to be so in the empire in Anatolian exile. The historian Pachymeres mentions that members of the court residing in Nicaea and Magnesia liked to play a ball game, certainly polo, as well as a jousting game.[44] Theodore was particularly fond of polo, which he described in verbose detail as "moving, spinning, throwing, turning, raising, passing, suspending, returning, shooting, and holding a little ball." The "beloved exercise ground" in which, as he wrote, soldiers practiced this and other games seems to have been a facility located in Nicaea or Magnesia.[45]

Theodore regarded generalship as the ruler's most essential duty. Curiously, he never mentioned that he had read texts about war strategy, a silence corresponding to the absence of surviving Byzantine military manuals after the tenth century. Instead, he remarked that the effective general was able to act by instinct. Clearly, however, he grew up receiving plenty of knowledge on what he calls "the laws of warfare." "Someone trained in generalship," he writes, needed to be able to conduct sieges, strengthen fortifications, and use deception in warfare.[46] His preparation for military leadership seems to have consisted in observation of and participation in army training and discussions with generals, including his father, just as in the twelfth century a young coemperor is reported to have learned the skills of generalship from the father, the senior emperor.[47] Knowledge about tactics and strategy seems to have been passed down orally from one generation to the next within royal and aristocratic households. When confronted with a war at the beginning of his sole reign, Theodore would use the winter-campaigning tactics favored by his father.

The head tutor ensured that Theodore read texts befitting his royal upbringing. Byzantine books of advice to princes – the so-called mirrors of princes – stress that the heir to the throne should be introduced to the wisdom literature of the Old Testament and to historical examples of royal virtue and the fragility of power.[48] That Theodore followed this traditional advice emerges from his wide-ranging knowledge of examples of good and bad rulers. He refers to leaders and monarchs from the Old Testament (Moses, David, Solomon) and draws his models of statesmanship mostly from Roman history: Brutus, Hannibal, Cato, Pompey, Caesar, Antony, Gaius, Nero, Titus, Trajan, Hadrian, and Marcus Aurelius. Paragons of justice for him were Caesar, the founder of "the monarchy," and Trajan. Late antique emperors appear less frequently in his writings: Maximian, Constantine, Licinius, Theodosius, and Justinian.[49] Greek heroic and historical figures (Achilles, Agamemnon, Odysseus, Cyrus, Alcibiades, Philip, and Demetrios Poliorketes) are even rarer, showing that he sought models for his rule chiefly in the Roman era.[50] The one exception is Alexander, whom Theodore saw as a world conqueror, an enlightened ruler trained by Aristotle, and a friend of philosophers.[51]

The adolescent Theodore was enthralled by the wisdom literature of the Old Testament and knew by heart passages from the books of Wisdom and Proverbs. In the *Satire*, he expressed his newly awakened passion for philosophy, meaning literally "love of wisdom" (*philosophia*), through a line from the Book of Wisdom (8:3): "The Lord of all fell in love with Her (Wisdom)." Lady Wisdom appeared to him in the flesh in his dreams.[52] Elsewhere he gave account of visions of female personifications of wisdom, virtue, and philosophy who guided him to the heavens and revealed to him celestial knowledge.[53] The pursuit of learning was an otherworldly, transcendental experience. In his mature years, at a time when he felt he was "spinning daily at the many different turns of life," he composed an oration commenting on one of his favorite scriptural sayings: "The beginning of wisdom is fear of the Lord, and all who practice it have a good understanding" (Proverbs 1:7; Psalms 110:10). Lady Wisdom, he wrote, was his divine bride who mediated in the journey toward God and helped him contemplate the "sun of Wisdom."[54]

Theodore approached the wisdom literature of the scriptures with an idiosyncratic personal touch. He was intrigued by the relativity of moral values. Bad people appeared to possess wisdom, for they had an intelligent way of thinking and spoke just like virtuous individuals.[55] He made the proposition that kings "rule through wisdom" and tyrants (*tyrannoi*) "oppress (*katadynasteuousi*) through wisdom," based on a slight modification of Proverbs 8:15–16 ("rulers (*tyrannoi*) rule (*kratousi*) through wisdom"). By substituting "oppress" for "rule" he brought the scriptural passage into agreement with the common understanding of the word *tyrannos*.[56] In classical Greek, *tyrannos* could refer to any king – hence *Oedipos tyrannos* – as well as an illegitimate ruler, but in Byzantium it designated a tyrant, a usurper, and an aggressor. The ambiguous polysemy of words, such as *tyrannos*, prompted questions about the diversity of human experience and the flexibility of moral principles. Commenting on the meaning of shrewdness (*panourgia*), he observed that the wisest king, Solomon, had used the word in the Book of Proverbs in a good and in a bad sense. Shrewdness meant cleverness as well as trickery. Fishermen, priests, emperors, and officials valued shrewdness greatly, but, as Theodore added, so did deceitful thieves and flatterers.[57]

Theodore was taught logic after, or concurrently with, rhetoric. The study of logic was traditionally based on Aristotle's treatises in the *Organon*. To judge from contemporary practice, it started with Aristotle's *Categories* and *On Interpretation*, with Porphyry's *Introduction to the Categories* being the essential guide. Theodore considered Porphyry's "five voices" (species, genus, difference, property, and accident) something that every educated person knew.[58] He knew, too, about John of Damascus' summation of Aristotelian logic, for he read a tenth-century manuscript containing the *Dialectica* and the *Exposition of Orthodox Faith* (Cod. Bodleianus, Cromwell, 13).[59] Thus, he approached the study of Aristotelian logic, partly at least, through derivative teaching texts, such as Porphyry, John of Damascus, and subsequently Blemmydes' *Epitome of Logic*. After logic, Theodore writes that he proceeded to mathematics and then to physics. He lists the disciplines covered in the course of his general or secondary education (*enkyklios paideia*) and higher learning in the following manner: "As I progressed from syllogistic to mathematics and hence to superior knowledge (earlier I had become well acquainted with physics and, above all, composition and rhetoric, thus studying poetics as well), I rose to higher subjects, even though he (the tutor) was going mad."[60] Grammar (called here "composition"), rhetoric, poetry, and logic ("syllogistic") form the usual sequence of disciplines in *enkyklios paideia*. Elementary mathematics was part of *enkyklios paideia*, but physics was an unusual subject for this level. Theodore may have been taught the basics of natural philosophy early on, but it is also possible that his retrospective description conflates the end of *enkyklios paideia* with the beginnings of higher studies, called here "superior knowledge" and "higher subjects."

The heir to the throne was in a unique position to take advantage of the best educational opportunities available in Byzantine Anatolia. Around the time when he was assigned to his head tutor, he met a sixteen-year-old youth named George Akropolites, who had just moved to the Nicaean court from Constantinople. Vatatzes, who was grooming the next generation of imperial civil servants, took a personal interest in the young man. Akropolites came from an old Constantinopolitan family. His father, a civil functionary in the service of the Latin emperor, provided the teenager with a strong recommendation and allegedly intended to follow his son to Nicaea, but never managed to carry out this plan. Born in Latin Constantinople, Akropolites brought with him useful insights into and knowledge about the captured city, and he knew conversational Latin – his long diplomatic career included an embassy to the Latin empire before 1254.[61] He had completed his *enkyklios paideia* in Constantinople, but he needed additional instruction to qualify for top careers.

Higher education in the empire of Nicaea paled in comparison with that of twelfth-century Constantinople. A few former instructors from the imperially funded "Patriarchal School" migrated to Anatolia after 1204, but neither the scale nor the structure of the capital's educational system was replicated.[62] The reason lay in the dispersal of teachers and books as well as the lack of an educational infrastructure that could match the churches and monasteries of Constantinople. The teaching position of the consul of the philosophers (*hypatos ton philosophon*) was revived in Nicaea, but its holder was sometimes charged with other responsibilities.[63] The preservation of higher education depended on the initiative of enterprising students and caring teachers, but most of all on imperial patronage. In 1234 the emperor John Vatatzes handpicked five youths – George Akropolites, Krateros, Romanos, probably Hagiotheodorites, and another unknown pupil – and sponsored their continued education at the highest level.[64] Theodore Laskaris would remember how his father supported the studies of the group of five, which he saw as a sign of the revival of philosophy in his times.[65] Most of the five students came from families with a history of imperial service. The Akropolites family was employed in the civil administration as judges and fiscal officials in the eleventh and twelfth centuries.[66] Hagiotheodorites came from a family of high functionaries in the twelfth century; Theodore would come to employ him as his private secretary. Krateros was a blood relative, possibly the son, of the chief chamberlain (*parakoimomenos*) Alexios Krateros, who was active in this capacity between 1216 and 1227.[67] The five youths studied initially with Theodore Hexapterygos, a teacher of poetry and rhetoric who had been educated in Constantinople. In about 1237, or shortly thereafter, they relocated to the monastery of St. Gregory the Miracle Worker near Ephesos to continue under its abbot Nikephoros Blemmydes who had the reputation of being the most accomplished philosopher of the time.[68] The senior emperor and the empress Irene kept an eye on the education of the five students, as emerges from a learned discussion at the court in the Periklystra palace. When a solar eclipse occurred on June 3, 1239, George Akropolites was asked to give the correct scientific explanation.[69]

The life and career of Nikephoros Blemmydes illustrate the difficulties of reviving and transplanting the twelfth-century educational institutions of Constantinople. He was born in 1197 into a doctor's family that migrated to Asia Minor after the fall of Constantinople. On completing his general education in Prousa and in Nicaea, he followed the family tradition and in 1217 embarked on seven years of medical study in Smyrna. Theodore would respect him for his knowledge and qualifications as a doctor, and medical writings under his name have survived.[70] After training as a physician, Blemmydes pursued his passion for philosophy and looked for a teacher in Smyrna, but there were none. He learned that a certain Prodromos, a one-time student of the ecumenical teacher (*oikoumenikos didaskalos*), known also as teacher of the Gospels, Constantine Kaloethes at the "Patriarchal School" in Constantinople, lived humbly as a monk in the Scamander region controlled by the Latins. He crossed the frontier – at great personal risk, he tells us – and completed his higher studies with Prodromos.[71] Blemmydes' educational qualifications secured the post of clerk (*logothetes*) in the patriarchal bureaucracy in Nicaea that he held between about 1225 and 1232, while at the same time giving private lessons in his house.[72] His reputation attracted the emperor's attention, and so did the debating skills he displayed in a disputation with visiting Latin friars held in Nicaea in January 1234. In his mid-thirties, however, Blemmydes came to realize that his true vocation was a life of quiet contemplation, reading, and writing. He took monastic vows and in due course (c. 1237) became the abbot of the monastery of St. Gregory the Miracle Worker near Ephesos, where he continued to offer instruction. With feigned humility (Blemmydes was a testy individual who held a high opinion of himself), he notes in his autobiography that he declined a state salary for teaching the five students.[73] It was in the same monastery that the emperor commissioned him to compose his influential and massive instructional handbook, the *Introductory Epitome,* consisting of *Epitome of Logic* and *Epitome of*

Physics.[74] Throughout the 1240s Blemmydes was preoccupied with founding his own private monastery of Christ Who Is, again in the vicinity of Ephesos, which took eight years to build (c. 1241–c. 1249). He spent the rest of his life as its abbot.[75]

The fame of Blemmydes as the foremost teacher of his time was like an irresistible magnet for Theodore. The teenage prince took the initiative to seek out instruction with him, probably with the cognizance of his father and certainly without the approval of his head tutor. These circumstances are echoed in letters. One of Theodore's letters to Blemmydes notes that he "has chosen" him to be his teacher and reassures him that his father would repay him with high honors for his services.[76] "You chose us out of this world," Blemmydes himself writes.[77] Theodore assigned greater importance than his teacher to the studies. There is indeed little evidence of teaching in Blemmydes' letters, which tend to heap praises on Theodore's intellect and deal with practical issues. The dedicatory letter of his mirror of princes *Imperial Statue* is the sole one implying a mentoring relationship.[78] In his autobiography Blemmydes writes enigmatically that before his journey to the Balkans (sometime between 1242 and 1244) he was "not unacquainted with the emperor's son" and afterward the latter became "rather well known" to him.[79]

When and where did Theodore take lessons with Blemmydes? Contemporaries finished their general education at the age of sixteen or seventeen years old, so Theodore would have first approached Blemmydes in 1238 or 1239.[80] Notably, in the *Satire* he expresses his admiration for an unnamed great philosopher from whom he began to receive instruction before the tutor's death in 1240. The learned man envied by the head tutor could have been no other than Blemmydes.

> [He was] possessed by the muse of Homer and also that of Socrates, knew the divine mathematics and God-inspired logic of Plato and Aristotle, and furthermore natural science and verbal subtlety, and was believed to know the philosophy of Pythagoras, the study of the elements by Euclid and Theon, as well as the fine arithmetic of Diophantus, the harmonics of Claudius, the astronomy of Ptolemy, and the movements of the visible stars.[81]

The passage is key to understanding the chronology and the content of Theodore's studies with Blemmydes. The *Satire* (which dates to 1240 or shortly thereafter) voices his eagerness to continue his lessons, now that there is no one to obstruct him from doing so. Theodore stresses that "education is a sort of second nature" and presents the six classic definitions of philosophy found in late antique school introductions to philosophy known as *prolegomena philosophiae* (and also in Blemmydes' *Epitome of Logic*) in order to demonstrate that the head tutor, in complete contrast to Blemmydes, fell short of being a philosopher.[82] His earliest letter to Blemmydes, dating to 1241 or earlier (around the time of composition of the *Satire*), refers to a recent experience and voices hopes that the studies would continue. "I came to hate," he wrote, "the treasures other people gave me, for they are material and perishable." Having affixed his "soul" onto his "real father," his teacher, he is "watered everyday" by the flood of his wisdom and is able "to rise above the salty and muddy waters of stupidity and ignorance." He urges Blemmydes to carry on instructing him by sending his writings. "Do give instruction in epistles," he exhorts him in the letter.[83] It is evident from this letter that the two men were separated. In another, undatable letter he appealed to Blemmydes to teach him philosophy as well as theology: "May you carry my intellect to its complete formation through lessons in both subjects."[84] Elsewhere Theodore noted that his next teacher, Akropolites, prevented his intellectual development from remaining unfinished in the manner of Penelope's web and taught him "the entire philosophy."[85] All indications, thus, point to relatively brief and incomplete studies with Blemmydes, which lasted from 1238 or 1239 until about 1241. The period coincided partly with that of the instruction of the five students, whose example Theodore wished to follow. In this period Blemmydes received from Vatatzes the commission to compose his *Introductory Epitome* on logic and physics, which served as teaching material for his lessons. Just like the five students, Theodore attended Blemmydes' classes in the monastery of St. Gregory the Miracle Worker, which was feasible during the winter season when the court resided in nearby Nymphaion.

According to the above-cited passage from the *Satire*, Blemmydes was versed in many philosophical subjects. His eager student mentions Aristotle and Plato first, and then highlights ancient mathematicians and astronomers: Euclid, Pythagoras, Diophantus (famous for his work on algebra), Theon of Smyrna (the author of *On Mathematics Useful for the Understanding of Plato*), and Ptolemy. The attention paid to mathematics and astronomy points in the direction of Theodore's own developing interests in numerology, geometry, and natural philosophy. He would refer frequently in his later writings to Pythagoras, Euclid, and Theon of Smyrna, and would come to favor a mathematical approach to theology, which he connected in the *Satire* with the "divine-speaking" mathematics of Plato.[86] Curiously, the *Satire* – a youthful work – displays Theodore's ignorance at that time of the fact that the "harmonics of Claudius" and "the astronomy of Ptolemy" belong to the same Claudius Ptolemy, the author of the *Harmonics* and the *Almagest*.

Aristotelianism was the foundation of his philosophical education under Blemmydes. In his writings, Theodore introduced Aristotle simply as the "divine philosopher" without naming him and reserved the expression "high knowledge" solely for Aristotelianism.[87] He was closely acquainted with a number of the Aristotelian treatises beyond the logical ones. He perused and glossed Aristotle's *Physics* and *On Heavens* in a manuscript decorated with gold headings and initials (Cod. Ambrosianus gr. M 46 sup.), whose production has been dated to the last quarter of the twelfth and the first quarter of the thirteenth century.[88] Concepts drawn from Aristotle's natural philosophy, such as motion, genesis, growth, diminution, corruption, and passing-away, abound in Theodore's writings. He had knowledge of the *Nicomachean Ethics* (Book 8 influenced his treatise on politics and friendship) as well as the Pseudo-Aristotelian treatise *De Mundo*.[89] Mentions of Aristotle, *On the Soul,* and Pseudo-Aristotle, *On Colors*, suggest acquaintance, no matter how cursory, with these works.[90]

An important point to make is that the inspiring teaching of Blemmydes was the main filter through which Theodore adopted and understood Aristotelian philosophy. For example, his curious attachment to the Aristotelian notion of "complete reality" or "actuality"(*entelecheia*) is owed to Blemmydes, who discusses it in his *Epitome of Physics*.[91] Citing the use of the concept in Aristotle's definitions of motion and the soul, Blemmydes explicated its meaning as "completeness" and "completed activity." Human beings, who develop out of an embryo and are first seen in their developed form with all their limbs and organs at the time of birth, illustrated the sense of the philosophical concept. Blemmydes went on to point out that *entelecheia* was also synonymous in simple language with the word *energeia* ("activity," "energy"), the antithesis to *dynamis* ("potentiality"), which has connotations of passivity.[92] Theodore would make frequent use of the concept in nonphilosophical contexts and would come to refer to his own accession as a sole emperor with the phrase "full completeness of my imperial rule" (*entelecheia tes basileias*).[93] Theodore's awareness of ancient philosophical schools corresponds to descriptions found in the *Epitome of Logic*. He speaks of Aristotelianism, Pythagoreanism, and Stoicism, and mentions the Platonic Academy, above whose gates stood the sign "Let No One Ignorant of Geometry Enter."[94] Similarly, Theodore's familiarity with key characteristics of the ancient philosophers may have come from classroom instruction and reading doxographical texts. Heraclitus was for him the lamenting philosopher.[95] The "wisest" and "divine" Plotinus was ashamed to live in a human body.[96] Plato was "the wisest" and "most divine" philosopher. Theodore flaunts his learning by quoting passages from Plato's *Sophist, Republic,* and the *Laws*.[97] How much of his knowledge of Plato and Platonic philosophy came directly from the dialogues rather than from later synopses is impossible to know. An experimentation with Socratic irony marked Theodore's philosophical thought, as we will see in Chapter 9. It is perhaps noteworthy that an essay written in the last years of his life comments on a proposition inspired by Neoplatonism ("nature does not revert on itself") found in Blemmydes' *Epitome of Physics*.[98] Blemmydes clearly influenced Theodore's reception of ancient philosophy.

A devoted and loyal student, Theodore came to take the side of Blemmydes in his rows with students and the authorities in Ephesos. Blemmydes was a notoriously difficult man and, in Akropolites' words, kept facing the hostility of "prominent people."[99] One of his five students, Romanos, accused the teacher of politically subversive and unorthodox writings.[100] Another student, Krateros, charged him with embezzlement from the estate of Manasses, the late metropolitan bishop of Ephesos, who had been Blemmydes' mentor in monastic practice. He made the accusation before the governor (*doux*) of the Thrakesion theme, Hikanatos, who is documented as holding this office in July 1239. The allegations were not proved, but the suspicion remained.[101] The head tutor added his voice to the denunciations of the philosopher, whom he saw as a competitor and feared his influence on the prince. In the *Satire* Theodore writes that the head tutor plotted to separate him from Blemmydes. "What need is there for me to describe his plots, his slanders, his libels, his insults, and everything else, which would have moved even a creature made of stone?"[102]

Vatatzes gave Blemmydes his unwavering support and acquitted him of the charges made by Romanos, but frictions with the local authorities dragged on.[103] The metropolitan bishop of Ephesos, Constantine Klaudioupolites, took the embezzlement charges seriously and forced Blemmydes to flee and take refuge at a monastic retreat on the island of Samos known as the Cave of Pythagoras. Again the emperor intervened and recalled Blemmydes back to his monastery.[104] The hatchet was not buried. John Komnenos Kantakouzenos, a later governor (*doux*) of the Thrakesion theme appointed sometime after June 1241 (he is attested in this capacity between November 1242 and 1249), detained Blemmydes as he was preparing to sail for the Balkans in order to study manuscripts unavailable in his library. Blemmydes was probably suspected of smuggling the stolen money to an area not controlled by the empire of Nicaea. His residence was searched for hidden treasure – even the cesspit was not spared. Blemmydes appealed to the emperor in writing and had a personal audience with him, whereupon Vatatzes took his side for the third time and forbade the metropolitan bishop Klaudioupolites to enter his monastery.[105] Theodore himself added his voice in support of Blemmydes by satirizing the avaricious and ambitious metropolitan, who hoped to become the patriarch of Antioch. In the end Klaudioupolites resigned from the see of Ephesos (probably not voluntarily) and took the monastic habit, after which he was disciplined by Manuel II, the new patriarch ordained in the second half of 1243.[106] Vatatzes provided Blemmydes with imperial letters of safe conduct and an escort of scouts for his extended book-hunting trip (sometime between 1242 and 1244), which took him to Mount Athos, Thessalonica, Ohrid, and Larissa. Vatatzes' policy of setting up libraries attached to schools explains the support that he offered to the scholar and teacher.[107]

After his return, Blemmydes was resolved to be a scholar and monk rather than a teacher. He declined the offer extended to him by the patriarch and the emperor (who himself had recalled him from the Balkans) to direct a school for boys and girls.[108] His letter of rejection reveals a strong sense of disappointment with ungrateful students and the employment opportunities available to the educated people. He complained that graduates were deemed worthy of the lowest positions and only the ignorant were promoted. Interest in learning ebbed, except for practical disciplines like agricultural science.[109] Faced with Blemmydes' Balkan journey and his unwillingness to offer instruction, Theodore turned to George Akropolites, who continued where his teacher had left off. Akropolites made the revealing remark in his *History* that Theodore "claimed" Blemmydes "to be his teacher," but not that Blemmydes *was* his teacher.[110]

Theodore's letters addressed to Blemmydes in the late 1240s and early 1250s show that he kept learning from the great philosopher by reading his works and paying him short visits, but not any longer in an instructional classroom setting. He writes that he saw him "in a customary manner" in his monastery in order to obtain his writings and that he rejoiced in receiving his most recent compositions.[111] He was captivated by the *Imperial Statue*, a mirror of princes addressed to him and his father in the late 1240s, perusing the work and readily citing memorable expressions and model figures.[112] Quite possibly Blemmydes had introduced the imperial prince already, between 1238 and 1241, to traditional theories of rulership, called "royal science" in the *Satire of the Tutor*, and had presented to him some of the material that found its way into the *Imperial Statue*. Blemmydes himself read some of the compositions of his student, such as the latter's imperial encomium on his father.[113] Theodore came to regard Blemmydes as the man chiefly responsible for his intellectual formation. He respected him as mentor, spiritual guide, political advisor, and much more: "Father, teacher, educator, intercessor before God, an expert in the affairs of the world, a comforter in sorrow, a guardian of the soul, a standard of goodness," and a truly holy, saintly and divine man.[114] Writing to Blemmydes as the sole emperor after 1254, he would praise him for laying the foundation of his learning. His teaching, compositions, and letters are said to have taught him the beauty of writing, natural philosophy, mathematics, ethics, and political principles.[115] He "created rivers with streams of noble words flowing in me and planted a tree bearing sweetest fruits."[116]

In advertising his association with Blemmydes, Theodore was doubtless motivated by a desire to fashion himself as a wise monarch. Great rulers needed to have great philosophers as their teachers and advisors. Alexander had his Aristotle and Marcus Aurelius his Hermogenes. Titus consorted with Apollonios of Tyana and opened the doors of the palace to wise men.[117] The imperial prince was at pains to portray himself as one of a distinguished series of enlightened rulers going back to antiquity. Above and beyond self-presentation, Blemmydes exerted a lasting influence on him and was a role model in spite of the brevity of the period of formal instruction. Like him, Theodore saw himself as a philosopher and wrote treatises on natural philosophy, rulership, and theology. Like him, Theodore considered himself a teacher and strove to instill knowledge in his companions and secretaries. He emulated Blemmydes in his sense of intellectual exclusivity, self-confidence, and contempt for people whom he saw as lacking reason. It was to Blemmydes that Theodore attributed his ability to "strike down human stupidity and give birth to the pearl of the intellect, that is, reason."[118]

Theodore demonstrated the special role Blemmydes played in his life when he chose to open his main epistolary collection with letters to the philosopher. These include his earliest surviving pieces of writing. The youthful letters to Blemmydes reflect efforts to ingratiate himself with his teacher. But they also alert us to differences in personality between the prince and the monk. Four of the letters ridicule two successive metropolitan bishops of Ephesos, Constantine Klaudioupolites and Nikephoros Pamphilos. We see Theodore taking the side of his teacher in attacking the money-loving Klaudioupolites, who had become the patriarch-elect of Antioch. His elevation was foiled only by the death in Nicaea of the patriarch of Constantinople, who was about to perform his ordination – probably Methodios, whose term in office in 1241 lasted only three months. When Constantine resigned from the sees of Ephesos and Antioch and wished to become the metropolitan bishop of his native Herakleia in Thrace, he estimated its annual revenue as 200 gold coins and asked Theodore to mediate with his father for a greater income. In a letter to Blemmydes, Theodore adopted an indignant attitude that closely matched that of his revered teacher. "Gold is everything, and virtue will not be achieved without it. Where is reverence today? Where is godliness? Where is active life in pursuit of good works? Where is simplicity? Everything strives for materiality, everything desires money."[119] Even more satirical is his portrait of the new metropolitan of Ephesos, Nikephoros Pamphilos, whom Theodore presents as an equally greedy and arrogant individual. A former deacon in the imperial clergy and a wealthy man, Nikephoros had difficult relations with the court.[120] In a letter to Blemmydes written at the time of Nikephoros' episcopal ordination, Theodore humorously compares the metropolitan with the Pharisee and the tax collector from Christ's parable: "The lowly Pharisee has welcomed the tax-collector presiding on high and has embraced with great desire the city of Ephesos as its bride." The joke was a memorable one and Theodore elaborated on it much later in his life. An essay composed ten years or more later, when he was the reigning emperor, exploits the comic coincidence that the metropolitan Nikephoros presented himself to the court precisely on the Sunday of the Pharisee and the Tax Collector during the pre-Lenten season.[121]

Blemmydes did not always approve of frivolous humor. Theodore apologized to him after he had jokingly asked Blemmydes to subject his sluggish servant to ecclesiastical punishment.[122] In a letter dating to about 1241, he confesses to his spiritual father the sinful appeal of court pleasures, such as hunting, and begs for forgiveness: "As we have been possessed by pleasure, we again went off course toward the pursuit of hunting . . . Do not condemn us!"[123] Unlike Theodore, Blemmydes had good relations with the metropolitan of Ephesos, Nikephoros Pamphilos, whom he described in his autobiography as "a real bishop, without pretense, without frills, and without falsehood."[124] The student tried to emulate the teacher, yet each man had his own values and way of life. In his early twenties, Theodore displayed his characteristic playfulness, *joie de vivre*, and sense of humor that would develop into a penchant for irony. In this regard Theodore stood worlds apart from Blemmydes, who was a strict disciplinarian, dour moralist, and reclusive man. Over time the prince came to favor different theological and social views than those held by his teacher, whom he nonetheless continued to respect and admire.

5 | Power-Sharing

Theodore played a growing role in royal governance in the 1240s. Evidence from his writings, documents, and seals allows us to gain a better understanding of this key aspect of his life in his twenties. The chapter reconstructs his responsibilities – fiscal, judicial, managerial, and other – in a power-sharing arrangement with his father. The division of duties between the senior and the junior emperor was a sign of the challenges the empire of Nicaea faced at a time of rapid territorial expansion and the rise of the Mongol menace from the East. Letters and other works of Theodore Laskaris give unique insights into practices of governance and aspects of Nicean society and the economy.

Before he turned twenty (in late 1241 or early 1242), Theodore experienced in quick succession the passing of his mother Irene, the remarriage of his father, and the death of his head tutor. His mother passed away most probably in December 1239, shortly before which she was tonsured with the name Eulogia.[1] A eulogist lamented her premature death. She was young, and her husband, in his early forties, was also still a young man – an observation perhaps alluding to his plans for remarriage. The emperor John Vatatzes was said to enjoy a powerful international position, for he controlled parts of the Balkans and the "Italians" were restricted to one sole fortress, the city of Constantinople.[2] Vatatzes quickly proceeded to choose a new wife. His goal was to strengthen his recent alliance with the Western Roman emperor Frederick II Hohenstaufen, who was to become his strategic partner for more than a decade in a trans-Mediterranean pact. The long partnership between the two rulers may seem paradoxical due to the traditional conflict between the eastern and the western medieval Roman emperors over the imperial title, yet it is fully understandable when account is taken of the powerful enemy they shared. Born in 1194 and raised in Palermo, Frederick inherited from his Sicilian Norman mother a fascination with the Mediterranean world and from his father, the emperor Henry VI from the Swabian Staufen family, a hostile relationship with the popes. An early letter of Frederick to Vatatzes – one among the several of surviving ones to the Nicaean ruler – shows that the two allies were united in their animosity toward the papacy. "All of us, kings and princes of the world, especially the zealots of the orthodox faith and religion," Frederick wrote, "have a common aversion and a special yet concealed disagreement with the prelates and primates of our church." The letter goes on to contrast the relations between emperors and the church in the East to the situation in "our Europe" and "the western region." "O fortunate Asia," the western Roman emperor exclaimed, "o fortunate rulers of the Eastern people who fear not the weapons of their subjects and the machinations of the popes!"[3]

Frederick benefited from the alliance with Vatatzes by receiving subsidies and military help. On his return from a crusade (1228–29) in the Holy Land, which he had led, ironically, as an excommunicate (the papacy would ban him from the church for the second and last time on Palm Sunday 1239), Frederick welcomed ambassadors from Nicaea, who brought him lavish gifts that included horses adorned with gold trappings, gold-embroidered silks, and "innumerable gold coins."[4] The next episode in the warming of the relations between the two emperors came in the 1230s, when Frederick was increasingly involved in warfare on the Apennine peninsula. On November 27, 1237, at Cortenuova, his troops inflicted a heavy defeat on the Lombard League of northern Italian cities.[5] Between July and October 1238, soldiers sent from Nicaea fought on Frederick's side during the siege of Brescia.[6] By that time the two emperors had reached an agreement and Frederick is reported to have acknowledged the legitimacy of John Vatatzes' claims to Constantinople.[7]

John Vatatzes initially used the alliance to undermine crusading efforts in support of the Latin empire, but his main agenda was to achieve the restoration of Constantinople. After the Nicaean-Bulgarian siege of Constantinople in 1235–36, Pope Gregory IX actively campaigned for a crusade against Nicaea. He charged Baldwin II, who was in western Europe at the time, with leading the large army, and appealed to lords and bishops, mostly in France and Hungary, to take up the cross. If they were unable to do so, they were to commute their crusader oaths into financial support for the Latin empire.[8] A brief letter from Pope Gregory IX issued in Viterbo on May 21, 1237, notified John Vatatzes of the imminent arrival of a large crusade.[9] Yet Frederick obstructed Baldwin's troops from sailing from north Italian ports. In the spring of 1238 Gregory IX complained to Frederick that he appeared to "favor the schismatics in their error."[10] The alliance seemed to produce its desired effect. It was only in June 1239 that Baldwin finally set off across the land route from central Europe and returned to his native city, Constantinople. John of Brienne had passed away in the meantime (March 1237), and Baldwin was crowned emperor around Easter 1240. His troops recovered Tzouroulos in Thrace and took captive many of its inhabitants, whom John Vatatzes later ransomed.[11] The Latin empire received a new lease of life.

In the late summer of 1240 John Vatatzes welcomed his young bride, Frederick's daughter Constanza, who was only around ten years old.[12] Constanza had been born out of wedlock from Frederick's long liaison with Bianca Lancia, a lady who originated from a noble family of imperial loyalists in Piedmont. Bianca Lancia's uncle Manfred II, the marquis of Busca (b. 1185/95–d. 1257/59), served Frederick as his vicar general in Piedmont after 1238.[13] Manfred's sons, Federico and Galvano Lancia, supported the emperor unstintingly in his struggle for control of Italy. After Frederick became a widower in 1241 on the death of his third and most recent wife, Isabella of England, he is reported to have wedded Bianca in order to legitimize their three children. Constanza's younger brother, Manfred, thus became eligible for the succession. In 1240, Constanza arrived in Asia Minor with a dowry consisting of precious jewelry and an entourage from her native Italy. She was accompanied by ladies-in-waiting and Greek monks from Calabria who took up residence in the monastery of Hyakinthos in Nicaea.[14] John Vatatzes presented his child bride with a generous gift consisting of landed estates and fortresses, which she named more than sixty years later in Latin as Quera, Stilar (probably Stylarion, on the Karaburun peninsula near Smyrna), and Cameres (Parion on the Sea of Marmara, not far from Pegai) in the kingdom of Natolin (that is, Anatolia). The annual revenue from the properties is said to have amounted to the fabulous sum of "thirty thousand *hyperpyra* of fine gold."[15] On becoming Nicaean empress, Constanza changed her name to Anna, which was more comprehensible to Greek-speakers. The wedding festivities in the palace of Nicaea were designed to broadcast a message of imperial might. John Vatatzes and the child bride made a ceremonial appearance in the palace courtyard on a platform brightly lit by torches (*prokypsis*). Verses chanted on this occasion glorified the sunlike emperor as "the eye of the inhabited world." Theodore himself found the celebrations worthy of mention in his *Satire of the Tutor*.[16]

The marriage that started with such pomp and circumstance proved unhappy and resulted in no offspring during its fourteen-year duration. Scandalously, the senior emperor became infatuated with an Italian lady-in-waiting of his bride, a woman by the name of Marchesina, with whom he had a lasting and publicly displayed relationship. Marchesina was granted the right to wear purple shoes and use purple horse trappings, symbolizing imperial status. Her retinue was larger than that of the empress.[17] The extramarital affair drew criticism in ecclesiastical circles. In about 1248, Blemmydes drove away Marchesina and her entire retinue when they entered to worship in the monastery of St. Gregory the Miracle Worker near Ephesos.[18] He issued an open letter in which he gave a detailed account of his righteous action. "Once again," he writes at the beginning of this public pamphlet, "I am in conflict with those in power and am accused of having a difficult character."[19] His relations with the court, strained already on account of his unwillingness to direct a state-funded school, reached their nadir. It was only his reputation as the leading philosopher of his age that prevented him from falling out of favor. Sometime after this scandal, between 1248 and 1250, Blemmydes presented John Vatatzes and Theodore Laskaris with his mirror of princes, *Imperial Statue*.[20] This critically written work warns against the misuse of public funds and crown wealth, and pays particular attention to moral misconduct, such as fits of anger and bouts of amorous passion. "How can a man be just," he asked, "who does injustice to himself and to the woman with whom he commits debauchery?"[21]

After the wedding celebrations in Nicaea, John Vatatzes and Theodore Laskaris went to Prousa with the assembled army. Military preparations were underway; battles with the Latins in Bithynia have been dated to 1240.[22] The tutor stayed in the meantime in Nicaea, where he fell ill. He left the city to visit Theodore for a week and then moved to the Thrakesion theme, where his health worsened further. His royal tutee was summoned to see him on his deathbed, but this plan was not fulfilled, because the gravely ill man passed away before the prince reached his residence. Theodore tells us that his crocodile tears barely concealed his joy at the demise of the hated tutor: "The 'dew of exultation' rose above 'Mount Zion' in my soul (Psalm 132:3). After shedding a few tears in a public capacity and saying a word of sorrow with the tip of my lips, I walked away in great joy."[23] The passing of the tutor, he wishes us to believe, enabled him to devote himself to philosophy without the tutor's suffocating oversight. Two impediments, however, remained: Blemmydes' reluctance to offer instruction and the growing burden of public responsibility that Theodore had to shoulder.

Viceroy of Anatolia

After the wedding John Vatatzes prepared for a siege of Constantinople. The attack was carried out between May and June 1241 by land and sea.

The Nicaean fleet, of around thirty galleys, was placed under a new commander, the Armenian Iophre.[24] The emperor Baldwin and his newly arrived troops defended the city well, and the Venetian *podestà* in Constantinople, Giovanni Michiel, led a naval counterattack, destroying many Nicaean battleships. The siege failed, and a two-year peace with Baldwin II was concluded on June 24, 1241. John Vatatzes and his son are both mentioned as representing the Nicaean side. Theodore Laskaris was, thus, perceived as having an official role in governance and already acting in the capacity of coemperor.[25]

The peace with the Latins gave John Vatatzes an opportunity to settle the score with the Epirote family of Komnenos Doukas. He viewed the rulers of the fragmented kingdom of Epiros-Thessalonica with undiminished suspicion after the blinded Theodore of Epiros, ever scheming against Nicaea, had managed to ingratiate himself with Ivan Asen II of Bulgaria. The widowed tsar married his daughter Irene and put great trust in her.[26] In around 1237 Theodore of Epiros entered Thessalonica in disguise, ousted his brother Manuel, and placed his son John on the throne as "emperor of the Romans." Exiled to the city of Attaleia in the sultanate of Rum, Manuel sought the assistance of John Vatatzes, swore an oath of allegiance to him, and received six armed galleys to assist him in reclaiming his rights. But Manuel changed his mind after disembarking in Thessaly and came to a compromise agreement with his blinded brother and nephews on the division of territories.[27] In an attempt to persuade the Epirote ruling family to accept his overlordship and abandon claims to the imperial office, John Vatatzes invited the blinded Theodore to Nicaea and entertained him as his dinner guest. Diplomacy proved fruitless, however, and the emperor had no choice but seek a military solution.

The Bulgarians no longer posed a formidable obstacle. In June 1241 Ivan Asen passed away and was succeeded by his underage son Koloman (Kaliman I), a brother of Theodore's wife Elena.[28] In late 1241 John Vatatzes mobilized the large land and sea army that had besieged Constantinople unsuccessfully and led it into the Balkans on a campaign against the "emperor of the Romans" in Thessalonica.[29] His twenty-year-old son Theodore was left behind in Pegai on the Marmara coast with the task of managing affairs in Asia Minor and sending reports to John Vatatzes, especially with regard to the Mongol threat. He would again remain in Asia Minor, and perform similar tasks, in 1246 and in 1252–53 while his father was campaigning in Europe.[30] His position can be described as a "viceroy of Anatolia" – the designated governor of the area in his father's absence. In the 1240s the emperor father and son had grave reasons for concern lest

Nicaea's military resources become overstretched. After a series of destructive raids, the Mongols appeared to be closing in on the empire of Nicaea. The Mongol horde of Batu, Genghis Khan's grandson, had established itself on the steppes of the lower Volga along the northern Caspian Sea and in December 1240 sacked Kiev, whose metropolitan received his ordination in Nicaea.[31] The Mongol army then invaded central Europe in the spring of 1241. Battles fought in April 1241 at Liegnitz (Legnica) in Silesia and at Mohi in Hungary resulted in crushing defeats of the Christian forces. It was only the death of the Great Khan Ögedei, a son of Genghis Khan, in December 1241 that led to the recall of the Mongol high command to Karakorum and interrupted the mighty incursion into Europe.[32] The victories of the invading Mongols had serious political consequences. The princes of the Rus fell under Mongol tributary dependence and some of them fled their homeland. One of them, Rostislav Mikhailovich (the son of the saintly Mikhail of Chernigov, martyred at the camp of Batu in Sarai on the Volga), migrated to Hungary in 1242 and married Béla IV's daughter Anna, a cousin of Theodore. Another fugitive grandee from Galicia, Jacob Svetoslav, moved to Bulgaria and acquired a lordship along the Balkan Mountains. The Bulgarian tsars themselves began to pay annual tribute to the Mongols of the Golden Horde after 1241.[33]

The Mongol horde based in the Mughan plain along the southern coast of the Caspian Sea was a greater source of trouble for Nicaea than Batu's horde along the northern Caspian. The sultanate of Rum under Ghiyāth al-Dīn Kaykhusraw II (r. 1237–45/46) was ill prepared to face the Mongol invasion. A fratricidal succession struggle at the beginning of Kaykhusraw's reign ushered in a period of internal strife, aggravated by population pressure due to the Mongols and warfare with Khorezmian warrior bands.[34] At the beginning of 1242 Chormaghun, the commander of the Mughan horde who was afflicted with an incapacitating illness, was replaced by the energetic Bayju. On the orders of Batu, Bayju immediately led an incursion deep into Asia Minor.[35] When his warriors reached Erzurum (Theodosioupolis, Karin) in early 1242, its Christian and Muslim inhabitants refused to surrender and shouted abuse at the enemy encamped outside the walls. The Mongols took the city by force, put its entire population to the sword, and returned to their pastures in the Mughan plain.[36] The news traveled fast through Asia Minor and reached Theodore at Pegai. He immediately alerted his father. The Nicaean troops were in front of the walls of Thessalonica and about to lay siege when the alarming message arrived. Vatatzes swore those around him who had heard the report to secrecy, so as to be able to negotiate with the ruler of

Thessalonica, John Komnenos Doukas, from a position of strength. He succeeded in convincing him to exchange the imperial title for the rank of despot, the second in the court hierarchy, and to swear an oath of allegiance. The Nicaean army then hastily withdrew to Asia Minor.[37]

In the spring of the following year (1243), Bayju returned. This time Kaykhusraw II gathered a large but undisciplined army of vassals and allies, including 2,000 Latins and 1,000 Greeks, some of whom came from Nicaea. According to a Western source, John Vatatzes had an agreement to supply the sultan with 400 fully armed warriors whenever a need arose.[38] A pitched battle, won by the Mongols, was fought at the defile of Köse Dağ on July 26, 1243. The defeated Seljuk sultan fled in panic to Ankara and his mother sought safety in Cilician Armenia. The Mongols sacked Kayseri (Caesarea in Cappadocia) and other cities before returning to Mughan at the end of the year. Kaykhusraw was obliged to pay an annual tribute to the Mongols and a diploma issued by Batu confirmed his rule.[39] He passed away in late 1245 and his powerful vizier enthroned his eldest son, 'Izz al-Dīn Kaykāwūs II (r. 1246–56, 1257–61), still a child, whose mother was the daughter of a Greek priest. The young sultan maintained close ties with Nicaea and seems at some point to have married a woman from the Nicaean aristocracy.[40] One of his two younger brothers, Rukn al-Dīn Kılıç Arslān IV (r. 1248–54, 1256–65), who had a Turkish mother, kept closer relations with the Mongols. After doing homage to the Great Khan Güyük (r. 1246–48) in Karakorum, Rukn al-Dīn returned with a Mongol decree that awarded him the status of sole sultan and started issuing coins influenced by Mongol types. In 1249 a military conflict between the two sultans flared up and resulted in an arrangement by which 'Izz al-Dīn ruled over central Anatolia and Rukn al-Dīn controlled the eastern parts of the realm closer to the Mongol overlords.[41] A Mongol protectorate was in effect established over almost all of Anatolia, with the sole exception of the empire of Nicaea. Seljuk grandees and the sultans were required to receive an official sanction of their authority from the Mongol overlords. The emperor of Trebizond and the king of Cilician Armenia were also tributaries of the Mongols, and were obliged to display in person their subordinate status and renew periodically their investiture by the supreme Mongol ruler. The Grand Komnenos Manuel (r. 1238–63) attended the inauguration of the Great Khan Güyük in 1246 in Karakorum. An Armenian high official, the Constable Smbat, set off in 1247 for central Asia and did not return until three years later. In 1253 the Armenian king, Hetoum, himself left for Karakorum disguised as a muleteer and also did not come back for three years.[42]

Theodore Laskaris feared that the empire of Nicaea might share the fate of its Anatolian neighbors. Pieces of information about Mongol customs and practices trickled in by hearsay. He was familiar, for example, with the skillful way in which the Mongols rode their small, sturdy horses. A certain Paktiares died, he wrote in a letter, after galloping "in a Tatar fashion."[43] He preferred to call the Mongols "Tatars" (as in "Tatar tribe" and "Tatar arrogance") in the manner of other thirteenth-century Byzantine authors rather than Scythians, a traditional name used for steppe nomads that he ascribed to the Cumans.[44] He designated the Mongols also as "Medes," probably in order to associate them geographically with north-western Iran (ancient Media), the base for their incursions into Asia Minor in the 1240s and 1250s.[45] Whether Theodore believed in the frightful and fantastic stories that the Mongols were dog-headed men and cannibals is not known.[46] But he must have been disquieted by their reputation for cruelty. The mere rumor of a Mongol incursion caused panic among the population, as it emerges from events in Nicaea in 1265. At that time, the residents of the city learned by word of mouth that the Mongols had made a sudden attack on the city and already breached the walls, slaughtering everyone on their way. Terrified people hid in fresh graves and in recesses of their houses. The report turned out to be false. After the citizens were calmed, an inquiry into the origins of the rumor was conducted and attributed to a Lenten street procession of women carrying an icon of the Holy Virgin. As the women were imploring the Mother of God to give them help against the Turks and the Mongols, bystanders misunderstood the prayer and started spreading the news that the Mongols were in the city.[47]

The defeat at Köse Dağ in July 1243 brought the Nicaean emperor and the Seljuk sultan even closer than before. Vatatzes and Kaykhusraw II met in the border fortress of Tripolis on the Maeander River, where they concluded a defensive pact against the Mongols.[48] The priority of Vatatzes was the security of the frontier. A Mongol invasion was considered imminent. Bayju was believed to have proposed through an embassy sent to Pope Innocent IV (1243–54) in 1248 a joint military operation against their common enemies, Frederick in Italy and Vatatzes in Asia Minor.[49] Vatatzes arranged for weapons – bows, arrows, shields, armor, and stone-throwing machines – to be stockpiled in public buildings in the cities. Ironsmiths were commissioned to manufacture additional arms. Wheat, barley, and other cereals were stored in granaries and depots for the eventuality of a poor harvest or a siege.[50] The grain was secured with lead seals, and newlywed husbands were required to list their arms in marriage contracts.[51] A panegyric of Vatatzes dating to 1252–53 refers to villages and cities being well supplied with inexpensive foodstuffs.[52] In this way the city population was made to prepare for Mongol incursions. The raids on the sultanate of Rum drove migrants across Nicaea's eastern frontier. In his speech in praise of his father (1250–52), Theodore wrote with pride that relations with the Seljuks had come full circle in his lifetime. The "Persian" (that is, the Seljuk Turks) no longer extracted tribute as in the past. His father John Vatatzes was receiving in his realm displaced individuals and money from the Seljuks.[53] Entire families residing in the sultanate are reported to have crossed into the empire of Nicaea during a great famine. They bought grain and chicken at high prices, bringing great profit to local producers.[54] According to Theodore's encomium, some of the newcomers migrated permanently and were made to exchange habitation with "the Scythians" (namely, the Cumans), who were transferred to frontier areas.[55] As a Eurasian steppe people, the Cumans understood the Mongol and Turkmen styles of warfare and were an effective first line of defense.

The need for the coemperor Theodore to take on ever-growing powers stemmed from the rapid expansion of Nicaea into the Balkans – an expansion that was largely the result of the weakness of the Latin empire and the Bulgarian kingdom. In 1243 or early 1244 the emperor Baldwin left on another tour of western courts and did not return until October 1248, creating a power vacuum.[56] In September 1246 John Vatatzes learned while carrying out an inspection along the Maritsa valley that the Bulgarian tsar Kaliman had been killed in a coup that placed on the throne his younger half-brother, Michael Asen, Ivan Asen II's son from his marriage to Irene, the daughter of Theodore of Epiros. The Mongols of Iran were engaged at the time in warfare with the remnants of the Abbasid caliphate and Theodore Laskaris had once again remained in Asia Minor. Vatatzes decided to advance with his small army toward Serres in Macedonia, even though it was late in the year and the weather was getting worse.[57] At Serres the walls of the lower town had been dismantled during the Bulgarian occupation, but the acropolis was still heavily fortified. Vatatzes' irregular troops occupied the defenseless lower town and the Bulgarian governor, Dragotas, who originated from Melnik (Melenikon), was persuaded to surrender. At this point, the urban elites in Melnik and Thessalonica approached John Vatatzes and agreed to switch their allegiance in exchange for imperial charters that guaranteed the safety and tax-exempt status of their properties.[58] Their example was contagious. The new acquisitions of John Vatatzes stretched from Verroia, west of Thessalonica, to northern Macedonia, including Skopje, Veles, Prosek, and the district of Velevousdion (Kyustendil), to the northern Rhodope Mountains, including Stenimachos and Tzepaina (Tsepena, near today's village of Dorkovo).[59] The ruler of Thessalonica, Demetrios Komnenos Doukas (another son of the blinded Theodore of Epiros), was betrayed by a group of conspirators who opened one of the gates of the city to let in Vatatzes' army. He avoided heavy punishment after the appeal of his sister Irene and was sent to Asia Minor as a prisoner. The Epirote ruling family was not fully removed from local authority, however. Theodore of Epiros was recognized as the master of Vodena (Edessa) and nearby areas. His nephew Michael II Komnenos Doukas (Michael of Epiros) ruled over Thessaly, Epiros, and areas of Macedonia that included Pelagonia (Bitolja), Ohrid, and Prilep. The new borders of Nicaea with the kingdom of Bulgaria were set by a treaty that stipulated the tsar was to assist the emperor with troops during campaigns.[60]

The westward expansion almost doubled Nicaea's territory and diverted much of the attention of the senior emperor away from Anatolia. In the summer of 1247 Vatatzes led his troops, along with Cuman and Bulgarian reinforcements, into eastern Thrace. The Cumans devastated the countryside, and the army reached the walls of Constantinople but suffered defeat on July 27. In August Vatatzes peacefully annexed Derkos (Durusu) and Medeia (Kıyıköy) on the Black Sea. He besieged Vizye (Vize), whose Latin garrison agreed to surrender. By contrast, Tzouroulos was taken by force, and many of its Latin defenders fell into captivity and were imprisoned in Nicaea.[61] In 1248 John Vatatzes was again fighting with the Latins, this time in the region of Nikomedeia, and posed a threat to Constantinople.[62] The absences of the senior emperor from Asia Minor could last for more than a year. For example, in early 1252 he left on a campaign against Michael of Epiros and did not return until the late autumn of 1253. Given the preoccupation of the senior emperor with events across the Hellespont, there was a pressing need for Theodore to take up an active role in governance in Asia Minor.

Coruler

In a self-referential passage of the *Satire*, a work written at the time of or shortly after the death of the head tutor in 1240, Theodore Laskaris gives the following self-description: "The son of rulers (*anakton*) who is about to rule through the Holy Spirit, a caretaker of many people, a protector of cities, a solace of the populace, and a midpoint of the state and coadjutor (*sylleptor kriseon*)."[63] He saw his position as a junior one. By saying that he

is "about to rule through the Holy Spirit," Theodore implies that he had
not yet been crowned and anointed, ceremonies that marked the beginning
of the divine ministry of kingship. In letters dating to the 1240s and early
1250s Theodore often spoke of himself as an emperor (*basileus*) and my
imperial majesty (*basileia mou*), while his father John Vatatzes styled
himself both *basileus* and *autokrator*, a combination of titles restricted to
the senior and crowned emperor only.[64] By describing himself as a coadjutor or co-decision-maker (*sylleptor kriseon*), he refers to a power-sharing
arrangement. Traces of this arrangement appear in his letters and on
his seals.

What were Theodore's responsibilities? An undated letter (Ep. 19) to
Blemmydes from the period of his coemperorship is a good place to start.
Theodore explains to Blemmydes that he was prevented from visiting him
"in the customary manner" in his monastery, because he needed to hold
court jointly with his father. His routine consisted of "the reception of and
obeisance to my holy master, the father and emperor, after which come the
daily discussion, the memoranda and petitions pertaining to beneficial
matters arising, and many other things of this kind appropriate to the
moment."[65] The "daily" court meeting took place on that occasion in
Nicaea. Theodore explains that he has just arrived in Nymphaion and is
preparing to travel onward to see his revered teacher near Ephesos.

His duties at court included participation in daily ceremonies in which
he performed obeisance (*proskynesis*) and led a ritual reception (*proypantesis*) of his father.[66] *Proskynesis* was enacted in different ways in Byzantium, ranging from a simple bow of the head to kneeling to full
prostration.[67] Strict protocol governed the public meeting between a junior
and a senior emperor. The custom followed in the fourteenth century when
the two emperors met outside the palace was for them to remain on
horseback, while their entourage dismounted. After removing his hat the
junior emperor bent down, clasped the hands of the senior emperor, and
kissed him on the face.[68] Theodore speaks of the customary nature of
performing *proskynesis* as a gesture of respect for the senior emperor and
himself received *proskynesis* from his subjects. In a letter dating to his
coemperorship he mentions that the "honorable *archontes*" from Ephesos,
whether local grandees or thematic officials, presented themselves to "do
obeisance to my imperial majesty, as is customary."[69] The setting of daily
reception of the imperial officials – whether by the two emperors or the
junior emperor alone – ranged from the hall of the palace to the palace
courtyard and the tent of the emperor. In the spring of 1256 Theodore
Laskaris, by then the sole ruler, received most of his officials at the end of

matins, the time "customary for them to enter," in his tent at the camp near Pegai.[70] The tradition attested in the tenth and in the fourteenth centuries was for the daily reception to be held twice, both at matins and at vespers. The practice seems to have been observed in the empire in exile. Theodore writes in letters dating to his coemperorship that he went into the palace immediately after the end of matins and exited the palace just before sunset.[71]

Some of the business conducted at the court emerges from the above-mentioned undated letter to Blemmydes (Ep. 19). What is meant by the word "memoranda" or "reminders" (*anamneseis*) becomes clearer when we consider the responsibilities of the imperial official of memorialist (*epi ton anamneseon*). His duties are reported in the fourteenth century to have traditionally consisted of "keeping record of those who excelled in campaigns and elsewhere, and making mention of them to the emperor, so that they could receive the appropriate honors."[72] In other words, some of the memoranda pertained to the granting of honors and economic rewards to soldiers, officials, and others. Making such decisions was part of the daily job of the emperor and the coemperor. Another task mentioned in the letter to Blemmydes (Ep. 19), a task especially important for Theodore as a coemperor, was receiving memoranda of petition (*hypomneseis*).[73] A Nicaean formulary for writing petitions to the emperor suggests a widespread practice. The text, which is short and simple, presents individuals complaining about injustice and expecting the emperor's intervention: "We, the unworthy subjects of our mighty and holy lord and emperor from the area so-and-so report daringly to our holy lord, emperor and master that we suffer injustice from so-and-so, when so-and-so, concerning such and such things."[74] Some of Blemmydes' letters to Theodore are elaborately written petitions and create the impression that John Vatatzes had ceded his son considerable executive authority. One letter requests a grant of arable land. Another asks for an annual salary (*roga*) to be paid to an unspecified individual. Elsewhere Blemmydes thanked his student for the speedy fulfillment of requests, exclaiming that this "shows that you will give us, if possible, the entire world."[75] In yet another letter, written between 1241 and 1249, Blemmydes drew Theodore's attention to the fiscal injustice done to the monastery of St. Gregory the Miracle Worker. Migrants from the island of Samos, now residing in Ephesos and the surrounding countryside, had been assigned in the past to "serve" the abbot Blemmydes, evidently as dependent peasants. Later they had been reassigned to a local soldier. Blemmydes appealed to the coemperor to authorize the soldier to collect only land tax (*telos*) from the Samians and require them again to render "service" to Blemmydes, whether through corvée labor, payment of rents, or some other obligation.[76] A letter from Theodore to the metropolitan of Ephesos Nikephoros responds to a petition by Blemmydes between 1244 and 1249. Blemmydes had asked Theodore to reverse the sale of a farm that had previously belonged to the monastery of St. Gregory the Miracle Worker on the grounds that its purchase by the metropolitan see of Ephesos was unlawful. Theodore ordered the annulment of the transaction and required the metropolitan of Ephesos to return the farm after getting back the purchase money, without compensation for any improvements of the property. Referring to himself as "my imperial majesty," he calls his letter to Nikephoros of Ephesos an ordinance (*prostagma*), the term used for a type of official imperial decree.[77]

Petitioning the emperor had a long history in Byzantium, whether on the Hippodrome in late antiquity, during imperial processions on the streets of Constantinople in the ninth century, during military campaigns in the tenth century, or on appointed days in the suburban Philopation palace in the early twelfth century.[78] What made the practice different in Nicaea was the itinerancy of the emperor. The petitions in Nicaea varied in their manner of delivery, some in person and others in writing, some in the palace and others outside. Theodore writes in 1257 that he had the habit of admitting petitioners to the royal residence at midday and riding his horse outside to "hear people unable to join those waiting at the gates of the palace."[79] His travels in Anatolia gave him the opportunity to hear the grievances of petitioners.

The logistics of his itinerancy deserve closer attention. As we have seen (Map 2), his tours focused on the core agricultural area of the empire of Nicaea. Theodore claimed that he had visited "the best part of Asia" and expressed an almost romantic wanderlust: "I like the change of places because of the different characteristics of locations."[80] Frequent and imaginative travel metaphors reinforce the impression of a fascination with mobility. He contrasted, for example, people who injure their feet and knees when they walk on difficult mountainous roads to those who take a smooth and divine path.[81] He moved among "irksome dogs," walked on "an ungrateful path" and "the path of ignorance," and described himself as "a dead man walking" in a moment of shame.[82] A phrase from Psalm 118, "walking in wide open space," was a metaphor for a carefree existence – before trouble and misfortunes.[83] The court usually wintered in Nymphaion and spent the summer in Nicaea, although the senior and junior emperors sometimes broke this rhythm. In January 1234 Vatatzes received four visiting friars in Nicaea rather than in Nymphaion. Theodore was in Nicaea in late January and early February on several occasions, for he describes as an eyewitness the feast day of St. Tryphon (February 1) in his encomiastic vita. The permanent royal residences – the palaces – functioned as economic units with their own food supply, staff, and storage facilities. In July 1239 the monks of the monastery of St. George Exokastritis in Smyrna complained that imperial food and wine caterers, who seem to have served the Perklystra palace, were encroaching on their properties. Vatatzes ordered the governor (*doux*) of the Thrakesion theme to investigate the situation.[84] Fine imperial clothes were stored in the palaces for ceremonial needs, and Theodore used them as gifts, which were highly valued by his companions.[85]

The tent was the temporary residence of choice when Theodore toured areas outside cities with royal palaces. Contemporaries were awestruck when they saw the cortege of John Vatatzes, with its numerous tents, stables, and horses.[86] Descriptions of twelfth-century aristocratic tents stress their size and ornate decoration.[87] Theodore's imperial tent was similarly large and well equipped for prolonged stays. His tent pitched in the vicinity of Pegai in the spring of 1256 accommodated many people, including officials and clergymen.[88] In one letter, Theodore describes his hunting tent as "a very small one," drawing an implicit contrast between his current humble dwelling and the large, sumptuous tent to which he was used.[89] A sense of its size can be inferred from the decision made by synod of the patriarch Germanos sometime during his term of office (1223–40), which gave permission for the placement within the imperial tent of "an easily portable tent" attached with ropes. The smaller tent was to serve as a chapel when the emperor was on the move.[90] An idea about this portable chapel-tent can be obtained from the diplomatic gift made sometime between 1261 and 1264 to the Mongol khan, Hülegü, in an attempt to foster Christianity at his court. Made of thick silk material with embroidered images of the saints, the tent was supported by crosses and ropes and contained the holy vessels of the liturgy.[91] Theodore Laskaris is silent about inns and guesthouses, possibly because they were unsuitable for royal tours of the country. Such facilities for travelers were maintained in thirteenth-century Byzantine Anatolia. The Sosandra monastery near Magnesia, founded by John Vatatzes, had facilities for the sick and for travelers.[92] The thirteenth century saw a flurry of caravanserai building in the sultanate of Rum. Whether this scale of construction was mirrored on the other side of the frontier is a question archaeologists are yet to address.[93]

The examination so far allows for a summary assessment of Theodore's duties. He held minor judicial powers that are seen in petitions addressed to him (for example, regarding the reversal of an illegal sale). His interest in the principles of royal justice is therefore fully understandable: royal justice was universal, scrupulous, and contributed to the well-being and preservation of the polity as a whole.[94] As a coemperor, he held powers over the distribution and management of tax resources. A piece transmitted among his letters to Blemmydes is a preamble to an imperial charter written during his coemperorship. It is followed in the Laurentian collection by a rhetorical elaboration on an unspecified grant, evidently to Blemmydes, in which he speaks of himself as "my imperial majesty."[95] Theodore had the power to make appointments. He nominated the monk Antony as the abbot of the monastery of the Virgin *tou Kouzena* in a letter to the metropolitan of Philadelphia, Phokas, in which he refers to himself as "my imperial majesty."[96] At times when his father was in the Balkans, Theodore had also the authority to receive foreign ambassadors, as we will see in the following chapter, and preside over deliberations of the privy council. In an undated pre-1254 letter to Mouzalon he mentioned presenting his views at the palace on questions of warfare and administration, concluding with the cryptic remark: "Nestor rather than Odysseus won. Think who he might be."[97] The Homeric figures served as code names for individuals who took part in a meeting of the council. The letter does not mention John Vatatzes, who seems to have been at a different location. Finally, Theodore played a part in implementing the agricultural, economic, and educational policies pursued by his father.

Lead seals provide additional clues as to Theodore's powers. A group of seals with an image of St. Theodore Stratelates (Figs. 17a and 17b) stand in stark contrast with his properly imperial seal, which was produced after his accession as sole emperor in November 1254 (Fig. 17c). The latter features his image standing, facing forward, and dressed in imperial regalia, according to the standard sigillographic representation of the emperor. The seals with the image of St. Theodore lack an imperial portrait, however, and are inscribed with the following prayer addressed to the military saint: "May you protect, athlete (of Christ), the emperor (*basileus*) Theodore, the ruler's son (*anaktopais*) and a Doukas." The inscription differs from that expected from a standard imperial seal. The designation "ruler's son" (*anaktopais*) corresponds to the way Theodore described himself in the *Satire* as "a son of rulers" (*hyios anakton*) and Akropolites' reference to him as "the ruler's son" (*hyios anaktos*) in verses composed during his coemperorship.[98] These seals, therefore, are evidence of Theodore's status as a coemperor before he assumed sole rule and served to authenticate ordinances and official letters. It is perhaps not insignificant that a number of his correspondents, all men close to him, were imperial secretaries (*grammatikoi*):

Balsamon, Kallistos, Kostomyres, Manikaites, George Akropolites, Joseph Mesopotamites, Hagiotheodorites, and the two brothers Phaix, one of whom was called John.[99] The secretaries worked at the imperial chancery and were also entrusted with ad hoc tasks, such as administering land grants.[100] They seem to have assisted either the father or the son emperor, or both, depending on need and occasion. Some of those mentioned in his letters are attested in other contemporary sources. Kostomyres was either John Kostomyres, an imperial secretary and head of the tax district (*katepanikion*) of Smyrna, or Nicholas Kostomyres, a correspondent of the teacher George Babouskomites.[101] Theodore's close friend and teacher Akropolites began his civil-service career as a *grammatikos*. Joseph Mesopotamites was one of Vatatzes' secretaries during his Balkan campaign of 1252–53.[102] Theodore rhetorically describes Mesopotamites' duties as "serving in beneficial matters and cutting off harmful things." The surgical metaphor, which elsewhere refers to the strictness of imperial justice, suggests that Mesopotamites enforced decisions of the central administration.[103]

Another seal of which a single specimen survives – an aniconic seal of poor quality – opens a window into the relationship between senior and junior emperor. The following inscription runs on both sides: "A seal of Komnenos Doukas of the Laskaris branch confirming the decisions of the father ruler (*patranax*)." The seal belonged to an imperial prince who clearly had official duties and who was descended from the families of Komnenos, Doukas, and Laskaris. Its owner could have been no other than Theodore. The expression "father ruler" (*patranax*) corresponds to the self-designation "the ruler's son" (*anaktopais*) on his seals made during his coemperorship and reminds us of his self-description as "the son of rulers" in the *Satire*.[104] The inscription on the aniconic seal presents a prince who carried out decisions and policies already set by his father, the senior emperor. The arrangement fits into the supreme command of Theodore Laskaris in Anatolia during his father's campaigns across the Hellespont. Notably, the family name Komnenos is added to those of Doukas and Laskaris, demonstrating Theodore's claim – one not expressed elsewhere – to be descended from the twelfth-century imperial dynasty.

The decisions of the senior emperor that his son confirmed, according to the seal, may have pertained to fiscal justice. Vatatzes had a reputation for selecting honest tax collectors and dismissing corrupt and rapacious ones.[105] Theodore was probably charged with enforcing his father's economic policies, which were aimed at improving the provisioning cities and stimulating agricultural and textile production.[106] Vatatzes is reported to have founded agricultural crown estates (*zeugelateia*) and farms.[107] His goal was to increase the security of cities in the face of an anticipated Mongol invasion. Peasants were settled on these estates with the task of provisioning the population of fortified towns in the vicinity.[108] Vatatzes' agenda was also to develop the economic self-sufficiency of the crown. The senior emperor took a personal interest in agriculture and viniculture, and is said to have handpicked knowledgeable estate managers.[109] He was admired in the fourteenth century for having presented the empress with a crown bought with revenues from imperial chicken farms.[110] Most of the sources are later and anecdotal, but there is contemporary corroboratory evidence. *Synopsis chronike* lauds Vatatzes for demonstrating to his subjects how to augment their agricultural wealth and flocks through the example of his animal farms breeding horses, cows, sheep, and camels. Blemmydes lamented that agricultural science was more valued in his own day than philosophy when he declined the teaching post offered to him by the patriarch Manuel II.[111] A document of 1231 gives an insight into the organization of crown lands. Following Vatatzes' order, Stephanos Kalopyros, the head of the imperial estate (*basilikon zeugelateion*) of Koukoulos, located on the plain of Memaniomenos near Smyrna, arranged for an agricultural plot of land belonging to this estate to be granted to the monastery of Lembos. One of the executors of the donation was Basil, the guardian of the palace (*palatophylax*), a title that suggests he was attached to the Periklystra palace in Smyrna. The official was charged during the Palaiologan period with the supervision of building and repair work in the palace, but if one judges from the document of 1231, in the empire of Nicaea he supervised the agricultural estates of the crown.[112] The crown estates supplied the emperors and the court with food and wine during their periodic visits, generated income, and had the additional function of cultivating and disseminating agricultural expertise.

Scattered references in letters and treatises indicate that Theodore exercised oversight over the imperial estates. Managers (*oikonomoi*) were placed under his control. He was familiar with specific villages and the quality of crops. He knew, for example, that the best barley for horse fodder came from the estate of Aristenos, which bordered Koukoulos.[113] He was well aware of the seasonality of agriculture. Fields were ploughed in springtime, he notes, when the Pleiades first rose in the night sky (their heliacal rising falls in late April). At that time, taxation weighed heavily on the peasants, who sometimes needed to borrow money to pay the tax collector.[114] In the summer, children harvested the crops on the plains of Asia Minor, and the elderly guarded the fields from wild animals.[115] The autumn was the season of collecting grapes and making wine. Grain and olive oil were deposited in storehouses by the heads of households.[116] He respected the skills and labor of the agriculturalist. The professions of the general, doctor, and farmer were linked, he argued, because they were all based on education and culture (*paideia*). To the counterargument that the farmer was no man of letters he objected by pointing out that the farmer's skill was rational. The tiller of the land inquired about seasons, places, and causes and ennobled his occupation through effort of the mind.[117]

The degree of Theodore's involvement in his father's efforts to stimulate domestic textile production is more difficult to gauge. The fourteenth-century historian Gregoras, our sole source, tells us that Vatatzes imposed a trade embargo on clothes imported from the Latin West and the Islamic East after he saw people around him wasting their money on foreign garments made of silk and other precious materials. The trade restrictions are said to have changed fashions, both elite and non-elite, and stimulated domestic textile production.[118] Unfortunately, we know neither when this economic policy was introduced nor how long it lasted (the years 1223, 1238–40 and 1243 have been suggested).[119] The embargo seems in particular to have targeted silk produced on a large scale in the Italian city of Lucca, which Genoese merchants sold in the eastern Mediterranean.[120] In any case, foreign tradesmen continued to visit the markets of the empire of Nicaea. Merchants from Egypt, India, and all over the world are said to have brought products to Magnesia during Vatatzes' reign. Venetian and Pisan merchants are attested, too, although it is not known whether the Venetians continued to enjoy the right to duty-free trade granted to them in 1219.[121] Theodore held an ambivalent attitude to luxury products. He believed that the exquisite clothes stored in the palaces were coveted by his circle of companions – an indication that the clothes were highly valuable. But he also displayed contempt for luxury on some occasions. The spirit of denial reflects the stoic ideals of the mirrors for princes, as well as his own self-fashioning as a man of virtue and a philosopher removed from material concerns. This self-fashioning was particularly prominent at certain moments of his life, such as the death of his wife Elena and his later years when he was the sole emperor.[122] One wonders whether the embargo on sumptuous foreign clothes sharpened such negative attitudes to luxury.

Theodore had firsthand knowledge of the urban economy of Byzantine Asia Minor. He notes that Philadelphia specialized in leather manufacturing and that Ephesos had money changers, fishermen, butchers, leather-workers, and tavern owners.[123] In the treatise *Representation of the World, or Life,* he observes that some silk merchants cheated when they weighed the raw material and that tailors who made silk clothes engaged in dishonest practices. These comments testify to the standardization and state control of weights and measures, as well as to Theodore's interest in silk trade and textile production.[124] The provenance of the silk, whether domestic or imported, is not mentioned.[125] Theodore specifies that Thessaly was an area famous for its textile production.[126] Epistolary evidence confirms that the Thessalian coastal town of Halmyros in the Gulf of Volos was known during the 1220s for its fine linen cloth. Halmyros had been a center of trade in the twelfth century when it was frequented by merchants from Venice, Genoa, and Pisa. The town had a sizable Jewish community at the time. Elsewhere in Greece, in Thebes, Jews specialized in different stages of silk production (dyeing, weaving, and tailoring).[127] In about 1238–39, Thessaly fell under the authority of Michael II Komnenos Doukas. He expelled the Venetians from the Gulf of Volos in 1246 and received the title of despot from John Vatatzes in that same year – or somewhat later.[128] Thessalian fabrics, whether made from linen, silk, or other fibers, were certainly appreciated in Nicaea and seem to have been exempt from the embargo on foreign textiles.

Theodore assisted his father in acts of philanthropy and public welfare. Blemmydes requested the intervention of his royal student on behalf of a paralyzed man. On learning that the metropolitan of Philadelphia had built a monastic hospital, Theodore wrote to congratulate him and advised him to finish the project by adding a bathhouse.[129] The leper hospital in Nicaea, which still functioned in the late thirteenth century, had evidently benefited from the patronage of the emperors in exile who emulated the imperial leper hospital in Pera (Galata) across the Golden Horn. Vatatzes funded poorhouses, nursing homes for the elderly, and hospitals. The Sosandra monastery he founded near Magnesia had medical facilities.[130]

Most importantly, Theodore supported his father in the creation of urban libraries (*bibliothekai*). This enlightened policy is known solely from a brief contemporary description in the *Synopsis chronike*.[131] John Vatatzes is said to have "collected" manuscripts "in every knowledge and science." His son also collected codices and officially "decreed" – evidently in the period of his sole rule (1254–58) – that the books be made available to those who wished to read and consult them.[132] The libraries were in cities and produced the desired effect of raising educational levels:

> Everywhere in the Roman territories and cities groups of wise people could be seen, theaters of Muses emerged, and almost every place was filled with assemblies of learned men occupied with juxtapositions and comparisons of scientific topics, who worked hard on logical premises and conclusions.[133]

The public libraries were linked with schools: the brief description implies that texts on logic were among the books copied and collected. Aristotelian logic was part of the curriculum of secondary education (*enkyklios paideia*). Notably, a letter from a certain George Babouskomites, a teacher of rhetoric and logic in the empire of Nicaea, to the imperial secretary John Makrotos, attested in this capacity in 1252–53, refers to the circulation of an Aristotle manuscript with unspecified content and shows that interested individuals in the mid-thirteenth century had access to Aristotle's works.[134] Unfortunately, the description in *Synopsis chronike* says nothing about the location of the libraries and the way readers accessed the books. Which cities had *bibliothekai*? Were the books deposited in monastic libraries? Who were the teachers involved? The collecting of manuscripts attempted to put right one of the negative consequences of the Fourth Crusade. Students in Byzantine Anatolia no longer had access to the great monastic and private libraries of Constantinople. The policy fits with the book hunt that Nikephoros Blemmydes undertook in the Balkans in the early 1240s with John Vatatzes' support.[135] Theodore supported his father in the collection of books and founded new schools when he became the sole emperor, such as a school on grammar and poetry in the church of St. Tryphon in Nicaea.[136]

We can glean indirect information on the division of duties between the senior and the junior emperor from a document issued less than fifteen years after Theodore's death. In 1272, the then senior emperor Michael VIII Palaiologos stipulated in a decree the responsibilities of his teenage son Andronikos, whom he had just crowned as coemperor.[137] Born and raised in the empire of Nicaea, Michael Palaiologos had no need to reinvent the wheel. The duties of Andronikos were remarkably similar to those of Theodore. Andronikos was assigned an entourage of guards and officials who included an attendant at his table (*epi tes trapezes*) and a carrier of his shield and spear (*skouterios*). Significantly, an *epi tes trapezes* also served Theodore.[138] As in Theodore's case, the junior emperor was given executive authority over the tax apparatus and was supposed to go on tours and receive petitions from wronged individuals. He had the right to dismiss corrupt tax officials and augment soldiers' lands (*pronoiai*) within set limits. The parallel with Theodore Laskaris' itinerancy and his custom of riding out of the palace to hear plaintiffs is once again remarkable. According to the ordinance, musicians accompanying the imperial cavalcade sounded trumpets and horns in order to notify the population that the junior emperor was nearby and ready to receive them.[139] Quite possibly this practice also goes back to the period of exile. The senior

emperor retained in 1272 exclusive judicial rights. While the son was
allowed to dispense justice to soldiers and commoners, powerful men were
tried and punished by the father alone. In a similar fashion, Theodore
concerned himself with minor matters of justice, such as the cancellation of
the land sale by Blemmydes' monastery. Charges of treason and lèse-
majesté were tried solely at the court of his father.

The origins of the itinerancy of the Nicaean emperors goes back to the
formative period of the reign of the elder Theodore Laskaris. We have seen
that the collapse of central authority in the aftermath of 1204 and the
proliferation of local lords had mandated the practice. Theodore's grandfather was on the move in order to communicate face-to-face with the
Anatolian elites and gain their allegiance. His grandson inherited an
already established custom, although royal travel now served to improve
the efficiency of government rather than being necessitated by the needs of
state building. His itinerancy differed also from that of the Seljuk sultan
ʿAlāʾ al-Dīn Kayqubād I, who was likewise on the move throughout his
reign (1219–37), whether residing in a mobile court of tents or in permanent royal residences. His winter palaces in Antalya and Alanya on the
Mediterranean coast resemble Nymphaion in concept.[140] Yet, as one
historian has noted, the movements of the sultan were largely dictated by
the requirements of warfare and the need to keep an eye on the politically
disruptive nomadic Turkmen.[141]

In his twenties Theodore journeyed between palaces and toured urban
and rural locations, hearing appeals, rectifying injustices, and carrying out
inspections. In this way he learned firsthand about the lives of a broad
social spectrum of the population. His findings informed the way he saw
the world and the material universe, as he described it in two of his
philosophical works, *Natural Communion* and *Representation of the
World, or Life*. It is doubtful that Vatatzes ever specified his son's prerogatives in a special decree. All indications point to accommodations that
developed out of necessity during his father's lengthy absences from
Anatolia. The regularity of royal travel on account of the lack of a fixed
capital, the ruler's proximity to the countryside, and the relatively small
core territory of the Anatolian Byzantine state are factors that converged to
give rise to governance by close monitoring. Theodore actively participated
in this governance, and his itinerancy contributed to the ultimate success
of the empire of Nicaea.

Figure 1 Portrait of Theodore II Laskaris in Codex Monacensis gr. 442 (14th century), f. 7v. The manuscript contains the *History* of George Pachymeres

Figure 2 Pen-and-ink portrait of Theodore II Laskaris in Codex Marcianus gr. 404 (15th century), f. VIr. The manuscript is a copy of the Monacensis (Fig. 1) and likewise contains the *History* of George Pachymeres. The inscription, the same as the partly faded one in the Monacensis, identifies the figure as "Theodore Doukas Laskaris in Christ and God faithful emperor and autocrat of the Romans"

Figure 3 Engraving of Theodore II Laskaris based on the portrait in the Monacensis (Fig. 1). It was included in Hieronymus Wolf's edition of the *History* of Nikephoros Gregoras printed in Basel in 1562

Figure 4 Seals of Theodore I Laskaris

4a Seal of Theodore Komnenos Laskaris, *protovestiarites* and *sebastos*, State Hermitage Museum, St. Petersburg. The seal presents St. George Diasorites on the obverse (top). The inscription on the reverse (bottom) identifies the owner and his title

4b Imperial seal of Theodore I Laskaris, Département des Monnaies, Médailles et Antiques, Bibliothèque nationale de France. The seal presents the elder Theodore dressed like a Byzantine emperor on the reverse (bottom), with a *labarum* and a cross-topped globe, and St. Theodore Stratelates, his namesake, on the obverse (top)

Figure 5 The walls of Nicaea

5a View of the walls of Nicaea in the 1930s

5b The south (Yenişehir) gate of the walls in 2015

Figure 6 The Babylonian Tower constructed by Theodore I Laskaris

6a The Babylonian Tower of the walls of Nicaea, constructed by Theodore I Laskaris and known today as Kız Kulesi (Maiden's Tower), shown here in the 1930s. The inscription runs: "This is the tower of Calneh (Genesis 10:10; Isaiah 10:9). It destroys the designs of the enemies." The words "Theodore Laskaris" and "wonder" are also visible

6b The Babylonian Tower in 2015

Figure 7 Church of the Dormition of the Virgin in the monastery of Hyakinthos, before the church's destruction in 1922 during the Greek-Turkish war. The photographs were published by Theodor (Fedor) Schmit in 1927

Figure 8 Church of St. Sophia in Nicaea

Figure 9 The Palace in Nymphaion (Kemalpaşa)

9a An engraving of the palace in Nymphaion published by Charles Texier in 1862

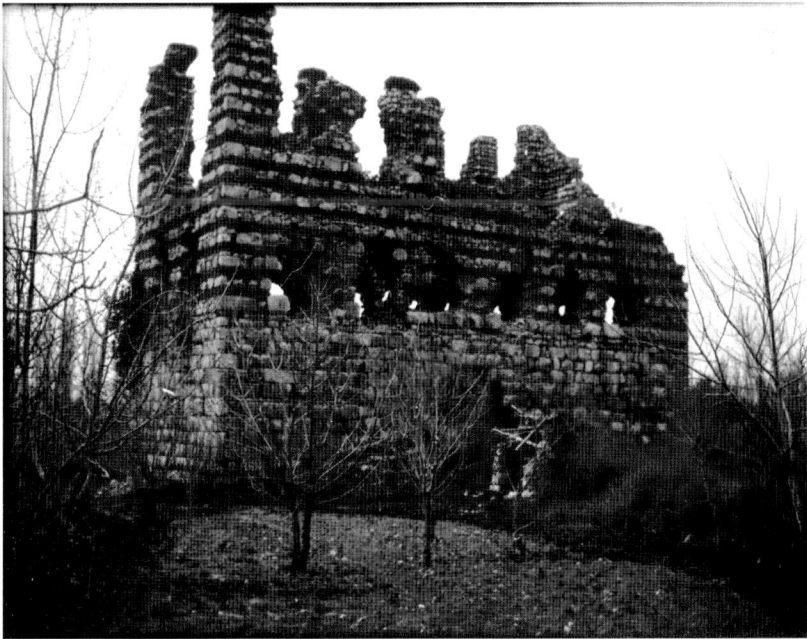

9b Photograph of the palace in 1907 taken by Gertrude Bell

9c Photograph of the palace in 1907 taken by Gertrude Bell

9d The palace in 2012

Figure 10 The fortifications of Magnesia

10a The fortifications of Magnesia

10b The fortifications of Magnesia with a view of the fertile plain and modern Manisa

Figure 11 Europe viewed from Asia at Lampsakos. Theodore Laskaris often stayed at Lampsakos where he could catch a sight of the Balkans less than 3 miles (5 kilometers) away across the straits of the Hellespont. Lampsakos was the place of his marriage in 1235

Figure 12 The fortifications of Pegai. Pegai was a strategic fortress on the Asiatic side of the Sea of Marmara, where Theodore Laskaris encamped as his father campaigned in the Balkans (1242) and as he prepared to cross into Europe in the spring of 1256

Figure 13 Seal of the emperor John III Vatatzes, father of Theodore II Laskaris. The emperor on the reverse (bottom) is dressed in imperial ceremonial attire and holds a cross-topped globe and a *labarum*. The image of Christ, identified as "Chalkites" by the inscription on the obverse of the seal (top), refers to a famous icon above the bronze gate of the Great Palace in Constantinople and symbolizes the political mission of reconquest of the empire in exile

Figure 14 Aniconic seal of the general Alexios Strategopoulos, a man much disliked by Theodore II Laskaris. Displaying pride in the owner's royal Komnenian ancestry, the inscription reads: "A seal validating the writings of Alexios Strategopoulos of the family of the Komnenoi"

Figure 15 Seal of Empress Irene, mother of Theodore II Laskaris. The empress on the reverse (bottom) is identified by the inscription as "Irene Komnene, most pious *augousta.*" The image of Christ the Redeemer appears on the obverse side of the seal (top)

Figure 16 The royal couple of Latin Constantinople

a.

b.

16a Seal of Baldwin II, Latin emperor of Constantinople (1217–73, r. 1240–61)
16b Funerary statue of Marie of Brienne (d. c. 1280), wife of Baldwin II. Black limestone. Ambulatory of the church of St. Denis, Paris

Figure 17 Seals of Theodore II Laskaris

a.

17a and 17b Theodore as a coemperor. The two seals feature St. Theodore Stratelates on the obverse (top) and an identical prayer to the military saint on the reverse (bottom): "May you protect, athlete [of Christ], the emperor Theodore, the ruler's son (*anaktopais*) and a Doukas"

b.

c.

17c Theodore as the reigning emperor depicted on the reverse (bottom) in full regalia, with the inscription reading "Theodore *despotes* Doukas Laskaris"

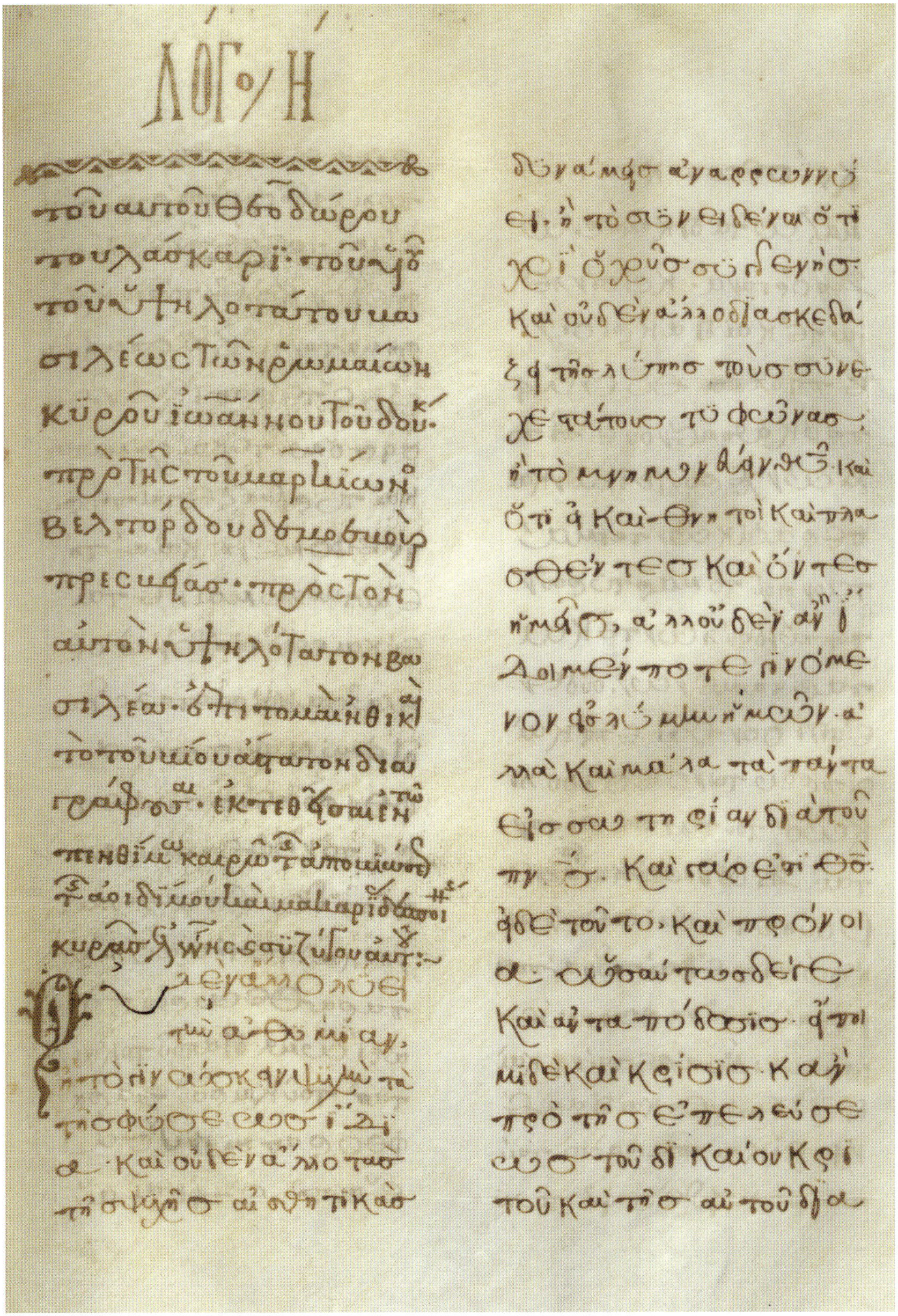

ΛΟΓ Η

Figure 18 The opening of the *Moral Pieces* in Cod. Ambrosianus gr. C 308 inf. (917), f. 78r. The heading mentions that the work – "Oration Eight" of the *Sacred Orations* – dates before the embassy of Marquis Berthold of Hohenburg

Figure 19 The Marquis of Hohenburg (Diepold of Vohburg or Berthold of Hohenburg, ambassador to Nicaea in the autumn of 1253) as depicted in Grosse Heidelberger Liederhandschrift (Codex Manesse), a collection of *Minnesang* poetry made in around 1300 in Zurich

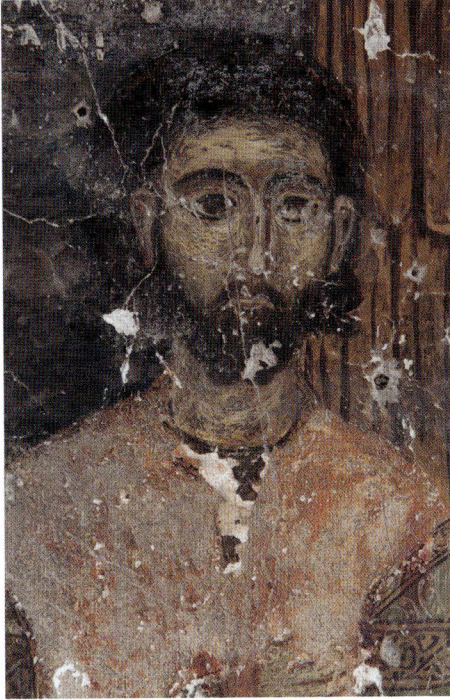

Figure 20 The Bulgarian tsar Michael Asen (?), Theodore's enemy in the Balkan campaign of 1255 with the tsarina Anna, daughter of Rostislav Mikhailovich of Mačva. Church of Taxiarches, Kastoria, 1254–55 (?)

Figure 21 Coins of Theodore II Laskaris

a.

21a Gold *hyperpyron*, Christ enthroned on the obverse (top) and the emperor in full regalia crowned by the Virgin on the reverse (bottom)

b.

21b Electrum *trachy*, St. Tryphon on the obverse (left) and the emperor on the reverse (right) in full regalia holding a cross-topped globe and a *labarum*

c.

21c Billon *trachy*, St. Theodore on the obverse (left) and the emperor on the reverse (right) in full regalia holding a cross-topped globe and a *labarum*

Figure 22 A view of the northern Rhodope Mountains from the hilltop fortress of Tzepaina (Tsepena), whose recapture was the prized goal of Theodore's Balkan campaign of 1255–56

Figure 23 The plain of Philippi, with a view of Pangaion, "the mountain of Orpheus." As Theodore encamped in Philippi during the campaign of 1255, he reflected on St. Paul's imprisonment and saw himself entering "the land of Philip and Alexander" (Macedonia). A campsite used by Theodore's father, Philippi was where Michael Palaiologos was put on trial in 1253

Figure 24 Seal of George Akropolites. Reflecting Akropolites' promotion at Christmas 1255 to *megas logothetes*, the seal features an image of St. George on the obverse (top) and the inscription on the reverse (bottom): "A witness to the writings of Lord Akropolites who bears the title of *megas logothetes*"

Figure 25 Theodore II Laskaris' eldest daughter Irene (right) as Tsarina of Bulgaria together with her husband Constantine Tikh. Fresco made in 1259 in the narthex of the small church of SS. Nicholas and Panteleimon in Boyana

Figure 26 Concentric circles of the four elements in BnF, Suppl. gr. 460, f. 17r, one of a number of diagrammatic drawings in the deluxe manuscript of *Natural Communion* that was produced during Theodore's lifetime as a presentation copy of this philosophical treatise

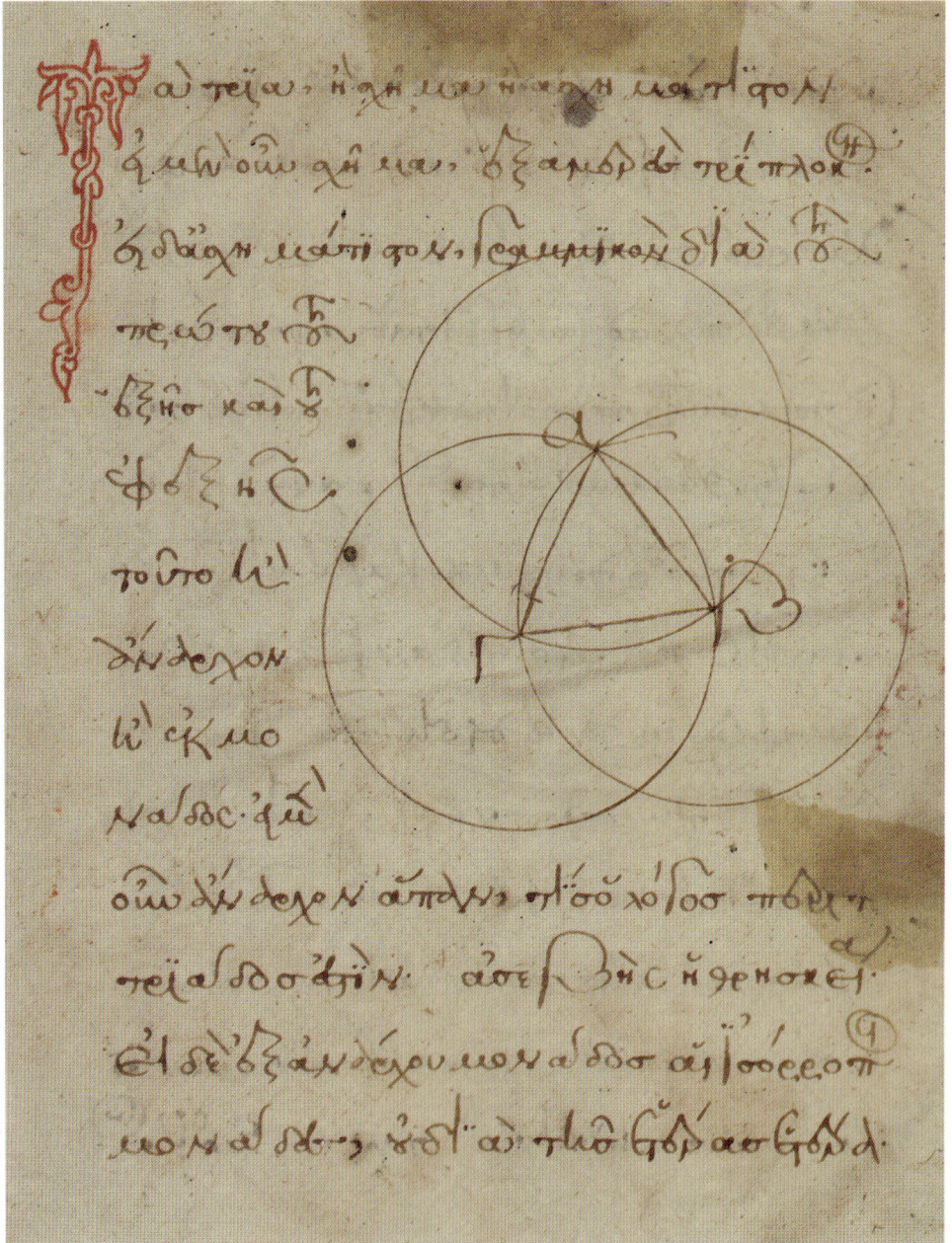

Figure 27 Diagrammatic drawing of the Holy Trinity in the *First Oration against the Latins* (sixth book of *Christian Theology*), Cod. Vaticanus gr. 1113 (13th century), f. 73v

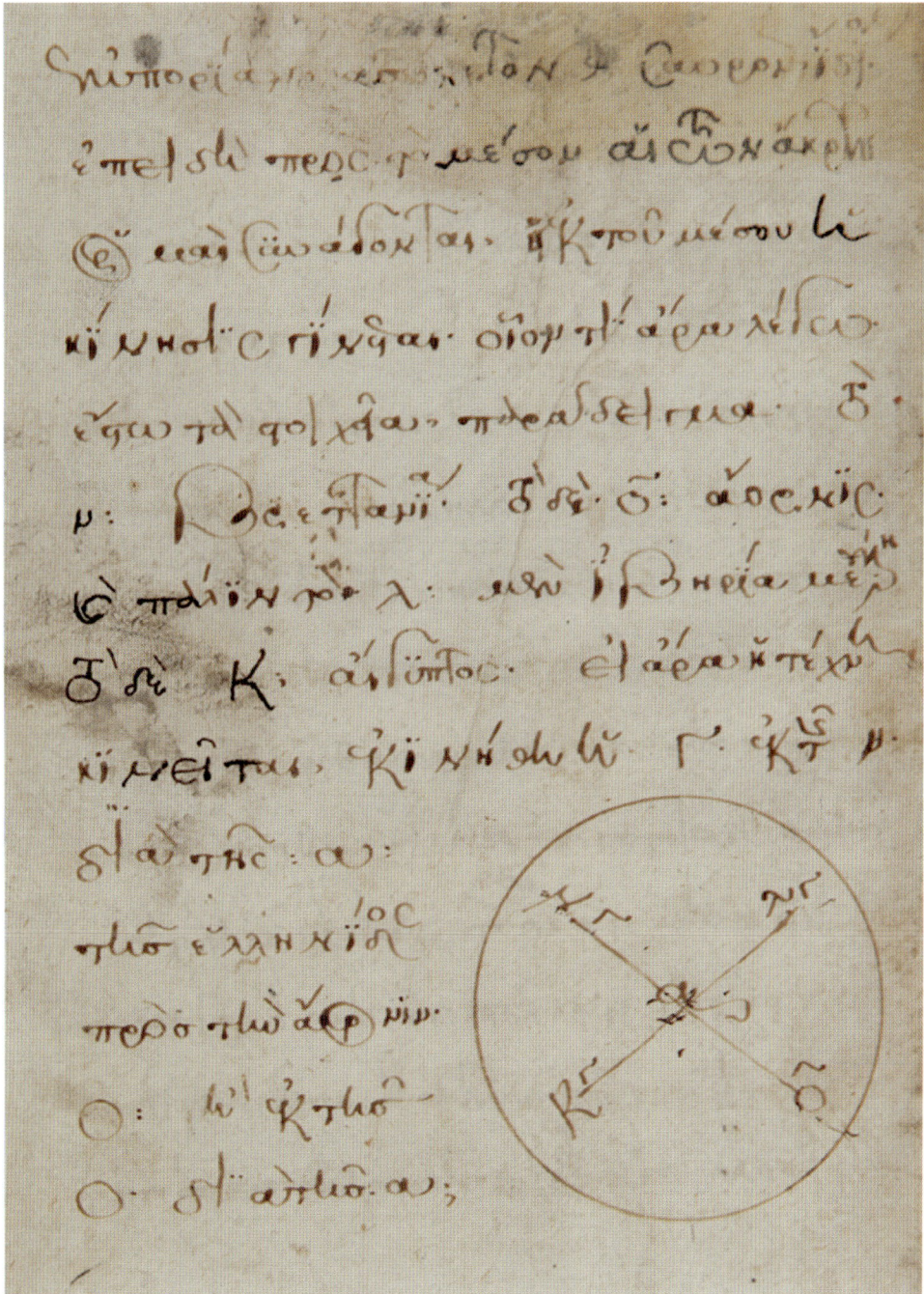

Figure 29 Hellas in the middle of the world. Drawing in the *Second Oration against the Latins* (seventh book of *Christian Theology*), Cod. Vaticanus gr. 1113 (13th century), f. 94v. The letter α at the center designates Hellas. **N** (upper left) is Britain. **Λ** (upper right) is Spain. **K** (lower left) is Egypt. **O** (lower right) is Aornis, a mythical land located in India. The letter **Γ** represents the skills and crafts that pass through α, Hellas, as they are disseminated throughout the world

Figure 30 Hellas in the middle of the world. Drawing in the *Second Oration against the Latins* (seventh book of *Christian Theology*), Cod. Barocci 97 (15th century), f. 80r. The drawing is nearly identical with that in the thirteenth-century Vatican manuscript (Fig. 29)

6 | Friends, Foes, and Politics

Theodore bonded during the years of his coemperorship with a close circle of companions. He called them his "friends," using a range of Greek words.[1] A scrutiny of this microcommunity at the court reveals aspects of his daily life and sheds light on the formation of his character, while exhibiting the network of individuals around him. Examining his companions at court also provides the background necessary to make sense of his confrontation with the top tier of the aristocracy and leads to a clearer understanding of his political and moral philosophy. The crown prince came to view friendship as a fundamental human value and a pervasive sociopolitical phenomenon. His interest culminated in a treatise on the role of friendship in society that he addressed to his long-term companion George Mouzalon. This special work represents the only articulation in Byzantium of a coherent theory of friendship, yet it is something of a conundrum. His investigation of friendship is as much theoretical as personal. A look at the profiles of his friends and foes illuminates both his promotion of what he called "friendship" and the political positions that he took as a reigning emperor.

The Youth Culture of the Court

Theodore's friends and companions shared a few common features. All were educated or had educational aspirations. In Theodore's own words, they were men whom "philosophy nourished to be good, agreeable, handsome, and desired by me, and to be brothers and comrades born by the same mother (that is, philosophy) and breathing the same spirit."[2] All sought patronage at the court and were employed in different ways in the imperial service. All were relatively young individuals born after the fall of Constantinople, usually but not always in Anatolia. They lacked the traumatized perspective of exile characteristic of what the patriarch Germanos called in one of his sermons the "humiliated generation" and brought plenty of youthful energy and *joie de vivre* to their interactions.[3]

The bonding between Theodore and his companions is explicable not only through their need for patronage but also through his longing for emotional support and human company in his busy, strenuous life. In a highly personal work composed before November 1254 titled an *Encomium on the Spring and the Charming Man*, Theodore reveals that he was often overcome by sadness and worries. He writes that "gloom, as if in a winter storm, and thoughts disturb my soul."[4] The reason for his low spirits is not given. The context implies an overall melancholic disposition, but it is quite possible that the author felt anxiety due to public duties or a stressful event. He makes clear that he found in friendship with his companions the psychological support needed to achieve a good and balanced existence. The charming man was a courtier capable of instilling joy and happiness in his heart in a way similar to the arrival of the spring. He was a musician with a pleasant voice, whose songs are said to surpass the lyre of Orpheus and his "speech is sweeter than honey" (*Iliad*, I 249). The courtier was attractive in appearance and sociable, yet with an air of simplicity. He drew attention to himself like a magnet and made onlookers admire him and wish to embrace and imitate him. The charming man, Theodore observes, causes no sadness and anger, and everyone emulating him would avoid negative thoughts. The courtier thus helped Theodore to overcome his own downcast disposition.

His closest companions and friends grew up in the court with him as pages and were known to him from his childhood years. The pages' daily chores taught them loyalty and instructed them in the inner workings of governance. On reaching maturity, pages remained in imperial service. In 1250, for example, a page was dispatched on a delicate mission to Frederick II in Italy in order to bring an imperial letter. Given the long journey and the important diplomatic task, the page must have been already a grown man rather than a child.[5] Such a former page close to Theodore was Valanidiotes.[6] But the best known and most prominent among the former pages in his entourage were the three Mouzalon brothers: Theodore (the eldest), George (the middle), and Andronikos (the youngest). Their father had "served the emperor" in an unknown capacity, which explains how his sons, born in Atramyttion, were introduced to the palace.[7] George Mouzalon, who was apparently somewhat younger than Theodore, became his most trusted confidant, correspondent, student, and reader of his works. Mouzalon was already acting as Theodore's agent and confidant in the early 1240s. Between 1241 and 1243 he followed the orders of his superior to present a mule to Blemmydes and bring barley for his pack horses.[8] We still see him acting as Theodore's confidant in the winter of 1253–54.[9] Theodore reminded him in a letter of how he had secured his upbringing and education: "You have been raised since a young age entirely among us. You cherish what we cherish because we nursed you with words of wisdom. And you love what we love because, as you grew up, we nourished you with the solid food of divine piety. And you do what we wish, because after you came of age we deposited in you all the thoughts of our intellect."[10] Theodore fashioned George Mouzalon as the perfect courtier. Their relationship was closer than that between a master and servant. His emotional letters to Mouzalon abound in powerful expressions of attachment between the two men: "my sweetest Mouzalon," "my desired son," "the sweetness of my eyes," "the joy of my soul," "my best solace," "my best and heavenly child," "the good offspring of our heart."[11] Using the language of kinship and love, Theodore designates George as his "son" and "child" and speaks of a "bond of love and adoption."[12] "Love does not permit me," he exclaims, "to be ever away from you, because I love you exceedingly."[13] He ended many of his letters to him, especially the later ones, by calling him "my strong bond indissoluble."[14]

The Mouzalon brothers were hardly new men in terms of pedigree, for the family had already gained prominence in the middle Byzantine period. In the tenth century, for example, a certain John Mouzalon was appointed military governor of Sicily. In the eleventh century Mouzalons entered the imperial civil service, and in the twelfth century Nicholas Mouzalon was an archbishop of Cyprus and later patriarch of Constantinople (1147–51).[15] The Mouzalons continued to be deemed worthy of high appointments in the empire in exile. One of them served as governor of the city of Nicaea, and another, John Mouzalon, was a private imperial secretary (*mystikos*), keeper of the imperial inkstand (*epi tou kanikleiou*), and eventually a monk. The snobbish attitude of this man born in Constantinople impelled the patriarch Germanos to deliver a polemical sermon on the meaning of nobility. In 1241–42 Theodore was left in his company in Pegai when his father crossed the Hellespont.[16] The relationship of the three pages to this man is not known. In any case, later historians are in agreement that they were born not noble – "of despicably low birth" in Blemmydes' words.[17] The meteoric rise of George Mouzalon – who was not only a former page but also a musician, and an entertainer at the court – to high military and civil office was something scandalous and unexpected for an outsider to aristocratic families of Komnenian descent.

Theodore found criticisms of Mouzalon's lack of noble blood disconcerting and reacted vehemently in his writings against this view. The treatise *Representation of the World, or Life*, addressed to Mouzalon, argued that contemporaries used the word "nobility" (*eugeneia*) wrongly and applied it to immoral, vain, and deceitful people. Nobility was, rather, a moral category. His examples of true nobility were Moses, who was born into a humble family, and Joshua, who became a leader by obeying Moses and through God's choice. Mouzalon, he pointed out, was "noble in his manners" and was "a philosopher, a friend, and a man noble in spirit." The "best" nobility was that which flowed from one's character.[18] Both as a coemperor and as the reigning emperor, Theodore was obsessed with refuting the view of nobility as nobility of blood. He argued that nobility of blood led to associations contrary to reason, being based on convention rather than nature. The "true and divine nobility" amounted to virtue and a life examined by people who are both wise and act wisely. "There is one true nobility in living creatures and soulless objects, nobility in nature."[19] Wisdom earned people respect and dignity "rather than the blood flowing from the parents."[20] He stressed that "nobility is measured not by blood, but by the way of virtue, simplicity of conduct, and purification for the purpose of apprehending and uniting with the existent."[21] An essay composed late in his life drives home the point that one arrives at virtue through a life blessed by God rather than noble blood and fleshly desires.[22]

The men who bonded with Theodore at the court were mostly secretaries and palace attendants. The chamberlain (*koubouklarios*) Constantine, whom he dubbed his friend, was a trusted servant like George Mouzalon and a messenger to Blemmydes, Akropolites, and Mouzalon.[23] Another messenger and go-between was Karyanites.[24] A certain Simon, together with George Mouzalon, carried out Theodore's orders to assist Blemmydes in his monastery.[25] Close to the coemperor was also an attendant by the name of Christopher, who had a distinctive hunch and was a repeated butt of jokes.[26] Two siblings bearing the surname Phaix – John and an anonymous brother – were part of his entourage. They served as messengers and secretaries.[27] As we have seen, several secretaries working for the imperial chancery – among them Akropolites, Hagiotheodorites, and Mesopotamites – had close personal relations with the coemperor.

Theodore was especially fond of people from his native Asia Minor. The Mouzalon brothers were born in Atramyttion. The page Valanidiotes evidently originated from Anatolia, for he bears a surname derived from the region of Valanida in the theme of Neokastra.[28] "Having traversed the best part of Asia," Theodore writes in a letter to the imperial secretary Joseph Mesopotamites, "I do not assign its pleasantries to a location, nor do I attribute its goodness to the land. But I assign its fame to the community of good people, its friendliness to its gentle people, and my affairs to my friends."[29] Not all of Theodore's favorites were ancestral Anatolians, however. George Akropolites was born in Latin-held Constantinople. Karyanites (Karianites) is a family name of twelfth-century imperial officials derived from a neighbourhood in Constantinople.[30] Joseph Mesopotamites was related in an unknown capacity to Constantine Mesopotamites, who was the keeper of the imperial inkstand (*epi tou kanikleiou*) under Isaac II Angelos and Alexios III Angelos. Ordained metropolitan bishop of Thessalonica shortly before 1204, Constantine resigned from his see in 1227 when he declined to perform the imperial coronation of Theodore of Epiros.[31] Theodore's private secretary Hagiotheodorites descended also from a powerful twelfth-century family of civil officials and churchmen, including two chief imperial ministers (*mesazontes*), the siblings John and Michael Hagiotheodorites, and a metropolitan of Athens, Nicholas Hagiotheodorites (a brother of John and Michael).[32] Members of this family relocated to Asia Minor after 1204. A certain John Hagiotheodorites was co-brother-in-law (*syngambros*) of the *mesazon* Demetrios Komnenos Tornikes. Their wives, two sisters from the Komnenos family, were maternal cousins of the *megas domestikos* Andronikos Palaiologos.[33] Theodore's private secretary may well have been a son of John Hagiotheodorites and thus a Komnenos by pedigree.[34]

The crown prince socialized with his friends and companions during leisure activities at the court. The vibrant culture of entertainment is truly astonishing, given the extraordinary historical circumstances of the emergence of the migrant court in Asia Minor and the itinerancy of the emperors. Theodore's descriptions of entertainment are sometimes marked by a spirit of denial, but this attitude cannot conceal his fascination with banqueting, music, and literature. He gives an account of the usual dinner parties at the court in a pre-1254 letter to Akropolites, which responded to the latter's advice that he should listen to music in order to overcome his despondency. Theodore countered this "indecent" suggestion by declaring his desire to flee from the material world and escape from the machinations of the devil. Elsewhere he noted that it was contrary to reason for the ruler to be associated with songs and flute-players, and praised his father for taking no care of his body and shunning musical performances, horse races, and other spectacles. It is with regret that he remembered reading erotic fiction in an essay addressing his weak and tempted human flesh.[35] The apologetic tone in all these texts stems from the religious disapproval of bodily pleasure and stoic conceptions about the ideal emperor.[36] He relished court entertainment, yet he was aware – and needed to make concessions to – disapproving views. At critical junctures of his life, he poured out genuine feelings of remorse. Social expectations also required a posture of distancing. He assumed a guarded, apologetic attitude, especially in letters to his teacher and spiritual father Blemmydes, but he felt far less constrained in letters to his childhood friend George Mouzalon.

Much of the socializing between the prince and his companions took place during musical performances and banquets. George Mouzalon and his brothers were singers and musicians. In the words of an eyewitness, they were "raised on the songs of the theater and took pleasure in the flute and strings and practiced singing to the lyre."[37] The description of the courtier in his *Encomium on the Spring and the Charming Man*, who was likewise a musical performer, was likely based on the Mouzalons. Addressing George Mouzalon, Theodore wrote that the music and songs resounding within the walls of the palace would captivate anyone who seeks the pleasures of life: "Does he love songs sung to tunes which enchant souls with their musical harmonies? 'When he hears the voice of the trumpet' (Daniel 3:5) in the imperial court, let him throw himself down on the ground and do obeisance to Pleasure."[38] The names of musicians other than the Mouzalons are not known, but it is clear that the performers were highly valued and that some of them were itinerant. Two wealthy musicians and actors – the brothers Basilikoi, born on the island of Rhodes – moved in the 1260s from the Seljuk to the Byzantine court and were appointed to the high position of chief chamberlains (*parakoimomenoi*).[39]

The musical performances usually took place during banquets at the court after the dinner guests finished their main course. Theodore records the exquisite food that was consumed at the court in the pre-1254 letter to Akropolites.[40] The guests drank delicate, clear wine from the island of Samos, valued in Byzantium in the twelfth century, and mulled wine from the domains of the Maliasenos family, large landowners in Thessaly. The *protovestiarites* George Zagarommates married at some point before 1252 the daughter of the Thessalian magnate Constantine Maliasenos, who maintained good relations with the authorities of both Nicaea and Epiros. The wine may therefore have been a gift.[41] The dishes and delicacies included oysters, "the food of angels," cabbage in brine ("another and more glorious food of angels"), pungent watercress seeds, caviar and bottarga, sausages and dried sturgeon.[42] There were other delicacies from "the property of Koites," a name or probably nickname of a well-off physician. Theodore connects the name etymologically with the island of Kos, the birthplace of Hippocrates (and possibly of the wealthy doctor himself), which was under the authority of the empire of Nicaea from the 1220s.[43] The availability of caviar and dried sturgeon from the Caspian can be explained by the flourishing international commerce in the northern

Black Sea after the Mongols became the dominant power of the region. A Dominican traveler reports that in 1253, merchants from Constantinople, probably Venetians, sailed to Matracha (Tmutarakan) on the Taman peninsula and from there entered the Sea of Azov on smaller boats in order to buy large quantities of salted sturgeon and other fish.[44]

The culture of court entertainment included the reading of erotic fiction, something Theodore remembered in an essay written in the later years of his life without specifying the novels. But it is worth noting that four ancient love novels by Longos, Achilles Tatios, Chariton, and Xenophon were copied in a thirteenth-century Laurentian manuscript, Conventi soppressi 627, along with Theodore's letters to George Mouzalon. Erotic fiction was not only read and appreciated but appears also to have been written in the thirteenth century, following the revival of the genre of the love novel in high-register Greek under the Komnenian emperors. The composition of the longest and most complex of the late Byzantine vernacular romances, *Livistros and Rodamne,* has been attributed to an anonymous author affiliated with the imperial court of Nicaea.[45]

Entertainment at the court also featured mime performances. While Mouzalon was recovering from illness, Theodore Laskaris tried to raise his spirits by dispatching to his residence several buffoons carrying wine and cheese. His accompanying letter offered a sneak preview of a slapstick show. Three of the men were to kick and slap the elderly letter bearer, who was to spit on their beards. There was certainly more to follow. Whether the mimes performing on this occasion were paid professionals or amateurs is not mentioned.[46] But what is certain is that some entertainers were mobile, like the Basilikos brothers, and sought new patrons. Theodore cultivated a community of laughter at the court guided by his own distinctive sense of humor. It is indicative in this regard that he addressed his *Satire of the Tutor* to his friends (*philoi*) and literati (*logioi*) "like a sweet delight from the imperial palace."[47] Mocking humor, such as that found in the *Satire* and in letters, served to strengthen the emotional bond with his companions. It drew an imaginary distinction between the microcommunity of those who laughed and those who were laughed at. The jibes were remembered and retold, which shows the sway they held over the community of jokers. He ridiculed the "pedagogue" Zabareiotes and the metropolitan bishop of Ephesos, Nikephoros, both before and after his accession as a sole emperor.[48]

The clergy was the social group that fared worst in the court culture of laughter and teasing. Bishops were targets of mockery on account of self-aggrandizement, greed, lack of secular philosophical education, and physical characteristics. Wishing to speed up Mouzalon's recovery from illness, Theodore reminded him about the comic features of the bishop of Monikos (Monoikos).[49] His letter to Mouzalon describes how he recently saw his "friends" after breakfast, as was his custom, and one of them remembered the bishop of Monikos, whereupon the company burst into almost uncontrollable laughter. Theodore urged Mouzalon to join the group of jokers in spirit and recall the bishop's funny physique, character, supposed musical abilities, and "over-smoothness" (*to polyglaphyron,* a neologism) of speech. A similar comical sketch is found in a letter to Akropolites. The letter, written in Philadelphia, told a funny story. As Theodore was entering Philadelphia, an unidentified high clergyman, mounted on a mule and surrounded by a crowd playing drums, approached him from the opposite direction. The cause of this grand ceremony is not mentioned, but it may have had to do with the welcoming of the visiting coemperor. Theodore asks rhetorically: "Who would describe his drab personality as a philosopher, his pious-sounding speech, the solemnity of his gait, and everything else as befitting the holy clergy?" When the churchman saw Theodore entering the city, he raised his brows, rode his mule faster, and shouted at him. Astonished by his croaking voice and the strangeness of the sight, the crowd laughed heartily.[50] In a letter to Blemmydes, Theodore ridiculed an anonymous bishop, whose speech was full of solecisms and barbarisms, and whose thoughts were heretical. In the scheme of the mythical ages of man, Theodore remarks, the bishop belonged to the era of bronze rather than that of gold or silver.[51]

A favorite object of derision was Nikephoros Pamphilos, the metropolitan bishop of Ephesos. As archdeacon of the imperial clergy, he had been a patriarchal candidate elected by the synod during the long vacancy (1241–43) before the appointment of Patriarch Manuel II, but John Vatatzes disapproved of him. Nikephoros was ordained instead as metropolitan of Ephesos in 1243 or 1244.[52] On learning the news, Theodore wrote to Blemmydes to warn him that an avaricious bishop was arriving at Ephesos who was about to despoil everyone: peasants and monks, widows and orphans, fishermen and money changers, tanners and butchers.[53] The satirical description presents Nikephoros as a closed-minded cleric interested only in religious learning and "unadulterated philosophy." Unversed in the dirt of grammar, he had not touched the evil of poetry or absorbed the filthy confusion of Aristotelian philosophy. After reaching heaven through purest philosophy, he was now descending among his parishioners in order both to edify them and deprive them of their gold and the skin off their backs.[54] This critique of poorly educated bishops was partly informed by

Theodore's sense of public duty, because many clergymen were cogs in the machine of government in Byzantine Anatolia. The bishops were high judges, and some of them, like Nikephoros, controlled large economic resources. Urban notaries were deacons in metropolitan churches, and all known village notaries in the empire of Nicaea were priests.[55]

Theodore's critique of the educational level of the clergy was the flipside of his cultivation of letters and learning among his companions. Several of his "friends" were linked in teacher-student relationships. Theodore himself was mentored by one of his closest associates. Not long after 1241, he continued his education by taking lessons from Blemmydes' student George Akropolites.[56] Akropolites was particularly well suited to the task, because he was continually present at the court in his capacity of imperial secretary and already complemented his income by teaching.[57] The account of a waking vision in Theodore's opening letter to Akropolites in the Laurentian collection is an allegory of the author's incomplete education.[58] Lady Virtue, philosophy's counselor, appears to Theodore one morning before sunrise and cautions him that he is not following the path of reason, intelligence, and philosophy.[59] Lady Virtue shows him a vision, which opens a story within the story. She leads him to a lavish feast in a royal palace constructed on seven pillars – the seven pillars of wisdom (Proverbs 9:1–6). Theodore alone is invited to the head of the table and is able to digest the delicacies: he is God's preferred choice to receive wisdom. After the meal he embraces two beautiful sisters in an erotic scene. They remove their magic belts and place them on Theodore's eyes, enabling him to gaze harmlessly at the sun, which abandons its daily course in the sky and enters the palace to join the feast. Theodore leaves the palace clothed in rags and accompanied by the two ladies, while Lady Wisdom hands him torches symbolizing newfound knowledge.[60] The celestial bliss contrasts to the poor reception that Theodore and his entourage, all wise and virtuous people, receive on earth after leaving the palace. A rough crowd encounters and mocks Theodore. Then a woman dressed in black appears, an embodiment of evil and death, and encourages the crowd to kill Theodore and his companions, who are likewise dressed in rags and, carrying torches, escort the two ladies they met in the celestial palace. The virtuous and the wise defend themselves with the torches and are saved in the end by a bolt of lightning, which kills the dark lady. The vision is rich in symbolism. The palace represents God's heavenly court. The two beautiful ladies are personifications of virtues. The sun is the "sun of wisdom," as Theodore calls it in his *Encomium on Wisdom*.[61] The fight between Theodore's companions and the crowd signifies the difficult destiny of wise people to

fight for their place under the sun. The letter expresses Theodore's combative sense of mission as a philosopher.

The period of study with Akropolites is alleged to have been intense, long-
lasting, and filled with sleepless nights.[62] What subjects did Akropolites
teach the heir to the throne? Theodore completed his education in logic
and mathematics, for which he thanked Akropolites as "a favor I could never
repay you."[63] Traces of Theodore's learning from these studies are found in
letters to Akropolites describing logical and mathematical problems. He
asked him whether a syllogism is categorical or hypothetical, posed a
mathematical question about an aliquot sequence, and engaged in a discussion on numerology indebted to Theon of Smyrna.[64] After the end of his
studies, he boasted before Akropolites that his grasp of mathematics
exceeded that of logic and physics, and even cracked mathematical jokes
thanks to his "most solid knowledge of mathematical theorems."[65] As
Theodore's confidence in his own abilities grew in the 1240s and early
1250s, he saw himself as the mentor of his younger and less educated
companions. We see Theodore inquiring from his secretaries, the Phaix
brothers, about the progress of their studies, urging Akropolites to complete
the education in rhetoric of the chamberlain Constantine, and reporting to
Akropolites his observations on the progress of the secretary Kostomyres.[66]
Questions asked by his companions prompted him to edify them on philosophical and theological matters. Thus, his treatise *On the Trinity* (the fifth
book of his *Christian Theology*) is a response to the request by the literati
(*logioi*) John Phaix and the chamberlain Constantine. Theodore took up the
task of instructing George Mouzalon in practical and theoretical philosophy.
He addressed to him letters of instruction and shared manuscripts with him,
such as a codex containing the orations of Gregory of Nazianzus.[67] Mouzalon's questions prompted Theodore's composition of his treatise on friendship and politics, and the philosophical compendium *Explanation of the
World*.[68] The latter work consists of four treatises on different subjects. The
first two books (*On the Elements* and *On Heavens*) present natural philosophical knowledge, but the third and fourth books are highly personal
works sharing the author's experiences and observations.[69]

Friendship and Politics

The elite group of urbane young laymen around the coemperor enjoyed
the pleasant lifestyle of the Anatolian palaces. They socialized in the course
of intellectual discussions and laughed and dined together. Gradually, as

the realities of power began to weigh heavily on his shoulders and exercise his mind, Theodore rethought the role of this tight-knit community. He saw in his trusted friends a valuable instrument for maintaining and consolidating authority in the face of factionalism and political danger.

Throughout the 1240s and the early 1250s he heard a chorus of critical voices. These criticisms were largely prompted by the high expectations that he faced as a public figure and heir to the throne. He was sometimes quick-tempered in his reactions, although he never lost the ability to differentiate between an innocuous and a harmful critique. First, he encountered people who found his love for philosophy objectionable, because they expected a full devotion to a life of action. He remembered how irrational people had raged against him for receiving instruction from Akropolites, just as in the *Satire* he complained about the machinations of the head tutor that were aimed at preventing him pursuing philosophical studies with Blemmydes.[70] There was also harmless banter around him that caught his notice. A certain Kalothetos, domestic of the *scholae* (an office traditionally held by military men), had reportedly spoken of him with derision, but Theodore preferred to ignore the episode in the spirit of mildness and clemency.[71] The court culture of laughter and teasing blurred the lines of authority and nourished a degree of free speech within an emotional community based on laughter and humor at the court. In addition, he accepted with good grace, as essentially well-intentioned, criticism from a loyal philosopher, articulated in a traditional literary form and in learned language. He did not reject differences of opinion expressed in this way, as seen in his admiration for Blemmydes' *Imperial Statue* in spite of its critical spirit.

Some critics, however, Theodore considered hurtful and malicious. An undated letter to Akropolites refers to the jokes of fellow students who mocked him for his way of reasoning (the precise nature of their playful comments is left unexplained). The coemperor found himself the target of a culture of laughter and making fun similar to the one he himself cultivated, but in this case he felt troubled and upset. His words are full of discontent and disappointment. "Raging against wisdom" and "far distanced from the philosophy" of their teacher, they dared to attack him, even though he had "learned everything by the providence of God." Theodore turned the derision into an opportunity to fashion himself as a misunderstood and under-appreciated philosopher – self-fashioning that emerged as a reaction to such unfriendly attitudes. He declared that he relished being ridiculed, "even if this appears somewhat paradoxical to all my friends," for the attacks on him were absurd and exposed the true character of his critics.[72] The philosopher is someone mad who is "dishonored by the unwise," he wrote elsewhere.[73]

This emotional attitude – self-ironizing and ironizing, defensive and polemical, self-confident yet fundamentally insecure – would develop into a mode of philosophical writing, as we will see in Chapter 9.

Opposition originating among the high clergy and aristocracy was particularly upsetting and dangerous. Theodore made a point of parrying accusations of sacrilege in his humorous letter to Akropolites that lampooned the high clergyman in Philadelphia, which suggests he considered accusations of impiety a real possibility.[74] That such accusations were in fact made against him emerges from his polemical letter to the metropolitan bishop of Ephesos, Nikephoros, one of the chief targets of his satirical humor. We learn from the letter that Nikephoros had accused the coemperor of vainglory and violation of the rules of fasting. In his response Theodore admitted his human imperfection, but also pointed to the hypocrisy of his opponent: "Why do you, who pride yourselves in virtue in words, belie it through your deceptive deeds?" Actions rather than appearances mattered in the pursuit of virtue. He patronized the bishop by instructing him in the three foundations and ladders of virtue and praise (education, experience, and good nature), and highlighted his own secular learning.[75] It is indeed extraordinary how seriously Theodore took the idea that he should acquire virtue and rule through virtue. He missed no occasion to flaunt his knowledge of important virtues, theorized about virtue, and presented himself as cultivating virtue. His oration *On Fasting* advertised his rigorous religious observance and can be read as his response to accusations like those aired by Nikephoros. Another work, his oration *On Virtue*, dispels doubts about his virtuous character. The piece is both apologetic and allusive. He admits to his sins: "Because I am flesh, because I am man, I seem often to be brought to perdition without perceiving doom." He voiced confidence that God will protect him from those who lay an ambush for him in the manner of a shameless robber envious of God's gifts, a pun on the name Theodore, meaning in Greek "the gift of God."[76] The same apologetic spirit is brought to a fever pitch in his *Response to Some People Who Trouble Him Malevolently, Demonstrating to Them That What God Has Established Is Stable and Indissoluble and That One Should Honor Those Honored by God*. The piece is polemical, supplicatory, and filled with quotations from the Psalms. Theodore presents himself as the victim of slander by greedy enemies accustomed to stealing the possessions of others.[77]

The complaint reflects his realization of the social dimension of the interpersonal conflicts in which he became involved. His perspective as a coemperor vested with public responsibilities came to clash, in particular, with two powerful adversaries descended from the imperial Komnenian aristocracy: Michael Palaiologos (Michael Komnenos Doukas Angelos Palaiologos) and Theodore Philes (Theodore Komnenos Philes).[78] Born in 1224 or 1226, Michael was a second cousin of Theodore – the emperor Alexios III Angelos was their shared great-grandfather through matrilineal descent. Michael united two branches of the powerful Palaiologos family who were intermarried with the Komnenoi, Doukai, and the Angeloi in the twelfth century. His mother, Theodora, was born from the union of Despot Alexios Palaiologos and Alexios III's daughter Irene.[79] His father was the *megas domestikos* Andronikos Palaiologos who had been the commander of the Nicaean field armies since the reign of the elder Theodore. His paternal uncle, also called Michael, was a high-standing palace official in the Nicaean empire with the title of *megas chartoularios*.[80] He was one among six siblings, some of whom were married into the Nicaean aristocracy. Michael's eldest sister, Maria, was the wife of Nikephoros Tarchaneiotes, a military commander and attendant at the imperial table *(epi tes trapezes)* from at least 1237. Tarchaneiotes succeeded Michael's father Andronikos Palaiologos between 1249 and 1252 in executing the duties of *megas domestikos*.[81] Another sister, Irene, was married to John Kantakouzenos, a man of Komnenian descent who served as governor of the theme of Thrakesion (c. 1242– c. 1249). Kantakouzenos performed the court duty of butler *(pinkernes)* and in 1248–50 warded off a Genoese invasion of the island of Rhodes.[82]

Theodore Komnenos Philes' ancestry is unknown, but he was a well-connected and wealthy aristocrat. He was the son-in-law of Irene Komnene Vranaina who owned landed properties near Smyrna and troubled the monastery of Lembos with claims over lands, olive trees, and animals – the kind of predatory social behavior that prompted Theodore to observe that his enemies augmented their wealth by illegal means. In the documentary evidence Theodore Komnenos Philes appears with the epithet "most noble."[83] Notably, a certain Leo Philes is called the "in-law *(gambros)* of emperors" on a seal found in Cyprus datable to the twelfth or thirteenth centuries.[84] Michael Palaiologos and Theodore Philes were both stationed in Macedonia after its reconquest by Nicaea. The *megas domestikos* Andronikos Palaiologos was the first Nicaean governor of Thessalonica after its annexation in the late 1246. He followed family tradition. A namesake, Andronikos Palaiologos, had administered Thessalonica in the early twelfth century.[85] Michael assisted his father, the *megas domestikos,* by commanding garrisons in Serres, Melnik, and adjacent areas in Macedonia.[86] The author of *Synopsis chronike*, a clergyman close to Theodore Laskaris, wrote dismissively that the *megas domestikos* accomplished nothing useful as governor of Thessalonica until his death (between 1249 and 1252). The assessment contrasts with that of Andronikos' eulogist, who commended him for strengthening the city's seawalls.[87] The eulogist drew attention to the prominent presence of his eldest and favorite son, Michael, at his deathbed and hoped that a successor would speedily assume the governorship of Thessalonica and the region around it.[88] The man dispatched from Anatolia was none other than Theodore Philes, who received the high provincial office of *praitor*.[89]

Philes had an intense personal conflict with Theodore marked by a flurry of mutual accusations. It is not known who first started the altercation. In 1253, Philes reprimanded Theodore Laskaris for having an affair and made this assertion public by circulating defamatory verses. Unfortunately, no details on the accusation and the nature of the alleged amorous liaison are provided. Theodore read the allegations near Nymphaion and angrily dismissed them as untrue.[90] On his part, he charged Philes with the murder of a close friend named Tribides, who apparently met his fate in Thessalonica.[91] The non-elite surname Tribides suggests a relatively humble Anatolian background. A certain Tribides is attested as the owner of a field with a ruined mill in the region of Philadelphia in the first half of the thirteenth century.[92] Blemmydes, who had only recently inveighed against Vatatzes' mistress Marchesina, took the charge of sexual misconduct seriously. His faithful student found himself compelled to profess his innocence in three highly emotional letters addressed to him.[93] He begged his teacher and spiritual father for forgiveness ("Forgive us, examine, and forgive us!"), and noted the irony that he himself struggled on behalf of maligned and persecuted individuals, but now was a victim of calumny. To prove that he was speaking the truth, he declared himself willing to undergo an ordeal by red-hot iron. "If you wish the discerning fire to carry out the inquest, as if it were some sort of cleansing, I accept."[94] Faced with the persistent entreaties, Blemmydes finally agreed to turn a blind eye to the accusation and granted Theodore his pardon.[95] In a letter to Akropolites, who was in the Balkans at the time, Theodore painted a grotesque portrait of the governor of Thessalonica, filled with rough sexual humor. Philes was a "many-headed and many-horned animal" who killed "anyone in his way," a "goat-stag" (*tragelaphos*), and "a scion of goats" (*tragophylon*). Another letter informed Akropolites that he would ask his father to punish the murderous slanderer. If Vatatzes refused, he himself would take a cruel revenge, imitating the tyrants of ancient Sicily.[96] The senior emperor indeed disciplined the Thessalonican governor without dismissing him.[97] The hatchet was not buried, however, and Theodore Laskaris and Theodore Philes remained deeply suspicious of each other, the former residing in Anatolia and the latter in the Balkans.

The conflict with Philes reveals two aspects of Theodore's thorny relations with the high aristocracy. First, the confrontations easily spilled over into violence, as we can see in the fate of Tribides and Theodore's desire for vengeance. In an encomium on his father composed between 1250 and 1252, Theodore voiced his fear lest the emperor becomes a victim of assassination "by those accustomed to his acts of generosity."[98] Second, the Philes affair shows that Theodore dispatched trusted men to the new Balkan territories. There were interlacing networks of loyalties, for Theodore's foes also had their confidants at court. In 1256 a certain Kotys warned Michael Palaiologos of Theodore's ill feelings toward him. Kotys is described as being "from the palace" and among Michael's "best friends."[99] Patronage networks of loyal followers were intertwined with the official structures of authority. Theodore valued loyalty greatly, but was also aware of its vulnerability – as can be seen in a composition he addressed to an anonymous friend who was concealing his true thoughts. The work is an allegorical comparison between the rose and the dung beetle. Envy was like a dung beetle burrowing near the root of the fragrant rosebush of friendship. Dung beetles were believed to die from the smell of roses, and the lesson Theodore wished to teach his secretive friend was that while friendship was not without its challenges, it emerged triumphant in the end.[100]

Theodore was conspicuously silent – a pregnant and uneasy silence – about the tense relationship with his second cousin Michael Palaiologos. The only direct reference to him is found in a letter to the patriarch Manuel II, in which Theodore points out that a certain Palaiologos continues to enjoy imperial favor.[101] This is most probably Michael, who was tried for treason in Philippi in the autumn of 1253. Indeed, Michael was quite well known to him, because he had spent time during his youth at the court and was only a few years younger.[102] During his Balkan campaign of 1252 and 1253, Vatatzes heard unverified rumors, originating in Melnik, that its governor Michael Palaiologos was plotting to break away from the empire. The allegations included his plans to marry the Bulgarian princess Thamar, Elena's sister, and thus legitimize the lordship. His judges, both laymen and ecclesiastics, convened in Philippi in eastern Macedonia, but were unable to confirm any of the reports, even after witnesses were questioned under torture. Michael is reported to have refused to go through ordeal by red-hot iron in order to prove his innocence.[103] He was brought in chains to Asia Minor for further investigation, but sometime in early 1254, on the initiative of the patriarch Manuel, he swore an oath of loyalty to the emperor and was released from prison, along with his companions. He was reappointed to military command, this time in Bithynia in Asia Minor, and was promoted to the rank of grand constable (*megas konostaulos*), held by the commander of the Latin mercenaries. The reconciliation led to the arrangement of his marriage to a grandniece of John Vatatzes named Theodora, a granddaughter of the emperor's brother, the *sebastokrator* Isaac Doukas, born through the latter's son John.[104] The family connection between the second cousins, Theodore Laskaris and Michael Palaiologos, was thus strengthened further.

The mounting confrontation with the high aristocracy of Komnenian descent is the backdrop to his treatise on politics and friendship composed before his accession as sole emperor in November 1254. This work represents an attempt by Theodore to adapt his experiences of socializing at the court and his philosophical knowledge to the question of societal structure. The theory of friendship in the treatise builds upon scattered thoughts in his letters regarding friendship, its place in the natural order of things, and its relations to kinship. Friendship obeyed "laws," he wrote in one letter. He noted in another letter that it was a force of nature holding the elements together in the animate and the inanimate world. "Everything assembled through reason is guarded by the bond of natural friendship."[105] "Everything akin to something has friendship as its main principle."[106] In both the treatise and in other works, Theodore Laskaris describes friendship as having two different sides. It was based on high ideals, but it also involved a reciprocal and mutual beneficial exchange. True friendship meant steadfast devotion stronger than one's life instinct. "A friend knows how to die for a friend."[107] In a letter to Akropolites he wrote that he had given him "all his soul and intellect," and added that friendship with the emperor had its material benefits in the form of generous gifts: gold, silver, precious stones, the protective company of servants (*hyperetai*), beautiful clothing, handsome horses, cold drinks, and delicacies.[108]

The treatise, thus, draws together ideas dispersed in his correspondence into a coherent discussion of elite solidarity, lordship, and the challenges of royal rule. Theodore envisaged a world with many lords (*kyrioi, despotai, hegemones*) below the emperor (*basileus*) occupying the top position in the social pyramid.[109] The most powerful force of social solidarity, in his view, was "friendship" (*philia*). Friendship was a reciprocal tie between two free but unequal individuals, a lord and his servant. Friendship with the emperor created an especially strong bond based on economic, social, and ideological incentives. The treatise is carefully structured. Mouzalon's query, which provided the occasion for its composition, is mentioned in the heading and again at the conclusion, serving as a framing device: "How should subjects serve their lords in all places, and how should they fittingly cater to their wishes?"[110] Another framing device is an anecdote about Alexander the Great borrowed from Blemmydes' *Imperial Statue*, which opens the treatise and recurs toward its end. When the king of ancient Macedon was asked to reveal his treasures, he pointed to his friends. Alexander's five friends, mirroring the five senses, are said to have been exemplary subjects, with qualities such as "pure fidelity," "undefiled love," and "blameless respect," on whom the great conqueror relied in his campaigns, which took him from Thrace "all the way to Lybia."[111] Theodore was inspired by the eighth book of Aristotle's *Nicomachaean Ethics*, according to which friendship was inherent in every polity. Kings and wealthy members of the community need to have friends to whom they are benefactors.[112] Theodore adopted Aristotle's categorization of friendship into three kinds: friendship based on the good, on benefit, and on pleasure. There are striking differences from his model, however. Aristotle's idea of equality as a key characteristic of friendship is missing from the treatise.[113] The Nicaean emperor changed "the good" of the *Nicomachean Ethics* to "the natural good" in order to stress that the legitimate monarchy was fully in harmony with nature (an idea developed in the fifth book of his treatise *Natural Communion*).

The reciprocal and practical character of friendship follows features of the understanding of the concept in Byzantium.[114] The benefits of being the emperor's friend are described in historically concrete terms understandable only in their Nicaean context. Friendship for the sake of the natural good, the highest form of friendship, meant that all subjects were – and needed to be – the emperor's friends, because the emperor is "clearly an image of God" and "governs over the fellow subjects (of God) in conformity with nature and by the lordly power of the Creator."[115] The "natural good" was synonymous with public welfare, which the emperor– who ruled by divine right – guaranteed. The ideological rationale is mixed with a practical one. The emperor secured the "peaceful state of the people" and the "glory of the fatherland." He led defensive wars, extended the frontiers, and welcomed refugees.[116] The lower forms of friendship, based on benefit and pleasure, were reciprocal. The picture is one of reciprocating favors in a dangerous world of multiple and intersecting loyalties, in which the emperor saw his friends as spies and confidants. His friends are utterly dedicated, patient, perseverant, industrious, discreet, and capable of serving as informants. The fear of factionalism and rebellion clearly shapes the description. In exchange for their loyalty, the friends gained from the emperor "forbidden knowledge" and the right of free expression. They also obtained material benefits in the form of money and property, and also preferential treatment by the emperor (and therefore, the imperial tribunal) when they were accused – a curious departure from the ideal of universal and impartial justice that Theodore espoused elsewhere.[117] The third kind of friendship, based on pleasure, brought the emperor's friends coveted access to the life of courtly pleasure. They received luxury clothes from the palaces, listened to musical performances, tasted exquisite food, and took part in exciting hunting expeditions. They hoped to receive praise from the emperor when they participated in gymnastic and military exercises, such as horseback riding, fencing, arrow-shooting, jumping, and running.[118] We hear the voice of Theodore complimenting his faithful friends: "Well done, my good and faithful servant!" "Call for me, my loyal and dear servant!" The reputation of being the emperor's friend was a valuable asset in itself and brought additional benefits. For, as the author argues, friends and relatives of the emperor's friend would respect that friend more, while the friend's enemies would try to establish good relations with him.[119]

Toward the end of the treatise Theodore delivered his punch line: "I will say something most unusual. The love of true friends surpasses that of many and great blood relatives!"[120] His proposition was "most unusual," because it went against the dominant family-based model of elite solidarity. Such a departure from core aristocratic values was occasionally voiced in court rhetoric in Nicaea.[121] Theodore went a step further, however, and sought an alternative to the paradigm of politics as one big family – a radical step for someone who was himself a product and beneficiary of this system. His realization that kinship by blood did not necessarily support centralizing policies and helped even less in the cultivation of a service aristocracy must have unsettled him deeply. Did not kinship bonds lead to fragmentation, entitlement, and rebellion in the Byzantine world that emerged after 1204? Was not his father's life threatened at the beginning of his rule by his scheming cousins from the Nestongos family? Was not the allegiance of his own second cousin Michael Palaiologos, and that of other relatives and descendants from the Komnenian dynasty, highly questionable?

Theodore Laskaris did not explain the implementation of his theories, but they are not a utopia. Clientelism seems a better word than friendship for the reciprocal relationship of dependence on the emperor outlined in the treatise. As scholars have noted, the notion of friendship was applied in

Byzantium to patronage networks and the description of feudal ties in the medieval West.[122] Theodore believed that his resources, both material and ideological, enabled him to harness the strong social bonds formed at the court and to create new ones on the same model for the purpose of centralizing royal authority. His hope was to govern through clients at the expense of aristocratic kinship groups. In this regard, the treatise set a political agenda for his independent rule. Revealingly, it called upon all lords and subjects to adopt the principle of friendship as the basis of their social interaction.[123] This appeal, along with the omission of crucial details, leaves the impression of a white paper. The treatise provokes the audience to fill in the blanks and think about the specific configurations of power in the future.

Governance by friendship presupposes a social consensus, yet was it realistic to expect a profound realignment of the governing elite to be accomplished in a peaceful and friendly way? In Chapter 8 we will see how Theodore put his ideas into practice during the period of his sole rule.

7 | Elena and the Embassy of the Marquis

Soon after Theodore Laskaris reached the age of thirty in late 1251 or early 1252, two events had a profound effect on him. The sudden death (1252) of his wife Elena led to an outpouring of grief and soul searching. One year after her passing (1253), the arrival of the embassy of Marquis Berthold of Hohenburg – a right-hand man of the emperor Frederick II Hohenstaufen and a patron of letters – impelled him to take stock of relations with the Latin West and to begin to prepare manuscript editions of some of his ever-growing literary and philosophical works. These episodes in his life have left many traces in his writings and were occasions for self-descriptive compositions. They deserve our close attention.

In the spring of 1252, possibly as early as March, John Vatatzes departed for a campaign in the Balkans that saw plenty of military and diplomatic action.[1] He headed a large army with many commanding officers. Theodore remained in Asia Minor in accordance with the usual practice, while his mentor George Akropolites joined the expedition. Continuing tensions with Michael II Komnenos Doukas (Michael of Epiros) caused Vatatzes' prolonged absence. Between 1248 and 1250, Michael of Epiros' wife, the saintly Theodora Petraliphina, had come in person to Anatolia in order to arrange for a treaty with Vatatzes. Theodora was well suited to the task of being a peace mediator. She and other members of the Petraliphas family were linked by marriage with powerful individuals in both states. Theodora was a daughter of John Petraliphas, a high provincial official in Thessaly and Macedonia before 1204, and her paternal aunt was the wife of the blinded Theodore of Epiros, the former self-proclaimed emperor. Her brother Theodore Petraliphas was married to a daughter of Demetrios Komnenos Tornikes, Vatatzes' powerful *mesazon*.[2] A certain John Petraliphas, who held the title of *megas chartoularios,* was a loyal and talented military officer of Vatatzes attested in the period 1240–42. Vatatzes welcomed Theodora Petraliphina and her young son Nikephoros in Pegai on the Sea of Marmara. An agreement was made on the imminent conclusion of a treaty that would provide a renewed recognition of Nicaea as the only legitimate successor to the twelfth-century empire. Michael of Epiros received the title of despot, either on that occasion or as early as 1246, and his son Nikephoros was betrothed to Maria, the second daughter of Theodore Laskaris. The Epirote ruler did not abide by his word, however, and by 1252 had risen in revolt with the assistance of his blinded uncle, the tireless and ever-scheming Theodore of Epiros.[3]

The Nicaean army reached Thessalonica, proceeded into western Macedonia, and besieged the fortress of Vodena (Edessa), which surrendered after its master, Theodore of Epiros, fled to the court of his rebellious nephew. Vatatzes encamped on the shore of Lake Ostrovo (Vegoritida) and dispatched his commanders, including Alexios Strategopoulos and Michael Palaiologos, to plunder areas controlled by Michael of Epiros. This strategy could not change the latter's mind. The decisive turn of the tide was the defection of powerful local lords who arrived at the Nicaean camp, such as Theodore Petraliphas (the son-in-law of Demetrios Komnenos Tornikes), Glavas of Kastoria, and Goulamos (Golem) of Albanon (a name for Albania used by Theodore and his contemporaries). Other grandees – Xeros, the metropolitan of Naupaktos; Constantine Maliasenos of Thessaly; and a certain Lampetes – convinced Michael of Epiros that his position was untenable and that he should cede more territories in Macedonia to Nicaea as the price of peace. Toward the end of the year, the emperor sent a delegation to him consisting of the metropolitan of Philadelphia, Phokas, the *primmikerios* of the court (*prim-mikerios tes aules*), Isaac Doukas Mourtzouphlos, Michael Hyaleas, and George Akropolites. They concluded the treaty in Larissa and returned to the winter camp in Vodena along with the blinded Theodore of Epiros, who was handed over to Vatatzes as a prisoner. His subsequent fate is unknown. The emperor remained in Vodena until Easter (April 20, 1253) and toured in the summer the newly annexed lands. He visited Ohrid and Kastoria, and secured the allegiance of local lords and towns. The empire of Nicaea came to extend westward to mountainous Albania and incorporated Kroia (Kroai), whose urban community received special privileges. Vatatzes finally returned to Anatolia in the late autumn of 1253 after an absence of a year and a half.[4]

In the spring or summer of 1252, shortly after Vatatzes' departure for the Balkans, Theodore's wife Elena Asenina passed away of unknown causes. She died most probably in the palace in Nymphaion, where her husband grieved over the sudden disaster. He felt devastated, deprived of a person for whom he felt the deepest love and affection: "a bond of incomparable love" in his own words. The couple had six children. The birth of his eldest daughter, who was named Irene after Theodore's mother, was followed by four other daughters: Maria, Theodora, Eudokia, and another girl whose name is not recorded. Their last child, John, was born around Christmas 1250.[5] Traces of Theodore's shattered state of mind are found throughout his writings, especially in letters, in his encomium on Cosmas and Damian, and in the *Moral Pieces*. He mourned Elena for a long period of time – longer, it seems, than the forty days prescribed by the church. It is only because of the order given by his father from the Balkans that he changed into his usual clothing, stopped fasting, and left Nymphaion on a tour that took him to Atramyttion, Troy, and probably the Hellespont, from where he could liaise more easily with the commanders of the army in the Balkans.[6] The senior emperor needed his trusted deputy to resume active duty and communicate sensitive information about the situation in Anatolia and along the eastern frontier. The change of clothing was the traditional practice, for bereavement was displayed in Byzantium through the wearing of black attire. One exception to the color code was the emperor. During the fourteenth century, an emperor who mourned the death of a spouse or another family member dressed himself in white for as long as he wished and subsequently put on a yellow garment until he decided to don his regular clothing.[7]

While lamenting the loss of his wife, Theodore composed ten heart-rending essays, the *Moral Pieces*, in which he pondered the fleeting nature of happiness and the transience of life (Fig. 18). He had been "journeying on the heights of happiness" only recently and had felt "utmost joy in my soul and in my soul mate – for speech cannot call her (Elena) by any other name than 'a like soul' and 'a sharer of my life.'" He writes that he had experienced no such suffering in the past.[8] His reflections on the fragility of human existence reveal towering sorrow:

> The lives of mortals are like the impulse of time, the flow of a river current, and the movement of a breeze. For all these resemble one another and ever flow inconstantly and make their way with no perman-ence whatsoever... Large is the sea of life and hard to cross, because the man who powerlessly sails on it is utterly unable to find harbor... Time flows, lives pass, customs slip away. The future is unpredictable, no one sees it, everyone is deluded: the possessors because they have no posses-sions, those who weep and those who laugh, the playful and the diligent.[9]

The lamentations and musings borrow themes from natural philosophy. Humans follow the fate of the elements. Once compacted, matter under-goes alteration, diminution, and decay "through the impulses and forces of time." The last essay of the *Moral Pieces* is a naturalistic depiction of the decomposition of the author's body and his descent into the under-world, where he wishes to join his beloved.[10] One of the main points of the work is that the author has come to the sad realization that the only constant in human life is change.[11]

The *Moral Pieces* echo a motif of religious literature in presenting sorrow as a step leading to salvation.[12] The author confesses that he has acquired knowledge of the self through grief and come to comprehend the paramount importance of virtue. He had been "running a course far distant from the true path" and "virtuous life" before Elena's passing, for even if he thought that he "possessed something, nothing was permanent." "Food, luxury, comfort, servants, honor, pomp, and everything else mortal nature is accustomed to value are of no benefit and use; none of them is for the sake of virtue and edification."[13] In this particular moment he understood virtue as a life of contemplation. There was fear among members of his entourage, both those staying with him in Anatolia and those in the Balkans accompanying the senior emperor, that the heir to the throne might embrace a life of solitude, reading, and writing. In a letter sent from the Balkans, Akropolites counseled the grief-stricken prince to seek solace in hunting and bathing, but Theodore rejected the suggestion by referring metaphorically to his spiritual ablution in the springs of salvation.[14]

Some people around Theodore saw speedy remarriage to be the best cure for his sorrow and the expected course of action for a widowed prince. Theodore cites their words in an elaborate literary piece titled *Response to Some Friends Pressing Him to Find a Bride*.

> You have the brightest power of wealth and a throne that reaches the clouds, the height of an imperial dignity exalted in its preeminence, the famous name of your family as an imperial offshoot and as a noblest lion cub. You should not withdraw from the cares of the world, because the hopes of many are anchored upon you.[15]

The *Response* comes close to the *Moral Pieces* in its musings on the transience of life and human existence. Thrones fall, lives end, and the honor of families changes in the course of time. The *Response* introduces the theme of philosophy, which takes the place of virtue. The earthly empire in all its glory is inferior to a life devoted to philosophy, just as matter ranks below immateriality.[16] It is the philosophical "contempt for everything" that makes one nobler.[17] The only ladies in his life from now, Theodore declares, were to be Wisdom (*sophia*) and Philosophy (*philosophia*). The erotic imagery of the first letter to Akropolites in the Laurentian epistolary collection became stronger here. Lady Wisdom, he writes, has kissed him with passion on the mouth. "She is my desire (*eros*). She is my housemate. She has embraced me, always embraces me, and will be embracing me." Even if he is compelled to dwell in the female quarters of the palace, she will continue to be his beloved and conceive literary offspring.[18] Theodore's statement in the *Response* that he would "draw on every teaching about flight from the world" seems to have worried Akropolites, who attempted to dissuade him from adopting the ascetic lifestyle of a monk.[19] In his lengthy response, Theodore pointed out that eremitic existence and flight from the world (*kosmos*) was the same as life in Christ, even though Akropolites might disagree; it meant avoidance of worldly pleasure. The "world" did not necessarily mean humankind and human company, but also pertained to worldly concerns about money, clothes, properties, and all the pomp and circumstance of his royal life. Everyone who renounced materiality was fleeing the world to take refuge in Christ, no matter whether he resided on Mount Sinai, Mount Carmel, in Nineveh, or elsewhere.[20] These reflections convey the spirit of the *Moral Pieces*, where he had written that a life of virtue was not necessarily ascetic: "Nothing else can implant virtue in the soul but her association with other good souls."[21] The circle of companions and courtiers – and especially George Mouzalon – mattered for him even more as a source of solace after Elena's death. Many of Theodore's later letters to Mouzalon close by calling his childhood friend "my strong bond indissoluble." This expression alludes to marriage and forms part of the vocabulary of kinship and the rhetoric of desire, with which Theodore signalled the strong connection and solidarity between the two men.[22]

The coemperor resumed his former lifestyle within months of his wife's passing. In 1253 we see him visiting cities in Asia Minor, such as Pergamon and Atramyttion, and receiving foreign embassies. The most lasting effect of the shock from Elena's death lies in his increasingly somber mood and his dedication to writing and philosophy. His letters show that he became more resolved than ever to combine his royal responsibilities with intellectual pursuits. Writing to Akropolites, he summarized the sobering effect of sorrow, which paradoxically led him to newfound knowledge about the meaning of human existence and hence to the joys of philosophy:

> Sorrow exceedingly saddened us, my friend, but it brought a greater fruit of knowledge. The former (sorrow) is caused by discernment, the latter (knowledge) by virtue, and all of it because of what has happened ... Do you see, my friend, how sorrow causes joy? And how sorrow especially does so when it rises to the level of knowledge and philosophy?[23]

In the *Response* Theodore highlights the intellectual offspring he has already conceived with Lady Wisdom. He refers to poetical pieces (probably ecclesiastical hymns) and writings inspired by Hermes, a phrase by which he could mean works of rhetoric as well as philosophy.[24] No specific compositions are mentioned, but it is clear that he was already an accomplished author and was resolved to continue on his chosen path. It is not a coincidence that most of his datable works and all of the authorized manuscript editions belong to the period after 1252.[25] Recovering from the loss of his wife, the thirty-year-old widower became painfully aware of his own mortality and came increasingly to think about his intellectual legacy.

The embassy of Berthold of Hohenburg in the following year (1253) gave Theodore the stimulus to embark on the first wave of publication of his writings. By the time this influential ambassador arrived, he had gained plenty of knowledge about the foreign world and the Latin West in particular. A look at his encounters with other visiting envoys helps to put this embassy into broader perspective and provides the necessary background for understanding Theodore's views on cultural and ecclesiastical relations with the West. A sense of familiarity with international affairs across the Mediterranean and Eurasia pervades the encomium on his father composed between 1250 and 1252.[26] Mention is made of Nicaea's most important neighbors and specific diplomatic maneuvers. The Seljuks of Rum ("the Persians") are presented as a shadow of their former self, the historical reality after the Mongol victory at Köse Dağ. Theodore alludes to a defensive pact caused by the Mongol menace. "The Persian (the Seljuks) holds out your mightiest hand" – he lauded his father – "as a threat against the arrogant Tatar army and presents the fear of you as his protector." As a result, "the shameful and foul wolf" (the Mongols) cohabited peacefully in the same pen with the "Persian lamb" (the Seljuks).[27]

Vatatzes engaged in cautious diplomacy with the new Great Khan Möngke (r. 1251–59), which is reflected in Theodore's encomium. In the account of his visit to Karakorum addressed to the French king Louis IX, who was on an ill-fated crusade in the Levant between 1248 and 1254, the Franciscan friar William of Rubruck refers to two Nicaean embassies to the Great Khan. The first embassy (1251–52) emerges from William of Rubruck's report that he met in Karakorum an Arab versed in several languages who had once served as the Great Khan's envoy to Vatatzes. The Nicaean emperor is said to have suspected a Mongol invasion and to have richly rewarded the Saracen envoy, on whose advice he dispatched his own ambassadors to Karakorum in order to play for time. After the Nicaean embassy to the Great Khan, Vatatzes is alleged to have ceased to fear the Mongols.[28] The most plausible chronological reconstruction of the reported events is that the Mongol envoy (the unnamed individual of Arab origin) came to the empire of Nicaea in 1251, soon after Möngke's accession, and that the resulting Nicaean embassy to Karakorum took place in 1251 or 1252.[29] The second Nicaean embassy was more recent. Between December 27, 1253, and January 4, 1254, William met in person in Karakorum Nicaean envoys who were at pains to stress the peaceful relations between Vatatzes and Louis IX in order to play down the divisions in Christendom. The envoys must have been dispatched in the course of 1253 and may have received instructions from Theodore, because John Vatatzes was then in the Balkans.[30]

Notably, Theodore mentions in his encomium that a certain Guneas the Arab intervened successfully in Vatatzes' efforts to appease the Mongols and the Seljuks.[31] One is immediately confronted with a curious problem of historical interpretation caused by Theodore's penchant for using code names. Guneas is a mythological figure found in the poem *Alexandra* by the Hellenistic author Lykophron and in Blemmydes' *Imperial Statue*. A Byzantine scholion on *Alexandra* states that Guneas was "an Arab famous for justice whom Semiramis made an arbiter between the Phoenicians and Babylonians."[32] Guneas, thus, symbolized the broker of a fair peace. It can hardly have been by chance that both Theodore Laskaris and William of Rubruck spoke of an Arab who was a diplomatic intermediary between the Mongols and Anatolian powers around the year 1251. The code name Guneas seems to have disguised a real person: a gifted multilingual Arab who served as a Mongol envoy across Eurasia and who came to assist John Vatatzes in his diplomatic agenda of averting a Mongol attack on Asia Minor.

More specific are Theodore's comments in the imperial encomium on Nicaea's relations with the West. The diverse Latin powers are compared to the many heads of a decapitated monster: Germans, Italians, Venetians, Lombards, Genoese, and Pisans. The titles of various Latin dignitaries are listed as *podestàs*, viscounts, consuls, first counsellors, and barons. The Latin emperor Baldwin II, who had returned to Constantinople in October 1248 without having procured the hoped-for support, was scoffed at as "the falsely crowned ruler."[33] The encomium expresses pride in the humbling and defeat of the formerly powerful enemies. The Latin empire continued to be plagued by financial problems in the late 1240s. Soon after Baldwin returned to Constantinople, his wife Marie of Brienne (Fig. 16b) herself left Constantinople on a fund-raising tour of western Europe that took her to France, the Low Countries, and Castile. Never to return to the Bosporus, she saw her only son, Philip, being mortgaged, probably as early as 1248, to

Venetian merchants. The child was brought up in Venice while Marie was trying to collect funds to pay off the debt. It was the decisive intervention of her cousin, the king of Castile Alfonso X, that led to the ransoming of Philip between June 1258 and May 1261.[34]

The encomium shows detailed knowledge of Vatatzes' dealings with the papacy, and especially the recent reception of a papal embassy at the church council held in Nymphaion in the spring of 1250. Vatatzes tried to undermine Baldwin's weak position by engaging Pope Innocent IV in negotiations on the status of Constantinople. His Janus-faced foreign policy was to adhere to the old alliance with his strategic partner Frederick II, while at the same time making overtures to the papacy. Pope Innocent IV – an able canon lawyer born in Genoa as Sinibaldo Fieschi – made the destruction of Frederick's power his mission and masterminded his dethronement from the imperial office at the Council of Lyons (1245). The all-out war against Frederick that followed and Innocent's interest in missionary activity among the Mongols, whose penetration into central Europe in 1241 was a cause for alarm, deflected attention from crusading against Nicaea. To be sure, Innocent still declared the weakness of the Latin empire of Constantinople to be among the "five afflictions" of Christendom at the Council of Lyons, during which the Latin emperor Baldwin played a prominent role and was seated at the right hand of the pope. Yet the papal call for a crusade against Vatatzes achieved nothing resembling the massive expedition that Baldwin led in 1239–40.[35] Innocent was more effective in his struggle with Frederick. His legates fomented rebellion against the supporters of the Hohenstaufens in Germany and Italy, and on February 18, 1248, the pro-papal forces led by Cardinal Ottaviano Ubaldini inflicted a massive defeat on the imperial army besieging Parma.[36] Vatatzes kept assisting his embattled father-in-law in spite of his setbacks. Greeks are attested fighting at Parma in 1247–48, and in the wake of the debacle, Vatatzes sent subsidies to Frederick.[37] In 1250 he dispatched aid in the form of archers and infantrymen. According to Frederick's letter to Michael of Epiros, which requested safe conduct for the Nicaean troops, Latin galleys were to welcome the soldiers in Dyrrachion and transport them to Apulia.[38] The troops seem to have taken the ancient *via Egnatia*, the trans-Balkan overland route connecting Constantinople and the Adriatic coast. This display of Nicaean power hardly had any consequence for the military operations in Italy, yet it had deep symbolic importance in Theodore's eyes. In the imperial encomium, he compared the "Hellenes" fighting in Italy to the conquering warriors of Alexander who had once upon a time campaigned far away from their homeland.[39]

In the summer of 1250 Frederick's troops began to turn back the tide and went on the offensive in the March of Ancona. On August 18, 1250, the imperial vicar-general of Lombardy, Hubert Pallavicini, defeated Parmesan forces and captured their *carroccio* (the wheeled vehicle with the city's standard), a victory that Frederick proudly advertised in a letter to Vatatzes. Two days later, Frederick's capable lieutenant Walter of Manupello captured the fortress of Cingoli in the March. Peter Capoccio, a Roman cardinal Innocent had appointed in April 1249 as his legate in Sicily and had entrusted with military command in the Italian peninsula, escaped from the town by disguising himself as a beggar. This humiliation, too, was deemed worthy of mention in a letter by Frederick to Vatatzes. The disgraced Capoccio was replaced with Ottaviano Ubaldini.[40] The two powerful cardinals became well known to Theodore Laskaris, who exchanged letters with them on ecclesiastical and political matters.[41]

Frederick could not derive much benefit from the military reversals, because he died from a dysenteric disease on December 13, 1250, in Castel Fiorentino in Apulia. Not long after his passing, Theodore honored his great Western contemporary by composing a speech in his memory. The work is a treatise on the challenges of kingship and conveys the spirit of solidarity between the two Mediterranean emperors evident in Frederick's epistles to Vatatzes. The text never mentions Frederick by name, yet he lurks behind the silence, for he is the model ruler on whose life and struggles the musings are based. Theodore kept abreast of events in Italy by various means: talking to the Greek-speaking companions of his step-mother; reading Frederick's letters; conversing with returning Nicaean soldiers; and possibly by perusing polemical pamphlets written during the struggle between the emperor and the papacy.[42] He felt empathy for the embattled emperor – "the emperor (*basileus*) of the Germans (*Alamanoi*)," ruling over the land of the Italians and the Germans.[43] The memorial speech presents the ruler and general – any ruler acting in the public interest like Frederick – as a deplorable victim of tragic misunderstanding. The principal feeling of subjects toward their ruler is not love, but hatred. This pessimistic observation echoes the hate campaign against Frederick after the Council of Lyons in 1245, but it also reflects Theodore's frustration at the hostility that his father – and he himself – faced in their dealings with segments of the aristocratic elite. The duty of the ruler was to bear up against ill-feelings and administer justice impartially for the sake of the preservation of the realm, incurring more resentment in the process. Kings, thus, had a lonely and thankless mission. They were maligned in their lifetime and their trials and tribulations were easily forgotten. Only trophies they left behind in certain places reminded later generations of their victories.[44]

While Frederick was fighting for his survival, Vatatzes approached his archenemy Innocent IV. His goal was to obtain papal concessions on the status of Constantinople, something he had already tried to achieve in the debates with the visiting friars in January 1234 in Nicaea. At that time, he had allegedly asked whether Pope Gregory IX would restore the patriarch "his rights" in the city if the latter acknowledged the primacy of the see of St. Peter.[45] Now Vatatzes was bolder in his requests. He employed Franciscans resident in the Greek East to make contact with the pope. By Lent 1249 two of them arrived at the papal curia in Lyons: Salimbene, a half Greek and half Latin, and Thomas, a Greek who was a lector in the Franciscan friary in Constantinople. They brought imperial letters addressed to both Innocent IV and John of Parma (Giovanni Buralli di Parma), the highly learned minister general of the Franciscan order, appointed to this position in July 1247, who had taught theology in Bologna, Naples, and Paris. Authorized by Innocent to discuss papal primacy and the Procession of the Holy Spirit in a local council, John of Parma departed for Anatolia in the company of other Franciscans, including Drudo, the minister of Burgundy, and the friars Salimbene and Thomas of Constantinople.[46]

The discussions with John of Parma took place at a church council convened in the spring of 1250 in Nymphaion. The council was well attended and multidenominational. The patriarch Manuel came from Nicaea, along with many metropolitan bishops. Blemmydes, who had excelled in the discussions with the Latins in 1234, was invited to participate – in spite of his uneasy relationship with Vatatzes on account of the recent public attack on his Latin mistress. At the request of Vatatzes, he once again formulated the arguments against the Latin position on the *filioque* (the Procession of the Holy Spirit from the Father and the Son), a key point of dispute between the Greek and the Latin church.[47] In his autobiography he boasts how he intervened at a crucial moment during the council in order to expose the falseness of a syllogism proposed by the Latins regarding the Procession of the Holy Spirit.[48] Representatives of the three Eastern patriarchs were present at the council along with a delegation of the Armenian church, probably headed by the doctor of the church (*vardapet*) Jacob. Blemmydes debated the Armenian addition to the *Trisagion* chant in the liturgy and the use of unmixed liturgical wine by the Armenian church.[49]

Theodore himself attended the deliberations, for he speaks as an eyewitness in the encomium on his father. According to him, Vatatzes cut a commanding figure at the council. Presiding over the doctors of the law and asking difficult questions, he resembled the Lord's Anointed.[50] Blessed with the gift of the Holy Spirit, he spoke the truth in the manner of a true philosopher and without the need for syllogisms.[51] The comment is worth keeping in mind. Dialectical inquiry into the holy scriptures was the core method of scholastic theology. John of Parma and his companions Drudo and Thomas were lectors – that is, teachers of theology in Franciscan houses. By witnessing the competitive disputations with the educated Latins, Theodore obtained firsthand knowledge of their way of arguing and, as we will see in Chapter 9, came to favor a critical approach to scholasticism and its use of syllogistic reasoning.

Theodore avoids mentioning in the encomium the compromise that Vatatzes and the orthodox patriarchs offered to make in return for political favors from the papacy. A document preserved in Latin in the papal archives, the so-called "chapters of recognition and petition" (*capitula recognitionis et petitionis*), represents the proposal for resolving the Eastern Schism adopted by the orthodox representatives at the Council of Nymphaion.[52] Their suggested concessions included the acceptance of papal primacy, the supreme position of the papal curia as a final court of appeal, and the right of the pope to preside in councils and make doctrinal judgments, which the rest of the bishops were to accept "as long as they do not depart from the evangelical and canonical regulations." In return, the Greek side requested the restoration of "the *imperium* of the city of Constantinople" to Vatatzes. The Latin emperor and patriarch were to leave Constantinople and the other Latin patriarchs were to abandon their sees, except for the patriarch of Antioch, Innocent's nephew Opizzo Fieschi.

A large Nicaean delegation consisting of four metropolitan bishops (among them Andronikos of Sardis and John Kleidas of Kyzikos), sixteen bishops, and a number of imperial officials was dispatched in the summer of 1250 to the papacy in order to present their "just requests."[53] Frederick II reluctantly agreed to transport the numerous envoys from Dyrrachion to Apulia (just as he did, although far more enthusiastically, with the Nicaean military contingent during the same summer), but declined to give the Franciscans a safe conduct.[54] His sudden death in December 1250 led to a long detention of the ambassadors in Apulia. Only in late 1251 or early 1252 did their audience with Innocent IV finally take place, in Perugia.[55] Innocent's oral response, a transcript of which survives, was that he had no legal reason to dispossess Baldwin of his crown unless the latter was accused and convicted by a law court. He assured Vatatzes that he would arbitrate between the two claimants to the throne of Constantinople. If an agreement could not be reached, he would try to offer a just settlement.[56] The negotiations understandably reached an impasse. Another large Nicaean embassy was dispatched in the second half of 1253 and after a long delay met the pope in 1254 in Rome, following him to Assisi and Anagni. According to the chronicler Matthew Paris, it took a confrontational stance on the Procession on the Holy Spirit and other issues, but returned nonetheless loaded with generous gifts.[57] Theodore remained sceptical during the negotiations. His lukewarm attitude is seen in a letter addressed to Blemmydes in 1252 after the return of Andronikos of Sardis from the first embassy. He compared the news he received to "a bitter bite, a badly sounding report, and venomous and indeed treacherous message." The pope is said to have demanded obedience in exchange for which he promised "to bring to fulfillment all our rights."[58] In another, probably earlier, letter to Blemmydes, Theodore complained that "people who have no spirit of truth" are "philosophizing about the Holy Spirit."[59]

The most impactful encounter of Theodore with a Latin ambassador and with current trends in Latin philosophy occurred during the disputations he held with the embassy of Berthold of Hohenburg. Berthold's diplomatic mission to Nicaea was connected with the succession struggle in Italy after Frederick's death. The testament of the dying emperor, which the papacy never recognized, declared his son Conrad, born from Yolanda of Jerusalem, to be the heir to the empire and the kingdom of Sicily, and designated another son, Manfred, born from Bianca Lancia, as Prince of Taranto and governor of the kingdom of Sicily as long as Conrad (King Conrad IV) remained in Germany. The guardian of the eighteen-year-old Manfred and plenipotentiary in the kingdom of Sicily was Berthold of Hohenburg.[60] Berthold was the son of Diepold of Vohburg (d. 1225), a nobleman from the March of the Nordgau in Bavaria who had acquired by marriage the title of marquis of Hohenburg and who had fought at the siege of Damietta (1218–19) during the Fifth Crusade. A trusted supporter of the emperor, Diepold assigned his four sons, one of whom was Berthold, as pages at his court.[61] Berthold rose to the position of captain of Como in 1239, served as general vicar of Pavia from 1244 onward, and held fiefs in Sicily. He married a daughter of Manfred II Lancia, the marquis of Busca in Piedmont, and thus acquired connection by marriage with Frederick's children born from his mistress Bianca Lancia, namely Manfred and Constanza-Anna, Vatatzes' wife.[62]

In early 1252 Conrad sailed to Apulia in order to secure his rights over Italy and the Kingdom of Sicily. He mistrusted the maternal relatives of his half-brother Manfred, the powerful Lancia family. Manfred II Lancia, the marquis of Busca, shared at the time with Hubert Pallavicini the governance of Lombardy and his son Galvano Lancia had been the imperial vicar of Tuscany since the last years of Frederick's reign.[63] The conflict deepened when on January 1, 1253, Manfred II Lancia was elected the *podestà* of Milan, the chief city of the anti-Hohenstaufen Lombard League.[64] In the winter of that year Conrad ordered the expulsion of the Lancias from his realm, except for Isolda Lancia, the wife of Berthold of Hohenburg, who found himself in a particularly delicate position.[65] Members of the Lancia family, including women and children, left en masse for the empire of Nicaea, where they sought asylum and the backing of their relative, the empress Constanza-Anna. They arrived in Anatolia in the spring or early summer of the year, at a time when Vatatzes was still campaigning in the Balkans. The political refugees included the brothers Galvano and Federico Lancia and their cousin Boniface of Agliano. A passage from the chronicle of Niccolò Jamsilla records these events:

> The king (Conrad) ordered Galvano Lancia – who had long served the emperor (Frederick) and whom the emperor had used for a long period of time as his vicar in Tuscia due to his steadfast loyalty and prudence – and also Federico Lancia and Boniface of Agliano, the uncle of the same prince (Manfred), as well as his (Manfred's) blood relatives and affines on his mother's side, because a favorable opportunity had presented itself against them, to leave the kingdom along with their wives, mothers, sisters, sons and daughters, older and younger . . . All left the kingdom and went to the sister of the same prince who was the empress of Romania.[66]

Theodore received the relatives of his stepmother in one of the royal palaces in the Thrakesion theme.[67] The defectors from abroad did not catch him fully by surprise, even if he hardly expected the arrival of such a large group all belonging to the same noble family. He was used to receiving elite foreigners, whether from the former Byzantine world or beyond, who were attracted to seek asylum by Vatatzes' reputation for generosity. In the summer of 1251, for example, Boniface, the marquis of Carreto, a Ghibelline supporter, arranged for a voyage to the empire of Nicaea for himself and his armed companions in order to escape from the political turmoil in Italy. In 1254 Ashraf Musa, the son of the Ayyubid ruler of Syria, An-Nasir Yusuf, left Egypt for the empire of Nicaea after having been expelled by the first Mamluk sultan, Aybak.[68] A letter from Theodore to Mouzalon informing the latter of various events at the court mentions the presence of a fractious and unruly group of Latins from the Lancia family, who were not allowed to proceed to Nicaea and

Thessalonica. In effect, their freedom of movement was restricted until the arrival of Vatatzes from the Balkans. The two brothers of Boniface of Agliano wished to leave and return to King Conrad in Italy, but Boniface insisted that they remain loyal to Galvano and Marquis Manfred Lancia:

> Boniface is presiding. Who will have an argument with him? For he has two brothers, the count Rigetos and *syr* Manfred. He is exhorting them daily not to return to the country of King Conrad. Indeed, they have *syr* Galvano and Marquis Lancia: let them listen to them. The crowd says to them: "If they will not listen to Galvano and Lady Bianca, they will not obey a certain *syr* Timbaldos (Diepold), even if he resurrects from the dead."[69]

A few months after the expulsion of the Lancias, Conrad reconsidered his policy and dispatched Berthold of Hohenburg on a diplomatic assignment in Byzantine Anatolia in order to convince them to return. Berthold arrived in the autumn of 1253 and was entertained by Theodore Laskaris.[70] He awaited there the arrival of the senior emperor later in the autumn and spent over a month at the Byzantine court in exile. His stay was long enough to give multiple opportunities for one-on-one interactions with the junior coemperor.[71] The success of Berthold's diplomatic mission is hard to assess. The chronicler Niccolò Jamsilla writes that Berthold arranged that Galvano Lancia and his brothers be "dismissed by the emperor of Romania (John Vatatzes)."[72] Galvano and Federico Lancia, and doubtless other members of the family, came back to Italy in the course of 1254, although their decision to return may have been due to Conrad's death in May rather than Berthold's powers of persuasion. The true significance of his embassy, both for the empire of Nicaea and the history of cultural interactions between the Latin West and the Byzantine East, lay in the discussions that took place at the Anatolian court.

An intellectually curious man and a patron of scholars, Berthold was a suitable match for the highly educated prince in Asia Minor. He is known to have held learned conversations with the Italian Jew Moses ben Solomon of Salerno, a commentator on Maimonides' *Guide to the Perplexed*, and came to Byzantine Anatolia in 1253 in the company of philosophers and physicians. He clearly anticipated that learned conversations would follow the official business of the diplomatic negotiations.[73] Berthold would acquire, soon after his death, the reputation of being a literary figure. Latin poetry under his name survives, and so do German Minnesang poems composed by a certain marquis of Hohenburg, with whom Berthold has been identified.[74] The portrait of the marquis of

Hohenburg graces the Codex Manesse, a splendidly illustrated collection of the works of minnesingers produced not long after 1300 (Fig. 19). Theodore describes his interactions with Berthold and his entourage in two letters, one addressed to Blemmydes and the other to the metropolitan bishop of Sardis, Andronikos, who was in Italy at the time on an embassy to the papacy. In the letter to Andronikos, Theodore painted a glowing portrait of Berthold as a charming and erudite interlocutor:

> A man has come to us who confirms the praises on his behalf. He is alert and shrewd, with a fine and well-tuned tongue, speaking to the point and quick in his responses, educated in Italian culture, but also in contact with the Hellenic, straightforward but not simple-minded, intelligent and with a good memory, kind and agreeable, sometimes saying quite a lot and sometimes speaking beyond what he means to say, skillful at examination and not fond of disputations (if he ever is, he does so in a gentle and piecemeal fashion), witty and fond of witticisms, very knowledgeable and gracious, fond of learning and scholars – I should say that he himself is not unversed in letters – with scholars and doctors in his company who pride themselves in philosophy. After we received him and were overwhelmed with joy on account of his virtue, we spoke and continue to be speaking with him.[75]

The language barrier evidently did not inhibit the depth and lively spirit of the discussions. There were a number of individuals around Theodore who were able to speak and understand both Greek and Latin. People born after 1204 in Latin-held cities, such as George Akropolites, had the opportunity to acquire a degree of knowledge of the Latin language at an early age. Franciscans resident in the East included children of mixed marriages, such as John Vatatzes' envoy to the papacy, Salimbene, who was able to communicate in both languages. The office of interpreters at the Nicaean court was staffed by experts in Latin. A certain Theophylaktos holding the court title of grand interpreter (*megas diermeneutes*) accompanied the two embassies to the papacy between 1250 and 1254. During his embassy to the papacy, the metropolitan bishop of Sardis, Andronikos, was able himself to translate from Latin.[76]

The letter to Andronikos describes a debate at the court modeled on the competitive theological disputations between Latins and Greeks (such as that in Nymphaion in 1250) and fully in the spirit of the pedagogical *disputationes* practiced at contemporary universities in western Europe. The disputation was entirely secular in content, however, and focused on the question of the genuineness of received philosophical knowledge. The touchstone of authenticity was the work of ancient philosophers, none of

whom are mentioned by name, yet it is implied that these revered authorities were Greek philosophers and that they were well known both to
Theodore and the learned members of his entourage:

> Because the philosophers who accompany him [Berthold] professed to
> know geometry and astronomy, arithmetic and music, the Organon and
> natural science, the theology of the Hellenes that ranks above them
> [metaphysics], and in turn ethics and politics, rhetoric and so many
> learned subjects and subjects pertaining to learning, which are useless
> for us to list by name, we who – as you know – have the knowledge of
> everything (I openly say this), we entered the stadium, and contests and
> prizes were at hand.[77]

The Latin scholars are said to have "scared many people with their
learning," yet were humiliated and shown to lack sufficient knowledge of
the mentioned subjects. In the same way in which the Rhine River tested
newborns by drowning the bastard offspring and preserving the lives of
legitimate children (a Byzantine proverb), so did the competitive discussion reveal the falseness of Latin learning.[78] Theodore exclaimed that "the
spectacle for the onlookers was great and the glory for the Hellenes was
immense."[79] His letter to Blemmydes describes a similar disputation on
philosophical questions. A mathematical theorem written on a single loose
sheet was brought by an Italian to the palace for examination. The solution
was known to Theodore and his entourage, but the Western scholars were
at an impasse. The coemperor shared with his teacher the joy felt by his
courtiers on account of the victory of the "Hellenes over the Italians."[80]

The philosophical discussions at the Anatolian Byzantine court in the
autumn of 1253 were just one brief historical episode within a long series of
encounters between Greek and Latin scholars in the Middle Ages, yet they
were hardly insignificant. The interactions between important patrons of
learning on this occasion had an impact on the Latin translation of Greek
philosophy. According to Theodore's letter to Andronikos, Berthold
"asked to receive and receives" gifts that he valued "more highly than
precious stones and pearls."[81] The gifts could have been nothing other
than Greek texts that he and the scholars around him obtained in Anatolia.
The thirteenth century saw an increased Western interest in the translation
of ancient philosophy from the Greek original, an interest that was already
on the rise in the twelfth century, both in Constantinople and in Norman
southern Italy and Sicily.[82] The anonymous philosophers and physicians
who accompanied Berthold helped to spread the reputation of the empire
of Nicaea as a center of learning and stimulated visits by other Latin

scholars eager to gain access to – and acquire – precious manuscripts, and translate philosophical texts from their authentic Greek version. Tangible results followed soon – ironically, after Berthold's tragic end. In August 1254 Berthold was forced to resign as regent of the kingdom of Sicily on behalf of Manfred, a position that he had assumed on Conrad's death in May. He went over to Innocent IV and took part in a military operation against Manfred. In the summer of 1255, the next pope, Alexander IV, gave him command over the papal army in Apulia, but Berthold wavered, surrendered to the victorious Manfred, and was sentenced to death in Bari in February 1256.

At the court of Manfred, who was crowned king of Sicily in August 1258, a number of new translations were produced from Greek. Bartholomew of Messina, who worked under Manfred's patronage, translated Pseudo-Aristotelian texts that were viewed as genuine parts of the Aristotelian corpus: *De Mundo*, *Problemata*, *Physiognomonica*, *De mirabilibus auscultationibus*, *De principiis*, *De signis*, *Magna Moralia*, and *De coloribus*.[83] In a letter addressed to scholars at the University of Paris Manfred presented recent translations from Greek and Arabic made by several translators.[84] Where did the manuscripts with the original Greek texts come from? Libraries with such texts were still available in Latin Constantinople.[85] Yet the empire of Nicaea acquired a strong pulling force for Western scholars, thanks to the intellectual exchanges during Berthold's embassy and the sustained patronage of education and book collection by John Vatatzes and Theodore Laskaris. The great Aristotelian translator and Flemish Dominican William of Moerbeke (d. c. 1286) visited Nicaea in April 1260, less than two years after Theodore's death, and completed in Nicaea the translation of Alexander of Aphrodisias' commentary on Aristotle's *Meteorology*.[86] It was in the city of Nicaea, as has been argued, that he gained access to a famous ninth-century Byzantine manuscript (Cod. Vindobonensis phil. gr. 100), from which he made the initial redaction of his translation of Aristotle's *Metaphysics* and in which he himself copied a list of the works of Hippocrates.[87] The presence of Moerbeke in Nicaea fits closely with Theodore's interest in Aristotle and the availability of Aristotle manuscripts in the empire in exile.[88] Moerbeke was active in continental Greece, as well. A few months after his visit to Nicaea, in December 1260, he was in Thebes, where a Dominican friary had been established since at least 1253, and translated Aristotle's *On the Parts of Animals* there. His first attempt at rendering Aristotle's *Politics*, a text hitherto unknown in the West, into Latin is also thought to date to his residence in the Greek East.[89]

The encounter between Theodore Laskaris and Berthold of Hohenburg in the autumn of 1253 had an impact on the Byzantine interlocutor, as well. It buttressed Theodore's conviction that ancient learning was a precious and sought-after cultural capital, a conviction that underpinned his sense of Hellenism. The feeling of pride was mixed with competiveness. Hellenic wisdom was his, not their, heritage and he saw himself as the gatekeeper and an heir of this tradition. The disputations during Berthold's embassy motivated him to launch the project of preparing manuscript editions of his own works, works he saw as belonging to the same age-old literary and philosophical tradition of Hellenism. The *Sacred Orations* (Fig. 18) and the Laurentian epistolary collection edited by George Akropolites on his return from the Balkans bear the headings "before the embassy of Marquis Berthold of Hohenburg to the great emperor John Doukas." The two collections were produced in the early months of 1254 and witness the pivotal role of the encounter with the Western diplomat and his retinue of scholars.[90]

The verses written by Akropolites as an introduction to the Laurentian collection warmly recommend to the reader the current "book" containing "letters of the emperor Theodore Laskaris, son of the renowned ruler John."[91] The preface mentions the existence of other editions of Theodore's works: "He publishes other long discourses, some on the examination of things whose place lies in nature, others on the elaboration of superior premises, and yet others which in turn boast to have encomium as their subject matter."[92] Akropolites seems to envisage the philosophical treatise *Natural Communion* and the *Sacred Orations*. The nine *Sacred Orations* open with a work on the Holy Trinity addressed to the chamberlain Constantine and the secretary John Phaix, and are followed by a speech of thanksgiving to Christ, hagiographical encomia on St. Euthymios and SS. Cosmas and Damian, *On Virtue, Encomium in Wisdom, Oration on Fasting*, the theophilosophical *Moral Pieces*, and the polemical *Response to Some People Who Trouble Him Malevolently*. The Laurentian epistolary collection starts with the letters to his teachers Blemmydes and Akropolites. The first letter to each of the two teachers comments on the beginning of his studies, and the penultimate letter to Blemmydes is a description of the discussion at the court with Berthold of Hohenburg, where Theodore poses as a philosopher and an established patron of learning. There are letters to other recipients, including satires of the metropolitans of Ephesos and the governor of Thessalonica, Theodore Philes. What is missing from the epistolary publication are letters to his minion George Mouzalon. The two collections prepared in the early 1254 –

the epistolary one and the *Sacred Orations* – presented the author as a devout and highly educated man with strong attachments to former teachers and current secretaries, as well as the patriarch. Theodore avoided advertising his closeness to the man whom he was grooming to become his chief minister. This precaution proved unnecessary, because his accession to the throne would take place in less than a year.

8 | Sole Emperor of the Romans

After his long absence in the Balkans, John Vatatzes spent the winter of 1254 in Nymphaion, close to his son. The month of February drew to a close and he took up residence in Nicaea in order to check the city's preparedness for siege warfare and improve its security.[1] The rumor of a massive Mongol invasion gave cause for concern. In 1254 the Great Khan Möngke dispatched one of his brothers, Hülegü, to lead a campaign of subjugation of Persia and the Nicaean state. Hülegü did not reach the Near East until 1256, but the timing and direction of this new wave of Mongol attacks were unknown – and profoundly unsettling for those living in western Asia Minor.[2] The senior emperor suddenly fell gravely ill in Nicaea, lying motionless and out of breath for two days. He never recovered fully, but began to suffer seizures, progressively lost his strength, and had to be carried on a litter. The illness was believed, at least by later historians, to be a severe form of epilepsy and his physicians applied bleeding. This diagnosis is highly unlikely, just as in the case of his son, because there are no indications that he suffered from epilepsy before he was stricken with illness. Epileptic symptoms can indicate other diseases and Byzantine doctors too readily assigned the diagnosis.[3] In early April Vatatzes returned to Nymphaion to celebrate Palm Sunday (April 5) and Easter (April 12). From there he moved to the Periklystra palace near Smyrna and came occasionally to pray to the miraculous icon of Christ kept in the Kamelaukas monastery in Smyrna dedicated to Christ the Savior.[4]

Theodore has not recorded his impressions of his father's grave illness. His whole upbringing from an early age had prepared him for the succession, but he could not foresee when the moment of transition would arrive and must have been deeply concerned by the uncertainty of his father's condition. He continued to regard him as the role model for his rule. Three years later he would write that Vatatzes' "truthful knowledge, patriotic reasoning and judgment regarding the subjects" set the example he followed.[5] In the spring and summer months of 1254, Theodore became, in effect, the reigning emperor, while making further progress with the project of preparing editions of his writings that had started earlier in the year with the epistolary collection and the *Sacred Orations*. In the course of 1254 he arranged for publication one more collection, consisting of ten secular works, in which he identified himself as "the son of the most exalted emperor of the Romans John Doukas."[6] The encomia on Vatatzes and Akropolites, as well as his encomium on the city of Nicaea, served to display him as an accomplished public orator. The autobiographical *Satire of the Tutor* and his long letter to Akropolites opening the collection bore witness to his thirst for knowledge. The treatise on politics and friendship addressed to Mouzalon pointed to the agenda for his reign.

In the autumn Vatatzes moved to Nymphaion in poorest health and breathed his last on Tuesday, November 3, 1254, in the imperial tent pitched in the gardens of the palace, leaving his thirty-two-year-old son as the sovereign.[7] Theodore was immediately acclaimed emperor seated on a shield, but could not be crowned right away because Patriarch Manuel II had also passed away in October and had not yet been replaced.[8] Vatatzes was buried in the imperial Sosandra monastery he had founded. Akropolites delivered the funerary oration, in which he captured the mood of the moment. Present in the audience were high officials, addressed collectively as the senate (*gerousia*), and Theodore Laskaris himself. The orator combined old clichés with comments on the political situation. The empire was the "ship of the world" (a phrase found in the popular sixth-century mirror of princes of Agapetos the Deacon), which the recently deceased captain had transformed from a small boat into a mighty vessel propelled by tens of thousands of oarsmen.[9] Asia Minor had been liberated from the Latins and the Turks had ceased their raids. The Bulgarians were no longer strong enough to determine state boundaries and the Serbs were clients obliged to provide soldiers during the emperor's campaigns. Only a small part of the former western provinces of the empire, the Peloponnese and Euboea, remained under the Latins.[10] The end of the speech introduces Theodore as the spitting image of his father and compares him rhetorically to Helen of Troy's drug of oblivion (*Odyssey*, IV, 220) – the young emperor cured the audience of its grief and diverted its attention away from public mourning. Akropolites aired hopes that the young emperor would lead the people of New Israel like a "pillar of fire" (Exodus 13:21) to recapture Constantinople.[11] The recovery of the old imperial capital was still considered by many to be the political mission of the Nicaean state, half a century after the Fourth Crusade. What perhaps mattered most for Theodore was that the eulogist proclaimed him both a philosopher enamored of books and a capable warrior – a fulfillment of the saying of an "ancient sage" (Plato) that the cities prosper when kings become philosophers.[12]

Akropolites made hints about political tensions. He marveled at Vatatzes' merciful handling of murderers and conspirators, whether proven or suspected.[13] The orator had in mind the plots of the Laskaris and Nestongos brothers at the beginning of his reign, as well as the recent acquittal of Michael Palaiologos and the lenient treatment of Theodore Philes, who remained the governor of Thessalonica. Akropolites expected justice to continue to reign in the peasant countryside. Nobody, he declared, will seize his neighbors' properties and "everyone will sit under their own fig tree" (Micah 4:4). For the new emperor already knew the best kind of imperial decrees, which order tax collectors to treat poor peasants fairly and prevent harmful individuals from wielding power in the countryside.[14] The comment is an allusion to Theodore's powers over the fiscal administration as a coemperor. In the account of Theodore's accession in his *History*, however, Akropolites mentions the rather different expectations that the landed aristocracy had of him at the beginning of his reign. Landowners whose properties had been confiscated pinned their hopes on the new emperor, charmed by "his young age, his congenial manner toward all, his gentle behavior with his companions and his cheerful discourse." It was not before long, however, that they changed their minds and began to wish for his death.[15]

Right after his accession Theodore visited the frontier town of Philadelphia in order to exchange information with the sultan 'Izz al-Dīn Kaykāwūs II and reaffirm the defensive pact against the Mongols.[16] 'Izz al-Dīn had just recently established himself as the sole ruler of the sultanate of Rum. In the course of 1254, the three brothers who shared sultanic authority among themselves – 'Izz al-Dīn Kaykāwūs II, Rukn al-Dīn Kılıç Arslān IV, and 'Alā' al-Dīn Kayqubād II – met in Kayseri to discuss Khan Batu's summons to 'Izz al-Dīn to present himself at his camp on the Volga. The youngest brother, 'Alā' al-Dīn, was sent instead of the eldest and passed away during the journey. The two remaining siblings and their supporters fought a battle at Ahmed Hisar, which led to the defeat and imprisonment of Rukn al-Dīn, who was favored by the Mongols. The internal strife gave to the emperor of Trebizond, Manuel I Grand Komnenos, the opportunity to annex Sinope on the Black Sea on June 24, 1254.[17] Theodore kept an eye on the fluid political situation in the sultanate, which served as a buffer against the Mongols but could also provoke dangerous Mongol interference in Anatolia.

After Philadelphia, the emperor came to Nicaea in order to address pressing matters. A letter to George Mouzalon, who stayed behind in the Thrakesion theme, conveys a sense of being overwhelmed. He voiced regret that he had no time for intellectual work. Instead of studying mathematics, he read accounting books filled with calculations about payments in gold coins. He attended to the words, manners, and opinions of the crowd. The air around him echoed with the hubbub of irrational individuals.[18] Two pressing concerns particularly occupied him. The first was the choice of a new patriarch. The electoral procedure mandated that the emperor pick the patriarch from three nominations proposed by the permanent synod of metropolitan bishops.[19] Accounts of the patriarchal election differ greatly because of the controversy that broke out a decade later around the figure of the successful candidate, the so-called "Arsenite Schism" (1265–1310).[20] Theodore's favorite was his teacher Nikephoros Blemmydes. In his auto-biography Blemmydes writes that the emperor insisted on his appointment and the synod backed him unanimously. Contrary to the canons, he was simultaneously the first, second, and third candidate. After he sought and failed to obtain a divine sign of approval for his elevation, however, Blemmydes declined the offer and rebuked Theodore for his arrogance in a personal meeting with him in the palace in Nicaea.[21] He accepted instead the lower position of supervisor of monasteries and continued to serve as the emperor's close advisor.[22] In another account, Theodore is said to have stopped cajoling his teacher after his choice fell on a meeker and submis-sive man, the monk Arsenios.[23] Arsenios was born in Constantinople into a prominent and well-connected family. His father, a certain Autoreianos, had been a high judge (*krites tou velou*) before 1204 and ended his days as a monk in the Peribleptos monastery in the Latin-held city. His mother was from the Kamateros family. Their son Arsenios relocated to Byzantine Anatolia and the patriarch, Germanos II, arranged for his secondary education. Drawn to eremitic life, Arsenios was tonsured and resided in monasteries on islands in the Sea of Marmara and Lake Apollonias, while keeping his connections with the circles of power. Thus, he was a candidate for the patriarchate of Jerusalem and was chosen to be an envoy to the papacy between 1250 and 1254.[24] His selection as a candidate for the patriarchate of Constantinople in exile was therefore hardly accidental. On his ordination in Nicaea, Arsenios performed the emperor's ecclesi-astical coronation and anointing.[25] He faithfully supported the domestic and foreign policies of his patron.

Another, very different, version of the events – originating from among Arsenios' zealous partisans – insists on the canonicity and providential character of the election. Several candidates are mentioned: Blemmydes; the metropolitan of Ephesos, Nikephoros; the abbot of the Sosandra monastery, Ioannikios Kydones; and the monk Arsenios. Theodore sought to obtain divine approval for his choice and to forge consensus by resorting to bibliomancy (*sortes biblicae*). An all-night vigil was held and the Gospel book was opened at sunrise at a random page for each candidate. The scriptural passage was read aloud and its relevance to the selection of the leader of the church was examined. Arsenios won the contest with the highly favorable phrase "He and His disciples" (John 18:1).[26] He was then ordained patriarch within a short space of time (the reports vary between a single day and a week). Did Theodore indeed resort to bibliomancy in order to break the electoral gridlock? The texts featuring this version of events promote the holiness of Arsenios and defend him against the accusation that he was a crony of Theodore Laskaris. The account may therefore have served to camouflage the emperor's willful choice of the new patriarch, although it is notable that Blemmydes refers in his autobiography to the search of a divine sign that he failed to obtain. It is impossible, therefore, to determine whether the story was fully or partly an invention. If it was indeed an invention, its creator and his audience would have found it entirely plausible because of Theodore's fascination with prognostication and the occult.

The second pressing concern that occupied Theodore in Nicaea in December 1254 and January 1255 was the drastically deteriorating situation in the Balkans. The young Bulgarian tsar Michael Asen (Fig. 20) – the son of Ivan Asen and Theodore of Epiros' daughter Irene – seized the opportunity of the power transition to deal the same crushing blow to Nicaea that he himself had suffered during his accession in 1246. Intent on restoring the territorial status quo under Ivan Asen, he raided Thrace and the Rhodope Mountains in November and December, and gained control of Stenimachos, Peristitza (Perushtitsa), Krytzimos (Krichim), Tzepaina (Tsepena), Perperikon, Kryvous, and other fortresses. Authority changed in Macedonia, too. The towns of Veles and Skopje on the Vardar (Axios) River reverted to Bulgarian control.[27] Thus, at the very beginning of his reign, Theodore Laskaris faced a military crisis of massive proportions that required his immediate attention. We see him summoning George Mouzalon to Nicaea in two letters, one certainly dating to December 1255, in order to discuss the emergency. The first letter opens with a nebulous reference to his political enemies, mentioning "illicit love affairs and very unjust plots and oppositions."[28] He designated Mouzalon as *megas domestikos* – the vacant position of commander-in-chief of the mobile army that had been held for more than twenty years by Andronikos Palaiologos and then by his son-in-law Nikephoros Tarchaneiotes as an interim incumbent. George's brother Andronikos Mouzalon came to occupy the military post of *protovestiarites*, an office filled for more than twenty years by George Zagarommates, who was promoted to the post of chief chamberlain (*parakoimomenos*).[29] A general much trusted by Theodore was Constantine Margarites, a former soldier from the Neokastra theme. Concentrating military power into the hands of the Mouzalons and Margarites was a snub at aristocrats with military tradition running in their families. Still, Theodore made a cautious attempt at reconciliation with a segment of the aristocracy that had fared poorly during his father's reign. He came to rely on his formerly exiled great uncles Michael Laskaris and Manuel Laskaris, and appointed as generals two individuals from the rebellious Nestongos family, the butler (*pinkernes*) George Nestongos and the attendant at the imperial table (*epi tes trapezes*) Isaac Nestongos.[30] All these acts of favoritism, and especially the promotion of the Mouzalon brothers, kindled tensions. Constantine Strategopoulos, the son of the elderly general Alexios Strategopoulos, is said to have publicly displayed his displeasure with the emperor at the beginning of his reign. Theodore kept complaining of disobedient army officers in letters written in 1255.

In the winter of 1254–55 the newly crowned emperor summoned all officials and generals to a council in Nicaea to discuss the timing of the counterattack. There was a clash of opinions. The majority of his advisors, with George Mouzalon being most outspoken in his insistence, favored an immediate military expedition modeled on Vatatzes' successful winter campaigns. Theodore's great uncles Manuel and Michael Laskaris considered this proposal reckless because of the weather and the absence of a battle-worthy army.[31] The hawkish approach carried the day. The emperor hurriedly assembled an army and left George Mouzalon as his deputy in Asia Minor with the responsibility of keeping him informed of the military situation along the eastern frontier, the very function that Theodore had himself performed at times when his father campaigned in Europe. His confidence that an attack by Hülegü was not imminent seems to have originated from the Mongol ambassadors who were detained in late 1254 as they passed through the empire of Nicaea. The leader of this embassy, dispatched by Khan Möngke to the king of France, Louis IX, was a certain Theodoulos, a Latin cleric from Acre who had fraudulently presented himself in Karakorum as a confidant of the papacy. In Nicaea, Theodoulos was detained as an imposter because he lacked an accreditation letter from the pope, and his fellow ambassador, a Mongol, passed away. The remaining Mongol envoys returned to Karakorum, probably carrying a communication from Theodore Laskaris, who had just acceded to the throne, and in late February or March 1255 met William of Rubruck in Erzurum along the way.[32]

On February 1, 1255, Theodore attended the feast day of St. Tryphon in Nicaea, praying for victory in the risky military enterprise, and then departed for the Hellespont. In his earliest campaign letter to Mouzalon, he mentioned the miracle of the blossoming winter lilies of Lake Askania and lauded the great martyr Tryphon for his "care, help, and encouragement."[33] The saint is reported to have appeared in a dream vision to him and to have approved of the campaign. Before departing, Theodore ordered the reconstruction of the flooded church of Tryphon in Nicaea and endowed a school of grammar and poetry attached to the ecclesiastical building with student stipends and salaries for the two teachers, Michael Senachereim and Andronikos Phrangopoulos.[34] His strong devotion to Tryphon was also displayed in other ways. He wrote before November 1254 an encomiastic *vita* of the saint, in which he described the miracle with the winter lilies, and composed a supplicatory text after his accession, in which he beseeched the patron saint of the city of Nicaea to give him the "prize of victory."[35] The image of Tryphon was placed on coins along with more traditional holy figures, such as the Virgin and St. Theodore, his namesake (Fig. 21b).

Lightning Victories

The emperor set up the army camp in Adrianople in Thrace. The generals Alexios Strategopoulos and Constantine Tornikes, the *megas primmikerios* and son of the late *mesazon* Demetrios Komnenos Torinikes, took up position in Serres in Macedonia. Reinforcements from Anatolia trickled in as the year progressed. Theodore had barely reached Adrianople when he received information from scouts about the proximity of the Bulgarian tsar. He decided to engage him on the very next day – a tactic of surprise assault that he would follow throughout the campaign. His vanguard defeated the startled enemy outposts and caused panic among the Bulgarians, who hurriedly abandoned their camp. Their retreat was so hasty that some of them rode off on unsaddled horses and the tsar badly scratched his face against some tree branches. Theodore pursued the enemy for more than 60 miles (100 kilometers) northward and plundered the town of Veroe (Stara Zagora), securing the necessary provisions for the army. The Bulgarians retreated beyond the Haimos (Balkan) Mountains, on whose northern slopes lay the royal residence Turnovo. The treacherous mountain terrain forced Theodore to turn back, and he encamped once again in Adrianople.

The campaign resumed before the end of the winter. Pushing forward along the Maritsa valley, after quick sieges he captured Peristitza, Stenimachos, and Krytzimos in the northern Rhodope Mountains. The only fortress to resist him was the stronghold of Tzepaina (Tsepena; Fig. 22).[36] The region of Achridos in the eastern Rhodopes also surrendered. On his return to Adrianople, the emperor ordered Alexios Strategopoulos and Constantine Tornikes to launch a spring offensive on Tzepaina from the south. The two generals proceeded cautiously from Serres through difficult passes in the Rhodopes. Along the way they panicked at the sound of the horns of shepherds and swineherds, which they mistook to be signals of a mountain ambush. Their disorderly retreat resulted in the abandonment of precious baggage and equipment.[37] The vexed emperor ordered Strategopoulos and Tornikes to return, but they defiantly disobeyed.

A series of fascinating letters addressed to George Mouzalon in early and mid 1255 open a window into the anxious state of Theodore's mind during the taxing campaign.[38] Theodore Laskaris has been considered a "tenacious military strategist in the Balkans" and a good student of tenth-century Byzantine military tactics, for he made effective use of surprise attacks, battle reconnaissance, and siegecraft during the war with the Bulgarians.[39] The winter mobilization of the army followed a successful tactical model set by Vatatzes, even though Theodore was well aware that this season was best suited for army training, improvement of fortifications, and logistical preparations.[40] The letters place us in the midst of the unfolding campaign and leave a slightly different impression, while in no way putting his highly competent military leadership in question. Writing to his best friend in Anatolia, whom he had just promoted to a supreme military position, Theodore shared a sense of confusion and uncertainty, antipathy to generals, and a deep desire to return to Anatolia. He notified him by letter that his victory had driven away the "unknown" enemies toward the mountains.[41] The reliability of his army was a source of worry. In his earliest campaign letter he mentioned that he had reached the flatlands of Thrace (the "Western fields") and was pursuing the Bulgarians.[42] He acknowledged that he had a duty to secure and protect the common people, his subjects, yet he voiced disappointment at his boorish and deceitful entourage. No one around him had enough education to be able to commemorate the events of the war. "Who will remember the toils and keep vigil with me in my sleeplessness? Who will put together in writing the difficulties which we suffered for the sake of reason? . . . Will a philosopher not bemoan this situation? Would not a close friend be struck with amazement?"[43] His characteristic obsession with legacy and remembrance shines through these words, as does a sense of distance from the illiterate masses. He saw himself as a new Noah, who sails in an ark tossed by "waves of wicked water (Kings IV 2:19) of my men, the Scythians, the Tauroscythians, the Mysians, the Phrygians, and the Persians."[44] Remarkably, the opponents he had in mind were almost entirely domestic. "My men" were his generals and officers. His ethnically diverse army was evidently hard to manage. According to Theodore's ethnographic vocabulary, the Scythians are Cumans who played an important role in his army during the campaign. The Tauroscythians, a name traditionally applied to the Rus (Tauric Chersonnesos was the Crimea), may also refer to the Cumans who migrated to the Balkans from the steppes of southern Russia and the Crimea.[45] The Mysians and the Phrygians appear to be soldiers from Anatolia.[46] The Persians, a word Theodore uses to designate the Turks, seem to have been the mercenaries in Nicaean service.

The main enemy, the Bulgarians, are described in terms of stereotypes mixed with firsthand impressions. As barbarians, they lacked reason and inhabited "the impassable Bulgarian mountains of folly" (the Rhodope Mountains).[47] Albania, too, was a barbarian land, even though a Nicaean governor, Constantine Chabaron, was in charge of the area.[48] Another negative image of the Bulgarians was their fondness for wine and drinking, a view that may have resulted from actual observations, given that his wife (and presumably her entourage) came from the Bulgarian royal house.[49] Theodore presented the Bulgarians as rough mountain people. His earliest campaign letter to Mouzalon speaks of the Bulgarian who "twists his body under the hollow precipices full of ravines of his places, concealing his head or his entire self in the orifices of rocks and dug-outs."[50] Elsewhere he states that the Bulgarians made "their residence in hollow places full of ravines" and that he pushed the enemy into the "mountain of oath-keeping and oath-observance."[51] He even attributed the arrogance of the Bulgarians "to their residence in the mountains."[52] The Haimos and Rhodope Mountains symbolized the frontier between the known, civilized world and the exotic wild land of the barbarians who practiced magic against him. The Bulgarians were said to cast spells on his army and his head tutor allegedly learned magic somewhere in the Haimos Mountains.[53]

A prolonged stay at the camp in Adrianople until the summer made Theodore increasingly exasperated. A letter to Mouzalon written at the camp speaks of continuing frictions in the army caused by "mean old men", one of whom was certainly Alexios Strategopoulos, on whose age he commented in another campaign letter. The Komnenian descent of

Strategopoulos advertised on his seal corresponds to the profile of other
dangerous adversaries of the emperor, such as Michael Palaiologos and
Theodore Philes (Fig. 14). In a letter to Akropolites, who – like Mouzalon –
stayed behind in Asia Minor, Theodore vented frustration with the broken
chain of command. If the top person in the hierarchy makes a correct
judgment, he reasoned, but the second in rank does not follow his order,
will not the error have a crippling effect on the entire army? The cowardice
and cunning of his generals were disappointing. "A hare seeing them," he
wryly remarks, "would laugh and a fox would be known as the most honest
animal . . . We speak, but who is there to listen? We reprimand, but no one
will understand. We act generously, and we throw the money at flocks of
sheep." The letter shows that Theodore was contemplating punishment:
honors needed to be taken away and tribunals set up.[54] He remained
nonetheless optimistic about the outcome of the war and voiced a belliger-
ent belief that the "guarding Hellenic spears" would prevail over the
Bulgarians and "remove their destructive and poisonous spirits from their
bodies."[55] He missed Anatolia and experienced nostalgic flashbacks,
reminding Mouzalon of the time the two spent together in Atramyttion,
the sound of the Aegean Sea, the mountainous landscape, the hot summer
weather not unlike that in Adrianople, the people they knew, and the
laughter they shared. In contrast to Anatolia, the Balkans appeared foreign
and offered no familiar excitements, such as hunting crane or gathering
fruit. He complained that the excruciating summer heat after the harsh
winter frost exceeded that of the torrid climate zone. "The broad and
mighty Hebros" (the Maritsa River) was so warm that it could not quench
the thirst of his soldiers.[56]

The situation in the summer worsened when Dragotas, a Bulgarian
grandee in Nicaean service, switched his allegiance. A native of Melnik
and former Bulgarian military commander stationed in Serres, he had
defected in 1246 when he came to support the authority of the Nicaean
emperor. Now he sided again with the tsar in Turnovo, gathered trusted
warriors, and laid siege to the upper fortress of Melnik – whose garrison,
commanded by Theodore Nestongos and John Angelos, refused to surrender. Theodore Laskaris, who was more than 125 miles (200 kilometers)
away in Adrianople, correctly judged that the situation demanded his
personal attention and led the rescue expedition himself.[57] He set off along
the main road to Macedonia, the ancient *via Egnatia*. In the longest
campaign epistle, written in Philippi during the summer march, he shared
with Mouzalon his seething anger at Alexios Strategopoulos and Constantine Tornikes. Their failure to lead an assault on Tzepaina from the south

was the reason for the current crisis. The "lawless Strategopouloi" and "ill-famed Tornikai," Theodore wrote indignantly, had ruined his victory. "The insubordination of the lawless people who left the army alone made the Bulgarian dogs devastate our lands, and the beginning of the current troubles thus fell upon us."[58] He complained of becoming a laughingstock after his father's death and carped at officials who challenged his authority on account of the bad turn of events. "Our people are fighting ours," he wrote and added that "everyone is defiantly against us, because the situation is against us."[59] He was particularly incensed with the "lawless *praitor*" Theodore Philes and the two disobedient generals. "Who is a just man in the West as much as Tornikes is unjust? Who is more courageous in wartime than this coward?" In the letter to Mouzalon he speaks of a "wicked old man" who fled toward Thessalonica because he was ill. The unnamed individual must be Alexios Strategopoulos, who was older than his fellow general Constantine Tornikes.[60] For a second time during the campaign, Theodore made manifest his perspective colored by intergenerational conflicts, which is traceable also in earlier works. Old age was almost a diagnosis and affected the brain like an illness, he wrote to Akropolites in a letter dating to his sole rule.[61]

Theodore's fascination with the ancient and apostolic history of Philippi contrasts to the gloomy presentation of the Adrianople camp. Was not Paul's imprisonment and beating in Philippi similar to his current troubles, he wondered? "We are grieved in our mind and we laugh with our lips, 'buying our time' (Ephes. 5:16, Coloss. 4:5) like Paul, because he suffered whipping in these districts."[62] Theodore saw himself as entering a land of ancient fame: "We see the fatherland of Philip and Alexander on one side, the mountain of Orpheus on the other (Mt. Pangaion), and the impassable Bulgarian mountains of unreason (the Rhodopes) before us (Fig. 23)." "The land once upon a time belonging to Alexander," he added, was "ravaged and ridiculed by a few weak Bulgarians, and insult has been added to injury."[63] The association of Philippi with memories of the ancient king and conqueror was probably inspired by standing antique monuments near the medieval fortress. Late medieval and Renaissance travelers report seeing the "manger" or "marble stable" of Alexander's horse Bucephalus, which is in reality a still-surviving Roman marble structure of enormous size with a Latin inscription. Cyriac of Ancona notes in the fifteenth century that local people linked the inscription with Alexander.[64]

Theodore reached Serres, where he spent just one day before hurrying off toward Melnik. The Roupel Pass along the Strymon River was so narrow that a single wagon could barely make its way along it. The situation was particularly difficult because the Bulgarians had constructed barriers that made passage impossible. Informed by scouts about the topography, Theodore made an astute tactical decision. Select troops climbed the hills overlooking the enemy and, during a moonless night, a formation consisting of archers and infantry advanced quietly along the pass. Volleys of arrows suddenly shot from two different directions forced the startled Bulgarian soldiers to abandon their position and retreat in panic in the darkness. Many of them perished in a stampede and the Bulgarian commander Dragotas died from his injuries after falling off his horse. Theodore's army reached Melnik on the following day and broke the siege. The undaunted Nicaean loyalists in Melnik, who had not surrendered to the Bulgarians in spite of the lack of provisions, applauded the emperor as a "swift eagle" and banished the enemy supporters from the town.[65] The victorious march from Adrianople to Serres had taken the emperor twelve days, the usual period for a land journey from Constantinople to Thessalonica along the *via Egnatia*.[66] The acclamation "swift eagle" therefore glorified Theodore's efficiency as commander-in-chief of the army rather than his extraordinary speed. On his return to Serres, Theodore visited the metropolitan church dedicated to his namesakes, the military saints Theodore Stratelates and Theodore Tyron. A story told in the town in the fourteenth century had the emperor praying in this church before the Battle of Roupel. The saints are said to have offered their support by joining his army in the guise of young and handsome warriors. After the victory, the emperor reportedly commissioned the composition of a hymn and made a donation of gold and silver for the production of a luxurious revetment for the stone-carved icon of the two Theodores that was kept in the church.[67]

Theodore continued the momentum of his victory and recovered other Bulgarian-controlled fortresses in Macedonia. His brief spell in Thessalonica may have been the occasion on which he discharged his old enemy, the *praitor* Theodore Philes. The disobedient generals Constantine Tornikes and Alexios Strategopoulos were also dismissed from army command. Tornikes was divested of the court office of *megas primmikerios*, for several months later the holder of this title was a certain John Angelos.[68] The mint of Thessalonica was closed down; Nicaean coins were struck from now on solely in Asia Minor. The creation of a new imperial treasury on the emperor's orders in Astritzion in the Troad, which lay close to the crossing point at the Hellespont, meant the concentration of monetary resources exclusively in Anatolia rather than in the rebellious

Balkans.[69] After leaving Thessalonica, Theodore encamped in Vodena, once a stronghold of Theodore of Epiros and the place his father had wintered two years earlier. The outbreak of a dysenteric disease delayed the soldiers in Vodena. Hence the army marched north toward Prilep and besieged Veles. There the garrison of 500 Bulgarian soldiers agreed to surrender the fortress in exchange for a sworn guarantee that they could leave unharmed. The troops headed by Theodore proceeded north along the Vardar River and reached the arid plain of Neustapolis (Ovche Polje), but the thirst and fatigue of the horses prevented them from continuing toward Skopje, and they returned to Serres via Stroumitza and the Roupel Pass. While he was residing in the area, Theodore confirmed his father's fiscal privileges for Kroia in Albania, and probably other cities and fort-resses in the area. His interest in the western borderlands is seen in the mention of the frontier regions of Skopje and Vranje, as well as Albania, in the newsletter of 1256.[70] He was playing a balancing game between enticing local elites and avoiding giving them excessive power. Strict measures were taken against the archbishop of Ohrid, Constantine Kabasilas, whose arrest and transferal to Anatolia he ordered in 1255 or 1256. A former metropolitan bishop of Dyrrachion, Kabasilas had strong links with the state of Epiros and his brothers were prominent supporters of Michael II Komnenos Doukas (Michael of Epiros).[71]

An alarming message from George Mouzalon about a Mongol invasion reached Theodore in Serres, whereupon he immediately left for the Hellespont with the army. Once he learned that the report was false, he redirected the soldiers to Didymoteichon and the Adrianople camp.[72] The autumn was drawing to a close, yet Theodore saw an opportunity for a surprise foray against the fortress of Tzepaina, the only remaining Bulgar-ian bastion of resistance in the northern Rhodopes – "most fortified, most troublesome ... and completely impregnable," as he described it.[73] The army plodded upstream along the Maritsa River on his orders, but the march stalled after the first snowfall. Most of his counsellors favored retreat and Theodore asked the officers to reaffirm their loyalty to him, a sign of his insecurity about the allegiance of leading army personnel. When the weather cleared, the army continued toward the well-provisioned fortress of Stenimachos, reached Vatkounion, and marched in the direc-tion of Tzepaina through a narrow and frosty mountain pass overgrown with trees.[74] The thick black smoke of the night campfire led to loss of orientation and caused panic. In the morning Theodore sounded retreat and the army made its descent along the same difficult path. The emperor ordered the sack of Vatkounion, and returned to Adrianople.[75] This setback notwithstanding, the campaign of 1255 had achieved its main goal of pushing back the Bulgarian tsar. In the course of eleven months Theodore had crisscrossed the Balkans, covering more than 1,250 miles (2,000 kilometers) in harsh weather and over difficult terrains. A letter to Mouzalon reveals his pride in his accomplishments: "Everyone who knows and reflects on the matter and its conclusion recognizes the greatest profit for the Roman state. My body was sacrificed to noble and diverse dangers. It rushed off as it was right to do. It was greatly exhausted. It devised stratagems and caused earlier sieges to be raised. It overcame ambushes and strengthened the state."[76]

As he prepared to cross into Asia Minor, Theodore stationed a military regiment in Thrace under the command of Manuel Laskaris and Constantine Margarites under strict orders to maintain a defensive line between Didymoteichon and Adrianople. He showered honors on the generals, naming Manuel Laskaris as *protosevastos* and appointing Margarites to the newly created military office of *megas archon*. Theodore and his mobile court celebrated Christmas at Lampsakos on the Hellespont, where he made a series of promotions that marked the point of no return in his confrontation with the aristocracy. He divested Alexios Raoul, a man married to Theodore's first cousin on his father's side, of the household office of *protovestiarios*, which Raoul had held for more than ten years, and instead appointed George Mouzalon. George Mouzalon also received the title of *protosevastos* and was given the newly introduced office of *megas stratopedarches*, whose holder was responsible for provisioning the army. In effect, George Mouzalon was entrusted with implementing the planned reforms of the army. Theodore granted George Mouzalon the special right to be addressed as "the emperor's brother," an honor that Vatatzes' long-standing *mesazon*, the late Demetrios Komnenos Tornikes, had enjoyed. Mouzalon seems to have also assumed the function of *mesazon*, the supreme minister coordinating all departments of the imperial service. George's brother Andronikos Mouzalon occupied the vacated post of *megas domestikos* and the third brother, Theodore Mouzalon, was appointed as "first hunter" (*protokynegos*), an official in charge of imperial game reserves. The Mouzalons obtained an authority unmatched by any family in the empire of Nicaea. Other imperial favorites were also highly decorated. Theodore's confidant Karyanites replaced Andronikos Mouzalon as *protovestiarites*. John Angelos rose from *megas primmikerios* to first imperial groom (*protostrator*). George Akropolites was elevated from logothete *tou genikou* to grand logothete (*megas logothetes*) (Fig. 24).[77] At a certain point during Theodore's reign, his secretary Hagiotheodorites was appointed logothete of the troops (*logothetes ton agelon*) and served as head of the treasury.[78]

The promotions were accompanied by various measures against distrusted generals and officials. Our sources list demoted and punished individuals without revealing the chronology.[79] Constantine Tornikes, called by Theodore "unjust" and "cowardly," was put on trial for insubordination and his partner Alexios Strategopoulos was imprisoned (whether with or without trial is not known). The emperor turned against his brothers-in-law married to female first cousins from the Vatatzes family, such as Alexios Strategopoulos' son Constantine and the ex-*protovestiarios* Alexios Raoul. Constantine Strategopoulos was blinded – a penalty for conspirators and rebels in Byzantium – for offending the emperor at the beginning of his reign.[80] The four sons of the *protovestiarios* Alexios Raoul (John, Manuel, Isaac, and an unknown fourth) were imprisoned.[81] The former imperial secretary Nikephoros Alyates, whom Theodore had promoted to the post of head of the imperial chancery (*epi tou kanikleiou*), was punished with cutting of the tongue and confiscation of his properties. The ex-governor of Thessalonica, Theodore Philes, was blinded, which marked the final resolution of the vendetta. The emperor tried to reshape aristocratic networks by making marital arrangements and ordered, in Pachymeres' words, his new appointees "to take in marriage noble ladies, even though these men often were not of noble parentage."[82] Many of the "noble ladies" belonged to the Palaiologos family. In early 1256 Akropolites was joined in matrimony to a certain Eudokia Palaiologina.[83] George Mouzalon wed Theodora Kantakouzene Palaiologina, a daughter of Michael Palaiologos' sister Irene and the *doux* of Thrakesion, John Komnenos Kantakouzenos.[84] Another of Michael Palaiologos' nieces also called Theodora – the daughter of his sister Maria-Martha and Nikephoros Tarchaneiotes – was married off to the former page Valanidiotes. The engagement had already taken place when the emperor ordered Theodora to marry a certain Basil Kaballarios.[85] A daughter of the ex-*protovestiarios* Alexios Raoul became the wife of the *megas domestikos* Andronikos Mouzalon.[86]

Marriages among the aristocracy had been tightly controlled by the emperor in the twelfth century. Permission by Manuel I Komnenos was needed for anyone to marry into the Komnenian elite consisting of his blood relatives and affines, who formed the backbone of the court hierarchy. Failure to obtain advance approval was a punishable offence.[87] Seen from a pre-1204 perspective, Theodore's marital policies were in line with Komnenian tradition. For all his idealization of friendship as a political principle, he could not entirely escape the power of the family and family

networks. He revealingly employed the language of kinship in letters to
Mouzalon after 1254, designating him as his "brother" and even describing their relationship (an emperor and his minister) as *homozygia*, a word
that refers also to the marital bond.[88] While the methods were old, the
goal was a new one: the cultivation and strengthening of a service elite at
the expense of an established and entrenched hereditary aristocracy
descended from the twelfth-century imperial families. The marriages of
"noble" ladies of Komnenian pedigree to men viewed by contemporaries
as lowborn would have been considered mésalliance in the twelfth century. Another difference from the marriages policies of the twelfth-
century emperors was that Theodore kept his immediate family above
the shifting aristocratic alliances. He delayed marrying off his daughters
to generals and dignitaries. The butler (*pinkernes*) George Nestongos was
rumored to be a future imperial son-in-law, but no engagement was
announced.[89]

In the late spring of 1256, while still residing in Nymphaion, Theodore
restarted the negotiations on the union of the churches in the hope of
extracting concessions from the papacy. He sent two laymen, Theodore
Dokeianos and Demetrios Spartenos, to Rome. His letter to Pope Alexander IV, filled with philosophical language and learned circumlocutions,
called attention to the continuing disagreements on the Procession of the
Holy Spirit. Theodore expressed willingness to mediate between Pope
Alexander and Patriarch Arsenios, who was described as an expert in
Trinitarian theology.[90] The "chapters of recognition and petition" formulated by the Nicaean side at the Council of Nymphaion in 1250 had
acknowledged the right of the Roman pontiff to make final pronouncements on doctrinal matters, but the two Nicaean embassies sent to Italy
after the council insisted that the Procession of the Holy Spirit be excepted
from the papal prerogatives and be examined through "scriptural testimonies and divine utterances." Pope Innocent IV had agreed at that time
that a future ecumenical council might make changes in the Nicene Creed
contingent upon prior agreement on the matter.[91] Arsenios, a former
envoy to the papacy and the author of a treatise on the schism, was in
Nymphaion on March 31, 1256, which suggests he and Theodore were
coordinating their positions in the negotiations with the papacy.[92]

Theodore himself displayed a degree of knowledge of Trinitarian doctrine
in his treatise on the Procession of the Holy Spirit, which he addressed to
Nicholas, a native of Dyrrachion who is usually known as Nicholas of
Croton. Nicholas had served as a cleric of the apostolic chamber of Pope
Innocent IV and may have played a role in the Nicaean-papal negotiations

of the early 1250s. On September 2, 1254, he was elected bishop of Croton (Cotrone) in Calabria. Fluent in Greek and Latin, he was the author of a list of testimonies from Greek church fathers on the Procession of the Holy Spirit, testimonies he often paraphrased and amplified in order to promote the Latin theological interpretation.[93] Between 1256 and 1258 Theodore composed his *Response* (*Antigraphe*) to Nicholas, which consists of a series of scriptural, patristic, and conciliar quotations on the same doctrinal subject.[94] The work followed the Photian tradition on the Procession of the Holy Spirit and made no effort to seek a common ground with the Latins, in contrast to the evolving position of Nikephoros Blemmydes.[95] At a time before the reopening of negotiations with the Latins (sometime between November 1254 and September 1256), Theodore Laskaris commissioned his former teacher and current patriarchal official, the holder of the post of supervisor of monasteries, to formulate the Byzantine doctrinal position as he had already done in 1234 and 1250. Blemmydes addressed to the young emperor a work justifying with scriptural and patristic quotations the Procession of the Holy Spirit from the Father through the Son, while continuing to adhere to the orthodox position that the Father was the only origin and cause of the Spirit.[96] Theodore preferred, however, to avoid this more conciliatory approach toward the *filioque*. He prepared himself carefully for the new round of negotiations. His choice of Demetrios Spartenos, a Nicaean loyalist from Thessalonica who had played a prominent role in the city's peaceful surrender to Vatatzes in 1246, as one of the envoys to Italy in the spring of 1256 suggests that the reception of the papal delegation in Thessalonica later in the year was planned in advance.[97] Pope Alexander IV warmly welcomed the initiative of the new Nicaean emperor and ordered the Dominican friar Constantine, bishop of Orvieto since 1250 who had already been Innocent IV's choice in 1254 as ambassador to Byzantine Anatolia, to prepare himself to depart in ten days or less.[98] Constantine was provided with Innocent's notes on "the chapters of recognition and petition" and was instructed to abide by them and, if possible, solicit further concessions. He was to accept the submission of the Greek church and hold a council "in those regions." If the Greeks made new demands, he was to bring their envoys to Italy for discussion.[99] Constantine of Orvieto carried a letter from the pope to his "dearest son in Christ, Theodore, emperor of the Greeks," which showered lavish praise on his erudition, "natural arguments, philosophical reasoning," and competent use of theological authorities.[100]

In the spring of 1256 Theodore was making preparations not only for negotiations with the papacy, but also for the resumption of the Balkan campaign. Once again, he needed assurance that the Anatolian frontier was secure before he could transfer troops into Europe. Envoys, among whom was an anonymous *pansebastos sebastos* close to the *logothetes ton agelon* Hagiotheodorites, were dispatched to the Seljuks on an information-gathering mission and apparently brought a favorable report, for Theodore decided to proceed with the campaign. The emperor mustered a larger army than that of the previous year and enlisted new recruits who included even hunters from the crown game reserves. The Mouzalon brothers were responsible for the recruitment, for Theodore Mouzalon managed the game reserves and George Mouzalon was charged with provisioning the army. The troops, led by the emperor, encamped near Pegai on the Sea of Marmara at a location called Mamas and then crossed the Hellespont at Lampsakos, taking up position at Boulgarophygon (Babaeski) east of the Maritsa River.[101] The situation in Thrace had taken a turn for the worse in early 1256. When the Bulgarian tsar incited 4,000 allied Cumans to make a plundering raid into eastern Thrace, Manuel Laskaris and Constantine Margarites disobeyed Theodore's parting injunction to maintain a defensive position and recklessly chased after the Cumans, which resulted in a heavy defeat at Varsakinai near Garella (Altınyazı), east of the Maritsa. Margarites was taken captive and the Cumans sacked Rhaidestos and Herakleia on the Marmara coast. Once in the Balkans, Theodore ordered his troops to seek out the invaders and put special trust in his own Cuman light cavalrymen, who were familiar with the fighting style of their compatriots. The division headed by the Cuman Cleopas and George Nestongos won a victory on the banks of the Regina (Ergene) River, an eastern tributary to the Maritsa. Another battle fought near Vizye resulted in the massacre of many invading Cumans, including their nobility.[102]

Theodore Laskaris set up the main army camp on the bank of the Regina. There he spent the entire spring and summer as he negotiated a peace treaty with the Bulgarians and finalized the long-planned marriage alliance with Michael of Epiros. Writing and reading kept him occupied in his tent. A letter addressed in the name of the patriarch Arsenios to the pope in October 1256 lauded Theodore for turning out literary works every day and for his wisdom, admired even by the man on the street.[103] Not all details of his negotiations with Michael Asen are clear. Theodore called for the return of Tzepaina and demanded monetary reparations, a claim that he later dropped.[104] He agreed to the Bulgarian proposal to involve the onetime prince of Chernigov, Rostislav Mikhailovich – "the ruler (*archon*) of the Rus," Theodore called him – as a peace mediator. Rostislav had sought refuge in the kingdom of Hungary from the Mongols, while he continued to title himself *dux* of Galicia. Marital connections with both

Theodore Laskaris and Michael Asen made him a suitable arbitrator. Rostislav's wife, a daughter of the Hungarian king Béla IV and Maria Laskarina, was Theodore's first cousin. Rostislav's daughter had recently married Michael Asen (Fig. 20). By 1254, the king of Hungary had invested Rostislav with the lordship of Mačva between the Danube and the Sava rivers, which made him a neighbor of the Bulgarian kingdom.[105] Rostislav arrived at the Regina camp in the early summer of 1256 accompanied by the grandees of "the Bulgarian people" in order to close the diplomatic deal.[106] On June 29, the feast day of the apostles Peter and Paul, or shortly thereafter, he confirmed the treaty drawn up by the *megas logothetes* George Akropolites and swore an oath on behalf of his son-in-law, Michael Asen. The prewar boundaries were restored and the fortress of Tzepaina was ceded back to the empire of Nicaea. For his services, Rostislav received on his departure a large quantity of gifts (reportedly numbering 20,000) that included precious clothes and horses.[107]

In an enthusiastic newsletter Theodore informed his subjects in Anatolia of the conclusion of the war. He followed an established propagandist practice of conveying the news of an imperial victory in a work intended for public reading. Trusted civil officials, such as Michael Psellos in 1059, Niketas Choniates in 1187, and the imperial secretary George Akropolites in 1246, were usually the authors of such news dispatches rather than the emperor himself.[108] In the newsletter Theodore marveled at God's miraculous act of bringing the war to a successful conclusion and awarding him the trophy of victory. Furthermore, Rostislav reportedly acknowledged him as "his father" and superior. The bulletin outlines the newly reestablished frontier. The border passed close to Sardike (Sofia) and Philippopolis (Plovdiv), which were held by the Bulgarians, as well as Velevousdion (Kyustendil), apparently also under Bulgarian control. The regions of Skopje and Vranje reverted to "their former status," which means a restoration of Nicaean rule in the case of the former city, for Vatatzes had gained control over Skopje in the last two years of his reign.[109] The border "went around" Albania and extended all the way to the kingdom of the Serbs.[110] Theodore expresses his attachment to Anatolia. God "brings every royal and peaceful word to the holy land, my mother Anatolia, like a most divine gift." He urged his audience – "you, my people (*hoi emoi*)" – to value the "profit of such great labors of the army and my imperial majesty." Animal comparisons and metaphors liven up the narrative and present the ending of the war as the fulfillment of a prophecy. A dog and a whelp are said to have begun a fight and to have later been joined by a bear, whereupon the dog was beheaded, the whelp fled, and the bear paradoxically became the mediator of peace. The dog evidently refers to the defeated Cumans in the spring of 1256; the whelp was the young Bulgarian ruler Michael Asen; and the bear was the "ruler of the Rus," Rostislav.[111]

Theodore was anxiously awaiting the handover of Tzepaina throughout July and August. According to an unverified rumor, Michael Asen did not accept the terms and Rostislav was a bogus ambassador, just like Theodoulos who had been detained in Nicaea less than two years earlier for lack of accreditation letter. The peace negotiator, the *megas logothetes* Akropolites, describes a dramatic scene in the army camp on the Regina River that served to illustrate Theodore's tyrannical tendencies. During the trooping of the color on Transfiguration Day (August 6), the emperor repeatedly questioned Akropolites about Rostislav's intentions and in a fit of fury ordered his public flagellation. Whipping was a punishment practiced at the late Byzantine court. Patriarch Germanos II mentions it in a sermon, and in the fourteenth century the imperial guard of the Vardariots had whips suspended from their belts for this gruesome task.[112] Theodore clearly lost his nerve despite all the advice he read in mirrors of princes, according to which the emperor ought to control his anger.[113] A diplomatic fiasco could deny him the fruits of hard-fought victories. He had already given up claims for reparations from the Bulgarians, and now it seemed that he had wasted precious resources on a Russian trickster. His imperial oration on his father had vilified Michael Asen as a perjurer, and his words now looked like a self-fulfilling prophecy.

His fears and suspicions proved unfounded, however. By early September Tzepaina had been peacefully handed over to him and the treaty went into effect. The Bulgarian kingdom was weakened in a series of coups and countercoups. The Peace of Regina undermined Michael Asen's authority. His paternal cousin Kaliman (Kaliman II) rebelled, assassinated him in the environs of Turnovo, and married his widow, Rostislav's daughter. Soon Kaliman himself fell victim to the revenge of the Bulgarian boyars, who punished him with death and took up the role of power brokers. Mitso (also known as Micho), the lord of Mesembria on the Black Sea who was married to Michael Asen's sister, put forth claims to be the legitimate tsar. He issued coins in his name and may have briefly entered Turnovo. A naval expedition organized by the Latin emperor Baldwin II and led by the Venetians against Mesembria in 1257 has been connected with the contest for the Bulgarian royal throne.[114] The conflict over the Bulgarian crown became even more entangled when Rostislav also assumed the title of tsar and made a foray into Bulgaria, but he did not establish himself in Turnovo and withdrew to Mačva along with his widowed daughter.[115]

The boyars threw their support behind Constantine Tikh, a descendant of the Serbian royal house, whom they selected as the new tsar. Tikh has been identified as a powerful local lord from the region of Skopje and therefore was a Nicaean client in the years 1253–54, when Skopje was temporarily under Nicaean rule.[116] Notably, the region appears not to have transferred its allegiance back to Nicaea as per the Peace of Regina: Akropolites' meticulous account of events in western Macedonia and Albania in 1257 conspicuously omits Skopje. Tikh had ambitions of his own and was enthroned in Turnovo, while his rival, Mitso, retained power in the eastern parts of the Bulgarian kingdom, including Preslav and Mesembria. The lack of blood connection with the Asenid dynasty prompted Tikh to send an embassy to Nicaea, requesting the hand in marriage of Theodore's eldest daughter Irene, a granddaughter of Ivan Asen II. The emperor gladly agreed to this proposal, which confirmed the Peace of Regina and marked the best possible conclusion of the exhausting two-year war. Irene was dispatched to Turnovo to become the new tsar's bride.[117] We can see her depicted along with her royal husband Constantine in a realistic fresco drawn in 1258–59 in the small church of SS. Nicholas and Panteleimon in Boyana near Sofia. She wears an open crown that resembles that of a Byzantine empress (Fig. 25).[118] In a letter to Blemmydes, Theodore shared his satisfaction at the steep decline of the Bulgarian kingdom. The assassination of the Bulgarian tsar Michael Asen was compared to the killing of a dragon: "The dragon came out and was truly beheaded, and the corpse of the dead man erected for us a massive victory monument."[119] Blemmydes was said to have prophesied the trophy and was urged to admire the "accomplishment of Hellenic bravery."

Theodore left the Regina camp on September 2, 1256, and set off – along with soldiers, officials, and bishops – for Thessalonica, where he was to conclude the long-planned marriage treaty with Michael of Epiros and receive the papal ambassadors led by Constantine of Orvieto. On the Day of the Elevation of the Cross (September 14), either in Lentza in the Voleron region of Thrace or in Langadas near Thessalonica, the emperor met with Michael of Epiros' wife Theodora Petraliphina. On behalf of her husband, Theodora finalized the provisions of the treaty and agreed to hand over to Nicaea two key towns, Servia in southern Macedonia and Dyrrachion on the Adriatic Sea at the westernmost end of the *via Egnatia*. The emperor and the accompanying dignitaries took up residence in Thessalonica, where they remained throughout the second half of September and most of October.[120] Patriarch Arsenios blessed the marriage of Theodore's daughter Maria to Michael of Epiros' son Nikephoros in one of the churches of the city. Nikephoros was granted the highest court title of despot and the newlyweds departed for the Epirote court. Animated discussions took place with the papal ambassador, Constantine of Orvieto, and the accompanying Dominican friars.[121] The letter of Arsenios to Pope Alexander IV, written by the metropolitan of Thessalonica, Manuel Disypatos, at the end of the negotiations, complains that the papal delegation had insufficient authority to address the Nicaean requests. The status of Constantinople seems to have been the main stumbling block.[122] Another impediment was the intransigent attitude of the emperor himself. His two *Orations against the Latins*, composed during the discussions in Thessalonica, show an implacably antagonistic position. He closed the second oration by urging the assembled Byzantine clergy of all ranks: "Do not consent in any way at all to the pointless or inopportune investigations of the Italians, do not take heed of their objections or the height of their arrogance. Those things are their custom and ours is to reject them!"[123] The recognition of papal primacy in the "chapters of agreement and petition" adopted in the Council of Nymphaion (1250) did not meet with Theodore's approval. In his *Response* to Nicholas of Croton he arrogated to himself the right to organize, fund, and chair the future unionist ecumenical council, an ambition that contradicted a privilege of the papacy recognized in the chapters. Theodore's idea seems to have been that a large number of eastern bishops should attend the ecumenical council: Arsenios' letter to Pope Alexander IV written by Manuel Disypatos mentions the figure of more than 500, even though just over thirty bishops came to Thessalonica in the autumn of 1256.[124]

The Latin envoys departed for Italy to consult with the pope on the points raised in the discussion. The *megas logothetes* Akropolites escorted them until Servia, one of the two towns ceded by Michael of Epiros to Nicaea. The rest of their land journey was disastrous. Constantine of Orvieto passed away under unknown circumstances in Greece and his body was transported for burial in Perugia.[125] His death brought to a halt the negotiations that had begun so unpromisingly. Theodore kept the channels of diplomatic communications open in case the papacy agreed to concessions. His approach is seen in his correspondence with the powerful and worldly Roman cardinals Richard Annibaldi, Peter Capoccio, and Ottaviano Ubaldini, Dante's *il Cardinale* punished in the sixth circle of Hell.[126] Capoccio and Ubaldini were previously known to him from reports about events in Italy, for they had led military operations against Frederick II. During Theodore's reign, Pope Alexander IV and two of the cardinals (Annibaldi and Ubaldini) asked the young emperor to set free an important Latin prisoner of war. This appeal was in keeping with the good-will gesture made in 1250 by John Vatatzes and Innocent IV, who had both released war captives kept in Nicaean and Latin prisons, respectively.[127] Theodore fulfilled the request, but did not miss the opportunity to teach Annibaldi a lesson about the unjust wars waged by the Latins in the eastern Mediterranean. The prisoner was "not fighting for his fatherland, not struggling against impiety, not leading a war on behalf of truth, and not slaughtering for the purpose of peace."[128] In a letter to his "best friend" Peter Capoccio, Theodore vowed that he welcomed his encouragement to bring the unionist negotiations to a successful ending.[129] It is unlikely, however, that he did anything to promote this cause during the rest of his reign beyond issuing polite assurances that he took the cause to heart.

Final Confrontations

The surprise news of a mighty Mongol incursion into Seljuk Anatolia cut short the emperor's stay in Thessalonica, which he hurriedly left on October 23, 1256.[130] At the beginning of the year Hülegü, the brother of the Great Khan Möngke, established himself in Iran with a large army he had led from central Asia. The local Mongol commander, Bayju, moved his hordes from the Mughan plain into the Anatolian plateau, which led to a confrontation with 'Izz al-Dīn Kaykāwūs II. A pitched battle was fought on October 14, 1256, not far from Aksaray. The sultan's contingent of Greek troops was under the command of none other than Theodore's second cousin, the *megas konostaulos* Michael Palaiologos. The latter had just defected to the sultanate, frightened by the incarceration on suspicion of disloyalty of his paternal uncle and namesake, the *megas chartoularios* Michael Palaiologos, after having received a warning by a palace official named Kotys.[131] The *megas konostaulos* and his retinue had stealthily crossed the Paphlagonian frontier, but ran into hostile Turkmen who detained and robbed the fugitives of their precious assets (gold, silver, horses, and luxury textiles), even depriving them of the clothes on their backs. Palaiologos made his way alone to Konya, where the sultan welcomed him and put him in charge of the Greek troops in his service. Other Nicaean aristocratic defectors – including Constantine Doukas Nestongos, the son the rebel Andronikos Nestongos – also received him warmly.[132] The Greeks under Palaiologos fought bravely at Aksaray, at least according to the Byzantine accounts, but in the end the Mongols were victorious. The Seljuk commander-in-chief Tavtaş escaped to Kastamon (Kastamonu) in

Paphlagonia, together with Michael Palaiologos.[133] The informal newsletter that Niketas Karantenos, a priest and notary in Palatia (Miletos), addressed to the abbot of the monastery of St. John the Theologian on the island of Patmos, bears witness to the distress caused by the Mongol invasion and the rapidity with which news traveled across Anatolia and the Balkans. On the basis of oral reports (the phrase "as they say" is ubiquitous), Karantenos recounts how the emperor "defeated every enemy and adversary" and restored "deep peace with Asen (Michael Asen) and with his co-father-in-law (Michael II of Epiros)." Karantenos mentions the wedding in Thessalonica, the annexation of "Dyrrachion and another great castle (Servia)," Michael Palaiologos' flight, and the departure of Michael's brother John Palaiologos for Rhodes (whether because of a new posting or due to fear of persecution), the Battle of Aksaray, and the flight of 'Izz al-Dīn to Antalya. The priest from Miletos could not explain the reason for the sudden incursion of the Mongols and could not predict their future movements. He implored the abbot to pray for peace.[134]

Theodore sailed across the Hellespont on December 1 and spent Christmas at Syrroia, not far from Prousa and Lopadion, where he received frequent messages from 'Izz al-Dīn, who was approaching the frontier with Nicaea. After the Battle of Aksaray, 'Izz al-Dīn fled from Konya, along with his wives and entourage, and took up residence in Antalya on the Mediterranean coast.[135] From there he moved to Laodikeia (Ladik), near the Nicaean border, in an area thickly inhabited by Turkmen who were among his most loyal supporters.[136] Bayju's grandson Besütay chased after the sultan with 1,000 mounted Mongol warriors, but the sultan persuaded his pursuer to turn back and he crossed the frontier accompanied by his entourage and children. In the meantime Bayju installed 'Izz al-Dīn's brother Rukn al-Dīn as sultan in Konya, where the city walls were leveled – with the sole exception of the citadel. 'Izz al-Dīn entered Nicaean territory in early January 1257, according to the *Synopsis chronike*. Theodore's army was on the move southward toward the Thrakesion theme, passing through Kalamos and the nearby fortress of Kavallares, when an emir arrived announcing that the sultan was already "around Tripolis." On Epiphany Day (January 6) the emperor sent off the army to encamp on the plain of Magnesia, while he himself went to Sardis to meet the sultan and escort him to Magnesia.[137] The sultan remained Theodore's guest throughout the winter and the spring. In the meantime, Bayju's Mongols withdrew to Iran to join the army of Hülegü, who issued a decree regarding the division of the sultanate: Rukn al-Dīn was to rule over its eastern part close to his Mongol protectors while 'Izz al-Dīn was permitted to return to Konya, which he re-entered in early May 1257.[138]

Theodore wrote a letter to George Mouzalon that captures the euphoria of the moment. He marveled at the reversal of relations with the Seljuks and the humbling of the sultan: "The great ruler of the Persians (the sultan) is under the authority of the Hellenic tribe." People around Theodore predicted an "utter destruction" of the Seljuk realm, while Theodore himself saw the fulfillment of a divine plan for the speedy and full restoration of the empire.[139] This assessment was mistaken. The sultan's weakness gave Theodore the opportunity to extract only minor territorial concessions. The imperial privy council and the emperor himself are said to have excluded the option of granting the sultan permanent asylum, which could further provoke the Mongols and weaken the eastern frontier.[140] Theodore agreed to provide 'Izz al-Dīn with 300 soldiers commanded by the *primmikerios* of the court, Isaac Doukas Mourtzouphlos, and 'Izz al-Dīn ceded to Nicaea the four fortresses of Laodikeia (Ladik), Chonai, Sakaina and Hypsele, which all lay in the borderlands along the Lykos valley.[141] Relations with Michael Palaiologos were patched up. In the course of 1257 the latter was reconciled with the emperor through the intervention of the metropolitan bishop of Ikonion as intermediary and returned from the sultanate in exchange for sworn guarantees for his safety.[142]

Alongside the agreement with the sultan Theodore adopted a policy of diplomatic engagement with the Mongols. The historian Pachymeres reports the reception of a Mongol embassy – arguably the embassy sent by Hülegü in the spring of 1257 to the empire of Nicaea in order to grant 'Izz al-Dīn permission to return to Konya.[143] The historian admires Theodore for his use of strategic deception. His agents were dispatched to select areas in the sultanate to spread rumors about the invincibility of his army. Once the Mongol envoys reached Nicaean territory, local guides took them through narrow passes and explained that the landscape of the entire realm was mountainous. Stationed along the route were soldiers in full armor and silk-wearing dignitaries, who took shortcuts in order to appear repeatedly in sight and created the impression of a vast and well-managed army. Theodore received the ambassadors in an elaborately staged ceremony that followed the best traditions of Byzantine diplomacy. Girt with a sword and seated on a tall throne, he was hidden behind a curtain, and once it was suddenly lifted, he uttered only a few words.[144] His diplomatic tactics were successful. Nicaea avoided the fate not only of the sultanate, but also of the remnant of the centuries-old Abbasid caliphate. In February 1258 Hülegü sacked Baghdad and closed a chapter in Near Eastern history by executing the last caliph. Theodore's rapprochement with the Mongols of Iran led to negotiations on a marriage alliance, which was concluded after his death.[145]

The territorial gains in the Balkans and Asia Minor in late 1256 and early 1257 marked the high point of Theodore's reign. Riding on the crest of the wave of his successes, he felt optimistic and energized. He sent an assertive letter to Blemmydes in 1257 that summarizes his achievements and lays out his agenda for army reform. He boasted that his empire now stretched from Cape Karambis on the Black Sea to Dyrrachion on the Adriatic, from Rhodes in the Aegean to Tripolis on the Maeander (Map 3).[146] The thirty-five-year-old emperor was confident that a new era was about to begin and believed himself to be in his prime, being "old" solely in his soul, which was steeped in wisdom.[147] He gave an account of his busy daily routine:

> When the sun rises, care for the soldiers is awakened from bed with us at the same time. As the sun mounts higher and is carried around loftier heights, we take care of ambassadors, of their reception and dismissal. While the sun is still rising, the order of the troops is arranged by us. When the sun is in the middle at noon, the task of dealing with petitioners is undertaken and performed, and we proceed on horseback in order to hear people who are unable to join those at the gates of the palace. When the sun is bowing low, we pass judgments for those who bow before us. When the sun sets, we taste food, as is usual, forced by the bond of soul and matter, and even then we do not cease to speak about our allotted duty. And when the sun turns and hides at the shores of the ocean, we make plans concerning campaigning and equipment.[148]

His experience during the Balkan campaign convinced him that he should strengthen the army with new recruits from among the native Anatolian population. Disparaging comments by Akropolites point unambiguously to the swelling of the army ranks. As we have seen, in 1256 Theodore enlisted soldiers more numerous than those who served his father, including hunters from the game reserves with no military preparation. The regiment sent to the Balkans in 1257 under the command of a certain Manuel Lapardas is dismissively described as a "rough mob of an army," ill-equipped and riding mares instead of horses.[149] The policy created tension with the Latin mercenaries under the command of the *megas konostaulos* Michael Palaiologos, who saw their salaries delayed by the order of George Mouzalon. It is incorrect, however, to assume that the emperor planned to disband the corps of foreign-born soldiers. Cuman warriors and the Varangian Guard were prominent in the years 1257 and 1258.[150] Theodore's aim, rather, was to shift the balance in the army and make it a larger and hence more formidable fighting force. To secure additional funding, his fiscal agents under the auspices of George

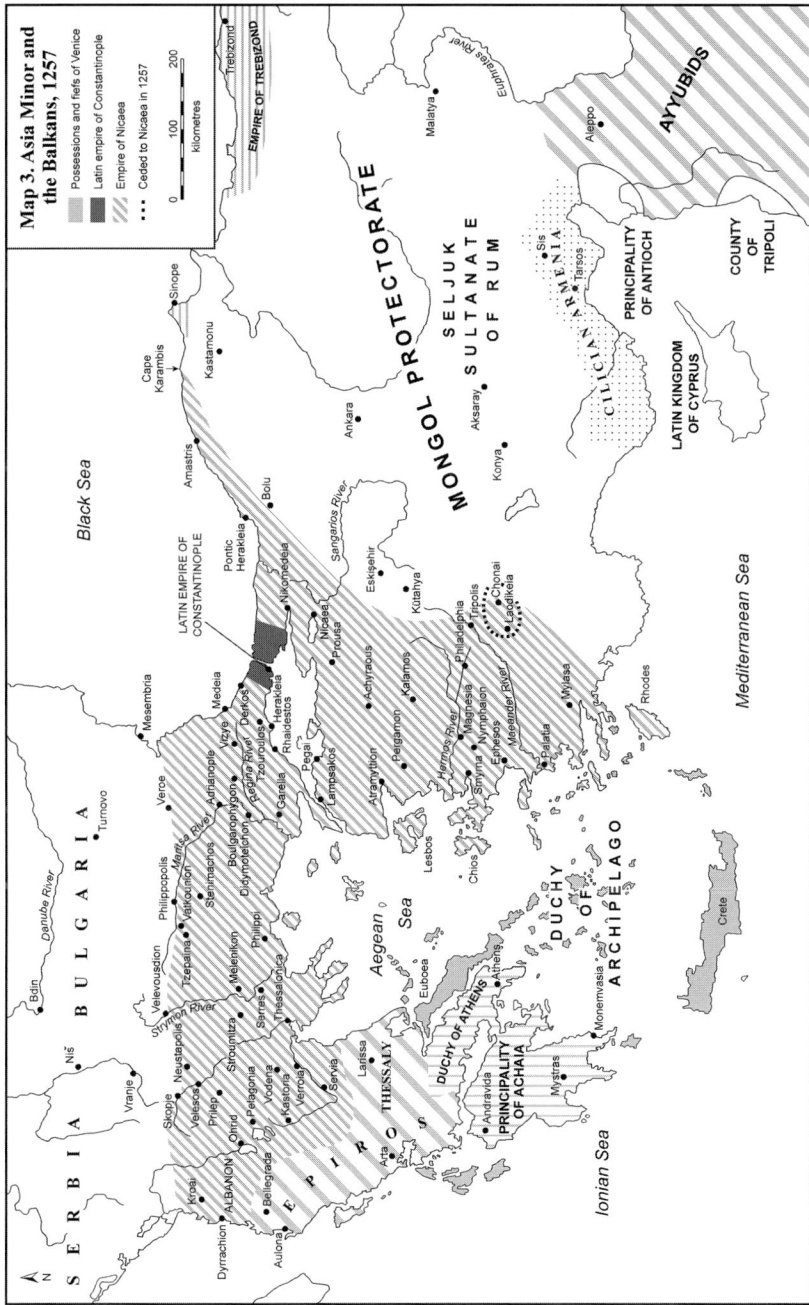

Map 3 Asia Minor and the Balkans in 1257

Map 3. Asia Minor and
the Balkans, 1257

Possessions and fiefs of Venice
Latin empire of Constantinople
Empire of Nicaea
····· Ceded to Nicaea in 1257

0   100   200
kilometres

Black Sea

Mediterranean Sea

Aegean Sea

Ionian Sea

MONGOL PROTECTORATE

SELJUK SULTANATE OF RUM

LATIN EMPIRE OF CONSTANTINOPLE

EMPIRE OF TREBIZOND

AYYUBIDS

CILICIAN ARMENIA

PRINCIPALITY OF ANTIOCH

COUNTY OF TRIPOLI

LATIN KINGDOM OF CYPRUS

SERBIA

BULGARIA

ALBANON

EPIROS

THESSALY

DUCHY OF ATHENS

PRINCIPALITY OF ACHAIA

DUCHY OF ARCHIPELAGO

Mouzalon scrupulously carried out their work. We hear remonstrations against the requisition or forced sale of grain for provisioning the army (a levy called *mitaton*) and complaints of Blemmydes about demands to pay a maritime tax (*naulos*) due from his monastery's properties.[151] The decision to site a new treasury at Astitzion in the Troad was a matter of logistics and military financing, for it was closer to the crossing point at the Hellespont than the old and still functioning treasury in Magnesia.

Theodore's assertive and upbeat letter of 1257 goes on to share with Blemmydes his conviction that a native army of "Hellenes" was more reliable than one consisting of foreign-born soldiers.

> Hostility against the common people is stirred up and foreigners are fighting against us. Who will be our helper? How will the Persian help the Greek? The Italian raged very much, the Bulgarian most manifestly. The Serb is forced into submission and suppressed. The person who is perhaps ours is not truly one of ours. Only the Hellenes (*to Hellenikon*) give aid to themselves, deriving motivation from within themselves.[152]

The letter is a response to Blemmydes' critical remarks, which had suggested that the emperor should use hoarded wealth consisting of coins and precious metals rather than public taxes in order to fund the army. Theodore's reply was that the treasury would be depleted if tax proceeds were not forthcoming and state finances would be driven into debt.[153] He closed the letter by appealing to later generations to evaluate the truth of his arguments. It was, thus, the future of the army that provoked Theodore Laskaris to call for the judgment of posterity. Was public financing of the army necessary? Was the army more effective if it was a larger fighting force with a greater proportion of native-born soldiers? The turn of events on the battlefield in the later thirteenth and early fourteenth centuries shows that Theodore made a valid point.

The spirit of optimism projected in the letter did not last long. The personal tragedy of Theodore Laskaris was that he saw the swift undoing of his military achievements, accompanied by the sudden, drastic deterioration of his health. Whether he lived long enough to witness the conquest by the Turkmen of the four frontier fortresses of Laodikeia, Chonai, Sakaina, and Hypsele ceded to him by 'Izz al-Dīn is not known.[154] But he certainly witnessed the reversal of the situation in the Balkans. On his hasty departure to Asia Minor he left Akropolites as the governor of Thessalonica and the region of western Macedonia and Albania, the position of *praitor* held earlier by Theodore Philes. Akropolites went on a three-month inspection (December 1256–February 1257) of the borderlands, which took him to Verroia, Servia, Kastoria, Dyrrachion (where he spent eight days in order to arrange the transfer of authority), Debre (Debar) and eventually Prilep.[155] Theodore's great uncle Michael Laskaris was stationed in Thessalonica as the commander of a regiment of Paphlagonian soldiers and 300 Cuman warriors. Theodore's local appointments suggest distrust of aristocratic families connected with the Balkans. He had already relieved of their duties individuals who had marriage ties to local lords in the state of Epiros. Constantine Tornikes – removed from army command and divested of the title of *megas primmikerios* – was a brother-in-law of Theodore Petraliphas, who had defected to the camp of Vatatzes in the spring of 1253. Theodore Petraliphas proved to be a man of fickle loyalty, however, and by 1259 he switched his allegiance back to Michael of Epiros.[156] The emperor also dismissed the *parakoimomenos* George Zagarommates, a long-serving official whose wife came from the Thessalian Maliasenos family.[157] Command over the Macedonian frontier areas was entrusted to men of humbler and Anatolian origin. The military governors of Veles and Prilep, Theodore Kalambakes and the *skouterios* Xyleas, had surnames attested in the region of Smyrna. Other newly appointed military officers, such as Manuel Ramatas, Poulachas, and Constantine Chabaron, came from relatively modest family backgrounds. Chabaron was stationed in Albania sometime before 1255. He had uneasy relations with Albanian lords who had accepted, nominally at least, rule from Nicaea.[158]

The outbreak of a new conflict with Michael of Epiros showed that Theodore Laskaris had made a critical error of judgment in making his local appointees. Not long after his departure for Asia Minor, the humiliated ruler of Epiros broke the agreement, fomented a rebellion among Albanian lords, and struck an alliance with the Serbian king Stefan I Uroš. The *epi tes trapezes* Isaac Nestongos and Akropolites attempted to quell the unrest in Albania, but accomplished nothing. Akropolites withdrew to Prilep, only to find himself surrounded by the numerically superior Serbs who made a foray from the north through Kičevo and plundered the environs of Prilep. Xyleas was defeated by the Serbs and barely escaped with his life. Chabaron was taken prisoner, allegedly after being tricked by fake love letters sent by Michael of Epiros' sister-in-law Maria Petraliphina.[159] Theodore kept sending military reinforcements from Asia Minor. The new recruits, under the command of Manuel Lapardas, suffered a heavy defeat in a mountain pass near Vodena (Edessa). The *megas konostaulos* Michael Palaiologos, who had just returned from the sultanate, was dispatched to lead troops stationed in Thrace. After linking up with the 500 Paphlagonians under Michael Laskaris, he finally defeated the Epirote forces and advanced toward the besieged fortress of Prilep. However, the order from the emperor in Anatolia was to withdraw and leave Akropolites to fight on alone.[160] As soon as the reinforcements left the area of Prilep, Michael of Epiros pressed on with the siege, the urban garrison surrendered, and Akropolites was imprisoned. The latter would observe bitterly in his *History* that Xyleas, Manuel Ramatas, Poulachas, and Isaac Nestongos – all of them Theodore Laskaris' protégés – readily switched their allegiance to the Epirote ruler. Only he and Constantine Chabaron resolutely declined to do so.[161] The Epirote-led coalition against the empire of Nicaea became even more dangerous when it drew in the prince of Achaia and the king of Sicily. In 1258 Michael of Epiros' daughter Anna married the prince of Achaia William II of Villehardouin and another daughter, Helena (the eldest), was betrothed to Manfred, who was crowned as King of Sicily on August 10, 1258.[162] Reviving the claims of his Norman ancestors over the Albanian coast, Manfred gained control between February 1257 and February 1258 of Dyrrachion, Aulona and Bellegrada (Berat).[163] In June 1258 he even dispatched a naval expedition to the Aegean. His experienced admiral Philippe Chinardo plundered the islands of Chios and Lesbos, and returned to Italy with captives and relics.[164]

Theodore was incapable of producing an adequate reaction to these military setbacks. A debilitating illness began to manifest itself in the late months of 1257 and prevented him from leading a campaign in person. The disease cannot be identified, but it certainly was not chronic epilepsy as traditionally assumed. It may have been cancer of the brain, the spine or the lungs, but this is just a hypothesis.[165] In a letter to Blemmydes describing its early symptoms, Theodore complained of numbness and pain in his arm radiating from his shoulder without there being any swelling. He criticized the inability of his doctors to cure him, calling them "stupid" and "human plagues," a Homeric phrase he used elsewhere to scoff at incompetent medics. His hope was that Blemmydes, a qualified physician, could find a remedy.[166] The confidence and optimism manifest in the letters he had sent to Blemmydes and Mouzalon just months earlier gave way to insecurity and growing despair. Two texts in particular, both dating to the last year of his life, reveal his anguished state of mind. In his *Supplicatory Canon* he prayed to the Mother of God to deliver him from illness and unnamed enemies, who had in the past pointed their weapons against him and who still "seek to tear apart my most wretched body and throw it down into earth." In an essay on the self-sacrifice of rulers, he observed that military campaigns fought in extreme weather conditions, both in the winter and the summer, damaged the health of the commander-in-chief. The healthy rulers were only those who took care of their bodies, just as their subjects did.[167] Feeling weakened by his illness, he looked back at the physical effects of the war with the Bulgarians as one of the causes of his worsening condition.

Theodore suffered weight loss and seizures as the disease progressed in 1258. He took up residence in Magnesia, rarely left the palace, and became increasingly gloomy and introverted. In his frustration he readily attributed his illness to magic and bewitchment – an understandable reaction of a man who was conscious of being surrounded by enemies and who was interested in occult sciences. Allegations of magic were easier to make than to prove in the absence of reliable witnesses. The only way in which an accused individual could clear his name was to agree to undergo an ordeal by red-hot iron. Pachymeres remarks that during his adolescence he saw people who passed unharmed through the procedure and were declared innocent after having been charged with practicing magic against the gravely ill emperor.[168] Interrogations by torture also took place. One of the individuals accused of magic was Maria-Martha, the eldest sister of Michael Palaiologos. Her daughter Theodora had married Basil Kaballarios at the emperor's bidding despite her earlier engagement to the ex-page Valanidiotes. The marriage remained unconsummated and Kaballarios blamed this on magic practiced by his mother-in-law, which led to suspicion that she was the cause of the emperor's mysterious illness. Maria-Martha was subjected to a gruesome procedure in order to determine whether she was a witch. She was stripped naked and locked in a sack full of straw and starved cats. The cats were poked with sticks from the outside in order to make them scratch the poor woman. The imperial tribunal seems to have followed a late antique and Byzantine law permitting the use of torture for the extraction of confession from imperial dignitaries who were charged with lèse-majesté, witchcraft, or subversive divination.[169] She did not confess, but suspicions remained. In late 1257 or early 1258 Theodore Laskaris ordered the arrest of Michael Palaiologos, her younger brother. The *komes* of the imperial horses Chadenos was dispatched to Thessalonica to take Palaiologos – who had recently led a relief expedition to Macedonia and had reached the beleaguered fortress of Prilep – into custody. According to Pachymeres, the accusations of magic against his sister Maria-Martha were only the pretext for his detention. The real reason was the emperor's continuing lack of trust and suspicions of rebellion. Palaiologos was incarcerated without an indictment. In the end the emperor, who was confined to the palace because of his illness, set him free, reminded him of his favors, and – according to Pachymeres – even called him a protector of his family.[170]

Here lies the ultimate irony of Theodore Laskaris. His reign began with the prospect of enlightened government by a young and educated emperor surrounded by a company of likeminded peers of a similar age. His belief in friendship as the cohesive force that could hold together the political elite, both the old aristocracy and the new men promoted by him, boded well for the changes that he intended to implement. The first two and a half years of his sole rule were marked by encouraging signs of political consolidation and imperial revival. Very soon, however, the situation spiraled out of his control. Not all of the individuals he trusted proved loyal to him and his enemies grew in number and in the intensity of their ill-feeling. His disease created a vacuum of authority at a critical moment. His reign became increasingly chaotic and resembled one of terror. Enemies, both real and imaginary, were purged. In his autobiography Blemmydes flaunts his brave stance in support of the unjustly accused. One of them was a member of the imperial guard.[171] Another was a long-serving palace official who was charged with *lèse majesté* and was about to be sentenced to death at the imperial tribunal because of an allegation that his subordinate had predicted the impending end of the emperor's reign. The poor individual was pardoned by Theodore only after Blemmydes intervened. We see how political prophecy had an unnerving effect on the emperor and people around him.[172] Blemmydes takes the credit also for preventing the imposition of an ecclesiastical interdict on the entire population of the state of Epiros, which would have led to the cessation of church services. He protested at the synod in Magnesia against the punishment of the innocent Christians and secured the modification of the interdict into an excommunication of the Epirote ruler.[173] On another occasion, he declined to add his name to a document absolving the ill emperor from his sins, which the patriarch Arsenios and the synod had already signed.[174] Blemmydes writes that he preferred to distance himself from his royal student by reducing his visits to the palace and even accused him to his face of ruling in a way displeasing to God.[175] The rupture does not appear to have been complete, however. The emperor continued to show respect and pay lip service to his teacher, spiritual father, and valued advisor until his death.

Theodore had time to settle his affairs in the spring and summer of 1258. He resided in the palace in Magnesia, next to the old treasury and not far from the family tomb at the Sosandra monastery. The transition of power was carefully orchestrated. In his testament he designated his only son, the

eight-year-old John Laskaris, as his sole heir and appears to have proclaimed him as coemperor. George Mouzalon was appointed regent, with
full executive authority until John came of age. Subjects were required to
take an oath to honor the succession arrangement – and when the will was
opened after Theodore's death, those present in the palace swore again to
abide by its provisions.[176] The emperor oversaw the production of two
more authorized manuscript editions of his works composed mostly after
the accession in 1254 – a period designated in the manuscript headings as
"full completeness of imperial rule." The collection *Christian Theology*
consists of eight religious discourses: Trinitarian treatises filled with geometrical and numerological reasoning, the treatise *On the Divine Names*,
the two polemical orations against the Latins, and an oration on the
Annunciation of the Virgin. The last months of his life saw the preparation
of another collection, which contained letters (including letters to Blemmydes in which he describes his fatal illness), essays, devotional texts, and
the treatise *Explanation of the World* in four parts.[177] Up until his last
breath Theodore continued to care deeply about his legacy and the preservation of his works and his voice.

Mortality had often preoccupied him. In his description of the change of
the seasons in the treatise *Representation of the World, or Life* (the third
part of *Explanation of the World*), the figure of the death appears out of the
blue during the spring.[178] He had voiced dark thoughts about the ineluct-
ability of death in 1252, at the time of the passing of Elena:

> The medicines are weak, the illness because of time's passing grows, the
> ship is wrecked, the cargo in the ship perishes, the soul at the helm falls
> asleep, the sail is torn asunder through carelessness, the rudder is tossed
> overboard, the wind is contrary, the sun sets, night advances, the storm
> intensifies, the burden is great, the road is long, time is short, things
> about to happen are unclear, all of them horrid, danger is near, perdition
> is inevitable.[179]

Six years later, Theodore approached his own "inevitable perdition" with
hopes of saving his own soul. Another word for "death" in Byzantium was
dormition (*koimesis*), namely, falling asleep before reawakening at the Last
Judgment. He became a monk without changing his birth name Theodore
and prepared to surrender his soul to God as a pious clergyman. Profound
and sincere repentance marks a late essay addressed to his sinful flesh. The
same spirit is reflected in his request from the patriarchal synod to absolve
him from sin and prepare a signed document to this effect. The metropolitan of Mytilene Gregory administered his last confession, at which the

emperor reportedly fell before his feet and wept, imitating the penitent sinful woman of the Gospel of Luke (7:37–47).[180]

Theodore Laskaris passed away on Friday, August 16, in the palace in Magnesia. He was thirty-six, still a relatively young man, one destined never to experience middle and old age. His age of death was below the average for Byzantine men of letters, which has been estimated as about seventy-one in the eleventh and twelfth centuries. He died younger even than most male peasants who survived the perilous years of early childhood.[181] His youthful perspective has consistently struck us. During his reign he promoted people of his generation and presented the conflicts with leading generals, such as Alexios Strategopoulos, as intergenerational. Only in 1257, one year before his death, he spoke of himself as being in the prime of life. Theodore Laskaris was buried at the Sosandra monastery of the Virgin Gorgoepekoos on Mount Sipylos – next to the grave of his father who had built the monastery and in close vicinity to his mother's resting place.[182] Nothing is left today of this important ecclesiastical complex. Byzantine rule in western Anatolia came to an end in the fourteenth century and the monastery, with its royal graves, was destroyed. A summer palace was built on its location at the second half of the fifteenth century for the Ottoman crown prince Mustafa, a son of Mehmed the Conqueror, although this structure has similarly not survived.[183] The only lasting monument of Theodore Laskaris are his written works – just as their author intended.

9 | The Philosopher

Theodore Laskaris made seminal contributions to intellectual life of his time as a philosopher and as a fervent advocate of Hellenism. Both by his training and in his frame of mind, he was a consummate philosopher. His interest in the principles governing the universe manifested itself in treatises and digressions on philosophical questions, in both letters and other works. His ideas point in different directions and resist facile classification into taxonomies of schools of thought. His originality has already attracted attention. In 1930 the historian of Nicaean court culture Maria Andreeva noted his empirical interests in nature and called his treatise *Representation of the World, or Life* (the third book of his *Explanation of the World*) "a major stride forward, a beginning of an evolution of thought – a turn toward experience and nature" that came to an abrupt end on account of the author's untimely death.[1] In 1949 the historian of philosophy Basil Tatakis added that Theodore opened a new chapter in Byzantine thought, because the treatise *Natural Communion* understood "nature in a purely philosophical way."[2] For another historian of philosophy, Gerhard Richter in 1989, *Natural Communion* showed that thirteenth-century Byzantine philosophy moved on a secular path well beyond the frameworks set in the late antique philosophical schools.[3] Theodore Laskaris' interests in nature and mathematics have led to comparisons to his Western contemporary Roger Bacon (c. 1220–c. 1292) as well as to Spinoza (1632–77), even though differences have also been noted.[4] Philosophers and philologists are yet to explore the richness of his thought and prepare much-needed editions of his two important philosophical treatises, *Natural Communion* and *Explanation of the World*.[5] The following discussion – by necessity brief and preliminary – aims to paint with broad brushstrokes a philosophical portrait of Theodore Laskaris through the analysis of salient strands of his thought: his views on nature; his empirical and humanistic approach; his fascination with the occult; the interest in geometry and numerology that led him to attempt a synthesis with theology; the related critique of scholasticism; and his cultivation of philosophical irony.

A basic question to ask ourselves at the outset is what Theodore meant by "philosophy." Like other highly educated Byzantines, he had no simple and uniform understanding of the concept. The complexity of his opinions follows the spirit of the six diverging definitions of philosophy found in late antique teaching texts, which Blemmydes reported in his *Epitome of Logic*.[6] Theodore himself listed the six definitions and explained that they pertained to the subject matter and goals of philosophy, its lofty status, and the etymology of the Greek word *philosophia*: (1) "knowledge of beings as beings," (2) "knowledge of divine and human matters," (3) "assimilation of man to God to the extent possible," (4) "preparation for death," (5) "the art of arts and the science of sciences," (6) "love of wisdom."[7] At the simplest level, Theodore saw philosophy as advanced-level knowledge of practical and theoretical subjects taught by a teacher of philosophy.[8] Philosophy was closely linked with the concept of *paideia* ("education," "culture"). Because philosophy dealt with things universal rather than particular, it could be imagined as the summit or eye of universal *paideia*.[9] Philosophical education involved studying the ideas of ancient philosophers, primarily the "divine" Aristotle. For Theodore Laskaris, Aristotle was the most important philosopher and an almost canonical philosophical authority. The natural philosophy of Aristotle's *Physics* and *On Generation and Corruption* captivated him, as we clearly see in his *Moral Pieces*, *Natural Communion*, and *On the Elements* (the first book of *Explanation of the World*). Aristotle's theories in the *Nicomachean Ethics* influenced the treatise on friendship he addressed to George Mouzalon. The pseudo-Aristotelian *De Mundo* (Περὶ κόσμου) left an imprint on Theodore's *Explanation of the World* (Κοσμικὴ Δήλωσις). The title echoes *De Mundo* and the first three books focus on subjects treated in *De Mundo*: the elements (book 1), the circular motion of the heavens (book 2), and the divine harmony of a changeable and diverse material universe (book 3).[10] Theodore frequently referred to Plato, as well, and made much use of Platonic and Neoplatonic ideas and language. He derived, for example, the connection between music and philosophy from Plato.[11]

Notably, the invocation of ancient authorities sometimes mattered more than the advocacy of ancient schools of thought. He gives the impression of flaunting the names of philosophers of old in order to support and even legitimize ideas and interpretations that were distinctively his own. He attributed the "divine fire" of investigating concealed matters (arguably an allusion to the fire of the ordeals by red-hot iron) to Plato and wrote that Plato advocated the notion of God as a "substantial-true number," but the term derives from Plotinus and refers to a number in the intelligible realm.[12] In his oration in memory of Frederick II, Theodore attributed the notion of the philosopher king to Aristotle rather than Plato. He fixed the error in *Explanation of the World.*[13] The important point to bear in mind is that Theodore did not uncritically follow ancient philosophers, nor did he always agree with his teacher Blemmydes. He had no hesitation, for example, in blaming Aristotle for ignoring the existence of the "unexpected," a comment based on the traditional Byzantine critique of Aristotle's denial of divine providence.[14]

Philosophy was not only knowledge rooted in ancient learning. It branched out into Christian theology, although not without tensions that were well recognized in Byzantium. Theodore maintained a notional distinction – and tried to keep a delicate balance – between a lower philosophy dealing with human matters and a "higher and divine philosophy" devoted to holy doctrines, that is, theology. The distinction corresponded to the traditional conceptions of "outer" (secular) and "inner" (religious) learning.[15] The Christian understanding of philosophy as assimilation with God through contemplation and flight from the world (a view connected with the third of the six classic definitions of philosophy) was well known to him. In his view, philosophy belonged to the divine scheme of salvation and was a means for humans to regain virtue and cleanse the eyes of their souls, whose spiritual vision was blurred after the Fall.[16] The fully educated person was someone who possessed both secular, outer learning based on the ancients and knowledge of the scriptures and the church fathers. In a letter to Blemmydes he scoffed at the "pure philosophy" of Nikephoros, metropolitan of Ephesos, which was not muddied by "Aristotelian confusion." Elsewhere he described the religious virtues and knowledge of the bishop as "analytic science," a phrase referring to the angels in Pseudo-Dionysios' *Celestial Hierarchy.*[17]

Theodore Laskaris pondered the possibilities of philosophical inquiry into divine revelation without offering a coherent epistemic solution. His opinions present a curious combination of pioneering spirit and conservatism. The one thing that is certain is that the line between faith and reason was fuzzy for him and that he kept redrawing it at different stages of his life. Discursive context and audience mattered. In an oration on the Virgin he wrote that the Hellenes (that is, the pagans in the context of this religious work) had once "irreverently" discussed the philosophical principles of nature and would have failed to comprehend miracles.[18] Works addressed to Latin clergymen or provoked by encounters with them made him adopt, as we will see soon, a traditionalist standpoint influenced by negative, or apophatic, theology. However, his treatises on nature and theology continually reconfigured the boundary between faith and philosophy, usually in the name – and for the benefit – of philosophy and without ever questioning his own Christian identity. His views sometimes bordered on an apology for the ancient Hellenes, for whom he could hardly conceal his profound admiration. In a letter to his secretary Mesopotamites that discussed the benefits of philosophy, he remarked that the Hellenes, a race of great thinkers, would have glorified the Creator and ceased to venerate the movement of the heavens if they had had the opportunity.[19] Their misfortune was to be born before the Coming of Christ.

Theodore Laskaris saw philosophy as something more than an intellectual inquiry. Philosophy was a quality.[20] It was nearly synonymous with virtue.[21] It was a way of life.[22] It provided tangible benefits for society.[23] Everyone acting in a beneficial manner for the community as a whole was said to philosophize: for example, the general, but not the leatherworker.[24] Philosophy's concern with things universal made it more necessary and valuable for the community – and hence more in tune with nature – than particular knowledge and specific skills. The knowledge of particular subjects, however, was nothing else but an invention of philosophy.[25] Philosophy and *paideia* were embedded in the communion of nature as Theodore saw it.

The Power of Nature

Theodore Laskaris saw nature as the chief unifying force in the universe. His two main philosophical works, the *Natural Communion* and *Explanation of the World,* are, in large part, disquisitions on nature. Composed during his coemperorship, *Natural Communion* is the earlier and more widely circulated of the two treatises. More than ten manuscript copies of the treatise are known, and they include a deluxe parchment codex with gold-decorated charts and drawings (BnF, Suppl. gr. 460), doubtless an authorized edition produced in a Nicaean scriptorium under Theodore's auspices.[26] Later on, during the period of his sole rule, Theodore published – and partly completed and redacted – *Explanation of the World,* a treatise addressed as a work of instruction to George Mouzalon that survives in a single manuscript.[27]

A summary of the content of the two treatises demonstrates Theodore's evolving thinking about nature and his quest to set the parameters of secular vis-à-vis divine knowledge. The first book of the *Natural Communion* lays out key principles of unity and communion, and the methods of philosophical inquiry, especially the use of geometry. The second book introduces the first among many diagrams: a drawing of four concentric circles, each representing the four elements (Fig. 26). The mixing (*krasis*) of the elements based on their properties generates soulless objects and living creatures. The third book discusses the formation of the human being as a mixture of its seven constituent parts: the three parts of the human soul (the appetitive, the angry, and the reasoning) and the four humors (blood, phlegm, and yellow and black bile). There are ninety-two possible mixtures beyond the full and perfect one of all seven components. The specific mixtures of the qualities of the humors and the parts of the soul, along with the increased or decreased intensity of each component in the mixture, produce individual human qualities.[28] His method of arguing here (as well as in the sixth book) involves geometrical parallels illustrated in charts and diagrams. The fifth book is devoted to humankind and discusses *paideia*. *Paideia* was inherent in nature and resembled the "form" assumed by humankind.[29] The author's interest in political and social issues marks this part of the treatise. The sixth book of *Natural Communion* discusses the concept of *episteme* ("knowledge," "scientific knowledge") and features an excursus on geometry.

Explanation of the World consists of four books, which are, in fact, four separate treatises on different topics. The first book, *On the Elements*, examines the four elements and the mixing that produces bodily humors and the human being itself, but in contrast to the *Natural Communion* omits the agency of nature and the typology of the human being. The universal, nondestructible elements are contrasted with particular, perishable elements that undergo generation and decay. The author reveals his Christian perspective in the statement that only "people truly and openly thinking in Hellenic fashion" can venerate the elements and ignore that they are corruptible and God-created.[30] The second book, *On Heaven*, deals with the circular shape and movement of the celestial sphere. Theodore forcefully rejects the theory that the heavens were shaped in the form of a dome. The idea of a hemispherical or vaulted universe had been espoused by some early Christian authors and had been elaborated in the sixth-century *Christian Topography*, attributed to Kosmas Indikopleustes ("the Sailor to India"), a work with which Theodore was evidently familiar. Michael Glykas, a learned author of the twelfth century, had felt the need to refute the misinterpretation and Theodore's polemical stance suggests that the view still had its adherents in his time.[31] He followed Aristotle and other ancients, as well as Byzantine philosophers, in arguing for the circular shapes and movements of the sun, the moon, and the stars. After proposing alternative theories about the movement of the thoughts in the intellect (*nous*), whether circular, triangular, or quadrangular, he concludes that the intellect is spherical and that thoughts move in a circle. The comparison between the rotational movements of the celestial sphere and the soul belongs to the Platonic tradition.[32] Life itself is cyclical, for generation gives way to growth, change, passing away, and renewed generation. "Oh, wondrous turnaround!" – he exclaims – "Oh, wondrous circular harmony of nature. Corruption gives birth to generation!"[33] The cyclical features of the material universe, an idea derived from Aristotelian natural philosophy, fits poorly into the Christian concept of the linearity of life, death, and the Last Judgment. The tension is never resolved in Theodore's thought.

The *Representation of the World, or Life*, the third book of the *Explanation of the World*, focuses on humankind as part of the natural universe. The treatise opens with the statement that the author has already studied "the things in nature and dependent on nature" (an allusion to the *Natural Communion*) and now wished to present to Mouzalon confidential know-ledge – an investigation into "secret matters" – revealed by Philosophy to him in a vision.[34] His starting point is that God gives a cohesive condition of stability to the universe, whose diverse particulars are in a constant state of flux. Order (*taxis*) and disorder (*ataxia*) are two features of the universe that complement and generate each other. "Order and disorder," he writes, "are the best things in life. For once the former is dissolved it constitutes the latter and the latter once again forms the former."[35] The work is structured around the succession of the seasons – an allegory for a divinely ordained and orderly inconstancy – and is filled with observations of real events, practices, and people, although the names of individuals are regrettably left out. Theodore makes his own imperfect actions an example of the wondrous diversity of life. His personal inadequacies – treated in a self-ironical and polemical way – are the theme of the final, fourth book of the treatise, *On What is Unclear, or A Testimony that the Author is Ignorant of Philosophy*.

The *Natural Communion* presents nature as a powerful force for gener-ation and movement. Everything comes from or revolves around nature in a way similar to the water cycle of rainfall and vaporization. Nature is the beginning and the midpoint of the four elements and their mixtures. The view is illustrated in the above-mentioned diagram that places nature in the middle of concentric circles of the four elements (Fig. 26). Above earth, the lowest element, lie water and air followed by fire, which forms the outer circle. Nature signified by the Greek letter Φ occupies the center of the universe.[36] All elements and mixtures are drawn toward and moved by nature. Elements close to each other in the diagram have strong mutual affinity with each other and a propensity for mixing: for example, water with earth, but not with fire.[37] In addition to the elements and their mixtures, nature produces knowledge and skills.[38] Theodore attacked the view that the unnatural was also a generative force. Evil and harm occur only due to the failure of nature and because of accident, for the goal of nature is always the good and the necessary.[39] The natural (*physei*) was a principle of communion or association that drew together the animate and the inanimate world. The natural operated alongside inferior and alternative principles, namely, communion and association established by setting or convention (*thesei*) and by mixture or temperament (*krasei*). Participation in the natural communion is always good, beneficial, and necessary, but associations by convention and temperament can lead to the good, as well as evil.[40] Humans are said to form associations by temperament, nature, and *paideia*. A thief is linked with another thief by temperament without the mediation of *paideia*. Nature and *paideia* are close partners in causing the best forms of association.[41]

The ideas of the treatise represent an original synthesis based on traditional concepts and ideas. In his study of its sources, Richter pointed out that there was no such discussion of the communion of nature in the Greek philosophical tradition.[42] The perspective is a deistic one insofar as nature emerges as an autonomous force that operates without divine interference. The author alludes in passing to the Christian doctrine of Creation, noting that "nature assumed its power (*dynamis*) from the first and all-supreme beginning (*arche*)."[43] God's agency is restricted to this initial and all-important moment, after which nature acts independently on her own. Theodore's silence about the relationship between the creative power of nature and God contrasts with the chapter on nature in Blemmydes' *Epitome of Physics*. Here, Aristotle's definition of nature as "the principle of motion and rest" (*Physics* 253b8–9) is supplied with the qualification that "nature moves by being moved" by God. Blemmydes went on to contrast the supreme creative power of God to the secondary one of nature, which carried out its work of creation "without knowledge and reversion upon itself."[44] Interestingly, the same proposition "nature does not turn on itself" – a proposition influenced by Blemmydes and going back to Neoplatonic philosophical sources – was the topic of a brief essay by Theodore Laskaris, who once again avoided broaching the question of the relationship between nature and God as the first mover.[45] The *Natural Communion* creates the impression of a work of intellectual experimentation, an impression confirmed by the hesitations bordering on agnosticism aired at the end of the treatise: "When our flesh is dissolved, then we will see whether philosophical things surpass unreason. Now we have written as we knew; and if in the meantime they will appeal to the judgment of wise people, we will ask for their leniency."[46] Theodore's approach changed in *Explanation of the World*, which is marked by an overt religious perspective. Here, he marveled at God as the "creator of nature" and frequently referred to his quest for union with God through philosophy. Indeed, one of the goals of the treatise stated in the general preface was to praise the Lord as the maker of the universe.[47]

Empiricism and Humanism

Theodore's interest in natural philosophy went hand in hand with an empirical mode of thinking. What is meant by empiricism here is not scientific experimentation, but a turn toward personal observation and sensory experience as a basis for philosophical theory. The first book of *Explanation of the World* states that "the demonstration is most forceful when it abounds in observed and sensed things."[48] The second book draws attention to how round stones fall to the ground faster than those with angular shapes, which explains the choice of disc-throwers and justifies the circular projectiles used by catapults.[49] Water poured into a container and left for a sufficiently long time evaporates and gives way to earth (namely, deposits), a phenomenon that served to show the dissolution and change of the elements. The climate of Syria causes lethal disease to people unaccustomed to heat. The metallic vapors abundant in the area's atmosphere demonstrate the invisibility of the elements and their transformation occurring in the sky.[50] He explained the economic specialization of the population of Balkan and Anatolian cities and regions as the result of custom. "Nothing drove apart the fame of cities other than habit, the powerful instrument of virtue and vice." Philadelphia, thus, was a center of leatherworking, Thessaly of cloth production, Corinth of music, and Nicaea of philosophy.[51] Theodore's fascination in *Representation of the World, or Life* with the wondrous diversity of and orderly change in the universe was based on observations of life's fragility and the seasonality of agriculture, warfare, taxation, and diplomacy. Seasonality confirmed the importance of right timing. An action beneficial on one occasion was disastrous on another. The successful farmer, the general, and the ship captain knew how to select the right season and time.[52]

   The empirical strand in Theodore's thought drove him toward a philosophy of life and theories of rulership that contradicted received wisdom. Experience, as he wrote in *Representation of the World, or Life*, resulted in "the clarification of many arguments."[53] By virtue of his royal birth and upbringing, his sense of public duty and order (*taxis*) was firmly ingrained in his mind. "Order (*taxis*), audience (*parastasis*) and ceremony (*katasta-sis*)" – he wrote using the vocabulary of court ritual – were features of the earthly and the divine kingdom.[54] Order, civil concord, and personal attachments were key to the formation and functioning of human communities, ranging from the family to the whole world.[55] The emperor had the duty to devote his full care and attention to the public good. The very name emperor (*basileus*) meant "foundation of the people" (*basis laou*), an etymology found in Blemmydes' mirror of princes. His subjects were "the Christ-named people" and "the chosen people."[56] The three most fitting associations of kingship mentioned in the *Natural Communion* were philosophy, generalship, and medicine.[57] Nonetheless, Theodore came to rethink many of these ideas. His speech in memory of Frederick II Hohenstaufen (1251) shows him reassessing the social ideal of civil concord. Rulers faced a hard choice when administering the scale of justice. They could fulfill the wishes of each of their subjects, but then they ran the risk of the disintegration of the realm on account of the subjects' discordant interests. The alternative was for rulers to pass impartial judgments and preserve the polity, which meant to generate hatred toward themselves in some of the subjects. This hatred was, paradoxically, "a good hatred," because it was in the name of the common good.[58]

His accession as sole emperor in November 1254 enhanced his pessimistic, but also realistic, view of politics. *Representation of the World, or Life* (the third book of his *Explanation of the World*) draws heavily on the confrontations and controversies of his reign. In the same way as order and disorder were in a dialectical relationship, the one generating the other, a failed law led to its correction – namely, justice that was not necessarily based on the word of the law – and the purity of the law led to the failure of court proceedings.[59] One comes to think immediately of the judicial ordeals, which were not part of Roman and Byzantine law. Theodore cast doubt on the ideal of the philosopher-emperor favored by Plato, an ideal he himself had embraced in the speech in memory of Frederick II and in the encomium on his father. He wrote that no philosopher was an emperor, no emperor was a philosopher, and philosophers were rare who reigned over the passions of their souls.[60] This puzzling observation seems to be related to the spirit of remorse and compunction seen, for example, in the essay addressed to his own flesh. In any case, Theodore did not abandon his philosophical quest and his desire to communicate philosophical knowledge to Mouzalon, which was the goal of *Explanation of the World*. The lack of perfect order in the universe meant that he himself was unable to introduce right order among his officials (*hoi en telei*).[61] But it also meant that using oppressive methods in order to establish order was in the nature of things and justified by God. He stated toward the end of the treatise that "the emperor rules" through God and "through Him the master (*dynasteuon*) tyrannizes the officials (*hoi en telei*)." The master (*dynasteuon*) is quite possibly an allusion to Mouzalon, who fulfilled the function of *mesazon*, which Byzantine authors writing in high-register Greek designated with the more elevated word *paradynasteuon*. The treatise therefore makes Mouzalon responsible for the measures against titled officials and explains them as part of the God-ordained and wondrous diversity of the world.[62] The reflections mark a departure from the moralizing spirit of court advice literature in Byzantium, yet the break with tradition was half-hearted. The political sphere was ultimately connected with Christian morality and eschatology. In the same treatise Theodore speaks of the accountability of rulers on Judgment Day and describes the punishment that ancient tyrants, such as Echetus and Phalaris, suffered in hell.[63] In the vision of *Representation of the World, or Life* divine order would eventually triumph.

The philosophy of Theodore Laskaris was humanist insofar as it put the individual and the human community in the spotlight.[64] His humanism was one of action, for as coemperor and emperor Theodore supervised the creation of libraries, the foundation of schools, and other philanthropic acts. His humanism was also a theoretical one: he frequently repeated the old saying that the human being was a microcosm (*mikros kosmos*).[65] *Natural Communion* discusses the formation of distinct human types and the role of *paideia*. The author displays remarkable appreciation for the skills of humble craftsmen and farmers, which in his view were ultimately derived from philosophy. These markedly humanistic tendencies did not, however, lead Theodore to idealize human nature and the innate creative powers of humankind. He had a skeptical attitude toward the crowd. A perceptive observer of the crowd's reactions, he was split between suspicion of the "vulgar" masses and an awareness of his royal duty to protect and care for the "people."[66] His elevated social position and his lone mission as a philosopher meant that he stood apart from the common folk.[67] The speech in memory of Frederick II expresses a deep-seated pessimism about the thinking and behavior of the masses. Theodore bemoaned the way in which the general public failed to comprehend that rulers acted for the benefit of the people at the cost of personal hardship and easily forgot this fact.[68]

Theodore's view of human nature was often dark and Machiavellian. It is true that virtue and friendship were high ideals for him and that the treatise on friendship and politics could not have been written without the author believing in the ultimate triumph of friendship. His allegorical oration on friendship and envy has a notably happy ending. The dung beetle, a symbol of envy, nestles at the roots of the rose, a symbol of friendship, but when the sun, namely, God's grace, shines on the blooming rose, the hideous insect perishes.[69] And yet, Theodore promoted the ideal of friendship as a corrective to the defects of humanity. One such defect was the kinship-based social structure of the aristocracy. His treatise on friendship and politics addressed to Mouzalon offered a solution to this perceived problem. Another defect lay in the deep flaws of human nature resulting from the Fall of Adam and Eve. The sins of humankind grew, he writes, when Cain, the evil "second human being," committed the heinous act of fratricide against the virtuous Abel.[70] Erring human nature rushed "toward pleasure in the manner of an unbridled horse and a mule." Its mortality differed "in no way from grass, the foliage of plants, and the withering of a flower."[71] His observations of the vicious world of politics and factionalism around him made his opinions even bleaker. *Representation of the World, or Life* marks the culmination of his pessimistic musings on human nature.[72] We see Theodore wondering at the beastly impulses of mankind and voicing amazement at how great rulers surrounded themselves with flatterers and slanderers. No matter how powerful, rulers had no control over the minds of their subjects. "The human being is more secretive in his speech than speechless animals, saying some things even when he is concerned with something else."[73] His long list of hypocritical actions and reprehensible behaviors is that of an outraged (and somewhat resigned) eyewitness. Seemingly modest people, he wrote, were arrogant and dissimulated like foxes. Shameless women controlled the actions of dignified individuals. Plotters concealed premeditated actions. Murderers received praise, poor people considered themselves wealthy, and rich men moaned pitifully. The descriptions are concrete enough to suggest that Theodore had real individuals in mind, although their identity is concealed – Mouzalon was certainly able to understand the allusions. One of the murderers is almost certainly Theodore Philes and Michael Palaiologos was probably one of the dissimulating well-off individuals, for he is said to have flaunted his poverty as evidence of his generous disposition.[74]

The Occult

In spite of his empirical perspective and interest in natural philosophy, Theodore Laskaris was not a rationalist. Nor, for that matter, were other

Byzantine philosophers. His fascination with the occult mirrors that of his teacher Blemmydes, the author of an alchemical treatise on making gold, and follows in the footsteps of the eleventh-century polymath Michael Psellos, who viewed the occult sciences as an integral part of philosophy. For Laskaris, as for Psellos, the occult represented the "secrets of philosophy."[75] He considered the heritage of Greek philosophy to include the occult sciences. His *Second Orations against the Latins* mentions the oracles, auguries, and palmistry of Calchas; John Laurentius Lydus' *On Celestial Signs*; Pythagoras' magic and his "special art of occult philosophy"; the works of magician, astrologer, and prophet Apollonios of Tyana; and the writings of the fifth-century physiognomist Adamantios.[76]

Theodore justified occult practices as an old philosophical tradition – and felt the need to do this. His approving view of ordeals exemplifies this line of reasoning. Judicial ordeals by red-hot iron took place in the thirteenth century in both Nicaea and Epiros in court cases of high treason and adultery, usually with the consent of the defendant, in which evidence by reliable witnesses was difficult to procure.[77] Theodore himself tolerated the use of ordeals at the imperial tribunal during his reign and dramatically declared in an earlier letter (Ep. 38) his willingness to go through an ordeal when Theodore Philes accused him of an amorous liaison. Contemporary critics of the practice dismissed it as barbarous and illegal, for it was not used in Roman or Byzantine law.[78] Theodore's response to such criticism was to claim that the ordeals were based on arcane philosophical knowledge. He opened *Representation of the World, or Life* by comparing his investigation to what Plato had named a "divine fire" (*theion pyr*) that divulged concealed secrets. The "divine fire" alludes to the red-hot iron of ordeals known by contemporaries as "sacred fire" (*hagion pyr*), also believed to unveil the hidden truth.[79] Elsewhere, in his allegorical comparison between the rose and the dung beetle, Theodore again linked the ordeals with philosophical knowledge. Describing how God put the dung beetle (that is, envy) ensconced in the rose of friendship to the test by exposing it to the heat of the sun, he added that people knew "on the basis of outer learning" how to prove a distinction (*diakrisis*) through fire.[80]

The occult was clearly more acceptable as learned philosophical tradition rather than popular superstition. To be sure, Theodore gives the impression that he was influenced by common belief in magic and divination. He complained that the Bulgarians were bewitching his army in the summer of 1255 and gave credence to the accusations of witchcraft against Maria-Martha Palaiologina.[81] In one of his letters he referred matter-of-factly to prognoses based on palmistry, cloud movements, and what he enigmatically called *hodoskopia*.[82] According to the author of *Synopsis chronike*, who was close to the emperor, Theodore approved of the use of bibliomancy during the tied patriarchal election of 1254: he is reported to have preferred the practice to casting lots as a way of seeking God's judgment.[83] The same author testifies to a contemporary belief that the emperor was endowed with the gift of augury. When a partridge chased by a falcon flew into the imperial tent pitched in the vicinity of Pegai in the spring of 1256, he is said to have explained correctly to those present that the partridge was the sultan 'Izz al-Dīn who would flee from the pursuing Mongols symbolized by the falcon. In another version of the story, Michael Palaiologos is said to have witnessed the omen without being able to comprehend its meaning, in contrast to the prophetic and farseeing Theodore.[84]

Theodore's dabbling in the occult was not, however, without its qualifications and limitations. His letter addressed after November 1254 to the metropolitan of Adrianople, Germanos, immerses us in a spirited debate on the acceptability of the occult and the distinction between theory and practice.[85] Theodore declared that he had "studied the secrets of philosophy thoroughly" and that he would have been accused of ignorance if he had not done so. Astrology and zodiacal predictions, both of which he saw as part of philosophy, met with his approval.[86] However, he rejected magic and lore about spells and omens as inane stupidities and "unscientific sciences." This critical attitude to magic follows the legal prohibitions.[87] It is significant that Theodore readily enforced the law when he and his chief minister George Mouzalon suspected magic being practiced against him. The emperor did not hesitate to undertake punitive action if he saw the occult subverting his own power and the established order.

Mathematics, Theology, and Critique of Logic

In his natural philosophy and theology Theodore Laskaris developed methods of arguing inspired by the study of mathematics. The techniques were chiefly based on numerology, proportionality, and geometry. The approach is most prominently featured in the *Natural Communion* (books 1, 2, 3, 4, and 6), *Explanation of the World* (books 1 and 2), and *Christian Theology* (books 2, 3, and 5). The approach he took to expressing the mathematically inspired arguments varies widely. A matrix of combinations of numbers establishes the ninety-two human types in the *Natural Communion*. Geometrical charts illustrate and explain specific arguments

in the same treatise. The second book of his *Christian Theology* contains
drawings that illustrate the composite nature of the cube and the circle as
geometrical shapes, something the author contrasts to the oneness of
Being.[88] The third book of his *Christian Theology* shows the relationship
among the three persons of the Trinity in a drawing of three partly
overlapping circles, or "suns," containing three different words. The circles
framing the words overlap insofar as these words have a self-defined and
equivocal meaning. The area that they share in common is the One (the
divine monad).[89] The shape and parts of the circle not only serve as
supporting evidence, but also help to generate and construct arguments.
Nature lies in the middle of the four elements just as concentric circles
share the same center.[90] Every skill is associated with *paideia* just as all
radii of a circle connect at the center.[91]

The turn to mathematics drew heavily on the symbolism of numbers.
The Trinitarian work addressed to the chamberlain Constantine and the
secretary John Phaix (the fifth book of his *Christian Theology*) posits three
causal principles of being in the universe: a numerical cause; a sensory
cause related to living creatures; and an intellectual or philosophical cause.
The three causes corresponded to the Trinity.[92] The same treatise assigns
symbolic significance to numbers. The divine monad, the beginning of
everything, is the subject of the first book of his *Christian Theology*. Two
and three, the first even and odd numbers, are the beginning, respectively,
of matter and intellect. Five, the sum of two and three, symbolizes the five
senses. Ten is significant, because it combines an odd and an even number
(its factors are five and two).[93] Indeed, Theodore attributed allegorical
meaning to all numbers until ten. Inspired by the Pythagorean system of
the tetrad (*tetraktys*), the treatise *On the Elements* (the first book of
Explanation of the World) describes the human being as the number four,
mentioning specifically the four humors and the four cardinal virtues that
lead to the divine monad.[94] *On Heaven* (the second book of *Explanation of
the World*) presents the circular harmony of nature as the number six,
namely, the six movements in Aristotle's *Categories* (genesis, corruption,
growth, diminution, alternation, and change of place).[95] One of his letters
calls philosophy the number seven (*septas*), the number that follows the six
definitions of philosophy. The symbolism of the number seven is derived
etymologically from the verb "to revere" (*sebesthai*).[96]

What were the driving forces behind this mathematically inspired
approach? Undoubtedly, Theodore Laskaris was influenced by strands in
Neopythagorean and Platonic philosophy, strands that had already had an
impact on early Christian authors such as Irenaeus of Lyons and Clement

of Alexandria.[97] There was an upsurge of interest in mathematics in his time. His teacher Blemmydes introduced him to ancient philosophers who wrote on mathematics, such as Diophantus, Pythagoras, and Theon of Smyrna, the author of *Mathematics Useful for Reading Plato*. Akropolites continued his instruction in mathematics. Theodore claimed in his correspondence with him that his knowledge of mathematics exceeded that of physics, logic, and metaphysics.[98] Notably, the earliest Greek treatise on the use of Arabic numerals (the Indian calculus), which was based on the Western usage adopted by Leonardo of Pisa's *Liber abaci* (c. 1202), dates to the year 1252.[99]

There is another important framework, however, that can explain Theodore Laskaris' inclination to use geometrical and numerological arguments. This framework is his negative reaction to and critique of scholastic theology. A way of defining doctrine through the use of logic, and in particular Aristotelian syllogisms, and a technique of learning through disputations and dialectical reasoning, scholasticism had become the dominant method of philosophy and university education in Western Europe by the middle of the thirteenth century. As we have seen, Theodore lauded his father for avoiding syllogisms during the discussions at the Council of Nymphaion in 1250. The two orations against the Latins occasioned by the debates in Thessalonica in 1256 rail against the Latin misuse of theological syllogisms. Theodore attacked the unscriptural syllogistic premises, and in particular the unscriptural middle term in the premises, which was instrumental in constructing the conclusion yet was absent from the conclusion. Demonstration through a middle term, he noted, has its use in other sciences, but not in "theology that surpasses all science." He equated "theology," which means literally "the word of God," with the scriptures and, by extension, with the doctrines of the fathers of the church.[100] He demonstrated this literal approach of adherence to the holy writ in his Trinitarian work on the Procession of the Holy Spirit addressed to Nicholas of Croton, which consists of a long list of scriptural and patristic testimonies. Theodore also criticized scholasticism from another angle. In his two orations against the Latins, he argued that the polysemy of language diminished the power of syllogistic reasoning. Language was an imprecise tool due to the many possible meanings, both literal and metaphorical, of the same word. The semantics of the word "generation" (*gennesis*), for example, varied depending on whether it referred to an animal or a water fountain. "We sense a shiver," he remarked, "when we converse about God and assess His nature, lest we put forward an interpretation of the divine texts other than that dictated by the voice of our God and Lord."[101] Too many commentaries corrupted the holy scriptures. "If Paul interpreted the Gospel, you interpret Paul, someone else interprets you again, another person interprets him, and if yet another man interprets the latter, how unsteady is the Gospel, how pointless!"[102]

Beyond the two polemical orations against the Latins, it is notable that the books of his *Christian Theology* that discuss the Trinity (books 3 and 5) employ diagrammatic reasoning and numerology at the expense of scriptural exegesis. The third book of *Christian Theology* explains the Trinity in terms of the correlation between three partly interlocking circles. In his other works, too, Theodore Laskaris moved toward reasoning based on ratios and geometrical correlations. Even numbers are said to relate to odd ones as the human body relates to the soul; as the body relates to the soul, so do humans relate to angels; and as the existent relates to the nonexistent, so does God to the angels.[103] The ratio between kingship and priesthood, body and soul, matter and immateriality is said to be the same. As the whole soul runs through the whole body, so is God present everywhere in nature.[104] The relationship between the different parts of the circle and the four elements served to differentiate the natural from the conventional as principles of communion.[105] Theodore went so far as to experiment in the *Natural Communion* with a syllogism based on proportions.[106]

The vehement critique of the use of syllogistic reasoning in theology sets Theodore in direct opposition to his teacher Blemmydes. Even though Blemmydes did not consider logic to play an epistemic and heuristic role in theological reasoning, he argued that logic was helpful for the study of the holy scriptures and used syllogisms masterfully in disputes with the Latins in 1234 and 1250.[107] He reacted negatively to Theodore's approach in the *Christian Theology*. In a short didactic work *On Theology* addressed to him as the reigning emperor, Blemmydes remarked that his royal tutee "accurately" saw that it was "very audacious to make examinations on the holy scriptures" (a reference to Theodore's critique of the Latins), but proceeded to rebuke him for the even more audacious manner in which he made assertions "on his own initiative."[108] Thus, the disagreement between Nikephoros Blemmydes and Theodore Laskaris during the latter's four-year reign not only concerned army finances and justice at the imperial tribunal but also pertained to theology. Teacher and student drifted apart in their approaches. Blemmydes was displeased with Theodore's way of reasoning in *Christian Theology*, while Theodore chose not to follow his teacher's reconciliatory Trinitarian approach to the Latins in his most recent works on the *filioque*.

Theodore's flirtation with negative, or apophatic, theology is also comprehensible in light of his encounter with scholasticism and his pessimism about the scope of syllogistic logic. His treatise *On the Divine Names* (the fourth book of his *Christian Theology*), composed after November 1254, consists of a long string of appellations of God imbued with the mystical spirit of Pseudo-Dionysios the Areopagite.[109] Significantly, Theodore adopted an apophatic perspective when he acted as an apologist for the tradition and distinctiveness of Byzantine theology in his exchanges with Latins. His *First Oration against the Latins*, notable for its critique of theological syllogisms, comments on the inadequacy of philosophical language in theology and engages experimentally in geometrical reasoning. Theodore proposes that the Trinity could be either a figure (*schema*) or something not represented by a figure. In the former case, the Trinity could be imagined – and was represented in the manuscript – as a threefold figure consisting of six parts (Fig. 27). Three interlocking circles encompass an equilateral triangle that lies in the middle and is formed by the centers of the circles.[110] The unstated implication is that the persons of the Trinity are fully equal and equally balanced. The author then goes on to consider the absurd proposition that the Trinity could not be represented by a figure. In his view, this proposition meant that the Trinity was a straight line. The reasoning serves to underscore the importance of geometry to Theodore's philosophical and theological thinking. A line without a beginning, he muses, would be a blasphemy on account of the doctrine of the Creation. But a straight line originating from the divine monad, itself without a beginning, would undermine the status of the other two equal monads, for a line would make them secondary in terms of chronology and value. Theodore continues the argument by remarking that those who carry out debates about the Trinity ought to realize that its characteristics lie beyond human comprehension. Terms, such as "time," "placement," "figure," "color," "quality," "substance," "quantity," and "number" cannot explain the mystery of the Procession of the Holy Spirit. The geometrical drawing of the Trinity, thus, serves to drive home the point that the Godhead lies beyond philosophical terminology and semantics. In a similar spirit, his letter to Cardinal Richard Annibaldi notes that "the inability to experience is the beginning of speaking about God" (*legein peri Theou*). God is described as imperceptible through the senses and resembled a master dwelling in a sealed house, where his slaves could not see him. It was "close to impossible" to extrapolate the principles of theology from scientific knowledge (*episteme*). Nor could someone explain God's words and actions in a "Hellenic manner" (that is, through ancient philosophy), because this approach would be built on flawed foundations.[111] Theodore issued a similar warning in his *Second Orations against the Latins*, where he accused his anonymous Latin opponent of making "the unrelated related" – that is, philosophy and theology. "Philosophy lies in scientific questions," he wrote, "but theology lies in doctrine."[112]

But were philosophy and theology incompatible? His Trinitarian treatise addressed to John Phaix and the chamberlain Constantine (the fifth book of his *Christian Theology*), which discusses the divinity of numbers and numerical causality, openly admits on two occasions that his approach is to combine theology with philosophy. In the context of mathematics and numerology, therefore, Theodore viewed this convergence to be a possibility.[113] Elsewhere, in the fourth book of his *Explanation of the World*, he wrote that an individual who sought divine illumination and union with God was able to do so through mathematics. In his own words, mathematics was an approach to "divine theology."[114] These reflections explain his willingness to use reasoning based on numbers, geometrical diagrams, ratios, and simple analogies, for this way of reasoning provided an alternative to the inadequacy of syllogistic logic and language. Mathematics – and in particular, numerological symbolism, geometry, and geometrical visualization – made possible a theology that differed radically from the dominant approaches in the Latin West. Theodore Laskaris himself took an important step toward such a theology, but never had the opportunity to develop and systematize his ideas due to his early death.

Humor and Socratic Irony

A rather different side of Theodore's thought is seen in the way he mixed humor and philosophy. He explicitly linked humor and laughter with philosophy in the *Satire of the Tutor*, where he explained the function of jokes (*asteismata*): "It is through jokes that wise people weave thoughts full of philosophy which are addressed and communicated to the wise, for every wise person sometimes jokes."[115] Humor was seen as a feature of ancient philosophers. Aristotle had once laughed even more than Democritus, who was known in antiquity as the laughing philosopher.[116] Socratic irony had a special potential for philosophical expression in the heated and polemical exchange of ideas, in which Theodore Laskaris was involved. He presented Socrates as his model in the fourth and "most theological" book of *Explanation of the World* entitled *On What Is Unclear, or A Testimony that the Author is Ignorant of Philosophy*. The general preface of *Explanation of the World* explains the agenda of the fourth book as follows: "Socrates who knew more than everyone else said he knew nothing and surpassed everyone . . . I show in this discourse that I know no philosophy. For I am a philosopher, and I am not ashamed."[117] Composed in the last two years of his life, *On What Is Unclear* makes a dramatic confession of the author's ignorance of logic, mathematics, music, rhetoric, allegory, grammar, government, and military art. His utterances are ironic, for the self-portrait is consistently undermined by highly learned descriptions of these disciplines. The treatise is described as theological, because the Socratic paradox comes close to the notion of divine unknowability, and also perhaps because, as Theodore explains in this work, the knowledge of mathematics can lead one to divine illumination and union with God.[118] The conclusion of the treatise unveils its powerful irony by stating that the Divine Logos has endowed the God-crowned author and emperor with the power of reason (*logos*).[119]

How did Theodore arrive at the posture of ignorance near the end of his life? His letters demonstrate that he was continually aware of the ambiguity of humor. Humor served to entertain as well as to convey serious messages. The same verbal expression, he observed, could have humorous and unhumorous meaning on account of the polysemy of language and the difficulties of epistolary communication. Was Akropolites serious or was he joking, Theodore asked, when his letter too much resembled his previous one? "I do not know whether you are playful or you are serious," he wrote, "but whatever you have written, whatever you now write and whatever you would write, I will not consider nonsense, but rather the best principles of philosophy." In another letter to Akropolites he shared his anxiety that readers might misinterpret his serious words as jokes: "There is no response to people to whom I appear to be joking when I am serious, lest serious things appear vice versa to be like jokes."[120] Theodore was aware of the ambiguity of his own playful attitude. His apologetic letter to Nikephoros of Ephesos, which reacts to the accusation that he was not living a life of virtue, lays out a theory about virtue and plays on numerology. Theodore poses a rhetorical question at the end: "Are we playful in order to make jokes or in order to be serious?"[121]

The ambiguity of Socratic irony allowed for the inversion of criticism and fitted well into the culture of laughter and teasing at the court. The posture seems to have started as a caustic response to jibes directed at him during the years of his studies with George Akropolites. A letter to Akropolites in the 1240s shows that unnamed fellow students – "people fond of scoffing," he calls them – laughed at his inability to reason correctly.[122] Theodore struck back by himself engaging in ridicule. He played the game of pretended ignorance in order to expose the absurdity of his critics' opinions:

> If therefore we are considered ignorant, we who have learned everything by divine providence, we should not be harmed by anyone ... But I know one thing, namely, I am joked about. And I will respect this, given that according to Plato (man) is a plaything of God because of a mixture and blending (of the elements). However, I know also another game where I will rather be the fittest subject of jokes: not to live from now on in philosophy, in love of wisdom and truth, and briefly said, not to live in fear of God.[123]

A letter to the Phaix brothers written at a time when they attended school shows Theodore feigning ignorance and vice in a dramatized fashion. The all-seeing Intellect leads Theodore to the Academy of Athens, but he cannot enter, because he fails the requirement inscribed over the door: *Let No One Ignorant of Geometry Enter*. The comment is particularly self-ironic in light of Theodore's training in mathematics. His self-description is worth citing:

> I am reluctant to record the characteristics of my simplicity, but I am compelled by force to say what kind and how many shortcomings I have. For I am exceedingly beastly, unapproachable, and unsociable ... If I wish to practice any virtue, unreason precludes me. If I wish to live in humility and silence, I am raised by the impulses of the unruly horses, anger and desire, to many heights, and yet I should have been humble, because I had no knowledge of the philosophy.[124]

At the end of the letter the author wittily asks his correspondents for help: "Give me, the country bumpkin, your opinion. Reveal to me your decision. I will help. Do not be afraid. For I am also God's creature. Even if am not good in every regard, I am by character very much in control of myself." The letter is filled with comic ambiguities and inversions. Its self-irony is also irony directed at those who mocked a wise man for his unreason and lack of virtue. Motifs of self-remorse are approached with humor. The author leaves the impression that he genuinely relished the literary game of self-deprecation and self-ridicule. The Socratic treatise that concludes his *Explanation of the World* represents the culmination of the epistolary tendency toward polemical self-irony. In the last years of his life Theodore was faced with a growing choir of critics. His response was to fashion himself as another misunderstood Socrates, which in turn allowed him to display his immense knowledge and prove his opponents wrong. The audience of this work seems to have included Blemmydes, with whom Theodore had disagreements on political and theological matters, and his detractors generally in the last two years of his life.[125]

The philosophical thought of Theodore Laskaris was moving along several interlaced trajectories in the years leading up to his early death. He availed himself of the vocabulary and approaches of the Greek philosophical tradition in order to weave new syntheses. His sense of rivalry with the Latin world led to a strong opposition to intellectual currents in the West. His critique was a constructive one, for he struggled to find a distinctively different mode of philosophical and theological reasoning. Theodore Laskaris can be considered a precursor of the anti-logical movement in Byzantium during the fourteenth century, which was similarly anti-Latin in spirit.[126] The young Nicaean emperor had a creative and ever-exploratory mind. He was prepared to build upon and modify his ideas in the light of new experiences. It is unknown, unfortunately, which one of the multiple tendencies in his philosophy he would have chosen to develop had he lived longer. The unfinished story of his philosophy resembles that of his passionate advocacy of Hellenism.

10 | The Proponent of Hellenism

Theodore Laskaris was the leading proponent of Greek identity and self-consciousness in medieval Byzantium. He saw his own subjects as Hellenes, described the land over which he ruled as Hellas, and used the words "Hellene" and "Hellenic" three times more frequently than "Roman." No one in his time was so daring in reassessing the traditional meaning of "Hellene" in medieval Greek as "pagan." His Hellenism was intellectually sophisticated, assertive, and passionate. The extent of its vision is on par with that of Julian the Apostate in late antiquity, with whom the thirteenth-century emperor, certainly a devout Christian, has been compared.[1] This concluding chapter unravels the different strands of this key aspect of Theodore's thought and offers an interpretation of its genesis and function.

Scholars have traditionally – and with a good reason – viewed Hellenic patriotism and protonationalism as a tendency characteristic of the period of the Nicaean empire.[2] The question of the medieval origin of the modern Greek nation and the *longue durée* have loomed large. Hellenic patriotism in Nicaea, one historian has remarked, was an ideology "oriented toward a model set in the past" and foreshadowing "developments to which the future belonged."[3] Theodore Laskaris has been seen as the seminal figure in this upsurge of Hellenic patriotism. In 1970 Apostolos Vacalopoulos wrote in his *Origins of the Greek Nation*: "Given his faith in the destiny of the Greek nation, which was symbolized by a steadfast ambition both to reconquer Constantinople and to reunite all Greeks under the imperial scepter, he (Theodore II Laskaris) may be regarded as the true originator of the 'Great Idea' (*megale idea*)."[4] A recent and more nuanced view holds that "none of the foundations on which the Greek nation was (re)imagined in modern times was lacking in his (Theodore Laskaris') conception" and proceeds to characterize his Hellenism as "an expression of his Roman nationalism."[5] The biographical approach of this book allows us to delve more deeply into the issue and extricate ourselves from the need to follow a diachronic perspective oriented toward historical origins or future developments. Seen from the inside out, Theodore's Hellenism emerges as a construct based on interpretations of ethnicity, culture, memory, territoriality, and imagined geography. A number of questions inevitably arise as we approach this complex and curious mixture. What was the interrelationship of the constituent components? Were there patterns dependent on the typology and audience of specific texts and on the typology and audience of his discourse? Was Theodore's Hellenism static or evolving over time?

At the outset, it is helpful to frame Hellenism conceptually, by discussing what it was *not*, and historically, by setting it within its time-specific cultural milieu. Theodore's Hellenism was not a fully fledged ideology that guided his policies and supported contemporary structures of power, even though, as we will see, he moved toward political interpretations at the end of his life. His Hellenism was, rather, a matter of identity – one prominent identity that he preferred at times to express and at other times to suppress. His Hellenism was not nationalism in the widely accepted sense of this term defined by Ernest Gellner as "a political principle which holds that the political and the national unit should be congruent." Nationalism, be it Roman or Hellenic, is a rigid and slippery analytical concept because of its associations with the modern world after the eighteenth century.[6] To be sure, Byzantium, like other premodern polities, displays some of the features of nationalism in an incipient form. There were foundation myths, such as Constantine's *translatio imperii*, and a strong awareness of the collective self as "the Romans." Ethnicity provided one form of communal identity. The wide-ranging semantics of the word *genos* ("family", "people," "race") included that of a community bound by shared blood, and Byzantine authors sometimes referred to the *Romaioi* as a *genos* or *ethnos*. Blemmydes reports a political argument made in Nicaea, according to which people belonging to the same *genos* (the *homogeneis*) should be ruled by one emperor, an emperor of the *Romaioi*.[7] At the same time, ethnicity did not function as a principle of state-building, nor was the establishment of ethnic or national homogeneity ever a goal of the authorities, nor was there a practice of drawing state boundaries along imagined or real national ones.[8] With all the innovative tendencies of his thought, Theodore Laskaris did not depart from the traditional model of an imperial state and its characteristic ethnic hierarchies. Furthermore, for him as for other Byzantines of his time, the key terms of collective self-identification – "Roman" and "Hellene" – were hardly set in their meaning, but had fluid semantics that depended on what has been called a cognitive "mechanism of naming."[9] A recent analysis has demonstrated, for example, that Akropolites used the appellation "Roman" to refer to ethnic as well as political identity determined by allegiance.[10] Another analysis has demonstrated that Blemmydes, Akropolites, and Theodore Laskaris each understood the words "Roman" and "Hellene" differently, and assigned varying importance to Roman and Hellenic identity.[11] Authorship, audience, and genre could lead to one meaning taking prominence over another.

Hellenism did not uproot or supplant Theodore's sense of Romanness, which he shared with his contemporaries in Nicaea and which continued to mark the political self-identification of the three main Byzantine states after 1204. Theodore designated his realm, land, cities, and subjects as "Roman" and "Ausonian."[12] As we saw in Chapter 4, he searched for historical models of rulership in the Roman rather than the Greek past, with Alexander the Great being the sole exception. He sometimes used "Hellenic" and "Roman" as self-identifiers side by side, a juxtaposition that he did not deem worthy of comment or explication. In a letter to Mouzalon, he wrote that "the Hellenic tribe" (*phyle*) rejoiced at the subjection of "the great ruler of the Persians" (the fugitive Seljuk sultan) and a few lines below referred to *Romais*, that is, his Roman state and land. Elsewhere he remarked that the robust "Hellenic chest" of Vatatzes' brave soldiers, which the enemy never succeeded in breaking, helped the emperor to reconquer "the Roman cities."[13] One prominent discursive pattern in the use of the two terms is that Theodore Laskaris felt more at ease giving expression to Hellenic identity in private than in public contexts. In a letter to Mouzalon written in 1255 during his Bulgarian campaign he referred to the successes of the "Hellenic troops" (*Hellenika strateumata*), but in his newsletter addressed to his Anatolian subjects (1256) during the same campaign he boasted of the achievements of the "Roman troops" (*Romaika strateumata*).[14] That "Roman" replaced "Hellene" in the newsletter shows that the words were, for him at least, interchangeable as signifiers of collective identity and that he operated more boldly within the mental framework of Hellenism when he wrote letters to his childhood friend. The same cognitive and discursive pattern has been observed by Erich Trapp in vocabulary choices. Theodore was predisposed to choose vernacular and low-register words more often in personal communications with Mouzalon than in letters to other correspondents.[15]

The novelty of Theodore Laskaris' approach lies not in his cultural Hellenism, but in his promotion of the Hellenism of the political community. This thesis needs to be explained. The confluence of Roman political and Hellenic linguistic, and hence cultural, identity is nothing unusual in itself. The Byzantines – a name used since the sixteenth century as a conventional designation for the Romans inhabiting the medieval empire centered on Constantinople – called themselves *Romaioi*. Their hybrid civilization was a merger of Roman politics, Greek culture, and the Christian religion. The interrogation of what it meant for one to be culturally and linguistically Greek, but at the same time a Roman citizen, goes back to the expansion of the Roman republic in antiquity.[16] Foundation myths told in antiquity, and also in Byzantium, attributed to the Greeks and the Romans a shared history and convergent genealogy.[17] Christianization gave the Greek word *Hellene* highly pejorative connotations. The *Romaioi* of Byzantium thus avoided identifying themselves as Hellenes, even while they remained acutely aware of the Hellenism of their language and literary culture. The cultural and political milieu of the empire of Nicaea was particularly propitious for the emergence of new types of self-consciousness because of anxieties about collective identity provoked by triumph of the Latins in 1204. While cross-cultural interactions with the conquerors who settled in the eastern Mediterranean intensified, concerns about purity and the preservation of tradition grew. The phenomenon can be observed on the Latin as well as the Byzantine side – and is known from other historical periods of mass migration.[18] The massacre of the Armenians of the Troad after 1204 and the proselytization of the Jews during Vatatzes' reign show hardening boundaries of religion and ethnicity. Patriarch Germanos II preached against the dualist Bogomils in Asia Minor and made an inquiry into their beliefs and practices. Bogomils repudiating their heresy were required to obtain a written document as a proof of their return to the orthodox Christian faith.[19] Political and religious leaders felt the need to draw firmer boundaries of communal difference in a period when there were good reasons to question them.

Hellenic self-identification meant a sharper demarcation of identity, for Romanness was more inclusive, theoretically universalist, and shared with the Latins. It is not coincidental that efforts to achieve an ecclesiastical union between the Byzantines and the Latins tended to invoke the common Roman past of the two religious communities. In two discourses on the schism and the Procession of the Holy Spirit written in Epiros during his captivity (1257–59), Akropolites highlighted a shared Roman identity. He addressed his Latin interlocutors as "Romans from the old Rome" or "my Roman friends." Once upon a time the Italians and the *Graikoi* had been two separate peoples (*ethne*), but the foundation of the New Rome meant that they were henceforward called "Romans" because of the two "greatest cities sharing a common name." They became one people and shared everything: "magistracies, laws, literature, city councils, law courts, piety itself." It was the schism that regrettably broke up the Christian and Roman unity.[20] On the opposite side of the Mediterranean, the emperor Frederick II toyed with the idea of shared Roman legacy in a letter to Vatatzes that reminded him of their alliance. Generally, Frederick titled himself "emperor of the Romans" and preferred to address Vatatzes as "emperor of the Greeks,"[21] yet his epistle of May 1250, filled with anger against the papacy, called the subjects of the Nicaean emperor "Romans." It was from "the most orthodox Romans," Frederick wrote, that "the faith of the Christians spread until the limits of the world."[22]

By contrast, Byzantine authors after 1204 who adopted confrontational positions toward the Latins focused on Hellenic identity in trying to make a strong case regarding age-old cultural difference. In the view of these authors, Hellenism marked the ethnic, ethnoreligious, and even political identity of their community. At a basic level, Hellenism distinguished the indigenous Greek-speakers from the "other" Romans who came from the West. Blemmydes named the empire of Nicaea (and specifically Byzantine Anatolia) "this Hellas" when he described the arrival of the four friars in 1234, whom he called "Romans."[23] Patriarch Germanos described his flock as the *Graikoi* and the Byzantine polity as that of these same *Graikoi*. A historical digression in a letter sent in 1232 to the Roman cardinals narrates how "the empire of the *Graikoi*" had once assisted Rome – the "old" and "great" Rome – and the popes in the struggle against heresy.[24] It must be added that the political concept of Romanitas easily morphed into and absorbed the timid manifestations of political Hellenism. The "empire of the *Graikoi*" became "our Rome" of the *Graikoi* in another letter by Germanos, in which he appealed to the Latin patriarch of Constantinople to release the "Greek priests" (*Graikoi hiereis*) held in the city from prison. Here Germanos remembered how "our Rome" had once helped rid old Rome of heretics and invaders such as Vandals and Goths.[25] John Vatatzes, or more probably the anonymous secretary in the imperial chancery, referred to his subjects both as Hellenes and as Romans in a letter addressed in 1237 to Pope Gregory IX in response to the announcement of an imminent crusade. The epistle followed up on Gregory's statement that wisdom originated and reigned in "our Hellenic race." This "was truly said," Vatatzes replied, and noted sarcastically that no Hellenic wisdom was necessary to refute the pope's false arguments. He boldly requested that Gregory IX recognize his historical rights over Constantinople, inherited from his ancestors belonging to the Doukas and Komnenos families, "not to mention other rulers from Hellenic families." The Roman church, he reminded the pope, had willingly proclaimed all of them "emperors of the Romans."[26]

Theodore Laskaris understood Roman identity as mostly political in meaning and pertaining to statehood, while Hellenism was predominantly an ethnic and cultural category. The distinction emerges clearly from his letter occasioned by 'Izz al-Dīn's flight to his court in 1257, where he used side by side the expressions "Hellenic tribe" and "Roman state or land" (*Romais*). He described the Bulgarians, who were Byzantine subjects in the twelfth century, as having maintained a "Roman loyalty" (*Romaike eunoia*) not a Hellenic one.[27] His attitude to Roman identity was competitive. He called the Westerners "Latins" (*Latinoi*) or "Italians" (*Italoi*), in contrast to his teachers Blemmydes and Akropolites, who sometimes designated them as Romans.[28] Still, just like his contemporaries, Theodore Laskaris was well aware that Roman heritage was shared with the Latin West and readily accepted the common historical memory about the emperor Trajan invoked by a Roman cardinal.[29] The allure of Hellenism in his eyes was that it could be used to set sharp and defined boundaries with the "other": Hellenism was a discourse of both identity and alterity. He designated his subjects as the Hellenes when they fought or competed with foreign powers, no matter whether these were Seljuks ("the Persians"), Bulgarians or Latins. Letters written during his Balkan campaign of 1255–56 against the Bulgarians and addressed to George Mouzalon speak of "the defensive Hellenic spears," "the Hellenic armies," "the achievement of Hellenic bravery" and the raising of a "Hellenic statue" on the summit of the mountains near Melnik as a trophy of victory.[30]

His most powerful annunciation of Hellenism was expressed in the context of confrontations with the Latins. Victories in battle against them made him speak with pride about the achievements of the Hellenes, and so did disputations on philosophical questions with Berthold of Hohenburg.[31] The *Second Oration against the Latins* (the seventh book of his *Christian Theology*), composed during the debates in Thessalonica in the autumn of 1256 with the papal embassy led by Constantine of Orvieto, is a veritable manifesto of Hellenism. The audience of the work consisted of his own clergy and bishops, including the patriarch, and an anonymous Latin interlocutor.[32] He urged the assembly of his coreligionists to avoid compromises with the Latins and boosted their morale by invoking their proud Hellenism. The speech is built on well-crafted antitheses. The Hellenes inherited antique philosophy, the Latins did not. The Hellenes preserved theological doctrine, the Latins made erroneous innovations. The Hellenes won battles, the Latins were weak and humiliated, and their empire (*basileia*) lay in ruins – presumably, the Western empire after Frederick's death rather than the pseudo-empire in Constantinople.[33]

Theodore's elaborate conception of Hellenic identity rested on three pillars: intellectual culture; geographical space; and collective memory embodied in historical figures and in specific sites imbued with the living spirit of the past. Other components – such as language and blood descent – mattered, too. He summarized his views in the *Second Oration against the Latins*, by addressing the anonymous Latin interlocutor as follows:

> You should know that philosophy belongs to the Hellenes, and that the Hellenes inhabit since ancient times the middle of the climate zones, and that the scientists are from us, and that their sciences are ours, and that the air we breathe now is the air then, and that we speak the Hellenic language, and we descend from their blood.[34]

The Hellenes, both ancient and contemporary, had an inalienable historical right to philosophy, for they "invented every philosophy and knowledge, not to name the specific sciences." The speech makes a long list of Greek philosophers (Socrates, Plato, Aristotle, Pythagoras, Thales, Euclid, Theon of Smyrna, Ptolemy, Proclus, and Plotinus), rhetoricians (Demosthenes and Hermogenes), the medical author Galen, the poet Homer, and authors on prognostication and the occult. Aristotelian metaphysics was "the theology of the Hellenes."[35] The same work makes the point that statehood was indispensable for the cultivation of learning. The reestablishment of government in Nicaea after the fall of Constantinople restored to the Hellenes their noble habit of mind and thirst for knowledge. Nicaea was both a political and an educational capital, and Theodore declared himself a Nicaean and an Athenian, exclaiming: "Now the city of the Nicaeans outrivals that of the Athenians."[36]

Latin admiration for Greek philosophy was a cause of both pride and anxiety. Theodore's concerns were that the Latins might harm philosophy through misunderstanding and that philosophy might find a new home in the West. When he observed Berthold of Hohenburg and the scholars in his entourage, he commented on the difficulties the Latins have in comprehending the intricacies of Greek philosophical thought:

> What is done this way, and is still being done, has brought fame to the Ausones (that is, the Romans, Theodore's compatriots) and those who will carry their fame far and wide, unless the saying "some things are published, yet others are unpublished" is brought to fruition in some way.[37]

The proverbial saying "some things are published, yet others are unpublished" refers to the obscurity of Aristotle's philosophy. Aristotle is reputed to have responded to Alexander's rebuke that he made his lectures public by assuring him that the lectures were "both published and unpublished," because only a narrow circle of initiates were able to understand them.[38]

Theodore was aware of the difficulties of cultural translation and realized that the Latin absorption of Greek philosophy was not tantamount to correct understanding, even less usage. The *Second Oration against the Latins* critiques, as we have seen, the improper theological syllogisms of the Latins. Theodore teased the Italian interlocutor sarcastically: "Do you wish to philosophize about fantasy? Come on, say new things, innovate, have no fear … If this is your custom, do innovate. I will remain with Christ."[39] A different kind of preoccupation was that the Latins might outdo the Hellenes and deprive them of their competitive edge. A pre-1254 letter to Blemmydes, structured around Isocrates' maxim that the roots of education are bitter and the fruits are sweet, aired frustration with the contemporary generation of students – a frustration that (probably intentionally) mirrored the sentiments of his teacher. Easygoing and motivated only under pressure, the students took no care of the vineyard of philosophy. Theodore made a gloomy forecast: "On this basis I estimate that philosophy will depart from us (for she belongs to the Hellenes who now dishonour her as a foreigner) in order to attach itself to the barbarians and glorify them, and I estimate that absurdities as those of the barbarians will appear among her persecutors."[40]

Theodore's Hellenism drew heavily on historical memory. Alexander the Great was a seminal figure: the "ruler (*anax*)" and "emperor (*basileus*)" of the Hellenes, as well as the "fellow soldier and commander of the Macedonians."[41] He was a world conqueror, a paragon of friendship, and a philosopher king who was part of the pre-Roman history of the Hellenes. The mere mention of Alexander in the panegyric of his father (1250–52) inspired Theodore to boast about the fame of the "children of the Hellenes" who fought in the distant land of the "Germans and Italians" ruled by Frederick II.[42] He was well aware of the idea of four world empires based on Nebuchudnezzar's dream in the second chapter of Daniel and the role of Alexander in the third, penultimate empire.[43] Early Christian and Byzantine scriptural exegesis usually identified the four empires as the Assyrian or the Mede, the Persian, the Macedonian, and the Roman, the last and eternal empire, which was destined to endure until Christ's Second Coming. In the encomium on his father, he divorced the theory from its eschatology and interpreted it as a historical pattern of the rise and fall of empires. The four empires were those of the Medes, the Persians, Alexander's Hellenes, and the Romans. Interestingly, in the same work Theodore called the Mongols "Medes" and the Seljuk Turks "Persians," so his description suggested that the success of the Mongols over the Seljuk Turks in his time was an act of historical retribution.[44] The unstated implication was that the Hellenes could do the same. His scheme of the rise and fall of great powers was a process, in which one ethnic group (*ethnos*) came to dominate over another through tribute and taxation without assimilating the subjugated people. In the past, he wrote, "the Hellene ruled over the Persian." The Persian in turn had imposed taxation on the Mede, and so "one ethnic group (*ethnos*) ruled over another and carried out its decisions." The description is remarkably close to the Mongol imperial system of tributary arrangements. Switching from the past to the present, the author observed that the Bulgarians "now paid tribute to the Romans" – a result of Nicaea's expansion into the Balkans in the 1240s – and reminded his audience of the "Roman loyalty" of the Bulgarians in the past.[45] We see here a clear articulation of both the ethnic and the political character of Roman identity.

Cities and locations famous in ancient history and with standing architectural remains stirred Theodore's Hellenic pride. While passing through Philippi in 1255, he thought he was entering the land of Philip and Alexander, and he kept referring to Alexander throughout the Balkan campaign, exclaiming that "the land belonging once upon a time to Alexander is pillaged and scorned by a very few weak Bulgarians."[46] He even identified with the Macedonians, without offering any explication. His newsletter (1256), composed at the conclusion of the war with the Bulgarians at the camp on the Regina River, spoke of "us, the Macedonians."[47] A letter to George Akropolites (1253) gives a remarkable account of his visit to Pergamon, along with an entourage that included his secretary Kostomyres and his attendant Christopher. The famous antique city was almost completely deserted in the seventh century and revived in the twelfth as a military stronghold of the Neokastra theme. The "city" consisted of a hilltop fortress and residences below it in close proximity to the ancient ruins. The population of thirteenth-century Pergamon has been estimated at no more than 2,400, in contrast to the more than 34,000 residents of antiquity.[48] Theodore wrote about the town from the perspective of an enthusiastic classicist. He reported seeing an arched bridge or bridges, probably over the Selinus River, and recorded his impressions from "the great theater" flanked by two round towers – whether the "Red Hall" (a large monumental temple built in the Roman period) or the Hellenistic theater adjacent to the fortress. He observed a hospital, which he compared to Galen's house, and was evidently aware that Pergamon was the birthplace of the physician. The ancient monuments aroused feelings of pride. They were "full of Hellenic genius" and "representations of its wisdom," bearing witness to "the past fame and magnificence" of their builders. His admiration was tempered by a gnawing sense of decline – an angst similar to his complaints about the slack students

of his time. The ruined "works of the dead" in the lower part of the city
looked grander and more appealing than the contemporary "humble huts,"
which resembled mouseholes. "If the analogy of the inhabitants is the same,"
he mused, "alas, what misfortune is there for the living!" Theodore's pessimistic assessment was no imaginary conceit. The archaeological discovery
of mud-plastered, one-floor stone houses built of reused ancient material on
the slopes of the hill confirms his words (Fig. 28).[49]

Figure 28 Theodore Laskaris contrasted the humble thirteenth-century houses in
Pergamon with the grandeur of the ancient theater, arches, and temples. Isometric
reconstruction of the Byzantine houses in Pergamon by Klaus Rheidt

One of the great ancient sites that Theodore saw was "the celebrated city of Troy" – not the Homeric town, but what was believed in the Middle Ages to be Troy, namely, the impressive ruins of the Hellenistic city of Alexandria Troas, opposite the island of Tenedos. In a letter written not long after Elena's death, he speaks excitedly of an imminent visit to Troy:

> After leaving the "three-gated Thebe" (Atramyttion), we are arriving at the celebrated city of Troy to see the deeds wrought by men of heroic repute and remind ourselves of Homer's muse, unless this, too, brings sorrow and awakens the memory of the suffering that I lament.[50]

Unfortunately, the author does not mention the ruins he saw. An early fifteenth-century Spanish traveler reports walls with gateways, ancient palaces, remains extending over many miles, and the fortress of ancient Ilion lying on a steep hill.[51] Nor does Theodore elaborate on the site in light of foundation legends linking Constantinople with Troy that were propagated during the early Byzantine period – for example, the transferal of Troy's palladium from Rome to Constantinople and its placement under Constantine's column. We do not know how he would have responded to the belief of the Frankish knights of the Fourth Crusade that they were the avenging descendants of the ancient Trojans.[52]

Places rich in historical associations belonged both to the Hellenic and the Roman past. Theodore commented on a Roman *lieu de mémoire* in a letter to Cardinal Peter Capoccio. Responding to an anecdote about the justice of the emperor Trajan, a story that was part of an earlier letter by the cardinal, he remarked that "there are many of his most wonderful cities (that is, cities founded by Trajan) among us."[53] He was thinking of Traianoupolis in Thrace along the *via Egnatia* and probably the city of Nicaea itself, whose foundation was attributed to the emperor Trajan. The story seems to have originated from a misinterpretation of stone-carved Greek inscriptions embedded into the fortifications of the city that describe building activities under the emperor Hadrian (designated in Greek as *autokrator kaisar Traianos Hadrianos*). The Renaissance traveler Cyriac of Ancona was shown "the tower of Trajan" when he visited Ottoman Nicaea in the fifteenth century.[54]

Reflections on geography and space are the most fascinating aspect of Theodore's imagined Hellenism. He referred to an area called *Hellas* or *Hellenis* and associated the concept of *to hellenikon* – literally "Greekness" and referring to the Hellenic people – with a territory inhabited by the Hellenes. For Theodore, as for Blemmydes, Hellas included the original Anatolian lands of the empire of Nicaea. Addressing the metropolitan of

Sardis, Andronikos, who was on a diplomatic mission in Italy, Theodore asked: "When are you going to come from Europe to Hellas? When might you glance at Asia from the inside after passing through Thrace and crossing the Hellespont?"[55] In another letter, Theodore considered Hellas as encompassing the region of Thessalonica.[56] This interpretation, too, is attested in his circle. Akropolites described as "our Hellenic land" the Nicaean-held areas lying east of the state of Epiros and the Pindos Mountains.[57] In fact, Theodore's territorial understanding of Hellas was broader than the state over which he ruled. He revived the ancient Hellenocentric climate theory of Herodotus, Plato, and especially Aristotle in the *Politics*, and elaborated on it at great length in his *Second Oration Against the Latins*.[58] The speech opens by presenting the biblical story of Creation, which the author links with the emergence of climate zones and ethnicities. Different ethnicities emerged over time and cultivated their own arts and skills, whether cruder or more refined, depending on proximity to the temperate climate zone.[59] The Hellenes occupied the middle of the climate zones "at the midpoint between all extremities in the inhabited world," which meant that they had a perfectly balanced temperament and surpassed other peoples in their natural aptitude for knowledge. "The Hellenic people (*genos*)," he wrote, equating language and people, "surpass all languages (*glossai*) in terms of location, mixture of temperaments, and therefore good disposition and knowledge."[60] Closeness to the sea was a special feature of the land of the Hellenes. Seawater and salubrious coastal breezes nurtured healthy bodies and minds, as well as natural intelligence.[61] The Hellenes were said to reside in a large territory in the eastern Mediterranean corresponding to the core and diasporic areas inhabited by the Greeks since antiquity and bordered by seas: the Gulf of Sicily (as he calls it), the Adriatic Sea, the Aegean (the "Cretan Sea"), the Sea of Marmara, and the Black Sea. The way in which Theodore outlined the shapes of the landmasses follows the tradition of ancient geography, yet the specificity with which he described regions of the Balkans and Asia Minor, as well as the surrounding seas, suggests that he may have followed contemporary works of cartography. He mentioned specific cities, rivers, and gulfs, such as Naupaktos, Epidamnos (that is, Dyrrachion), Sebastoupolis (Sukhumi), the Don River, the Danube, the Sava River, the Halys (Kızılırmak) River, the Tigris, the Euphrates, and the Persian Gulf ("the Syrian Gulf").[62]

The Hellenes benefited in another way from the centrality of their geographical location between East and West. Thanks to patterns of sea travel, they attracted like a magnet skills and knowledge from all over the world.[63] The argument was illustrated and explained with a diagram in the form of a circle containing two inscribed diametrical lines crossing each other at a right angle (see Figs. 29–30). The center of the circle, the Greek letter α, is the land of the Hellenes (*Hellenis*). At one extremity of the world lies Britain, designated by the Greek letter ν. At the opposite end, marked as the letter ο, is Aornis ("the birdless land") in India. The ancient geographer Dionysios Periegetes had described Aornis as a majestic mountain in southern India located on a peninsula that projected into the sea.[64] The other diametrical line in the drawing connects Spain, marked as λ, and Egypt, marked as κ. The letter Γ stands for any art, craft, and expertise (*techne*). The Hellenes were able to draw upon all human skills that evolved after the Creation as these skills were exported from one edge of the inhabited world to another – whether from Spain to Egypt, Egypt to Spain, Britain to India, or India to Britain. This simple drawing of world travel and communications in the *Second Oration against the Latins* is not a fantasy. For one, it is a sign of broadening geographical horizons after the establishment of the Mongol empire in Eurasia. It also reflects contemporary patterns of Mediterranean sea voyages. Favorable coastal features and wind patterns made the northern shoreline of the Mediterranean Sea more suitable for navigation than the southern.[65] This is why ships bound from Spain to Egypt tended to sail along the coast of Sicily and through the Aegean Sea (part of *Hellenis*) rather than along the littoral of North Africa. According to Theodore Laskaris, this navigational pattern made the Hellenes the winners in a world of shared knowledge. In spite of his animosity to the Latins and his advocacy of rigid cultural boundaries, he came to attribute the wisdom of the Hellenes to cultural borrowing. Expertise flowed from West to East and East to West. Just as the Latins wished to adopt the wisdom of the Hellenes in his own times, so did the Hellenes, presumably in the distant past, gather knowledge from their neighbors and from people far distanced from them. Paradoxically, Theodore thus undermined his own static notion of an indigenous and age-old tradition.

The imagined geography of Hellas as the center of the world took on features of Constantinople, which was known as the eye and midpoint of the inhabited world.[66] Theodore's writings erode and implicitly question the traditional place of the imperial metropolis in Byzantine political and geographical imagination. In his encomium on Nicaea, he adopted literary motifs from the traditional rhetoric about Constantinople and called Nicaea "the queen of cities" that "surpasses truly all cities." He contrasted Nicaea's recent military successes to Constantinople's abysmal failure in 1204.[67] To be sure, Theodore did not entirely forget about Constantinople as "the queen of cities" and still viewed it as a symbol of the Byzantine polity, although he added the revealing remark that in his time Constantinople was "named after the parts," namely, the territorial states that emerged after 1204.[68] His lukewarm attitude to Constantinople contrasts sharply to his warm attachment to his "mother" Anatolia and his moving descriptions of the natural features of the Hellenic land.

The last three years of his life saw an evolutionary tendency in his thought toward a more intensified and sophisticated Hellenism. To this period date his letters written during the Bulgarian campaign (1255–56), his *Second Oration against the Latins* (1256), and the polemical epistle to Blemmydes (1257) defending the recruitment of patriotic Hellenes in the army. His speech against the Latins rallies his audience behind the cause of Hellenism and makes an overtly political point. The Hellenes are presented as having a resurgent state, a large diaspora along the eastern Mediterranean and the Black Sea, and an ancient and venerable culture. Why did he choose to voice these ideas in a speech addressed to clergymen assembled for negotiations with Latin ecclesiastics? For one thing, Hellenism stood for native tradition, and Theodore was making an appeal for adherence to religious tradition in the face of a temptation to make concessions. Compromises had already been made in the "chapters of recognition and petition" adopted by the Council of Nymphaion (1250). His teacher and leading advisor, Nikephoros Blemmydes, had begun to adopt a more conciliatory view on the *filioque*. The leader of the papal embassy, Constantine of Orvieto, had a mandate to extract further concessions, but, as we have seen, Theodore remained unyielding and raised his own counterdemands.[69]

But there were other, equally important causes for the politicization of Hellenism. In those years Theodore was struggling to find an ideology of unity to counterbalance fragmentation and centrifugal forces in the Byzantine world and to inspire and mobilize the population of his rapidly expanding state, which straddled Anatolia and the Balkans. In turning toward Hellenism, Theodore proved himself a leader of keen political intuition. The thirty or so bishops who attended the disputations with the Latins in Thessalonica must have included high clergymen from the state of Epiros, who came to celebrate the marriage of Theodore's daughter Maria to Michael of Epiros' son Nikephoros, a marriage blessed by the patriarch Arsenios. The pre-1204 Byzantine theme of Hellas included Thessaly, which lay at the time under the political control of Michael of Epiros. Hellenism, therefore, would have been appealing to Greek ecclesiastical leaders and lords in the Balkans. As a public orator, Theodore proved able to capture the pulse of his audience and formulate its aspirations. He judged correctly that alternatives to Hellenism were not viable at this historical moment. Constantinople was an occupied city and Constantinopolitan patriotism could not galvanize and inspire a generation born in exile. Romanness was contested by the Latins. Anatolian patriotism was unattractive to the population of the Balkans. Revealingly, Theodore praised Anatolia as "the holy land, my mother" in a text addressed to his subjects in Asia Minor.

As Hellenism rose in political importance, it understandably took on some of the characteristics of Romanness. Hellenism became imperial and irredentist. It is unknown in which direction Theodore would have developed his views if he lived long enough to witness and take credit for the reconquest of Constantinople. His Hellenism would probably have become more nuanced and conscious of its inner tensions and a complex relationship with Constantinople. As with his philosophical thought, so with his Hellenism, Theodore's untimely death deprives us from reading the final chapters of a book that was still in the making.

Epilogue

Theodore Laskaris is a historical figure who defies convention, one of stark contrasts and unfulfilled dreams. His intellectual accomplishments were extraordinary, yet they belonged to an unsuccessful leader, whose failure was not entirely of his own making because of his premature death. His passing on August 16, 1258, led to the collapse of the new configuration of the political elite and the undoing of his reforms, which were just beginning to take shape. It released bottled-up forces with an immediate destructive effect. Many of his right-hand men were assassinated or removed from power. His family was dispersed. The Laskaris dynasty was overthrown and his archenemy Michael Palaiologos seized power. The empire in exile itself disappeared from the pages of history less than three years later when, on July 25, 1261, Constantinople was restored as the capital. The eagerly anticipated and yet strikingly sudden recapture of the city consigned Nicaea to the margins of history – a strange interlude and an aberration in the centuries-long history of Byzantium.

The Mouzalon brothers fell victim to a bloody vendetta within days of Theodore's passing.[1] The regent, George, faced the implacable hostility of the aristocracy and was suspected of coveting the throne. He is alleged to have volunteered to resign, but was hypocritically dissuaded and took residence at the Sosandra monastery in order to prepare the memorial service at Theodore's tomb, a fateful event that different accounts report to have taken place on the third (August 18, 1258) or the ninth (August 24, 1258) day after the emperor's death.[2] The service was well attended. Present were the child-emperor John IV Laskaris, high clerics, officials and their spouses, as well as men recently demoted or punished by Theodore Laskaris. While the hymns were being performed, Latin mercenaries stationed outside the monastery mutinied. They bore a grudge against George Mouzalon for the delay in their payments and were further aggravated on account of a rumored threat to the rights of John IV Laskaris. When the child-emperor tried to calm the uproar, his hand gesture was misinterpreted as a sign of approval. The soldiers broke into the church, hunted down the three Mouzalon brothers who in desperation hid in the sanctuary, and slaughtered them mercilessly. One Latin warrior named

Karoulos (Charles) dissected the body of George Mouzalon into so many pieces that the remains had to be collected in a bag for his burial.[3] The murderous spree of the Latins had the silent approval of the crowd. The commander of the Latin mercenaries, Michael Palaiologos, who was present in the church, did nothing to stop the bloodshed. According to one account, he even prevented his niece Theodora, George Mouzalon's wife, from protesting lest she herself fall victim.[4] In the aftermath, members of the crowd are said to have assembled around Theodore's grave and rebuked the dead man for having surrounded himself with worthless individuals.[5] Karoulos himself continued to enjoy a place in Palaiologos' guard and proved his fidelity several years later, in 1265, when he forewarned him of a conspiracy.[6]

Palaiologos, the champion of the aristocracy, exploited the urgent need for a strong hand. In the West, the anti-Nicaean coalition of Michael of Epiros, Manfred, King of Sicily, and William II of Villehardouin, Prince of Achaia, was poised for an invasion. In the East, the pressure exerted by the Mongols on the divided sultanate of Rum intensified again after the fall of Baghdad in February 1258 and the establishment of the Ilkhanid empire in the Near East. Restless Turkmen of the Lykos valley who crossed the Seljuk-Nicaean frontier posed a threat that demanded immediate attention.[7] With his proven military record in Asia Minor and the Balkans, Palaiologos was the right man at the right time. A public assembly was convened in Magnesia consisting of people arranged by rank and ethnicity – *Romaioi*, Latins, and Cumans – and legitimated his selection as the regent and promotion from *megas konostaulos* to the rank of *megas doux*. When the patriarch Arsenios arrived from Nicaea to Magnesia he discovered a fait accompli that he endorsed in a signed document.[8]

Henceforward the rise of Palaiologos to power was meteoric. On about November 13 he was appointed despot. On January 1, 1259, in the palace in Nymphaion, he was proclaimed emperor, having committed himself under oath on penalty of excommunication to observe a power-sharing arrangement.[9] He swore to recognize the underage John Laskaris as his "senior" colleague and only successor. The child emperor was to enjoy precedence on ceremonial occasions, and the two coemperors declared that they would not conspire against one another. All imperial subjects took an oath with their hands on the gospel that they would honor the constitutional arrangement and, in the eventuality of either coemperor scheming against his colleague, would rebel and kill the culprit. The agreement turned out to be a ploy and was already being ignored at the coronation ceremony, which took place in the early months of 1259 in Nicaea. Palaiologos was crowned first and John

Laskaris was humiliated to wear a cap with pearls rather than a proper crown. In the second half of the year Arsenios resigned in protest from the patriarchate and withdrew to a monastic retreat in the region of Nikomedeia. Palaiologos' choice for his replacement – Nikephoros Pamphilos, the metropolitan bishop of Ephesos – was a vindication of a man with whom Theodore had strained relations.[10]

Palaiologos rapidly consolidated his power base. While still the regent, he designated his brother John as *megas domestikos* and dispatched him in early 1259 to the Balkans at the head of the Nicaean army against Michael of Epiros, elevating him later in the year to the ranks of *sebastokrator* and despot. Another brother, Constantine Palaiologos, was given the high honorary titles of Caesar (*kaisar*) and later *sebastokrator*.[11] Officials punished or dismissed by Theodore Laskaris regained prominence. The general Constantine Tornikes was restored to the title of *megas primmikerios* and was promoted to *sebastokrator* in the course of 1259. He gave his eldest daughter in marriage to John Palaiologos on the eve of the campaign in the Balkans.[12] Andronikos Tornikes, who was probably Constantine's brother, came to serve Michael Palaiologos as head minister (*mezason*).[13] The formerly disgraced general Alexios Strategopoulos became *megas domestikos* on Palaiologos' coronation and later in 1259 was elevated to *kaisar*.[14] In the same year, we find the blinded ex-governor of Thessalonica, Theodore Philes, serving as an ambassador to Michael of Epiros. The alliance between the Palaiologos and the Philes family was strengthened through the marriage of Theodore Philes' son Alexios to the emperor's niece Maria, a daughter of his sister Irene-Eulogia.[15] Companions and protégés of Theodore Laskaris disappear from the historical record. The *protovestiarites* Karyanites fled to the sultanate, but was ambushed and killed along the way by Turkmen.[16] Nothing more is heard of Theodore's chamberlain Constantine, his secretaries, the brothers Phaix, the generals George and Isaac Nestongos, and the "new men" Kalambakes, Xyleas, Ramatas, and Poulachas, whom the emperor had appointed to high military positions in Macedonia in the autumn of 1256. Some of Theodore's more opportunistic civil officials, however, rapidly switched their loyalty in the new political situation. Palaiologos promoted the treasurer and *logothetes ton agelon* Hagiotheodorites to the title of *logothetes ton oikeiakon* at his imperial coronation and welcomed the services of the *megas logothetes* George Akropolites, a man married to his relative Eudokia, once he was released from Epirote captivity in 1259.[17]

Military victories, crowned by Constantinople's reconquest, buttressed the argument that Palaiologos ruled by God's favor. In the spring or early summer of 1259, the Nicaean troops under the command of his brother John inflicted a crushing defeat on the plain of Pelagonia in Macedonia on the joint forces of Michael of Epiros, Manfred of Sicily, and the prince of Achaia, William II of Villehardouin.[18] William was captured, along with the 400 Latins dispatched by Manfred of Sicily. Palaiologos attacked the fortress of Pera (Galata) next to Constantinople in the spring of 1260, sending a message about his resolve to succeed where his predecessors had failed. In March 1261 he won the military assistance of the Genoese by granting them far-reaching commercial privileges in various ports in the Aegean and the Sea of Marmara, including Constantinople in the eventuality that it was restored as his capital.[19] A fortuitous accident led to the recapture of the city. In the summer, Palaiologos put the *kaisar* Alexios Strategopoulos in charge of a small force consisting of native soldiers and Cumans, and sent him on a relief and reconnaissance expedition in Thrace. Michael of Epiros had broken a recent agreement and the Bulgarian tsar Constantine Tikh was rumored to be preparing a punitive incursion at the instigation of his wife Irene, Theodore's eldest daughter, who resented the mistreatment of her younger brother John Laskaris. The local population outside the city walls known as "the volunteers" (*thelematarioi*) informed Strategopoulos that all thirty ships of the Venetian navy guarding Constantinople were away on campaign in the Black Sea. The *kaisar* saw a window of opportunity and ignored the emperor's instruction to avoid battle with the Latins. His proclivity for insubordination that had only recently incensed Theodore Laskaris and bordered on recklessness – the *kaisar* was captured twice by the Latins, in 1260 and the autumn 1261, but was speedily released on both occasions – worked to his advantage at this pivotal historical moment.[20]

During the night of July 25, 1261, a small group of armed men broke through the walls of Constantinople, probably by crawling through an abandoned aqueduct.[21] The Latin guards were killed and the blocked Gate of Pege was thrown open. The Nicaean soldiers under Strategopoulos' command poured into the city before the break of dawn. When Baldwin II learned about the presence of the enemy, he left the Blachernae Palace in panic and sailed along the Golden Horn for the Great Palace. The discovery of his abandoned crown and sword in the Blachernae instilled courage among the soldiers and their Constantinopolitan sympathizers. The Venetian fleet returned speedily from the Black Sea only to discover that the Latin neighborhoods along the Golden Horn had been set on fire. The Venetians rescued the distraught crowd fleeing from their burning houses, with Baldwin in their midst, and sailed away. The fugitive Latin emperor would never see Constantinople again. As an honorary guest of Charles of

Anjou, King of Sicily (r. 1266–82) and Naples (r. 1282–85), he long planned a victorious comeback to his native city, now capital of the restored empire of Michael Palaiologos, but he was to pass away in 1273 in Naples without ever taking his revenge. On August 15, the church feast of the Dormition of the Virgin, Palaiologos entered Constantinople through the Golden Gate in a public procession of penance and thanksgiving to the Mother of God. He brought his coup to a conclusion by removing Theodore's children from the palace. In the autumn, he arranged for the marriage of three of Theodore's daughters who were still single (Theodora, Eudokia, and an anonymous third) to foreign husbands. Theodora wed the Latin nobleman Matthew of Véligourt, Count of Velingosti and Damala in the Peloponnese. The latter passed away by 1263, and Theodora was then due to marry the Byzantine general John Makrenos, who had fallen into Latin captivity, but the remarriage never took place because of Palaiologos' disapproval.[22] Her subsequent fate is unknown. Eudokia wed William Peter (Guglielmo Pietro), the Count of Ventimiglia in Liguria and the fortress of Tende in the French Alps, and had an eventful life in the West, as we will soon see.[23] An unnamed daughter, whose existence is reported solely by Pachymeres, became the wife of Despot Jacob Svetoslav, a Russian nobleman who had migrated to the Balkans and who now became a contender for the Bulgarian crown from his base in Bdin (Vidin) on the Danube.[24]

John Laskaris, Theodore's only son, had the most unfortunate fate of all the royal siblings. Soon after the recapture of Constantinople, Michael Palaiologos placed him under arrest and ordered his blinding on Christmas Day 1261. Also incarcerated was Manuel Laskaris, the great uncle, general and trusted advisor of Theodore Laskaris.[25] Deprived of his sight, the dethroned child-emperor and last male descendant of the Nicaean royal line spent his life imprisoned in fortresses near Nikomedeia, first in Chele (Şile) and then in Dakibyze (Gebze), until his death in around 1305. His place was duly taken by Michael's son Andronikos Palaiologos, who was proclaimed coemperor in his early childhood after the recapture of Constantinople, and was anointed and crowned in 1272. Andronikos succeeded his father on the throne in 1282, which marked the establishment of the longest-reigning Byzantine dynasty, the Palaiologoi. The Laskaris family lost its political prominence, even though it is well attested until the final fall of Constantinople in 1453. Michael Palaiologos drove a wedge among the loyalties of its members in the same way he had done with the inner circle of Theodore Laskaris. The other elderly great uncle of the late emperor, Michael Laskaris, enjoyed Palaiologos' favor and supported political reconciliation. He even led an embassy to Hungary in 1271–72, which prepared the marriage of the coemperor Andronikos to Anna of Hungary, great-granddaughter of the elder Theodore Laskaris via his daughter Maria.[26] The more than sixty members of the Laskaris family counted in the prosopography of the Palaiologan period include middle-ranking holders of court titles, land-owners, governors of cities and fortresses, military officers, a writer, a composer, a physician, and a merchant, yet no Laskaris held a top court title or the position of high general – in contrast to representatives of other families, such as Palaiologos, Tarchaneiotes, and Kantakouzenos.[27]

The pro-Laskarid sentiments of the population of Anatolia were troub-ling for Palaiologos. There were rebellions whose goal was to topple the usurper in accordance with the oaths sworn before his imperial proclam-ation. In 1262, the villagers of Trikokkia and Zygos in Bithynia took up arms and proclaimed as their leader a man who claimed to be the unjustly treated John Laskaris. In 1273, another pseudo-John Laskaris appeared, this time in the West. He sought the support of Charles of Anjou, the king of Naples, who was planning a crusading expedition against Constantin-ople. As late as 1305 John Drimys, a priest from the Balkans, rebelled and attracted a large following by presenting himself as the legitimate emperor John Laskaris.[28] The period of the empire in exile was remembered by many Byzantine Anatolians as a time of peace and prosperity before a new wave of Turkish invasions in the late thirteenth and early fourteenth centuries led to the chaotic collapse of the once stable land frontier. Two of the Nicaean emperors were venerated as saints. The cult of St. John Vatatzes, known as St. John the Merciful, was centered on Magnesia. His relics were moved from the Sosandra monastery to the city before its conquest in 1313 by Saruhan Bey and were believed to continue to perform miracles after its fall to the Turks.[29] The relics of the unjustly dethroned child emperor, St. John Laskaris, were kept in the fourteenth century in the monastery of St. Demetrios of the Palaiologoi in Constantinople, a sym-bolic act of political reconciliation.[30]

The downfall of the Laskaris dynasty was not the only ironic twist of history after Theodore's death. His concern with establishing a legacy contrasts with the persistently bad press that he received in the works of historians, both medieval and modern. The unforgiving negative assess-ment by his teachers Nikephoros Blemmydes and George Akropolites stemmed from the fact that they wrote their narratives of the past in the years after the recapture of Constantinople in 1261. At that time, they faced the stark choice of throwing their support behind the new regime or falling out of grace. Blemmydes had the added preoccupation of securing the future of his monastic foundation of Christ Who Is at Emathia near Ephesos and felt the need to dispel doubts about his loyalty to the new emperor after one of his monks and the governor of the Thrakesion theme accused him at court of subversive remarks.[31] In his autobiography he glosses over his proximity to Theodore. He claims that he "dreaded his youth, his quick temper and his stubbornness" and highlights his heated confrontations with the young emperor.[32] The *megas logothetes* George Akropolites served his new master faithfully as a high imperial minister and diplomat, and was heavily involved in arranging the union with the papacy concluded in Lyons (1274). In his *History* he mentions Theodore Laskaris only a few times before 1254 and portrays all of his political protégés, apart from the author himself, in a highly negative way. The lengthy description of his beating in the army camp on the Regina River in the summer of 1256 served to portray Theodore as an irascible and unstable man unfit to rule, in contrast to Michael Palaiologos, the hero of his account.

The negative opinions of Akropolites were not shared by other Byzantine historians, yet they came to cast a long shadow. Akropolites' silences and censures were reversed by the author of *Synopsis chronike*, a clergyman close to the late emperor. His additions to and revisions of Akropolites' account, which he otherwise closely followed, portrayed the emperor in a glowing light. According to his laudatory assessment of his reign, contemporaries admired Theodore Laskaris for his philosophical and military accomplishments, his dealings with foreign powers, and his generosity. The author of this chronicle chose to focus on the emperor's support for learning and the establishment of public libraries, which he compared to Ptolemy's legendary library in Alexandria.[33] The politically motivated urge to voice disapproval of the Nicaean emperor waned over time. The fourteenth-century historians Ephraim of Ainos (d. between 1323 and 1332) and Nikephoros Gregoras (d. between 1358 and 1361) avoided any criticism of Theodore Laskaris. Ephraim added an encomiastic description of the ruler and Gregoras praised the succession arrangements of the Nicaean emperors in contrast to those of the Palaiologoi.[34]

The Nicaea-born historian George Pachymeres (d. in or after 1309) also painted a mostly positive portrait of Theodore Laskaris in stark contrast to his criticisms of Michael and Andronikos Palaiologos.[35] His account of Theodore's last moments was modeled on the Passion of Christ: the emperor passed away on Friday and his death was accompanied by an eclipse of the sun.[36] The emperor is described as a patron of learning, a philosopher, and a talented author, and is praised for his quick-wittedness, military prowess, generosity, and especially for recruiting officials according to merit rather than nobility of blood and kinship by marriage with the imperial family. The historian mused that "this policy was, upon close scrutiny, the deed of a ruler who fosters virtue and incites his subjects toward good repute."[37] Theodore's heavy-handedness and his approval of trials by ordeal were attributed to the effects of his debilitating disease toward the end of his life. "Everyone was a suspect to the suffering man, if anyone brought an accusation about acts of magic."[38] But Pachymeres' most influential description was his explanation of Theodore's gifted mind as a medical phenomenon. His account of the epileptic disease that led to the death of Theodore Laskaris draws heavily on medical and philosophical literature. The cause of illness is reported to have been excessive heat of the heart, which led to his exceptional intelligence and talent.[39]

The accounts of Akropolites and Pachymeres saw their first printed editions in the seventeenth century and came to influence modern historians.[40] Akropolites' critique and Pachymeres' presentation of Theodore Laskaris as a gifted epileptic gave Edward Gibbon the basis for his devastating verdict on the young emperor in the sixth volume of his *History of the Decline and Fall of the Roman Empire* (London, 1788). It is unlikely that Gibbon read any of the works of Theodore Laskaris. "A strong shade of degeneracy," Gibbon wrote, "is visible between John Vataces and his son Theodore; between the founder who sustained the weight, and the heir who enjoyed the splendour, of the Imperial crown ... His (Theodore's) virtues were sullied by a choleric and suspicious temper: the first of these may be ascribed to the ignorance of control; and the second might naturally arise from a dark and imperfect view of the corruption of mankind." Gibbon elaborated on the effects of Theodore Laskaris' fatal illness. "The cruelty of the emperor was exasperated by the pangs of sickness, the approach of a premature end, and the suspicion of poison and magic. The lives and fortunes, the eyes and limbs, of his kinsmen and nobles, were sacrificed to each sally of passion; and before he died, the son of Vataces might deserve from the people, or at least from the court, the appellation of tyrant."[41] Gibbon's negative judgment did not go unchallenged. In 1894, in an article discussing Theodore as a philosopher and literary figure, the German scholar Johannes Dräseke objected to it, pointing to the extenuating circumstance of the emperor's epilepsy.[42] This interpretation comes straight from the pages of Pachymeres. So does Krumbacher's fascination with the psychology of Theodore Laskaris, whom he did not hesitate to call "a type of degenerate" in his *History of Byzantine Literature* published three years later. The account by William Miller in the *Cambridge Medieval History* (1923) represents a summation of what by then had become the traditional assessment, which is made even harsher due to stereotypes about the unoriginality of Byzantine authors.

> But as a writer he (Theodore Laskaris) was too academically educated to be original; his ideas are overwhelmed in a jungle of rhetoric; and his style, on which he prided himself and eagerly sought the judgment of the critics, strikes us, even in his private letters, as frigid and jejune. His correspondence, to which we naturally look for interesting sidelights on his temperament and times, abounds in commonplaces, but, with the exception of the letters written after his accession, is singularly barren of historical facts. Upon his character his studies had made no real imprint; like Frederick the Great, he affected philosophy as a Crown Prince, only to discard it as mere theory when he was brought face to face with the realities of government. Feeble in health and fond of solitude, he had abnormally developed one side of his nature. He was, in a word, a mass of nerves, an "interesting case" for a modern mental specialist. His short reign not only falsified the maxim of Plato that all would be well if kings were philosophers and philosophers kings, but afforded one more instance of the truism that the intellectual type of monarch is not the most successful, even for a nation which, in its darkest hours, by the waters of Nicaea or in the Turkish captivity, has never ceased to cherish the love of learning.[43]

Every single point in this destructive description is contestable. The reported lack of a "real imprint" of learning on Theodore's character – the character of a self-reflective and accomplished philosopher – could not be further from the truth. The call for a mental specialist to perform an examination comes straight from Gibbon and Krumbacher, thus harking back to Pachymeres' learned account of the effects of disease on the emperor. The truism that "the intellectual type of monarch is not the most successful" fails to take into consideration that Theodore Laskaris did not live long enough to see his reforms through and reap the benefits of his achievements. It also ignores the fresh ways in which he approached received tradition and cultivated a fiery political rhetoric of Hellenism.

The efforts of Theodore Laskaris to "gain an icon of remembrance" among the future generations and secure "the clearing" of his name through the dissemination of his writings met with a limited success. A flurry of manuscript production accompanied the preparation of editions of his works in his lifetime under his auspices. There are thirteenth-century codices of the *Natural Communion* (BnF, Suppl. gr. 460, Vat. gr. 1938), the *Sacred Orations* (Ambr. gr. C 308 inf.), the collection of ten secular works (BnF, Suppl. gr. 472), and the *Christian Theology* (Vat. gr. 1113).[44] Yet his works were never as widely copied and read as their author intended. Interest in them declined over time. Some have survived in one single codex. A miscellany copied after 1261 in Constantinople by a well-connected teacher of rhetoric – Codex Vindobonensis Phil. gr. 321 – is the sole extant manuscript of his *Explanation of the World*, letters dating to the period of his rule, devotional texts, and six essays.[45] The epistolary collection prepared by Akropolites survives in one fourteenth-century manuscript copied alongside the letters of Synesius of Cyrene. The manuscript circulated among Constantinopolitan literati in the 1320s and is kept today in the Laurentian Library in Florence (Laur. Plut. 39, 65).[46] A codex of his ten secular orations copied in Florence in 1486 (BnF, Cod. gr. 3048) by Michael Souliardos, a Greek from Nauplion, attests to a modest interest in the figure of the Byzantine author and emperor during the Renaissance.[47] Only a few of Theodore's works held the interest of later generations. His hymn of supplication to the Virgin, known as the Great Supplicatory Kanon, entered the liturgical cycle of the church and is still regularly performed during Marian feasts. Congregations of orthodox churches and connoisseurs of Byzantine music can hear today the moving words of the emperor imploring the Virgin at the end of his life to restore his health, dispel his gloom, and overcome his enemies. His orations for the Feast of the Akathistos and St. Tryphon were put to liturgical use in Byzantine churches during the fourteenth century, as manuscripts in which they were copied indicate.[48] The treatise *Natural Communion* was his most disseminated secular work and was copied in more than ten manuscripts produced before and after 1453. A Latin translation by Claude Aubery, a physician and professor of philosophy in Lausanne, appeared in print in 1571.[49]

A totally unintended legacy of Theodore Laskaris in the West was the introduction of the surname "Lascaris" among the European nobility through the marriage of his daughter Eudokia.[50] Her husband William Peter, Count of Ventimiglia and Tende, was in the service of Genoa in the eastern Mediterranean around 1261, when he fell into Byzantine captivity. Michael Palaiologos considered him a suitable match for Eudokia, granted her a sizable dowry of 20,000 *hyperpyra*, and requested from the authorities of Genoa to give the newly married couple a safe conduct to William Peter's native country.[51] Eudokia and her husband had six children. In 1278 or thereabouts she relocated to the kingdom of Aragon. There she met another famous lady from the Nicaean court, Constanza-Anna of Hohenstaufen, Theodore's stepmother, who had similarly been sent away to the West in 1261 by Michael Palaiologos. After the death of her brother Manfred at the Battle of Benevento (1266), Anna moved eventually to the court of her niece Constance, Manfred's only daughter, who was the wife of King Peter III of Aragon (r. 1276–85) and mother of Alfonso III (r. 1285–91) and James II (r. 1291–1327).[52] When Eudokia first arrived in Spain, her cortege traveled from Catalonia to Aragon through the village of Montblanc, where her horse cart, carrying an icon of the Virgin, is said to have become stuck on the road. Eudokia felt that a miracle had occurred and commemorated it by founding in Montblanc the convent of Santa Maria de la Serra, which is still in existence today.[53] In 1281 the widowed Eudokia married her second husband, Arnold Roger, the count of Pallars, who passed away in 1288. Eudokia herself died in 1309 in Saragossa, where she was buried in the convent of St. Dominic. Her daughter Vatatza (Vataça), born from her first marriage with William Peter, was the wife of a Portuguese nobleman and a lady-in-waiting of the saintly Elizabeth of Aragon, Queen of Portugal. Vatatza devoted herself to works of charity in Santiago do Cacém and Coimbra, passing away in 1336. Her sculpted tomb, an artistic masterpiece featuring double-headed eagles that symbolize her Byzantine pedigree, can be found today in the old cathedral in Coimbra.[54]

The counts of Ventimiglia and Tende, starting with Eudokia's eldest son Giovanni Lascaris, adopted the family name of the Byzantine royal dynasty throughout the late Middle Ages and well into the modern period. The surname "Laskaris" came to carry more prestige outside rather than within the frontiers of Byzantium. Arab historians of the late Middle Ages referred to any Byzantine emperor, including Michael Palaiologos, as "al-Ashkari."[55] In the West, the name Laskaris has been perpetuated in sumptuous mansions in France and Italy owned by the Lascaris de Vintimille. The Palais Lascaris in Nice, built for the family in the seventeenth century, was in their possession until the French Revolution. It is a museum today, housing a splendid collection of musical instruments. The Palazzo Lascaris in Turin, also constructed in the seventeenth century, received its name because the family owned it briefly in the early nineteenth century. The building is the seat of the regional government of Piedmont in Italy.

The literary and philosophical output of Theodore Laskaris is his most powerful legacy, regardless of its mixed reception over the centuries, and it still provides us today with the best way to understand this complex historical character. His intellectual accomplishments are many and diverse. We see a man with a creative and liberated mind, an active participant in medieval philosophical debates in Byzantium and in the

West. We see an intellectual rebel against the established system that brought his family to power. His theories of social solidarity based on clientelism ("friendship") rather than kinship set him against the dominant mode of elite formation in his time, of which he was a product, both social and biological. His writings on Hellenism make him one of the most interesting historical figures in the politics of identity in the Middle Ages and over the many centuries of Hellenic tradition. Theodore Laskaris should not be idealized as a human being. He was a complex person – not black and white, but with multiple shades of gray, just as in real life. Lack of realism and blind trust in individuals sometimes clouded his judgment and cost him dearly. He overestimated his ability to transform the aristocratic elite around him and underestimated its powers of resistance. In a way, he and his dynasty fell victims to his ideas and ambitions. For all his idealization of friendship and belief in the triumph of virtue, he had a dark side to his character. He readily resorted to violence, although he was not alone in this in the precarious and brutal world of court politics.

Even though Theodore Laskaris often appears to us to have been a man ahead of his times, he belonged firmly to the era in which he lived. His perspective was that of the generation of Byzantines born in exile after 1204, too late to have witnessed the fall of Constantinople and too early to see its recapture. Theodore responded to the call of history that this generation should assume two very different roles: tenaciously holding on to old, endangered traditions while entering uncharted territories of thought and action. His fervent Anatolian patriotism and his emotional distancing from Constantinople reveal a strikingly new mental outlook. Equally striking is his conscious and persistent desire to display and declare that he was a member of a young and restless generation. He lost no opportunity to underscore that he was different from his elder contemporaries. Nor did he conceal his fondness for innovation, even though the "innovation" was sometimes for the sake of defending tradition (for example, his attitude to Latin theology). His sensibilities and his philosophical thought present idiosyncratic features, yet these features are grounded in the historically concrete context. His novel positions on communal identity, for example, were a sign – one among many – of the depth and extent of the consequences of the Fourth Crusade for a leader who, paradoxically, never himself experienced this watershed event.

The life of Theodore Laskaris was marked by dramatic polarities. He was torn between the active and contemplative life. His royal birth loaded him with confidence and boldness, yet he was crushed by sincere Christian contrition, a painful awareness of sin, and an anxiety about the salvation of his soul. He would have been a worthy character for an ancient Greek tragedy. A man prone to forming strong attachments, he was destined to lose and alienate those dearest to him. A reforming emperor who wished to strengthen royal authority in the face of an entrenched aristocracy, he saw mounting opposition in the final year of his life and lost out to his principal political rival, who abolished his reforms, punished and banished his children, and reaped the reward of the hard-won accomplishments of the emperors in exile. His teachers chose to distance themselves from him. The polity in which he was born and lived soon ceased to exist. His ideas became irrelevant in the restored empire on the Bosporus. With the establishment of the Palaiologos family on the throne, the twelfth-century methods of governance by family privilege triumphed once again. Theodore's militant and romanticized form of Hellenism was no longer the order of the day. With the recapture of Constantinople, the city of New Rome resumed its pulling force in state-building and imperial imagination. Theodore's *Second Oration against the Latins* was forgotten and consigned to the dusty tomes of the collection in which its author had included it shortly before his death.

Theodore Laskaris did not change history and his story was largely a dead end. One of the main lessons to draw has to do precisely with the way his life and work came to an abrupt conclusion. A series of hypothetical "what-if" questions arise, which in turn raise unsettling questions about the making and logic of dominant historical narratives. Would Theodore Laskaris have been able to crush the power of his aristocratic opponents had he lived longer? Would he have modified his policies had he succeeded in retaking Constantinople? Would he have presided over the recapture of Constantinople so soon, given that he had discharged and disgraced the fortunate general who accomplished its reconquest, Alexios Stratego-poulos? And what would have been the consequences for the history of the Byzantine and the eastern Mediterranean world if Theodore had not died prematurely and if the Laskaris dynasty remained in power? None of these counterfactual questions can, of course, be given an answer. Historians prefer, rightly, not to ask them, lest they damage the foundations and credibility of their craft. After all, history is about the past as it happened, not about the past as it could have happened. Yet the unique life and legacy of Theodore Laskaris have this special quality about them, that they inspire us to imagine alternative histories. His story and its aftermath make us ponder the complexity of events, the role of contingency, and the way in which dominant narratives have come to be constructed, creating in the process the illusion of teleology and inevitability. This illusion is all the more powerful in studying the premodern past, because the temptation to focus on historical processes and impersonal motive forces is stronger on account of the limitations of the surviving evidence. That history did not happen differently does not mean, however, that it could not have happened differently. We view the past with hindsight, but this privileged position does not always work to our advantage. It can impoverish our perspective and leads us to lose sight of the broad horizon of multiple and alternative paths to the future that once lay open. These paths were very much alive in the dreaming minds of individuals who felt and thought, lived and died, just as we do today.

Notes

Introduction

1 Ep. 44.119–20 (p. 59).

2 Or. Fr., 86.6–7.

3 Sat., 165.255–57. See also Or. Fr., 94.204–09 (the ruler's trophies prevent oblivion); Ad Georg. Mouz., 137.421–24 (the ruler and his friends are compared to a statue).

4 On his official name, see Ep. 143.1–5 (p. 202), 205.44 (p. 256). See also the inscription accompanying his manuscript portrait and his representation on his seal as sole emperor (Figs. 1, 2, and 17c). On the shorter version of his name used in his lifetime, see Akrop. II, 8.19.

5 Alberic of Trois-Fountaines (Scheffer-Boichorst 1874:906.35–36) calls the elder Theodore Laskaris *imperator Nicee.* In vol. 6, Chapter 61 of his *Decline and Fall of the Roman Empire* (1788), Edward Gibbon spoke of the "emperors of Nice." See also the term *Nicanus imperator* in the portrait of Theodore Laskaris in the edition of the *History* of Nikephoros Gregoras by Hieronymus Wolf published in Basel in 1562 (Fig. 3).

6 καινότατον: Or. Fr., 88.66; Apol., 118.187, 118.197; KD, I, 112.4; Ad Georg. Mouz., 137.435 (καινοπρεπέστερον); Ep. 282.87.

7 Ep. 39.22–24 (p. 50). In the *Satire* he mocked his tutor's old age and blamed his parents' old age for muddying their minds when appointing him. See Sat., 161.166–67, 161.181.

8 Warren 1982:15. See also the observations of Fleming 2009.

9 Kaegi 2003:317.

10 Hinterberger 1999. On Michael Psellos, see Papaioannou 2013. See also the volume edited by Pizzone 2014.

11 The autobiographic, or autographic, texts of Theodore Laskaris, especially his personal letters, essays, the *Satire* and the *Moral Pieces*, differ in their subjectivity from literary autography as studied by Spearing 2012 on the basis of the I-voice in medieval fictional narratives. I follow the definition of autography given by Abbott 1988 (612–13) as "nonnarrative self-writing" distinguished from narrative autobiography.

12 The value of Byzantine letters as sources on daily life has been recognized by Mullett 1981:81–82.

13 See Laiou 1996 on the insights historians can gain into the mechanisms of governance from the letters of Patriarch Gregory of Cyprus (1283–89).

14 See Appendix 2.

15 Ep. 172 (p. 225): the letter to George Mouzalon announces a composition that Mouzalon was expected to read on his return. Ep. 187 (p. 236): a letter of dedication of the *Representation of the World, or Life,* to George Mouzalon. Ep. 209.30–38 (p. 261): a composition is sent to Mouzalon. Ep. 29 (pp. 38–39): the letter addressed to Blemmydes seems to refer to a work written by Theodore. Blemmydes read Theodore's encomium on his father, John Vatatzes (see Agapitos 2007:1–6). Ep. 51.69–93 (pp. 74–75): the letter to George Akropolites accompanies a work by Theodore, possibly his encomium on Nicaea. See Appendix 1, 334. Ep. 56, 66, 68 (pp. 84–85, 94–95, 96): works on mathematics and philosophy are sent to Akropolites. Ep. 141.50–56 (p. 200): the letter to the metropolitan bishop of Kyzikos, Kleidas, accompanies an oration in praise of the Virgin. On the secretary John Phaix and the *koubouklarios* Constantine as addressees of the Trinitarian work opening the collection *Sacred Orations,* see Appendix 1, 326, n. 10.

16 Ep. 136 (p. 192) addressed to Neilos, the abbot of the monastery *tou Stylou.* In Ep. 140 (p. 197), we learn that Theodore has read a hymn composed by Demetrios Iatropoulos, the *prokathemenos* of Philadelphia. On Blemmydes' works addressed to Theodore, see Blem., Ep. 13 (p. 303); Stavrou 2007–13 I: 275–353; Stavrou 2007–13 II:155–211.

17 On the main features of Byzantine epistolography as a genre, see, in general, Karlsson 1959; Littlewood 1976; Mullett 1981. See also Hatlie 1996a.

18 On Theodore's epistolary editions and the chronology of the letters, see Appendix 2.

19 See the revealing analysis of Demetrios Kydones' letters by Hatlie (1996b).

20 On Ep. 142.17 (p. 202), see Appendix 2, 376. For another example of de-concretization (Ep. 10), see Appendix 3, 387, n. 28. On "de-concretization" as a phenomenon in Byzantine epistolary collections, see Karlsson 1959:14–17; Hatlie 1996b:86–87 (an example of a pre-edited and an edited letter of Demetrios Kydones). The details of an unspecified grant to Blemmydes were probably removed from the preamble and summary of the grant once the texts were included in the Laurentian collection. See Ep. 25 (pp. 34–35).

21 The usual eschatocol of a *prostagma* is the so-called *menologem* consisting of the month and indiction of its issuance. See Dölger and Karayannopulos 1968:109–12. In 1272, the junior coemperor Andronikos II was given the right to issue ordinances, whose ending was to be his official signature rather than a *menologem.* See Pach. II, 415.3–6; Greg. I, 109.20.23 (the latter uses the word *prostagma*). According to Dölger-Wirth, *Regesten,* 1995, the coemperor was authorized in 1272 to issue and sign chrysobulls. Neither a signature nor a *menologem* is found in Theodore's ordinances included into the Laurentian epistolary collection.

22 Ep. 107 (pp. 146–48) addressed to Nikephoros of Ephesos (Dölger-Wirth, *Regesten,* 1823), 116 (pp. 162–63) addressed to Phokas of Philadelphia (Dölger-Wirth, *Regesten,* 1823a). Franz Dölger (Dölger-Wirth, *Regesten,*

V–VI) thought that the two ordinances were issued by Theodore's chancery as a coemperor, but under his dictation, as evidenced by their philosophical language.

23 Ep. 205.43–45 (p. 256). See Appendix 2, 373. The letter has his signature but omits the date (an incomplete eschatocol). It features the characteristic literary ending ("my strong bond indissoluble") of many of Theodore's epistolary communications to George Mouzalon. See 289–90, n. 22.

24 Ep. 143.1–5 (p. 202). According to the terminology of Byzantine diplomatics, the letter has a protocol consisting of *inscriptio, intitulatio,* and *salutatio.* See Appendix 2, 376.

25 The diplomatic records published between 1852 and 1861 by Jean-Louis-Alphonse Huillard-Bréholles fill six volumes. They include the official register kept for 1239–40.

26 Ep. 27.30, 30.20–21 (pp. 37, 40). See also Ep. 41.15–17 (p. 53).

27 Ep. 168.6–8, 171.3 (pp. 223, 224).

28 On hunting trophies, see 265, n. 42; on gifts of food, Ep. 52.38–40, 70.24–27, 177 (pp. 77, 97–98, 228–29); on exchange of manuscripts (works of Gregory of Nazianzus), Ep. 172.12–14 (p. 225); on exchange of compositions, see above nn. 15–16.

29 Ep. 199.32–33 (p. 245) contains, for example, the following enigmatic words: "the whelp tears the lamb and the fox tears the pure dove."

30 Sat., 155.41–42; Ep. 52.1–2 (p. 75); KD, III, 22.19. For the origin of this idea, see 263, n. 16.

31 *Tragophylon*: Ep. 77.32–33, 77.42, 80.38–44 (pp. 104, 108). I have adopted the hypothetical translation of the neologism in LBJ, 8 (2017), 1794. The *kriophoros* ("ram-bearer") in Ep. 171.5–6 (p. 224), called *aigophoros* (also meaning "ram-bearer") in Ep. 173.46 (p. 227), seems to have been Christopher, a man from Theodore's entourage with a distinctive hunch (see 282, n. 26) who is mentioned in Ep. 171. The person called *strongylophilosophogrammatographos* in Ep. 128.2–3 (p. 179) cannot be identified.

32 Nicol 1996:139.

33 For the influential description of the letter as an "icon of the soul," see Demetrios, *On Style,* 227, in Roberts 1902:174. The author adds: "In every other form of composition it is possible to discern the writer's character, but in none so clearly as in the epistolary." See Littlewood 1976:216–219; Mullett 1981:80–81.

34 Ep. 58.4–5 (p. 86).

35 Karlsson 1959:21–23; Mullett 1981:79, 1988:9–10.

36 Hörandner 2012:106.

37 Friends as alter ego: Ep. 75.2–3 (p. 102); friends as soul mates: Ep. 206.16–19 (p. 257), 214.45–46 (p. 266); friends share everything together: Tartaglia, Op. rhet., 7.131–133; Ep. 62.10–11 (p. 91), 173.1–3 (p. 225).

38 Ep. 36.61–64 (p. 46).

39 Ep. 132.14–23 (p. 187).

40 See Aphthonios' guidelines in Rabe 1926:27–31 (*psogos* of Philip). Cf. Baldwin 1982.

41 Mor. P., XII, 268.510–11. A free spirit, he notes, was characteristic of the philosopher. See Apol., 112.51–59, 114.96–101.

42 Pach. I, 59.14–16: οὐ μᾶλλον ἐκ μαθήσεως ἢ φύσεως τὴν περὶ τὸ γράφειν δύναμιν ἔχων, ὡς καὶ πολλὰ ἐπιρρύδην ἐκτιθέναι, εἰ μόνον ὁρμήσειεν. The word ἐπιρρύδην is a hapax.

43 Satirical letters and his *Satire of the Tutor* abound in unusual words, which the author seems to have chosen for an added comic effect.

44 Papageorgiu 1902:29.

45 Ep. 180.1–6 (pp. 230–31) dating to 1253 and addressed to George Mouzalon; Ep. 70.1–7 (p. 97) addressed to Akropolites before November 1254 mentions the objections of physicians.

46 Ep. 27.18–20 (p. 37).

47 Essay 6 in **V**, ff. 67v–68r. See Agapitos and Angelov 2018. The phrase in question is ὄμματι τηλεσκόπῳ: Aristophanes, *Clouds*, 290; Blem., *Imperial Statue*, 48, Chapter 18. On the date of the sixth essay, see Appendix 1, 346.

48 Imperial newsletters (*epanagnostika*) and speeches on the emperor's behalf (*selentia*) were written by literati close to the court, such as Michael Psellos and Niketas Choniates. See Psellos in Littlewood 1985:nos. 1, 2, 3, 5; Choniates, *Orationes*, nos. 2, 13, 17. The composition of letters by professional *dictatores*, as in the high and late Middle Ages in the West (Constable 1975:32–44), does not appear to have been an important feature of letter writing in Byzantium.

49 For a survey of the collections, the time of their preparation and the chronology of composition of the works, see Appendix 1. On the date of *Satire of the Tutor* and Ep. 1, see Appendix 1, 331–33; Appendix 2, 356–57.

50 On this collection which can be reconstructed hypothetically, see the analysis of the Laskaris dossier in **V** by Agapitos and Angelov 2018; Appendix 1, 326–27.

51 Rashed 2000.

52 On BnF, Par. Suppl. gr. 472, see Astruc 1965:400–02; Rashed 2000:298–99. On the deluxe edition that was probably the archetype manuscript of **A**, the thirteenth-century codex of the *Sacred Orations*, see Angelov 2011–12:246–51.

53 See the editorial preface to Manuel's *Dialogue with the Empress-Mother on Marriage* by Angelou (1991:13–20) on BnF, Cod. gr. 3041, one of the working copies of his writings.

54 For the term "hagiographical autobiography," see Munitiz 1992. See also the analyses by Munitiz 1988:1–42; Angold 1998:246–51; Hinterberger 1999:361–66.

55 On the life and career of Akropolites, see Macrides 2007:11–12, 22–26.

56 *Synopsis chronike*, 514.6–13, 530.17–18 (where the author suddenly switches to the first person plural when describing the movements of the army led by Theodore), 534.16–21, 535.5–536.12, esp. 536.9–12. On the open question of authorship of this work, see Macrides 2007:65–69; Zafeiris 2011.

57 On the figure of Gregory of Mytilene, see Akrop. I, §74 (p. 153.12–20); *Synopsis chronike*, 534.7–15; Pach. II, 347.26–349.4. On Pachymeres' life, see Lampakes 2004:19–38.

58 On the way *Kaiserkritik* influenced the presentation of the Nicaean emperors by Pachymeres and Gregoras, see Angelov 2007:253–85.

59 Published by Ferrari della Spade 1913. The formularies are found in Cod. Vaticanus gr. 867, copied in 1259. Nikos Oikonomides (1964:162) has shown that one of the officials in the formulary on the allocation of a *pronoia* grant, the *stratopedarches* of a theme, is attested solely in the empire of Nicaea.

60 MM, IV, 220–21 (Dölger-Wirth, *Regesten*, 1839a); MM, IV, 247–48 (Dölger-Wirth, *Regesten*, 1839b).

61 Krumbacher 1897:478. On Krumbacher's intellectual biography, see most recently Agapitos 2015.

62 Heisenberg 1900:211. In 1927, the Russian historian Maria Andreeva echoed this view and dubbed Theodore Laskaris "one among the most interesting rulers and scholars of the thirteenth century." See Andreeva 1927:99.

63 Krumbacher 1897:478.

64 Pach. I, 53.14–21. See Epilogue, pp. 223–25.

65 On Theodore's supposed chronic epilepsy, see Appendix 3.

66 See the classic biographies of Frederick II by Kantorowicz 1927, 1931; Van Cleve 1972; Abulafia 1988.

67 On the alliance, see Chapter 5, pp. 88–90. On learning at Frederick's court, see Van Cleve 1972:299–318.

68 See the critical review by Festa 1909.

69 Hellenism: Vacalopoulos 1970:36–43; Angelov 2005:299–305; Kaldellis 2007:272–79. On political thought: Svoronos 1951:138–9; Angelov 2007:204–52.

1 Byzantium in Exile

1 In the absence of any demographic data, I have adopted a conservative number for the population of Constantinople and have followed the estimate of Magdalino (2002:535) for the twelfth century, which comes close to that of Jacoby (1961) for the sixth based on a solid methodology. Modern estimates have varied widely.

2 Madden 1991/92.

3 *Devastatio Constantinopolitana* in Andrea 2000:221, 337; Robert of Clari in Lauer 1924:§98 (p. 96); trans. McNeal 1936:117.

4 Choniates, *Historia*, 647–55, esp. 649.84–650.9. On Choniates' description of the destroyed statues, see Cutler 1968.

5 See Choniates, *Historia*, 576, and John III Vatatzes' letter of 1237 to Pope Gregory IX (Pieralli 2006:124.56–63).

6 Choniates, *Historia*, 558–59. The identification is discussed by Jenkins 1947.

7 See the partition documents, including Boniface's cession of his rights to Crete, in Tafel and Thomas, I, 1856:444–88, 512–15. For a critical edition of the *Partitio*, see Carile 1965. I have adopted here the interpretation of Oikonomides (1976a:23–27) that the *Partitio* was drafted on the basis of annual tax registers. On its likely date, see Oikonomides 1976a:8–11. On the way Venice acquired its rights over Crete, see Saint-Guillain 2010.

8 Magdalino 2005a.

9 Ep. 82.5 (p. 109); Sat., 160.161 (βασιλὶς τῶν πόλεων), 164.233; Tartaglia, Op. rhet., 101.136; Chr. Th., VII, 142.157.

10 Sat., 164.242.

11 Chr. Th., VII, 142.157–59. On the date of this work, his *Second Oration against the Latins*, see Appendix 1, 342.

12 Simpson (2013:11–23) gives a useful summary of the known events of his life.

13 Choniates, *Historia*, 592.

14 On Michael Komnenos Doukas, who never assumed the title of despot, see Polemis 1968:91–92.

15 For an account of its history, see Nicol 1957; Nicol 1984; Bredenkamp 1996.

16 According to Vasiliev (1936:32), the title was assumed by Alexios, the first ruler of Trebizond. Vasiliev is followed by Karpov (2007:109), who argues for April 1204 as the time of the imperial coronation. The imperial title of Manuel I Grand Komnenos (r. 1238–63) is solidly attested. For a critical discussion of the issue, see Prinzing 1992:171–76. On the fourteenth-century title, see Oikonomides 1978.

17 On Nicaea as a crossroads of communications, see Ramsay 1890:240–42.

18 Enc. Nic., 80.303–04. See also his pride at being the grandson of an emperor in Ep. 80.40–41 (p. 108).

19 Akrop. I, §18 (p. 31.19–22), says that at the time of his death in November 1221, Theodore Laskaris was "more than forty-five years old but less than fifty" (hence born between 1171 and 1176). Greg. I, 13.14–16, notes that at the time of his proclamation (1205) he was "around thirty years old," from which we can infer a birthdate of c. 1175.

20 The names of the brothers are conveniently listed by Savvides 1987:144, n. 6. Ilias Giarenis (2008:33) considered that the "most illustrious" (*panendoxotatos*) Michael Laskaris, who served as a witness to a document preserved in the Vatopedi archives, lived around 1180 and would therefore have been a representative of the Laskaris family during the twelfth century. This document, however, has been redated to 1239/40. See Vatopedi, I, no. 14, 131, 134.

21 Pachymeres (Pach. I, 91.21–23, 107.13) calls the two brothers "the Tzaman-touroi from among the Laskaris family." In addition, the same historian (Pach. I, 153.20–21) refers exclusively to Manuel Laskaris as Tzamantouros. For the suggestion that the father of the elder Theodore had a second wife from the Tzamantouros family, see Saint-Guillain 2006:220, n. 250. By contrast, Macrides (2007:284, n. 3) has proposed that Tzamantouros was a nickname derived from the town of Tzamandos in Cappadocia and alluding to the exile of Manuel Laskaris in Seljuk-held Cappadocia during John Vatatzes' reign. Tzamantouros is, in fact, a rare family name attested during the fourteenth century in both Anatolia and the Balkans (PLP 27725–29). Thus, a certain Michael Tzamantouros defended Philadelphia against the Turks and was killed in 1348. See Couroupou 1981:73.38. Different hypotheses regarding the origin of the family name have been raised. For one suggestion, see Zachariadou 1994:286. For a derivation from the noun *tzamandas* ("leather bag," "suit-case"), a medieval Greek word borrowed from Persian via Turkish, see LBJ, s.v. As discussed above, the family name may originate from the town of Tzaman-dos in the manner of other Byzantine surnames, such as Neokaisareites (from Neokaisareia) and Antiochites (from Antioch).

22 The seal of elder Theodore Laskaris, apparently a unique one, is kept in the Hermitage Museum. See Sabatier 1858:90; Shandrovskaia 1975:no. 26. On the seal of Constantine Laskaris (of which several specimens survive), see Campagnolo-Pothitou 2009:209–10. On both seals, Wassiliou 1997:416–18. On the monastery in Pyrgion, see Amantos 1939; Wassiliou 1997:418–20. For the monastery and a possible link of the family with Pyrgion, see Campagnolo-Pothitou 2009:213–14 (who suggests also a military engagement near Pyrgion celebrated on the seal). See also Puech 2011:70.

23 Ep. 96.19–25 (p. 131).

24 MM, VI, 153. On the date, see *Engrapha Patmou*, II, 142, n. 1. See also Angold 1975a:62; Ragia 2008:142–46. On the introduction of the title of *panhyperse-bastos* and the degree of kinship by marriage to the emperor, see Stiernon 1965:223, n. 12.

25 Theodoridis (2004) examines theories about the Persian and even Greek derivation of the name, proposing an Arabic origin. The thirteenth-century historian Ibn al-Athir referred to the senior Theodore Laskaris as al-Ashkarī. See El-Cheikh 2001:62, n. 54.

26 Vryonis 1957:271; Lemerle 1977:26.192–27.212.

27 On the Shaddadids, including Abu l'Aswar of Dvin and his nephew Lashkari ibn Musa (the son of Abu l'Aswar's brother Musa), see Minorsky 1953:46–47. The story of the hostage is reported by John Skylitzes (Thurn 1973:464.25–27; Constantine IX, 20), who calls him "Artaseiras" and reports that he was transferred to Byzantium when Lashkari ibn Musa's uncle Abu l'Aswar, emir of Dvin and one-time Byzantine ally, adopted confrontational policies toward Constantinople. Minorsky 1953:49 (see also Felix 1981:153, 172) has shown

that Skylitzes errs in identifying Artaseiras as the son of Fatloum, who was not his father but his great-grandfather. For the seal, see Maksimović and Popović 1990:226–28.

28　For this pattern and other examples, see Cheynet 1987, reprinted in Cheynet 2008 I:133–44. On Tornikes or Tornikios, see Kazhdan, ODB, vol. 3, 2096–97. On Raoul, see Kazhdan, ODB, vol. 3, 1771. On Nestongos, see Cheynet 2008 II:599–607. The first known Nestongos was a brother of the governor of Sirmium, an area annexed in the first half of the eleventh century after the defeat of Samuel of Bulgaria.

29　Heisenberg 1923b:25.15, 1923c:12.25; Tafel and Thomas, II, 1856:207; Oikonomides 1967:123.31. On the inscription, see 248, n. 38 (Nicaea) and 254, n. 115 (Pontic Herakleia). Theodore's brother Alexios is called "Alexios Komnenos" in an ordinance of 1207. See MM, IV, 217. See also Cheynet 1990:443–44.

30　Choniates, *Historia*, 483–84. On the devaluation of the title of *sebastos*, see Magdalino 1993:182–83.

31　Guilland 1967a; Oikonomides 1976b:129–30; Kazhdan, ODB, vol. 3, 2163. Anna Komnene, *Alexiad*, 4, 4, 3 (Reinsch and Kambylis 2001:127) describes them as the guards closest to the emperor.

32　Choniates, *Historia*, 508.81–82; Heisenberg 1923b:27.3–4 (appeal of the Constantinopolitan clergy for the election of a new patriarch drafted by Nicholas Mesarites that outlines the career of the elder Theodore).

33　See, for example, the case of the *protovestiarites* Leo Kephalas (landowner in Macedonia and governor of Larissa during the passage of the armies of the First Crusade): Lavra, I, no. 44, 243–44 (dating to 1082); Anna Komnene, *Alexiad*, 5, 5, 3 in Reinsch and Kambylis 2001:155–56. In 1181 the *vestiarites* Andronikos Vatatzes was in charge of delivering tax revenues to Cuman soldiers in the theme of Moglena in Macedonia. See Lavra, I, no. 65, 337–41. On the fiscal function of the *vestiaritai* in the empire of Nicaea, see Angold 1975a:233–34. The *protovestiarites* ranked between seventeenth and twentieth in the court hierarchy during the fourteenth century, when he performed the function of master of ceremonies. See Pseudo-Kodinos in Verpeaux 1966:176–77; Macrides, Munitiz, and Angelov 2013:88–91, 456.

34　Choniates, *Historia*, 498.

35　Choniates, *Historia*, 508–09. I am following the dating of the marriage suggested by Van Dieten in his edition of Choniates' *History* rather than early spring 1199, as proposed by Brand (1968:130). Just after the marriage celebrations, Alexios Palaiologos, the elder Theodore Laskaris, and Manuel Kamytzes campaigned against the Bulgarian rebel Ivanko. Kamytzes was captured, but Alexios III then led the troops in person and took Ivanko as his prisoner. The fall of Ivanko is traditionally dated to 1200. See Zlatarski 1940:132; Brand 1968:131.

36　See 239, n. 41.

37 Choniates, *Historia*, 465–71, 473, 497–98. See Varzos 1984 II:437–39, 742. Isaac Komnenos Vatatzes, the son of Alexios Komnenos Vatatzes, passed away during imprisonment in Bulgaria in the spring of 1196.

38 Vannier 1986:170–72.

39 Choniates, *Historia*, 525–26, 534.

40 Zacos and Veglery I.3 1972:no. 2752 (pp. 1568–69); Jordanov 2001:446; Carile 1965:219.59–60. The estate was in the *orium* of Patra and Methone, on which see Zakythenos 1941:248–49.

41 The high rank of despot was introduced into the court hierarchy as a title designating the successor in 1163, when the emperor Manuel I granted it to his son-in-law and heir, Béla. Akrop. I, §7 (11.5–6), mentions explicitly that Theodore Laskaris held the title of despot before becoming emperor. For the seal, see Zacos and Veglery I.3 1972:no. 2753 (pp. 1570–71). Therefore, I have adopted Ostrogrosky's view (1951:458–59) that Theodore was named despot only when he became the heir to the throne on the death of Alexios Palaiologos. The sources do not make it clear when exactly Theodore was granted the title. Guilland (1959:56) and Ferjančić (1960:30) prefer to leave the matter unresolved.

42 For this estimate, see Riley-Smith 2005:81. For the events of the Fourth Crusade and the individuals involved in its diversion, see McNeal and Wolff 1969; Angold 2003a:3–108 (Part 1).

43 For these events, see Choniates, *Historia*, 544–47. On Theodore's role in the events (which Choniates preferred to suppress in the final version of his *History*), see apparatus at 544.19, 546.65. On the capture of Constantine Laskaris, see Villehardouin, §167 (I, 168–69).

44 Choniates, *Historia*, 550–56. See 239, n. 50 on Choniates' speech referring to the elder Theodore's escape from prison.

45 The account of these events is based on Choniates, *Historia*, 562–64.

46 Tartaglia, Op. rhet., 164.236–39. Choniates, *Historia*, 564, mentions the fate of Alexios IV but is silent on that of Isaac II.

47 Blem., *Imperial Statue*, 52, Chapter 28. On the poor administration of the empire by the Angeloi, see *Synopsis chronike*, 432.1–8, which here follows Choniates, *Historia*, 538. The bad reputation of the Angelos family persisted in later times. An anonymous chronicle of the fall of Constantinople composed in 1391 mocks them as "an ill-bred, bastard breed." See Matzukis 2004:1119. 320–23.

48 Choniates, *Historia*, 571–72. On Constantine Doukas, who may have been a half-brother of Michael Komnenos Doukas, see Polemis 1968:195.

49 Robert of Clari in Lauer 1924:§79 (p. 79); trans. McNeal 1936:100.

50 Choniates, *Orationes*, 126.33–127.1. On the date of the speech (*selention*), see Van Dieten 1971:140–43.

51 Heisenberg 1923b:26.26–31. For an analysis of this passage, see Lampsidis 1977.

52 Michael Choniates in Kolovou 2001:285.32–33 (ep. 179). On the date (after 1217), Kolovou 2001:149*.

53 See the appeal of the Constantinopolitan clergy in Heisenberg 1923b:27.3–4, 29.32–32.35. See also Villehardouin, §313 (II, 122–23).

54 The presence of his daughters is explicitly mentioned in Akrop. I, §6 (p. 10.19–21).

55 Nicholas Mesarites (Heisenberg 1923b:39.6–8) calls Pylai the "beginning of Asia."

56 Choniates, *Historia*, 277. A good number of the fifty-eight rebellions counted in the period 1180–1204 broke out in Asia Minor. See Cheynet 1990:110–45 (nos. 150–207).

57 The event is related in Akrop. I, §6 (p. 10.23–25).

58 Choniates, *Historia*, 281–88. Severe punishments were meted out also to rebels in neighboring Prousa and Lopadion. A subsequent revolt in Bithynia near Nikomedeia during the reign of Isaac II Angelos led by a certain Basil Chotzas was also crushed mercilessly. See Choniates, *Historia*, 423.

59 Choniates, *Historia*, 245, 262–64; Cheynet 1984:40–44.

60 Choniates, *Historia*, 399–401; Hoffmann 1974:66–68; Cheynet 1984:45–53; Hendy 1999:392–96.

61 Choniates, *Historia*, 529; Polemis 1968:91–92; Cheynet 1990:134 (no. 190).

62 Villehardouin, §301 (II, 108–10).

63 Ahrweiler 1965:7; Oikonomides 1976a:18–19, 20. By contrast, *Provincia Phyladelphye* is mentioned in Alexios III's privileges to Venice of 1198. See Tafel and Thomas I, 1856:271.

64 Choniates (*Historia*, 639) says that in the aftermath of 1204 Rhodes had an independent lord, but does not specify his name.

65 Carile 1965:217–18. The loyalty of Mylassa and Melanoudion to Constantinople is confirmed by the ordinance of Alexios IV of January 1204 protecting an estate of the monastery of Saint Paul on Mount Latros. See MM, IV, 327–29.

66 Choniates, *Orationes*, 127.1–4.

67 On the treaties with the Seljuk sultans, see Ibn Bibi, in Duda 1959:32, 38. On the Seljuk troops, see Choniates, *Orationes*, 132.21–33. Akrop. I, §6 (pp. 10.26–11.4), refers to the elder Theodore's alliance with the Seljuks and his efforts to convince the population of Nicaea and Prousa to recognize him as emperor instead of his father-in-law.

68 Villehardouin, §304 (II, 112–13), §316 (II, 124–25).

69 Herakleia, Rhaidestos, and Kallipolis are mentioned in the *Partitio*. On Lampsakos, attested in Venetian possession in 1214 and 1219, see Jacoby 1993:165–66. See Jacoby 1993:199–201 (the Venetian fiscal survey).

70 Choniates, *Orationes*, 131.17–22. On the efforts of the elder Theodore to gain legitimacy, see the observations of Prinzing 1992:135–40.

71 Choniates, *Historia*, 602; Villehardouin, §319–20 (II, 126–29). The Latins accepted the surrender of Lopadion and captured the fortress of Apollonia on Lake Apollonias.

72 Choniates, *Historia*, 603–04; Villehardouin, §322–23 (II, 130–33). Sinogowitz (1952:355–56) suggests that Constantine Laskaris was killed at the Battle of Atramyttion. *Contra*, see Savvides 1987:164–65.

73 Villehardouin, §340–42 (II, 150–53).

74 Or. Fr., 90.109–10.

75 Villehardouin, §360–61 (II, 168–171).

76 Villehardouin, §306–08 (II, 114–17). He was thrown from the column of Theodosius in the Forum of the Bull.

77 Choniates, *Historia*, 612, 620, comments caustically that Alexios III exchanged his insignia "for a ration of bread and allowance of wine."

78 Choniates, *Historia*, 626; Choniates, *Orationes*, 135.32–136.22.

79 Choniates, *Historia*, 640–41; Choniates, *Orationes*, 139.13–146.16. See Van Dieten 1971:146–52.

80 Manuel Mavrozomes' father has traditionally been identified as Theodore Mavrozomes, a right-hand man of Manuel I, who married Manuel's illegitimate daughter. See Varzos 1984 II:496–502. Métivier (2009:205) raises the possibility that Manuel was a son of the *sebastos* John Mavrozomes, a Byzantine general active in about 1185. On Manuel's descendants in the sultanate of Rum, see Yıldız 2011; Métivier 2012:236–37.

81 Choniates (*Historia*, 626) explicitly associates the elevation of Theodore Laskaris as emperor with the defeat of Mavrozomes. See also Choniates, *Orationes*, 127.15–16, 136.33–137.14. For the spring of 1205 as the time of his imperial proclamation (based on the sequence of events in Choniates' first encomium on Theodore Laskaris), see Sinogowitz 1952:348–51. Theodore's treaty with Kaykhusraw, mentioned by Choniates (*Historia*, 638), which recognizes Mavrozomes as the lord of Chonai and Laodikeia, is traditionally also dated to 1205. See Dölger-Wirth, *Regesten*, 1668b.

82 The quotation is from Akrop. I, §7 (p. 12.19–21). See also *Synopsis chronike*, 453.7–8.

83 A certain Athanasia Mangaphina and her husband, named Mangaphas, are known to have owned houses in Philadelphia and rural estates in its environs before 1247. See Vatopedi, no. 15, 155.81–87.

84 On Asidenos, see Wilson and Darrouzès 1968:14–15 (Dölger-Wirth, *Regesten*, 1688); MM, IV, 292. On Kontostephanos, see MM, IV, 291 (Dölger-Wirth, *Regesten*, 1694, 1695). See also the *Partitio* in Carile 1965:218.24; Angold 1975a:61–62.

85 The letter by Michael Choniates, Niketas' brother, to Theodore I Laskaris is in Kolovou 2001:123.23–24 (ep. 94). See also Kolovou 2001:223.25–35 (ep. 136, on the case of the *sebastos* Chalkoutzes from Chalkis in Euboia).

86 Ad Georg. Mouz., 125.137–126.139; Blem., Ep. 16 (pp. 305–06), on the case of a certain Vililides from Thessalonica.

87 On the landed estates of the Raoul family in Thrace and on the Vranas and the Kantakouzenos families in the western Peloponnese, see the *Partitio* in Carile

1965:219.40, 219.57–58. On the connections of the Palaiologos family with Thessalonica, see Chapter 6, p. 121. Vincent Puech (2011:74–76) has called this segment of the Nicaean elite "the European aristocracy."

88 Choniates, *Historia*, 482; Villehardouin, §476 (II, 290–92), §479 (II, 294–95); Ahrweiler 1966:289–90, 304–13.

89 On the *megas droungarios tes vigles* and *epi ton deeseon* Andronikos Doukas Kamateros, the author of the *Sacred Arsenal*, see Polemis 1968:126–27; Magdalino 1993:259–60, 345, 348, 369, 461, 471, 476.

90 On Basil Kamateros, see Polemis 1968:130–31. On his blinding, see Choniates, *Historia*, 266–67. On his powerful role after 1204, see Michael Choniates in Kolovou 2001:208.1–209.46 (ep. 129). On the embassy to Armenia, see Dölger-Wirth, *Regesten*, 1684a.

91 Vannier 1986:176–78. Greg. I, 69.10–12, is the only source on Andronikos' appointment as *megas domestikos* during the reign of Theodore I Laskaris.

92 On the career of the elder Demetrios Tornikes and his son Constantine, see Darrouzès 1970a:32–35. On the connection with Thebes, see Darrouzès 1968:96. On the fate of Constantine Tornikes, see Choniates, *Historia*, 643. For the imperial document of 1216 in which Demetrios Komnenos Tornikes is attested as *mesazon*, see *Engrapha Patmou*, II, no. 61, 138 (Dölger-Wirth, *Regesten*, 1696a). On this historical figure, see also Macrides 2007:254–55.

93 Darrouzès 1965:152–55.

94 On the election of Michael Autoreianos and its connection with the anointing of the elder Theodore, see the texts from the dossier of Nicholas Mesarites published by Heisenberg (1923b:25–35). On the date of the election, see Heisenberg 1923b:10–11. According to Ostrogorsky 1955, royal anointing was first adopted in the empire of Nicaea under Western influence. But see the different view of Nicol 1976. See also Angelov 2007:387–92 (with further bibliography on this vexed question); and the call for caution by Macrides 1992.

95 On the fiscal surveys, see Angold 1975a:211–12. On the imperial treasury, see Hendy 1985:440–43.

96 Hendy 1999:453.

97 KD, III, 30.16–24.

98 See the comments of Theodore in the encomium in praise of his father: Enc. John, 40.384–88.

99 Ahrweiler 1958:59–63; 1965:39, 99. See the reference to an estate "once belonging" to the church of Saint Sophia in MM, IV, 15.

100 Published by Oikonomides (1967:123.7–11).

101 Constantine's title of despot is mentioned in colophons (published by Volk 1955:170–72) in three manuscripts that he presented to the monastery. See also Förstel 2005:132. The location of the monastery in Nicaea is specified by the note in Vat. gr. 805, f. 1v, a hagiographical codex donated in 1208 by Abbot Petros Philanthropenos. The fugitive emperor Alexios III named as

despots Leo Sgouros (*Synopsis chronike,* 453.27–28) and possibly also Leo
Chamateros (Magdalino 1977:321–22, n. 6), two lords in the Peloponnese.

102 On the *doux* and *sebastokrator* George Laskaris, see MM, IV, 35, 38; Ahrweiler 1965:138–39. On the title of *sebastokrator* of Alexios and Isaac, see Akrop.
I, §22 (34.22–23).

103 Villehardouin, §486 (II, 300–01). On Alexios Komnenos and the *vestiariatai*
under his authority, see MM, IV, 217–18; Dölger-Wirth, *Regesten,* 1676. The
"brotherhood" of Alexios has been considered a symobolic one by Ahrweiler
1965:179.

104 For the concept of a "household government," see Angold 1975a:147–81. On
the influx of "foreign" titles first attested in Nicaea, such as *konostaulos*
("constable") and *tzaousios* (a title of Turkish origin referring in Byzantium
to military commanders), see Macrides, Munitiz, and Angelov 2013:304–06.

105 Choniates, *Historia,* 645.71–83 (see also Choniates, *Historia,* 635, text in the
apparatus, lines 95–97). See also the preface to his *Treasury of Orthodoxy* in
Van Dieten 1970:57.7–19. For Choniates' complaints from this period, see
Simpson 2006:218–20; 2013:22–23.

106 The source on the delayed elections is Nikephoros Kallistos Xanthopoulos,
PG, vol. 147, col. 465AB. See Laurent 1969:133–34. The death of Michael
Autoreianos in 1213 (on this year, see Macrides 2007:160, n. 2, with references
to the sources) led to a delay of ten and a half months. The patriarch who died
in 1216 was Theodore Eirenikos. Michael Hendy was the first to suggest that
the Thrakesion theme became a center of governance during the reign of the
elder Theodore. See Hendy 1985:444–45; Hendy 1999:470–71.

107 Akrop. I, §15 (p. 27.16–18).

108 PL, vol. 216, cols. 353–54, esp. 354A.

109 Villehardouin, §480–89 (II, 294–305); Dölger-Wirth, *Regesten,* 1674.

110 See Pope Innocent's letter of response in PL, vol. 215, cols. 1372C–1373B.

111 Métivier (2012:243–45) has recently reexamined the disputed chronology of
the battle and argued for its traditional dating (1211). On Kaykhusraw as
Alexios III's adopted and baptized son, see Akrop. I, §8 (p. 14.4–23); Macrides
2007:128, n. 20. In an oration written specially for the occasion, Choniates
praises the elder Theodore for killing the sultan, but Akropolites is uncertain
who did it. See Choniates, *Orationes,* 171.17–18, etc.; Akrop. I, §10 (p.
17.10–13). According to Ibn Bibi (Duda 1959:49), it was a Latin in Theodore's
army who killed the sultan.

112 Prinzing 1973:914.90–915.94.

113 Prinzing 1973:416–17, esp. 417.153–58.

114 Akrop. I, §15 (pp. 27–28). On the treaty of 1212–14, see Dölger-Wirth, *Regesten,*
1684; Hendrickx 1988:no. 129 (which suggests a date around December 1214).

115 For the inscriptions on the walls of Nicaea and Prousa, see 248, n. 38 and 250,
n. 67. For the inscription in Pontic Herakleia that dubs the elder Theodore
"the tower maker," see CIG, vol. 4, 8748. On the archaeological context, see in

general Buchwald 1979; Foss 1979b: esp. 316–20; Foss 1987. See the fascinating formulary published by Ferrari della Spade 1913:55–56 (no. 18). On the settlement of peasants in the vicinity of fortresses for the purpose of supplying them with produce, see also the testimony of Pachymeres cited in 278, n. 108.

116 Okoinomides 1967:123.44–124.45. On the name of the sons, see *Synopsis chronike*, 465–66.

117 The son of this marriage was "not yet eight years old" at the time of Theodore's death in November 1221 and must have been born in 1214. See Akrop. I, §18 (p. 31.15–17). On the chronology of the marriage, see Van Dieten 1971:181–86. In October 1213 the synod declared that the marriage between the elder Theodore and Leo's daughter would be conducted by full observance of the canons. See Pavlov 1897. Armenian sources identify the bride as Leo's niece Philippa. See Constable Smbat §49 in Dédéyan 1980:92.

118 On these events and Robert of Courtenay's reign, see Longnon 1949:153–68; Van Tricht 2013.

119 Akrop. I, §15 (p. 26.13–15); Kosztolnyik 1996:60–68.

120 Akrop. I, §18 (p. 31.1–13); Macrides 2007:158, n. 4.

121 Akrop. I, §15 (p. 26.16–19), §16 (p. 29.4–7).

122 The title of a Lenten sermon by Nicholas Mesarites mentions that he conducted the marriage ceremony and gives the name of the bridegroom as Constantine Doukas Palaiologos. See Heisenberg (1923c:59–60) for a discussion of the date of the marriage (February 1216). Traditionally historians have considered Irene to have been married only once, to a Palaiologos. Polemis (1968:156, nn. 3, 4) preferred the name Constantine, and Vannier (1986:172–74) preferred Andronikos. According to the hypothesis of Mitsiou (2011b), Irene's husbands Andronikos Palaiologos and Constantine Doukas Palaiologos were in fact two different individuals.

123 The title is mentioned by Akrop. I, §15 (p. 26.19–22) and is adopted here. *Synopsis chronike*, 462.3–4, claims he held the title of *protovestiarios*.

124 Akrop. II, 15.12–15 (burial oration for John Vatatzes). For the rhetorical comparison to David, see Jacob of Bulgaria as cited in 256, n. 8. In his *History*, Akropolites notes simply that Theodore I Laskaris bequeathed the imperial office to John Vatatzes. See Akrop. I, §18 (p. 31.11–13). Later accounts and legends present John Vatatzes as the chosen successor and depict his marriage to Irene in heroic colors. He is said, for example, to have defeated a Latin contender for her hand in single combat. See the fourteenth-century *vita* by George of Pelagonia in Heisenberg 1905:212–17 (on its authorship, see Moravcsik 1927; Angelov 2007:253–57); and the eighteenth-cenury *vita* based on legends collected by Nikodemos the Hagiorite in Langdon 1992:94–103.

125 See the report by Choniates quoted in 245, n. 132.

126 Choniates, *Historia*, 95.16–21. The marriage of Constantine and Theodora, the daughter of Alexios I, is said to have resulted from a romantic liaison rather than an arrangement. See Zonaras in Büttner-Wobst 1897:739.18–740.2.

127 In the early eleventh century a certain Vatatzes was prominent enough to propose to deliver his native city of Adrianople to Samuel of Bulgaria. See Skylitzes in Thurn 1973:451–52. A John Vatatzes joined the rebellion of his relative Leo Tornikes centered on Thrace in 1047/48. Another representative of the Vatatzes family is attested in Rhaidestos on the Thracian coast of the Sea of Marmara. See Skylitzes, in Thurn 1973:169, 175, 195; Skylitzes Continuatus, in Tsolakis 1968:174. See also Cheynet 1984:40–44. According to the fourteenth-century *Life* of John Vatatzes (Heisenberg 1905:197–201), the urban endowments by the Vatatzes in Adrianople lay in ruins after the city's conquests by the Ottomans in 1369.

128 See Varzos 1984 I:419–20; 1984 II:382 (no. 147). On his son, the Philadelphian rebel John Komnenos Vatatzes, see 240, n. 59. On his grandson, the *sebastokrator* Isaac Komnenos Vatatzes, who was the first husband of the empress Anna before her marriage to Theodore I Laskaris, see 239, n. 37.

129 According to Akrop. I, §52 (p. 103.15–19), whose eyewitness testimony I have preferred, Vatatzes was sixty-two on his death in November 1254. According to Greg. I, 50, he died in his sixtieth year and therefore would have been born in 1194 or 1195. Akrop. I, §15 (p. 26.20–22) writes that he "came from Didymoteichon." See also *Synopsis chronike*, 462.2–4.

130 The most plausible hypothesis has been advanced by Polemis (1968:106–07). It has been adopted by Varzos 1984 II:576–77, no. 75 (genealogical table), 851–57. According to Amantos (1951), John Vatatzes was the grandson of the Philadelphian rebel John Komnenos Vatatzes and was raised in secret in order to elude the vengeance meted out to his family. The theory was based on the story of the rebellion told in John Vatatzes' fourteenth-century *vita* by George of Pelagonia (Heisenberg 1905:200.12–13, 205.8–27, 206.19–31). According to Choniates (Choniates, *Historia*, 264; *Synopsis chronike*, 328–29), after John Komnenos Vatatzes' rebellion was crushed, his two sons, Manuel and Alexios (they are called Nikephoros and Theodore in the fourteenth-century *vita*) fled to the Seljuks and hence tried to sail to the Norman court in Sicily, but were apprehended on Crete and blinded at the order of Andronikos I, who died in 1185, seven years before John Vatatzes' birth. This makes the theory improbable on chronological grounds. Another hypothesis, as much tantalizing as implausible (Langdon 1978:40–42), makes John Vatatzes the illegitimate son of a military commander stationed in Bithynia in the 1190s, who had an affair with the empress Euphrosyne, Alexios III's wife, and was punished with death (Choniates, *Historia*, 486). The bastard son of a disgraced father could hardly have become the head of the imperial guard, much less an heir to the throne.

131 MM, IV, 319–20, confirming the possessions and exemptions of the monastery of Saint Paul on Mount Latros. See also MM, IV, 292.

132 Choniates, *Historia*, 400.4–6 (Βατάτζης Βασίλειος, γένους μὲν ἀσήμου βλαστῶν, διὰ δὲ τὸ εἰς γυναῖκά οἱ γαμετὴν συναφθῆναι τὴν τοῦ βασιλέως πρὸς πατρὸς ἐξανεψιὰν δομέστικος τῆς ἀνατολῆς τιμηθείς). See also Choniates,

Historia, 435, where the rebel Constantine Doukas Angelos is identified as a brother of Basil Vatatzes' wife. On the rebellion, see Cheynet 1990:127 (no. 176). Polemis (1968:107) correctly interprets *exanepsia* as "cousin." On the term see also Laiou 1992:47. In his genealogical study, Konstantinos Varzos has identified Basil Vatatzes' wife as an anonymous daughter of Isaac Angelos Doukas and a granddaughter of Constantine Angelos and Theodora: Varzos 1984 I:673–74; 1984 II:576–77 (table), 851–57.

133 Pieralli 2006:121–26.

134 Theodore was not oblivious of his descent from the Komnenoi, which he did not advertise to the extent he did his ancestry leading back to the Doukai. See the sigillographic evidence discussed in Chapter 5, p. 103.

135 Choniates, *Historia,* 440, 446.

136 Patriarch Germanos II mentions that he was the younger brother in a sermon (Lagopates 1913:275.2–25).

137 On the emperors of the eleventh and twelfth centuries practicing *oikonomia* in matters of marriage, see Laiou 1992:35–36, 45–46, 56. On the "custom" in the empire of Nicaea, see Akrop. I, §50 (p. 100.5–14). See also Puech 2011:72, n. 19.

138 Ferrari dalle Spade 1913:59 (no. 29). On the semiofficial epithet *oikeios*, see Verpeaux 1965; Macrides, Munitiz, and Angelov 2013:299–300.

139 Akrop. I, §14 (pp. 24.12–25.7). See also the polemical letter (1228) addressed to the Nicaean patriarch, Germanos II, by the metropolitan bishop of Corfu, Bardanes, in Loenertz 1970:499.427–29. The kinship of the Epirote ruling family with John III Vatatzes explains the statement in Akrop. I, §38 (p. 61.21) that a third brother, Manuel Doukas Komnenos, was "related by family" to Vatatzes.

2 "The Holy Land, My Mother Anatolia"

1 For the first two expressions, see Ep. 111.16–17 (p. 155). For the latter, see his newsletter of 1256 to his Anatolian subjects edited by Festa as an appendix to the letters: Ep., 281.74.

2 Akropolites places the capture of these cities after the defeat of the Seljuk sultan in 1211. See Akrop. I, §11 (p. 18.1–4); Heisenberg 1923c:25–26, 33 (Mesarites' report of events in 1214). On the chronology, see Oikonomides 1967:141, n. 67; Macrides 2007:134, n. 1.

3 Chr. Th., VII, 138.50–52.

4 Angelov 2013a.

5 Michael Choniates in Kolovou 2001:122, 222, 284 (the titles of letters 94, 136, and 179); Maltezou 1989; Tafel and Thomas II, 1857:312–13.

6 Ep. 199.44 (p. 246); Sat. 160.165, 164.241; Enc. John, 28.111.

7 Choniates, *Orationes*, 128.26, 147.5, 175.32–34. For more examples, see Angelov 2005:297. On Constantinople as the promised land of milk and honey, see

Akrop. II, 28.15–20. For the inscription that compared the Nicaean wall tower
with the tower of Calneh (the location of the tower of Babel in the Septuagint
version of Isaiah 10:9), see Schneider and Karnapp 1938:52; Schneider 1938:442
and plate III.

8 Ap. Mal., p. 283.1–2. Theodore compares Nicaea to Babylon also in Enc. Nic.,
69.30–31. For another allusion to Psalm 136:9, see Ad Georg. Mouz.,
139.469–471. In one of his orations composed after 1204 Choniates (Van
Dieten 1973:205.26–30) compares Lake Askania to the "waters of Babylon."

9 Pieralli 2006:125–26.

10 On the endowment of the churches, see *Synopsis Chronike* 508.24–509.6. See
Patriarch Germanos II's letters to the Constantinopolitans and the monks of
the Petra monastery of St. John the Baptist: Lagopates 1913:350–53; Gill 1974.

11 Oration for the feast of the Akathistos during Lent in Giannouli
2001:273.22–24. Theodore engages here in an etymological wordplay between
the words ὁ Ῥῶς ("the Rus") and ὁ ῥοῦς ("the current") that drowned the Rus
who attacked the city with their boats. On the belief that the Virgin was the
protector of Constantinople, see Cameron 1978.

12 Kantorowicz 1963:136–49. The frontier hero in the twelfth-century Byzantine
epic romance *Digenis Akritis* prays eastward. See Grottaferrata version, I.142,
II.250, IV.685, VIII.150 (Jeffreys 1998:10, 38, 106, 224). For the author contemporary to Theodore Laskaris known as "Theognostos," who completed in
1252 or 1253 his book of edification entitled *Treasury*, see Munitiz
1979:55.67–70.

13 Heisenberg 1923b:39.6–11.

14 Lagopates 1913:286–87 (sermon in Nicaea), 352–53, esp. 353.16–17 (letter to
the Constantinopolitans referring to the "second paradise"). See also Germanos
II's hymn (Horna 1905:32) and his letter of 1227 to Demetrios Chomatenos
describing John Vatatzes as the "one who planted the paradise of the church in
the East" (Prinzing 1983:35.40–41).

15 Ep. 93.18–20 (p. 124); KD, II, 4.4–6.

16 Ep. 143.45–47 (pp. 203–04); *Oration of Gratitude to Our Lord Jesus Christ
Composed upon Recovery from a Terrible Illness*, **A**, f. 16v, BnF, Cod. gr. 1193,
f. 30r.

17 Hendy 1985:26, 108–14; Geyer 2002:32–33. According to a modern estimate,
between 30 and 50 percent of the land of the empire of Nicaea in 1242
(including its outpost in Thrace) was suitable for agriculture. See Mitsiou
2010:228–29.

18 Constantine Manasses in Horna 1904:328.29.

19 Enc. Nic., 75.186–76.193.

20 *Encomium on Wisdom* in Paléologou 2007:82.18–20 (ἡ δὲ οἷα γῆ πίων καὶ
ἀγαθή). See also Apol. Mal., 284.22.

21 See Chapter 5, pp. 104–5. For the leaves of the olive trees, see Chr. Th., VII,
139.60–61.

22 Ep. 111.1–2 (based on *Iliad* II, B 461), 111.13–17 (p. 155).

23 Ep. 112.8–9 (p. 156), 15.4 (p. 21), 17.1 (p. 22); Apol. Mal., 284.32–34; Ep. 204.45 (p. 252).

24 Pach. I, 29.5, 29.16, 29.21, 33.13.

25 *Synopsis chronike,* 507.29–508.7 (focuses entirely on livestock); Pach. I, 101.10–16; Greg. I, 42.1–12.

26 On pastoralism along the Maeander valley in the Byzantine period, see most recently Thonemann 2011:179–83.

27 Chr. Th., IV, 103.126–27.

28 "Many-waved sea": Ep. 94.1–2 (p. 125), 202.21 (p. 248); Chr. Th., VII, 137.10. "Surging wave" (*klydasmos*): Ep. 23.5 (p. 28), 49.1 (p. 67); Apol., 110.7. See also the *Supplicatory Canon to the Virgin* in PG, vol. 140, col. 777C. For the other sea metaphors, see Sat., 162.198–201; Mor. P., III, 257.11–12.

29 On the fleet, see Ahrweiler 1966:301–27; Angold 1975a:196–200; Macrides 2007:100–01. On John Vatatzes' Cretan expeditions, see Langdon 2001. On his offer to transport the Latin friars after the disputation held in Nymphaion, see Golubovich 1919:452.

30 *Encomium on the Spring and the Charming Man* in Tartaglia, Op. rhet., 142–52, esp. 145–46, showing his aversion to the winter season. For winter-based metaphors and other impressions from the season, see also Ep. 122.15–16 (p. 171), 195.4–8 (p. 241); KD, III, 33.30–32.

31 Essay 6 in **V**, ff. 67v–68r (see Agapitos and Angelov 2018); KD, III, 30.8–19, 31.23–32.2, 32.24–33.3.

32 Enc. Nic., 72.100–101, 82.349. Theodore engages in the etymological wordplay when he writes, in a passage referring to military victories, that "we are Nicaeans not by family descent (*genos*), but due to our resolve on behalf the people (*genos*)." See Chr. Th., VII, 142.164–65.

33 Enc. Nic., 68.17–18 (πόλις πόλεων καὶ βασιλὶς βασιλίδων καὶ ἄρχων ἀρχόντων), 71.76 (βασιλὶς ὑπάρχουσα πόλεων), 75.183–85. In a letter to the monks of the Evergetes monastery in Constantinople, Nicholas Mesarites described already in 1208 Nicaea as an "imperial city" (βασιλεύουσα). See Heisenberg 1923b:36.6–7.

34 Cahen 1948. On the political history of the twelfth-century Seljuks in Anatolia, see Cahen 1988:11–48.

35 Ahrweiler 1960.

36 See Nicholas Mesarites in Heisenberg 1923b:43.17–19, 46.9–11.

37 Twelfth-century Nicaea caught the attention of Latin and Arab observers: see William of Tyre, *Chronicon*, 3.1, in Huygens 1986:197; al-Idrisi in Jaubert 1840 II:302, 304. Some of al-Idrisi's comments are found also in the work of the ninth- and tenth-century geographer Ibn Khordadbeh, ed. and trans. M. J. de Goeje, 77–78. See also Foss 1996:31–34, especially the material drawn from the *Life* of Saint Neophytos.

38 CIG, vol. 4, 8745, 8746, 8747; Schneider and Karnapp 1938:52–53. On the walls of Nicaea, see Schneider 1939; Foss and Winfield 1986:79–121.

39 Foss 1996:94–95.

40 Enc. Nic., 75.190–76.195, 76.304–78.239, 79.277.

41 On the cemetery, see the *Life* of St. John the Merciful, in Polemis 1973:45.19–23. The area was probably named after the monastery of Agalma outside the city walls. See Polemis 1973:39. Blemmydes speaks of native and migrant population in the city. See Blem., *Autobiographia,* I, 12.27–28 (p. 8).

42 Enc. Nic., 78.241–42. For Choniates' complaints, see 243, n. 105.

43 The imperial palace is mentioned, for example, in Blem., *Autobiographia,* I, 12.7–8 (p. 8); Golubovich 1919:430. Blemmydes uses the plural *oikoi,* which suggests a palace complex of several buildings. According to Foss (1996:119), the palace may have been built on the site of the ancient theater, where the foundations of a large building have been identified.

44 Greg. I, 44.19 (St. Anthony); Pach. III, 193.2–5 (monastery built by the Tornikes family); *Synopsis chronike,* 512.3–11 (St. Tryphon). On the churches of Nicaea, see Foss 1996:104–10 (with a suggested identification of the church of St. Tryphon).

45 Chatzipsaltis 1964:142 (Laurent, *Regestes,* 1210). On the Hyakinthos monastery, see Schmit 1927; Foss 1996:97–101.

46 Angold 2003b:36.

47 MM, III, 65 (Laurent, *Regestes,* 1261) dating to August 1232. Foss (1996:111–14) identified the church with the one mentioned in the document and suggested that it served as the patriarchal cathedral at the time.

48 Logopates 1913:214–17.

49 Golubovich 1919:428; Mango 1994:354–56.

50 On the palaces of Magnesia and Smyrna (Periklystra) see 250, n. 61 and 250, n. 64 and Chapter 5, pp. 101, 104. A fourteenth-century Greek text describing the siege of Philadelphia by the Turks of Aydin in 1348 designates a segment of the fortifications as "the palace" (*to palation*). See Couroupou 1981:71.19, 72.3, 73.11. Lemerle (1984:66) notes that this area of Philadelphia has not been identified.

51 Ad Georg. Mouz., 131.268–69 (*oikoi*). For the singular *anaktoron,* see Ep. 40.26 (p. 52). For *ta anaktora* (grammatical plural but with singular meaning), see Ep. 172.2 (p. 225), 174.4 (p. 227), 179.29–30 (p. 230). For *ta basileia* ("the palace"), see Ep. 121.24 (p. 168). On May 4, 1250, the patriarchal synod met in the residence (*oikia*) of the emperor in Nymphaion. See Laurent 1934:23 (Laurent, *Regestes,* 1312).

52 On Magnesia, see Laurent, *Regestes,* 1335 (1257–58). On Nymphaion, see 249, n. 51 and 250, n. 60.

53 Blem., *Autobiographia,* I, 12.9–10 (p. 8); Akrop. I, §41 (pp. 67.26–68.2), §47 (p. 85.1–2), §84 (p. 176.10–21). On the location of Klyzomene, see the hypothesis of Ahrweiler (1965:71–72).

54 On Nymphaion, see Foss 1979b:309–12.

55 Nicaea: Ep. 3.25 (p. 7), 51.88 (p. 75), 84.5 (p. 111), 194.22 (p. 241); Nymphaion: Ep. 19.9 (p. 25), 36.34 (p. 45), 59.44 (p. 89).

56 Eyice 1960.

57 This little-known bath complex has been discussed in the PhD dissertation by Naomi Pitamber (2015:226–28). On bath construction, see Theodore's letter to the metropolitan bishop of Philadelphia in Ep. 118.7–12 (pp. 164–65). On the metaphor, see his letter to Akropolites cited in 289, n. 14.

58 Çağaptay 2010 suggests that the palace was surrounded by gardens and pavilions. On the Seljuk palaces, see Redford 1993.

59 On Kubadabad, see Otto-Dorn and Önder 1966:173. On the palace in Turnovo, see Georgieva, Nikolova, and Angelova 1973:109–12. On the northwest wing of the palace in Mystras, see Bouras 1997:242.

60 This monastic foundation was the venue of the patriarchal synod held on March 31, 1256. See MM, I, 118–19 (Laurent, *Regestes,* 1331).

61 On the physical remains of Magnesia and the likely location of the palace, see Foss 1979b:306–09. Blem., *Autobiographia,* I, 83.1–2 (p. 41), explicitly says that he entered "the imperial palace" (τὰ βασίλεια) to protest against the decision by the synod, which convened in Magnesia. On the treasury, see Pach. I, 97.21; 101.20. Hendy (1969:231–35) suggested on the basis of coin finds that Magnesia was the location of the main royal mint as early as the reign of the elder Theodore. See also Hendy 1985:443–45. On "golden Magnesia," see Ep. 213.18 (p. 265). See also Ep. 71 (p. 98.1–10). On the treasury and the international market, see *Synopsis chronike,* 507.13–18.

62 Doukas in Bekker 1834:13.2–4.

63 See the excellent historical detective work by Mitsiou (2011:674–81) based on the report by the seventeenth-century Ottoman traveler Evliya Çelebi.

64 On Periklystra, see Akrop. I, §39 (p. 63.1–2); §52 (p. 103.8–11). On the fleet, ibid., §48 (p. 87.14–17). On Smyrna generally in the period, see Ahrweiler 1965:34–43, esp. 35–37, where Periklystra is localized at the modern Halka Pinar neighborhood of Izmir. By contrast, Ramsay (1890:116) identifies Periklystra as Pınarbaşı (Bunar Bashi) in today's Borova metropolitan district of Izmir. On the *neon* and *palaion kastron* ("new and old fortress"), see also MM IV, 9, 25, 55. See also the inscription on Mount Pagus in CIG, vol. 4, 8749.

65 Anna Komnene, *Alexiad,* 11, 5, 6; 14, 1, 5–6; 14, 3, 1; 14, 3, 7 in Reinsch and Kambylis 2001:338, 426–27, 434–35, 437; Akrop. I, §53 (p. 105.22–24).

66 Choniates, *Historia,* 95, 135.

67 Theodore refers to being Prousa along with his father in Sat. 192.917–919. On the hot baths, see Constantine Porphyrogennetos in Moravcsik 1967:246–8. On the inscription, see CIG, vol. 4, 8744. On the Byzantine monuments of Prousa, see Pralong and Grélois 2003.

68 On Lopadion, see Foss in ODB, vol. 2, 1250–51; Ahrweiler 1960:185–86. On the walls of the fortress of Achyraous, see Foss 1982:161–66. On the identification of Kalamos with Gelembe, see Robert 1962:66–69. On the fortress of Meteorion (Gördük Kale), see Foss 1987:95–99.

69 Golubovich 1919:464–65.

70 Ahrweiler 1965:137. According to Cheynet (2014:104), Ephesos was the reli-
gious, Smyrna the economic, and Philadelphia the military center of the
Thrakesion theme.
Foss 1979a:110.

71 Kirakos of Gandzak in Brosset 1870:158; Khanlarian 1976:196; Bedrosian
1986:266.

72 Ep. 106.20–21 (p. 146).

73 Blem., Ep. 14.1–2 (p. 310).

74 Ep. 11.27–33 (pp. 15–16). On middle and late Byzantine Ephesos, see Foss
1979a 116–37.

75 Rheidt 1990, 1991, 2002. See Chapter 10, pp. 210–11.

76 Ep. 59.26–27 (p. 88). On the treasury, see Pach. I, 97.25. Astritzion has been
identified as Kız Kalesi. See Cook 1999:319; Bieg, Belke, and Tekkök
2009:178–79.

77 Ep. 59.26 (p. 88) ("three-gated Thebe"), 202.16–17 (p. 248) (reminding his
friend George Mouzalon, a native of Atramyttion, of "Thebe under Plakos").
Theodore Laskaris never mentions Atramyttion by its contemporary name.
Herodotus, *History*, 7.42, locates Thebe under Plakos on the plane of Atramyttion. The Byzantine author John Pediasimos identified Thebe under Plakos
with Atramyttion. See his scholia on Hesiod in Gaisford II 1823:616.14–15.

78 On the restoration of Atramyttion under Alexios I, see Anna Komnene,
Alexiad, 14, 1, in Reinsch and Kambylis 2001:425.44–52; Ahrweiler:1960:184.
See also al-Idrisi in Jaubert 1840 II:303; Villehardouin, §321 (II, 128–30).

79 Akrop. I, §61 (p. 125.13–19), §83 (p. 173.19–20). On the little that is known
about Byzantine Lampsakos, see Bieg, Belke, and Tekkök 2009:167–68, 173–74.

80 Akrop. I, §41 (p. 68.3–19), §49 (p. 88.19–22); Macrides 2007:100. On the
fortifications, see Aylward 2006. On the merchants from Monemvasia in Pegai,
see Schreiner 1978:20. On the vexed question about the date of the Latin
conquest of the city during Vatatzes' reign, see Saint-Guillain 2015.

81 For the soldiers from Paphlagonia, see Akrop. I, §66 (p. 139.5–6), §71
(p. 147.23), §77 (p. 161.6–7). For the mention of Cape Karambis, see
Ep. 44.34 (p. 57). For the little known about Nicaean Paphlagonia, see
Booth 2004.

82 Ep. 44.33 (p. 57).

83 Ep. 87.47–48 (p. 114); *Natural Communion*, PG, vol. 140, col. 1349A; Chr. Th.,
VII, 141.131. On Palatia, see Foss, ODB, 2, vol. 1372–73.

84 Akrop. I, §28 (p. 45.22); Ep. 44.34 (p. 57).

85 Ahrweiler 1965:125–27.

86 Angold 1975:247–48, 252. A *stratopedarches* (second-in-command after the
doux) of the "theme of Philadelphia and Thrakesion" is attested in 1234. See
MM, IV, 18. For the list of the *doukes* of Thrakesion, see Ahrweiler
1965:137–54.

87 Darrouzès and Wilson 1968:13–14, 20–21.

88 On the formation of the theme in the twelfth century, see Ahrweiler 1965:128–29.

89 Choniates, *Historia,* 150.

90 According to Akrop. I, §15 (p. 28.6–7), the city of Kalamos marked the boundary of Neokastra. See Angold 1975a:245; Macrides 2007:152–53. The inclusion of Meteorion in the Neokastra theme is hypothetical. On the suggested location of Magedon, see Foss 1979b:302–03. On archery, see Pach. I, 291.3–8. See also Angold 1975a:191.

91 In 1284 Magnesia was in the theme of Neokastra. See MM, IV, 262–63. On this basis, Ahrweiler (1965:134–35) places Magnesia in Neokastra throughout the thirteenth century. But see the reservations of Mitsiou (2010:227, n. 40).

92 Akrop. I, §7 (p. 11.23).

93 Pach. I, 43.6–7.

94 Sat., 192.931–32; Ep. 194.21–22 (p. 241). On the proverb, see Ep. 45.46 (p. 61), 55.21–23 (p. 82); Leutsch and Schneidewin II 1851:730. Thrakesion theme: Sat. 193.950–51.

95 Darrouzès, 1981:386 (Notitia 15). The chronology of the elevation of the sees is not entirely clear, because the rank of Philadelphia had been raised before 1204. See Darrouzès 1981:131, 165.

96 On the notaries, see Ahrweiler 1965:103–21 (the notaries in the metropolitan bishopric of Smyrna); Angold 1975a:273–74.

97 Nicole 1894:80.10–28; Ep. 11.10–11 (p. 15).

98 On this expression, see the sermon of Patriarch Germanos II in Lagopates 1913:282, esp. 282.27–29. On the ethnic communities in thirteenth-century Byzantine Asia Minor, see Charanis 1953.

99 On Tzys, see Ep. 10.11 (p. 14). On Cleopas, see the sources cited in 253, n. 110. Ahrweiler (1965:24, n. 121) considered Tzys to be a name of Latin origin, while Nicola Festa (1898:458) hypothesized that Tzys was the *tzaousios* Constantine Margarites. Tzys might also be a variation of the family name of John Tzykes, *doux* of the theme of Mylassa and Melanoudion, who is reported as deceased in an act of 1216. See MM, IV, 291; Dölger-Wirth, *Regesten,* 1693.

100 On Latin mercenaries in Nicaea, see Kyriakidis 2014. Latin mercenaries in Nicaea are well attested in the 1250s. On February 12, 1253, for example, Pope Innocent IV granted his cardinal legate the right to annul the excommunication of the mercenaries provided they leave the service of John Vatatzes. See Berger 1897 III:no. 6337 (p. 176). On the important political role the Latin mercenaries played in 1258, see Akrop. I, §76 (p. 158.15–17). On western envoys and refugees, see Chapter 7, pp. 137–43.

101 Golubovich 1919:430.

102 Pach. I, 101.22, refers to the Varangians ("the axe-bearing Celts") guarding the treasury at Magnesia in 1258. On the ἐγκλινοβάραγγοι, see the imperial ordinance of 1272 in Heisenberg 1920:39.49. See also Dawkins 1947; Bartusis 1992:273–76.

103 See the canonical responses of John of Kitros in PG, vol. 119, col. 977.

104 Choniates, *Historia,* 601–02, 617; Villehardouin, §310 (II, 118–19), §322 (II, 130–31), §380–381 (II, 188–91), §385 (II, 194–95). On the Armenians near Smyrna, see MM, IV, 78 (document of sale of 1232).

105 On the Jews of Mastaura and Chonai along the Maeander valley, see Prinzing 1998b:156, 163–67 (with references to the sources). See the travels of Benjamin of Tudela in Adler 1907:14. On the date of his journey through Byzantium (between 1159 and 1163), see Jacoby 2002. On the epigraphic monument in Nicaea and its likely date, see Schneider 1943:36; Foss 1996:71 and n. 27. For the Jewish fabric dyers of Pyrgion(?) who were Christian converts, see the fascinating contract formulary in Kourouses 2002–2005:547, 573–75. On Bare, see MM, IV, 25.9.

106 Akrop. II, 24.24–32. The unspecific taxes may have included the so-called Jewish tax, on which see Starr 1939:11–17; Charanis 1947b:77. The references to preaching are contradicted by a letter written in about 1270 in Valencia by Rabbi Jacob ben Elia of Carcassonne, who reported that John Vatatzes had issued an edict on the forced baptism of the Jews in his last regnal year. See Mann 1926; Dölger-Wirth, *Regesten,* 1817. For a translation of the section of the letter dealing with Byzantium, see Bowman 1985:228–31. Jacob ben Elia's claim regarding forced baptism seems exaggerated and echoing Michael Palaiologos' anti-Laskarid propaganda after Theodore's death, as Günter Prinzing (1998b:167–73) has argued.

107 *On Virtue* in Paléologou 2007:77.262–63; Ep. 128.12 (p. 179). The Hypsistarians were an ancient Judaizing community. On the converted Jews, see the contract formulary cited in 253, n. 105.

108 Akrop. I, §35 (pp. 53–54) (note the mention of Cuman slaves, on which see also Chapter 3, p. 63); Greg. I, 36.16–37.9 (the settlement of Cumans in Asia Minor). On the baptism of the Cumans, see Akrop. II, 24.17–19. On the Cumans in the Nicaean army in 1241, see Akrop. I, §40 (p. 65.24–26). On their knowledge of Greek, see Akrop. I, §76 (p. 158). On the Cuman community near Smyrna, see MM, IV, 167. A fourteenth-century descendant of a high-born Cuman leader (Sytzigan) was Syrgiannes, a key figure in the civil war of 1321–28. See John Kantakouzenos in Schopen 1828 I:18. That Sytzigan may have been the Cuman "king" Saronius, whose two daughters were married to knights from the Latin empire. See Vásáry 2005:63–68, esp. 67–68.

109 Joinville in De Wailly 1874:§495–496 (pp. 271–72). The story was told by Philippe de Toucy, the bailiff of the Latin emperor of Constantinople, to King Louis IX of France during the latter's stay in Caesarea in Palestine (March 1251–May 1252). On the dog in Cuman religious belief, see Golden 1997:93–97.

110 Akrop. II, 24.20–22; Ep. 207.28–33 (p. 259); *Synopsis chronike,* 527.5–11.

111 See the testament of 1247 by the founder of the Voreine monastery: Vatopedi, I, no. 15, 159.217, 159.238, 161.299. On personal names of "Oriental" origin and Byzantine demography, see Shukurov 2008a.

112 Akrop. I, §71 (p. 148.10): a Turk in the entourage of Michael Palaiologos during his Balkan expedition in 1257; §81 (pp. 170.23–171.2): the Christianized Turk Nikephoros Rimpsas, a high-ranking officer in 1259. Rimpsas commanded a Turkish mercenary contingent in the 1270s. See Macrides 2007:361 and 364, n. 20; PLP 24292.

113 Ep. 44.34 (p. 57). See the delineation of the frontiers by Charanis 1947a. Future archaeological and epigraphic data, if forthcoming, could certainly contribute to a more precise assessment.

114 Wirth 1962; Magdalino 1993:98–99, 124.

115 Belke and Mersich 1990:238–42 (Dorylaion); 222–25 (Chonai); 232–36 (Laodikeia); 312–16 (Kotyaion).

116 Choniates, *Historia,* 639. On Aldebrandinos, see also Hoffmann 1974:69–71; Cheynet 1990:147–48 (no. 210).

117 Synopsis in Métivier 2012:238–40. On one of the inscriptions, see Kiourtzian 2008.

118 See his hagiographic encomium on St. Tryphon in Delehaye 1925:353.

119 Laurent, *Regestes,* 1297–98 (on the burial of Michael Xeros in a church constructed by him in Konya); Lagopates 1913:358–59 (Patriarch Germanos II's letter to a certain Nicholas Grammatikos who resided under the Seljuks). On the presence of metropolitan bishops from central and eastern Anatolia at the synod, see Laurent, *Regestes,* 1242 (March 1226: Christophoros of Ankara; discussing matters pertaining to Melitene); 1251 (September 1229: signed by the metropolitan bishop of Pisidia); 1312 (May 1250: the metropolitan bishops of Ankara Gregory and Pisidia Makarios); 1314–15 (July 1250: Metrophanes of Caesarea).

120 The embassies are known from a dossier of three letters dispatched by the patriarch and the synod preserved in Vat. gr. 1455, Vat. Ottob. gr. 77 (a copy of the former), and Monac. Gr. 207. See a synopsis in Devreesse 1939. For the first letter sent by the patriarch Germanos II to *katholikos* Constantine (the letter has been dated to 1239–40), see Lagopates 1913:354–57; Bartikian 2002:63–71 (Laurent, *Regestes,* 1290). The second letter was issued by the synod in May 1241 at a time of vacancy in the patriarchate after Germanos' death. I have consulted it in Vat. gr. 1455, ff. 27r–29v; Vat. Ottob. gr. 77, ff. 28v–33v. The third letter, one prompted by the arrival of Armenian envoys during the winter season, was issued in 1248 by the patriarch Manuel II. It addresses the *katholikos* Constantine and the Armenian king Hetoum, and summarizes the exchange of embassies in past years: Bartikian 2002:75–85 (Laurent, *Regestes,* 1309).

121 See Patriarch Manuel II's letter in Bartikian 2002:83. Phokas was close to the emperor John Vatatzes. See the acerbic comment by Akropolites: Akrop. I, §50 (p. 96.21–22); Macrides 2007:266. He was given the honorary see of Syracuse in Sicily. See the patriarchal act dated July 10, 1250, in Rhalles and Potles 1852–59, V:116; Laurent, *Regestes,* 1316.

122 Métivier 2012:236–37 (with further references to the several sources on John Komnenos Mavrozomes, d. 1292).

123 Vryonis 1971:229–44, esp. 233–34. See the sworn declaration of the Latin king of Cyprus on July 19, 1216, in Beihammer 2007:171–72 (no. 20) and the mention of the *apokrisiarios* Alexios at 171.10–11.

124 Choniates, *Historia,* 118–21; Magdalino 1993:76–78, 118. See also the observations of Lilie (1991:96–130).

125 In the late twelfth century, the trade fair at the annual feast day (September 6) commemorating the miracle of the Archangel Michael at Chonai attracted the Turks from Konya and elsewhere. See Michael Choniates in Lampros 1879–83, I:56.14–18; Magdalino 1993:129–32.

126 See Chapter 1, p. 25; Beihammer 2011:617–27, 630–32, 649–51 (table).

127 See the interpretation by Peacock 2006, who dates the expedition to between 1220 and 1222.

128 The main source on the border conflicts is the historian Ibn Nazif. See Cahen 1971:147–48. A letter by the Nicaean patriarch Germanos II in 1228 refers to John Vatatzes fighting "face to face with the faithless Hagarenes." See Prinzing 1983:35.42–43. On the basis of a post-Byzantine hagiographical text, Langdon (1992:25–33) has suggested that John Vatatzes recovered Tripolis and Laodikeia. See also Korobeinikov (2014:157–60 and n. 310, 170).

129 On Chormaghun, see Jackson 1993.

130 Cahen 1988:66–97. On the defeat of the Khorezmians, see Barthold 1928:393–462. On the Mongol conquests in western Asia before the battle of Köse Dağ in 1243, see Saunders 1971:54–62, 77–89.

131 Ibn Bibi in Duda 1959:175–76.

132 Saunders 1971:78–80.

133 This is the elaborate explanation offered by George Pachymeres in the opening section of his *History*: Pach. I, 23–33. For a recent analysis, see Korobeinikov 2014:236–43.

134 Cahen 1974:42–43; Akrop. II, 18.15–16.

135 *Oration on Wisdom* in Paléologou 2007:77.261–62; 77.771–78.773; Sat., 186.779–80.

136 Egypt and Kos: *Natural Communion*, PG, vol. 140, col. 1345B; India: Sat. 190.866 ("Indian ant"); Syria: KD, I, 110.7–15. On the meaning of Syria in Byzantine texts, see Durak 2011.

137 Ep. 214.20–21 (p. 266). The letter dates to 1257.

3 "I Was Brought Up as Usual for a Royal Child"

1 The chronology can be reconstructed solely through Byzantine short chronicles. On the elder Theodore's death in November 1221, see chronicle 19/2 of Peter Schreiner's edition (Schreiner 1975–79, I:173; II:187–88). The accession of John

III Vatatzes can be dated backward through the reported years and months of his reign at the time of his death (November 3, 1254). According to chronicle 8/2 (Schreiner 1975–79, I:74), he passed away after a reign of thirty-three years: that is, his reign would have begun around November 3, 1221. According to chronicle 22/1 (Schreiner 1975–79, I:180), he passed away after a reign of 32 years and 10 months (the text in the manuscript has been emended to 11 months by the editor): that is, he would have acceded to the throne around January 3, 1222. Commenting on the puzzling short chronicle 19/3 (Schreiner 1975–79, I:173; III:174), Darrouzès (1978:276–77) dates the accession to around December 15, 1221, but the logic of his calculations is questionable.

2 Akrop. I, §52 (p. 104.19–23), notes that at the time of Vatatzes' death (November 3, 1254) Theodore was still "completing his thirty-third year" (τριάκοντα καὶ τρία ἔτη διανύοντι) and that he "was as old as his father's reign was long, for his birth almost coincided with his father's proclamation as emperor." The same comment is found in *Synopsis chronike,* 506.3–5. Therefore, he must have been born not long after November 3, 1221. In an encomium on John Vatatzes, Jacob of Bulgaria (Mercati 1970:91.14) praises Theodore as "born in the *porphyra,*" which suggests birth in the palace. The word *porphyrogennetos* featured on his gold coins conveys the same impression, even though the presence of the title may simply be due to an imitation of twelfth-century numismatic issues. See Hendy 1999:516. A poem by Nikephoros Blemmydes (written by the "monk Blemmydes," according to the manuscript title) refers to the birth of an imperial successor around Christmas (Heisenberg 1896:110–11). Traditionally, the poem has been seen as referring to the birth of Theodore's son John IV Laskaris in 1250, which is most likely; Macrides (2007:276) has suggested the possibility that the poem celebrates Theodore's birth.

3 Sat., 191.908–09; Enc. Nic., 83.367–70.

4 Lagopates 1913:214–17, esp. 215.30.

5 Akrop. I, §31 (p. 48.20–21); Andrea Dandolo in Pastorello 1938:299.7.

6 On the date of the battle, see Macrides 2007:167. The winter season emerges from Akropolites' description (cited in 257, n. 14), who links the battle with winter campaigning.

7 Akrop. I, §55 (pp. 109.19–110.2); *Synopsis chronike,* 513. Michael Laskaris resided in Thessalonica in 1246. On the meaning of Tzamantouros, see 237, n. 21.

8 Jacob of Bulgaria in Mercati 1970:83.27–31. Cf. Angelov 2007:66–67 (on the date of the speech), 90–91, 127–31 (on David as a model).

9 See the account of the conspiracy of the Nestongos brothers in Akrop. I, §23 (pp. 36–38); *Synopsis chronike,* 470–71, adds that John Vatatzes grew increasingly suspicious of his own relatives after the planned coup. On representatives of the family in the thirteenth century, see Polemis 1968:150–52.

10 Akrop. I, §51 (p. 101.6–18). This John Angelos seems to have been different from his namesake, who was Theodore's protégé when he became the sole emperor. See Macrides 2007:269–70, n. 5; Ahrweiler 1965:142.

11 On the marriage of Constantine Strategopoulos, see Pach. I, 41.17–18; Pach. III, 173.2–20. See also Pach. III, 172, n. 29 (by Albert Failler). On John Strategopoulos, see MM, IV, 295 (Dölger-Wirth, *Regesten,* 1693). On the family name Komnenos Strategopoulos, see also MM, IV, 390. The sixteenth-century historian Makarios Melissourgos-Melissenos, the author of the *Chronicon Maius* (misattributed to Sphrantzes), identifies Alexios Strategopoulos as the son of a victorious general in Paphlagonia, although his report is suspect. Makarios forged his genealogical descent from the Melissenos family in Byzantium and included the Strategopouloi among his fictitious ancestors. See Grecu 1966:275.

12 Akrop. I, §40 (p. 66.18–20), §49 (p. 92.17–18); Fassoulakis 1973:15–16; PLP 24110.

13 Tafel and Thomas, I, 1856:572.

14 On the Battle of Poimanenon, the subsequent conquests in Asia Minor, and winter campaigning, see Akrop. I, §22 (pp. 34–36), §37 (p. 59.7–10); Akrop. II, 15.34–16.6, 17.6–15. On the role of Holkos and the interruption of traffic along the straits, see Akrop. I, §22 (p. 36.9–15); *Synopsis chronike,* 469–70, with the valuable additions on 470.19–22.

15 Greg. I, 28.20–29.4.

16 Lagopates 1913:265.26–31. The date emerges from Germanos' statement that he delivered the sermon one year after his ordination.

17 Akrop. I, §24 (p. 38.6–12). The Nicaean-Latin treaty has been assigned different dates: c. 1225 (Dölger-Wirth, *Regesten,* 1711; Hendrickx 1988:no. 158) and 1227–28 (Van Tricht 2013:1028, n. 135).

18 Nicole 1894:77.5–7; Laurent, *Regestes,* 1251.

19 Enc. John, 28.94–96.

20 Enc. Nic., 83.368–69.

21 Ep. 35.2–8 (p. 43); Sat., 167.311–19.

22 Ep. 26.3–5 (pp. 35–36); Enc. John, 25.37–38.

23 Greg. I, 44.7–12. The Armenian historian Kirakos of Gandzak (Brosset 1870:158; Khanlarian 1976:196; Bedrosian 1986:266) reports a marriage alliance (c. 1250) of a Seljuk sultan of Rum, whom he misidentifies, and "the daughter of Laskaris, the Greek king in Ephesos." Modern historians have sometimes seen here evidence that Theodore Laskaris had a sister who was married to the young sultan 'Izz al-Dīn Kaykāwūs II. See, for example, Langdon 1998:120. But see the well-founded doubts of Shukurov 2008b:106–07; Thomson 2011:205.

24 On mother-empresses, see Mary of Alania (late eleventh century) and her son Constantine Doukas (Theophylaktos of Ohrid in Gautier 1980:191.27–29), and the empress Irene Doukaine (late eleventh and early twelfth centuries) and her daughter Anna Komnene (George Tornikes in Darrouzès 1970a:263.16–19). See also Herrin 1999.

25 Akrop. I, §34 (p. 52.13–14).

26 The women's quarters (*gynaikonitis*) are mentioned by Theodore in Apol., 115.137. See also Blem., Ep. 5.26–31 (p. 297), which describes the gift of a capon to Theodore and alludes to eunuchs serving in the *gynaikonitis,* and Blem., Ep., 2.37–38 (p. 293) (mentioning well-guarded women's quarters). On the *gynaikonitis* as a palace tradition in Constantinople, see John Skylitzes in Thurn 1973:279.3–280.2; Zonaras in Büttner-Wobst 1897:753.12–15.

27 Pach. II, 395.5–8. The empress' clergy is well attested alongside that of the emperor in the fourteenth century. See Pseudo-Kodinos in Verpeaux 1966:265–66; Macrides, Munitiz, and Angelov 2013:230.

28 Polemis 1968:139–40 (no. 115), who shows that on one occasion Irene was identified with the surname Doukas. See Akrop. II, 3.21–22; Beihammer 2007:179 (no. 28). In 1232 a village priest and notary from Mantaia near Smyrna spoke of the joint rule of John Vatatzes and Irene: "the reign (*basileia*) of the most pious and great emperors crowned by God." See MM, IV, 77.

29 Her ordinance is mentioned in a document of 1264: *Engrapha Patmou,* I, no. 33, 275.3–4. On her seals, see Nesbitt 2009:no. 103.1; Zacos and Veglery I.1 1972:no. 119.

30 On the church in Prousa, see Greg., I, 44.19–22; Janin 1975:174–75. On its Ottoman conversion into Sultan Orhan's mausoleum, see Çağaptay 2011. On the monastery of the Virgin *tou Kouzena,* see the fourteenth-century *vita* of George of Pelagonia in Heisenberg 1905:217.28–34; Ahrweiler 1965:96.

31 Ep. 69.9–10 (p. 96), 116.15–18 (p. 163).

32 Sat., 161.173–74.

33 Mor. P., XII, 267.483–85.

34 See the encomiastic comments by Jacob of Bulgaria (1252–53) in Mercati 1970:91.15; and by Akropolites (1254) in Akrop. II, 26.12–15. In his *History,* George Akropolites calls Theodore an emperor when he gives account of events in 1235–37 and 1242. See Akrop. I, §34 (p. 52.23), §40 (p. 67.5). Macrides (2007:39–40) suggests that Theodore Laskaris was a coemperor at least from 1234. On his coemperorship, see also Zhavoronkov 2006.

35 On the twelfth-century pattern, see Christophilopoulou 1956:157–63. On Nicholas Laskaris as a coemperor, see 244, n. 116.

36 For the treaty with the Latins, see Alberic of Trois-Fontaines cited in 273, n. 25.

37 See the letters cited in 276, n. 64.

38 Pach. I, 61.19–22, followed at length by Greg. I, 53–55. Notably, both historians were critical of the Palaiologoi and constructed the image of Theodore Laskaris as their antithesis, including the supposed lack of entitlement to the imperial title cultivated by his father. See Angelov 2007:269–82.

39 Ep. 26.2 (p. 35), 59.43–44 (p. 89), 108.20 (p. 149); Sat., 161.178, 167.312; Enc. John, 24.8. On Theodore's duties as coemperor, see Chapter 5, pp. 98–108.

40 Ep. 84.3–6 (p. 111). Comparisons between the earthly and divine kingdom: *On Fasting,* **A,** f. 66r; **P,** f. 96r (God's ordinances were mandatory, just as the decision of the emperor was the law); Apol. Mal., 287.128–288.130.

41 *On Virtue* (written before 1254) in Paléologou 2007:73.122–23. The echo from
   Psalm 2:7 is not noted by the editor. He presented his father John Vatatzes as
   "the son of God": Enc. John, 35.253.
42 Ep. 62.11–14 (p. 91); Ad Georg. Mouz., 131.264–69.
43 Mor. P., XII, 267.484–85. The scriptural context implies that he was raised for
   sacrifice (that is, sacrificing his own soul) under the corrupting influence of
   pleasure.
44 Ep. 51.5 (p. 72): τὸ πολὺ τῆς δεσποτείας καὶ τῆς δουλείας διάστημα.
45 See Chapter 5, pp. 101, 104, Chapter 6, p. 112. On the presence of physicians,
   see the discussion in Appendix 3, pp. 387–88.
46 Ep. 62.12 (p. 9); Mor. P., XI, 267.468.
47 Akrop. I, §23 (pp. 37.25–38.5).
48 The two units of the palace guards were probably functioning by the 1230s. The
   presence of Englishmen in Nicaea in 1234 suggests the recruitment of Varangians. See 252, n. 101. A Vardariot who was not a Turk is mentioned in an
   undated act of the patriarch Germanos. See Oudot 1941:no. 15, 78–79; Laurent,
   Regestes, 1299. In 1256 the Vardariots accompanied Theodore Laskaris on
   campaign in the Balkans. See Akrop. I, §63 (pp. 131.25–132.3). See also
   Pseudo-Kodinos in Verpeaux 1966:181–82, 210; Macrides, Munitz, and Angelov 2013:100–02, 154. Cf. the reference to whipping at the court in 260, n. 75
   and 260, n. 76.
49 Ahrweiler 1965:177–78. See MM, IV, 31.
50 On the role of pages in the fourteenth-century court, see Pseudo-Kodinos in
   Verpeaux 1966:174, 176, 226; Macrides, Munitz, and Angelov 2013:81, n. 138;
   84, 88, 172.
51 On George Mouzalon as Theodore's page and playmate, see Greg. I, 62.3–12.
   On knucklebones and collecting fruits, see Akrop. I, §76 (p. 157.2–4) (based on
   the childhood of John Laskaris, the eight-year-old son of Theodore). On
   surviving material evidence of knucklebones (a favorite children's game in
   Byzantium), see Pitarakis 2009:234–36.
52 Mor. P., II, 256.74–78; III, 258.133–35; XI, 267.468. The head tutor is said to
   have incited Theodore's *douloi* to slander their teenage master. See Sat.,
   168.330–38.
53 Ferrari della Spade 1913:62–64 (formularies no. 37 and no. 38).
54 Akrop. I, §35 (pp. 53–54).
55 On slave trade between Crimea and Seljuk Anatolia, see Peacock 2006.
   According to Zhavoronkov 1982:82, the presence of Nicaean merchants should
   not be excluded. On Innocent IV's letter, see Berger 1884 I:no. 2122 (p. 316).
   Cf. Jacoby 2005:209.
56 Longnon 1950; Stavridou-Zafraka 1988; Bee-Seferli 1971–76. On the title,
   claims, and territorial extent of the archbishopric of Ohrid, see Prinzing 2004.
57 The "Adrianople affair" has been dated differently. The traditional date
   (Macrides 2007:176–77) is 1225. Bredenkamp (1996:109) prefers 1227 on the

basis of Akropolites' explicit reference to the imperial status of Theodore of Epiros.

58 Akrop. I, §24 (pp. 40.1–41.4).

59 For the treaty, see Predelli 1872:184–85.

60 The schism has been analyzed by Karpozilos 1973. See also the chronological analysis of the correspondence between Nicaean and Epirote ecclesiastics in Prinzing 1983:25–30, 58–60.

61 See Chapter 4, p. 72.

62 Longnon 1949:166–68; Van Tricht 2013.

63 On this treaty, see Marinus Sanutus Torsellus, *Liber secretorum fidelium crucis* in Bongars 1611:72–73. See discussion in Dancheva-Vasileva 1985: 123–24.

64 Tafel and Thomas, II, 1856:265–70, esp. 267 (the investment of Baldwin with domains from the *regnum Nicenum*). As late as 1252, a Venetian estate owner in Lampsakos transferred his rights over properties in the city to his two sons. See Jacoby 1993:166, n. 77; 167 (Giberto Querini).

65 Longnon 1949:169–71. For a discussion of the date of Marie's marriage to Baldwin, see Wolff (1954:47, n. 6), who suggests that it could have been postponed to 1235, when the bride would have been ten years of age.

66 Akrop. I, §26 (pp. 43–44). On Manuel, see Ferjančić 1979. On Michael II of Epiros, see Nicol 1957:128–40.

67 Zlataraski III 1940:592–93; translation in Petkov 2008:425.

68 Browning 1997:101.

69 Philosophy: Ep. 123.36–37 (p. 173) (ἐξ ἀπαλῶν ὀνύχων); Apol., 117.181–118.185; warrior skills: *Response* to Nicholas of Croton on the Procession of the Holy Spirit in Chr. Th. (reprint from Swete 1875), 182.548–52, especially lines 548–49 (ἐκ βρέφους); the church: Chr. Th., VI, 126.70–71 (νηπιόθεν).

70 Praying: Ep. 152.1–2 (p. 215). Readiness to die for the Church: Ep. 99.61–73 (p. 135) addressed to Patriarch Manuel I.

71 Delehaye 1925: col. 356.

72 On the chronology of Germanos' term in office as patriarch (January 1223– summer 1240), see Nystazopoulou 1964a; Laurent 1969:136–37. On his family origins, see Nikephoros Kallistos Xanthopoulos, PG, vol. 147, col. 465C.

73 Lagopates 1913:216.10–19.

74 For the attribution, see Xintaras 1999:I–V (unpaginated introduction); see also Bernard Flusin's review in REB, 60 (2002), 293. Geramnos was one among several ecclesiastics in Nicaea working on liturgical texts. Akakios Sabaites produced commentaries on the Great Canon of Andrew of Crete in Nicaea between 1219 and 1261. See Giannouli 2007:76–86.

75 Lagopates 1913:224.27–33.

76 Lagopates 1913:226.28–30.

77 Lagopates 1913:227.15–20.

78 Lagopates 1913:230.27–35, 304.9–20.

79 Ep. 141.47–49 (p. 200). Addressed to Kleidas, the metropolitan bishop of Kyzikos, this letter was written after 1254. The oration to the Virgin was either that written for the feast of the Akathistos (Giannouli 2001) or the oration dedicated to the Annunciation of the Virgin composed after 1254 (Chr. Th., VIII, 149–55).

80 The sermon speaks of Germanos' humble origin without giving more details. A report regarding his birth in a family of fishermen in Anaplous on the Bosporus is mentioned in the historical account of the patriarchs of Constantinople by Nikephoros Kallistos Xanthopoulos. See 260, n. 72.

81 Lagopates 1913:281–83.

82 Lagopates 1913:283.

83 On the idea of nobility as a quality of the soul in Gregory of Nazianzus, monastic florilegia, and mirrors of princes, see Angelov 2007:229–30. For Theodore's polemical reflections on nobility, see Chapter 6, pp. 111–12.

84 Lagopates 1913:286–87.

85 Lagopates 1913:217.5–7, 347.16–348.27 (see Joshua 9:3–27).

86 See Germanos' letters to the inhabitants of Latin Cyprus (1229), Pope Gregory IX (1232), the Roman cardinals (1232), and the Latin patriarch of Constantinople, Nicholas of Castro Arquato (after 1234): PG, vol. 140, col. 617D (Laurent, *Regestes,* 1250); Sathas, MB, II, 41 (Laurent, *Regestes,* 1256); Arampatzis 2004–06:376.63–65 (Laurent, *Regestes,* 1257); Uspenskii 1879:75–78 (pagination of the appendices; Laurent, *Regestes,* 1277). In early and middle Byzantium the word *Graikoi* (found in Aristotle, *Met.* 352b2) is rarely attested; it appears in Procopius' *Wars,* the Acts of the Sixth Ecumenical Council, Theophanes' *Chronicle,* and the *Tactics* of Leo the Wise. See Magdalino 1991:9–10, nn. 41–43; Koder 2003:305.

87 PG, vol. 140, col. 620A (Laurent, *Regestes,* 1250). See also his letter to the orthodox residents of Latin Constantinople: Lagopates 1913:352.34–353.1.

88 Blemmydes was eight years old when he began to study with a grammarian in Prousa; he progressed to the study of rhetoric in a little less than four years. See Blem., *Autobiographia,* I, 3–4 (p. 4); I, 24 (pp. 14–15); Munitiz 1988:14–15. Browning (1997:101) sets the beginning of instruction in grammar at the age of nine or ten.

89 On the content of *enkyklios paideia,* based mostly on evidence drawn from saints' lives, see Lemerle 1986:112–20. See the list of subjects forming the *enkyklios paideia* in Theodore's letter to the teachers Michael Senachereim and Andronikos Phrangopoulos (ep. 215.116–18 [p. 275]); and his autobiographical reminiscences in Sat., 171.407–10.

90 On grammar studies, especially the role of etymology and George Chroiroboskos' *epimerismoi* (grammatical explications) on the psalms, see Robins 1993:21–22, 130–38.

91 Long letter to Akropolites in Tartaglia, Op. rhet., 5.72–6.106, 20.435–21.452. See also Chapter 4, pp. 77–78; Chapter 7, p. 132, Chapter 9, pp. 189–90.

92 On the "new" schedography of the twelfth century, see Agapitos 2014. See the humorous *schedos* by Theodore Prodromos published by Polemis 1995:297–98 (on the authorship, see Polemis 1995:287–90). On schedography in the thirteenth century, see Vassis 2002 (description of the content of Vat. Palatinus gr. 95, a late thirteenth-century schedographic codex containing twelfth-century *schede*). On the systematization of schedography by Manuel Moschopoulos (fl. c. 1300), see Keaney 1971.

93 Panagiotis Agapitos will be discussing the schedographic source of inspiration for thirteenth-century authors in a forthcoming publication. On Theodore's occasional use of demotic words, see, for example, Ep. 216.45–47 (pp. 269–70). The editor, Festa, has often emended Theodore's language to make it look more classical. See the examples of vernacular words highlighted by Trapp 1993:124; 2003:141–42.

94 Browning 1975.

95 Konstantinopoulos 1984; PLP 25154. He is one of the addressees of Ep. 217 (pp. 271–76).

96 For example, "ten tongues" (*Iliad* II, 484): Sat., 155.34–35. See Akrop. II, 24.33–34.

97 ἄρνησις κόρης: Ep. 51.60 (p. 74), within Homeric context; 202.23 (p. 249), without Homeric context. The recipients of the two letters are Akropolites and George Mouzalon, respectively. On the *schedos* that discusses this episode (part of Manuel Moschopoulos' collection), see Stephanus 1545:191–94.

4 Pursuit of Learning

1 Sat., 161.174–75. The dating depends on whether Theodore's counting here is inclusive (as I have inferred from the expression) or exclusive.

2 On the hat, see Sat., 183.729–184.752. On the title, see Laurent 1953. See the court hierarchies published by Verpeaux 1966:300, 307, 321 (the appendix to the *Hexabiblos* of Constantine Harmenopoulos, the versified list of Matthew Blastares, and the list in Vaticanus gr. 952); Macrides, Munitiz, and Angelov 2013:455–63 (tables). See Macrides, Munitiz, and Angelov 2013:323–25, on the introduction of headgear at the court.

3 Sat., 190.866–69.

4 Sat., 162.202–03, 175.500–01.

5 Sat., 163.215–16.

6 Sat., 185.753–55.

7 Sat., 166.284–86. "Gates of the wise people" means their lips, as Theodore explains in *Natural Communion*, PG, vol. 140, col. 1394AB. The proverbial expression connected with Plato, *Laws*, 953d is found in other authors, such as Gregory of Nazianzus and Nicholas Mesarites. Theodore uses it elsewhere: KD, IV, 46.15–16.

8 Sat., 161.181, 164.240, 192.924.

9 Zabareiotes is mentioned in Ep. 216.28–40 (p. 269), where Theodore ridicules an unknown person seen by him one day earlier. His balding (literally "exposed to the air") and dry head is said to have had as its "pedagogue" Zabareiotes. As Theodore writes jokingly, Zabareiotes had been born dry, conceived when his father's moisture had withdrawn from his genitalia. The dryness of Zabareiotes is also mentioned in Ep. 202.17–19 (p. 248). Pappadopoulos (1908:17, n. 1; 1929:27) has suggested that the first name of Zabareiotes was Christopher, but there is not enough evidence to support this conclusion. Christopher mentioned in Epp. 80, 168, and 216 was a member of Theodore's entourage who was active *after* the death of the head tutor. See 282, n. 26. Theodore calls Christopher κυρτόφορος ("a hunchback," a pun on his name) in Ep. 80.32–33 (p. 108), describing a visit to Pergamon in 1253. In Ep. 216.49–51 (p. 270), where Zabareiotes is mentioned, Theodore jokes that he wishes that the hunched back of Christopher could be straightened: this is important, because the latter man is clearly different from Zabareiotes. In Ep. 168.10–12 (p. 223) he jokes that Mouzalon could give a beating to Hagiotheodorites and Christopher. This Christopher may be the hunched man to whom Ep. 171.5–6 (p. 224) jokingly alludes. Theodore's *baioulos* was satirized for having a hunch, but this is only one of many aspects of his grotesque appearance. The possibility of the head tutor having the surname Eirenikos emerges from the only allusion to his name in the *Satire*. According to Sat., 196.1020–21, he was homonymous with peace (*eirene*) and thus deceived simple-minded people.

10 On the *kouropalates* and *logariastes* Gregorios Zabareiotes, see his seal published by Stavrakos 2000:155–56 (no. 85). On Theodore Eirenikos, see Choniates, *Historia*, 271; Nikephoros Kallistos Xanthopoulos in PG, vol. 147, col. 465AB; Laurent 1969:133–34; Simpson 2013:31–32 (based on two letters by Niketos Choniates written in Nicaea). On Nicholas Eirenikos, an author of occasional poetry, see 272, n. 16.

11 Sat., 169.376–81.

12 His life before 1204 is described in Sat., 154–60 (§1–§6). Mutilation of the nose was a punishment meted out to adulterers from the eighth century onward. See *Ecloga*, 17.27.

13 Sat., 164.240–41.

14 Around the age of twelve, Blemmydes started his own study of rhetoric, followed by the first parts of logic. See Munitiz 1988:14. On Theodore's description of the sequence of subjects covered in his general education, see Chapter 4, 78–79.

15 KD, IV, 45.2–46.8.

16 The idea derives from an interpretation of Hermogenes, *On Issues*, 11 (Rabe 1913:88.11–14). See Sat., 155.141–42; Ep. 52.1–2 (p. 75); KD, III, 22.19. For a reference to Hermogenes' "six circumstances," see Sat., 163.216–18; Hermogenes, *On Invention* III, 5 (Rabe 1913:140.16–19). For Hermogenes as an authority, see Chr. Th., VII, 141.135.

17 For a mention of Demosthenes, see Enc. Nic., 72.117. For Polemon of Laodicea, see the encomium on Akropolites in Tartaglia, Op. rhet., 102.162–66. It is perhaps noteworthy that Cynaegirus is mentioned by Blem., *Imperial Statue*, 88, Chapter 137.

18 Ep. 90.26 (p. 118), 172.12–15 (p. 225).

19 On the dates of Elena's birth, betrothal, marriage, and death, see Angelov 2013b:274–82.

20 Angelov 2011b:113–15.

21 Akrop. I, §31 (pp. 48–49). On the termination of the union with the papacy, see Cankova-Petkova 1968; Gjuzelev 1977:148–49.

22 Arampatzis 2004–06:377.101–08.

23 See the hagiographical account of the transfer of the relics of Saint Petka in Kozhukharov 1974:128, translated by Petkov (2008:438–40). On his way to Nicaea, Ioakim obtained in Kallikrateia, around 9 miles (15 kilometers) west of Constantinople along the Sea of Marmara, liturgical texts related to the cult of Saint Paraskeve (Petka), a tenth-century local holy figure especially popular in the Slavic Balkans, whose relics had recently been transferred to Turnovo. See also the Slavic *vita* of Saint Petka in Kałużniacki 1899:52–54.

24 Golubovich 1919:446.

25 See the account in the *Synodikon of Boril,* §113 in Bozhilov, Totomanova, and Biliarski 2010:156–61; translated by Petkov 2008: 256–57; Akrop. I, §33 (pp. 50–52); Laurent, *Regestes,* 1282. On the elevation in status of the Bulgarian church, see Cankova-Petkova 1968. An identical concession to a Balkan Slavic church had been made in 1219, when Sava, a former Serbian prince and one-time Athonite monk, was consecrated in Nicaea as autocephalous patriarch of Serbia. Sava served as a model: Ivan Asen II invited him to Bulgaria on his return from a pilgrimage to Jerusalem, and he passed away in Turnovo in January 1235 or 1236. See Stanojević 1933; Obolensky 1988:168.

26 Enc. John, 29.128–32. See Angelov 2013b:282–83.

27 See the observations of Laiou 1984:279–80 (based on the court records of the dossier of Demetrios Chomatenos).

28 For the patriarch's sermon on the subject of the human body and soul, see Lagopates 1913:257.13–259.24. See Akropolites (as cited in 257, n. 25) on the role of the empress mother.

29 Browning 1975:27 (on Tzetzes' *Allegories of the Iliad* dedicated to Empress Bertha of Sulzbach); Robert of Clari in McNeal 1964:117 (on Agnes of France, who married Theodore Branas after 1204).

30 *Encomium on the Holy Anargyroi,* **A**, f. 42r; **P**, ff. 63v–64r. See below, Appendix 1, 336–37.

31 Mor. P., XII, 269.516–18, 269.542–44; Ep. 58.17–19 (p. 87).

32 On Pope Gregory IX's letter of December 16, 1235, see Theiner 1859:140–41 (Auvray II 1907:no. 2872). On the Venetian fleet, see Martin da Canal, I, 83–84, in Limentani 1972:82–85; Morreale 2009:32–33; Andrea Dandolo in Pastorello

1938:295.1–13. On the role of Geoffrey II of Villehardouin and his troops, see Alberic of Trois-Fountaines in Scheffer-Boichorst 1874:938.39–939.3; Philippe Mouskes in de Reiffenberg 1838 II:vs. 29238–53 (pp. 620–21). On the chronology of the siege, see the analysis by Langdon (1985).

33 Longnon 1949:178–82; Wolff 1969:221–22.

34 Detailed discussion in Nicol 1988:168–71. On hearing this news, the French king, Louis IX, redeemed this famous relic. Nicaean galleys are said to have tried in the winter of 1238–39 to intercept the boat carrying the Crown of Thorns to Venice. See the story of the *translatio* to Paris by Gautier Cornut, archbishop of Sens, in Riant 1877:52.

35 The legal rules were ambiguous. Sixth degree of affinity had been a ground for marriage prohibition since 997. In 1088 and 1092, respectively, Alexios I first outlawed and then authorized the marriage of an uncle and a nephew with an aunt and a niece. See Laiou 1992:13–15, 37–39; Pitsakis 2000:684. In the fourteenth century Matthew Blastares considered this kind of marriage permissible: Rhalles and Potles 1852–59, VI:131.

36 Akrop. I, §34 (pp. 52–53), §36 (pp. 54–57); Enc. John, 30.142–51 (referring to Michael Asen of Bulgaria).

37 Sat., 172.446–49.

38 Sat., 163.210–11.

39 Akrop. II, 27.25–30; KD, IV, 50.20–26.

40 Ep. 2.79–88 (p. 6).

41 Ep. 112.9–17 (p. 156).

42 Ad Georg. Mouz., 131.274–75. See also Ep. 71 (p. 98), 155 (p. 217), 202.24–25 (p. 249).

43 Blem., *Imperial Statue*, 84, Chapter 128. The fourteenth-century paraphrase of *The Imperial Statue* (Blem., *Imperial Statue*, 85, Chapter 128) names the game explicitly as polo (*tzykanion*).

44 Pach. I, 95.8–12 (Magnesia after Theodore's death), 147.20–21 (Nicaea after the coronation of Michael VIII in the early 1259). See Wirth 1961. The expression κοντῶν συντριβή used by Pachymeres echoes the description of jousting games. See Schreiner 1996. Andreeva (1927:22–23) locates the polo ground in Magnesia. On polo at the Byzantine court, see also Angelov 2009:105–06.

45 KD, IV, 50.26–30, esp. line 29: ἐν γυμνασίῳ τούτῳ τῷ ποθεινῷ.

46 On generalship and rulership, see Or. Fr., 86.5; KD, IV, 50.16–18; Essay 6 in **V**, ff. 67v–68r (see Agapitos and Angelov 2018). On the successful general acting by instinct, see *Natural Communion*, PG, vol. 140, cols. 1353B–1354A.

47 See the panegyric of the emperor John II Komnenos by Michael Italikos in Gautier 1972:283.14–21.

48 See the mirror of princes by Pseudo-Basil, attributed to the patriarch Photios, in Emminger 1913:69–70 (Chapter 56), 73 (Chapter 66).

49 Old Testament: Enc. John, 59.823–30; KD, III, 31.1–2. Roman and late antique history: *Natural Communion*, PG, vol. 140, cols. 1355–56; Enc. John,

54.709–55.735, 58.807–61.875; KD, III, 26.10–25, 30.28–30; Ep. 147.27–40
(p. 210: the anecdote of Trajan's just treatment of the widow, ultimately
derived from Dio Cassius).

50 Enc. John, 55.736–58.805; KD, III, 24.14–15.

51 *Natural Communion,* PG, vol. 140, col. 1358AB; Ad Georg. Mouz.,
120.6–121.27; Enc. John, 53.685–54.708; KD, III, 26.25–26; Ep. 122.4–5
(p. 170: the example of the cynic Kalanos, who was in reality a gymnosophist,
may be based on Plutarch, *Alexander,* 65.2).

52 Sat., 168.345–49. For the rare word "initiate" (*mystis*) in the same line of the
Book of Wisdom (Wisdom as an initiate in the knowledge of God), see
Theodore's *Oration on Wisdom* in Paléologue 2007:84.81; Ep. 49.72 (p. 70);
Enc. Nic., 80.285–86; KD, III, 26.6. For other references to the Book of Wisdom
and the Proverbs embedded in descriptions of his love of learning, see Ep.
1.15–16 (p. 2), 2.44–45 (p. 4), 53.41–42 (p. 72), 199.11–12 (p. 245).

53 See Chapter 6, 117–18, for the account of his vision in Ep. 49 addressed to
Akropolites. See also his vision of Lady Philosophy in KD, III, 34.10–35.27.

54 The author makes clear (Paléologue 2007:88:195–96, 88.218–19) that he composed the *Oration on Wisdom* during his mature years rather than as practice
school essay (*chreia*). The scriptural saying appears paraphrased often in his
letters. See Ep. 1.9–18 (pp. 1–2), 2.44–45 (p. 4), 53.41–42 (p. 78), 103.43–46
(p. 141).

55 Paléologue 2007:84.90–85.113.

56 Paléologue 2007:83.30–31. For his views on tyranny, see Angelov 2007:245–50.

57 Long letter to Akropolites in Tartaglia, Op. rhet., 5.72–6.106.

58 Blem., *Autobiographia,* II, 7 (p. 49), mentions studying logic "before the
Analytics" at this level. In KD, IV, 40.20–27, Theodore refers to Aristotle's
ten categories and to syllogisms of the three figures. See also his letter to the
secretary Balsamon, Ep. 115.30–32 (p. 160).

59 A note states that emperor read the manuscript (Cod. Bodleianus, Cromwell, 13):
"This book, too, was read in its entirety by the wisest emperor Theodore Doukas
Laskaris." See Hutter 1977–1997 3.1 (*Oxford Bodleian Library. Textband*):16. See
Prato 1981 for an identical manuscript note in an Aristotle manuscript.

60 Sat., 171.407–411.

61 For Akropolites' background and biography, see Macrides 2007:5–29. On
Akropolites as an ambassador to Constantinople in Theodore's lifetime, see
Ep. 82 (pp. 109–10).

62 On the structure of the so-called "Patriarchal School," see Magdalino
1996:325–30. On the migration of twelfth-century teachers to Nicaea and the
scaling down of the educational system, see Constantinides 1982:5–8.

63 The *hypatos ton philosophon* Demetrios Karykes, a teacher of logic, was in
charge of a fiscal survey in the Thrakesion theme in around 1226. See Blem.,
Autobiographia, I, 20 (pp. 12–13); Munitiz 1988:17, 54–55; Constantinides

1982:114–15. On the first known *hypatos ton philosophon* in Nicaea, Theodore Eirenikos, a high civil servant (*epi tou kanikleiou*) before 1204 and subsequently a patriarch (1214–16), see 263, n. 10.

64 Akrop. I, §32 (pp. 49–50); Akrop. II, 19.29–32. On Hexapterygos and a plausible hypothesis regarding Hagiotheodorites' being one of the five students, see Constantinides 1982:10–11, n. 33 (based on Ep. 27.22–23 [p. 37]). In Ep. 168.8–9 (p. 223), Theodore comments on the philosophical education of Hagiotheodorites. The hypothesis that the judge Sergios was the fifth student is based on a letter not written by Blemmydes. See Munitiz 1988:71, n. 91. Two of the students bore the names Romanos and Krateros. See Blem., *Autobiographia*, I, 49–50 (pp. 26–27).

65 See Theodore's encomium of Akropolites in Tartaglia, Op. rhet., 103.187–104.207.

66 Macrides 2007:7, n. 21.

67 On the *parakoimomenos* Alexios Krateros, see MM, IV, 240–41 (Dölger-Wirth, *Regesten,* 1714), 295; Ahrweiler 1965:140. On the family prominent since the ninth century, see Cheynet 2001 (reprinted in Cheynet 2008 II:583–98). On the Hagiotheodorites family, see 283, nn. 32–34.

68 Akrop. I, §32 (p. 50.2–6). Assessments of the chronology of the five students' instruction have varied. Munitiz (1988:20–21) suggests Blemmydes taught them in the years 1237–39, while Macrides (2007:194, n. 6; 212, n. 6) proposes that in 1239 Akropolites might have just begun his studies with Blemmydes. What is certain is that in around 1239 Blemmydes fell out with his student Krateros because of the embezzlement controversy.

69 Akrop. I, §39 (pp. 62.23–64.5), with a description of the clash of opinions between George Akropolites and the chief court physician Nicholas (Nicholas Myrepsos).

70 Texts published by Kouzis 1944. See also Theodore's letters: Ep. 30.15–16 (p. 40): "a doctor for the sick"; Ep. 48 (pp. 64–66).

71 Prodromos' teacher has been identified as Constantine Kaloethes by Constantinides 1982:6 n. 6, 8. Blem., Ep. 23 (p. 310.17–18) refers to his teacher Prodromos as a student of the "late Kaloethes of Madyta"; Constantine Kaloethes was appointed as a bishop of Madyta (near Eceabat) in the Gallipoli peninsula before 1204.

72 Blem., *Autobiographia*, I, 27 (p. 16).

73 Blem., *Autobiographia*, I, 49 (pp. 26–27).

74 On the title of the two textbooks on logic and physics (PG, vol. 142, cols. 675–1004, 1005–1320) as *Introductory Epitome,* see Lackner 1972:161. Blemmydes updated and revised the textbooks in the course of his teaching career. The preface of the *Epitome of Logic* refers to the two editions; in the case of the *Epitome of Physics*, the final edition dates to about 1260. See PG, vol. 142, col. 687–89; Lackner 1981:353, 362–63.

75 These dates follow the reconstruction of his life suggested by Munitiz (1988:21–25).

76 Ep. 16.7–15 (p. 22).

77 Blem., Ep. 9.10 (p. 300).

78 Blem., Ep. 12 (pp. 302–03).

79 Blem., *Autobiographia*, I, 67.2–4 (p. 34). On the Balkan journey of Blemmydes, see 269, n. 107.

80 Akropolites was sixteen when he completed his *enkyklios paideia*. See Akrop. I, §29 (p. 46.13–15). Blemmydes was seventeen when he began his medical studies in Smyrna after finishing his secondary education: Blem., *Autobiographia*, I, 4, 19; II, 7 (pp. 4, 12, 49); Munitiz 1988:14–15. The traditional date for the beginning of Theodore's tutorials with Blemmydes is 1240 (see Heisenberg 1896:XIX; Constantinides 1982:14).

81 Sat., 171.422–30. According to the editor Tartaglia (note in the apparatus at lines 422–23), the philosopher was Akropolites, but this is impossible on chronological grounds.

82 Sat., 159.143–160.144; 173.464–181.657. Blemmydes, *Epitome of Logic*, §4, in PG, vol. 142, cols. 719–24.

83 Ep. 1.40–49 (pp. 2–3).

84 Ep. 8.20–21 (pp. 11–12).

85 *Encomium* on George Akropolites, in Tartaglia, Op. rhet., 105.225–28.

86 Pythagoras: KD, III, 33.24; Chr. Th., VII, 141.129, 141.145; Sat., 171.427; Ep. 141.31 (p. 199); Tartaglia, Op. rhet., 8.157; *On Virtue* in Paléologou 2007: Euclid: Sat. 171.427–28; Ep. 130.1–3 (p. 181), 143.50–51 (p. 204); Chr. Th., VII, 141.13, 141.144.

87 Ep. 130.2–3 (p. 181); KD, IV, 47.29–30. In 32.5–6 (p. 41), he called himself a peripatetic. He alluded to the peripatetic school of Aristotle when he described his own penchant for philosophy by using the Greek verb *peripateo* ("to walk"). See Ep. 49.11 (p. 67), 53.40 (p. 78).

88 A note states that the emperor read the manuscript (Cod. Ambrosianus gr. M 46 sup). In the early fifteenth century, the Byzantine scholar and book-collector John Chortasmenos added a colophon and claimed that he could identify Theodore's scholia. For a detailed discussion, see Prato 1981, esp. pp. 252–53 regarding the date of the manuscript on paleographical grounds. On this rare deluxe philosophical manuscript produced before the Renaissance, see also Rashed 2000:301.

89 On the *Nicomachean Ethics*, see Chapter 6, p. 125. Ep. 80.10–11 (p. 107) to Akropolites echoes *De Mundo*, 391a18–b3, as identified by Wilson 1996:220, n. 7; see also 306, n. 10; 308, n. 58.

90 *On the Soul: Natural Communion,* PG, vol. 140, col. 1277AB. See also Ep. 202.4–8 (p. 248); *On Colors*: Sat., 170.388–89; Ep. 55.14–18 (p. 82), 59.8–9 (p. 88).

91 *Physics*, 201a10–1: "the actuality (*entelecheia*) of what exists potentially (*dynamei*), in so far as it exists potentially"; *On the Soul*, 412a27–28.

92 Blemmydes, *Epitome of Physics*, Chapter 4, in PG, vol. 142, Chapter 4, col. 1049.

93 On the words ἐντελέχεια, ἐντελεχής, and ἐντελεχῶς, see, for example, Ep. 44.3 (p. 56), 63.3 (p. 92), 109.14 (p. 151), 130.45 (p. 182), 133.9 (p. 188), 156.6 (p. 218), 184.24 (p. 235). On the expression used for his accession as sole emperor, see Appendix 1, 325–26, 328–30.

94 Blemmydes, *Epitome of Logic*, §6, in PG, vol. 142, cols. 725–28. Platonism and Aristotelianism: Enc. Nic., 72.114–15; KD, IV, 41.21–26; Inscription: Ep. 121.19–20 (p. 168); KD, IV, 41.23–24; Pythagoreans: Ep. 135.17–18 (p. 191), 216.8 (p. 268); Stoics: Ep. 32.7 (p. 41), Chr. Th., VII, 142.176.

95 Mor. P., III, 257.116–17. Cf. Ep. 32.4–5 (p. 41).

96 Apol., 112.60–64. See also Ep. 96.33 (p. 131), Chr. Th., VII, 141.140.

97 *Sophist:* Ep. 23.22–23 (p. 29); Sat., 174.480–81; *Republic:* Ep. 59.12–15 (p. 88); *Laws:* Ep. 57.37–40 (p. 78).

98 Essay 3 in **V**, f. 67r. See Agapitos and Angelov 2018. The proposition of the essay that "nature does not turn on itself" goes back to Proclus and reflects the generative power of nature discussed by Blemmydes, *Epitome of Physics*, Chapter 7, in PG, vol. 142, col. 1089BC.

99 Akrop. I, §53 (p. 106.13–15). See also his reputation among people of Ephesos reported by Gregory of Cyprus in Lameere 1937:181.15–23. An excellent assessment of Blemmydes' personality can be found in Munitiz 1988:29–42.

100 Blem., *Autobiographia*, I, 54 (p. 29).

101 Blem., *Autobiographia*, I, 49–53 (pp. 26–29). On Hikanatos, see MM, IV, 215; Ahrweiler 1965:143; Angold 1975a:250–51. The next governor of the Thrakesion theme, Manuel Kontophre, is attested in the spring of 1240.

102 Sat., 185.753–67, esp. lines 764–67.

103 See Blemmydes' poem praising Vatatzes for turning a deaf ear to slanderers in Heisenberg 1898:102.68–103.91.

104 Blem., *Autobiographia*, I, 55–57 (pp. 29–30).

105 These events are told by Blem., *Autobiographia*, I, 58–62 (pp. 30–32). On the *doux* John Komnenos Kantakouzenos, see Ahrweiler 1965:144–45; Angold 1975a:210–11. He was already *doux* of Thrakesion on November 1, 1242. See the document published by Wilson and Darrouzès 1968:20–21. The previous *doux*, George Kammytsoboukes, is last attested in June 1241, which is the *terminus post quem* for the appointment of Kantakouzenos.

106 Ep. 2.53–78 (p. 5), 8.35–53 (p. 12); Appendix 2, 357–63.

107 The journey – described in Blem., *Autobiographia*, I, 63–64 (pp. 32–33) – took place during John Kantakouzenos' term as *doux*, that is, after June 1241 (see 269, n. 105). Time needs to be allowed for the investigations against Blemmydes, the return of Vatatzes from his military expedition against Thessalonica (1242) (see 273, n. 29), and the resulting agreement, after which the Nicaean emperor was in a position to support Blemmydes' trip to the area. The earliest year, therefore, when Blemmydes could have departed is 1242. In the preface to his edition of Blemmydes, Heisenberg (1896:XVIII), followed by Munitiz (1988:21; 77, n. 107), dates the journey before Patriarch

Germanos' death in 1240, but this date does not fit with the documentary evidence. The revised date for Blemmydes' journey to the Balkans would remove the necessity to cluster many events in Blemmydes' life into the period 1239–40. On the imperially sponsored creation of libraries, see Chapter 5, p. 106–07.

108 Blem. Ep., 329.113–16. He also declined to become the mentor to Patriarch Manuel II who was ordained between August and October 1243. See Blem., *Autobiographia,* I, 69.15–18 (p. 35).

109 Blem. Ep., 325–29. The letter is translated by Munitiz (2003:370–74), who has suggested 1244 as the year when Blemmydes likely received the teaching offer.

110 Akrop. I, §53 (p. 106.15–18).

111 Ep. 19.5–6,19.11–12 (p. 25), 14.51–52 (p. 20).

112 For borrowed phrases, see Blem., *Imperial Statue,* 48, Chapter 14.2 and Tartaglia, Op. rhet., 7.123–124, 104.205–206 ("double-edged weapon"); Blem., *Imperial Statue,* 44, Chapter 4.2–3, and Or. Fr., 91.149 ("preservation of the realm"); Blem., *Imperial Statue,* 48, Chapter 14.2–3, and Or. Fr., 89.90–91; Blem., *Imperial Statue,* 84, Chapter 130.2, and Or. Fr., 91.145. See Chapter 7, p. 134, for a borrowed mythological figure. For other examples, see Angelov 2007:212, n. 34; 222, n. 80; 240, n. 151.

113 Agapitos 2007:1–6, esp. 5 (short poem by Blemmydes).

114 Ep. 41.6–9 (p. 53).

115 Ep. 45.7–15 (p. 60).

116 Ep. 42.8–9 (p. 54).

117 *Natural Communion,* PG, vol. 140, cols. 1355–56.

118 Ep. 42.12–14 (p. 54).

119 Ep. 2 (pp. 3–6), 8 (pp. 11–12), esp. Ep. 8.48–51 (p. 12). On these letters and their chronology, see Appendix 2, 357–61.

120 Ep. 10 (p. 14), 11 (pp. 15–16). See Appendix 2, 362. On Nikephoros' family name, Pamphilos, see Darrouzès 1984:186. On his wealth, see Pach. I, 167.19–21. On Theodore's portrayal of Nikephoros, see also Chapter 6, pp. 116–17.

121 Ep. 11.5–7 (p. 15); Essay 5 in **V**, f. 67r–v (see Agapitos and Angelov 2018).

122 Ep. 9 (p. 13), 15 (pp. 20–21).

123 Ep. 2.79–88 (p. 6).

124 Blem., *Autobiographia,* I, 68.15–17 (p. 34).

5 Power-Sharing

1 Akrop. I, §39 (p. 64.1–5). On the date of her death, see Macrides 2007:213–14, n. 12. On her monastic name Eugenia, see the document of 1269 published in *Engrapha Patmou,* I, no. 36, 286.2–3.

2 Akrop. II, 5.69–75, 6.96–101. The text was reedited by Hörandner (1972). On the anonymous author, a *megas logariastes* traditionally identified with Akropolites for no plausible reason, see Macrides 2007:20.

3 Huillard-Bréholles 1852–61, VI, 2:685–86. A clue as to the chronological terminus of the letter is the reference to "a concealed disagreement" with the papacy, which suggests that Frederick's second and final excommunication on Palm Sunday 1239 had not yet taken effect. See Wellas 1983:24–25, 137. Wellas' view that Vatatzes planned to make a state visit to Italy is far-fetched. In any case, as Acconcia-Longo (1985–86:230–43) has shown, the addressee of the Greek poem by George of Kallipolis mentioning the visit is not the Nicaean emperor but a certain John Komnenos Vatatzes from Corfu.

4 Richard of San Germano (Garufi 1937–38:164.3–5 [November 1229]) refers to the embassy as *de Romania quidam Greci*. Traditionally, this expression has been interpreted as referring to envoys sent by John Vatatzes, an interpretation confirmed by the fact that John Vatatzes struck gold coins (from 1227, according to Michael Hendy's hypothesis), whereas Theodore of Epiros did not. See Hendy 1999 II:473–75, 545–49; cf. the doubts of Kiesewetter 1999:246–48, n. 12. Frederick's familiarity with Byzantine and Muslim gold coins may have been an inspiration for the *augustalis* he issued in 1231 (Grierson and Travaini 1998:174–75).

5 Van Cleve 1972:391–409. The *podestà* of Milan, Pietro Tiepolo, a son of the Venetian doge, was captured, and an extravagant imperial triumph was staged in Cremona.

6 *Annales Placentini Gibellini* in Pertz 1863:479.32–37.

7 According to the versified chronicle of Philippe Mouskes (De Reiffenberg 1838 II:vs. 29860–29883, pp. 642–43), John Vatatzes was to become a vassal of Frederick if the latter ensured that Constantinople was delivered to him and Baldwin left for France. Although the arrangement for vassalage is unlikely, it is highly probable that John Vatatzes provided military help to Frederick in return for recognition of his legitimate claims, if not necessarily full rights.

8 Theiner 1859:140–41 (same as Auvray II 1907:no. 2872). See also Auvray II 1907:nos. 2873–79; nos. 2909–11 (January 1236), nos. 3395–96 (December 1236). On Gregory IX and his busy crusading agenda in support of Latin Constantinople, see Chrissis 2012:99–133.

9 Grumel 1930:455–56 (letter by Gregory IX); Pieralli 2006:121–26.

10 See the pope's letter dated March 17, 1238, in Huillard-Bréholles 1852–61, V, 1:181–83, esp. 183.

11 The estimate of the army's size varies from 20,000 to 40,000. On the return of Baldwin, see Akrop. I, §37 (pp. 57.20–59.3); Alberic of Trois-Fountaines in Scheffer-Boichorst 1874:946–47; Longnon 1949:181–83.

12 On the date of the wedding, see Appendix 1, 331–33. Constanza was born c. 1230. See Kiesewetter 1999:241, n. 9.

13 This is the most plausible theory of Bianca Lancia's kinship with Manfred II, based on the testimony of the contemporary Genoese annalist Bartolomeo Scriba: MGH SS, vol. 18, 228. See Ferro 1992; Settia 2004a. On Manfred II, see Van Cleve 1972:445; Settia 2004c.

14 The jewelry is mentioned in her testament (see the note below). On the ladies-in-waiting, see 272, n. 17. On the Greek monks from Calabria, see the patriarchal document published by Oudot (1941:no. 16, pp. 80–83) and the additions from Codex Iviron 381 in Laurent, *Regestes*, 1308 (p. 114).

15 See the testamentary provisions of August 15 and 16, 1306, by which Constanza-Anna ceded her rights to the crown of Aragon: Miret y Sans 1906:695–96 (in Catalan), 717–18 (in Latin). On the identification of the place names, see Ahrweiler 1965:54–55, 68–69; Bieg, Belke, and Tekkök 2009:168, 174. See also Dölger-Wirth, *Regesten*, 1780, 1781.

16 Sat., 191.911–192.913; poem by Nicholas Eirenikos in Heisenberg 1920:100–05, esp. 104.103.

17 Akrop. I, §52 (p. 104.1–10). See also Blemmydes' *Open Letter,* whose title states that the *archontissa* Marchesina "took precedence even more than the empress": Blem., *Autobiographia*, 91.

18 The affair is described also in Blem., *Autobiographia*, I, 70–71 (pp. 35–36), II, 49 (p. 67); Greg. I, 56–57. Blemmydes writes that the quarrel with Marchesina occurred "recently" (ὑπόγυον), before the disputation in the spring of 1250, which makes c. 1248 a plausible date. See Blem., *Autobiographia*, II, 50.11–14 (p. 67). A similar date has been suggested for different reasons by Munitiz (1988:24–25 and 141, n. 9), who proposes Pentecost 1248 as the time of the confrontation in Blemmydes' monastery.

19 Blem., *Autobiographia*, pp. 91–94. For a translation of the open letter, see Munitiz 1988:139–43; see also Munitiz 1982.

20 Blem., *Autobiographia*, II, 76.1–2 (p. 79), writes that he presented the mirror of princes "before the emperors." The letter of dedication to Theodore survives: Blem., Ep., 13 (pp. 303–04). The *Imperial Statue* postdates the Marchesina affair c. 1248 (see 272, n. 18) and predates the *Memorial Speech* for Frederick II (d. December 13, 1250), whose language it influenced. See 270, n. 112.

21 Blem., *Imperial Statue*, 62, Chapter 66.1; Ševčenko 1978:225, n. 20. See also chs. 1–5 on taxation (p. 44).

22 Akrop. I, §37 (p. 59.4–10). See Longnon 1949:183.

23 Sat. 194.981–85.

24 The estimate of the number of the Nicaean galleys varies. According to Akrop. I, §37 (pp. 59.11–60.2), Iophre commanded thirty galleys, of which he lost thirteen. According to Andrea Dandolo, the Nicaeans attacked the city with twenty-five galleys, of which Giovanni Michiel captured ten. See Andrea Dandolo in Pastorello 1938:298.10–14. According to Martin da Canal, Vatatzes attacked with one hundred and sixty galleys (the number is certainly

exaggerated), of which Giovanni Michiel captured ten. See Martin da Canal, I, 85–86, in Limentani 1972:84–87; Morreale 2009:33–34.

25 Alberic of Trois-Fontaines in Scheffer-Boichorst 1874:950.23–24: *in biennium firmaverunt Constantinopolitani treugas ad Colmannum Alsani filium et ad Vastachium et eius filium.*

26 Akrop. I, §38 (p. 61.13–14), remarks that he "loved her exceedingly, no less than Antony did Cleopatra."

27 These events are related by Akrop. I, §38 (pp. 60–62).

28 Alberic of Trois-Fontaines in Scheffer-Boichorst 1874:950.12–15.

29 The campaign of John Vatatzes against Thessalonica (Akrop. I, §40) is traditionally dated to 1242. See Macrides (2007:219, n. 24, with references to the historiography), who suggests the possibility of late 1241 (Macrides 2007:216, 221, n. 4); the campaign is re-dated on the basis of Akropolites' narrative and the assumption that the encounter in Tripolis and the treaty between John Vatatzes and Kaykhusraw II (reported in Akrop. I, §41) dates to the second half of 1243, not long after the Battle of Köse Dağ on July 26, 1243. The traditional date for the campaign against Thessalonica (1242) is nonetheless not to be dismissed, because the campaign was interrupted by the alarming news of a Mongol incursion and victory "over the Muslims" in Anatolia. The event was most probably the bloody sack of Erzurum/Theodosioupolis (1242). See 274, n. 36. One can reconcile the discrepancy of the sources by proposing a winter campaign of 1241–42, which would fit into Vatatzes' strategy of out-of-season warfare. Korobeinikov (2014:11, n. 21) argues correctly that the battle between Mongols and Seljuks referred to by Akropolites cannot have taken placed in late 1241, as suggested by Macrides (2007:219, n. 18) on the basis of Vincent of Bouvais, because Vincent's source, Simon of Saint Quentin, gives the correct date (1242). But it is doubtful that Akropolites speaks not of a real battle, but a possible battle-to-be, when he reports in §40 the hasty withdrawal of John Vatatzes from Thessalonica (Korobeinikov 2014:11). The information is too specific, and given by an eyewitness, to be dismissed. Zhavoronkov (2001) has suggested that Vatatzes' campaign against Thessalonica took place in 1243 and was interrupted by the Seljuk defeat at Köse Dağ. The hypothesis is less likely, because it cannot account for the highly specific report of Ivan Asen's death in June 1241 by Alberic of Trois-Fontaines.

30 Akrop. I, §42 (p. 71:20): the case of the campaign of 1246. For the campaign of 1253, see Chapter 7, pp. 128–29.

31 Thus, the metropolitan bishop Joseph, a Greek, was ordained in Nicaea in 1237. His fate after the Mongol sack of Kiev is unknown. The next metropolitan, Peter, served for more than thirty years and was a native. An appointee of the prince of Galicia, he was ordained in Nicaea in 1248–49. See Meyendorff 1981:39–44; Zhavoronkov 1982.

32 For the Mongol campaigns against Kiev and in Europe, see Saunders 1971:81–89; Morgan 1986:136–41.

33 On the beginnings of the Mongol domination in Russia, see Fennell 1983:76–96. On the flight of Rostislav Mikhailovich, see Dimnik 2003:360–66. On Jacob Svetoslav, see Pach. I, 243.20–21; and Epilogue, p. 221. On Bulgaria's reduction to tributary dependence on the Golden Horde, see Zlatarski 1940:424–25; Cankova-Petkova 1969:63–65.

34 Cahen 1988:90–98. The Turkmen rebellion led by the charismatic mystic Baba Ishaq, which broke out in 1240, was not suppressed for two years.

35 Jackson 1990.

36 Kirakos of Gandzak, Chapter 34 in Khanlarian 1976:175–76; Bedrosian 1986:240–42; Vardan Arewelts'i in Thomson 1989:216. The attack occurred at the beginning of the year 691 of the Armenian era (January 20, 1242), namely, in early 1242. See Grumel 1958:259. Simon of Saint Quentin (Richard 1965:75) says that Erzurum was sacked after the population first submitted peacefully to the Mongols. See also Jackson 1978:216–17.

37 Akrop. I, §40 (pp. 65–67).

38 On the number of soldiers John Vatatzes was obliged to provide to the sultan, see Simon of Saint Quentin in Richard 1965:70. On the Latin and Greek troops in Kaykhusraw II's army, see Ibn Bibi in Duda 1959:227. See also Langdon 1998:116.

39 Cahen 1988:227–30; Korobeinikov 2014:176–78. On the Battle of Köse Dağ, see Ibn Bibi in Duda 1959:224–30; Kirakos of Gandzak, Chapter 35, in Khanlarian 1976:176–78; Bedrosian 1986:243–47; Bar Hebraeus in Budge 1932:406–07; Simon of Saint Quentin in Richard 1965:78–80.

40 For different opinions on the name of 'Izz al-Dīn's mother, see Shukurov 2008b:90–92 (Prodoulia, an otherwise unattested name); Korobeinikov 2014:186, n. 108 (a Greek woman from a fortress on Lake Burdur). The Armenian historian Kirakos of Gandzak describes 'Izz al-Dīn's wife as the "daughter of Laskaris, the ruler of Ephesos." See 257, n. 23. I am adopting here the suggestion of Korobeinikov (2014:186) that she was "a member of the Byzantine aristocracy."

41 On these events, see Cahen 1988:230–35; Korobeinikov 2014:181–89. According to Cahen, Rukn al-Dīn journeyed to the court of Batu, but see now Korobeinikov 2014:182, n. 84. On Rukn al-Dīn's coins, see Lindner 1974.

42 On the Grand Komnenos, see Bryer 1994. On the king of Cilician Armenia, see Constable Smbad §56, §58, in Dédéyan 1980:98–100; Boyle 1964; Der Nersessian 1969:652–53. On the new system of tributary rulers in Mongol-dominated Eurasia, see Allsen 1987:63–76.

43 Ep. 179.26 (p. 230).

44 Enc. John, 27.82–83, 28.104, 31.175. On Theodore's involvement in Mongol diplomacy, see Chapter 7, p. 134; Chapter 8, pp. 152, 170–71. Akropolites calls the Mongols Tacharoi and Pachymeres prefers the name Tocharoi. By contrast, the fourteenth-century historian Gregoras calls them Scythians and engages in an ethnographic discussion. See Greg. I, 30–40.

45 Enc. John, 29.133, 32.182.

46 As reported in Pach. I, 187.19–21. On the Mongol reputation for cruelty see also Michael Palaiologos' autobiography: Dmitrievsky 1895:791.

47 The story is reported by Pach. I, 317.19–323.30.

48 Akrop. I, §41 (pp. 69.23–70.12), according to whom the two rulers "affirmed more strongly the earlier agreements, so that they might fight the enemy jointly"; Greg. I, 41, who in hindsight ascribed to Vatatzes the strategic motive of using the sultanate of Rum as a buffer; Dölger-Wirth, *Regesten*, 1776, dates the treaty to the autumn of 1243.

49 Matthew Paris in Luard 1872–84, vol. 5:37–38. On the context of this Mongol embassy to the papacy, see Guzman 1971:238–39. In 1254 William of Rubruck overheard that John Vatatzes had greatly feared and still suspected an imminent Mongol invasion. See Chapter 7, pp. 133–34.

50 *Synopsis chronike*, 506.19–507.9.

51 Pach. I, 187.12–19. See Pach. IV, 475.30–477.3 (the case of Tripolis).

52 Jacob of Bulgaria in Mercati 1970:89.24–25.

53 Enc. John, 28.97–103.

54 Greg. I, 42.

55 Enc. John, 28.107–29.116. See the discussion and translation in Angelov 2011:30–32. Greg. I, 37.9, refers to Cumans being settled in Phrygia (the borderlands with the sultanate) and along the Maeander valley. The same conclusion about the settlement of Cumans as *akritai* is reached by Langdon (1992:19–20; 62, n. 87), who prefers to see in Theodore's words evidence of John Vatatzes' campaigns in 1225–31 rather than, as suggested here, of a migration from the sultanate after 1243.

56 Longnon 1949:185; Wolff 1969:224–25.

57 The events are narrated by Akrop. I, §42–§45 (pp. 70–83).

58 Choniates, *Historia*, 599; Villehardouin, §280 (II, 88–89). See Patlagean 1998. The privileges granted to Verroia also date to this period. See Kyritses 1999:230–31.

59 On these borders, see Akrop. I, §44 (p. 78.14–22); §46 (p. 84.16–22).

60 On the treaty with Bulgaria, see Akrop. I, §44 (p. 78.22–25); Zlatarski 1940:439; Dölger-Wirth, *Regesten*, 1787.

61 The confrontations in Thrace in 1247 are mentioned by Akrop. I, §47 (p. 85) and in two manuscript notes published by Polemis (1966) and Evangelatou-Notara (1989). While Akropolites mentions the release of the Latin prisoners of war captured in Tzouroulos (including John Vatatzes' sister-in-law Eudokia, the wife of Anselm de Cahieu), one of the notes (Polemis 1966:171.18–21) refers to all imprisoned Latins being sent to Nicaea. See also Cankova-Petkova 1969:65–68; Dancheva-Vasileva 1989:158–59; Macrides 2007:245–46.

62 Akrop. I, §48 (p. 86.1–7). In 1248 the prince of Achaia, William of Villehardouin, headed a relief expedition in defense of Constantinople. See Saint-Guillain 2014:21–23, 49.

63 Sat., 179.597–99.

64 On Theodore's use of the words *basileus* and *basileia*, see, for example, Ep. 25.28 (p. 35), 107.16 (p. 147), 107.43 (p. 148), 116.21 (p. 163). Contemporaries refer to Theodore Laskaris as a *basileus* during his coemperorship. See Blem., Ep. 23.1 (p. 309), 24.22 (p. 311). See also the imperial oration of Jacob of Bulgaria in Mercati 1970:91.15. On the title of John Vatatzes, see, for example, the signature in his chrysobull of 1228: MM, IV, 4. A crowned coemperor in the fourteenth century could be – and often was – named *basileus* and *autokrator* by his father on his coronation. According to Pseudo-Kodinos, if the father did not grant his permission to his son and coemperor to use both titles, the latter had the title of *basileus* only. See Pseudo-Kodinos in Verpeaux 1966:252–53; Macrides, Munitiz, and Angelov 2013:212.1–5; Franz Dölger in BZ, 33 (1933):136–44.

65 Ep. 19.5–9 (p. 25): ἡ πρὸς τὸν ἅγιόν μου αὐθέντην πατέρα καὶ βασιλέα προϋπάντησις καὶ προσκύνησις, μετὰ δὲ ταύτας ἡ καθ' ἑκάστην ὁμιλία καὶ αἱ πρὸς τὰ τοῦ καιροῦ χρήσιμα ἀναμνήσεις καὶ ὑπομνήσεις καὶ ἄλλ' ἄττα πολλὰ καὶ κατάλληλα τῷ καιρῷ.

66 On the rare word *proypantesis,* encountered in the works of Anna Komnene, Pachymeres, and a few other authors, see LBJ, s.v.

67 Guilland 1946–47; Macrides, Munitiz, and Angelov 2013:386–87.

68 John Kantakouzenos in Schopen 1828 I:167.21–168.4.

69 On Theodore performing *proskynesis*, see Ep. 83.22–27 (pp. 110–11); and also Ep. 26.2–3 (p. 35), which describes Theodore meeting his father at the Hellespont and greeting him with obeisance. Pach. I, 61.25–28, assumes that *proskynesis* was a gesture Theodore would have performed on meeting his father. On the *archontes* of Ephesos, see Ep. 106.20–23 (p. 146).

70 Ceremony in the courtyard: Nicole 1894:78.19–20; Laurent, *Regestes*, 1251. In September 1229 the bishops of the synod are said to have "glorified the emperor in the church and rendered *proskynesis* in the holy courtyard" (*hagia aule*). Daily reception in a tent: *Synopsis chronike*, 522.14–29.

71 Macrides, Munitiz, and Angelov 2013:395–98; Ep. 172.1–3 (p. 225), 174.1–4 (p. 227), 179.29–30 (p. 230).

72 Attested first in the Palaiologan period. Kazhdan, ODB, vol. 1, 724, corrects the opinion of Guilland (1967b:147–48) that the title existed in the reign of Alexios I.

73 The word *hypomnesis* can mean any official notice and memorandum, but in particular a memorandum of petition. See MM, IV, 36–37 (no. IV), 291, 327–28 (petition to the emperor Alexios IV in 1204). The word is used also in the formulary cited in the note immediately following. See also Ep. 107.8 (p. 147).

74 Ferrari dalla Spade 1913:61 (no. 33).

75 Blem., Ep. 10.22–24 (p. 301), 12.10–13 (p. 303), 23.13–16 (p. 310).

76 Blem., Ep. 8 (pp. 298–99). See especially the reference to a prior decree of Theodore at lines 29–30 (καθὼς προεθέσπισε). The date of this letter emerges

from the mention of the *doux* of the Thrakesion theme and *pinkernes,* John Kantakouzenos, whom Blemmydes presents as being on his side in the dispute. On Kantakouzenos, see 269, n. 105. On dependent peasants (*paroikoi*) paying both the land tax (*telos*) and rent, see Laiou-Thomadakis 1977:45–48.

77 Ep. 107 (pp. 146–48); Dölger-Wirth, *Regesten*, 1823. Theodore's letter is longer and more elaborate than the usual chancery *prostagma*.

78 Cameron 1976:162–79, 285–86; Haldon 1990:124.491–126.495. Middle Byzantine examples have been gathered by Macrides (2004:356–61, 366–70). On petitioning in Byzantium, see also Feissel and Gascou 2004.

79 Ep. 44.67–70 (p. 58).

80 Ep. 111.4–6 (p. 155), 167.1 (p. 222).

81 KD, II, 9.28–33. He walks toward "the clearest fountain of virtue and letters" (referring to his quest for knowledge) and "on a rough and untrodden path" (referring to his encounter with the unknown). See Tartaglia, Op. rhet., 100.113–14; Ep. 19.1–2 (p. 25), 39.27–28 (p. 50).

82 Sat. 162.197–98; Enc. John, 24.23; KD, IV, 41.16.

83 Psalm 118:45. See Ep. 36.65–66 (p. 46), 57.10–11 (p. 85).

84 MM, IV, 215; Ahrweiler 1968:143.

85 Ad Georg. Mouz., 131.268–69. According to one anecdote told by Pach. I, 62.25–63.11, Vatatzes insisted on gold-decorated imperial silk robes being used only on public occasions, such as the reception of foreign ambassadors, and scolded his son for donning them during a hunting expedition.

86 *Synopsis chronike*, 508.

87 Anderson and Jeffreys 1994 (the tent of the *sebastokratorissa* Irene); *Digenis Akritis*, Grotofarrata version, IV.908–810 (Jeffreys 1998:120–121). See the extensive written evidence gathered by Mullett (2013a:274–284). On tented ceremonies, see Mullett 2013b.

88 *Synopsis chronike*, 522.14–29 (spring 1256).

89 Ep. 71.17 (p. 98).

90 Oudot 1941:no. 12, pp. 72–73, Laurent, *Regestes*, 1302. The decision is justified as a return to tradition. The statement can be taken either at face value or with a grain of salt as a way of justifying innovation.

91 See Pach. I, 235.12–18 and n. 7, by the editor, Albert Failler, on the date of the embassy to Khan Hülegü. On King Louis IX's diplomatic gift of a decorated chapel tent to the Mongols in an earlier period, see Joinville in De Wailly 1874:§134 (p. 74), §471 (p. 258).

92 See Blemmydes' poetic description of the Sosandra monastery near Magnesia in Heisenberg 1896:118.104–08.

93 Erdmann 1961–76.

94 Or. Fr., 91.145–92.153; Enc. John, 35.264 (note the adjective ἀκριβοδίκαιος). Both texts date to his coemperorship. See also Essay 4 in **V**, f. 67r, written during his sole rule (Agapitos and Angelov 2018).

95 Ep. 25 (pp. 34–35). The editor, Festa, decided to unite two pieces transmitted separately in the Laurentian codex.
96 Ep. 116 (pp. 162–63); Dölger-Wirth, *Regesten*, 1823a.
97 Ep. 174.1–5 (p. 227).
98 In addition to the Fogg seals kept at Dumbarton Oaks (Figs. 17a and 17b), see other examples in Zacos and Veglery I.3 1972:no. 2755abc (pp. 1574–77); Stavrakos 2000:234–35 (no. 142). See the text from his *Satire* cited in 276, n. 63 and Akrop. II, 8.20 (verses written on the occasion of the publication of Theodore's collected letters in early 1254).
99 Ep. 115 (pp. 159–61), 119–22 (pp. 166–71), 135 (pp. 190–91), 137 (pp. 193–94), 138 (p. 195). On Hagiotheodorites, see Introduction, p. 8, Chapter 6, p. 113. On Mesopotamites, see Chapter 6, p. 113.
100 On the title *grammatikos* given to imperial secretaries after the twelfth century, see Oikonomides 1985:172. On the administration of imperial land grants, see MM, IV, 232–33 (the *grammatikos* Phrangopoulos); Ahrweiler 1965:161.
101 For the former identification (John), see Ahrweiler (1965:159) based on documentary evidence (MM, IV, 85–86, 247; cf. MM, IV, 215). For the latter (Nicholas), see Laurent 1935a:90, 98; Constantinides 1982:22. Kostomyres was a young man in the early 1250s (on his ongoing education at the time, see Chapter 6, p. 118), which makes the identification with John unlikely, if Ahrweiler's dating of the documents to 1238–39 is accepted.
102 Akrop. I, §44 (p. 79.1–7), §49 (p. 91.1–5). On Akropolites' career and promotions (he seems to have become *logothetes tou genikou* by 1252 or 1253), see Macrides 2007:19–23.
103 On the surgical metaphors, see Ep. 111.28 (p. 156) addressed to Mesopotamites; Enc. John, 35.264–266; Or. Fr. 89.85–88. Ep. 112 (pp. 156–157) voices particular closeness to Mesopotamites by calling him ὁ ἐμός.
104 Cheynet and Theodoridis 2010:121–22, no. 108. The seal belongs to the private collection of Dimitris Theodoridis. Jean-Claude Cheynet, who published the collection, considered the seal enigmatic and has hypothesized a fourteenth-century date. The combination of surnames militates against this possibility, however, and the forms of the letters on the seal are already attested on thirteenth-century seals.
105 *Synopsis chronike*, 507.21–24; Jacob of Bulgaria in Mercati 1970:89.20–27; Enc. John, 40.383–88; Pach. IV, 325.21–327.6.
106 On the economic policies of John Vatatzes, see Ahrweiler 1958; Mitsiou 2010b.
107 Greg. I, 42.1–12.
108 Pach. I, 99.6–11. On the settlement policy pertaining to fortifications, see the formulary cited in 243–44, n. 115.
109 Pach. I, 101.10–16; Greg. I, 42.6–8.
110 Greg. I, 43.10–15.

111 *Synopsis chronike*, 507.29–508.7; Blem., Ep., 329.116–17.

112 MM, IV, 142 (*prostagma* of 1231: Dölger-Wirth, *Regesten*, 1725), 142–44 (*periorismos* at the order of the Stephanos Kalopyros, head of the *zeugelateion* of Koukoulos). See Gounaridis 1988:620–21; Ahrweiler 1965:162. On the *palatophylax* in the Palaiologan period, see the formulary of his appointment in Sathas (MB VI:649). In 1234 we find the heads of the households (*oikodespotai*) of Koukoulos witnessing another land grant to the monastery. The documents of 1234 are an imperial *prostagma* (MM, IV, 146–47; Dölger-Wirth, *Regesten*, 1737) and a *paradosis* issued by the *prokathemenos* of Smyrna. See MM, IV, 147–50, esp. 147. Michael Papadopoulos, called *oikodespotes* from the *zeugelateion* of Koukoulos in the *paradosis* of 1234, appears as a witness in the *periorismos* of 1231. It is possible that the *palatophylax* Basil of 1231 is Basil Kretikos, who is identified as being "from Palatia" in the *paradosis* of 1234. The Kretikos family were large landowners in Silleon, near Smyrna. See Nicholas Dermatas Katzibarenos Kretikos in MM, IV, 150, 152–58, 163–68, 174; PLP 13748. The region of Palatia near Smyrna is related to crown lands mentioned in MM, IV, 9, 20, 24, 30. See Ahrweiler 1958:54.

113 For the *oikonomoi*, see Ep. 134.10 (p. 189), in response to a request from the monk Akakios. Ep. 71.14 (p. 98): village of Mountokome. For a hypothesis on its location, see Ahrweiler 1965:70–71. Ep. 216.45 (p. 269): village of Achladeron. On the best barley from the estate of Aristenos, see Ep. 8.28–32 (p. 12). On the location of the estate (*proasteion*) of Aristenos, see Ahrweiler 1965:64. The *proasteion* is mentioned as bordering the *zeugelateion* of Koukoulos in MM, IV, 144, 148.

114 KD, III, 23.17–20, 30.19–23. According to *Geoponica* I, 9.4 (Beckh 1895:18.5–6), the helical rising of the Pleiades occurred on April 23.

115 KD, III, 31.23–26.

116 KD, III, 32.27–33.3. The same word for heads of households (οἰκοδεσπόται) is found in documents preserved in the cartulary of the Lembos monastery that date to Theodore's lifetime. See MM, IV, 81–83, 147.

117 *Natural Communion*, PG, vol. 140, col. 1358B.

118 Greg. I, 43.15–44.6.

119 Brezeanu 1979; Mitsiou 2010a:196; Dölger-Wirth, *Regesten*, 1777.

120 Jacoby 1999:20–25.

121 *Synopsis chronike*, 507.13–18; Tafel and Thomas, II, 1856:205–07 (treaty of 1219); Thomas and Predelli I 1880:141. On a Pisan who passed away in Atramyttion before 1244, see Davidsohn 1896–1919, II:295.

122 See Chapter 7, pp. 129–33; Essay 2 in **V**, f. 66r–v (Agapitos and Angelov 2018).

123 *Natural Communion*, PG, vol. 140, col. 1348b; Ep. 11.27–33 (pp. 15–16). See also Ep. 157 (p. 218), where Theodore uses the market as a metaphor.

124 KD, III, 34.28–35.2.

125 Jacoby (2001:19), based on Metochites, *Nicene Oration*, which refers to the flourishing art of weaving in Nicaea (Foss 1996:§18, 190.15–192.17), has suggested that some of the silk industry of twelfth-century Constantinople was relocated to Nicaea.

126 *Natural Communion*, PG, vol. 140, col. 1345A.

127 On the linen cloth of Halmyros, see John Apokaukos in Vasil'evskii 1896:282.21. On Halmyros in the twelfth century, see Benjamin of Tudela in Adler 1907:11. On the participation of Jews in the silk production amply attested in Thebes, see Jacoby 1991–92:485–8.

128 Nicol 1957:141–42. See Akrop. I, §39 (p. 64.20–22); Macrides 2007:40, 97, 214 nn. 18 and 20, 244 n. 9.

129 Blem., Ep. 20 (p. 308), 22 (p. 309); Ep. 118.7–12 (pp. 164–65).

130 Greg. I, 42.4–6. On the Sosandra monastery, see Blemmydes' poem cited in 277, n. 92. On John Vatatzes' care for lepers, see Akrop. II, 24.2–6. On the leper hospital, see Metochites, *Nicene Oration*, in Foss 1996:§8, 176.11–25. See also Theodore's passing mention of the cultivation of medical knowledge in Nicaea in Enc. Nic., 73.124–25. On imperial patronage of the leper hospital in Pera, founded in the late fourth century by Saint Zotikos, see, for example, Leo the Deacon VI, 5 in Hase 1828:99.20–100.4 (the reign of John I Tzimiskes); Janin 1950:566–67.

131 *Synopsis chronike*, 507.19–20, 535.26–536.6 (= Akrop. I, 186.12–14, 297. 18–298.4). The description is made succinctly at the end of his account of Vatatzes' reign and somewhat more extensively in the historian's concluding remarks on Theodore Laskaris.

132 *Synopsis chronike*, 507.19–20, 535.26–30 (note the use of the verb ἐθέσπισε, which suggests a royal decree).

133 Translation is based on the critical edition by Heisenberg in Akrop. I, 297.27–298.4. For "theater of the muses," see Themistius, Or. 21, 243a; Or. 24, 302a (with echoes from Plato, *Laws*, 953a).

134 Letter published in Laurent 1935a:93.12 (n. 4): βίβλος ἀριστοτελική; Akrop. I, §49 (p. 91.4–5). See Constantinides 1982:15.

135 On Blemmydes' book-hunting trip to the Balkans, see Chapter 4, pp. 84–85. On its connections with Vatatzes' policy, see Constantinides 1982:12–13.

136 See Chapter 8, p. 107.

137 Heisenberg 1920:37–41.

138 Blem., Ep. 5.26–28 (p. 296), where he jokes that the capons presented to Theodore could be judged worthy of the court title of attendant at the dinner table (*epi tes trapezes*).

139 Heisenberg 1920:39.29–44. The fourteenth-century ceremonial book adds that an imperial official, the master of petitions (*epi ton deeseon*), collected petitions during the emperor's tours. See Pseudo-Kodinos in Verpaux 1966:172–73, 183; Macrides, Munitiz, and Angelov 2013:80–82, 106.

140 Redford 1993. See also Çağaptay 2010.

141 See the observations by Peacock 2013.

6 Friends, Foes, and Politics

1 In addition to φίλοι (the most common word), he also called them συνήθεις, γνήσιοι, ἐμοί and ἡμέτεροι.

2 Ep. 52.29–31 (p. 76).

3 Patriarch Germanos II, *Sermon for the Elevation of the Holy Cross and Against the Bogomils*: PG, vol. 140, col. 641B.

4 Tartaglia, Op. rhet., 151.251–152.260.

5 Merendino 1974–75:322. The name of the page is given as Paidrytes in an earlier edition (see MM, III, 72). Merendino pointed to a textual problem and emended the manuscript reading to παιδάριον.

6 Pach. I, 55.17–21, 155.6–10.

7 Akrop. I, §75 (p. 155.16–19); Pach. I, 65.25–29 (note the reference to their father); Greg. I, 62. On the relative age of the siblings, see Macrides 2007:342–43, n. 16.

8 Ep. 8.28–34 (p. 12) (on the date, see Appendix 2, 361), 9.1–13 (p. 13). The beasts of burden were used in the construction of the monastery of Christ Who Is.

9 Ep. 185 (p. 235). See Appendix 2, 370.

10 Ep. 179.7–12 (p. 230). See also the preface to the four books of Theodore's treatise *Explanation of the World*: KD, I, 101.1–2.

11 Ep. 150.1–3 (p. 214), 161.1–2 (p. 220), 184.18–19 (p. 234).

12 Ep. 164.1 (p. 221), 165.1–2 (p. 221), 179.22 (p. 230).

13 Ep. 175.1–2 (p. 227). See also Ep. 153.4–5 (p. 216), 171.1 (p. 224), 173.38–41 (p. 227).

14 Ep. 155.7 (p. 217), 191.8–9 (p. 238), 192.14 (p. 239), 193.17 (p. 240), 194.23 (p. 241), 202.61–62 (p. 250), 204.134–35 (p. 255), 205.44–45 (p. 256), 207.42–43 (p. 259), 213.23 (p. 265), 214.49 (p. 266).

15 John Skylitzes in Thurn 1973:263. See the seal of Eugenios Mouzalon, *krites* (eleventh century), in Wassiliou and Seibt 2004:no. 41 (p. 68). Cf. Wassiliou and Seibt 2004:68, n. 267, for seal of Leo Mouzalon, *spatharios* and *basilikos notarios* (eleventh century).

16 On the governor of Nicaea, see Blem., *Autobiographia*, I, 30.1–4 (p. 17). On the monk and ex-*mystikos* John Mouzalon, see Akrop. I, §40 (p. 67.6–9). Angold (1975a:161, n. 70) has plausibly identified him with the deacon, *mystikos*, and *epi tou kanikleiou* mentioned by the patriarch Germanos in a polemical sermon: see Chapter 3, p. 67.

17 Blem., *Autobiographia*, I, 88.6–7 (p. 44). See also Akrop. I, §60 (p. 124.10–11), §76 (p. 160.13–14). Pach. I, 41.14; Greg. I, 62.4–5.

18 KD, III, 31.1–14, 38.5; Ep. 199.27–28 (p. 245).

19 *Natural Communion*, PG, vol. 140, cols. 1357A, 1362B (written before November 1254).

20 *Encomium of Wisdom*, in Paléologou 2007:83.39–40 (written before November 1254).

21 Mor. P., IX, 264.382–265.385 (written in 1252).

22 Essay 2 in **V**, f. 66r–v, written after November 1254 (Agapitos and Angelov 2018).

23 This man who appears in five letters (Epp. 30, 34, 51, 160, 192) is the addressee, along with John Phaix, of a treatise on the Trinity, the opening work of the collection *Sacred Orations*. See 285, n. 66; Appendix 1, 325 and 326, n. 10. Theodore's use of the word *koubouklarios* may suggest a family name, but the phrase "my own *koubouklarios* Constantine" in Ep. 160.2–3 (p. 219) shows that the position of chamberlain is meant. On his role as a messenger, see Ep. 30.18–20 (p. 40) to Blemmydes, 51.88–91 (p. 75) to Akropolites (Constantine was to report Theodore's activities in Nicaea), 160.1–4 (p. 219) to George Mouzalon.

24 Ep. 174.8–9 (p. 227).

25 Ep. 9.2 (p. 13), 15.20–25 (p. 21), 16.19–24 (p. 22). It is not impossible that Simon, a butt of jokes, was the nickname of Blemmydes' servant Peter known from his autobiography. See also Ep. Blem., 30.12–14 (p. 317), where Blemmydes asked Theodore to permit Peter to return to his monastery and tend to his sickness; the letter has been connected with the disputations with the friars in 1250 (Stavrou 2007–13 I:242, n. 3) and thus postdates Theodore's letters mentioning Simon.

26 Ep. 80.32–33 (p. 108), 168.10–13 (p. 223), 216.47–50 (p. 270). This interpretation differs from that of Nigel Wilson (1996:221), who spots in Ep. 80 a reference to Saint Christopher. When Theodore refers to saints in his letters (Tryphon, Demetrios, George, Spyridon, and Onouphrios), he identifies them as such, whereas in this case he refers humorously to one Christopher. See Ep. 136.7–8 (p. 192), 150.11 (p. 215), 163.2 (p. 220), 164.2–3 (p. 221), 166.3 and 167.2 (p. 222), 194.16 (p. 241), 199.42 (p. 246), 217. 154–55 (p. 276). Notably, Theodore calls Christopher ὁ ἡμέτερος ("our man") in Ep. 80. This word refers to close friends and companions: see Ep. 44.82–83 (p. 58), 53.47 (p. 78), 74.10 (p. 101), 77.38 (p. 104). None of the *Various Invocatory Hymns* in **V** is dedicated to Saint Christopher. See Appendix 1, 322–23. On Christopher's not being the first name of his head tutor Zabareiotes, see 263, n. 9.

27 Ep. 7.9–11 (pp. 10–11), 71.14–16 (p. 98). See also Ep. 72.14–16 (p. 99), in which Theodore urges Akropolites to bring him news about the two brothers. Ahrweiler (1965:70) suggests that they owned land near Magnesia.

28 MM, IV, 268–69; Ahrweiler 1965:70.

29 Ep. 111.4–8 (p. 155).

30 For a Karianites who was a civil servant, see, for example, *Engrapha Patmou*, 1, no. 46A, 329.336 (*pittakion* of Alexios I of 1087). Macrides (2007:300, n. 9) suggests that the name derives from the *Ta Karianou* region of Constantinople. A Karyanites served as a tax official in the empire of Nicaea. See MM, IV, 176; Ahrweiler 1965:161.

31 On Constantine Mesopotamites and his association with Niketas Choniates, see Simpson 2013:32–34.

32 On the *mesazontes* John and Michael Hagiotheodorites, see Magdalino
   1993:254–57; Choniates, *Historia*, 58–59; Madariaga 2017:61–69 (John
   Hagiotheodorites).

33 On John Hagiotheodorites being *syngambros* of the *mesazon*, see the document
   published by Criscuolo 1982:126–30, esp. 126.11–13; Laurent, *Regestes*, 1232.
   Demetrios Komnenos Tornikes is reported to have married a first cousin of
   Andronikos Palaiologos by Akrop. I, §50 (p. 93.14–15). On his wife's identity
   (an anonymous maternal cousin of Andronikos Palaiologos, the daughter of an
   unknown sibling of the latter's mother Irene Komenene), see Vannier
   1986:183–85. The *mesazon* arranged for the betrothal of his brother-in-law's
   orphaned daughter, but Patriarch Manuel I Sarantenos (1216/17–1222)
   annulled the marriage on the grounds of consanguinity and the ages of the
   spouses, tearing the marriage agreement into pieces. On the figure of John
   Hagiotheodorites and a plausible hypothesis that he was the father of Theodore's secretary, see Madariaga 2017:72–78.

34 The first name of the secretary has traditionally been considered to be Konstas
   (PLP 241; Madariaga 2017:78–86), but this identification is uncertain, because
   the individual named as Konstas by Theodore may have been yet another
   representative of the Hagiotheodorites family. Theodore refers to his private
   secretary solely by his family name. See Ep. 27.19–20 (p. 37), 70.24 (p. 97),
   168.8 (p. 223). Only on one occasion, in a letter to Akropolites (Ep. 71.12–13
   [p. 98]), he mentions the first name Konstas, but he also specifies that Konstas
   Hagiotheodorites was an in-law (*gambros*) of the metropolitan bishop of
   Ephesos, Nikephoros Pamphilos. Quite possibly the specification was needed
   because a different individual from the family was meant.

35 The letter to Akropolites is Ep. 54 (pp. 78–81). See *Natural Communion*, in PG,
   vol. 140, col. 1356A; Enc. John, 47.546–63; and 284, n. 45 for the essay
   mentioning erotic fiction.

36 On the stoic ideal, see Angelov 2007:81–82, 92, 192.

37 Akrop. I, §60 (p. 124.1–17), §75 (p. 156.8–18).

38 Ad Georg. Mouz., 131.269–273. The allusion spotted by the modern editor
   Tartaglia is to the worship of the golden statue at Nebuchadnezzar's court in
   Babylon.

39 Pach. I, 183.1–19.

40 Ep. 54 (pp. 78–81).

41 Loukaki 1996.

42 Elsewhere, Theodore marvels at the craft of fishermen who hunted oysters and
   shellfish. See Tartaglia, Op. rhet., 5.76–86.

43 In addition to Ep. 54.85 (p. 81), Koites appears also in Ep. 70 (pp. 97–98) in the
   capacity of a doctor recommending medicines. In the letter, Theodore alludes to
   Hippocrates (line 7 ὁ ἐκ τῆς Κῷ). Festa (Ep., Index, 406) thought that Koites was
   an alias for Hippocrates, who was born on Kos. By contrast, Ahrweiler (1965:24,

n. 121) considered Koites to be a Latin individual, although it is unclear what would have been the Latin name from which "Koites" is derived. What is clear is that Theodore engages in wordplay between "Koites" and the island of Kos. Whether the physician was really named "Koites," a *hapax*, is far from certain, given Theodore's propensity for neologisms. See also Appendix 3, 387.

44 On some of the delicacies mentioned by Theodore (Ep. 54.47–85 [pp. 80–81]), see Karpozilos 1995:71, 73, 77. Wine from Samos, Chios, and Lesbos is mentioned in the twelfth century by Ptochoprodromos, and in the early thirteenth century we again hear of wine from Chios and Lesbos. See the evidence collected by Jacoby 2010:137. On the sturgeon trade, see William of Rubruck, chapters 1,3 in Van den Wyngaert 1929:166; trans. Jackson 1990:64. According to Jacoby (2009:352), the merchants who brought caviar from the northern Black Sea to the empire of Nicaea were Venetians. See also Jacoby 2005:206–07.

45 On Theodore as a reader of love fiction, see Essay 2 in **V**, f. 66r–v (edition, translation, and analysis in Agapitos and Angelov 2018). For a series of different arguments on the Nicaean context of composition of *Livistros and Rodamne*, see Agapitos 1997:131–34, 2006:51–53 (preface); see also Agapitos 2013:412–15. There are striking similarities between the vocabulary of Theodore Laskaris and *Livistros and Rodamne.*

46 Ep. 188 (p. 237). According to Andreeva (1927:171–72), the buffoons were itinerant professionals. Ep. 160 (pp. 219–20) probably also refers to a comic performance at the court.

47 Sat., 182.701–183.704.

48 In Ep. 202.18–19 (p. 248), addressed to Mouzalon from the Bulgarian front in 1255, reminded him of the joke about the dry Zabareiotes, which we find in Ep. 216.36–43 (p. 269) to Hagiotheodorites. A comic sketch on the metropolitan bishop of Ephesos Nikephoros dates to the period 1254–58, long after the satirical Epp. 10 and 11 addressed to Blemmydes. See Essay 5 in **V**, f. 67r–v (edition, translation, and analysis in Agapitos and Angelov 2018).

49 Ep. 158 (pp. 218–19). Monoikos has been identified with modern Menemen near Smyrna. See MM, IV, 31, 262–63; Ahrweiler 1965:64–65; Angold 1975a:54.

50 Ep. 73 (pp. 99–101). One cannot agree with Andreeva (1927:78–79) that the mocked individual is the *prokathemenos* of Philadelphia.

51 Ep. 6 (pp. 9–10), esp. lines 20–21, with a possible allusion to Philadelphia.

52 Pach. I, 165.18–23. In Ep. 108 (pp. 148–49), addressed to Nikephoros of Ephesos, Theodore refers to a letter by the metropolitan bishop to John Vatatzes that contained inappropriate words.

53 Ep. 10 (p. 14), 11 (pp. 15–16), esp. lines 26–33.

54 Ep. 11.40–53 (p. 16).

55 On the notaries, see 252, n. 96.

56 Traditionally, Akropolites has been considered to have begun instructing Theodore in 1246. See, however, the discussion of the chronology of Epp. 26

and 49 in Appendix 2, 362–64; see also the well-founded call for caution by Macrides (2007:10–11).

57 Ep. 63.17–19 (p. 93) reveals that Akropolites had students other than Theodore.

58 Ep. 49 (pp. 67–71).

59 Ep. 49.1–17 (p. 67–68), 49.109–10 (p. 71).

60 Ep. 49 (pp. 69.71–70.73). The description echoes Wisdom of Solomon 8:4.

61 In the romance *Livistros and Rodamne,* the female personifications of Truth and Justice stand by King Eros in his court (*Livistros and Rodamne* in Agapitos 2006:276–77). See Agapitos 2013:395–403, esp. 400, n. 32, for interesting parallels of personifications of virtues flanking the emperor's portrait in Byzantine illuminated manuscripts. On the sun of wisdom, see *Oration on Wisdom* as referenced in 266, n. 54.

62 Tartaglia, Op. rhet., 105.235–106.248. In his *History* Akropolites never comments on the teacher-student relationship and only reports Theodore's words that he (Akropolites) "was source of many benefits to me – referring to his learning – and I am much indebted." See Akrop. I, §63 (p. 131.5–7).

63 See his encomium on Akropolites in Tartaglia, Op. rhet., 108.287–90.

64 Ep. 64 (p. 93), 66 (pp. 94–95). See also the geometrical discussion in Ep. 83 (pp. 110–11), 84 (pp. 111–12). Cf. Constantinides 1982:18.

65 Tartaglia, Op. rhet., 8.158–12.261, esp. 12.244–52, where he expresses his great confidence in mathematical knowledge.

66 Ep. 51.88–91 (p. 75: the chamberlain Constantine), 80.33–37 (p. 108: Kostomyres' progress), 119 (p. 166: the Phaix brothers). The Trinitarian treatise addressed to John Phaix and the chamberlain Constantine, originally part of the collection *Sacred Orations,* became the fifth book of the collection *Christian Theology,* which was prepared after Theodore's accession in November 1254. Note that a reference to the two dedicatees is made in the title of the work only in the *Sacred Orations.* See Chr. Th., V, 109 (*apparatus criticus*).

67 Ep. 173 (pp. 225–27), long letter about the nature of the human body and soul; Ep. 172.12–15 (p. 225), through which he sent the manuscript.

68 KD, I, 98.1–8. Questions by Mouzalon are mentioned, too, in Ep. 152 (pp. 215–16).

69 See Appendix 1, 338–42.

70 Op. rhet., 105.235–106.240.

71 Ep. 139 (p. 196). Ahrweiler (1965:146–47) suggested the possibility that he was identical with Theodotos Kalothetos, *doux* of the Thrakesion theme in 1259. See also Ep. 138 (p. 195), where Theodore tries to bring closer or reconcile the secretary Kostomyres with Kalothetos, who is jovially called "Kakothetos."

72 Ep. 53.36–47 (p. 78).

73 Apol., 115.121–23.

74 Ep. 73.3–5 (p. 100). See also lines 35–36 (p. 101) where the author associates, somewhat defensively, Akropolites with jokes about arrogant individuals.

75 Ep. 103 (pp. 140–43), esp. 103.64–66 (p. 142).

76 Paléologou 2007:75.178–92, 76.210–17.

77 Apol. Mal., esp. 283.7–8, 286.71–74.

78 On the full names of the two men, see the documentary evidence in MM, IV, 28 (the imperial signature of Michael Palaiologos), 225 (see also 286, n. 84).

79 On the family of Michael Palaiologos, see Vannier 1986:178, 185–86 (genealogical tables). The *megas domestikos* Andronikos Palaiologos had six children by two different wives. See Jacob of Bulgaria in Mercati 1970:77.59–63, 79.27–30, 79.6–7. It emerges from Pach. II, 667.7–8, that Michael was born in 1224, but 1226 is also a possibility: Akrop. I, §50 (p. 98.16).

80 Pach. I, 43.15–16.

81 Akrop. I, §36 (p. 55.14–21), §49 (p. 89.15–16). See Macrides 2007:252, n. 8.

82 He has been considered to be the son of a daughter of the *sebastokrator* John Doukas (brother of the emperors Isaac II and Alexios III), which made him the nephew of Theodore of Epiros and his brothers. See Nicol (1968:14–16), who disagrees with the identification proposed by Ahrweiler (1965:144–45). See also Angold 1975a:210–11; and here 269, n. 105.

83 Ahrweiler 1965:169, 174. See the fragmentary imperial ordinance regarding a land dispute in MM, IV, 213, which Dölger (1927:314) (Dölger-Wirth, *Regesten*, 1741) dated to the year 1234 on the basis of the seventh indiction. See also the two documents in MM, IV, 225–26.

84 Metcalf 2004:no. 119.

85 On the date of the death of the *megas domestikos*, see 286, n. 87. His namesake Andronikos Palaiologos, son of George Palaiologos, has been identified as the anonymous governor of Thessalonica in the early twelfth century described by the satiric dialogue *Timarion*. See Vannier 1986:147–49.

86 Akrop. I, §46 (p. 84.1–6).

87 Andronikos Palaiologos died after October 1248, because at that time Jacob of Bulgaria, his future eulogist, was still the archbishop of Ohrid. Subsequently, Jacob abandoned his see and sought refuge with Andronikos in Thessalonica. See Duichev 1960; Macrides 2007:243, n. 6. For the negative view of Andronikos, see *Synopsis chronike*, 498.1–2. For more positive ones, see Jacob of Bulgaria's monody in Mercati 1970:68.30–70.5; Akrop. I, §46 (p. 83.17–22).

88 Jacob of Bulgaria in Mercati 1970:67.26–68.24.

89 On Theodore Philes as governor of Thessalonica and the new Balkan provinces, holding the title of *praitor*, see Akrop. I, §46 (p. 84.15–16); Macrides 2007:99; 242, n. 2; 244, n. 7.

90 On the accusation of *eros*, see Ep. 78.18–19 (p. 105) addressed to Akropolites. On the defamatory verses, see Ep. 36.32–35 (p. 45) addressed to Blemmydes. On the date of the "Philes affair" and the convergences found in Theodore's letters to Blemmydes and Akropolites, see Appendix 2, 368–69.

91 The murder of Tribides, called his "friend" (ὁ ἡμέτερος), is mentioned in two letters to Akropolites, which are our main source on the conflict: Ep. 77 (p. 104.34–35), 78 (p. 105.22–23).

92 See the testament (1247) by Maximos, the founder of the Boreine monastery: Vatopedi, I, no. 15, 159.233–34.

93 Ep. 36, 37, and 38 (pp. 44–49).

94 Ep. 36.59–60 (p. 46), 37.9–10 (p. 48), 38.11–13 (p. 48).

95 Ep. 39 (pp. 49–51).

96 Ep. 78.24–32 (pp. 105–06).

97 See Ep. 80 (p. 108.38–44), the famous letter from Pergamon, at the end of which Theodore informs Akropolites of the imperial chastisement of the individual codenamed *tragophylon*.

98 Enc. John, 50.625–29.

99 Pach. I, 43.8–9.

100 *To a Secretive Man Who Was Deceiving Him*, in Tartaglia, Op. rhet., 199–202. The allegorical story interprets old sayings and literary images. For dung beetles dying from the smell of roses, see Pseudo-Aristotle, *Mirabiles auscultationes*, 845a35–b3. Envy is compared to a dung beetle in a saying reported in Plutarch's *Moralia* and hence included in *florilegia*, such as *Melissa* (PG, vol. 136, col. 969C). I thank Martin Hinterberger for the latter reference.

101 Ep. 95.71–74 (p. 130).

102 See Michael Palaiologos' autobiographical *typikon*: Grégoire 1959–60:451. See also the reference to sons of officials taking part in fourteenth-century court ceremonies in Pseudo-Kodinos: Verpeaux 1966:212; Macrides, Munitiz, and Angelov 2013:156.18–20.

103 Akropolites and Pachymeres report the trial of Michael Palaiologos with differences in detail and interpretation: Akrop. I, §50 (pp. 92–100); Pach. I, 37.3–41.3. For a critical comparison, see Macrides 2007:263–68. See also Czebe 1931. The suggestion that Michael should prove his innocence through an ordeal is found only in Akropolites' account. Pachymeres (I, 37.21–39) omits this detail and writes that Michael Palaiologos agreed to the "old custom" of a judicial duel.

104 Akrop. I, §51 (pp. 100.15–101.18), §64 (p. 134.10–12). See Michael Palaiologos' *typikon* for the monastery of Saint Demetrios in Constantinople in Grégoire 1959–60:451. On Michael's wife Theodora, see Talbot 1992.

105 Ep. 14.31–44 (pp. 19–20).

106 Ep. 179.1–2 (p. 229).

107 Sat., 172.453–54.

108 Ep. 62.10–18 (pp. 91–92). For a similar idea, see Ep. 51.63–66 (p. 74); also Ep. 187.3–5 (p. 236), the letter of dedication of the *Representation of the World, or Life*, where he mentions many gifts – "material delights, wealth, pleasure and luxury together with food" – that he had already granted Mouzalon.

109 Ad Georg. Mouz., 134.352–55, 137.423–24.

110 Ad Georg. Mouz., 140.486–92. This question of Mouzalon, as it appears in the conclusion, differs from that found in the manuscript title: *To George*

Mouzalon Who Asked How Should Subjects Conduct Themselves vis-à-vis Their Lords and Lords vis-à-vis Their Subjects.

111 Ad Georg. Mouz., 120–22, 134.360–136.403; Blem., *Imperial Statue*, 66, Chapter 75. The anecdote has a long history. See Theon (first–second century AD), *Progymnasmata*, in Spengel 1853–56, II:100; Themistius (fourth century), Or. 16, 203bc.

112 Aristotle, *Nicomachean Ethics*, VIII 1, 1155a6–10.

113 Aristotle, *Nicomachean Ethics*, VIII 5, 1157b36; VIII 7, 1158b27–28. Echoes are found in a letter to Blemmydes, where he writes that the best tie of friendship was based on "giving and receiving that is equal in value," and in the comparison between the rose and the dung beetle. See Ep. 16.1–2 (p. 21); Tartaglia, Op. rhet., 200.33.

114 Mullett 1988:13–14.

115 Ad Georg. Mouz., 126.164–68, 133.314–16, 134.355–57.

116 Ad Georg. Mouz., 125.128–126.154.

117 Ad Georg. Mouz., 127.169–130.251. See 277, n. 94.

118 Ad Georg. Mouz., 130.252–132.296.

119 Ad Georg. Mouz., 127.188–89, 132.297–307, 134.338–40.

120 Ad Georg. Mouz., 137.435–37.

121 Angelov 2007:105–10.

122 See the similar observations, but different conclusions, by Kazhdan and Constable (1985:26–28) and Mullett 1988 (16–21). On the ideas of the treatise in the context of feudalism in the medieval West and with oath-taking in Byzantium, see Svoronos 1951:138; Angelov 2007:224–26.

123 Ad Georg. Mouz., 137.421–28.

7 Elena and the Embassy of the Marquis

1 Heisenberg (Akrop. II, VIII) suggested that the emperor departed as early as March 1252.

2 On the *sebastokrator* John Petraliphas, see Choniates, *Historia*, 451; *Life* of Saint Theodora of Arta, in PG, vol. 127, cols. 904AB, 905AB. On Theodore Petraliphas, see Akrop. I, §49 (p. 90.19–22); Macrides 2007:254, n. 18; 358, n. 3. On the *megas chartoularios* John Petraliphas, see Akrop. I, §37 (p. 58.18–21), §40 (p. 66.22). On the thirteenth-century members of the Petraliphas family, see Macrides 2007:175–76, n. 12.

3 For an account of these events, see Akrop. I, §49 (pp. 88.15–89.19). On the chronology of the designation of Michael of Epiros as despot, see Macrides 2007:251.

4 See the detailed eyewitness account of the campaign of 1252–53 by Akrop. I, §49 (pp. 89.20–92.24); Appendix 2, 352–53. The privileges to Kroia are mentioned in the later chrysobull of Andronikos II: Solovjev and Mošin 1936:316.10; Dölger-Wirth, *Regesten*, 1810. On the meaning of the term Albanon, see Macrides 2007:320, n. 8.

5 That Irene was the eldest daughter can be inferred from Akropolites, who reports a total of four daughters and a son: Akrop. I, §50 (p. 100.6–8), §74 (pp. 153.25–154.6). Pach. (I, 243.20–21) adds a fifth, unnamed daughter. In 1253 Irene was considered a possible bride for Michael Palaiologos, so she was probably then in her early teens. In 1248–50 Maria was engaged to Nikephoros of Epiros, and the marriage was celebrated in 1256. See Akrop. I, §49 (p. 88.17–19); Macrides 2007:251. On Theodore's children, see also Failler 1980:65–77, esp. 73, n. 34. The converging testimonies of Akropolites and an anonymous chronicle (Schreiner 1975–79, I:75.4) show that John was born around Christmas 1250.

6 On the date of Elena's death, see Angelov, Mor. P., 237–41; Appendix 2, 365–66. On Theodore leaving Nymphaion at the command of the senior emperor, see Ep. 59.43–45 (p. 89).

7 Pseudo-Kodinos in Verpeaux 1966:284–85; Macrides, Munitiz, and Angelov 2013:262–65. See Macrides, Munitiz, and Angelov 2013:263, n. 769; 320.

8 Mor. P., III, 257.106–08, 258.142–47, XII, 268.491–93.

9 Mor. P., I, 255.56–58, II, 256.61–63, 256.89–94.

10 Mor. P., VIII, 263.314–19, X, 266.420–25, XII, 269.522–42. The mourner's wish to die is a literary motif in Greek laments. See Alexiou 1974:189.

11 Mor. P., VII, 262.277–79.

12 The idea of grief (*penthos*) as a step toward union with God is laid out in Chapter 7 of John Klimakos' *Ladder of Divine Ascent* and was one of the main themes of katanyctic liturgical poetry of contrition, such as Andrew of Crete's great canon. See Giannouli 2007.

13 Mor. P., I, 254.10–19, II, 256.74–78, IV, 258.149–54, V, 260.201–09.

14 Ep. 61.6–9 (p. 90), 61.21–23 (p. 90). He followed the patriarch Germanos who compared Christ to a "bath-man" cleansing the human soul in a sermon. See Lagopates 1913:225. On the baths in the palace in Nymphaion, see 250, n. 57. See also Mor. P., X, 265.398–99: "only the contemplator of God finds stability."

15 Apol., 112.64–113.70. In a letter to the patriarch Michael, a former chief priest (*protopapas*) of the emperor John Vatatzes, Theodore also confessed that he has removed every pleasure from his life. See Ep. 90 (pp. 118–19).

16 Apol., 113.81–83.

17 Apol., 112.60–64, 113.70–77, 117.177–78. The comparison with Plotinus goes back to his *vita* by Porphyry.

18 Apol., 115.135–116.140, 118.190–91.

19 Apol., 113.89–92. Akropolites' letter from the Balkans has not survived, but its tenor can be gleaned from Theodore's response.

20 Tartaglia, Op. rhet., 19.415–21.463.

21 Mor. P., X, 265.411–13. He drew in his audience: "We ought to fit ourselves to virtue." See Mor. P., VIII, 264.349–51.

22 The expression "strong bond indissoluble" (ἐρρωμένος δεσμὸς ἀλληλένδετος) is first found in Ep. 155 addressed to Mouzalon. From Ep. 191 onward (Epp. 192,

193, 194, 202, 204, 205, 207, 213, 214), it is used with great consistency. Ep. 193 is the first one dating after his accession (see Appendix 2, 371). The word ἐρρωμένος, which refers to someone who has regained his strength, sounds like ἐρώμενος ("beloved"). A "bond" is reminiscent of a marriage bond. For the language of love and desire (the noun ἔρως and derivative words) in letters to Mouzalon, all composed after Theodore's accession as sole emperor, see Ep. 195.29–30 (p. 242), 200 (pp. 246–47: a comparison between the general and the lovesick man), 204.7–9 (p. 251). For Theodore as well as for other Byzantines, *eros* could mean divine love (Ep. 30.11–12 [p. 40]) as well as carnal desire (Ep. 49.53 [p. 69]). On the double meaning, see Cameron 1997:11–14.

23 Ep. 72.1–3, 72.10–12 (p. 99). A similar idea is found in a letter to the monk Akakios, where Theodore exclaims: "Oh, good sorrow!" See Ep. 132.30–34 (p. 187). In the long letter to Akropolites (Tartaglia, Op. rhet., 4.59–60), Theodore connects knowledge and sorrow with Isocrates' maxim about the bitter roots of knowledge. There is no basis for the contention by Andreeva (1927:168) that after his wife's passing Theodore became increasingly fascinated with ancient poets and music, acquiring a new *joie de vivre*.

24 Apol., 116.139–48. As the cunning god, Hermes was considered in Byzantium the inventor of rhetoric. See, for example, John Doxapatres in the eleventh century in Rabe 1931:90. As Hermes Trismegistus, Hermes was regarded as the originator of secret philosophical knowledge and the author of the Greek Hermetic corpus. See the translation and commentary by Copenhaver 1995. Revealingly, Theodore describes his mind paying a visit to the god Hermes when he wrote a composition that he made obscure and embellished. See Ep. 172.5–8 (p. 225). Uneducated people are blamed for destroying the "offspring of Hermes" (Sat., 166.282). The head of Alexander is said to have had Hermes-like desires (Ad Georg. Mouz., 121.28–30).

25 See Appendix 1, 324–27.

26 On its date, see Appendix 1, 335–36.

27 Enc. John, 28.104–06, 31.174–80. Theodore refers to the defensive alliance between Nicaea and Rum struck after the Battle of Köse Dağ rather than to events of 1241–43, as argued by Korobeinikov (2014:178–80). The defensive pact between Nicaea and the Seljuks was, therefore, not short-lived, even though its exact provisions are not specified.

28 William of Rubruck, 33,3 in Van den Wyngaert 1929: 290; trans. Jackson 1990: 227–28. William of Rubruck met the Arab on May 23, 1254.

29 Langdon 1998 (127, n. 181) suggests 1251 and 1252.

30 See William of Rubruck 28,10 in Van den Wyngaert 1920:247; trans. Jackson 1990:175.

31 Enc. John, 31.181–32.184.

32 Lykophron, *Alexandra*, 128–29; on the scholion attested in the twelfth century, see Scheer 1881–1908, II:62 (scholion on line 128); Blem, *Imperial Statue*, 98, Chapters 159–60. See Angelov 2011:29–30.

33 Enc. John, 27.85–28.96.

34 Wolff 1954; Wolff 1969:225.

35 *Relatio de Concilio Lugdunensi* in Weiland 1896:514.11–14. On Innocent IV and crusading in Romania, see Chrissis 2012:139–59. See also Wolff 1969:226–27; Gill 1979:78–86.

36 On these events, Van Cleve 1972:484–512; Abulafia 1988:355–400.

37 Salimbene de Adam (Scalia 1998–99 I:296) mentions the presence of *Greci* in Frederick's army. For the subsidies, see Collenuccio 1929:141; Van Cleve 1972:514–15.

38 Merendino 1974–75:300 (the letter is dated to March 1250), 317–20 (text) (=MM, III, 68–69). For the Latin version of the letter dated by the editor to February 1250, see Huillard-Bréholles 1852–61, VI, 2:759–61.

39 Enc. John, 54.701–02. Given the date of the speech, it is possible that the Nicaean infantry and archers remained in Italy for some time after Frederick's death in December 1250.

40 For Frederick's two Greek letters of July and September 1250 informing John Vatatzes about these and other successes against the papacy, see Merendino 1974–75:332–41, esp. 338–41. On these events, see Van Cleve 1972:498–530; Abulafia 1988:400–07.

41 His surviving letters date to the period 1256–58. See Appendix 2, 374–77.

42 Frederick's encyclical letter *Audite gentes* (March 1249) may have reached the Nicaean court. See Huillard-Bréholles 1852–61 VI, 2:705–07; Schaller 1965:72–74.

43 Or. Fr., 86.3–4 (manuscript title); Enc. John, 54.701–02. Both texts were written after Frederick II's death.

44 Or. Fr. throughout, esp. 86.6–87.35, 91.139–92.166, 94.204–09.

45 Golubovich 1919:445. The tactful and optimistic answer Vatatzes is said to have received was that the patriarch could obtain even greater concessions from the Roman church. See Langdon 1994.

46 Salimbene de Adam in Scalia 1998–99 I:489–90. According to him, there were "many" friars who took part in the embassy. See also the documents published by Franchi 30–31, 33–35. On the composition of the embassy, see Franchi 1981:18–27. On the Nicaean-papal negotiations of 1250–54, see Gill 1979:87–96. See also the recent interpretation of John Vatatzes' overall aims by Chrissis 2012:161, 166. The Nicaean emperor did not, however, fully "turn his back" on Frederick.

47 See the text published by Stavrou 2007–13 I:239–42 (date and context) and 258–73 (text).

48 Blem., *Autobiographia*, II, 50–60 (pp. 67–73); recently reedited and commented by Stavrou 2007–13 II:260–70.

49 Blem., *Autobiographia*, II, 61–66 (pp. 73–75). An Armenian historian (Kirakos of Gandzak, Chapter 58, in Khanlarian 1976:223; Bedrosian 1986:302–03) reports that the *katholikos* of the Armenian church and King Hetoum I dispatched the *vardapet* Jacob to "the Greek king John who ruled in Asia"

sometime before 1253. Jacob is said to have effectively defended the Armenian position on the nature of Christ and the *Trisagion*, which contradicts Blemmydes' claim of his own success in the disputation on the *Trisagion*.

50 Enc. John, 36.293–37.297. See Luke 2:46.

51 Enc. John, 37.310–38.320, 38.341–40.371.

52 Critical edition in Franchi 1981:84–87 (date discussed Franchi 1981:90–110). Pope Alexander IV (r. 1254–61), Innocent IV's successor, included the *capitula* as well as Innocent's response in his letter of 1256 to Constantine of Orvieto. See Haluščynskyj and Wojnar 1966:no. 28 (pp. 39–42), 28a (pp. 44–46); see Chapter 8, pp. 163, 167–69.

53 On the members of the embassy, see Franchi 1981:135–39. On its mandate, see the ending of Patriarch Manuel II's letter to Innocent IV in Franchi 1981:168–71, esp. 170.

54 See the ending of Frederick's letter of May 1250 to John Vatatzes in Merendino 1974–75:330. The friars in fact returned via Dubrovnik. See Franchi 1981:187–88.

55 Niccolò da Calvi, *Life* of Innocent IV, in Pagnotti 1898:107. On the chronology, see Franchi 1981:189–90, 214–15.

56 Critical edition of Innocent IV's oral response in Franchi 1981:194–99. According to Franchi 1981:202, the substance of his response had already been communicated to the Nicaean delegation in 1251 or 1252. For an analysis of the legalistic language, see Stolte 1990.

57 Franchi 1981:231–46; Niccolò da Calvi, *Life* of Innocent IV, in Pagnotti 1898:112, 114; Matthew Paris in Luard 1872–84, vol. 5:456.

58 Ep. 18 (pp. 24–25), esp. 18.10–13 (p. 24).

59 Ep. 6.18–20 (p. 9).

60 Döberl 1894–95:213–14; Niccolò Jamsilla in Muratori 1726:518D.

61 Döberl 1894–95:205–07.

62 On Berthold of Hohenburg's life, see the extensive discussion Döberl 1894–95: 207–71. See also Kantorowicz 1931:274, and especially Walter 1967; Schaller 1977.

63 On Galvano Lancia, see Settia 2000b. For some of these events, see Karst 1897:1–10; Döberl 1894–95:215–27. See also Runciman 1958:26–30.

64 Böhmer, Ficker, and Winkelmann, *Regesten*, 4592, 13908a, 13913a.

65 Böhmer, Ficker, and Winkelmann, *Regesten*, 4593, 4594; Capasso 1874:323–24, no. 522.

66 Niccolò Jamsilla in Muratori 1726:506BC.

67 Ep. 180 (see 293, n. 69) reveals that he was in an Anatolian palace other than Nicaea.

68 On Vatatzes' reputation for generosity to foreigners, see Akrop. I, §52 (p. 103.20–23). On Boniface of Carreto, see Balard 1966:485–86, 490–502 (documents). In Balard's opinion, the *Romania* mentioned in the Genoese documents is the empire of Nicaea. See also Angold 2003a:161. On Ashraf Musa, see Makrizi in Quatremère 1837–40 I:56; Holt 1986:82–87.

69 Ep. 180.13–20 (p. 231). As has been noted by Koutouvalas in a PhD dissertation (2014:210–11), the passage playfully borrows phrases from the parable of
the Rich Man and Lazarus in Luke 16:24–31. Festa (1898:225) corrected his
edition and thought that the name "Bianca" refers to Manfred's sister Constanza, but this is unlikely. She seems to be a different individual and may have
been Boniface's wife, as suggested by Berg (1988:269). The identity of Diepold
mentioned by the letter is unknown. He could have been Berthold's late
brother (see 293, n. 74) or father.

70 Addressing Andronikos of Sardis (who was at the time in Italy on an embassy
to the papacy) and describing Berthold's arrival at the Anatolian Byzantine
court, Theodore called his letter an "autumnal heron." This indicates that
Berthold was already there in the autumn of 1253. See Ep. 125.1–2 (p. 174).
The emperor John Vatatzes returned to Anatolia in the late autumn of 1253,
visiting first Nicaea and then moving southward to his winter quarters in
Nymphaion. See Appendix 2, 352–53. The manuscript titles of all works in
the *Sacred Orations* specify that John Vatatzes received the embassy. See, for
example, Paléologou 2007:69.6, 83.5; Angelov 2011–12:254.4–6. On the
embassy, see also Andreeva 1927:144–46; Tinnefeld 1979:254–60.

71 On Berthold's activities in Italy in April 1254, see Döberl 1894–95:228. It is
possible that he departed as late as the winter of 1254. Pappadopoulos
(1908:53) dated Berthold's stay in Anatolia to the spring of 1254 without
any basis.

72 Niccolò Jamsilla in Muratori 1726:506C. According to Döberl (1894–
95:226–27), Berthold failed in his mission.

73 Kantorowicz, 1927:318, 1931:151, referring to Güdemann 1884:228 (who in
turn refers to a manuscript in Munich). See Ep. 125, as quoted in 293, n. 75.

74 He purportedly wrote his poetic *Lamentacio*, filled with quotes from Ovid and
Boethius, in prison at the end of his life. Anna Moscati, who published the text
(1953:122–5), has argued (1953:127) that it was a rhetorical exercise without
much historical value. The poem serves to show Berthold's reputation as a
tragic figure in thirteenth-century schools of rhetoric. His authorship of Minnesang poetry is also unlikely. See Walter 1967:586. The Minnesang poems by
the marquis of Hohenburg are more likely to have been associated with
Berthold rather than another member of the family. See Neumann 1955–56.
For Berthold's brother Diepold (killed in the siege of Parma in 1248) as
"possibly" the minnesinger, see Kantorowicz 1931:275. See also Döberl 1894–
95:272–74.

75 Ep. 125.10–21 (pp. 174–75).

76 On Theophylaktos, see Franchi 1981:138; on Salimbene, see Chapter 7, p. 137;
on Andronikos of Sardis, see Ep. 125.57 (p. 176). Under what circumstances he
acquired this expertise is not known. On the knowledge of Greek among
mendicants in the period, see Altaner 1934:449–54.

77 Ep. 125.21–28 (p. 175).

78 See *Corpus paroemiographorum Graecorum*, in Leutsch and Schneidewin 1839–51 II: 569.10. The proverb was Theodore's favorite: see Sat., 161.180; Tartaglia, Op. rhet., 144.73–145.74. It is found in late antique and Byzantine authors, such as Gregory of Nazianzus, George of Pisidia, John Tzetzes, Demetrios Chomatenos, and Manuel Philes.

79 Ep. 125.28–38 (p. 175). On this section of the letter, see the notes by Papadopoulos-Kerameus 1899:552–53.

80 Ep. 40 (pp. 51–52), esp. lines 18–19 (p. 52).

81 Ep. 125.43–44 (p. 175).

82 Berschin 1988: 217–25, 231–35.

83 On Bartholomew of Messina and his translations, see Minio-Paluello 1950:232–37; Brams 2006:103–05; De Leemans 2014. On his translation of *De Mundo*, see Minio-Paluello 1950:232–37 and Lorimer and Minio-Paluello 1965: XVI–XIX (*Aristoteles Latinus*, XI 1–2).

84 The letter is edited and discussed by Gauthier 1982:323–24. A previous edition can be found in Huillard-Bréholles 1852–61 IV,1:383–85.

85 See the report of the four friars published by Golubovich 1919:434. According to Wolff (1944:230), the Greek books mentioned were kept in the Franciscan friary in Constantinople.

86 For an overview of Moerbeke's translations produced in the Greek East and in Italy, see Minio–Paluello 1974; Fryde 2000:103–44; Brams 2006:105–12.

87 The theory has been developed by Gudrun Vuillemin-Diem. For the view that Moerbeke came across the Greek manuscript in Nicaea, which is supported by a note in a Latin manuscript of the translation, see Vuillemin-Diem 1987:159–67; Vuillemin-Diem 1995:253–54 (*Aristoteles Latinus*, XXV 3.1). On the list copied by Moerbeke in this manuscript, see Vuillemin-Diem 1989.

88 See Chapter 4, p. 83; Chapter 5, p. 107 and 280, n. 134.

89 For a hypothesis that the *Politica imperfecta* dates to this period, see Bossier 1989:282, n. 21; 288, n. 28.

90 Appendix 1, 324–25.

91 Akrop. II, 7.14–8.20.

92 Akrop. II, 8.31–34.

8 Sole Emperor of the Romans

1 The events of 1254 and the death of Vatatzes are related by Akrop. I, §52, although there are a number of details reported solely by *Synopsis chronike*. On the emperor's fears of a Mongol invasion and the security of Nicaea, see *Synopsis chronike*, 504.14–18; Macrides 2007:272, n. 1.

2 William of Rubruck, Chapter 32, 4 (Van den Wyngaert 1929:287; trans. Jackson 1990:222–23 and 223, n. 1) reports that he learned in May 1254 in Karakorum that Hülegü had already departed on this expedition.

3 A possible diagnosis with epilepsy is implied by the accounts of Pach. I (99.27–101.3); Greg. I, 49.21–50.23. Akrop. I, §52 (pp. 101.19–103.19), a close eyewitness, is conspicuously silent. See Macrides 2007:272–73. Makris (1995:384–93) casts well-founded doubts on the alleged epilepsy of Byzantine emperors, including John Vatatzes. Jeanselme (1924:261–67) took the historians' reports of epilepsy at face value.

4 The icon is mentioned solely by *Synopsis chronike,* 505.8–15. On this monastery, known from documentary evidence, see Ahrweiler 1965:93.

5 Ep. 44.28–32 (p. 57).

6 See Appendix 1, 325.

7 The date of John Vatatzes' death is given in manuscript notes. See Schreiner 1975–79 II:608 (chronological notes 17, 20,2). See the commentary in Schreiner 1975–79 II:195. See also Macrides 2007:274, n. 12.

8 Akrop. I, §53 (p. 105.18–22). On this late antique inauguration ceremony of Germanic origin practiced occasionally in middle Byzantium, see Macrides, Munitiz, and Angelov 2013:217, n. 620; 418–20. On the date of Patriarch Manuel II's death, see Laurent 1969:138–39.

9 Akrop. II, 15.1–9, 26.15 (κοσμικὴ ὁλκάς). Agapetos the Deacon, §2 in Riedinger 1995:26. On the learned language in the memorial speech, see Valdenberg 1929–30.

10 Akrop. II, 14–18.

11 Akrop. II, 28.15–20.

12 Akrop. II, 27.25–28.14. The allusion is to Plutarch, *Likourgos,* 5, 3.

13 Akrop. II, 22.1–15.

14 Akrop. II, 26.11–27.24.

15 Akrop. I, §52 (p. 105.3–17).

16 Akrop. I, §53 (p. 105.21–22). Dölger–Wirth, *Regesten,* 1825, 1826, on which see Nystazopoulou 1964b:244, n. 15 (one and the same event).

17 Ibn Bibi in Duda 1959:61–69; Cahen 1988:238–39; Korobeinikov 2014:190–91. On Synope, see Nystazopoulou 1964b. See also Ibn Bibi in Duda 1959:286; Cahen 1939:137–38.

18 Ep. 193 (pp. 239–40). On its date, see Appendix 2, 371.

19 The procedure is reported in the fourteenth century by Pseudo-Kodinos, Chapter 10 (Verpeaux 1966:252–83; Macrides, Munitiz, and Angelov 2013:250–61, with translation and commentary). The tenth-century description in Constantine Porphyrogennetos' *Book of Ceremonies,* II, 14 (Reiske 1829:564.13–16) is broadly similar, with the significant addition that the emperor could ignore the three candidates and propose his own candidate.

20 See Epilogue, pp. 291, 221–23.

21 Blem., *Autobiographia,* I, 74–80 (pp. 37–40).

22 Blem., *Autobiographia,* II, 77 (p. 80). On this office, see Darrouzès 1970b:312–13.

23 Akrop. I, §53 (pp. 106.4–107.13).

24 On the offer of the patriarchate of Jerusalem, see Nikolopoulos 1981–82:456.192–96. On the embassy to Rome, see the unique testimony in *Synopsis chronike*, 511.11–14.

25 Historians have traditionally dated Theodore's anointing and coronation to Christmas 1254 without adducing evidence. See Pappadopoulos 1908:65; Gardner 1912:212. Laurent (1969:139–40 and n. 42) examined older views and suggested instead the feast of the Entry of the Virgin into the temple on November 21, but this is unlikely given Theodore's visit to Philadelphia after his father's passing and the need to arrange the patriarchal election.

26 The two accounts of Arsenios' election written by his partisans are found in the *Synopsis chronike* and his *vita*. There are minor discrepancies. According to *Synopsis chronike* (509.23–512.2), the synod did not agree with Theodore's nomination of Blemmydes; Arsenios was proposed at the electoral assembly after the first three candidates had failed the test. The *vita* of Arsenios (Nikolopoulos 1981–82:457–58) presents Arsenios as the third candidate and adds the detail about the prayer vigils before the morning ceremony.

27 Akrop. II, 27.2–5 (the reign of peace); Akrop. I, §54 (pp. 107.14–109.5) (Michael Asen's offensive in Thrace and the Rhodopes). On Veles, see Chapter 8, p. 159. On Skopje, which was to be restored under Nicaean rule in 1256 (but in fact it was not), see Chapter 8, pp. 165, 167.

28 Epp. 194 and 195 (pp. 240–42), esp. Ep. 194 (p. 240.1–3). See Appendix 2, 371.

29 George Mouzalon was already *megas domestikos* before the onset of the Bulgarian campaign in early 1255. See *Synopsis chronike*, 514.3–6 (missing from Akropolites' *History*). By Christmas Day 1255, Andronikos Mouzalon had been appointed *protovestiarites*, which means that George Zagarommates no longer held this title. Elsewhere in the *History* Akropolites reports his promotion as *parakoimomenos*, after which he fell out of favor. See Akrop. I, §60 (p. 124.7–8); §75 (p. 155.5).

30 On Manuel and Michael Laskaris, see Akrop. I, §55 (p. 109.9–11), §59 (p. 122.1–5). On Constantine Margarites, see Akrop. I, §60 (p. 123.6–15). On George and Isaac Nestongos, who were appointed to high positions by 1256, see Chapter 8, pp. 164, 175.

31 For an account of these events, see Akrop. I, §55 (pp. 109–11); *Synopsis chronike*, 513.5–514.15. Akropolites omits the detail about George Mouzalon.

32 William of Rubruck, Chapter 29,7–13; Chapter 37,24–38,13 (pp. 253–55, 321–28); trans. Jackson 1990:184–87, 264–73. William of Rubruck does not mention Theodore Laskaris by name, but the chronology of the Nicaean encounter with the Mongol envoys implies his involvement.

33 Ep. 199.41–44 (pp. 245–46). The letter suggests that the feast of St. Tryphon was a recent event that he had just witnessed in Nicaea.

34 *Synopsis chronike*, 512.3–11, 514.3–12. See his letter to the two teachers: Ep. 217.152–57 (p. 276); Constantinides 1982:20.

35 The encomium has been published by Delehaye 1925:352–57. For the devotional text, one of his *Invocatory Hymns,* see **V**, f. 107r. On these two works, see Appendix 1, 322–23.

36 Akrop. I, §57 (pp. 113.10–114.1). Ep. 201 (pp. 247–48), accompanies a gift to Mouzalon and refers to an imminent arrival at Kryvous and Stenimachos. For the place names, see Soustal 1991:160–61 (Achridos), 325–26 (Kritzimos), 327 (Kryvous), 393 (Peristitza), 460–61 (Stenimachos); 488–89 (Tzepaina). On Tzepaina (Tsepena), see also Končev 1959.

37 Akrop. I, §57 (p. 114.2–19).

38 These are Epp. 199–206 (to Mouzalon) and Ep. 87 (to Akropolites).

39 Langdon 2003:205; Kanellopoulos and Lekea 2007:66–68.

40 These thoughts are recorded in KD, III, 23.26–24.2.

41 Ep. 200 (p. 247.26–29). Note the word ἀγνώστους.

42 Ep. 199 (pp. 244–46).

43 Ep. 199.20–27 (p. 245).

44 Ep. 199.34–37 (p. 245). The biblical phrase has not been noted by the editor Festa.

45 On the Cumans being called "Scythians," see, for example, Chapter 5, p. 95. On the Tauroscythians as the Rus, see Leo the Deacon in Hase 1828:63.9; John Kinnamos in Meineke 1836:115.16, 232.4; Choniates, *Historia*, 523.10.

46 Mysia, a Roman province along the lower Danube, is sometimes used to refer to Bulgaria in the works of Byzantine authors. But Theodore notably calls the Bulgarians *Boulgaroi,* including in this very letter, and never designates them as *Mysoi.*

47 Ep. 200.20–21 (p. 247), 202.1–2, 202.13 (p. 248), 202.26–27 (p. 249), 204.44–47 (p. 252). On Theodore's presentation of the Bulgarians in his campaign letters, see in greater detail Angelov 2013b:285–93.

48 Ep. 203.8–11 (p. 250).

49 Ep. 202.13–15 (p. 248), 202.30, 202.35–36 (p. 249).

50 Ep. 199.45–50 (p. 246). On the Bulgarians as inhabiting a mountainous land, see Angelov 2013a:49–50.

51 Ep. 200.26–29 (p. 247) (the sole surviving codex of the campaign letters to Mouzalon, Laur. Conventi soppressi 627, f. 7v, has ὄρος, "mountain," rather than ὄρον, "boundary," "category" in the accusative), 202.28–30 (p. 249).

52 Ep. 204.57–58 (p. 253).

53 Ep. 202.3–4 (p. 248), 202.30–33 (p. 249); Sat., 169.376–381.

54 Ep. 202.42–43 (p. 249) (to Mouzalon), 87 (pp. 113–15) (to Akropolites). For another comment on Strategopoulos' old age, see Ep. 204.117 (p. 254).

55 Ep. 202.54–58 (p. 250).

56 Ep. 202.17–35 (p. 249).

57 Akrop. I, §58 (pp. 114.20–115.15). On the basis of the destruction layer in archaeological excavations of the upper city, Popović (2007) has plausibly reconstructed the battle. See the similar approach of Tsvetkov 1985.

58 Ep. 204.52–64 (pp. 252–53), esp. Ep. 204.59–62 (p. 253). For editorial suggestions regarding this letter, see Papageorgiu 1902:25. On the identification of Philippi as the place of composition of Ep. 204, see Angelov 2013b:287–88.

59 Ep. 204.81 and Ep. 204.86–87 (p. 253).

60 Ep. 204.105–120 (p. 254).

61 Ep. 88.3–4 (p. 115). The letter dates to Theodore's sole rule.

62 Ep. 204.40–43 (p. 252). For the whipping of the apostle Paul in Philippi, see Acts 16:23.

63 Ep. 204.68–70 (p. 253).

64 On the monument in Philippi, see *Descriptio Europae Orientalis* in Górka 1916:10 ("marble stable"); Francesco Scalamonti's *vita* of Cyriac of Ancona in Mitchell and Bodnar 1996:58 (§76) ("mangers" and partial transcription of the inscription).

65 Akrop. I, §58 (pp. 115.16–117.17).

66 Villehardouin §302 (II, 110–11). The Latin emperor Henry also managed to travel from Constantinople to Thessalonica in twelve days in c. 1210 (see his letter in Prinzing 1973:412.24–25). A twelve-day journey is reported also by Harun ibn Yahya (ninth or tenth century). See Vasiliev 1932:162.

67 Theodore Pediasimos in Treu 1899:21.17–22.2; newly edited by Odorico 2013:138–39. See Dölger 1961. On the icon, see Drpić 2012.

68 On the title of John Angelos on Christmas 1255, see Akrop. I, §60 (p. 124.9). At that time, the *megas primmikerios* John Angelos was given a higher title.

69 Noting the issue of a single billon coin in Thessalonica during Theodore's reign, Hendy (1999 II:615) suggested 1254/55 as the time of the closure of the mint.

70 On the confirmation of the privileges to Kroia, see Solovjev and Mošin 1936:316.10; Dölger-Wirth, *Regesten*, 1850. For the newsletter, see Ep. 281.71–72; on its date, see Appendix 1, 344–45.

71 Akrop. I, §80 (pp. 166.11–167.5). The detention of Constantine Kabasilas in Anatolia is mentioned solely in *Synopsis chronike*, 542.25–543.2. On the episcopal career of Kabasilas, which included the sees of Grevena and Stroumitza, see Pitsakis 2005; PLP 10097.

72 Akrop. I, §59 (pp. 117.18–119.8).

73 See his newsletter in Ep., 281.51–59.

74 On the fortress of Vatkounion, near today's village of Patalenitza, see Soustal 1991:194–95.

75 Akrop. I, §59 (pp. 119.9–121.24).

76 Ep. 205.3–9 (p. 255).

77 On these appointments, see Akrop I, §60 (p. 124.1–24). On Alexios Raoul, see Chapter 3, p. 59. On *megas stratopedarches* as a new office, see KD, I, 97.9–12 (manuscript heading of *Explanation of the World*); on its function in the fourteenth century, see Pseudo-Kodinos in Verpeaux 1966:174; Macrides, Munitiz, and Angelov 2013:84.5–6. For the bestowal of "brotherhood" on

George Mouzalon, see the headings before the treatise *Explanation of the World* and letters: KD, I, 97.6–8; Ep. 150 (p. 214), 211 (p. 263). For the designation of the *mesazon* Demetrios Komnenos Tornikes as a "brother" of John Vatatzes, see Akrop. I, §49 (p. 90.20–23). For the title of Theodore Mouzalon, see Akrop. I, §75 (p. 155.18–19); Greg. I, 66.2. By contrast, Pachymeres (I, 41.13–14) calls him first falconer (*protoierakarios*).

78 He was *logothetes ton agelon* and head of the treasury in 1258. See Pach. I, 77.28–31, 155.22.

79 Akrop. I, §75 (pp. 154.26–155.10), followed by *Synopsis chronike*, 536.23–537.5; Pach. I, 41.6–43.3. While it is possible that some of the punitive measures were taken in early 1256, it is notable that Pachymeres links them with Theodore's illness. In the case of Constantine Strategopoulos, however, he is explicit that the event occurred at the beginning of his reign (see the following note).

80 Pach. I, 93.3–8.

81 On the punished members of the Raoul family, see Fassoulakis 1973:17–23.

82 Pach. I, 55.11–23.

83 Macrides 2007:27. Akropolites' conspicuous silence on Theodore's policy can be explained by the fact that he married his wife through an arrangement ordered by the emperor, the anti-hero of his *History*.

84 Pach. I, 41.10–11, 153.21–155.5. Theodore sent his good wishes for the wedding. See Ep. 212 (p. 263–64).

85 Pach. I, 55.17–26.

86 Pach. I, 41.11–13, 155.15–16.

87 On Manuel I's punitive measures, see Rhalles and Potles 1852–59, IV:189 (the case of the imperial *grammatikos* Theodore Mesarites who was punished for marrying without imperial permission). For further evidence and discussion, see Laiou 1992:44; Magdalino 1994:210–12. For an arranged marriage at the emperor's order dating to the early eleventh century (the *protospatharios* Himerios marrying a daughter of the *protospatharios* Gregory Solomon by imperial order), see the *Peira* of Eustathios Romaios in Zepos 1931, IV:198; Laiou 1992:105.

88 Ep. 206.38–39 (p. 258).

89 Pach. I, 95.1–12, 107.12–16. *Synopsis chronike* (524.6) calls his office *epi tou kerasmatos*, which is a different way of describing the *pinkernes*.

90 Ep. 143 (pp. 202–04). Dölger-Wirth, *Regesten*, 1835–39, have dated this letter, along with the other four epistles by Theodore to the papacy found in **V**, to the winter of 1256 (before March 21). See Appendix 2, 374–77.

91 Franchi 1981:86, 195–96; Haluščynskyj and Wojnar 1966:no. 28 (pp. 39–40).

92 On Arsenios' presence in Nymphaion, see MM, I, 118–22 (Laurent, *Regestes*, 1331). On his participation in an embassy to the papacy, see 296, n. 24. His treatise on the schism has been published by Gedeon 1911:330–43.

93 For Nicholas' biography, see PLP 20413; Appendix 1, 343–44. See the comments by Dondaine on Nicholas' use of sources in his edition of the *Libellus de fide Trinitatis* (Dondaine 1967:14–18). The *Libellus* would be given eventually to none other than Thomas Aquinas for examination and verification.

94 See Appendix 1, 343–44, on this work.

95 Stavrou 2007–13, I:284–85.

96 Blemmydes' work addressed to Theodore has been edited by Stavrou 2007–13, I:304–53. See Stavrou 2007–13, I:285 for the *termini* 1254–56. Blemmydes' letter to Jacob of Bulgaria, which is a more developed defence of the view of the Procession of the Holy Spirit *per Filium*, has also been edited by Stavrou 2007–13, II:74–153, who suggests 1256 as the date of composition (Stavrou 2007–13, II:61).

97 Akrop. I, §45 (pp. 79.19–82.7); Macrides 2007:238, n. 6; PLP 26495.

98 Haluščynskyj and Wojnar 1966:no.28a (pp. 44–48). Earlier edition in Schillmann 1918:113–9.

99 Haluščynskyj and Wojnar 1966:no. 28 (pp. 39–44); the chapters were edited earlier by Schillmann (1918:113–9), as incorporated in the papal letter to Constantine of Ovieto.

100 Haluščynskyj and Wojnar 1966:no. 28b (pp. 48–51); earlier edition in Schillmann 1918:119–23.

101 Akrop. I, §61 (pp. 124.25–125.20). On the embassy of the *pansebastos sebastos* who brought back a garment made of camel wool, see Kourouses 2002–05:542–44, 557–58. On the camp at Mamas near Pegai, see *Synopsis chronike*, 522.6–29.

102 Akrop. I, §61 (pp. 125.21–126.28); *Synopsis chronike*, 522.30–524.11. Only *Synopsis chronike* gives information regarding the Cuman victory at Varsakinai, on which see Külzer 2008:281 (Varzachanion), as well as regarding the victory of the Nicaean troops under Cleopas and George Nestongos.

103 Pieralli 1998:180.48–181.67.

104 Theodore's newsletter in Ep. 280.34–40.

105 For an early case (1245) when he titled himself as *dux Galiciae*, see Nikov 1920:61–62. On Rostislav, see Hösch 1979:103–04; Chapter 5, p. 93 and 274, n. 33.

106 Ep. 280.42–46.

107 Akrop. I, §62 (pp. 126–27). The time of the treaty is suggested only by *Synopsis chronike*, 524.31–525.5, which adds that Theodore waited until the end of August for its implementation and the delivery of Tzepaina.

108 On Theodore's newsletter (*epanagnostikon*) published in Ep. 279–82, see Appendix 1, 344–45. For other examples of this genre, Michael Psellos in Littlewood 1985:16–17 (Or. 5); Choniates, Or. 2, in Van Dieten 1973:6–12, esp. 7.8–12 (Or. 2) (on the date, see Van Dieten 1971:77–78); Akrop I, §44 (p. 79.1–7). Akropolites mentions that he followed the "ancient custom" of composing victory letters addressed to the Balkan cities incorporated into

the empire of Nicaea in 1246. Other examples: the emperor Tiberius II (574–82) announced his choice of a successor through an *epanagnostikon* read in a public space in Constantinople (Theophanes in De Boor 1883:252.9); the logothete of the drome Stephanos Meles authored news bulletins about John II Komnenos' campaigns in Cilicia (Michael Italikos, Ep. 40, in Gautier 1972:232–34; Gautier 1972:248.8; Magdalino 1994:313–14); after the Battle of Antioch-on-the-Maeander, the elder Theodore Laskaris is said to have dispatched "letters to all the provinces mentioning the extent and gains made by his victory" (Prinzing 1973:414.90–415.94).

109 On the status of Skopje according to the peace agreement, see Zlatarski (1940:461–62), who does not mention that the city had already fallen under Nicaea's authority in 1253. See Akrop. I, §44 (p. 78).

110 Ep. 280.46–281.73. See Papageorgiu (1902:27) for corrections.

111 Ep. 282.83–94. The animal metaphors can be considered a play on the tradition of political prophecies. On the lion-whelp oracle, see Alexander 1985:120–22, 172–74. Blemmydes is said to have prophesied the Nicaean victory. See Ep. 46 (pp. 62–63).

112 Pseudo-Kodinos in Verpeaux 1966:181–82; Macrides, Munitiz, and Angelov 2013:100.13–15.

113 See Blem., *Imperial Statue*, 56–58, Chapters 45–48, for a naturalistic description of a fit of anger that the emperor was advised to avoid. See also Theodore's own words in Enc. John, 42.421–24.

114 On Mitzo (or Micho), see Gjuzelev 1975; Jordanov 1981 (the rich numismatic evidence). For a discussion of the name of Mitso's wife, see Mladjov 2012:486–90.

115 On Kaliman, see Bozhilov 1985:113–14. On Rostislav's assumption of the title of tsar of the Bulgarians, see Nikov 1920:66–77.

116 The complex problem of Constantine Tikh's origin has recently been addressed by Pirivatrić 2009; Pirivatrić 2011:13–17. See also Zlatarski 1940:474–75.

117 Akrop. I, §73 (pp. 152–53).

118 On the patron of this church, *sebastokrator* Kaloyan (a local lord, a grandson of the Serbian king Stefan the First-Crowned, and a relative of Tikh), see Pirivatrić 2011:17–33.

119 The coup has been traditionally dated to the second half of 1256 in order to accommodate the claims raised by multiple pretenders to the Bulgarian crown in 1257. See Zlatarski 1940:467.

120 *Synopsis chronike*, 526.22–527.7, specifies that he left on a Saturday at the beginning of the month and speaks of Lentza in the Voleron area as the place of the meeting with Theodora, while Akrop. I, §63 (pp. 132.30–134.2) refers to Langadas as the venue.

121 *Synopsis chronike*, 529.11–15; Laurent 1935b:42–44; Pieralli 1998:183.91–102 (note the explicit mention of the Dominican friars).

122 Pieralli 1998:183.104–184.108; Gill (1979:97–100) stresses the issue of Constantinople as the stumbling block. See also Chrissis 2012:172–75.

123 Chr. Th., VII, 147.332–35. On date and context of this work, see Appendix 1, 342.

124 *Response* to Nicholas of Croton on the Procession of the Holy Spirit in Chr. Th. (reprint from Swete 1875), 180.506–182.547; Pieralli 1998:184.120–25.

125 *Annales Urbevetani* in Carducci and Fiorini 1903:128 and n. 1. See Kaeppeli 1940:288–89.

126 On the letters to the three cardinals, see Appendix 2, 374–77; Dante, Hell, canto X, lines 119–20.

127 A letter of Innocent IV from August 1250, at the height of the Nicaean-papal negotiations, refers to the reciprocal release of prisoners. See Franchi 1981:162.22–163.28.

128 Epp. 142, 144, 146 (pp. 201–02, 205–06, 208), especially Ep. 144.7–9 (p. 205).

129 Ep. 209 (pp. 209–11), esp. lines 29–30 (p. 210) and lines 50–53 (p. 211).

130 *Synopsis chronike*, 529.9–10.

131 Akrop. I, §64 (pp. 134–36), §65 (p. 136.8–137.8); Pach. I, 43.6–45.4. See Prinzing 1998a.

132 For the encounter with Constantine Doukas Nestongos (PLP 20201), *parakoimomenos tes megales sphendones* and provincial official in the later thirteenth century, an encounter known solely from a poem by Manuel Philes (Miller 1855–57 II:261.21–35), see Korobeinikov 2011.

133 Akrop. I, §65 (pp. 137.9–138.20); Pach. I, 43.4–45.3; Nystazopoulou 1966:288.10–289.14.

134 Nystazopoulou 1966:288–89 (text); 298–307 (line-by-line commentary).

135 Ibn Bibi in Duda 1959:273–76. Ibn Bibi mentions Antalya as the place where the sultan fled after the battle, but the newsletter by Niketas Karantenos refers to Kalonoros (Alaye, Alanya). See Nystazopoulou 1966:288.11, 301–02. According to Aspanovich (2007), it is probable that two members of his entourage – the constable (*kundastabl*) and his brother – were identical with ʿIzz al-Dīn's Christian maternal uncles. See also Turan 1953:82.

136 On the Turcomans of the area, see Cahen 1974:42–43.

137 The account of *Synopsis chronike* (530.12–29) is far more detailed than Akrop. I, §66 (p. 138.21–25), §69 (pp. 143.23–144.2). *Synopsis chronike* alone reports the whereabouts of the emperor at Christmas at a location callled τὰ Σύρροια (the *Testament* of Patriarch Arsenios refers to this place name alongside Prousa and Lopadion: PG, vol. 140, col. 952C) and mentions his route.

138 On Hülegü's decree, see Bar Hebraeus in Budge 1932:425. On the date of his entry into Konya, see Cahen 1988:244; Korobeinikov 2005:94, n. 130.

139 Ep. 214 (pp. 265–66); Angelov 2011a.

140 Pach. IV, 671.21–673.8.

141 *Synopsis chronike*, 530.29–531.9; Akrop. I, §69 (p. 144.2–19). Akropolites reports only the ceding of Laodikeia and does not mention the other three

fortresses. I have accepted the figure of 300 given in the *Synopsis chronike*, whose author was an eyewitness to the events, rather than 400 according to Akropolites, who was in the Balkans in 1257. On Sakaina and Hypsele (location unknown), see Belke and Mersich 1990:124.

142 Akrop. I, §69 (p. 144.20–23), Pach. I, 45.4–12; Greg. I, 59.13–14.

143 Pach. I, 187.22–189.25. The word ἀρχή in the phrase Θεοδώρου δὲ τὴν ἀρχὴν βασιλεύοντος (Pach. I, 187.22) has been interpreted differently by scholars. For a dating of the embassy at the beginning of Theodore's reign (in this interpretation, ἀρχή means "onset"), see Lippard 1984:180–85; Langdon 1998:131–32. For a different view (ἀρχή means "realm"), which is adopted here, see Andreeva (1926:192) who dated the embassy to late 1257 or early 1258. Korobeinikov (2005:95; 2014:195–97) has adduced plausible arguments based on Bar Hebraeus (see Budge 1932:425) for the arrival of the Mongol embassy in the spring of 1257. Discussions so far have overlooked that Pachymeres very often uses ἀρχή to refer to "realm" or "empire." See, for example, Pach. I, 25.24–25, 31.13, 33.14–15, 37.11–20, 43.13–19, 61.19–20, 105.23, 109.10–26, 129.2, 133.20, 135.1–2, 141.12, 179.18–19, 187.27–28. Failler translates the above phrase as *sous le règne de l'empereur Théodore.*

144 The elevated position of the emperor, the display of his sword, and the raising of the curtain are all elements of the *prokypsis* ceremony as described in detail in the fourteenth century. See Pseudo-Kodinos in Verpeaux 1966:195–204; Macrides, Munitiz, and Angelov 2013:126–46.

145 Pach. I, 189.26–30, notes that the reception of the Mongol embassy was the beginning of a series of embassies and "right away" a marriage alliance was planned. See Andreeva 1926:200.

146 Ep. 44 (pp. 56–59). On the date of the letter, see Appendix 2, 377–78.

147 Ep. 44.61–63 (p. 58).

148 Ep. 44.63–75 (p. 58).

149 Akrop. I, §61 (pp. 124.25–125.20), §70 (p. 146.25–26).

150 Delay of the payment of the salaries of Latin mercenaries: Pach. I, 79.18–24. Cumans (active in 1257 in the Balkans): Akrop. I, §68 (p. 141.21); the Varangians (the treasury in Magnesia entrusted to them on Theodore's death); Pach. I, 101.22.

151 See the novel issued by Michael Palaiologos correcting injustices connected with the collection of *mitaton*: Burgmann and Magdalino 1984. On the *naulos*, see Ep. 44.41–42 (p. 57); Antoniadis–Bibicou 1963:134.

152 Ep. 44.79–84 (p. 58).

153 Ep. 44.44–49 (p. 57). The word *hellenikon* refers here to the Hellenes in accordance with ancient usage found, for example, in Herodotus, *Histories*, 1, 4, 16; 1, 58, 1; 7, 139, 24; 8, 144, 13. See also Chr. Th., VII, 146.306, 147.309.

154 *Synopsis chronike* and Akropolites (see 302, n. 141) report that the fortresses fell "soon" after their cession to Nicaea. On the Turkmen presence near

Laodikeia-Denizli and Michael Palaiologos' campaigns in the area in 1260 and 1261, see Korobeinikov 2014:221–27.

155 Akrop. I, §67 (pp. 139–40).

156 Akrop. I, §49 (p. 90.19–22), §80 (p. 166.1–4). Theodore Petraliphas was the sister of the saintly Theodora Petraliphina, wife of Michael II Komnenos Doukas. See Chapter 7, p. 128.

157 Akrop. I, §75 (p. 155.3–6); Loukaki 1996.

158 Akrop. I, §66 (pp. 138–39); §72 (p. 151.6–8). On a representative of the Kalambakes family who served as *doux* of the Neokastra theme, see Ahrweiler 1965:138, n. 89; 165. On a certain Balsamon Xyleas (PLP 20952) who was a peasant near Smyrna in the early fourteenth century, see MM, IV, 260; Ahrweiler 1965:154 (on the date of the document). Ramatas (PLP 24069–71) and Chabaron (30328–36) are rare family names; Poulachas is rarest. Ep. 203 (p. 250), a campaign letter of 1255 to Mouzalon, refers to Chabaron's gift of a horse from Albanon.

159 Akrop. I, §68 (pp. 140–43), §70 (pp. 145.16–146.12).

160 Akrop. I, §70 (pp. 144.24–145.15), §71 (pp. 146–49); Pach. I, 45.15–47.6. An illegitimate son of Michael of Epiros, Theodore fell in the battle against Michael Palaiologos and Michael Laskaris, in which many captives were taken.

161 Akrop. I, §72 (pp. 149–53), §79 (p. 164.15–19).

162 Nicol 1957:170–73. For a discussion of the date of Helena's marriage in the following year (1259), see Berg 1988:273–83.

163 MM, III, 240; Nicol 1957:160–67.

164 Berg 1988:263–67. The source on these raids is the account of the translation of relics of St. Thomas to Ortona and the delivery of Greek prisoners from Chios and Lesbos; it has been excerpted in Capasso 1874:144–46. The daring attack seems to have been related to the presence of Manfred's widowed sister, Constanza-Anna, at the Nicaean court.

165 See Appendix 3, 381–89.

166 On the letter to Blemmydes describing his symptoms, see Ep. 48.22–37 (p. 65). On this letter and other descriptions of his illness, see Appendix 3, 383–85. On the doctors as "human plagues" (βροτολοιγοί), see Ep. 45.65 (p. 62) (the letter dates from the time of his terminal illness). See also Ep. 20.32 (p. 27), 70.22 (p. 97).

167 On the date of these two texts and their content, see Appendix 1, 345–46. See PG, vol. 140, col. 772AB; Essay 6 in **V**, ff. 67v–68r (Agapitos and Angelov 2018).

168 Pach. I, 53.13–55.10.

169 *Basilika*, LX, 39, 28 (= *Codex Iustianianus*, IX, 18, 7).

170 Pach. I, 47.8–12, 51.3–53.10, 55.17–57.29, 155.6–10. Identifying Michael Palaio-logos as the anonymous Greek constable mentioned by the historian Aqsarayi, Korobeinikov (2014:201–03) hypothesizes that Michael Palaiologos had a second stint in the sultanate and was in Konya in February or March

1258, when Sultan 'Izz al-Dīn appointed him as a military commander. The assignment of Michael Palaiologos to the Balkans (1257) and his arrest by Theodore Laskaris (late 1257 or early 1258) makes the proposed identification problematic. Traditionally, the Greek constable has been identified with one of 'Izz al-Dīn's Christian maternal uncles. See Turan 1953:82; Aspanovich 2007.

171 Blem., *Autobiographia*, I, 89 (p. 44). The member of the imperial guard was a certain Drimys, who had once threatened to kill Blemmydes during his confrontation with Marchisina and is said to have died later.

172 Blem., *Autobiographia*, I, 87–88 (pp. 43–44), Laurent, *Regestes*, 1329 (the suggested date of December 1254 is unlikely). George Mouzalon is said to have taken a prominent part in the high tribunal of laymen and ecclesiastics chaired by Theodore. Another prophecy reported by Pachymeres as originating in Thessalonica in 1258 predicted the imminent imperial elevation of Michael Palaiologos. See Pach. I, 49.1–51.31.

173 Blem., *Autobiographia*, I, 81–84 (pp. 40–42); Laurent, *Regestes*, 1335.

174 Blem., *Autobiographia*, I, 85 (p. 42).

175 Blem., *Autobiographia*, I, 86 (pp. 42–43); II, 78 (p. 80).

176 *Synopsis chronike*, 536.13–20, 537.13–17. In his *Testament* (PG, vol. 140, col. 949C), Patriarch Arsenios agrees with *Synopsis chronike* in mentioning oaths sworn to John IV Laskaris as the successor both before and after Theodore's death. John IV Laskaris is called emperor when first mentioned by historians. See Pach. I, 63.15; *Synopsis chronike*, 536.19. According to a short chronicle, John Doukas Laskaris was proclaimed emperor being not yet fully eight years of age in August of the first indiction (August 1258). See Schreiner 1975–79, I:75.4 (no. 8).

177 On these two collections, see Appendix 1, 325–27.

178 KD, III, 30.12.

179 Mor. P., II, 256.94–257.105. See also Mor. P., III, 258.128.

180 On the monastic name Theodore, see Cappuyns 1935:491 (no. 59); Polemis 1968:110, n. 10. The essay (Essay 2 in V, f. 66r–v) has been edited and translated by Agapitos and Angelov 2018. On his request from the synod, see Blemmydes' autobiography cited above, 305, n. 174. On his last confession, see Akrop. I, §74 (pp. 153–54); *Synopsis chronike*, 533.27–534.27 (a more detailed account, based on the eyewitness testimony of the patriarch Arsenios who was close to the author).

181 For the former estimate, see Kazhdan 1982:117 (based on a statistical pool of fifteen literati of the eleventh and twelfth centuries, mostly Constantinopolitans). The average lifespan of fourteenth-century peasants in Macedonia who survived early childhood has been estimated as forty-two and a half years by Laiou-Thomadakis (1977:294–95). See also Bourbou 2010:40–41. If early childhood survival is taken into consideration, the average life expectancy becomes lower.

182 The date of death is given by a chronological note in Vat. Palat. gr. 25 (153v), in Schreiner 1975–79, II:608 (no. 22). For Magnesia as place of his obit, see Blem., *Autobiographia*, II, 80 (p. 81).

183 Mitsiou 2011:674–81. On his supposed marble sarcophagus, see the interesting but doubtful hypothesis of Henri Grégoire discussed in Appendix 5, 392.

9 The Philosopher

1 Andreeva 1930:34.

2 Tatakis 2001:194–97.

3 Richter 1989:208–09, 229.

4 Dräseke 1894:503; Tatakis 2001:197; Richter 1989:230–33 (with a discussion of the similarities and differences between Spinoza and Bacon).

5 See Dräseke 1894:503; Tatakis 2001:197; Richter 1989 (230–33) has summed up some of the problems with these comparisons.

6 Blemmydes, *Epitome of Logic*, §4 and §6, PG, vol. 142, cols. 720–24, 729–36. On the classic six definitions and the rival Christian view, see Ierodiakonou and O'Meara 2008:712–13, 715–16.

7 Ep. 123.1–18 (pp. 172–73). See also Sat., 179.610–181.648.

8 Ep. 7.12–14 (p. 11), 105.29 (p. 144), 121.39–40 (p. 168), KD, III, 25.14.

9 *Natural Communion*, PG, vol. 140, cols. 1342A, 1343A, 1344B, 1352A, 1353A. See Ibid. 1342A.

10 Compare also KD, III, 21.3 with *De Mundo*, 397b9–10. *De Mundo* (396a33–b11, 397a11–14) refers to the union of opposites in the universe and the orderly procession of seasons, ideas prominently featured in *Representation of the World, or Life*.

11 Ep. 23.21–24 (p. 29).

12 Letter to Akropolites: Tartaglia, Op. rhet., 12.255–56: οὐσιώδης ἀριθμός. The view goes back to Plato, *Epinomis*, 977e3–978a6. On the Neoplatonic term, see Plotinus, *Enneads*, 6, 6, 9; 6, 6, 16. On Plato and his "divine fire," see Chapter 9, p. 192 and 310, n. 79.

13 Or. Fr., 90.121–91.132 (mistake); KD, III, 25.20 (correction). The misattribution may originate from the opening chapter of Blemmydes' *Epitome of Logic*, where Aristotle's concept of a definition (*horos*) is introduced through the example of the proposition "the king philosophizes." See Blemmydes, *Epitome of Logic*, §1, in PG, vol. 142, col. 692A. See Richter (1989:203) on the way Theodore quotes Aristotle, *On the Soul*, without having a deep familiarity with the work.

14 Ep. 32.5–7 (p. 41), 36.75–77 (p. 47); Bydén 2013:159–62. See also Apol., 111.24–25.

15 Ep. 129.4–6 (p. 180), addressed to the patriarchal officials Xiphilinos and Argyropoulos, speaks of two kinds of philosophy. See also Ep. 217.12–13

(p. 272). On outer (θύραθεν, ἔξω) learning, see, for example, Chr. Th., V, 112.83; Tartaglia, Op. rhet., 12.264.

16 Ep. 109.30–31 (p. 151). See also Chr. Th., V, 114.170–115.175. On the true philosopher as the monk, see Dölger 1953.

17 Ep. 11.40–45 (p. 16) addressed to Blemmydes; Ep. 105.47–52 (p. 145) addressed to Nikephoros of Ephesos.

18 Giannouli 2001:53.14–15.

19 Ep. 107.47–47 (p. 152).

20 *Natural Communion*, PG, vol. 140, col. 1345B. The treatise describes philosophy as a quality subject to increase and decrease in intensity. Universal *paideia* is also a quality: *Natural Communion*, PG, vol. 140, col. 1355B.

21 Ep. 39.57–58 (p. 51), 40.30 (p. 52), 53.40 (p. 78).

22 Ep. 47.4–5 (p. 63).

23 *Natural Communion*, PG, vol. 140, col. 1351B.

24 *Natural Communion*, PG, vol. 140, cols. 1353A–1354A, 1342A (leatherworker), 1358A.

25 *Natural Communion*, PG, vol. 140, cols. 1348A–1351A. See also col. 1347B.

26 Rashed 2000.

27 On the relative chronology of *Natural Communion* and *Explanation of the World*, and on the date of the four parts of *Explanation of the World*, see Appendix 1, 338–42.

28 *Natural Communion*, PG, vol. 140, col. 1313A.

29 *Natural Communion*, PG, vol. 140, cols. 1341B, 1354A.

30 KD, I, 112.23–27.

31 KD, II, 18.7–26. Or. Fr., 87.28–35, mentions the Indian buffalo (*taurelaphos*), an exotic animal unique to the *Christian Topography*. On the influence of the early Christian Antiochene tradition regarding a vaulted or domed sky and the discussion by Michael Glykas, see Caudano 2008:70–86, esp. 85–86.

32 KD, II, 5.22–14.26. On the circle as the most natural shape, see *Natural Communion*, PG, vol. 140, cols. 1271A–1272B. On some of the philosophical background, see Plato, *Phaedrus*, 247b–d, *Republic*, 616b–617d, *Timaeus* 34a–b, *Laws* 897; Plotinus, *Enneads,* V.1.4.17–19.

33 KD, II, 15.2–16.12, esp. 16.9–10.

34 KD, III, 21.5–7, 34.10–36.1.

35 KD, III, 21.1–3, 25.22–24, 26.30–27.1.

36 *Natural Communion*, PG, vol. 140, cols. 1281B, 1284A, 1364B.

37 *Natural Communion*, PG. vol. 140, cols. 1281B, 1284A. On nature as a foundation, see col. 1364B.

38 *Natural Communion*, PG, vol. 140, cols. 1277A, 1281B, 1347A, 1352B, 1393B–1394A. On the differences from Neoplatonic metaphysics, see Richter 1989:17–18.

39 *Natural Communion*, PG, vol. 140, cols. 1343A–1344B, 1393A.

40 *Natural Communion*, PG, vol. 140, cols. 1298AB, 1363A. An athletic context is natural, but the drinking bout – and the award given by the referee – are a matter of convention. See *Natural Communion*, PG, vol. 140, col. 1357A.

41 *Natural Communion*, PG, vol. 140, col. 1352A. See also *Natural Communion*, PG, vol. 140, cols. 1354B, 1356B.

42 Richter 1989:211. See Richter 1989:17–18, on the differences from Neoplatonic metaphysics.

43 *Natural Communion*, PG, vol. 140, col. 1297A.

44 Blemmydes, *Epitome of Physics*, PG, vol. 142, col. 1089BC.

45 Essay 3 in **V**, f. 67r. For an edition, translation, and analysis, see Agapitos and Angelov 2018.

46 *Natural Communion*, PG, vol. 140, col. 1396A.

47 KD, I, 98.18–99.4 (general preface); union with God: KD, I, 102.19–103.2, 112.26–114.3, KD, II, 2.5–9; God as the "creator of nature": KD, II, 14.22, 20.4–5.

48 KD, I, 108.25–26.

49 KD, II, 3.13–22.

50 KD, I, 109.30–110.1, 110.7–15.

51 *Natural Communion*, PG, vol. 140, cols. 1345B–1348B.

52 KD, III, 23.20–24.8.

53 KD, III, 23.1–2.

54 *Oration on the Annunciation*, in Chr. Th., VIII, 152.123–153.124. On the meaning of *katastasis,* see, for example, Constantine Porphyrogennetos, *De Cerimoniis*, I,1 in Reiske 1829:28.10. For *parastasis*, see Pseudo-Kodinos in Verpeaux 1966:140; Macrides, Munitiz, and Angelov 2013:32.7; 33, n. 7.

55 *Natural Communion*, PG, vol. 140, cols. 1346A, 1350AB. See also cols. 1346B–1347A. On *taxis* as Byzantine political ideal, see Kazhdan and Constable 1982:60–61.

56 On "foundation of the people" (βάσις λαοῦ), see Enc. John, 36.285–87 (with the addition that the emperor is "fundament of the church"). On the etymological wordplay, see Blem., *Imperial Statue*, 46, Chapter 8; Angelov 2007:193, n. 52. For the "Christ-named people", see Ep. 99.69 (p. 135). On the "chosen people," see Enc. John, 61.876. On the duty of the emperor to secure the well-being and protection of the subjects, see KD, IV, 49.17–18; Or. Fr., 90.110–111.

57 *Natural Communion*, PG, vol. 140, col. 1361AB.

58 Or. Fr., 91.133–92.160. Theodore's musings reflect his own observations, although it is interesting that Pseudo-Aristotle's *De Mundo* (396a32–b22) also presents social concord as the outcome of conflict among people of different ages, ethnic origin, economic status, and moral characteristics.

59 KD, III, 24.29–25.3.

60 KD, III, 25.16–22.

61 KD, III, 25.22–24.

62 KD, III, 36.24–37.3. The identification with Mouzalon has been proposed by Andreeva 1930:11–12. The word *paradynesteuon* was used in the middle and

occasionally in the later Byzantine period to refer to the emperor's "prime minister," the *mesazon*, which is the position that Mouzalon held during Theodore's rule. See Beck 1955:310–20; Kazhdan in ODB, vol. 3, 1548. The historian Gregoras (Greg. I:170) calls George Mouzalon *paradynasteuon*.

63 KD, III, 33.21–24.

64 See the observations by Richter 1989:215–16.

65 Letter to Akropolites in Tartaglia, Op. rhet., 20.442–45 (see the *apparatus fontium* for an allusion to Gregory of Nazianzus); KD, I, 112.1–4; Enc. Nic., 69.36–37. He attributed the saying to an unnamed church father rather than Democritus who is usually credited with its authorship.

66 Observation of the reaction of the crowd: Ep. 73.28 (p. 100), 214.34–37 (p. 266). Protection of the "crowd" (πλῆθος): Ep. 44.79 (p. 58). Well-being of the "people" (λαός): KD, IV, 49.17–18; Or. Fr., 90.110. On "the vulgar crowd" (βάναυσοι, χυδαῖοι), see Ep. 49.78–97 (p. 70); Ep. 199.5–16 (pp. 244–45).

67 Mor. P., V, 259.192–195; VI, 260.235–261.240.

68 Or. Fr., 86.22–88.53, 93.180–187.

69 *To a Secretive Man Who Was Deceiving Him*, in Tartaglia, Op. rhet., 199–202.

70 *On Virtue* in Paléologou 2007:78.290–303. On the Fall of humankind, see also Chr. Th., V, 120.332–39.

71 Mor. P., IV, 259.173–179; XI, 267.452–55.

72 KD, III, 26.21–28.17.

73 KD, III, 27.25–26.

74 KD, III, 28.23–25; Pach. I, 97.2–4, 103.1–6, 107.5–9. Andreeva (1930:15–18) suggested allusions in this part of *Representation of the World, or Life* to prominent individuals, such as Blemmydes, Akropolites, the patriarch Arsenios, Theodore Philes, Alexios Strategopoulos, Constantine Tornikes, and the emperor himself.

75 On "rationalism" as an anachronistic concept and on Psellos' views, see Magdalino and Mavroudi 2006:15–20, 27–31. Blemmydes' alchemical treatise has been published by Berthelot and Ruelle 1887–8 II:452–9. On the expression "secrets of philosophy" (τὰ ἄρρητα τῆς φιλοσοφίας), see Ep. 131.23 (p. 184); Chr. Th., VII, 141.145. See also Ep. 216.7–9 (p. 268) referring to the oracles of Pythia. Elsewhere (KD, III, 34.12–14), Theodore explained to Mouzalon that he had learned "the mysterious mysteries" (μυστηριώδη μυστήρια) of philosophy.

76 Chr. Th., VII, 141.140–45. On Apollonios of Tyana in Byzantium, see Dzielska 1986:107–11. Astrological texts were ascribed in Byzantium to Pythagoras who, according to Iamblichus' biography, had learned secret arts from the magi.

77 On the Philes affair, see Chapter 6, pp. 122–23. I will be discussing in detail Theodore Laskaris' views on ordeals in a forthcoming publication. There is a long bibliography on judicial ordeals by red-hot iron in Byzantium. See especially Geanakoplos 1976; Angold 1980; Macrides 2013. Most scholars have considered the practice to be an importation from the Latin world around 1204, but the issue seems more complex. Macrides (2013) rightly leaves the question open.

78 See the court cases heard by Demetrios Chomatenos (Prinzing 2002:no.87 [pp. 302–03], no. 127 [397–99]) and John Apokaukos (published and analyzed by Fögen 1983). Summary by Macrides 2013:35–38. The ordeals are explicitly characterized as a foreign and barbarian custom by Chomatenos (Prinzing 2002:303.20–21, 399.47–48) and Apokaukos (Fögen 1983:95.25–26).

79 KD, III, 21.1–8. For *hagion pyr* as the fire of ordeals, see Pach. I, 55.4–5.

80 Tartaglia, Op. rhet., 199.17–200.23. The word διάκρισις alludes to the "discerning fire" (πῦρ διακρίσεως), namely, the ordeal by fire to which Theodore volunteered to subject himself in order to dispel libelous charges of adultery. See Ep. 38.11–13 (p. 48).

81 See Chapter 8, p. 155.

82 Ep. 147.1–7 (p. 209). The meaning of *hodoskopia*, a hapax, might refer to prognostication of travel or divinations based on accidents occurring during travel. See also Ep. 176.1 (p. 228).

83 *Synopsis chronike*, 510.6–10. Approving attitudes to bibliomancy are attested in early Byzantium. Anastasius of Sinai had noted in the seventh century, for example, that the fathers of the church favored bibliomancy in order to prevent worse offences, such as sorcery and divination. See Anastasios of Sinai, Question 57, in Richard and Munitiz 2006:108–09.

84 *Synopsis chronike*, 522.6–29; Nikolopoulos 1981–1982:459.276–85.

85 Ep. 131.1–33 (pp. 183–84). The emperor criticized the "great scientists" of his time, experts in arithmetic, geometry, music, and astronomy (the *quadrivium*), for devoting themselves to practice rather than theory, which was a more appropriate pursuit for the philosopher. In the eleventh century Michael Psellos had espoused a similar view. See Magdalino and Mavroudi 2006:27–28.

86 Ep. 131.17–24 (p. 184).

87 On the legal background (late antique laws repeated in subsequent Byzantine law collections), see Troianos 1990. See Matthew Blastares' fourteenth-century summary of canons and laws in Rhalles and Potles 1852–59, VI:356–62.

88 *Natural Communion*, PG, vol. 140, cols. 1323–24; Chr. Th., II, 88.27–89.51.

89 Chr. Th., III, 96.50–98.96.

90 *Natural Communion*, PG, vol. 140, col. 1327.

91 *Natural Communion*, PG, vol. 140, col. 1350A.

92 Chr. Th., V, 111.79–112.80, 115.179–181, 116.232–117.241.

93 Chr. Th., V, 112.92–114.166. On the symbolism of the number ten, see the discussion of Clement of Alexandria's anthropological decalogue by Kalvesmaki 2013:128–36.

94 KD, I, 110.23–111.12 (and also KD, II, 6.28–9.13). The theory is developed by Theon of Smyrna and fourth-century Christian authors. See Kalvesmaki 2013:175–86.

95 KD, II, 15.6–8, 16.13–15. Aristotle, *Categories*, 15a13–33; Blemmydes, *Epitome of Logic*, §21, in PG, vol. 142, col. 840BC. On the symbolism of the number six in Philo of Alexandria, see Kalvesmaki 2013:9–10.

96 Ep. 123.16–23 (p. 173). Theodore assigned symbolic meaning also to the numbers eight and nine. See Ep. 103.69–72 (p. 142), 109.24–27 (p. 151), KD, IV, 47.13–17.

97 On Theodore's approach and the Greek philosophical background, see Richter 1989:179–97, esp. 186–91. On number symbolism among early Christian Greek authors, see Kalvesmaki 2013:103–51.

98 See his long letter to Akropolites in Tartaglia, Op. rhet., 12.244–52. He presented ideas derived from Theon of Smyrna and asked Akropolites to solve mathematical problems. See Tartaglia, Op. rhet., 9.170–10.202; Ep. 66.11–14 (p. 95). See also his encomium on Akropolites in Tartaglia, Op. rhet., 108.287–90.

99 Published by Allard 1978. On the Latin influence on the Arabic numerals in this work, see Wilson 1996:226. It is not known whether Theodore was familiar with this work.

100 Chr. Th., VII, 146.292–94. See also Chr. Th., VI, 127.111–24.

101 Chr. Th., VI, 128.128–42, 132.265–134.333, esp. 134.318–20.

102 Chr. Th., VII, 146.297–300.

103 Chr. Th., V, 117.258–67.

104 Ep. 130.19–25 (p. 182); KD, III, 36.24–26.

105 *Natural Communion*, PG, vol. 140, col. 1343A.

106 As noted by Richter 1989:191–92, based on *Natural Communion*, PG, vol. 140, col. 1355B. The ratio between philosophy and rhetoric is the same as that between Aristotle and Hermogenes (first syllogistic premise). The ratio between Aristotle and Hermogenes was that between Alexander and Marcus Aurelius (second syllogistic premise). Hence philosophy and rhetoric stood in the same relationship as Alexander and Marcus Aurelius. Richter did not notice Theodore's dislike for the use of syllogistic logic in theology.

107 Blemmydes, *Epitome of Logic*, preface, in PG, vol. 142, col. 688C. On Blemmydes' approach to theological epistemology, see Stavrou 2009.

108 *On Theology*, 12.13–18 in Stavrou 2007–13 II:198–200. For the imperial addressee and a suggestion that Blemmydes reacted to Theodore's Trinitarian speculations based on numerology and geometry in some of the books of his *Christian Theology*, see Stavrou 2007-13 II:155–166.

109 The idea of the unknowability of God makes its appearance in other works, too. See Apol. Mal., 286.89–92, where Theodore writes that only "the man who penetrates into God's ineffability after passing through the darkness of divine unknowability by means of purification and simple manners" can conceive of God's justice.

110 The part of the treatise of interest to us here is Chr. Th., VI, 129.148–131.244.

111 Ep. 145.26–47 (p. 207).

112 Chr. Th., VII, 145.263–65.

113 Chr. Th., V, 110.43–45, 120.332–34.

114 See his reflections in KD, IV, 41.30–44.11, esp. 43.15–17.

115 Sat., 165.259–62.
116 Apol., 111.24–26. One Heraclitus as the weeping philosopher, see Mor. P., III, 257.116–17.
117 KD, I, 100.9–12.
118 KD, IV, 43.15–17, 44.5–6.
119 KD, IV, 52.5–8.
120 Ep. 62.1–6 (p. 91); long letter to Akropolites in Tartaglia, Op. rhet., 12.258–61.
121 Ep. 103.74–75 (p. 142).
122 Ep. 53.4–6 (p. 77).
123 Ep. 53.13–15 (p. 77), 53.36–42 (p. 78).
124 Ep. 121 (pp. 167–70), esp. 121.2–5 (p. 167), 121.8–12 (pp. 167–68).
125 Connecting the treatise with the polemical Ep. 44 to Blemmydes and with *Representation of the World, or Life*, Andreeva (1928) suggested that the work responded to Blemmydes' accusations that he fell far short of the ideal ruler. On the date of the work, see Appendix 1, 340–41.
126 Ierodiakonou 2002.

10 The Proponent of Hellenism

1 On Julian's Hellenism and its fourth-century contexts, see, for example, Bowersock 1978:84–93; Elm 2012; Johnson 2012:445–51. In 1894 Konstantinos Sathas (MB VII:23, preface) fancied that Theodore had renounced his Christianity, probably in a pagan ceremony in the church of St. Tryphon in Nicaea, and that Hellenism in Nicaea came to undermine the Christian faith and the church. There is no evidence in support of this thesis.
2 Ahrweiler 1975; Angold 1975b; Angelov 2005:293–94; 300–03 (on protonationalism); 2007:97–98; Koder 2003:310–13. On protonationalism as an analytical category, see Hobsbawm 1992:46–79.
3 Irmscher 1972:115, 137.
4 Vacalopoulos 1970:36–43, esp. 40.
5 Kaldellis 2007:378–79.
6 Gellner 1983:1. On the view of Byzantium as a nation state of the Romans, see Kaldellis 2007.
7 Blem., *Autobiographia*, I, 23.8–9 (p. 14). On *genos* and *ethnos* in an ethnic sense, see Page 2008:41–42; Constantine Porphyrogennetos famously refers in the tenth century to the Romans as an *ethnos* and describes them as *homogeneis* ("people of the same stock"). See his *De Administrando Imperio*, 13, in Moravcsik 1967:74.
8 See Stouraitis 2014:185–89.
9 Angelou 1996:16.
10 Page 2008:99–107.
11 Kaldellis 2007:383.

12 Enc. John, 27.93–28.94 ("Roman land"), 34.227–28 ("Roman cities"); Enc. Nic., 79.257, 80.303 ("realm of the Romans"). On the Ausones, see Ep. 125.46 (p. 175), 205.6 (p. 255), 214.32 (p. 266); Enc. John, 27.84–85. Continuity of Romanness: Theodore's mother Irene was praised as the "empress of New Rome" (Akrop. II, 3.18); Manuel Komnenos Doukas, the brother of Theodore Komnenos Doukas of Epiros, spoke of "us, the Romans," in his letter of 1232 to Patriarch Germanos II (MM, III, 60.26–27).

13 Ep. 214.34–35 and 214.40–41 (p. 266); Enc. John, 34.225–30.

14 Ep. 204.59 (p. 253); newsletter in Ep., 281.63.

15 Trapp 1993:124.

16 For two different approaches to the blending of Roman and Greek identity in antiquity, see Woolf 1994 and Wallace-Hadrill 1998.

17 For example, the Augustan Greek author Dionysios of Halicarnassus tells the story that Rome's founders were Greeks. See Fox 1996:49–95. According to a legend found in the influential seventh-century *Apocalypse of Pseudo-Methodios*, Romulus married a daughter of King Byzas, the eponymous founder of the ancient city of Byzantion. See Alexander 1985:42, 57–58.

18 See McKee 2000 regarding the Venetians on the island of Crete.

19 Blem., *Autobiographia*, I, 27.7–8 (p. 16). See Germanos' sermon delivered on the Day of the Holy Cross: PG, vol. 140, cols. 664–65. The Nicaean formulary for the confession of Bogomils has been published by Ferrari dalle Spade 1913:51 (no. 9). On Bogomils (*phoundagiagitai*) active in Asia Minor in the eleventh century, see the polemical work published by Ficker 1908:62.10–13, 66.13–68.4; Obolensky 1948:174–183, 222.

20 Akrop. II, 30.1, 31.4, 64.9–24. See Kaldellis 2007:381–83.

21 Merendino 1974–75:322.1–2, 332.1–2, 336.1–4 (see Merendino 1974–75:320.23–24).

22 Merendino 1974–75:322.12–21.

23 Blem., *Autobiographia*, II, 25 (p. 57). He calls the pope "the chief of the Romans." See Blem., *Autobiographia*, I, 72.7 (p. 36); II, 28.12 (p. 58). For the expression "scepter of the Hellenes," see Blem., *Autobiographia*, I, 6.11–12 (p. 6); Angold 1975b:65, n. 48.

24 Arampatzis 2004–06:376:63–65. Laurent, *Regestes*, 1257.

25 Uspenskii 1879:75–78 (pagination of the appendices); incomplete edition based on Cod. Barocci 91, ff. 17r–20v (Laurent, *Regestes*, 1277). On the word *Graikoi* often used by the patriarch, see 261, n. 86.

26 Letter in Pieralli 2006:121–26, esp. 123.18–124.52; Dölger-Wirth, *Regesten*, 1757; partial translation in Kaldellis 2007:370.

27 Enc. John, 29.128–32. *Mutatis mutandis*, Akropolites implied in his *History* that Romanness was politically defined. The subjects of the emperor of Nicaea were Romans, but the inhabitants of the rival kingdom of Epiros–Thessalonica were not. See Akrop. I, §45 (p. 83.13–14); Macrides 2007:94–95; 241, n. 25.

28 Latins: Enc. John, 27.80; Italians: Enc. Nic., 80.284, 80.292; Ep. 125.13 (p. 174), Chr. Th., VII, 146.304. Kaldellis (2007:379–81) has shown the differences between Theodore Laskaris and Blemmydes.

29 On his letter to the cardinal (Ep. 147), see 315, n. 53. In his *Response* to Nicholas of Croton he noted that his duty as an emperor – an emperor of the Romans – was to be tolerant and impartial to speakers of different languages: "The emperor does not favor those who speak the same tongue as his, but is equal to everyone and disposed in the same manner to all his subjects." See Chr. Th (reprint from Swete 1875), 181.529–538, especially lines 532–534.

30 Ep. 202.55–57 (p. 250), 204.59–60 (p. 253), 204.124–130 (p. 255). See also Ep. 46.8–9 (p. 63) addressed to Blemmydes after the end of the war. On the Hellenes and the Persians (in the context of the theory of the four empires), see Enc. John, 29.132–34; and Chapter 10, 209–10.

31 See, for example, Chr. Th., VII, 142.157–161; Ep. 40.18–19 (p. 52), 125.38 (p. 175).

32 See the address to the assembled clergy: Chr. Th., VII, 147.331–34. See also the address to an anonymous Latin interlocutor in the second person singular: Chr. Th., VII, 142.152.

33 Chr. Th., VII, 143.190–92.

34 Chr. Th., VII, 142.179–83.

35 Chr. Th., VII, 141.125–49, 142.179; Ep. 5.14–15 (p. 8), 109.47–57 (p. 152). On the "theology of the Hellenes," see also Ep. 125.23–24 (p. 175). On metaphysics as theology in Aristotle, see *Metaphysics*, 1064b.

36 Chr. Th., VII, 142.155–165; Enc. Nic., 71.90–72.110.

37 Ep. 125.44–46 (p. 175).

38 See Aristotle's spurious letter to Alexander in Hercher 1873:174 (ep. 6). Use of the phrase: Photios, *Amphilochia*, 142.3, in Laourdas and Westerink 1983–88 V:158; John Zonaras, *Annals*, IV,8, in Pindar 1841 I:331.22–332.4; Michael Choniates in Kolovou 2001:3.12–14 (ep. 1).

39 Chr, Th, VIII, 145.268–271.

40 Ep. 5 (p. 8), esp. Ep. 13–17 (p. 8). See Blem. Ep., 329.116–117, on his dissatisfaction with the value placed on learning voiced in a letter to Patriarch Manuel II declining the offer of a teaching position.

41 Enc. John, 53.685–86; Ad Georg. Mouz., 120.6–7. See also Blem., *Imperial Statue*, 50, Chapter 20.

42 Enc. John, 53.688–54.708.

43 Podskalsky 1972. See Theodore's comic commentary on Nabuchudnezzar's vision in Ep. 10 (p. 14).

44 Enc. John, 29.132–30.138, 32.182.

45 Enc. John, 29.117–32, 30.138–42.

46 Ep. 204.43–44 (p. 252), 204.58–59, 204.67–69 (p. 253), 205.41 (p. 256).

47 Ep., 281.69–70: πρὸς τοὺς Μακεδόνας ἡμᾶς. One wonders whether he envisaged here an identity derived from the Byzantine theme of Macedonia centered on

Adrianople in Thrace rather than the ancient historical region. On Macedonia as Thrace, see Akrop. I, §13 (p. 21.10), §59 (p. 120.4); Macrides 2007:141, n. 2.

48 On the history of Pergamon in the Byzantine period, see Rheidt 2002.

49 Rheidt 1990.

50 Ep. 59.26–29 (p. 88).

51 Ruy González de Clavijo in López Estrada 1943:29; trans. Le Strange 1928:54. For the impressions left by other medieval travelers, see Wood 1985:37–38.

52 John Malalas 5.12, 5.22, 5.23, 5.24, 5.25, 5.29, 7.1, 13.7 in Thurn 2000:81–82, 93–95, 100, 132, 245–246; Zonaras in Büttner-Wobst 1897:18. On the Trojan legend in Byzantine chronicles, see Jeffreys 1979:206, 208, 211–12, 214, 216–17, 224, 232, 234, 236, 237. On one Frankish view, see Robert of Clari in Lauer 1924:§106 (p. 102); trans. McNeal 1936:122. Benoît de Sainte-Maure's *Roman de Troie* was translated and reworked in Greek after 1204. See the discussion by Shawcross 2003.

53 Ep. 147.27–42 (p. 210), especially lines 36–37.

54 On the emperor Trajan as the founder of Nicaea, see Metochites' oration in Foss 1996:§3, 168. Cf. Foss 1996:197–98, n. 14. On the inscriptions, see Schneider and Karnapp 1939:44–45. On the tower of Trajan, see Francesco Scalamonti's *vita* of Cyriac of Ancona in Mitchell and Bodnar 1996:127–28 (§84). On Traianoupolis, see Soustal 1991:482–84.

55 Ep. 125.52–54 (p. 176). See also Ep. 118.23–24 (p. 165), where he juxtaposes Europe to *hellenikon*. See Angold 1975b:64. Papageorgiu (1902b) saw similarities with the way in which eastern Europeans of his time, especially Greeks, viewed Europe as "the other." On Blemmydes' use of the expression "this Hellas" as the Anatolian territory of the empire of Nicaea, see Chapter 10, p. 206 and 313, n. 23.

56 Ep. 77.1–4 (p. 103).

57 Akrop. I, §80 (p. 166.6–7). See Angold 1975b:64. According to Macrides (2007:358, n. 4), "our Hellenic land" refers to the old theme of Hellas.

58 Herodotus, *History*, 3.106; Plato, *Timaeus* 24c; Aristotle, *Politics*, 1327b20–36. For some of the key assumptions, see also Hippocrates, *On Airs, Waters, and Places*, 12. Another Byzantine author, also a late one, to employ Hellenocentric climate theory is Theodore Metochites. As Theodore Laskaris does, he links the Hellenes with the sea, although in a discussion on ancient history. See his *Sententious Remarks (Miscellaneous Essays)*, no. 113 in Müller and Kiessling 1821:757–68, esp. 758–79.

59 Chr. Th., VII, 137.5–138.33. The view that climate determined the character of different peoples is seen also in a joke Theodore made in a letter to Andronikos of Sardis. He joked that the bishop, who was in Italy on a diplomatic mission, would not be "transformed by the difference of climate and air" and begin to speak Latin instead of Greek. See Ep. 125.55–57 (p. 176).

60 Chr. Th., VII, 138.34–35.

61 Chr. Th., VII, 139.59–77. The proximity of the Hellenes to the sea is noted already in Aristotle's *Politics*, 1271b34–35.

62 Chr. Th., VII, 138.34–139.58.

63 Chr. Th., VII, 139.78–140.113.

64 Dionysios Periegetes, *Description of the World*, 1146–51. Choniates, *Historia*, 78.8, refers to the great height of the "celebrated Aornis." Spelled differently, Aornos was believed to be one of Alexander's conquests in India. See, for example, Arrian, *Anabasis of Alexander*, 3, 29, 1; 4, 28, 1–8; *Indica*, 5, 10; Strabo, *Geography*, 15, 1, 8. Lake Avernus in Italy was also known in Greek as Aornos or Aornis.

65 Pryor 1988:20–24; Broodbank 2013:75–76, 572.

66 Fenster 1968:30, 102, 133, 141, 146, 189, 198, 205, 212, 287; Magdalino 2005b.

67 Enc. Nic., 68.17–18, 71.76, 75.183–85, 79.272–77, 81.309–17. On the tension between Nicaea and Constantinople in this work, see Delobette 2006. See also Chapter 2, pp. 39–40, 42.

68 *Encomium* on George Akropolites in Tartaglia, Op. rhet., 101.134–38. On Constantinople as the "queen of cities," see Sat., 160.161.

69 See Chapter 8, pp. 167–69.

Epilogue

1 The events are recounted at length, with made-up speeches given by George Mouzalon and Michael Palaiologos, by Pach. I, 63.14–89.26. For other reports with differences in detail and interpretation, see Akrop. I, §75 (pp. 154.20–156.18); *Synopsis chronike*, 536.13–537.27; Greg. I, 63.15–66.11. For a historical reconstruction of the "revolution" of 1258, see Geanakoplos 1953a.

2 Akropolites and *Synopsis chronike* refer to the assassination happening on the third day after the memorial service, while Pachymeres and Gregoras mention the ninth day. See Akrop. I, §75 (p. 154.20–21), *Synopsis chronike*, 536.20–21; Pach. I, 81.5–6; Greg. I, 65.9.

3 I have chosen the version of Pachymeres (Pach. I, 81.5–89.26) rather than that of Akropolites, not only because it is more detailed, but also because the historian was well informed of the tragic event. As Pachymeres writes, a murdered secretary of George Mouzalon by the name of Theophylaktos was his relative and the story must have been told in his family. The account by Akropolites, who was still a captive in Arta, is understandably partisan.

4 Pach. I, 89.17–20.

5 Akrop. I, §75 (p. 156.8–18). *Synopsis chronike* omits this detail. Both imply that the murder happened with the approval of the assembled crowd.

6 On Karoulos' role as an informant during the conspiracy of Phrangopoulos in 1265, see Pach. II, 371.8–15; PLP 30093.

7 In the autumn of 1260, Michael Palaiologos fought a punitive campaign against the Turkmen of the Maeander valley, who already seem to have retaken Chonai and Laodikeia, fortresses conveyed to the empire of Nicaea in 1257 by 'Izz al-Dīn Kaykāwūs II. See Korobeinikov 2014:226–27.

8 Akrop. I, §76 (pp. 158.5–159.4), followed by *Synopsis chronike*, 538.18–28, reports the assembly. For a different account, see Pach. I, 91.18–99.3. In his *Testament* (PG, vol. 140, cols. 949C), Arsenios stressed that he was absent at the time of the election of Palaiologos to the regency; this agrees with Pachymeres, but contradicts Akropolites and *Synopsis chronike*.

9 On the dates and venues of Michael Palaiologos' imperial proclamation and coronation, see Wirth 1961 (based on a short chronicle, the *History* of Pachymeres, and one of Manuel Holobolos' imperial encomia). See also Failler 1980:39–42; 1986:237–42; Macrides 2007:348, n. 1; 348, n. 3; 349, n. 5. On the oath, see Pach. I, 135.6–137.16; Arsenios, *Testament*, in PG, vol. 140, cols. 952A–953A. Arsenios reports (col. 949 CD) that Palaiologos swore oaths also when he was promoted to the regency and was made a despot.

10 On the chronology of Arsenios' withdrawal and the patriarchal election of Nikephoros c. January 1, 1260, in Kallipolis, see Failler 1980:45–53. See the pro-Arsenios account by *Synopsis chronike*, 548.27–549.15.

11 Akrop. I, §77 (pp. 160.16–19, 161.4–6); Pach. I, 153.10–16.

12 Pach. I, 137.19–24; Akrop. I, §82 (pp. 173.1, 173.8–9).

13 He had left the customary mark of the *mesazon* (the *dia*-mark) on an imperial ordinance by Michael Palaiologos issued in July 1259. See MM, IV, 222; Dölger-Wirth, *Regesten*, 1877; Schmalzbauer 1969:122; PLP 29121. The dating of the document to the last years of Vatatzes' reign by Korobeinikov (2014:73, n. 262) is impossible, because the emperor was clearly Michael Palaiologos.

14 Akrop. I, §77 (p. 161.3–4); §82 (p. 173.15–18); Pach. I, 153.19.

15 Akrop. I, §79 (pp. 163.18–165.3); Pach. I, 153.21–155.6.

16 In an effort to exonerate Palaiologos, Akrop. I, §77 (pp. 159.19–160.3), writes that he imprisoned Karyanites because the latter man was responsible for the murder of the Mouzalons. None of this is mentioned by Pach. I, 89.29–91.9. See Macrides 2007:249, n. 7.

17 Pach. I, 155.21–157.1.

18 On the date of the Battle of Pelagonia, see Nicol 1959; Failler 1980:30–39. For the historical context, see Geanakoplos 1953b; Nicol 1957:170–82; Berg 1988:276–89.

19 On the siege of Galata, the privileges to Genoa, and the recapture of the city, see the account by Akrop. I, §83 (pp. 173–75); Pach. I, 171.25–177.10; see also Geanakoplos 1959:75–115. The privileges to Genoa issued in Nymphaion in March 1261 have been edited by Pieralli 2006:130–42. On the chronology of events in 1260, see Failler 1980:46–53.

20 He was captured during two battles against Michael of Epiros: the first one at Trikoryphos in 1260 and the second one in the autumn of 1261, after which he was sent to the court of Manfred but was released by December. See Pach. I, 125.17–127.7, 151.20–21, 249.6–7; Nicol 1957:188–9. On the chronology, see Failler 1980:79–80, 82–83.

21 Akrop. I, §85 (pp. 181–83), followed by other Byzantine sources, speaks of gaining access through an opening in the walls. By contrast, Pach.

I (191.2–203.29) describes the local population of the "volunteers" scaling the wall at night. For a critical comparison, see Geanakoplos 1959:103–09.

22 PLP 7304; Pach. I, 243.15–17, 275.22–277.16 (the marriage did not take place because of suspicions in Constantinople that Makrenos was plotting against Palaiologos, suspicions resulting in Makrenos' blinding); Greg. I, 92.21–93. On the daughters of Theodore Laskaris, see Failler 1980:65–77.

23 PLP 91888; Pach. I, 243.17–20; Greg. I, 93.1–5. On Eudokia's life in the West, see 319, nn. 50–53.

24 Pach. I, 243.20–22. On Despot Jacob Svetoslav who gained prominence after 1261, see Nikov 1920:114–90. See also Chapter 5, p. 93 and 274, n. 33.

25 PLP 14551; Pach. I, 113.20–21, refers to his imprisonment in Prousa in 1259.

26 PLP 14554; Pach. II, 401.18–19, 413.7–11.

27 PLP 14487–14556, 93962.

28 On the three rebels who claimed to be John Laskaris, see (1) Pach. I, 259–67 (rebellion in 1262); (2) Geanakoplos 1959:217; Shawcross 2008:212 (Pseudo-John Laskaris in the West); (3) Pach. IV, 653; Failler 1996 (John Drimys).

29 Pach. IV, 347–49, 439–41 (evidence of the saint's cult in Magnesia in 1303); Heisenberg 1905:232–33 (the miracles wrought by the relics in Magnesia after its fall to the Turks). On the fate of Magnesia in the early fourteenth century and the emperor-saint, see Ahrweiler 1975:46–47; Macrides 1981:69–71.

30 Macrides 1981:71–73; Shawcross 2008:218–23.

31 Blem., *Autobiographia*, II, 82–85 (pp. 82–83). The governor of Thrakesion, Theodotos Kalothetos, was a relative of Michael Palaiologos. See Ahrweiler 1965:146–47; On Blemmydes' ultimately unsuccessful attempts to establish the independence of his monastery, see Failler 1981:205–07; Munitiz 1988:28.

32 Blem., *Autobiographia*, I, 74.19–20 (p. 37), 81–88 (pp. 40–44), esp. I, 88.1–18 (p. 44); II, 77–78 (p. 80).

33 *Synopsis chronike*, 535.5–536.12. On the issue of authorship, see Introduction, p. 10, and 235, n. 56.

34 Ephraim of Ainos in Lampsides 1990:327.9295–328.9308; Greg. I, 53–62. On Gregoras' views, see Angelov 2007:281–82. The fourteenth-century author Theodore Pediasimos described Theodore as a "most pious and wisest man" in his account of the miracles in 1256 of the two saints Theodore, the heavenly patrons of the metropolitan church of Serres. See Treu 1899:21–22; Odorico 2013:138.

35 Angelov 2007:269–80.

36 The description is based on Luke 23.44–45. See Albert Failler's note at Pach. I, 59, n. 2.

37 Pach. I, 57.32–61.22, esp. 61.10–11 and 61.19–22. Pachymeres, followed by Gregoras, errs in stating that Theodore did not hold the imperial title during his father's reign. See Chapter 3, p. 61 and 258, n. 38.

38 Pach. I, 53.26–27.

39 Pach. I, 53.14–21. See the discussion in Appendix 3, 381–83.

40 The *History* of Akropolites was edited with a Latin translation by Leo Allatius in Paris in 1651. The *History* of Pachymeres appeared in Rome one decade later, between 1666 and 1669, in an edition and Latin translation by Pierre Poussines.

41 Gibbon 1788 VI:224–25.

42 Dräseke 1894:514.

43 Miller 1923:501.

44 Appendix 1, 324–27.

45 On the texts preserved in **V** and the manuscript itself, see Agapitos and Angelov 2018; Appendix 1, 326–27.

46 Appendix 2, 349–50.

47 Vogel and Gardthausen 1909:318–20.

48 Giannouli 2001:270–71. See 327, n. 12.

49 See 321, n. 1.

50 On the peripatetic life of Eudokia, see Miret y Sans 1906; Pano 1958; Origone 1988.

51 See the letter by Michael Palaiologos to Genoa in Belgrano 1885:227–29.

52 Miret y Sans 1906; Diehl 1908:223–24; Marinesco 1924:454–55.

53 On the foundation of the convent, see Palau y Dulcet 1931:114–15, 118.

54 MacLagan 1975.

55 For example, the thirteenth-century historian Ibn Nazif calls John III Vatatzes al-Ashkari, while the biographer of the Mamluk Sultan Baybars (1260–77) uses the name with reference to the emperor Michael VIII Palaiologos. See Cahen 1971:147–48; Sadeque 1956:112, n. 6. The same usage persisted in the fourteenth century, for example, in the works of Ibn Khaldun.

Appendix 1 | The Chronology of the Works of Theodore Laskaris

The rich and diverse writings of Theodore Laskaris are the principal source for reconstructing his life and thought. The historical detective work involved in this reconstruction could not be carried out without establishing, wherever possible, a chronology of composition of his works. The first two appendices discuss chronological issues and serve as an essential guide to the narrative presentation and analysis in the chapters. Appendix 1 lays out the methods for assigning dates to individual works – apart from his letters, which are treated in Appendix 2. The discussion proceeds in four steps: (1) creating a list of the surviving works of the author; (2) surveying the authorized collections prepared under the author's auspices; (3) establishing the termini of composition of works included in the authorized collections vis-à-vis key events mentioned as chronological markers in manuscript headings (*lemmata*) in the collections – that is, *before* the embassy of Berthold of Hohenburg and *before* or *after* his accession as sole emperor; (4) investigating more specific timeframes for individual works.

The Surviving Writings

Letters

1 Festa, *Epistulae* (c. 217 letters).
2 Tartaglia, Op. rhet. (no. 1), 1–22 (long letter to George Akropolites).

Orations

3 *Encomium on His Father, the Most Exalted Emperor Lord John Doukas* (= *Encomium* on John Vatatzes): Tartaglia, Op. rhet. (no. 2), 24–66; previous edition: Tartaglia 1990.
4 *Encomium on the Great City of Nicaea*: Tartaglia, Op. rhet. (no. 3), 68–84; previous edition: Bachmann 1847.
5 *Encomium on the Great Philosopher Lord George Akropolites*: Tartaglia, Op. rhet. (no. 5), 96–108; previous edition: Markopoulos 1968.
6 *Encomium on the Spring and the Charming Man*: Tartaglia, Op. rhet. (no. 8), 142–52.

7 *On Virtue: A Speech of Gratitude to God While He was Troubled with Some Problems, Which Dispels a Few Suspicions and Condemns Evil*: Paléologou 2007:69–81.
8 *Encomium on Wisdom*: Paléologou 2007:82–88.
9 *Oration on Fasting*, in **A**, ff. 66r –77r; **P**, ff. 95v–111r.

Satire

10 *A Satire of His Tutor, a Most Evil and Worst Man*: Tartaglia, Op. rhet. (no. 9), 154–97; previous edition: Tartaglia 1992.

Polemical Works

11 *Response to Some People Who Trouble Him Malevolently, Demonstrating to Them That What God Has Established is Stable and Indissoluble and That One Should Honor Those Honored by God*: Festa, *Epistulae*, 283–89.
12 *To a Secretive Man Who Was Deceiving Him*: Tartaglia, Op. rhet. (no. 10), 199–202.
13 *Response to Some Friends Pressing Him to Find a Bride*: Tartaglia, Op. rhet. (no. 6), 110–18; previous edition: Tartaglia 1991.

Politics

14 *To George Mouzalon Who Asked How Should Subjects Conduct Themselves vis-à-vis Their Lords and Lords vis-à-vis Their Subjects* (= *Response to George Mouzalon*; treatise on friendship and politics): Tartaglia, Op. rhet. (no. 7), 120–40; previous edition: Tartaglia 1980–81.
15 *Memorial Discourse in Honor of the Emperor of the Germans, Lord Frederick*: Tartaglia, Op. rhet. (no. 5), 86–94; previous editions: Pappadopoulos 1908:183–89; Dragoumis 1911–12:404–13.

Philosophy

16 *Natural Communion* (Φυσικὴ κοινωνία), in J. P. Migne, PG, vol. 140, cols. 1259–1396 (includes the Latin translation by Claude Aubery published in 1571).[1]

---

[1] The heading *Natural Communion* (Φυσικὴ Κοινωνία) is found in the main thirteenth-century manuscript prepared in the author's lifetime: BnF, Cod. Parisinus Suppl. gr. 460. The heading differs in other manuscripts. In volume 140 of *Patrologia Graeca* (1865), Jacques Paul Migne

17 *Explanation of the World* (Κοσμικὴ Δήλωσις): Festa 1897–98:97–114 (book 1); 1899: 1–52 (books 2, 3, and 4).

18 *Moral Pieces Describing the Inconstancy of Life:* Angelov 2011–12; previous edition: Tartaglia 2008. The twelve essays can be regarded generically also as a theophilosophical work.

Hagiography and Orations to Holy Figures and Saints

19 *Oration of Gratitude to Our Lord Jesus Christ Composed upon Recovery from a Terrible Illness:* **A**, ff. 13r–25r; **P**, ff. 24r–42r.

20 *Encomium on St. Euthymios:* **A**, ff. 25r– 35r; **P**, ff. 42r–55v.

21 *Encomium on the Holy Anargyroi* (SS. Cosmas and Damian): **A**, ff. 35v–43v; **P**, ff. 55v–66v.

22 *Encomium on the Great Martyr of Christ Tryphon: Acta Sanctorum Novembris IV,* ed. H. Delehaye (Brussels, 1925), cols. 352–57.

23 *Oration on the Virgin to be Read in the Celebration of the Akathistos,* Critical edition in Giannouli 2001; earlier editions: Σωτήρ, 16 (1894), 186–92; T.P. Themelis, Νέα Σιών, 6 (1907), 826–33.

24 *Oration on the Annunciation of Our Holiest Lady, the Mother of God, That Is, Concerning the Incarnation of Our Lord Jesus Christ (Christian Theology,* VIII): Krikonis 1988:149–55.

Hymnography

25 *Supplicatory Canon* to the Virgin (παρακλητικὸς κανὼν εἰς τὴν ὑπεραγίαν Θεοτόκον) (= *Great Supplicatory Canon* or μέγας παρακλητικὸς κανών) J. P. Migne, PG, vol. 140, cols. 771–80; published also in Ὡρολόγιον τὸ Μέγα, ed. M. I. Saliveros (Athens, 1922), 516–25.

26 Canon to the Virgin: S. Eustratiades, *Theotokarion,* I (1931), 39–42.

27 Canon to the Virgin: Nikodemos Hagiorites and G. Mousaios, Στέφανος τῆς Ἀειπαρθένου, ἤτοι Θεοτοκάριον (Constantinople, 1849), 93–96.

28 *Various Invocatory Hymns* (ὕμνοι διάφοροι προσφωνητήριοι), **V**, ff. 103r–107r. The seventeen hymns (in reality, works of personal devotion) are dedicated to the Holy Trinity, Jesus Christ, the Holy Cross, the Mother of God, the Archangels, St. John the Baptist, St. Peter, St. Paul, St. John the Evangelist, St. George, St. Theodore Stratelates, St.

transcribed the text from the fourteenth-century Cod. Parisinus gr. 2004, rendering the title as Τῆς Φυσικῆς Κοινωνίας Λόγοι Ἕξ and reprinting the Latin translation published in Basel in 1572 by Claude Aubery.

Theodore Tyron, St. Demetrios, St. Prokopios, St. Tryphon, the Forty Martyrs, and St. Nicholas.[2]

Theological and Theophilosophical Works

29 *On Being* (*Christian Theology*, I): Krikonis 1988:85–87.
30 *Being is One* (*Christian Theology*, II): Krikonis 1988:89–94.
31 *The One is Three* (*Christian Theology*, III): Krikonis 1988:95–98.
32 *On the Divine Names* (*Christian Theology*, IV): Krikonis 1988: 99–108; previous edition by A. Mai, *Bibliotheca Nova Patrum*, 6, part 2 (Rome, 1853), 259–63; hence reprinted in J. P. Migne, PG, vol. 140, cols. 763–70.
33 *On the Trinity* (*Christian Theology*, V): Krikonis 1988:109–23.
34 *First Oration against the Latins, or, on the Procession of the Holy Spirit* (*Christian Theology*, VI): Krikonis 1988:124–36.
35 *Second Oration against the Latins, or, on the Procession of the Holy Spirit* (*Christian Theology*, VII): Krikonis 1988:137–48.
36 *Response to the Bishop of Croton against the Latins and on the Holy Spirit*: Swete 1875 (reprinted in Krikonis 1988:161–82).

Other

37 Newsletter: Festa, *Epistulae*, 279–82; published also by Balaschev 1911 with a Bulgarian translation.
38 Six Essays: Agapitos and Angelov 2018 (based on **V**, ff. 65v–68r).

Anepigrapha

39 Three Essays (transmitted anonymously in BnF, Parisinus Suppl. gr. 1202, f. 9v): Paramelle 1979:320–25; new edition and attribution to Theodore Laskaris by Mineva (2018).

Collections Produced in the Lifetime of Theodore Laskaris

Authorized collections of Theodore Laskaris' writings were produced under the auspices of the author. These collections are of considerable

---

[2] An edition by Antonia Giannouli is under preparation.

interest, even though they have only recently begun to receive due attention, for they demonstrate how this author and ruler wished his works to
be disseminated among his contemporaries and future generations.[3] In
each collection, his works were arranged in a specific order and were
supplied with manuscript headings (*lemmata*) that feature authorial and
chronological formulas. In two cases – the collections *Sacred Orations* and
Christian Theology – the works were numbered consecutively as λόγος α′,
β′, γ′, etc. Four collections (I–IV) have come down to us in their entirety
in manuscript copies reflecting, in varying degrees, the original editions
prepared during Theodore's lifetime. The existence of another such collection (V) can be ascertained, a collection which, unfortunately, has not
survived in full; it was broken up and was copied in different codices. Not
all of Theodore's works seem to have been incorporated into collections, or
at least into these five collections: the hymns to the Virgin and the *Response
to Nicholas of Croton* have a manuscript transmission that is unrelated to
any collection. The five collections are as follows.

I. The main epistolary collection edited by Theodore's tutor George
Akropolites survives in a single fourteenth-century manuscript in the
Laurentian Library in Florence: Laur. Plut. 59, 35. It has been designated
"the Laurentian epistolary collection." The letters (most of **1**) were grouped
in it by addressee. The headings of batches of letters to each recipient
specify, with a few exceptions, a date "before the embassy of the marquis
Berthold of Hohenburg" (autumn 1253).[4] Appendix 2 below proposes
early 1254 as the date this collection was produced. The versified preface
by Akropolites remarks in the present tense that the author also "publishes" (ἐκφέρει) other "discourses" (λόγοι), some of which deal with nature,
while others have a superior premise, and yet others are encomia.[5] The
poem probably envisages the treatise *Natural Communion* (**16**) and certainly the *Sacred Orations*. The latter collection has a marked religious
spirit, contains encomia of saints (**20, 21**), and was likewise produced after
the departure of the embassy of Berthold of Hohenburg.

---

[3] In 1903 August Heisenberg argued that two thirteenth-century manuscripts containing different
selections of Theodore Laskaris' writings – Ambros. gr. 917 (C. 308 inf.) (=**A**) and BnF,
Suppl. gr. 472 – represented a two-volume edition. See Akrop. II, XVII, n. 2. This theory was
rejected on solid grounds by Charles Astruc (1965:400–01), who pointed to paleographical and
codicological differences. Recently, there has been a renewed interest in the collections in the
context of critical editions of Theodore's works. See the editorial remarks by Paléologou 2007;
Angelov 2011–12; Agapitos and Angelov 2018.

[4] On the date of the embassy, see Chapter 7, p. 141 and 293, n. 70.   [5] Akrop. II, 8.29–35.

II. The collection entitled *Sacred Orations* (Λόγοι ἱεροί) contains nine numbered works. They are arranged in the following sequence: **33, 19, 20, 21, 7, 8, 9, 18, 11**. The collection survives in two manuscripts: **A** (Ambros. gr. 917 [C. 308 inf.]), a thirteenth-century parchment codex that is arguably based on a lost deluxe manuscript, and **P** (BnF, Cod. gr. 1193), a fourteenth-century paper codex.[6] The heading before each work specifies a date of composition before the embassy of the marquis Berthold of Hohenburg and identifies the author as "the son of the most exalted emperor of the Romans Lord John Doukas." As with the epistolary collection, the heading should be interpreted as an indication of the time of production of the authorized edition in early 1254.

III. The third collection contains ten important secular works of Theodore Laskaris. They are arranged in the following sequence: **2, 3, 4, 15, 5, 13, 14, 6, 10, 12**. It survives in four manuscripts:[7] (1) the thirteenth-century BnF, Parisinus Suppl. gr. 472 copied in the same Nicaean scriptorium in which BnF, Parisinus Suppl. gr. 460 (the deluxe codex of *Natural Communion*) (**16**) was produced;[8] (2) the fifteenth-century codex BnF, Parisinus gr. 3048 copied in 1486 by Michael Souliardos; (3–4) two sixteenth-century codices: BnF, Parisinus Suppl. gr. 37 and Scor. gr. 432 (Y-I-4). The heading of all ten works identifies the author as "Theodore Doukas Laskaris, the son of the most exalted emperor of the Romans Lord John Doukas." This heading demonstrates that the work was produced before November 1254, that is, during Theodore's coemperorship. For one thing, Theodore is called the son of "most exalted emperor," a designation already found in *Sacred Orations*. Conspicuously missing is the term ἐντελέχεια τῆς βασιλείας, which Theodore preferred to use in headings of works in the next two collections put together during his reign. The collection must have been produced in the summer or autumn of 1254, because it includes the encomium on George Akropolites (**5**), which dates to the spring of 1254 (see below).

IV. A collection named *Christian Theology* contains eight numbered religious works (**29, 30, 31, 32, 33, 34, 35, 24**). It has been preserved in its entirety in the thirteenth-century Cod. Vat. gr. 1113, the fifteenth-century Cod. Barocci 97, and the seventeenth-century Vat. gr. 1942 (an apograph

---

[6] On the content of the two manuscripts and codicological description, see Paléologou 2007:60–63; Angelov 2011–12:246–50. On the lost exemplar of **A**, see Angelov 2011–12:251–52.

[7] The codices transmitting the ten secular works of Laskaris have been described by Astruc 1965; Georgiopoulou 1990:68–85.

[8] Rashed 2000:298–300.

of Vat. gr. 1113).[9] The first three works and the fifth are Trinitarian treatises. The fourth is the treatise *On the Divine Names*, which consists of a long list of appellations of God and is written in the mystical tradition of Pseudo-Dionysios the Areopagite. The sixth and seventh works are orations against the Latins; they bear the manuscript title *First* and *Second Oration against the Latins, or, on the Procession of the Holy Spirit*. The eighth work is an oration on the Annunciation of the Virgin. All but one of the eight books of the collection *Christian Theology* contain in their heading the phrase "after the full completeness of imperial rule" (μετὰ τὴν ἐντελέχειαν τῆς βασιλείας). The sole exception is the fifth discourse (**33**), a Trinitarian treatise filled with sacred numerology that had previously been the opening work of the collection *Sacred Orations,* where its heading had featured the chronological marker "before the embassy of Berthold of Hohenburg."[10] Now that the work was included into another collection, it was given the heading "before the full completeness of imperial rule" (πρὸ τῆς ἐντελεχείας τῆς βασιλείας). The production of *Christian Theology* dates late in the reign of Theodore Laskaris, for the *First* and the *Second Oration against the Latins* (**35** and **36**) were prompted, as we will see below, by an event that took place in the autumn of 1256.

V. Another authorized collection, which has not come down to us in a single manuscript, was prepared during the last year of the author's life (see below regarding the date of the last of the six essays featured in the collection). The existence of the collection can be gleaned from codicological and textual peculiarities of two thirteenth-century codices: Cod. Vindob. phil. gr. 321 (=**V**) and Cod. Laur., Conventi soppressi 627.[11] The headings of the works in the collection feature a chronological formula oriented toward "the completeness of imperial rule" (ἐντελέχεια τῆς βασιλείας) – the same formula as that in the collection *Christian Theology*. Works addressed to George Mouzalon found in the collection, both letters and the treatise *Explanation of the World* (these works have survived solely in Laur., Conventi soppressi 627 and **V**), designate in their headings the addressee as the emperor's "brother" and a holder of the titles

[9] Krikones 1988:41–44.
[10] The heading of the work in the collection *Sacred Orations* adds one further detail that is found in the *pinakes* of **A** and **P,** but which was dropped when the text was included in the collection *Christian Theology*: "Oration *On the Trinity* addressed to the literati Constantine the *koubouklarios* and John Phaix who both made the request" (Λόγος [om. **P**] περὶ Τριάδος πρὸς τοὺς λογίους τόν τε Κωνσταντῖνον τὸν κουβουκλάριον καὶ Ἰωάννην τὸν Φαῖκα αἰτησαμένους τὸ αἴτημα). The *pinax* of **A** has been published by Paléologou 2007:61.
[11] This argument is laid out in detail by Agapitos and Angelov 2018.

protosebastos, protovestiarios, and *megas stratopedarches* granted to him on Christmas Day 1255. The collection contained miscellaneous works that survive only in **V**, such as letters and essays, a philosophical treatise (namely, *Explanation of the World*), and devotional texts (**1, 17, 28, 37,** and **38**). The encomium on St. Tryphon (**22**) was quite possibly included in the collection.[12] In addition, the collection arguably contained sixty-five letters addressed to George Mouzalon (surviving in Laur., Conventi soppressi 627 and **V**), most of which date to the period before the emperor's accession in November 1254 and are conspicuously missing from the Laurentian epistolary collection.[13]

The philosophical treatise *Natural Communion*, in six books, which was not included in any collection, in contrast to *Explanation of the World*, was an integral part of the same editorial project. A deluxe parchment manuscript of *Natural Communion*, BnF, Parisinus Suppl. gr. 460, was produced during Theodore's lifetime in a Nicaean scriptorium.[14] It features headings, initials, and geometrical drawings executed in gold. Letters and numbers are written in red ink. The *Natural Communion* was much copied in later centuries. Eleven manuscripts are known, including two codices that were destroyed during the fire at the Escorial Library in Madrid in 1671, which makes it the most widely circulated text among Theodore's secular works.[15] The *Supplicatory Canon* to the Virgin (**25**) was his most copied religious work. A study of the manuscript transmission of both works is a desideratum.

---

[12] The encomium was copied on a separate quire (321r–327[a]v) appended to the end of the eleventh-century Vaticanus gr. 516, which contains homilies by John Chrysostom. The scribe crudely reproduced an ornamental headpiece and copied the formula πρὸ τῆς τῆς βασιλείας ἐντελεχείας in the heading. The heading on f. 321r is followed by the formula εὐλόγησον δέσποτα, signaling to the priest the beginning of a reading. This standard formula resembles the heading of another religious oration by Theodore Laskaris in a fourteenth-century liturgical manuscript: his oration on the feast of the Akathistos in Codex Atheniensis 331, f. 101v. See Giannouli 2001:271, 272 and *apparatus criticus.*

[13] In his edition, Festa published these letters consecutively from Cod. Laur., Conventi soppressi 627, and from **V**: sixty-one letters from the former manuscript (Epp. 150–210) and four letters from **V** (Epp. 211–214).

[14] Discussed by Rashed 2000.

[15] (1) BnF, Parisinus Suppl. gr. 460 (13th c.); (2) Vaticanus gr. 1938 (13th c.). The scribe who copied this manuscript also copied the thirteenth-century manuscript of the collection of ten secular works: BnF, Suppl. gr. 472. I owe this information to an oral communication from Christian Förstel, who is planning a critical edition of the *Natural Communion*; (3) BnF, Parisinus gr. 2004 (14th c.); (4) Cod. Laur. Plut. 55, 11 (15th c.); (5) Cod. Laur. Plut. 58, 02 (15th c.); (6) Cod. Iviron 837 (Athos 4957) (15th c.); (7) Cod. Iviron 388 (Athos 4508) (16th c.); (8) Cod. Ambros. D 85 inf. (924) copied in 1566; (9) Cod. Basiliensis F IX 17 (16th c.) copied by Andreas Darmarios. The two lost manuscripts are (10) Cod. Escorial B.V.19; (11) Cod. Escorial Γ.IV.18. See De Andrés 1968:133, 205.

Chronology vis-à-vis Key Events Mentioned in the Manuscript Headings

There are three main types of manuscript headings (*lemmata*) with which Theodore's works have been transmitted: (1) Some headings identify the author as "Theodore Doukas Laskaris, the son of the most exalted emperor of the Romans Lord John Doukas" – the heading demonstrating that the works date to the lifetime of his father and before his accession as sole emperor in November 1254. (2) Another kind of heading mentions the period before "the embassy of Berthold of Hohenburg" in the autumn of 1253. (3) The third type of heading contains the formula "full completeness of imperial rule" (ἐντελέχεια τῆς βασιλείας). The Aristotelian terms ἐντελέχεια and ἐντελεχής are characteristic of Theodore's vocabulary. An essay composed during the period of his sole rule shows that he interpreted his accession in November 1254 through this philosophical language.[16] Usually, the formula in the heading runs as follows: "after the full completeness of imperial rule" (μετὰ τὴν τῆς βασιλείας ἐντελέχειαν). But in a few rare cases this type of headings refers to composition "before the full completeness of imperial rule" (πρὸ τῆς τῆς βασιλείας ἐντελεχείας). Each of the three kinds of headings (1), (2), and (3) is characteristic of a specific collection (authorized edition) and provides a valuable clue as to the period of composition of the copied works. By contrast, works that circulated independently from the collections, primarily hymns and other religious works, do not seem to follow the above pattern. Their manuscript headings refer to the author as the *autokrator* or *basileus* Theodore (Doukas) Laskaris, sometimes adding his monastic habit and designating him as *aoidimos* (meaning "celebrated" or "ever-remembered," a word used in reference to a deceased person).[17] These headings appear to have been added by scribes

---

[16] Essay 1 in **V**, ff. 65v–66r (edition, translation, and analysis in Agapitos and Angelov 2018).

[17] Thus, the heading of his oration for the Feast of the Akathistos (**23**) refers in one of the manuscripts (the fourteenth-century Cod. Athen. 331) to the "*autokrator* Theodore Doukas Laskaris"; however, another fourteenth-century manuscript (Ms. Barocci 197) misattributes the work to Andrew of Crete. See Giannouli 2002:253 (discussion of authorship) and 272 (apparatus with the manuscript headings). The reference to the author in the *Response* to Nicholas of Croton (**36**) varies in the manuscripts: "the monk and *basileus* Theodore Laskaris," "the *aoidimos* monk and *basileus* Theodore Laskaris" or simply "the *basileus* Theodore Laskaris." See Chr. Th. (reprint from Swete 1875), 161 (apparatus). The heading of the *Supplicatory Canon* to the Virgin (**25**) refers to "the *basileus* Theodore Doukas Laskaris." See PG, vol. 140, cols. 771–72; Saliveros 1922:516. No critical edition of the hymns exists. A similar designation of the author is found in the titles of two other hymns: "the *basileus* Theodore Laskaris" in the canon (**27**) published by Hagiorites and Mousaios (1849:95) and the "most pious *basileus* Theodore Laskaris" in the canon (**26**) published by Eustratiades (1931:39).

who copied the texts in liturgical manuscripts or other miscellanies, and therefore do not necessarily have chronological implications in contrast to the *lemmata* of the authorized collections. Therefore, the works bearing these headings are omitted from the list below.

COMPOSED BEFORE THE EMBASSY OF BERTHOLD OF HOHEN-BURG (AUTUMN 1253)

*The formula πρὸ τῆς πρεσβείας features in the manuscript headings

1 Most letters in the Laurentian epistolary collection (see Appendix 2)

The nine numbered *Sacred Orations* arranged as follows:

33 *On the Trinity* (as per the heading in the *Sacred Orations,* which specifies that the work is addressed to the *koubouklarios* Constantine and John Phaix)

19 *An Oration of Gratitude to Our Lord Jesus Christ*

20 *Encomium on St. Euthymios*

21 *Encomium on the Holy Anargyroi*

7 *On Virtue*

8 *Encomium on Wisdom*

9 *Oration on Fasting*

18 *Moral Pieces*

11 *Response to Some People Who Trouble Him Malevolently*

COMPOSED BEFORE THEODORE'S ACCESSION (NOVEMBER 1254)

*The author is titled in the headings as "the son of the most exalted emperor of the Romans Lord John Doukas"

16 *Natural Communion*

17 *Explanation of the World.* The heading of the general preface identifies the author as "the son of the most exalted emperor Lord John Doukas" and dates it to "before the full completeness of imperial rule" (πρὸ τῆς ἐντελεχείας τῆς βασιλείας). In fact, only the first and the second part, *On the Elements* and *On Heaven,* are datable to the period before November 1254: see below the chronological discussion of *Explanation of the World.*

Collection of ten secular works in the following order:

2 Long letter to George Akropolites

3 *Encomium* on John Vatatzes

4 *Encomium on Nicaea*

15 *Memorial Discourse* for Frederick II Hohenstaufen

 5 *Encomium* on George Akropolites
13 *Response to Some Friends Pressing Him to Find a Bride*
14 Treatise on friendship and politics
 6 *Encomium on the Spring and the Charming Man*
10 *A Satire of His Tutor, a Most Evil and Worst Man*
12 *To a Secretive Man Who Was Deceiving Him*

*The formula "before the full completeness of imperial rule" (πρὸ τῆς τῆς βασιλείας ἐντελεχείας) is featured in the manuscript headings of the following works:

33 *On the Trinity* (as per the new heading of the work in *Christian Theology*)
22 *Encomium* on St. Tryphon
 1 Forty-three (Epp. 150–92) of the sixty-one letters to George Mouzalon surviving in Laur., Conventi soppressi 627. A note on f. 5v between Epp. 192 and 193 states: αἱ τοιαῦται ἐπιστολαὶ πρὸ τῆς τῆς βασιλείας ἐντελεχείας· αὗται αἱ ἐπιστολαὶ μετὰ τὴν τῆς βασιλείας ἐντελέχειαν, μεθ᾽ ἣν καὶ τὴν αὐταδελφότητα τούτῳ ἀπεχαρίσατο.[18]

COMPOSED AFTER THEODORE'S ACCESSION (NOVEMBER 1254)
*The formula "after the full completeness of imperial rule" (μετὰ τὴν τῆς βασιλείας ἐντελέχειαν) is featured in the manuscript headings.

 1 All fourteen letters from **V** published by Festa. The sequence in **V** is as follows: Epp. 141, 131, 142, 144, 146, 143, 147, 145, 148, 149, 211, 212, 213 and 214.[19] Eighteen (Epp. 193–210) of the sixty-one letters to George Mouzalon surviving in Laur., Conventi soppressi 627.
28 *Various Invocatory Hymns*
38 Six Essays

The collection *Christian Theology*, except for the fifth book (**33**):
29 *On Being* (*Christian Theology*, I)
30 *Being is One* (*Christian Theology*, II)
31 *The One is Three* (*Christian Theology*, III)
32 *On the Divine Names* (*Christian Theology*, IV)
34 *First Oration against the Latins, or, on the Procession of the Holy Spirit* (*Christian Theology*, VI)

---

[18] The note has been indicated by Festa in the apparatus to his edition of Theodore's letters (p. 239).
[19] No heading is preserved before the two letters to Philip (Epp. 148, 149), which can be explained with the lacuna in **V** before the fragmentary Ep. 148.

35 *Second Oration against the Latins, or, on the Procession of the Holy
   Spirit* (*Christian Theology*, VII)
24 *Oration on the Annunciation* (*Christian Theology*, VIII)

The Chronology of Individual Works

The chronology of individual works can be based only on internal
evidence, that is to say, references and allusions to historical events that
can themselves be dated on the basis of other sources, such as Byzantine
and Latin historical narratives as well as documents. The discussion
below of the complex chronology of the four books of the treatise
Explanation of the World serves to remind us that the assignment of
dates is based, by necessity rather than preference, on the texts that have
come down to us after their publication in the collections. No traces
are left of earlier textual versions, redactions, or drafts made for oral
recitation.

10   *Satire of the Tutor* (in or after Autumn 1240)

The *Satire* was composed shortly after the death of Theodore's head tutor
(*baioulos*): it opens with the exclamation that "evil has departed from
amidst the good things" (ἀπέστη μέσον τῶν καλῶν ἡ κακία). According
to the text, the head tutor passed away following the marriage of the
emperor John Vatatzes and his second wife Constanza-Anna celebrated
in Nicaea. After the wedding festivities, the elderly man lingered on in
Nicaea and fell ill. He visited Theodore in "Mysia" for a week and moved to
the Thrakesion theme, where he passed away.[20] When did the wedding of
John Vatatzes and Constanza-Anna take place? The question can be
answered on the basis of the testimony of the Venetian chronicler Andrea
Dandolo when it is compared with information gleaned from the *Satire*
itself. Dandolo reports the marriage without assigning a date and places his
report *before* the Nicaean assault on Constantinople in the months of May
or June 1241.[21] May–June 1241 is, thus, a *terminus ante quem* for the

---

[20] Sat., 191.908–194.980.
[21] Andrea Dandolo in Pastorello 1938:298. Casting doubt on the chronology of Dandolo, John
   Langdon (1985:114–15, 130–31, n. 44) dated the attack on Constantinople to 1242, but the
   interpretation rests on questionable assumptions.

wedding. In a seminal article (1999) Andreas Kiesewetter used the testimony of the Venetian chronicler in order to refute two older interpretations.[22] The first and dominant one – based on the chronicle of Matthew
Paris (the Benedictine monk at St. Albans Abbey, Hertfordshire) – held
that the wedding took place in 1244. However, the date in the chronicle of
Matthew Paris is a *terminus ante quem*.[23] Another hypothesis proposed by
Stelian Brezeanu – based on the mention of the emperor John Vatatzes and
his Italian bride in a private document from the chartulary of the Lembos
monastery (a document dated by its nineteenth-century editors to March 1,
1242) – held that the wedding took place in late 1241 or early 1242. Once
again, however, we are confronted with a *terminus ante quem*.[24] Kiesewetter
countersuggested that the marriage of John Vatatzes must have taken place
at the end of 1240 or the beginning of 1241, for it preceded the earliest
terminus ante quem: the Nicaean assault on Constantinople.

The *Satire* provides a clue that allows us to refine the dating suggested by
Kiesewetter. After the wedding, John Vatatzes is said to have left Nicaea at
the head of the army and in the company of his son, while the tutor
remained in Nicaea. At that time the Dog Star was "wandering" in the
sky.[25] The reference to the Dog Star, which rises during the hottest days of
the summer (the "dog days of summer"), enables us to identify the season.
The Byzantine agricultural treatise *Geoponika*, assembled in the tenth century, gives the heliacal rising of the Dog Star between July 19 and 24, and its
setting on November 22.[26] The wedding, thus, could not have taken place in
the spring of 1241 just before the Nicaean assault on Constantinople. Notably,
the *Satire* is conspicuously silent about any military operation against
Constantinople, but speaks of the movement of the army toward Prousa
and Theodore's residence in "Mysia," followed by a trip to the Thrakesion
theme in order to see his terminally ill tutor.[27] The mention of the Dog Star
in the *Satire* is accompanied by a reference to the zodiac constellation
Virgo. If this chronological indicator is also taken into consideration, the

---

[22] Kiesewetter 1999: 240–41 (dating of the Nicaean assault on Constantinople), 243–45 (suggested
a date for the wedding).

[23] For the traditional interpretation, see, for example, Dölger-Wirth, *Regesten*, 1779 (c. 1244).

[24] Brezeanu 1974. For the document, see MM, IV, 66: ἐπὶ τῆς βασιλείας τῶν εὐσεβαστάτων καὶ ἐκ
θεοῦ ἐστεμμένων κοσμποθήτων αὐθεντῶν καὶ βασιλέων ἡμῶν, κυροῦ Ἰωάννου τοῦ Δούκα καὶ
Ἄννης. As Kiesewetter (1999:243, n. 13) has pointed out, there is a mismatch between the first
indiction, which falls between September 1, 1242, and August 31, 1243, and the reported year
6750 since the Creation (September 1, 1241–August 31, 1242).

[25] Sat., 192.917–20.

[26] *Geoponica* I, 8.1, 9.7, 9.11; II, 15.2 in Beckh 1895:15.15–16, 18.12–23, 55.10–11.

[27] Sat., 192.917–18, 192.930–31, 193.949–52.

wedding must have been celebrated in late August or September 1240, a little less than one year after the likely time of the passing of John Vatatzes' first wife Irene in December 1239.[28] The head tutor also passed away in the late summer of 1240. Theodore composed the *Satire* not long afterward. The presence of many *hapax legomena* in this work confirms the impression of youthful experimentation, in which the author voices his commitment to continue his philosophical studies with Blemmydes, now that one of the chief impediments, the hated head tutor, was dead.

4 *Encomium on Nicaea* (1246–50)

Theodore Laskaris addresses the citizens of Nicaea at the beginning of the oration and creates the impression that he wrote the work in the presence of his father John Vatatzes. Close to the end, he remarks that "just now" (ἄρτι) his father has offered the city the "brood of vipers of the western powers" (γεννήματα ἐχιδνῶν τῶν δυτικῶν ἀρχῶν), who have escaped the emperor's wrath and justice.[29] Elsewhere in his writings Theodore designates the Balkan Peninsula – the space beyond the Hellespont – as the "west" and as "western."[30] The encomium, thus, was written euphorically on the return of John Vatatzes from a victorious campaign in the Balkans, when he apparently brought prisoners to the city. John Vatatzes is praised for conquering large territories and bringing the empire "somewhat close" to its ancient greatness. Unfortunately, it is impossible to pinpoint which campaign and enemy Theodore had in mind. The campaign of 1246 is the most likely one, for it led to a massive expansion of the empire of Nicaea in Macedonia and the Rhodope Mountains. In December 1246, John Vatatzes brought to Asia Minor the last independent ruler of the kingdom of Thessalonica, Despot Demetrios Komnenos Doukas, who was imprisoned in the fortress of Lentiana.[31] However, there is no reason to exclude the possibility of later Balkan campaigns. Following his return in 1246, John Vatatzes wintered in Nymphaion and in the spring of 1247 crossed the Hellespont to campaign in eastern Thrace.[32] A manuscript note of August 1247 describes how John Vatatzes "went to the west," reached the walls of Constantinople, captured Tzouroulos, and sent the captives to Nicaea.[33]

---

[28] Macrides 2007:213–14, n 12.   [29] Enc. Nic., 82.342–47.
[30] Enc. John, 28.107–08; Ep. 93.17–20 (p. 124), which informs Patriarch Manuel II of the imminent arrival of the victorious emperor to Nicaea and uses imagery found also in the encomium on Nicaea. See Ep. 199.43–44 (p. 246).
[31] Akrop. I, §46 (p. 84.9–12).   [32] Akrop. I, §46–47 (pp. 83–85).   [33] Polemis 1966:270–71.

These prisoners could have been the "brood of vipers of the western powers." In 1248 John Vatatzes was campaigning again against the Latins of Constantinople, this time in the region of Nikomedeia in the vicinity of Nicaea.[34] In 1248, 1249 or 1250 he was in the region of Pegai, where he struck an agreement with Michael II of Epiros.[35] John Vatatzes campaigned against Michael II Komnenos Doukas of Epiros in 1252 and 1253, but it is highly unlikely that this was the occasion for the encomium. As we learn from Epp. 83–85 to Akropolites, John Vatatzes visited Nicaea on his return in the late autumn of 1253, while Theodore was in the Thrakesion theme at the time. The senior emperor then departed for his winter residence and Theodore met him along the Nicaea-Nymphaion road. Theodore seems to have shared the encomium on Nicaea with Akropolites. The long and playful Ep. 51, addressed to him, accompanies a newly composed work, which the author describes enigmatically as δῶρον λογικόν. At the end of the letter, Theodore refers to Akropolites as being away from "the city of Nicaea which is celebrated by me" (ἐπειδὴ τῆς ὑμνουμένης ἐξ ἡμῶν Νικαέων ἀπέστη πόλεως).[36] Notably, Ep. 51 is one of the first letters to Akropolites according to its placement in the Laurentian epistolary collection, a circumstance that strengthens the argument for a date of composition in the 1240s.

15   *Memorial Discourse* for Frederick II Hohenstaufen (Early 1251)

The emperor Frederick II passed away on December 13, 1250, in Castel Fiorentino, Apulia. The news would have reached Theodore Laskaris around the beginning of the following year, 1251. The Nicaean prince seems to have written the text with the event still fresh in his mind. The oration includes his idiosyncratic musings on kingship, the difficult decisions facing rulers, and the negative public opinion in store for them during their lifetime and after their death. The work contains no biographical information on Frederick whatsoever, yet it displays awareness of the propaganda war declared on Frederick by the papacy. News about Frederick's troubles easily reached the Nicaean court. Frederick's daughter Constanza-Anna, Theodore's stepmother, was surrounded by an entourage from her homeland and kept in touch with her family in Italy. Frederick himself had the habit of informing John Vatatzes of his struggles against

---

[34]   Akrop. I, §48 (pp. 86–88); Macrides 2007:248, n. 4.
[35]   Akrop. I, §49 (pp. 88.15–89.2); Macrides 2007:251.   [36] Ep. 51.73 (p. 74), 51.88 (p. 75).

the papacy: for example, in his Greek letters to the Nicaean emperor dating to the summer of 1250.[37] The large Nicaean ecclesiastical delegation that left for Italy in 1250 and was detained in Apulia – Theodore was in epistolary communication with at least one of the ambassadors (Andronikos of Sardis) – may also have transmitted information by way of letters about opinions critical of Frederick in pro-papal circles.

3   *Encomium* on the Emperor John III Vatatzes (1250–52)

The editor Luigi Tartaglia has proposed convincing *termini* for the composition of the encomium: 1250–54.[38] The *termini* can be narrowed down further. The speech postdates the spring of 1250. In a lengthy section (Enc. John, 36–40), Theodore lauds his father John Vatatzes for his debating skills in refuting Latin theological views. The emperor is alleged to have done this "oftentimes" (πλειστάκις),[39] yet Theodore mentions a specific encounter that he himself witnessed: "I saw you also seated in the midst of the council and imagined you as the Lord's Anointed, presiding amidst the teachers of law and questioning them about the inexplicable."[40] The author envisages a recent event, which could only have been the debates with John of Parma's delegation held in Nymphaion during the spring of 1250.[41] The *terminus ante quem* for the encomium can be moved earlier than the death of John Vatatzes. For one thing, the speech could not have been given in the period between spring 1252 and late autumn 1253, because at that time John III Vatatzes was in the Balkans on campaign against Epiros, while Theodore Laskaris remained in Asia Minor. The year 1254 is also highly unlikely, for one would then expect the encomium to make prominent references to the recent successful campaign against Michael II Komnenos Doukas of Epiros. However, greater attention is given to other enemies: the Latins, including the doctrinal disputes in Nymphaion in the spring of 1250, the Turks ("Persians"), the Cumans ("Scythians"), the Mongols, the Bulgarians, and the Serbs. The conflict with Epiros is mentioned in passing as a μερικὴ Ῥωμαϊκὴ δύσνοια.[42] The suggested narrower timeframe is confirmed by the allusion in the speech to a diplomatic intermediary

---

[37] Merendino 1974–75.

[38] See the preface to the first edition of the text: Tartaglia 1990:16–17. Here Tartaglia refuted the view of Maria Andreeva who had argued that the work was a burial eulogy. In his Teubner edition of the text, Tartaglia (Op. rhet., 23) preferred to date the work to "c. 1250."

[39] Enc. John, 36.284, 37.297, 38.336.

[40] Enc. John, 36.294–37.296. Note the allusion to Luke 2:46.   [41] See Chapter 7, pp. 137–38.

[42] Enc. John, 27.83.

between the Mongols and the Seljuks. The author presents this individual as "Guneas the Arab," a mythological figure borrowed from Lykophron's *Alexandra* through Blemmydes' *Imperial Statue*. The figure corresponds in historical reality to an Arab polyglot who went on an embassy to Nicaea on behalf of the Great Khan Möngke during the years 1251–52.[43] One further consideration supports dating the work to 1250–52. Joseph Munitiz has plausibly suggested that Theodore wrote the speech on his thirtieth birthday, because he described it as a "tithe" (ἀποδεκάτωσις).[44] The birthday, which fell in late 1251 or early 1252, coincided with the time of exchange of embassies with the Great Khan Möngke. A response to the panegyric by Nikephoros Blemmydes has survived in the form of seven verses copied in the thirteenth-century Cod. Barocci 131 immediately after Blemmydes' *Encomium on St. John*, which has been dated to May 8, 1250.[45]

18   *Moral Pieces* (1252)

The *Moral Pieces* are twelve essays on theophilosophical topics, which, as the manuscript heading specifies, the author "composed during the period of mourning for the passing of the ever-remembered and blessed empress Lady Elena." The death of his wife Elena occurred in the spring or early summer of 1252.[46]

21   *Encomium on the Holy Anargyroi Cosmas and Damian* (1252)

This hagiographical work is a very personal one. The author thanks the healing saints for assisting him in overcoming illnesses. Toward the end of the text, he mentions the death of a woman close to him who had prayed in a church dedicated to the healing SS. Cosmas and Damian. Theodore is mourning the deceased lady and prays for the salvation of her soul in this same church. Unfortunately, his description is brief, allusive, and based on wordplay. "For also the icon of virtue, my soul partner by the law of human nature, who had God's law in her soul, often offered here services to the Creator, having them (SS. Cosmas and Damian) as protectors and assistants" (Καὶ γὰρ ἡ τῆς ἀρετῆς εἰκών, ἡ ἐμοὶ μὲν νόμῳ φύσεως ἀνθρωπίνης ἰσόψυχος, ψυχὴν δὲ αὕτη ἔχουσα νόμον τὸν τοῦ θεοῦ, πλειστάκις ἐνταυθοῖ

---

[43] See Chapter 7, p. 134.   [44] Enc. John, 25.32–33; Munitiz 1995:56 and n. 34.
[45] Agapitos 2007:3–4.   [46] Appendix 2, 365–67.

λατρείας τῷ κτίστῃ προσέφερε, τούτους ἔχουσα προστάτας καὶ συνερ-
γούς).[47] There are two possible identifications of the pious woman: his
mother Irene, who passed away in December 1239,[48] and his wife Elena.
Notably, the word ἰσοψυχία in the above passage refers to his late wife in
the *Moral Pieces*.[49] Elena's death looms large in many works of the author
dating to early 1250s: letters, the *Moral Pieces*, and *Response to Some
Friends Pressing Him to Find a Bride*. Therefore, it is probable that the
text dates also to the period after her passing.

13   *Response to Some Friends Pressing Him to Find a Bride* (1252–53)

This polemical work is a response to unspecified individuals ("friends"),
who advised Theodore Laskaris to remarry after the death of his wife
Elena and argued that this was the expected course of action for the heir to
the throne.[50] Indeed, there was an important precedent to follow: his
father John Vatatzes had remarried within a year following the death of
his wife Irene. In the *Response* the author vehemently opposes remarriage
and voices ascetic attitudes, which he presents as a passion for Lady
Wisdom. The work dates not long after Elena's passing – within a year
at most.

5   *Encomium* on George Akropolites (Early 1254)

The encomium on George Akropolites was occasioned by Akropolites'
edition of the epistles of Theodore Laskaris of the "Laurentian epistolary
collection" (Cod. Laur. Plut. 59, 35). The encomium opens by alluding to a
laudation written by Akropolites – that is, the verses that he composed as a
preface to the letters of his student.[51] As we will see in Appendix 2, the
preparation of the Laurentian epistolary collection dates to early 1254,
which must also be the date of the encomium.

---

[47] *Encomium on the Holy Anargyroi* (the healing saints Cosmas and Damian), **A**, f. 42r (with the
prior folio missing), **P**, ff. 63v–64r.
[48] See 270, n. 1.   [49] Mor. P., XII, 268.495.   [50] Tartaglia, Op. rhet., 112.64–113.70.
[51] Tartaglia, Op. rhet., 96.5–15. In his edition of the encomium, Athanasios Markopoulos
(1968:107, n. 7 and the apparatus to pages 110 and 116) indicated cases of similar phraseology
in the two texts. Already in 1900 August Heisenberg had remarked that the encomium was
Theodore's response to Akropolites' verses, suggesting 1251–53 as the date for the encomium.
See Heisenberg 1900:213.

14 *Response* to George Mouzalon (Treatise on Friendship and Politics) (1250–54)

The exact time of composition of the work is difficult to pinpoint. Eurydice Lappa Zizicas suggested that Theodore Laskaris authored it in November or December 1254, after his father's death but prior to his coronation.[52] In assigning a date, she tried to reconcile the divergent indications found in the manuscript heading, which refers to Theodore as "the son of the most exalted emperor Lord John Doukas," and in Ep. 209, addressed to George Mouzalon after Theodore's accession, an epistle which she considered to be the letter of dedication of the treatise. The letter indeed accompanies an oration (λόγος) that the author shared with Mouzalon, but nothing suggests that this work was the treatise on politics and friendship. The letter rhetorically contrasts the oration sent to Mouzalon with entertainment at the court and implies that the oration was marked by a religious spirit. The treatise on politics and friendship clearly postdates Blemmydes' *Imperial Statue*, for it is also described as a "statue" (ἀγαλματουργία), and it opens with an anecdote about Alexander the Great told in the *Imperial Statue*.[53] The *Imperial Statue* was written in 1248–50, not long after Blemmydes' confrontation with Marchesina, the mistress of John Vatatzes, in around 1248.[54] The treatise on politics and friendship could, thus, have been composed at any time in the early 1250s.

17 *Explanation of the World* (before and after November 1254)

The dating of this four-partite treatise, which the author addressed to George Mouzalon as a work of instruction, confronts us with a chronological puzzle. The opinions of modern scholars have tended to contradict the manuscript title. Alice Gardner has suggested in passing that the treatise belongs to the period after Theodore Laskaris acceded to the throne in 1254.[55] Maria Andreeva dated the third book of the treatise – *Representation of the World, or Life* – to Theodore's rule, specifically to the last two years of his life after his return to Asia Minor from the Balkans in early 1257, on the basis of references and allusions to events and tensions from

---

[52] Lappa-Zizicas 1950:121–22.
[53] Ad Georg. Mouz., 137.424. On the anecdote, see Blem., *Imperial Statue*, 66, Chapter 75.
[54] Echoes from the *Imperial Statue* are found already in the *Memorial Discourse* for Frederick II, so the *Imperial Statue* must have been written by 1250. On the chronology of the confrontation with Marchesina alluded to in the *Imperial Statue*, see 272, nn. 18, 20.
[55] Gardner 1912:287.

this period. She identified in the third and also the fourth book of the treatise – *On What is Unclear, and A Testimony that the Author is Ignorant of Philosophy* – the polemical spirit of Theodore's combative Ep. 44 to Nikephoros Blemmydes.[56] There are solid reasons to keep the dating of the third and fourth book proposed by Andreeva. Gerhard Richter has rightly observed that *Explanation of the World* postdates the treatise *Natural Communion.*[57] *Explanation of the World* shows familiarity with *Natural Communion*: Theodore opened the third book of *Explanation of the World – Representation of the World, or Life* – with the statement that he has already studied "the things in nature and dependent on nature" and that his current line of inquiry was different.[58] As we have seen in Chapter 9, the four books of *Explanation of the World* display a more religious spirit than the *Natural Communion* in presenting God as the creator of nature continually involved in the universe. Seen from this angle, the *Explanation of the World* reflects the evolving views of the author at a later stage in his life. The relative chronology of the two works does not, however, shed light on the date of composition of the *Explanation of the World*. All we know about the *Natural Communion* is that it dates to the period of Theodore's coemperorship, in all probability before early 1254.[59]

The manuscript heading before the general preface of the treatise explicitly mentions that "the wisest *autokrator* Theodore Doukas Laskaris, the son of the most exalted emperor John Doukas" wrote *Explanation of the World* "before the full completeness of his imperial rule" (πρὸ τῆς τῆς βασιλείας αὐτοῦ ἐντελεχείας) and addressed it to George Mouzalon, to whom "the wisest emperor" (βασιλεὺς σοφώτατος) granted brotherhood "after the full completeness of imperial rule" (μετὰ τὴν τῆς βασιλείας ἐντελέχειαν). According to the heading, "this wisest *autokrator*" (ὁ τοιοῦτος αὐτοκράτωρ σοφώτατος) promoted Mouzalon to the ranks of *protosebastos* and *protovestiarios*, and also honored him with the dignity of *megas stratopedarches,* which he newly (ἐκ νέου) introduced into the court hierarchy.[60]

Composition before November 1254 mentioned by the heading does not fit, however, with the internal chronological clues found in books 3 and 4 of the treatise (see below), as well as the multiple promotions of Mouzalon

---

[56] On the third book of *Explanation of the World*, see Andreeva 1930: *passim*, esp. 4, 8–9. On the fourth book, see Andreeva 1928.

[57] Richter 1989:198–99, 228.   [58] KD, III, 21.1–5.

[59] Akropolites' poem opening the Laurentian epistolary collection (early 1254) mentions that Theodore has composed a work on nature. See Akrop. II, 8.30.

[60] KD, I, 97.9–11.

(Christmas 1255) mentioned by the same heading. The inconsistency can be resolved in the following fashion. Theodore Laskaris began writing the work during his coemperorship as part of his ongoing effort to educate George Mouzalon and groom him for public service. The general preface mentions a query by Mouzalon that resembles the question that prompted the treatise on politics and friendship: the author was evidently concerned with showing that George Mouzalon took the initiative first. He wrote books 1, 2, and 3 during the period of his coemperorship, as per the heading of the general preface. It is notable that the letter of dedication of the third book (*Representation of the World, or Life*) falls within the section of the letters to George Mouzalon copied in Laurentianus, Conventi soppressi 627, which are marked as dating "before the full completeness of imperial rule" (specifically in the period January–October 1254).[61] After his accession, in 1256–58, Theodore revised the third book and probably wrote the fourth book, which is filled with polemical sarcasm and self-irony, from scratch. He then wrote the general preface addressed to Mouzalon, which drives home the point that the four-part oeuvre forms a coherent whole, even though the parts are in fact self-contained treatises. The edition of the *Explanation of the World* represents a revised product prepared in the last two years of his life. The entire treatise appears, thus, to have been composed over a period of time before and after his accession.

*On Elements and *On Heaven*, books 1 and 2 of *Explanation of the World* (before November 1254)

*Representation of the World, or Life (Κοσμικὴ στήλη ἢ βίος),[62] book 3 of *Explanation of the World* (before November 1254 and revised in 1257–58)

In the letter of dedication (composed before November 1254) of this discourse (λόγος) to George Mouzalon, Theodore remarks that the work discusses questions of "matter and immateriality" (περὶ δὲ τῆς ὕλης καὶ ἀυλίας).[63] The content of the treatise does not match this summary. The author is more on target, even if equally laconic, in the general preface written during his reign: *Representation of the World, or Life* is a book "about everything" (περὶ τῶν ὅλων).[64] Indeed, the lens moves rapidly and haphazardly from topic to topic as it examines the wondrous variety of life. The most important reason for dating the final revised version of

---

[61] Ep. 187 (p. 236). Note the dating of Epp. 183–85 to late 1253.

[62] The word στήλη has meanings, such as a "buttress," "pillar," "monument," but in particular it referred to a "statue" or "an image, a visual representation." See Pseudo-Kodinos in Verpeaux 1966:167; Macrides, Munitiz, and Angelov 2013:72.1.

[63] Ep. 187.5–7 (p. 236).   [64] KD, I, 99.13–15, 100.23–24.

Explanation of the World to the period of his sole rule (1254–58) is that it conveys Theodore's preoccupations as a reigning emperor fully in charge of governance. He makes explicit his difficulties with high officials who resist his authority. He has exposed, he writes, the disorder and inconstancy of his judges, has brought order among some grandees (ἄρχοντες), but has been led astray about "those in office" (οἱ ἐν τέλει).[65] He revisits the subject about "those in office" toward the end of the work, where he remarks: "The emperor reigns through Him (God) and through Him the *dynasteuon* tyrannizes those in office."[66] The allusion is to the *paradynasteuon*, namely, the chief imperial minister or *mesazon*, known as *paradynasteuon* in high-register Greek. George Mouzalon held this all-powerful position after Christmas 1255.[67] In the treatise, Theodore makes an effort to justify his selection of George Mouzalon as his all-powerful minister by embarking on a polemical discussion of nobility as a moral rather than social category. The author adopts the posture of an experienced and mature man. "Experience," he writes, is "an elucidation of many arguments."[68] Vivid descriptions of hypocritical conduct illustrate the point that the human being is a most deceptive creature. The examples include a conspirator who misappropriated money, a swarthy person ("an Ethiopian") who was in fact "an angel of light," a murderer who claimed that he was redressing wrongs as a divine retribution and received praises for his action, murderers who fixed the blame on others, poor men who thought to be rich, and rich men who considered themselves to be poor.[69] It is difficult to identify the individuals envisaged.[70] The specificity of the complaints suggest that the author produced the final version of the work in 1257–58 when he prepared the four books of *Explanation of the World* for inclusion in a collection of his works.

On What Is Unclear and A Testimony that the Author Does not Know Philosophy, Book IV of *Explanation of the World* (1257–58)

The author presents himself at the end of the treatise as "crowned by God," which indicates a date during his sole reign.[71] He assumes a Socratic posture of ignorance while laying out in impressive detail his knowledge in subjects such as rhetoric, logic, mathematics, governance, etc. The treatise is full of sarcasm against unnamed critics. Andreeva thought that

[65] KD, III, 25.22–24.   [66] KD, III, 37.1–2.
[67] The suggestion was made first by Andreeva 1930:10. On *paradynasteuon* as a designation of the *mesazon* in high-register Greek, see Beck 1955:318.
[68] KD, III, 23.1–2.   [69] KD, III, 27.25–28.17.   [70] See Chapter 9, p. 191.
[71] KD, IV, 52.5–8.

the work targeted Nikephoros Blemmydes, because many of the imperial virtues that the author claimed to lack are those found in the *Imperial Statue*.[72] It is more probable that the chorus of hostile voices that Theodore heard near the end of his life – criticising his personality, choices for ministerial appointments, and proposed military reforms – provoked in him the bitter frustration that marks this work. Theodore sought to prove the absurdity of the accusations by comparing himself to the unjustly treated Socrates.

34, 35   First and Second Orations against the Latins, or, on the Profession of the Holy Spirit, Sixth and Seventh Books of *Christian Theology* (Autumn 1256)

The two orations are occasioned by Theodore's encounter with a delegation from the papacy, in which a disputation on the *filioque* took place. The first oration addresses "the most learned and wonderful legate" and speaks of the "ambassadors of the holiest pope and their companions honored with the dignity of official representatives (*topoteretes*)."[73] In the second oration, Theodore speaks of the interlocutors as "Italians from Rome" (the legate and his companions) and addresses in the second person an unnamed "Italian."[74] He also addresses his own deacons, priests, bishops, and the patriarch, all of whom he urges to avoid idle disputes with the Latins and encourages not to fear their counterarguments.[75] The author refers to political turmoil in the "empire" (*basileia*) of his opponents, which corresponds to the situation in Italy after the deaths of Frederick II (December 1250) and his son Conrad IV (May 1254).[76] The setting corresponds closely to the reception of the papal embassy led by Constantine of Orvieto in Thessalonica in September and October 1256 by Theodore, Patriarch Arsenios, and leading bishops.[77] The emperor addressed the two speeches to Byzantine churchmen attending disputations in Thessalonica in an effort to discourage them from making doctrinal concessions. He used the opportunity to make a critique of scholasticism. The second oration stands out for its feelings of Hellenic pride evident in Theodore's letters from the Bulgarian campaign of 1255–56.

[72] Andreeva 1928.   [73] Chr. Th., VI, 127.92–94, 128.141.
[74] Chr. Th., VII, 142.152, 146.303–304.   [75] Chr. Th., VII, 147.331–334.
[76] Chr. Th., VII, 143.190–192.   [77] As observed already by Christos Krikonis, Chr. Th., 61–63.

36 *Response* to the Bishop of Croton (1256–58)

The treatise defends the orthodox doctrine of the Procession of the Holy
Spirit through a series of quotations from the scriptures, the Greek fathers,
and the ecumenical councils. Only a few hard facts are known about the
addressee, Nicholas, the bishop of Croton (Cotrone) in Calabria. He was a
native of Dyrrachion and was versed equally in Greek and Latin. He served
as a cleric of the apostolic chamber of Pope Innocent IV who ordained him
on September 2, 1254, as bishop of Croton. It is unlikely that Nicholas
assumed his pastoral duties: the bishopric was occupied by a usurper by the
name of Maur, and Calabria was controlled until 1266 by the papacy's rival
Manfred of Sicily.[78] Nicholas often volunteered as an intermediary in
unionist negotiations between the Greek and the Latin church during the
1250s and 1260s. For example, he held doctrinal discussions with the
emperor Michael VIII Palaiologos in 1263 and conveyed his letters to
the papacy. He probably took part in the Council of Lyons in 1274. He
made his will in Venice on October 2, 1274, and donated his manuscripts
to the monastery of San Giorgio Maggiore.[79] As the *Response* makes clear
at the beginning, Theodore Laskaris already knew Nicholas. In the past
Theodore had asked him to "answer to my imperial majesty in what ways
does the holiest great church of God, the old Rome, profess its doctrine
regarding the Procession of the Holy Spirit" and had already received
Nicholas' answer. Now the emperor responded by presenting doctrines
of "our holiest great church of God."[80] According to Antoine Dondaine,
Theodore Laskaris composed his *Response* to Nicholas of Croton after he
received the latter's *Libellus de fide Trinitatis*, a treatise of 113 chapters
composed in Greek and Latin (the Latin texts only survives today), which
Pope Urban IV (r. 1261–64) would present for close scrutiny to none other
than Thomas Aquinas, who wrote on its basis his *Contra Errores Graecorum*. The last chapter, 113, addresses a learned Byzantium emperor,
identified by Dondaine as Theodore Laskaris, who had been eager to learn
about Latin doctrines.[81] Most recently, however, it has been argued that

---

[78] Berger 1897 III:no. 7984 (p. 501).
[79] On Nicholas of Croton, see Dondaine 1950; Sambin 1954; PLP 20143. See also Alexakis 1996:234–70.
[80] Chr. Th. (reprint from Swete 1875), 161.1–7.
[81] Nicholas of Croton, *Libellus de fide Trinitatis*, ed. Dondaine 1967:§113 (p. 150). According to Dondaine (1950:328), Nicholas may have traveled to the empire of Nicaea to present the treatise. Most of *Libellus* contains quotations from Greek fathers and synodal acts supporting the Latin view on the Procession of the Holy Spirit. There also are a few chapters on papal primacy, the use of unleavened bread in the liturgy, and purgatory.

Nicholas composed the *Libellus* in 1263 and addressed it to Michael VIII Palaiologos rather than Theodore Laskaris.[82]

A *terminus post quem* for the composition of Theodore's *Response* is the September 1254, because Theodore addressed Nicholas as ἱερώτατε ἐπίσκοπε Κοτρώνης ("holiest bishop of Cotrone"). I exclude the possibility of the year 1255 as the time of composition, because Theodore Laskaris was campaigning in the Balkans and had no access to a library in order to collect the testimonies. The termini of the work, thus, are 1256–58. There is no evidence as to when Nicholas became first known to the emperor in his capacity as an intermediary in the unionist negotiations.[83] In the preface to his *Response* to Nicholas, Theodore states: "We say that It (the Holy Spirit) does not proceed from the Son, but we believe and think that It is bestowed on us through the Son for the sake of purification and sanctification."[84] Nikephoros Blemmydes addressed to Theodore a doctrinal work on the Procession of the Holy Spirit "through the Son," which its recent editor has dated to between 1254 and early 1256: it was written, that is, in preparation for the encounter with the papal delegation in Thessalonica.[85] Theodore does not follow Blemmydes' argument in the *Response*, nor does he adopt his more conciliatory tone, yet an echo from his teacher's most recent work on the Trinity can perhaps be detected in the preface.

37 *Newsletter* on the Peace of Regina (June 29, 1256, or Soon Thereafter)

The newsletter informs the subjects in Anatolia of the provisions of the peace treaty concluded between Theodore Laskaris and Michael Asen of Bulgaria through the intermediacy of the Russian prince Rostislav Mikhailovich, who came in person to the camp of the emperor on the Regina (Ergene) River in eastern Thrace. The pact was prepared on June

---

[82] Alexakis 1996:251, n. 35. Dondaine (1950:316 n. 3, 336) noted that Thomas Aquinas was aware of the *Libellus* by 1256–57, because in a work composed in 1256 he quoted from it a passage attributed to Cyril of Alexandria. The question needs further examination.

[83] Christos Krikonis (Chr. Th., 63–64) has suggested that Nicholas resided in the Greek East in 1255–56. It is equally possible that Nicholas played a role in receiving the Nicaean embassies to the papacy in 1250–54.

[84] Chr. Th. (reprint from Swete 1875), 161.11–162.13.

[85] According to Stavrou (2007–13 I:284–85), Theodore composed the *Response* to Nicholas of Croton in 1254 or 1255, and Blemmydes wrote the doctrinal work addressed to Theodore between 1254 and 1256.

29, 1256, the feast day of Peter and Paul, or shortly thereafter.[86] The euphoric spirit of the newsletter suggests that it was composed not long after the conclusion of the treaty. There is no sign in the text of Theodore Laskaris' mounting frustration at the delay in the implementation of the agreement and the delivery of the fortress of Tzepaina to him, which occurred only in August.

25 *Supplicatory Canon* Addressed to the Virgin (*Great Supplicatory Canon*) (Late 1257–58)

The themes and motifs of this moving hymn strongly suggest that Theodore Laskaris composed it in the months leading up to his death on August 16, 1258. The themes are found in earlier works, yet they are articulated with particular intensity and with flashbacks into the past. Each of the odes of the canon ends with a prayer to the Virgin to look favorably upon "the grievous affliction of my body" (τὴν ἐμὴν χαλεπὴν τοῦ σώματος κάκωσιν) and "the pain of my soul" (τῆς ψυχῆς μου τὸ ἄλγος).[87] The connection between physical and spiritual illness harks back to orations in which he expressed his gratitude to Christ and the saints Cosmas and Damian (the Holy Anargyroi) for his recovery from illnesses.[88] Theodore confesses in the hymn that he has approached Hades in the past and that he has been pulled back to life thanks to the mediation of the Virgin,[89] who he already knows to be a reliable "doctor of diseases" (τῶν νόσων ἰατρόν σε γινώσκω).[90] The theme of the descent to Hades is found in the *Moral Pieces* (the last essay), but here it is linked with his illness and the intervention of the Virgin. Theodore prays to the Mother of God to deliver him from "malevolent enemies" (ἐχθρῶν δυσμενῶν).[91] In addition, he beseeches the Virgin to save him from "those who hate him" (οἱ μισοῦντες), who have in the past pointed their weapons against him and who still "seek to tear apart my most wretched body and throw it down onto the earth" (ἐπιζητοῦσι τὸ πανάθλιον σῶμα σπαράξαι μου καὶ καταβιβάσαι πρὸς γῆν).[92] The notion of the subjects feeling hatred (μῖσος) for the ruler is a theme of the *Memorial Discourse* in honor of Frederick II, but here the author confesses that he felt that he himself was the object of hate.

---

[86] The date of the Peace of Regina is specified only by *Synopsis chronike* (524.31–525.5). In his *History*, George Akropolites omits this detail and focuses instead on his beating at the camp on the Regina River on August 6 (the feast of the Transfiguration).

[87] PG, vol. 140, cols. 772B, 773B, 776B, 777B, 777D, 780C.   [88] See Appendix 3, p. 388, n. 33.

[89] PG, vol. 140, col. 773B.   [90] PG, vol. 140, col. 776C; see also col. 777CD.

[91] PG, vol. 140, col. 772A.   [92] PG, vol. 140, col. 776AB.

Murderous individuals denying their crime are mentioned in *Representa-tion of the World, or Life*, but here their target is the emperor himself. The *Supplicatory Canon* is a highly personal and dramatic poem. Theodore's angst is vividly conveyed as he speaks about a "tempest of disasters" and a "storm of painful things."[93] One can imagine him composing the hymn not too long before he passed away, when he was increasingly ill and believed that he was surrounded by ill-wishers.

38   *Six Essays,* Sixth and Last Essay (Late 1257–58)

The six essays date to his sole rule, as is clear from the heading of the first essay (μετὰ τὴν τῆς βασιλείας ἐντελέχειαν). The topic of the sixth and last essay is the physical decline of rulers due to their selfless efforts to take care of their subjects and fulfill their responsibilities. In this essay Theodore reflects on his experiences in the Bulgarian campaign. He comments on the exhaustion of the commander-in-chief who is exposed to freezing cold in the winter and scorching heat in the summer. The same complaint is found in letters to Mouzalon written from the front lines in 1255.[94] In the essay, Theodore generalizes about the way in which the hard life of rulers causes disease. Only the ruler who takes care of himself and not of his subjects can be healthy. The essay dates to a time after the end of the Bulgarian campaign, when Theodore already felt symptoms of bodily weakness (that is, the onset of his terminal illness) and looked for an explanation.

---

[93]   PG, vol. 140, col. 773AB. Theodore used often the word τρικυμία ("mighty wave," "sea storm"). See Ep. 18.3–4 (p. 24); Mor. P., II, 256.100; Sat., 162.200; *On Virtue* in Paléologou 2007:73.135–36. For similar vocabulary in the oration for the feast of the Akathistos, see Giannouli 2001:268.

[94]   Ep. 202.30–36 (p. 249) written in the summer of 1255 contains complaints about extreme weather conditions. In Ep. 205.6–8 (p. 255), Theodore writes that he has sacrificed his body for the subjects during the campaign.

Appendix 2 | Chronology of the Letters

In 1898 the Italian philologist Nicola Festa published an edition of 217 letters by Theodore Laskaris. The total number is larger, because Festa counted two letters to the Phaix brothers as one letter (Ep. 121) and merged into a single letter (Ep. 25) what in fact are two separate pieces: a preamble (*prooimion*) to a donation to Theodore's teacher Nikephoros Blemmydes and a rhetorical recapitulation of this unspecified grant. The total of the letters grows to 220 when one adds the lengthy letter to George Akropolites that Theodore Laskaris included into the collection of his ten secular works. The letters were addressed to twenty-seven correspondents – one more than the twenty-six counted by Festa (who registered the metropolitan of Kyzikos, Kleidas, and Pope Alexander IV as the same correspondent, numbered as 19). Unfortunately, letters addressed to Theodore Laskaris have rarely survived. The exceptions are Blemmydes' twenty-nine letters to his royal tutee and a letter by Pope Alexander IV.[1]

The letters have come down to us without any date in an edited version prepared under the author's auspices, sometimes with the help of an editor, as is the case with the Laurentian epistolary collection. Establishing the chronology of the letters is a challenging task that involves the same detective work as with the author's other writings. More than a century ago, August Heisenberg made a few hasty suggestions that he later retracted. In a review of Festa's edition, he assigned all letters to Akropolites in the Laurentian epistolary collection to the second half of the year 1246 at a time when Akropolites accompanied the senior emperor

---

[1] Festa published thirty-one letters by Blemmydes as an appendix to the edition of Theodore Laskaris' epistles, but the number can be reduced safely to twenty-nine: Blem., Ep. 4 refers to an emperor in Constantinople and is addressed to Michael Palaiologos (see Andreeva 1929); Blem., Ep. 27 is addressed to the patriarch Manuel II (see Munitiz 2003 for the attribution and a translation). Common subjects and themes occasionally link the letters sent and received by Theodore. Thus, in Ep. 8 he promises Blemmydes a mule that he has not yet sent, Blemmydes responds that he is awaiting the mule (Blem., Ep. 15), and in Ep. 9 Theodore dispatches the pack animal. The letter of Pope Alexander IV to Theodore has been published by Schillmann 1918:119–23; Haluščynskyj and Wojnar 1966:48–51 (no. 28b).

on a campaign in the Balkans.[2] He argued that the letters follow a chronological order and proposed 1253–54 as the timeframe of Theodore's letters to George Mouzalon: during an absence, probably of only one or two months, when Mouzalon was away recovering from illness.[3] In the preface to the second volume of the edition of Akropolites' works, however, Heisenberg rightly pointed out that there was no *prima facie* reason for this simple chronology.[4] References to known historical events and episodes in the life of the author are the main method for assigning a date to a single letter. Fortunately, the existence of thematic-chronological clusters (see below) expands the number of datable letters. Valuable clues are added by the codicological context. The discussion below begins with the manuscript transmission of the letters, with a special focus on the Laurentian collection. A series of thematic-chronological clusters are then identified. A list of dated letters and arguments favoring specific timeframes follows.

The Manuscripts

Festa edited the letters on the basis of the three manuscripts and grouped them according to their addressees, adhering to the sequence of correspondents in the Laurentian epistolary collection, which served as the backbone of his edition. In one exceptional case (two letters to Hagiotheodorites), he rearranged the order.[5] After reaching the last letter to each correspondent in the Laurentian collection, Festa edited letters addressed to the same recipient (if such letters have survived) from Cod. Vindob. philol. gr. 312 (**V**). In addition, Festa edited letters to two recipients from another Laurentian manuscript: Laurentianus, Conventi soppressi 627. Most of Theodore's letters are transmitted by a *codex unicus,* that is, by only one of the three manuscripts, with a small number of them addressed to Blemmydes and Akropolites being copied both in the only surviving codex of the Laurentian collection and in **V**.[6]

---

[2] Heisenberg 1900:216. The year is wrongly printed as 1245. As Heisenberg himself pointed out on the margin of his edition of Akropolites' *History*, this expedition took place in 1246. See Akrop. I, §43– §45 (pp. 72–83).

[3] Heisenberg 1900:220.   [4] Akrop. II, VIII n. 1.

[5] The letters to Blemmydes and Akropolites in Cod. Laur. gr. 59, 35 are immediately followed by two letters to Hagiotheodorites, the first of which lacks a heading and is jointly addressed to Hagiotheodorites and Mouzalon on the occasion of the marriage of the latter's sister. Festa preferred to edit the two letters near the end of his edition as Epp. 215 and 216.

[6] On the letters to Blemmydes and Akropolites, which the copyist of **V** selected from a manuscript of the Laurentian epistolary collection, see 350, n. 17.

Laurentianus Plut. 59, 35 (14th c.), or the Laurentian Epistolary Collection[7]

A total of 133 letters on ff. 42r–178r (a total of 131 in Festa's numeration due to the above-mentioned manner in which he treated Epp. 25 and 121). The letters address nineteen recipients. The headings before most of the groups of letters assign them to the period "before the embassy" of Berthold of Hohenburg. (However, there are some exceptions – see the section below discussing accretions to the Laurentian collection.) Verses written by Theodore's teacher and editor of the letters, George Akropolites, precede the collection on ff. 39r–40v. Akropolites praises the letters for their style and content, and recommends them warmly to the reader.[8] A table of contents (*pinax*) follows on f. 41r–v just before the opening group of letters addressed to Nikephoros Blemmydes. Interestingly, a letter by Theodore Xanthopoulos to an anonymous *megas logothetes* (f. 40r–v) – who has been identified as Theodore Metochites, appointed to this high position in 1321 – appears immediately after the verses and just before the table of contents; this letter was copied after the production of the manuscript by a different scribal hand in the scant space available.[9]

Cod. Laur. Plut. 59, 35 is a miscellaneous paper manuscript produced in the early fourteenth century. The bulk of the codex consists of letters by Synesius of Cyrene and Theodore Laskaris; it contains also an oration by the Maximos Planoudes on the entombment of Jesus and the lamentation of the Virgin, and a few other minor texts. The date of production of the manuscript is confirmed by colophons mentioning the death of Irene of Brunswick, first wife of Andronikos III, on August 16, 1324 (f. 38v); the name of Hélion de Villeneuve, grand master of the Knights of St. John on Rhodes (in the years 1319–46) (f. 178r); and the passing of a certain nun, Martha, on March 14, 1330 (f. 188v).[10] The manuscript circulated among scholars and teachers in Constantinople in the 1320s. Clear indications are the copying of Xanthopoulos' letter to a *megas logothetes* (Theodore Metochites) and another contemporary letter addressed by the astronomer Nicholas Rabdas to Andronikos Zarides, which predicts the solar eclipse on June 26, 1321, and the lunar eclipse on July 10 that year.[11] The manuscript made its way to Florence in the fifteenth century when the

---

[7] Described by Bandini 1768: 555–68; most recently also by Riehle 2016:161–63.

[8] Akrop. II, 7–9.   [9] Edited and translated by Riehle 2016:251–52.

[10] The notes have been published by Bandini 1768:566–67; one of them has been republished by Trapp 1978:200.

[11] Published by Riehle 2015.

humanist Politian wrote marginal scholia on the letters of Synesius.[12]
A note written in Greek and Latin in brown ink on f. 40r states that "the
codex was a property of Angelus Politianus and friends."

Vindobonensis Philol. gr. 321 (13th c.)[13]

A total of forty-nine letters (ff. 310r–v, 59r–64v, 318r, 68r–71v, 311r–v,
72r–73v, 108r–114v) copied in a section of the codex that contains works
of Theodore II Laskaris. Some single folios (ff. 310, 318, 311) have been
bound at the end of the manuscript. There is a lacuna, with missing folios,
between f. 311 and f. 72.[14]

The headings before the epistles to individual recipients copied on ff.
310r–v, 59r–64v, 318r, 68r–71v, 311r–v, 71r–73v – a total of twenty-four
letters – tend to assign a date after "the full completeness of imperial rule"
(μετὰ τὴν τῆς βασιλείας ἐντελέχειαν) or, in the case of the letters to George
Mouzalon, identify the recipient as "brother" of the emperor and holder of
the titles *protosebastos*, *protovestiarios* and *megas stratopedarches*. These
twenty-four letters all date to the period of Theodore's rule as a sole
emperor and seem to have been part of an authorized edition of his works
prepared at that time.[15] They include: seven epistles to Blemmydes; three
to Akropolites; one to Kleidas, the metropolitan of Kyzikos; one to
Germanos, the metropolitan of Adrianople; six to representatives of the
Roman curia (Pope Alexander IV and the cardinals Peter Capoccio,
Richard Annibaldi, and Ottaviano Ubaldini); two letters to a certain Philip;
and four addressed to George Mouzalon.[16]

An additional twenty-five letters addressed solely to Blemmydes and
Akropolites are copied on ff. 108r–114v.[17] Notably, the epithets of

---

[12] Maïer 1965:335.
[13] The manuscript has been described by Hunger 1961:409–18. On the section with the Laskaris
texts, see Agapitos and Angelov 2018.
[14] The lacuna, noticed by Festa, falls between Ep. 145 to Cardinal Richard Annibaldi and Ep. 148
addressed to a certain Philip.
[15] See the analysis of **V** in Agapitos and Angelov 2018. Appendix I, 326–27.
[16] Their order in Festa's edition is as follows: Epp. 42–48 (to Blemmydes), 87–89 (to Akropolites),
141 (to Kleidas, the metropolitan of Kyzikos), 131 (to Germanos, the metropolitan of
Adrianople), 142 (to Pope Alexander IV), 144 (to Richard Annibaldi), 146 (to Ottaviano
Ubaldini), 143 (to Pope Alexander IV), 147 (to Peter Capoccio), 145 (to Richard Annibaldi),
148–49 (to Philip), 211–14 (to Mouzalon).
[17] Epp. 1, 3, 9, 10, 11, 14, 15, 26, 33, 36, 40, 41 (addressed to Blemmydes), 49, 56, 57, 58, 60, 67, 69,
71, 72, 76, 81, 82, 85 (addressed to Akropolites). On the paleographical peculiarities of this
section of **V**, see Agapitos and Angelov 2018. Festa did not always note the presence of a letter
in **V** in his edition.

Blemmydes in the headings in the Laurentian epistolary collection and in this section of **V** are identical: πρὸς τὸν ἐν φιλοσόφοις μέγαν διδάσκαλον καὶ ἁγιώτατον ἱερομόναχον κῦρ Νικηφόρον τὸν Βλεμμύδην (Βλεμμίδην in **V**). This circumstance suggests that the copyist had a manuscript of the Laurentian collection in front of him.[18] He chose to copy letters to Blemmydes and Akropolites that focused on the student-teacher relationship.

Laurentianus, Conventi soppressi 627 (13th c.)[19]

A total of sixty-two letters (1r–11v) copied at the beginning of the manuscript. The heading before the sixty-one letters to George Mouzalon (Epp. 150–210) identify the recipient as the "brother" of the emperor and a holder of the titles *protosebastos, protovestiarios* and *megas stratopedarches*. A note on f. 5v separates the preceding letters (Epp. 150–92, forty-three in total), dating them to the period "before the full completeness of imperial rule" (πρὸ τῆς τῆς βασιλείας ἐντελεχείας) from the letters that follow (Epp. 193–210, eighteen in total), which it assigns to the period "after the full completeness of imperial rule" (μετὰ τὴν τῆς βασιλείας ἐντελέχειαν). A letter to "the learned teachers of rhetoric and poetry" Michael Senachereim and Andronikos Phrangopoulos (Ep. 217) follows the Mouzalon dossier. The heading of this letter seems to be a scribal addition: "Another letter by the same, that is, the wisest emperor Lord Theodore Doukas Laskaris."

The miscellaneous paper codex is important for the transmission of antique love novels by Longus, Achilles Tatius, Chariton, and Xenophon of Ephesos. In addition, the manuscript preserves specimens – sometimes unique ones – of eleventh-, twelfth- and thirteenth-century poetry, various Nicaean and early Palaiologan texts, letters of Gregory of Nazianzus and Basil of Caesarea, and other works.

The Laurentian Epistolary Collection (Early 1254)

This edition of the letters postdates the embassy of Berthold of Hohenburg (autumn 1253), because the embassy is mentioned in the headings of letters to individual recipients, just as the same embassy appears in the headings of individual works in the collection *Sacred Orations*. As we have

[18] For this argument, see also Agapitos and Angelov 2018.
[19] Described by Rostagno and Festa 1893:172–76.

seen in Chapter 7, the stimulating intellectual discussions during Berthold's visit to the Anatolian Byzantine court gave Theodore the impetus to publish the two collections, which could have been produced either during or, most probably, in the intermediate aftermath of the embassy. Scholars have traditionally dated the epistolary collection on the basis of the career and movements of its editor, George Akropolites, who was a civil official in the service of the emperor John Vatatzes at the time. In his *History of Byzantine Literature* Karl Krumbacher remarked in passing that Akropolites edited the letters in 1252.[20] In the review of Festa's edition, Heisenberg noted briefly that the publication of the letters took place before 1253.[21] Elsewhere he elaborated that the publication could have been prepared at any time between 1246 and 1252, and in any case before March 1252 when, according to Heisenberg, Akropolites departed for the Balkans along with John Vatatzes on a military expedition in the Balkans.[22] Another scholar has suggested that, perhaps, the editing started at the end of 1251 and finished in the spring of 1252.[23]

None of these views takes into account the date of the embassy of Berthold of Hohenburg. In fact, two letters in the collection (Epp. 40 and 125, the latter clearly dating to the autumn of 1253) explicitly mention the arrival of Berthold and the philosophical discussions at the court. Also datable to 1253 is a cluster of letters occasioned by the "Theodore Philes affair" (Epp. 35–39, 77–78, 80; see below). Notably, in his prefatory poem Akropolites uses the expression Θεοδώρου Λάσκαρι τοῦ βασιλέως ἄνακτος υἱοῦ παγκλεοῦς Ἰωάννου, which refers to Theodore as the heir and coemperor: the preparation of the epistolary collection by Akropolites clearly predates November 1254.[24] Akropolites accompanied John Vatatzes on his Balkan campaign in 1252 and 1253 against Michael II Komnenos Doukas of Epiros. He left Anatolia in the first half of 1252, wintered in the Balkans, and returned to Asia Minor along with the senior emperor in the late autumn of 1253, after the public treason trial of Michael Palaiologos during the autumn of the same year in Philippi in eastern Macedonia. Berthold of Hohenburg must still have been in Anatolia at the time, awaiting the return of the senior emperor. After crossing the Hellespont, John Vatatzes briefly visited Nicaea and was reunited with his son on the main road to the

---

[20] Krumbacher 1897:287.   [21] Heisenberg 1900:213.
[22] Heisenberg in Akrop. II, VIII. On the departure of the campaign in the spring of 1252, see Chapter 7, pp. 128–29.
[23] See the preface by Markopoulos (1968:107, n. 3) to his edition of Theodore's encomium on George Akropolites.
[24] Akrop. II, 8.19–20.

Thrakesion theme (see below the thematic cluster of Epp. 83–86). The court then wintered in Nymphaion. John Vatatzes was back in Nicaea at the end of February 1254 in order to take care of the city's defenses because of an anticipated Mongol invasion.[25]

It is during the winter sojourn of the court in Nymphaion that Akropolites had the opportunity to edit the collection. Notably, none of the letters in the collection is datable to the year 1254. Therefore, I would like to suggest the early months of 1254 as the date for the preparation of the Laurentian epistolary collection and the *Sacred Orations*. One can imagine Theodore and Akropolites, a student and a teacher, discussing the arrangement of the letters and deciding to begin with those addressed to their common mentor, the monk and philosopher Nikephoros Blemmydes. The epistolary collection was in large part intended to be a record of the education of the author and his evolving relationship with his teachers. The first letter to Blemmydes (Ep. 1) documents the beginning of Theodore's studies and the penultimate letter (Ep. 40) describes a discussion during Berthold's embassy. An overall – but not uninterrupted – chronological arrangement is noticeable, as are thematic clusters of letters. The degree of Akropolites' editorial intervention is, of course, impossible to gauge. The letters to Akropolites were placed after those to Blemmydes. The first epistle in this section, a dream vision, presents the author as still needing instruction; the last letters refer to the return of Akropolites after a long period of separation (1252–53). Once again, there is an overall chronological arrangement and there are thematic clusters. The letters to Hagiotheodorites, Patriarch Manuel II, and other correspondents follow those to Blemmydes and Akropolites.

One possible counterargument against dating the Laurentian epistolary collection to early 1254 is the surprising presence of divergent headings. The letters preserved in Laur. gr. 59, 35 address a total of nineteen recipients, including a few joint recipients. In the majority of cases (in ten cases), a reference is made in the heading to a period before the embassy of the marquis Berthold of Hohenburg. In four cases, the headings lack any chronological or authorial marker whatsoever, something that may result from a scribal omission: the letters to Hagiotheodorites, the secretary Kostomyres, the domestic of the *scholae* Kalothetos, and Demetrios

---

[25] According to Akrop I, §49 (p. 92.22–24), John Vatatzes encamped in Philippi in the autumn (that is, the autumn of 1253) and convened a high tribunal at which Michael Palaiologos was put on trial. The senior emperor then crossed into Anatolia and wintered in Nymphaion, as was his custom, for he came back "from the East" to Nicaea in late February. See Akrop. I, §52 (p. 101.19–23); *Synopsis chronike*, 504.14–16.

Iatropoulos, the *prokathemenos* of Philadelphia.[26] Three headings, however, refer to a period before the "full completeness of imperial rule" (πρὸ
τῆς τῆς βασιλείας ἐντελεχείας), a type of heading found in collections
produced during the emperor's reign: letters to the patriarchal officials
Xiphilinos and Argyropoulos, letters to the monk Akakios, and a letter to
the secretary Kallistos.[27] Finally, there are two cases of headings referring
to the period "before the full completeness of imperial rule and the
embassy of the marquis" (πρὸ τῆς τῆς βασιλείας ἐντελεχείας καὶ τῆς τοῦ
μαρκίωνος πρεσβείας): a letter to the monk Neilos, abbot of the monastery
tou Stylou, and a letter to the secretary Manikaites.[28]

Two important features unite the letters with divergent headings that
mention the period "before the full completeness of imperial rule" and "before
the full completeness of imperial rule and the embassy of the marquis." First,
they are all copied (Epp. 126–137 in Festa's edition) *after* the letters whose
headings refer to the embassy. Second, they are mostly single letters per
recipient (and, in any case, never exceed four letters), which is far less than
the letters to Blemmydes, Akropolites, and the patriarch Manuel II. A very
probable scenario is that these relatively few letters (none can be dated down
to a specific year through internal evidence) were copied, or were inserted, as
an appendix after the letters edited by Akropolites. The collection, thus, grew
by accretion. The resulting expanded collection was recopied during the sole
reign of Theodore Laskaris in a sort of a second edition, with some of the
headings now featuring the phrase πρὸ τῆς τῆς βασιλείας ἐντελεχείας, whether
alone or in combination with the standard formula referring to Berthold's
embassy. As we have seen, the phrase πρὸ τῆς τῆς βασιλείας ἐντελεχείας was
preferred to the formula referring to Berthold's embassy in editions produced
during the emperor's rule. This preference is clearly seen in the Trinitarian
treatise opening the *Sacred Orations* once the treatise was included into the
collection *Christian Theology* as its fifth discourse.

The fourteenth-century Laurentian codex shows evidence of disruption in
the original edition. For one thing, the table of contents (*pinax*) placed
before the letters suggests omissions and additions in the process of copying.[29] It lists forty-eight letters addressed to Blemmydes instead of the forty-

---

[26] See pp. 195, 196, 197, 267, 268 of Festa's edition (Epp. 138, 139, 140, 215–216).
[27] See pp. 177, 188, 190 of Festa's edition (Epp. 126–129, 132–134, 135).
[28] See pp. 192, 193 of Festa's edition (Epp. 136, 137).
[29] This *pinax* found on f. 41r–v is published by Festa, Ep. IV–V. A similar *pinax* precedes the ten
Sacred Orations in both **A** and **P**. The note following the *pinax* counts the letters, correctly, as
totaling 133, but it may have been added by a copyist rather than have formed part of the
original edition of early 1254. It runs as follows (in Festa's edition): Ὁμοῦ ἐν τῇδε τῇ βίβλῳ

two copied: six missing letters that were once part of the collection have
since been lost. I am inclined to agree with Heisenberg that one of the letters
to Akropolites, according to its placement in the Laurentian manuscript
(Ep. 55 in Festa's edition), may actually have been addressed to Blemmydes,
but somehow entered the Akropolites dossier.[30] Furthermore, the table of
contents lists one letter to the Phaix brothers instead of the actual four
copied and one letter to Hagiotheodorites instead of the actual two copied.
A sign of the intervention by a copyist is seen in the successive simplification
of headings mentioning the embassy of the marquis Berthold of Hohenburg.
The heading of the forty-two letters to Blemmydes runs as follows: Ἐπιστολαὶ τοῦ υἱοῦ τοῦ μεγάλου βασιλέως κυροῦ Ἰωάννου τοῦ Δούκα, Θεοδώρου τοῦ
Λάσκαρι, πρὸς τὸν ἐν φιλοσόφοις μέγαν διδάσκαλον καὶ ἁγιώτατον ἱερομόναχον κυρὸν Νικηφόρον τὸν Βλεμμύδην πρὸ τῆς τοῦ μαρκίωνος Βελτόρδου Δε
Ὀεμβούργ πρεσβείας πρὸς τὸν αὐτὸν μέγαν βασιλέα κυρὸν Ἰωάννην τὸν
Δούκα. The heading of the letters to Akropolites lacks the phrase πρὸς τὸν
αὐτὸν μέγαν βασιλέα in the chronological formula. Subsequent headings are
simpler and shorter. Those preceding the letters to the Phaix brothers and to
the metropolitan bishop Andronikos of Sardis and Germanos of Adrianople
do not mention the name of the marquis at all, referring simply to a period
πρὸ τῆς τοῦ μαρκίωνος πρεσβείας.[31] There were, therefore, losses, additions,
scribal interventions, and some rearrangement. The growth of the collection
by accretion and its copying during Theodore's reign could explain this
phenomenon. Nonetheless, these disruptions appear to have been minor
ones, and the letters in the Laur. gr. 59, 35 generally reflect the order and
authorial intent of the original edition.

Thematic Clusters

At first glance, the letters appear to follow chronological sequence both in
the Laurentian collection and in the other manuscripts.[32] An overall
chronological order is observable in the batches addressed to Blemmydes
and Akropolites, and also in those to George Mouzalon copied in Laur.,

ἐπιστολαὶ ἑκατὸν τριάκοντα τρεῖς· Ἐγράφησαν δὲ πᾶσαι πρὸ <τῆς > τῆς βασιλείας ἐντελεχείας
καὶ τῆς τοῦ μαρκίωνος πρὸς τὸν μέγαν βασιλέα κυρὸν Ἰωάννην τὸν Δούκαν πρεσβείας.
Significantly, the note shows that the letters formed a single manuscript volume (βίβλος).

[30] Festa (Ep. VI) suggested that Epp. 55, 62, 66, and 68 addressed to Akropolites may, in fact, have
been intended for Blemmydes. Heisenberg (1900:216) agreed with the reattribution of letter 55
only, connecting it – reasonably in my view – with Blemmydes' Ep. 15 to Theodore.

[31] See pp. 166, 172, 188 of Festa's edition.   [32] See the view of Heisenberg 1900:215.

Conventi soppressi 627 and dating to the Bulgarian campaign (1255–56). The chronological arrangement of letters is a phenomenon traceable in other Byzantine *epistolaria*.[33] However, a careful examination shows an organizing principle other than chronology. The letters were grouped as dossiers of texts addressed to an individual recipient. Within each dossier, the letters were arranged thematically. It is only in the thematic units that the chronological ordering of the letters becomes relevant, for the letters were arranged in such a way as to show development over time. The thematic clusters themselves tended to follow each other chronologically. However, there were letters outside the main thematic clusters. These "stand-alone letters" can be dated only rarely on the basis of references to important events, such as foreign embassies or Theodore's activities as a sole emperor after November 1254. Sometimes these stand-alone letters disrupt the overall chronological sequence. This is the case with Epp. 18 and 24, addressed to Blemmydes, both datable to 1252 (and both part of the Laurentian epistolary collection), which frame letters of invitation to Blemmydes that cannot belong to the year 1252.

The mention of a datable event in a letter that is part of a thematic cluster makes possible the assignment of chronology to other epistles in the cluster. This approach can be applied to the following thematic units: letters critical of Constantine Klaudioupolites, the metropolitan bishop of Ephesos; letters critical of Nikephoros, the metropolitan bishop of Ephesos; letters occasioned by the death of Theodore's wife Elena; letters pertaining to the Theodore Philes affair; letters to George Mouzalon from the Bulgarian campaign. Not all thematic clusters, however, can be assigned a date. More than thirty letters from Ep. 150 until at least Ep. 186, occasioned by the absence of George Mouzalon due to illness, present a particular difficulty I cannot resolve. Ep. 180 is datable to early to mid 1253 and Epp. 183–85 belong to the late autumn of 1253. It would appear that at least this section of the letters to Mouzalon, as well as the letters to him from the Bulgarian campaign, follow chronological order.

The Datable Letters and Clusters of Letters

Ep. 1: before autumn 1241. This letter to Blemmydes is the opening one in the Laurentian epistolary collection and speaks (lines 40–44) of the

---

[33] See the observations by modern editors on the collections containing the letters of John Mauropous and the emperor Manuel II Palaiologos: Karpozilos 1990:30; Dennis 1977:xx.

beginning of Theodore's education. It was copied before the earliest datable letter (Ep. 2) and appears to be the earliest piece in the correspondence with Blemmydes and in the entire Laurentian collection.

Thematic cluster (Epp. 2 and 8): Constantine Klaudioupolites, metropolitan bishop of Ephesos and patriarch-elect of Antioch (1241–43). Epp. 2 and 8 to Blemmydes ridicule an anonymous metropolitan bishop of Ephesos. Ep. 2 describes him as a venal man who "wished to be a bishop over the eparchies of Cilicia" – that is, the Greek orthodox patriarch of Antioch – but says his ordination was postponed due to the death of the consecrator.[34] Ep. 8 continues the story. Theodore notifies Blemmydes that he read on Wednesday of Cheesefare Week the letter of resignation of a certain bishop, nicknamed "Grand Hammerer" (*megas sphyristes*), from the sees of Ephesos and Antioch.[35] The letter was brought to the meeting of the court by his nephew nicknamed "Little Hammerer" (*smikros sphyristopoulos*). The person about to be ordained patriarch of Antioch in Ep. 2 was, therefore, also a metropolitan bishop of Ephesos. According to Ep. 8, he wished to return to his homeland in Herakleia in Thrace in "order to reside on Mount Ganos and converse in a more hermitic fashion with John." Mount Ganos, on the European side of the Hellespont, had a well-known monastic community, and the resigning bishop evidently wished to enter a monastery dedicated to John the Baptist. Epp. 10 and 11 continue to ridicule an anonymous metropolitan of Ephesos, although these letters make clear that the individual has recently been ordained and is about to assume his episcopal functions.

Scholars have traditionally interpreted all four letters (Epp. 2, 8, 10, and 11) as referring to the metropolitan of Ephesos, Nikephoros, a correspondent of Theodore and briefly patriarch (1260) of Constantinople in exile.[36] Theodore had strained relations with Nikephoros over a long period of time, something that is seen both in letters addressed to him written during his coemperorship and in a satirical sketch that he composed during his sole reign (the fifth of his six essays).[37] Yet the career of Nikephoros also

---

[34] The region of Cilicia and the kingdom of Cilician Armenia formed part of the ecclesiastical province of the patriarchate of Antioch. See Devreesse 1945; Korobeinikov 2003:202–05. Blem., *Autobiographia*, I, 72 (p. 36), refers to the Armenians in the area as "Cilicians."

[35] The *hapax* σφυριστής seems derived from σφῦρα, "hammer," and the rare adjective σφυριστός, "hammered," attested in the hymnographic commentaries of Akakios Sabaites from the Nicaean period. See LBJ, 7 (2011):1726. A similar use of allusive language is found in Ep. 11. The individual who occupied the see of Ephesos is said to have had an "iron staff" (Psalm 2:9), with which he "beat with a hammer" (ἐσφυρηλάτησε) his flock and other bishops.

[36] See, for example, Heisenberg 1900:215.

[37] Ep. 105, addressed to Nikephoros, is filled with irony. Ep. 108 mentions that Theodore has read the bishop's letters to John Vatatzes that offended the emperor and the patriarch. See also

not correspond with the information found in Epp. 2 and 8. Nikephoros Pamphilos, as was his full name, was an archdeacon in the imperial clergy of John Vatatzes. He was one of the three candidates proposed by the synod sometime between 1241 and 1243 for the vacancy in the office of patriarch of Constantinople. John III Vatatzes, just like his son, disapproved of this choice: "How could someone tolerate him as patriarch when one cannot do so as an archdeacon?"[38] The emperor instead selected another member of the imperial clergy, the head chaplain (*protopappas*) Manuel, who was ordained between August and October 1243 as Patriarch Manuel II (r. 1243–54).[39] Nikephoros was compensated, probably in 1243 or 1244, with selection as the metropolitan bishop of Ephesos.[40] Nikephoros' career knew no election to the patriarchate of Antioch, subsequent resignation, or monastic vocation.

The target of Theodore's critique in Epp. 2 and 8 emerges from a little-known canonical text. Commenting on canons 3 of St. Cyril and 16 of the Council in 861, convened by the patriarch Photios in the church of the Holy Apostles, the metropolitan of Kyzikos, Theodore Skoutariotes (second half of the thirteenth century and possibly identical with the author of *Synopsis chronike*), pointed out that an erring bishop should not be permitted to adopt the monastic habit in order to avoid an ecclesiastical sanction. One of the two recent examples he gave was the metropolitan bishop of Ephesos, Constantine, who had adopted the monastic habit under the name Cyril, but the synod of Patriarch Manuel decided to recall him and subjected him to an unspecified sanction.[41] The decision of

---

Ep. 32.4 (p. 41) addressed to Blemmydes. The satirical Essay 5 in **V**, f. 67r–v, has been edited and translated by Agapitos and Angelov 2018. By contrast, Blemmydes has only good words to say about Nikephoros in his *Autobiography*: "a real bishop, without pretense, without frills, and without falsehood."

[38] Pach. I, 165.22–23.

[39] Nikephoros Kallistos Xanthopoulos in PG, vol. 147, col. 465D; Laurent 1969:138–39.

[40] On Nikephoros' career, see Blem., *Autobiographia*, I, 68 (p. 34); Pach. I, 165.18–23. On his name, see Darrouzès 1984:184. Blem., *Autobiographia*, I, 69.1 (p. 35) writes that Patriarch Germanos' death (1240) occurred before the appointment of Nikephoros as metropolitan bishop of Ephesos.

[41] Lauriotes 1901:54. Laurent, *Regestes*, 1327, doubted that the patriarch was Manuel II and preferred instead Arsenios, but there is no reason to explain away the phrase ἐπὶ τοῦ πατριάρχου κῦρ Μανουήλ. The other example, in addition to Constantine of Ephesos, is Nicholas, the bishop of Vonditza in southern Epiros, who adopted the monastic habit and resided "for years" in the monastery of St. Michael in Anaplous, until Patriarch Arsenios and his synod recalled him from his monastery and restored him to his bishopric without the right to consecrate. Laurent, *Regestes*, 1369, dated this episode to second patriarchate of Arsenios (1261–64), yet it could have occurred during his first patriarchate (1254–60) as well, because the monastery of St. Michael in Anaplous on the Bosporus functioned during the

the resigning metropolitan of Ephesos to become a monk on Mount Ganos fits closely with the canonical commentary. The patriarch must be Manuel II (r. 1243–54) rather than Manuel I (r. 1217–22), because no bishop of Ephesos by the name of Constantine is known during the latter's patriarchate.[42] The metropolitan Constantine in question was none other than Constantine Klaudioupolites, a vengeful personal enemy of Nikephoros Blemmydes. According to the latter's autobiography, Klaudioupolites was a different character than his predecessor, the metropolitan of Ephesos, Manasses, who had initiated Blemmydes in monastic life and eventually appointed him as abbot of the monastery of St. Gregory the Miracle Worker near Ephesos. Klaudioupolites gave credence to slanders circulated by Blemmydes' student Krateros, who charged his teacher with stealing money from the estate of the deceased Manasses. Blemmydes was cleared by Hikanatos, the governor of the theme of Thrakesion, but Klaudioupolites kept giving him trouble and forced him to relocate to a monastery on the island of Samos. In addition, Klaudioupolites took seriously the accusations made by the deacon Leo Adralestos that Blemmydes had murdered Manasses and was a Manichean. Only after the emperor John Vatatzes intervened and banned Klaudioupolites from entering in the monastery of St. Gregory the Miracle Worker did Blemmydes return from Samos.[43] Subsequently, another governor of the Thrakesion theme, John Komnenos Kantakouzenos, connived with Klaudioupolites and renewed the charges of embezzlement. Blemmydes was detained and his residence was searched for a hidden treasure. Once again, John Vatatzes offered support and banned the metropolitan from Blemmydes' properties. The emperor then provided for Blemmydes' seaborne voyage to Mt. Athos and the Balkans.[44]

The careers of the governors (*doukes*) of the Thrakesion theme point to Klaudioupolites' term in office in Ephesos: he was a metropolitan bishop from 1238–39 until *at least* 1241, the earliest possible time for Kantakouzenos to have assumed the post.[45] As we will see shortly, Klaudioupolites seems to have become the patriarch-elect of Antioch in 1241 and submitted his resignation

---

period of the Latin rule and received donations from the emperor John Vatatzes. See *Synopsis chronike*, 509.3–4.

[42] See the survey of metropolitans of Ephesos by Pargoire 1905.

[43] Blem., *Autobiographia*, I, 50–57 (pp. 27–30).

[44] Blem., *Autobiographia*, I, 58–59 (pp. 30–31).

[45] The documentary evidence has been surveyed by Ahrweiler 1965:142–45. Hikanatos is attested as governor in July 1239. The previous governor is reported as deceased in September 1238. Between March and May 1240, the governor was Manuel Kontophre. In June 1241 the function was performed by George Kammytzovoukis. See MM, IV, 254–55 (Dölger-Wirth, *Regesten*, 1772). Kantakouzenos is attested as governor already on November 1, 1242 (see the document

in 1242 or 1243, when he took the monastic habit. He was subsequently recalled, disciplined by Patriarch Manuel II, and replaced as metropolitan bishop of Ephesos by the archdeacon of the imperial clergy, Nikephoros.

Ep. 2: autumn 1241. This letter describes how "the person who wished to be a bishop over the eparchies of Cilicia" (Klaudioupolites) – a greedy clergyman practicing simony – was about to receive ordination when his consecrator passed away. The consecrator was the patriarch of Constantinople who normally ordained the patriarch of Antioch in this period.[46] Given that Klaudioupolites was metropolitan of Ephesos from 1238–39 to at least 1241, the date of the letter can be narrowed down to the deaths of two successive patriarchs of Constantinople in exile: Patriarch Germanos II, who died in the summer of 1240, and his successor, Methodios, who passed away in the autumn of 1241.[47] Methodios' death is more probable insofar as we can judge from the ecclesiastical negotiations with the king of Cilician Armenia and the Armenian *katholikos*, negotiations known from three letters sent to Armenia by the patriarchate in Nicaea over a period of almost ten years.[48] A letter addressed by Patriarch Germanos shortly before his death (Vitalien Laurent dates the letter to 1239 or 1240) to the *katholikos* of Armenia, Constantine, mentions the arrival of an embassy sent by King Hetoum I carrying a letter from the patriarch of Antioch, who encouraged the negotiations and was still alive.[49] It is unlikely, therefore, that Germanos arranged for the ordination of a new patriarch of Antioch. Germanos dispatched the metropolitan of Melitene, John, to Cilician Armenia. On his return, after Germanos had passed away, an embassy arrived from Armenia. This Armenian embassy evidently came in the spring of 1241, because in May 1241 the patriarchal synod, in the absence of a patriarch, addressed a letter to the king of Armenia, Hetoum, and dispatched the metropolitan of Melitene back to Armenia.[50] Either John of Melitene or the Armenian embassy could have brought the news of the death of the patriarch of Antioch, a key intermediary in the exchange. Regrettably, little is known about the history of the orthodox (Melkite) patriarchate of Antioch in the early 1240s. The patriarch who passed away

published by Wilson and Darrouzès 1968:20–21). Pargoire (1905:289–90) dated the ending of Klaudioupolites' episcopate to "1239 or a little later."
[46] On the twelfth-century practice, see Pitsakis 1991:92–94.
[47] Laurent (1969:136–39) based these dates mostly from the patriarchal *pinakes*.
[48] For the dossier of the three letters, see 254, n. 120.
[49] Lagopates 1913:354–57; Bartikian 2002:63–71 (Laurent, *Regestes*, 1290).
[50] The letter of May 1241, see Vat. gr. 1455, ff. 27r–29v. The exchange of embassies in the 1240s is summarized in Patriarch Manuel II's letter of the winter of 1247–48. See Bartikian 2002:79–81.

may have been the long-serving Symeon, who divided his time between Antioch, Cilician Armenia, and the empire of Nicaea. Symeon is last attested in the period 1234–36, and the next known patriarch, David, is documented in 1246.[51] In the second half of 1241, Germanos' successor as patriarch of Constantinople in exile was ordained: Methodios, the abbot of the monastery of Hyakinthos in Nicaea. Methodios served for only three months before he passed away.[52] He evidently intended to ordain Constantine Klaudioupolites as the new patriarch of Antioch. As we learn from Ep. 2, he died before performing the inauguration ritual.

Ep. 8: early 1242 or early 1243. This letter dating to the pre-Lenten season gives the next stage in the story: Klaudioupolites resigns from the metropolitan bishopric of Ephesos and his position as patriarch-elect of Antioch. In his letter of resignation, the repenting bishop expressed a desire to take up residence as a monk on Mount Ganos. He also wished to return to, and even become the bishop of, nearby Herakleia in Thrace, his native city. One wonders whether Klaudioupolites' decision to become a monk with the name Cyril was voluntary, given that John Vatatzes took the side of Blemmydes in the dispute between them. Klaudioupolites was later disciplined by the new patriarch, Manuel II, whose appointment between August and October 1243 is a *terminus ante quem* for the letter. This dating fits with the mention in the letter of Blemmydes' new monastic foundation at Emathia, called here ἡσυχαστήριον, which is also how Blemmydes describes it. In the letter Theodore reports hearsay to the effect that this site was at "a difficult place, hard to access" (information confirmed by Blemmydes) and sends barley for Blemmydes' horses. It is known from Blemmydes' autobiography that the building of the monastery at Emathia took seven years and nine months. Joseph Munitiz has hypothetically dated its foundation to the summer of 1241.[53]

[51] For example, in 1206–07 Symeon was in Antioch and in 1217 in Armenia. See Cahen 1940:612, 619; Rey 1896:388–89. He accepted the primacy of the papacy, because a manuscript note in an Athonite codex states that a decision of the synod of Patriarch Manuel I reappointed him to his office (Laurent, *Regestes*, 1220, dates the note to 1217–18). Symeon is last attested in 1234–36. He took part in the religious disputes in Nymphaion in 1234 and gave his permission for the elevation of the rank of the Bulgarian church to that of an autocephalous patriarchate in 1235. The metropolitan of Corfu Bardanes wrote to him in the winter of 1235–36 when he was surrounded by schismatics (Armenians?). See Golubovich 1919:444; Laurent, *Regestes*, 1282; Hoeck and Loenertz 1965:205–06. Pope Innocent IV sent a letter on August 9, 1246, to David, the earliest known successor of Symeon. See Haluščinskyj and Wojnar 1962:74–75; and also Cahen 1940:684, nn. 15–16; Nasrallah 1968:4, n. 10.
[52] Nikephoros Kallistos Xanthopoulos in PG, vol. 147, col. 465D; Laurent 1969:137–38.
[53] Munitiz 1988:23–24.

Thematic cluster (Epp. 10 and 11): Arrival of Nikephoros as the new metropolitan of Ephesos (late 1243–44). These letters, addressed to Blemmydes, ridicule a newly ordained metropolitan bishop of Ephesos. Ep. 10 is a playful commentary on the dream vision of Nebuchadnezzar in the second chapter of the book of Daniel. Ep. 11 derides the greed and lack of education of the bishop about to arrive in Ephesos. The man could be either Constantine Klaudioupolites, in the eventuality that he was simultaneously subjected to ecclesiastical punishment and temporarily reinstated, or his successor Nikephoros. The expression "spirit of the North" (Ep. 11.11–12, based on Ezekiel 1:4) can allude either to Klaudioupolites returning from Mount Ganos or the archdeacon of the imperial clergy, Nikephoros, coming to Ephesos from Nicaea, the seat of the patriarchate. The letter makes an allusion to the troubles of Blemmydes during Klaudioupolites' term of office in Ephesos. Blemmydes writes in his *Autobiography* that his accusers even searched the cesspit of his monastery in the hope of finding hidden gold.[54] In a similar manner, Ep. 11.16–17 states that "all the power of the garbage-collectors will shudder before his (that is, the metropolitan's) face, and the *bows* of the abbots are to be *destroyed*" (Ps. 36:15). To whom, then, does this letter refer? The recognizable faults of Klaudioupolites, such as his arrogance and fondness for money, are criticisms Theodore levied against other ecclesiastics. Two considerations tilt the balance in favor of Nikephoros. First, Theodore creates the impression of a new incumbent: "the person who is from now onward the metropolitan of Ephesos."[55] Second, Theodore describes the metropolitan as a man who has embraced "pure, genuine philosophy" and stands above the filth of grammar, poetry, and "Aristotelian confusion."[56] In a letter addressed to Nikephoros filled with unease and tension (Ep. 105), Theodore referred to the religious learning of his addressee and revealed that he himself was different: he knew Plato and kept reading philosophy. At the same time, he assured Nikephoros that he valued the Holy Scriptures more highly and that "inner learning" was true wisdom.

Ep. 49 (1241–46). This long and fascinating letter to Akropolites, which opens the dossier of epistles addressed to him in the Laurentian collection, refers to the beginnings of Theodore's studies with him. The letter is a veiled appeal to Akropolites to take over Theodore's unfinished education in philosophy. It describes a celestial vision, in which Lady Virtue tells Theodore that he has not yet adopted the ways of philosophy, reason, and

---

[54] Blem., *Autobiographia*, I, 61 (pp. 31–32); Blemmydes' letter to Patriarch Manuel II, in Blem. Ep., 327.63–64. See Munitiz 1988:78; Munitiz 2003:372.
[55] Ep. 11.57 (p. 16).   [56] Ep. 11.41–45 (p. 16).

intelligence (lines 10–17). The date of the letter, therefore, depends on the timing of Akropolites beginning to tutor the heir to the throne. Scholars have traditionally adopted Heisenberg's view that Theodore Laskaris took lessons from Akropolites after the latter's return from the Balkans in 1246.[57] However, given that Theodore received instruction under Blemmydes from 1238 or 1239 until about 1241 (see Chapter 4, pp. 81–82), it is implausible that the heir to the throne would have waited several years before attaching himself to Blemmydes' student Akropolites, who was already a teacher. The letter was most probably written not long after 1241, with 1246 being a *terminus ante quem*.

Thematic cluster (Epp. 21, 22, and 26): Invitations to Blemmydes (1244–46?). These three letters bid Blemmydes to present himself at court without mentioning the reason. The dating can be only hypothetical and hence is followed by question marks.

Epp. 21 and 22: 1244–45 (?). These two letters – of similar length and copied next to each other – ask Blemmydes to appear before the emperor John Vatatzes. Blemmydes is called "our father and teacher" (Ep. 21.6). His presence at the court is said to be capable of bringing "a great profit" (Ep. 22.7–8). Costas Constantinides has connected the two epistles with the offer of a teaching post extended by Patriarch Manuel II and emanating from the emperor.[58] The offer is known solely from Blemmydes' letter of response to the patriarch, in which he resolutely declined the honor to head an education establishment for boys and girls.[59] Blemmydes notes that he faced an ecclesiastical penalty if he did not accept the appointment, which fits with the strong language in one of Theodore's letters to Blemmydes (Ep. 21.2: ἀναγκάζομεν). In the letter to the patriarch, Blemmydes points out that he returned from his journey in the Balkans (1242–44) only because he was summoned (again, a noteworthy correspondence with Theodore's epistles), vents his frustration with the behavior of his former students Krateros and Romanos, and criticizes the opportunities available to educated individuals in the empire of Nicaea.[60] The teaching offer extended to Blemmydes has traditionally been dated to 1244.[61] If this

---

[57] For Heisenberg's view, see Akrop. II, VII–VIII.   [58] Constantinides 1982:14 n. 54, 15 n. 58.

[59] The letter has been published by Festa, Ep., Appendix III, 325–29, and translated by Munitiz 2003.

[60] Festa, Ep., Appendix III, 325.5–7, 328.92–329.117. On the chronology of Blemmydes' journey to the Balkans, see 269, n. 107.

[61] Laurent, *Regestes*, 1305 (the teaching offer of 1244 is seen as a compensation after Blemmydes did not become the patriarch: see Blem., *Autobiographia*, I, 69 [p. 35]). The teaching offer has been dated similarly to 1244 by Munitiz 2003:369. Constantinides (1982:14–15) preferred 1245–46.

was the reason why Theodore wrote the two urgent letters of request, as it seems likely, then the two letters date to 1244–45.

Ep. 26: 1246–47 (?). This letter to Blemmydes mentions Theodore welcoming John Vatatzes and George Akropolites back to the Hellespont, and once again invites Blemmydes to the court. A philosophical discussion with Akropolites is said to have taken place, which suggests that instruction under his direction had already begun. Costas Constantinides has dated the letter to late 1246, when John Vatatzes and his secretary Akropolites campaigned in the Balkans and secured the peaceful territorial expansion of the empire of Nicaea over large areas in Macedonia and Thrace. The date is possible, yet not certain, because the letter makes no reference to this historic event. John Vatatzes campaigned in Thrace in 1247, as well, and Akropolites may have accompanied the senior emperor in the Balkans on another unknown occasion – for example, when he went on a diplomatic mission to Constantinople.[62]

Ep. 107: 1243–49. Following a petition by Blemmydes, abbot of the monastery of St. Gregory the Miracle Worker, this letter, addressed to the metropolitan bishop of Ephesos, Nikephoros, annuls the illegal sale of an agricultural plot of land (named Anachoma) by a former abbot of the monastery to a cleric of the metropolitan church of Ephesos. The reason for the illegality of the sale is not given. The monastery (that is, its abbot Blemmydes) was to reimburse the buyer for the money paid at the time of the transaction. In case the land plot had been converted into a vineyard, the monastery was not to be asked to reimburse the buyer for the agricultural improvements, because the profit from the vineyard already provided sufficient compensation. The *termini* for the letter are the appointment of Nikephoros as metropolitan of Ephesos (the earliest possible date is the second half of 1243, the time of ordination of Patriarch Manuel II) and the transfer of Blemmydes to his new foundation at Emathia, which has been dated to around the spring of 1249.[63] The letter uses the technical term "ordinance" (πρόσταγμα), a type of imperial document, even though it lacks the usual diplomatic features.

Ep. 18: 1252. This letter to Blemmydes mentions the return of an embassy from the papacy that brought proposals for a union of the churches. These proposals can be identified as Pope Innocent IV's response to the Nicaean chapters of recognition and petition (*capitula recognitionis et petitionis*) resulting from the discussion with John of Parma in Nymphaion in the

---

[62] Constantinides 1982:14 n. 57, 15 n. 58, 17–18. See the call for caution by Macrides 2007:10.
[63] Munitiz 1988:24. Dölger-Wirth, *Regesten*, 1823, date the letter to the period 1241 (?)–48.

spring of 1250.[64] The metropolitan bishop of Sardis, Andronikos, is reported in the letter to have been particularly enthusiastic about accepting papal primacy. Andronikos took part in the Nicaean delegations to the papacy in 1250–52 and in 1253–54.[65] In the summer of 1250, the first Nicaean embassy departed to meet Innocent in Lyons, but was detained in Apulia in the aftermath of Frederick II's death (December 1250) for a year and a half; it finally met Innocent IV in Perugia in early 1252 and then returned to the empire of Nicaea with the pope's answers.[66] This is the time of composition of Ep. 18. A reference to the return of the second Nicaean embassy of 1253–54 to Pope Innocent IV is impossible. Ep. 18 dates before the embassy of Berthold of Hohenburg, but the second embassy came back in the middle of 1254 when Berthold had already departed.[67] The mention of a shipwreck in the author's life, with which the letter opens, is probably a reference to the death of his wife in the same year.

Ep. 118: 1252. This letter, to the metropolitan bishop of Philadelphia, Phokas, mentions the return "from Europe" of Andronikos of Sardis, an ambassador to the papacy. As in the above case, the first Nicaean embassy of 1250–52 is the only possibility, because the letter predates the embassy of Berthold of Hohenburg. The letter was dispatched from Anatolia to the Balkans, because in 1252 Phokas accompanied John Vatatzes during the long campaign against Michael of Epiros.[68]

Thematic cluster (Epp. 24, 57–61, 72, 94, 132): Death of his wife Elena (spring or early summer 1252). A number of letters in the Laurentian collection – one to Blemmydes, five to Akropolites, one to the patriarch Manuel II, and one to the monk Akakios – communicate, or echo, Theodore's deep distress caused by the death of his wife Elena. She passed away sometime between Christmas 1250 (the birth of her son John Laskaris) and the autumn of 1253 (Berthold of Hohenburg's embassy mentioned by the heading of Theodore's *Moral Pieces*).[69] The precise chronology emerges from Theodore's letters to Akropolites.[70] Four consecutively copied letters (Epp. 57–60) reveal the shock of the author after the sudden passing of his wife. According to Ep. 58, Theodore's grief is made even more unbearable due to the absence of his father and Akropolites. The author alludes to his deceased spouse: "My resplendent light has set in a dark abode, leaving to

---

[64] Franchi 1981:83–87, 193–99.   [65] Franchi 1981:136–7, 232 n. 366.
[66] Franchi 1981:180–92, 214–15.
[67] Franchi (1981:249) dates the return to June or July 1254 on the basis of a papal document.
[68] Akrop. I, §49 (p. 92.4).   [69] On the birth of John Laskaris, see 289, n. 5.
[70] The chronology has already been discussed by Angelov, Mor. P., 237–41.

me no hope of its rising."[71] He asks rhetorically: "Where is the flower of my youth? Where is the beehive of the words and wishes of my heart? Everything has disappeared, everything has gone leaving me behind truly alone."[72] Ep. 59 presents Akropolites and John Vatatzes still being away from Theodore. Akropolites has already comforted the author in writing. A similar reference to a comforting epistle from Akropolites is made in Ep. 61, which must form part of the thematic cluster. In Ep. 59, Theodore writes that by the command of his father he has left Nymphaion (the site of his mourning), changed his clothes (his mourning clothes), and resumed eating meat. Theodore was already on the move, refers to his departure from the "three-gated" Thebe (Atramyttion) for the "celebrated Troy," and mentions his expectation of laying his eyes on the Hellespont, which, he states, separated him from Akropolites.

The military campaign against Epiros in the years 1252 and 1253 is the only lengthy period spent by John Vatatzes and Akropolites in the Balkans in the period between Christmas 1250 and autumn 1253. The emperor left Anatolia in 1252, wintered in the Balkans, and returned to Anatolia in the late autumn of 1253 immediately after the public trial of Michael Palaiologos in Philippi in the autumn of that year.[73] In Ep. 58 Theodore gives rhetorical emphasis to his sorrow with the proverb "things last year are always better." The Byzantine year began on September 1 and, therefore, Elena could have died either before September 1, 1252, or September 1, 1253. September 1252 is the only valid *terminus ante quem*, because otherwise Epp. 59–61, as well as Akropolites' comforting letters, would have had to have been written within the span of two months at most, which is impossible. Furthermore, none of Epp. 57–61 mentions Theodore's expectation of meeting his correspondent, which contrasts with letters to Akropolites in which the author rejoices at his imminent arrival (Epp. 83–85). The death of his wife Elena in Nymphaion must have occurred in the spring or early summer of 1252, soon after the beginning of the campaign. Theodore felt incapacitated by towering grief and his sorrowful messages reached his father. The insistence of John Vatatzes (Ep. 59) that his son ought to stop mourning and resume his usual lifestyle is explicable by his concern that the junior coemperor should be effective in performing his duties during his father's absence.

Ep. 57: 1252. This letter to Akropolites mentions a divine retribution that has befallen the author who declares his wish to die, just as in the dramatic closure of the *Moral Pieces*.

---

[71] Ep. 58.14–15 (p. 87).   [72] Ep. 58.18–19 (p. 87).   [73] See Chapter 8, pp. 123–24.

Ep. 58: 1252. This letter to Akropolites alludes to the passing of his wife and mentions the absence of both Akropolites and his father.

Ep. 59: 1252. This letter reveals that Akropolites has already comforted Theodore, who asks him to keep him informed whether his father has been pleased by the fact that he has left Nymphaion, changed his clothes, and resumed eating meat.

Ep. 60: 1252. This brief letter to Akropolites speaks of inconsolable sorrow and thoughts of death.

Ep. 24: 1252. This letter to Blemmydes echoes the sorrowful mood of Epp. 57–60 and is especially close in spirit and motifs to the *Moral Pieces.* Noteworthy are the mentions of his recent separation from his soul mate, a tomb, and the author's dramatic wish to die.

Ep. 61: 1252–53. This letter to Akropolites speaks of a "flood of sorrow" that Akropolites had encouraged Theodore to cure with frequent bathing. The letter continues the theme of Epp. 57–60, but it postdates these letters, because it implies a second comforting epistle by Akropolites.

Ep. 132: 1252-53. This letter to the monk Akakios refers to the great sorrow of the author, which Akakios had tried to dispel in a consolatory work, and resembles Ep. 72 in arguing that sorrow can lead to philosophical thinking and knowledge of God.

Ep. 72: 1252-53. This letter to Akropolites is related to Epp. 57–61 to the same addressee and makes the further point that sorrow has had a sobering effect on the author, leading him to philosophy.

Ep. 94: 1253. This comforting letter to Patriarch Manuel II is provoked by the death of the latter's son and mentions that the patriarch had offered solace to the author one year earlier on a similar occasion. The letter, therefore, was written one year after Elena's death.

Long letter to Akropolites (Tartaglia, Op. rhet., 2–22): 1253. Toward the end of the letter, Theodore mentions Akropolites' worries about his desire for flight from the world (κόσμος). Akropolites had evidently understood that the heir to the throne intended to become a monk. Theodore dismissed the concerns by stating that flight from the world does not necessarily mean a monastic vocation.[74] This is not the first time that Theodore spoke about flight from the world in a letter to Akropolites.[75] However, the exchange reflected in the letter seems to be linked with the death of his wife and, in particular, with the expression of preference for a life of solitude and contemplation in his *Response to Some Friends Pressing*

---

[74] Tartaglia, Op. rhet., 19.415–21.463.   [75] See Ep. 54.22 (p. 79).

Him to Find a Bride (1252–53). This dating is supported by the allusion in the long letter to the slanderous machinations of Theodore Philes (see below).

Thematic cluster (Epp. 36–39, 77–78, 80, long letter to Akropolites): the Theodore Philes affair (1253). A series of letters to Blemmydes and Akropolites relates to the bitter conflict between the heir to the throne and Theodore Philes, who was appointed between 1248 and 1252 as the Nicaean governor of Thessalonica and the region around it holding the title of *praitor*. Philes succeeded the deceased *megas domestikos* Andronikos Palaiologos in this position.[76] The outlines of the conflict emerge most vividly before our eyes in Epp. 77, 78, and 80, all addressed to Akropolites. Ep. 77 is a satire filled with sexual innuendo lampooning a powerful man residing in "present-day Hellas" and the "land of the Myrmidons," whom Theodore Laskaris blames for the murder of his close associate Tribides. In Ep. 78 we discover the identity of the derided individual (Philes) and learn that he has charged Theodore Laskaris with an amorous liaison (*eros*). No specific details of this allegation are given. The coemperor vows in Ep. 78 to punish Philes and notifies Akropolites that he has complained to his father, the senior emperor John Vatatzes. The sequel is found in Ep. 80, a famous letter in which Theodore Laskaris shares his impressions from a visit to the ruins of ancient Pergamon. Here, he refers in passing at the end to an unspecified sanction by the senior emperor against Philes, nick-named "scion of goats" (*tragophylon*). When did the exchange of accusations between Theodore Laskaris and Theodore Philes take place? A clue can be found in his long letter to Akropolites, datable to 1253. Addressing his tutor, who was in the Balkans at the time, Theodore speaks of a scheming and deceitful person trying to drive a wedge between the two of them. He was confident that Akropolites would ignore the calumny.[77] This calumniator must be the governor of Thessalonica, Theodore Philes, with whom Theodore Laskaris was trading accusations. It was, therefore, in 1253 – at a time when John Vatatzes and his generals were in Macedonia during the campaign against Michael of Epiros and visited Thessalonica – that the conflict between Theodore Laskaris and Theodore Philes flared up.

Four letters to Blemmydes (Epp. 36–39) pertaining to the Philes affair also date to 1253. In Ep. 36 Theodore writes that he read allegations against

---

[76] Acrop. I, §46 (p. 84.15–16); Macrides 2007:99, 242 n. 2, 244 n. 7.
[77] Tartaglia, Op. rhet., 7.124–26. Theodore wrote: "Who would say or do something against me and you would not devour him? For there is no one who can do this whom you will not tear apart. Therefore, nobody approaching you will say anything against me."

him composed in the form of defamatory verses (tetrastichs) near Nym-phaion and professes his innocence. In Ep. 37 he asks Blemmydes to "examine and forgive." In Ep. 38 Theodore dramatically declares his willingness to go through an ordeal by red-hot iron, which was sometimes used in the thirteenth century for the judicial examination of cases of adultery.[78] Finally, we see in Ep. 39 Theodore rejoicing as he has regained the favor and trust of Blemmydes who has finally decided to ignore the slanderous allegation. The following convergences between Epp. 77 and 78 to Akropolites and the four letters to Blemmydes indicate that the unnamed accuser of Ep. 36 is Philes. First, the letters to Akropolites and Blemmydes use similar language in referring to "a stupid man" (λῆρος) who speaks "stupidities" (ληρήματα): see Ep. 36.33 (p. 45), 39.16 (p. 49), 78.23 (p. 105). Second, Theodore informs Blemmydes (Ep. 36.20–23 [p. 45]) that his accuser has charged him with a type of offense of which the opponent himself is guilty, which relates to the sexual slurs about Philes in Ep. 77 to Akropolites. Third, in Ep. 78.12 (p. 105) Theodore complains to Akropolites of his teacher's unforgiving harshness, which is Blemmydes' attitude emerging from the three letters to him.

Ep. 180: early to mid 1253. This epistle, addressed to Mouzalon, is the only firmly datable piece among the forty-three letters to Mouzalon attrib-uted by a manuscript note (placed after Ep. 192 in Laur., Conventi soppressi 627) to the period before Theodore's "full completeness of imperial rule." Ep. 180 mentions, among other things, a discussion at the court with members of the Lancia family, including Galvano Lancia and Boniface of Agliano. These are the Lancias expelled by King Conrad IV in the early months of 1253, who fled en masse to Byzantine Anatolia and sought the assistance of their relative, the empress Constanza-Anna.[79] We learn from the letter that there were disagreements among them as to the best course of action and that Theodore prevented them from traveling to Thessalonica (evidently in order to meet the senior emperor) and even to the city of Nicaea.

Ep. 125: autumn 1253. This letter to Andronikos, metropolitan of Sardis, refers to the arrival of Berthold of Hohenburg and explicitly mentions the autumn season.

Ep. 40: autumn 1253. This letter to Blemmydes describes a disputation with Berthold of Hohenburg that took place in one of the Anatolian palaces.

---

[78] See Chapter 6, p. 122.
[79] On the date of their flight to Nicaea, see Chapter 7, p. 140.

Thematic cluster (Epp. 83–86): Return of John Vatatzes and Akropolites from the Balkans (late autumn 1253). These four letters conclude the epistolary dossier addressed to Akropolites in the Laurentian collection and focus on the encounter in Asia Minor between Theodore and the returning senior emperor John Vatatzes accompanied by Akropolites. Theodore filled Epp. 83–84 with discussions of geometry and mechanics aimed at impressing his teacher Akropolites. Ep. 83.18–21 encourages Akropolites and John Vatatzes (still in Nicaea as Ep. 84 explicitly mentions) to take the direct route and be reunited with the author: Theodore is evidently in Nymphaion or Magnesia. According to Ep. 84, Theodore has been notified that the senior emperor has left Nicaea and has ordered Theodore to come and greet him. Theodore has already embarked on the journey. The expression ἔστ᾽ ἂν τοῖς τῶν μετεωρίων ὁρίοις πλησιάσειας may be a reference to a meeting point at the fortress of Meteorion along the main route from Nicaea to Magnesia. Ep. 85 is an expression of joy at the imminent encounter. In Ep. 86 Theodore sends his confidant Mouzalon to do obeisance to the senior emperor, announcing that he himself was about to arrive.

Ep. 183: late autumn 1253. This letter to Mouzalon announces that Theodore has dispatched his teacher – evidently Akropolites, who has just returned from the campaign in the Balkans – to see Mouzalon at an undisclosed location. The season of composition of Ep. 183 emerges from Epp. 184–185, with which it is closely related, and from the arrival of Akropolites from the Balkan campaign in the late autumn. It would appear, therefore, that at least some of the pre-1254 letters to Mouzalon were arranged chronologically. Ep. 180 can be dated securely to 1253 and Ep. 184 dates to December 12, 1253. The late autumn of 1254 is impossible, because of the emperor's accession in November 1254 (the cut-off point, indicated by a manuscript note, lies between Ep. 192 and Ep. 193).

Ep. 184: December 12, 1253. This letter informs Mouzalon of the improvement of the weather after a storm and mentions the commemoration of St. Spyridon, which falls on December 12 in the Byzantine liturgical calendar. The December date is also suggested by the allusion to the forthcoming feast of the Nativity of Christ (the expression used is ἔλευσις τοῦ Κυρίου).

Ep. 185: December 1253 or winter 1254. This brief letter mentions the return of Akropolites (see Ep. 183), who has already met with Mouzalon and has brought the joyful news of their encounter.

Ep. 187: January–October 1254. This letter of dedication of *Representation of the World, or Life* (first redaction), is probably to be dated to this period due to the chronological sequence of the letters.

Ep. 193: November–December 1254. This letter is the first one after the manuscript note in Laur., Convent soppressi 627 referring to the emperor's accession and therefore dates after November 3, 1254. It conveys the author's preoccupations as the reigning emperor after the major transition.[80]

Ep. 194: c. December 12, 1254. This letter, which precedes the letters from the Bulgarian front line, invites Mouzalon to Nicaea – probably in order to attend the emperor's advisory council mentioned by Akropolites and *Synopsis chronike*. Mouzalon is known to have advocated a surprise winter counterattack against the Bulgarians, contrary to the advice Theodore received from his great uncles Michael and Manuel Laskaris.[81] The mention of St. Spyridon suggests a date of around December 12. The letter opens with enigmatic references to plots and opposition against the emperor.

Ep. 195: December 1254–January 1255. This letter renews the invitation to Mouzalon. Mention is made of the winter season and the difficult travel conditions.

Thematic cluster (Epp. 199–210): Letters during the Bulgarian campaign (1255–56).

Theodore addressed more than ten letters to Mouzalon from the front line. The ordering of the letters follows the known sequence of events during the campaign against the Bulgarian tsar Michael Asen.[82] We see Theodore crossing the Hellespont and entering Thrace (Ep. 199), fighting with the Bulgarians, setting camp, and marching westward (Epp. 200–04), and summarizing his achievements before returning to Asia Minor at the end of the first year of campaigning (Ep. 205).

Ep. 198: winter 1255 (after February 1). According to this letter, the time for battles has now arrived. The emperor appears to be bound for the Hellespont, together with the army.

Ep. 199: winter 1255 (after February 1). This letter presents the emperor as having reached Thrace ("the western fields") and thanking St. Tryphon for his miracle with the winter lilies in Nicaea. Theodore evidently left Nicaea on or after the feast day of Tryphon (February 1). Noteworthy are the complaints he makes against his simpleminded military companions and about the motley ethnic composition of the army.

---

[80] A loose English translation can be found in Gardner 1912:307.

[81] Akrop. I, §55 (pp. 109–11). Details unreported by Akropolites are found in *Synopsis chronike*, 513.5–514.15.

[82] The letters have been discussed in more detail by Angelov 2013b:284–89.

Ep. 200: winter 1255. This letter speaks of a victory and confesses the author's unawareness of the identity of his enemies, who have fled into the mountains. The advancing Nicaean troops in the winter of 1255 defeated the surprised watch posts of the Bulgarians in Thrace who, along with the Bulgarian tsar, fled to the Haimos Mountains.[83]

Ep. 201: winter 1255. This letter mentions Theodore's expectation of arriving at Kryvous (Krivo) and Stenimachos, which is known to have occurred in the winter of 1255 after the battle with Michael Asen's army mentioned in the previous letter.[84]

Ep. 202: summer 1255. This emotional letter complains of the scorching heat at the army camp on the Maritsa River, which the author contrasts to the freezing cold weather at the beginning of the campaign.

Ep. 203: summer 1255. This letter accompanies the gift to George Mouzalon of a handsome horse bred in Albania. Its date emerges from its position between Ep. 202 and Ep. 204, as well as the mention of the campaign against the Bulgarians.

Ep. 204: summer 1255. This letter, the longest one written during the campaign, narrates recent events during the war and mentions the author's current location: Philippi along the *via Egnatia*. Theodore alludes to the experiences of St. Paul in Philippi and describes (lines 43–45) the sight in front of his eyes: the Rhodope Mountains ("the impassable Bulgarian mountains of folly"), the mountain of Orpheus (Mount Pangaion), and the land of Philip and Alexander (Macedonia). The author writes that he is in a hurry to reach Serres and hopes that in four days he will arrive in Melnik, achieving a victory over the Bulgarians. The historical context is well known from the *History* of Akropolites. In the spring of 1255, Theodore Laskaris had requested the support of the troops stationed in Macedonia. The generals Alexios Strategopoulos and Constantine Tornikes advanced from Serres toward Tzepaina (Tsepena) in the Rhodope Mountains, but turned back after they were frightened during the march, abandoning their baggage to Bulgarian shepherds and swineherds. They refused to follow Theodore's order to resume the march.[85] Ep. 204 lampoons the cowardly conduct of the two generals, making a general reference to their families: "the lawless Strategopouloi" and "ill-famed Tornikai" (lines 52–56, 109–20). Theodore writes that "the disobedience of the lawless individuals, leaving the army

---

[83] Akrop. I, §56 (pp. 111.21–112.16).
[84] Akrop. I, §57 (p. 113.19–25) explicitly mentions Stenimachos, but not Kryvous.
[85] Akrop. I, §57 (p. 114.2–19).

alone, made the Bulgarian dogs devastate our lands, and for this reason now a beginning of troubles fell upon us" (lines 59–61). Mention is made of the "lawless *praitor*," that is, Theodore Philes (line 106) who is evidently still in office. According to Akropolites, the rebellion of Dragotas in the region of Melnik in Macedonia and his siege of the Nicaean garrison in the town forced Theodore Laskaris to lead a relief expedition. Setting off from Adrianople sometime in the summer of 1255, he managed in twelve days to reach Serres, defeat the Bulgarians at the Rupel Pass (where Dragotas perished), and raise the siege of Melnik. Subsequently, Theodore visited Thessalonica and made a tour of western Macedonia, returning to Serres. Ep. 204 was written during a stopover in Philippi before Theodore reached Serres and Melnik.[86]

Ep. 205: late autumn 1255. This letter celebrates the achievements of the campaign in 1255. It must date to a time not long before Theodore crossed the Hellespont late in the year and returned to Asia Minor. He spent Christmas 1255 in Lampsakos, where he had made a series of promotions and appointments.[87]

Ep. 206: late autumn 1255. This letter announces to Mouzalon the author's imminent return.

Ep. 207: late autumn 1255. This letter, too, notifies Mouzalon of Theodore's imminent return, partly in the form of an imaginary dialogue between the two correspondents. He mentions the "Scythian Cleopas" (that is, his trusted Cuman general Cleopas), whom the author has sent to Asia Minor ahead of his own arrival. Cleopas is the same man who in the spring of 1256 would lead a detachment of Cuman troops against fellow Cumans allied with the Bulgarians and inflict a crushing defeat on them along the Regina River in eastern Thrace.[88]

Ep. 208: late autumn 1255, or 1256. This letter mentions that Theodore has sent to Mouzalon in Asia Minor an individual whose "shameful deeds" (αἶσχη) are compared to the fall of Adam and Eve. In addition, it reports that the bishop of Didymoteichon preached to the night guards of the fortress. Mouzalon was told to correct this individual's errors but also to grant a pound of gold coins to the "mentioned" person. Whether the rewarded person was the reprimanded man referred to in the rest of the letter, or another individual known solely to the letter-bearer, is not clear. Theodore Laskaris visited Didymoteichon in late 1255 before his

---

[86] Akrop. I, §58 (pp. 114–17), §59 (pp. 117.18–118.22).
[87] Akrop. I, §60 (p. 124.1–24). On this letter, see Dragoumis 1911–12:213.
[88] This information is found solely in the *Synopsis chronike*, 524.5–11.

unsuccessful attack on Tzepaina. But he may have toured the area again in the spring and summer of 1256 while the army was encamped along the Regina River in eastern Thrace.[89] Both late 1255 and 1256 are, therefore, possible dates for the letter.

Ep. 87: 1255. This letter is one of the three epistles to Akropolites (Epp. 87–89) preserved in **V** that date to Theodore's reign. Ep. 87 complains of the insubordination and cowardice of the generals, whom the author compares to tortoises, dung beetles, foxes, and frightened hares (lines 41–45). In spirit it resembles Ep. 204 and seems to have been written in the summer of 1255 when Akropolites evidently stayed in Asia Minor. Akropolites is known to have accompanied Theodore in 1256 during the two-year-long Bulgarian campaign.

Thematic cluster (Epp. 142–47): Letters to the papal curia (1256–58). The six letters are transmitted solely in **V**, along with epistles dating to the sole reign of Theodore Laskaris. Epp. 142–43 are addressed to Pope Alexander IV. The recipient of Epp. 144–45 is Cardinal Richard Annibaldi – a relative of Pope Alexander IV, a former archpriest of St. Peter, a cardinal since 1237, and the founder of the Augustinian order.[90] Ep. 146 addresses Cardinal Ottaviano Ubaldini, a former bishop of Bologna from a Florentine Ghibelline family who had served as Roman cardinal since 1244, and Ep. 147 addresses Cardinal Peter Capoccio, a member of a noble Roman family who had also been a cardinal since 1244.[91] In his *Regesten der Kaiserurkunden*, Franz Dölger linked the dossier with the resumption of the negotiations with the papacy after the death (December 7, 1254) of Pope Innocent IV and dated all six letters to the early months (January–March 21) of 1256: that is, before Theodore departed for the Balkans during the second year of his Bulgarian campaign.[92]

A fuller picture of the new round of negotiations emerges from additional sources: a rich dossier of letters and documents issued by the chancery of Pope Alexander IV; and the letter in Greek that Manuel Disypatos, metropolitan bishop of Thessalonica, composed on behalf of Patriarch Arsenios and addressed to Pope Alexander IV after the

---

[89] Akrop. I, §60 (p. 123.3). The strategic importance of Didymoteichon in 1256 is illustrated by the fact that the Cumans plundered its environs early in that year. See Akrop. I, §60 (pp. 125.27–126.1).

[90] Roth 1954:5–18.

[91] On Ubaldini, see Hauss 1912; Van Cleve 1972:505–6. On Capoccio, see Reh 1933.

[92] Dölger–Wirth, *Regesten*, 1835–39. An entry for the emperor's second letter to Cardinal Richard Annibaldi (Ep. 145) is missing.

conclusion of the debates in Thessalonica in the autumn of 1256.[93] Alexander IV's Latin letters show that the initiative to reopen the negotiations came from Theodore, who sent his agents Theodore Dokeianos and Demetrios Spartenos to the papal curia. The two envoys brought with them a letter from the emperor to the pope, and the pope wrote a letter in reply to Theodore, which has survived without its date of issue.[94] After receiving Dokeianos and Spartanos, Alexander IV asked Constantine, bishop of Orvieto – a Dominican who had already been selected by Pope Innocent IV for a unionist embassy to the Nicaean court – to prepare himself for the embassy to the Greek East within ten days.[95] By September–October 1256, Constantine of Orvieto had arrived in Thessalonica and held discussions there with Theodore Laskaris and high Byzantine ecclesiastics.[96]

Legitimate doubts have been raised as to whether all six letters of Theodore Laskaris were composed in early 1256, at the very beginning of the negotiations, because the subject matter and content of most of them presupposes prior contacts.[97] In fact, only Ep. 143, addressed to Pope Alexander IV, can belong to the initial stage of the epistolary exchange. The remaining letters seem to be later. Three of them (Epp. 142, 144, and 146) respond to a petition for the release of an important Latin prisoner of war. Vitalien Laurent has connected this request with the skirmishes around Constantinople in the summer of 1257 attested in Pope Alexander IV's register (entry for July 15, 1257).[98] This is certainly a possibility. In addition, students of Byzantine diplomatics have been puzzled by the peculiar style and form of the letters. Franz Dölger thought that they were private letters rather than products of the chancery.[99] Luca Pieralli observed the conspicuous absence of standard diplomatic components (for example, a *dispositio* or an eschatocol), the unusual *salutatio* of the protocol of Ep. 143, and the high rhetorical language and philosophical content of all letters. He proposed that the epistles, as preserved in **V**, were

---

[93] The Latin dossier has been published by Schillmann 1918 and reedited by Haluščynskyj and Wojnar 1966. On the basis of these documents and Theodore's letters, Laurent (1935) made a number of interesting observations on the unionist negotiations at the time. For a critical edition and commentary of the letter composed on behalf of Patriarch Arsenios, see Pieralli 1998.

[94] Schillmann 1918:119–23; Haluščynskyj and Wojnar 1966:48–51.

[95] Schillmann 1918:113–14; Haluščynskyj and Wojnar 1966:44–46.   [96] See Chapter 8, p. 168.

[97] Thus, Pieralli (2006:11, n. 46) proposed a date of 1256–57 for Ep. 145 to Richard Annibaldi and Laurent (1935:44, n. 1) suggested a date after November 1256 for Ep. 147 to Peter Capoccio.

[98] Laurent 1935b:55, n. 1; De la Roncière et al. 1902–59, II:no. 2072 (p. 637).

[99] Dölger-Wirth, *Regesten*, V–VI (Dölger's preface to the first edition of 1932).

revised by a rhetorician, perhaps by the emperor himself, and therefore have little to do with the original letters sent to the papacy. In his view, no one in Nicaea was able to render Theodore's elaborate prose into Latin.[100] Yet Alexander IV's letter of response to Theodore Laskaris makes clear that the pope had in front of him a letter not unlike Ep. 143. The pope admires the emperor's natural arguments, philosophical reasoning, and recourse to theological authorities. Theodore is praised fulsomely for "the grandeur of sententious eloquence" (*sententiosi eloquii maiestas*) and "the abundance of a learned command of language" (*doctae dissertitudinis affluentia*).[101] The Latin translation of Theodore's letter evidently conveyed well enough the form and content of the Greek, and Alexander IV's letter of response seems to imitate on purpose its rhetorical style.[102] It is, of course, impossible to say what version of Ep. 143 reached the papacy, and it is reasonable to assume that this letter, like all letters, was edited before its incorporation into the authorized collection. The removal of chancery usage was a component of the editorial process (see above, p. 5). In any case, there is no reason to doubt that the emperor's pen was responsible for the six letters.

Ep. 143: January–March 1256. This letter, to Pope Alexander IV, expresses the hope for the termination of the schism and asks the pope to dispatch someone "strong in his views" to carry out the negotiations. The letter dates to the initial stage of reopening of communications with the papacy and seems to have been written during the emperor's stay in Nymphaion before the resumption of the Bulgarian campaign in 1256.

Ep. 142: October 1256–58. This letter to Pope Alexander IV mentions the fulfillment of the pope's urgent request and the sending of a Latin prisoner, evidently a prominent enough individual, back to his homeland. The pope's prayers were in lieu of the payment of a ransom (lines 15–18). Ep. 142 thus shares the same subject with Epp. 144 and 146. The name of the Latin individual is missing. He is called "so and so" (ὁ δεῖνα), a clear sign that the name was removed when the letter was edited for publication.[103]

Ep. 144: October 1256–58. This letter, to Cardinal Richard Annibaldi, notifies him of the release of the prisoner of war.

---

[100] Pieralli 2006:10–11, 128, n. 2.
[101] Schillmann 1918:120; Haluščynskyj and Wojnar 1966:48–49.
[102] As noted by Laurent 1935b:46, n. 2.
[103] For a similar example from the correspondence of Nikephoros Choumnos when the expression ὁ δεῖνα was introduced in the editorial process, see Riehle 2011:49–50.

Ep. 145: October 1256–1258. This letter to Cardinal Richard Annibaldi, of which a fragment survives, discusses the relationship between human and divine (theological) knowledge, and points to the unknowability of God on the basis of first principles. It is close in spirit to polemical arguments made in Theodore's *Orations against the Latins*.

Ep. 146: October 1256–1258. This letter, to Cardinal Ottaviano Ubaldini, notifies him of the release of the prisoner of war.

Ep. 147: 1257–58. This letter, to Cardinal Peter Capoccio, responds to exhortations mixed with remonstrations on the part of the cardinal about Theodore's silence. Theodore writes diplomatically that "patience together with examination brings the most peaceful rewards" (lines 45–46) and urges his addressee to write to him with any requests.[104] The letter presupposes prior correspondence between the two men and seems, therefore, to date after the discussions in Thessalonica in the autumn of 1256.

Ep. 212: 1256. This letter, to George Mouzalon, congratulates him on his marriage to Theodora: the daughter of the governor (*doux*) of Thrakesion, John Komnenos Kantakouzenos, and Irene Palaiologina, the sister of Michael Palaiologos. The marriage was arranged following Mouzalon's promotions in Christmas 1255 in Lampsakos. The letter dates, therefore, to 1256 and seems to have been addressed to Mouzalon from the Balkans.

Ep. 214: January 1257. This letter to Mouzalon was written on the occasion of the flight of 'Izz al-Dīn Kaykāwūs II to the empire of Nicaea. According to the eyewitness account of *Synopsis chronike*, Theodore welcomed the sultan to Sardis in person shortly after Epiphany Day (January 6) 1257 and brought him to Magnesia, in whose vicinity the Nicaean troops were encamped. The letter captures the euphoria of the moment and must have been composed in Magnesia in January 1257, not long after the initial encounter.[105]

Ep. 44: 1257. This long polemical letter to Blemmydes mentions that the borders of the empire of Nicaea extended to Dyrrachion (line 33). There-fore, the letter dates after the treaty with Michael of Epiros in September 1256 that ceded the city to Nicaea, but before the loss of Dyrrachion to Manfred in 1258.[106] It was written after the emperor's return to Asia

---

[104] Laurent 1935:44, n. 1.

[105] *Synopsis chronike*, 530.12–29. For a discussion of the letter and a translation, see Angelov 2011a. Note that the immediately preceding Ep. 213 (with which Theodore sent from Magnesia six luxurious, gold-decorated and foreign-looking items of clothing to Mouzalon) may also have been written in January 1257 during the same stay in Magnesia.

[106] Akrop. I, §63 (pp. 133.12–15), §67 (pp. 140.1–9); MM, III, 240. See Chapter 8, p. 176.

Minor in 1257.[107] Theodore describes his daily routine (lines 63–75), and makes an impassioned argument for an increase in army finances and the recruitment of native, Hellenic troops (lines 80–84).

Ep. 45: autumn 1257–58. This letter to Blemmydes praises the rhetorical style of the latter's most recent laudatory epistle. It mentions the author's ill health and the pain in his hand (lines 28 and 60–63), which he hopes that his "spiritual doctor" (νοερὸς ἰατρός), Blemmydes, will be able to cure. Theodore complains about the incompetence of physicians who make his condition worse. The pain in his hand is the same symptom as in Ep. 48, which gives a detailed description of the illness. Theodore's disease manifested itself in the late months of 1257 (see Appendix 3), hence the suggested *terminus post quem* of the letter.

Ep. 46: autumn 1257–58. This letter to Blemmydes can be dated on the basis of its position between Epp. 45 and 48 referring to the author's illness. It speaks cryptically of the beheading of the dragon in accordance with Blemmydes' prophetic words and mentions with pride the author's victory and the accomplishment of "Hellenic bravery," which Blemmydes is called to admire. To whom does the metaphor of the decapitated dragon refer? The most likely possibility is that the author envisages the weakening of the Bulgarian kingdom after the victorious war of 1255–56. After the treaty of Regina, the Bulgarian king, Michael Asen, was assassinated outside Turnovo. The period of political turmoil (see Chapter 8, pp. 166–67) ended with the accession of Constantine Tikh, a nobleman from Skopje, who sent an embassy to Nicaea in the late 1257 or 1258 to ask for the hand in marriage of Theodore's daughter Irene and legitimize his power. The reference to "Hellenic bravery" parallels the Hellenic pride in letters written during the Bulgarian campaign: Epp. 202.55–59, 204.58–59, 204.124–130.

Ep. 47: autumn 1257–58. This letter comments on the brevity of a letter by Blemmydes and states that it accepts its unspecified prophetic words. Its position between Epp. 45 and 48 suggests its date.

Ep. 48: 1258. This letter to Blemmydes gives a detailed description of Theodore's terminal illness (see partial translation in Appendix 3, 384). The author complains of a "bodily pain which no one has ever seen or heard," criticizes again the incompetence of his doctors, and asks for Blemmydes' prayers, informing him at the end that he has carried out his request transmitted through an anonymous *protonotarios*. The letter dates to the last several months of the life of Theodore Laskaris.

---

[107] For this dating, see Angelov 2007:193.

Datable Letters

Letters datable within a delimited timeframe, including Theodore's sole
rule (November 1254–August 1258)

Ep. 1	before autumn 1241
Ep. 2	autumn 1241
Ep. 8	early 1242 or early 1243
Ep. 10	late 1243–44
Ep. 11	late 1243–44
Ep. 18	1252
Ep. 21	1244–45?
Ep. 22	1244–45?
Ep. 24	1252
Ep. 26	1246–47?
Ep. 36	1253
Ep. 37	1253
Ep. 38	1253
Ep. 39	1253
Ep. 40	autumn 1253
Ep. 42	1254–58
Ep. 43	1254–58
Ep. 44	1257
Ep. 45	autumn 1257–58
Ep. 46	autumn 1257–58
Ep. 47	autumn 1257–58
Ep. 48	1258
Ep. 49	1241–46
Ep. 57	1252
Ep. 58	1252
Ep. 59	1252
Ep. 60	1252
Ep. 61	1252–53
Ep. 72	1252–53
Ep. 77	1253
Ep. 78	1253
Ep. 80	1253
Ep. 83	late autumn 1253
Ep. 84	late autumn 1253
Ep. 85	late autumn 1253
Ep. 86	late autumn 1253
Ep. 87	1255
Ep. 88	1254–58
Ep. 89	1254–58

Long Ep. to Akropolites	1253
Ep. 94	1253
Ep. 107	1243–49
Ep. 118	1252
Ep. 125	autumn 1253
Ep. 131	1254–58
Ep. 132	1252–53
Ep. 141	1254–58
Ep. 142	October 1256–58
Ep. 143	January–March 1256
Ep. 144	October 1256–58
Ep. 145	October 1256–58
Ep. 146	October 1256–58
Ep. 147	1257–58
Ep. 180	early to mid 1253
Ep. 183	late autumn 1253
Ep. 184	December 12, 1253
Ep. 185	December 1253 or winter 1254
Ep. 187	January–October 1254
Ep. 193	November–December 1254
Ep. 194	c. December 12, 1254
Ep. 195	December 1254–January 1255
Ep. 198	winter 1255
Ep. 199	winter 1255
Ep. 200	winter 1255
Ep. 201	winter 1255
Ep. 202	summer 1255
Ep. 203	summer 1255
Ep. 204	summer 1255
Ep. 205	late autumn 1255
Ep. 206	late autumn 1255
Ep. 207	late autumn 1255
Ep. 208	late autumn 1255, or 1256
Ep. 211	1254–58
Ep. 212	1256
Ep. 213	January 1257
Ep. 214	January 1257
Ep. 217	1254–58

Appendix 3 | The Mystery Illness

One of the most enduring myths about Theodore Laskaris is that he was an epileptic. His epilepsy is thought to have been chronic (that is, he suffered from it throughout his life or a large part of his life) and hereditary (he inherited the illness from his father), and to have led to his premature death.[1] Historians of disease have been sufficiently intrigued to explore the issue, although they have reached opposite conclusions. In 1995 Georgios Makris examined cases of Byzantine emperors alleged to have been epileptics and concluded that neither Theodore Laskaris nor his father John Vatatzes suffered from the disorder.[2] In 1998, however, John Laskaratos and Panagiotis Zis argued on the basis of the *History* of Pachymeres that Theodore was afflicted with chronic epilepsy of the tonic-clonic (grand mal) type, which the emperor developed possibly before his thirties.[3] Retrospective diagnosis of a famous historical figure based solely on written sources – in the absence of skeletal remains to be analyzed by bioarchaeologists – is notoriously difficult. The only contemporary author to diagnose Theodore with epilepsy is George Pachymeres, whose testimony is not confirmed by any other Byzantine historian and contradicts Theodore's own description of the symptoms of his lethal disease. We will begin, therefore, with a critical analysis of Pachymeres' description and will address the question as to whether Theodore Laskaris was affected by a chronic illness. The discussion of the evidence on his health leads us to assess the possible causes of his early death.

The historian Pachymeres, who was born and raised in Nicaea, was sixteen years of age (and thus still a student pursuing secondary education following the curriculum of *enkyklios paideia*) at the time of Theodore's death. Later in life, when he was employed in the patriarchal bureaucracy, he

---

[1] William Miller (1923:506) spoke of "a hereditary malady" and Donald Nicol (1966:321) wrote that Theodore "was an epileptic, and his affliction made him vacillate between the extremes of nervous diffidence and blind self-confidence."

[2] Makris 1995:390–92.

[3] Laskaratos and Zis 1998. A similar argument was made by Jeanselme (1924:267–73), who took Pachymeres' report at face value. He also did so with earlier reports by Byzantine historians attributing the disease to emperors.

became close to the metropolitan of Mytilene, Gregory, the confessor of the dying emperor, and may have well derived some information from him. Notably, a relative of George Pachymeres by the name of Theophylaktos was a secretary to the regent George Mouzalon and was assassinated in the Sosandra monastery, together with his patron, in August 1258 within days of the emperor's passing.[4] The account of the disease is found in Chapter 12 of the first book of his *History*, entitled "How the ailing emperor was suspecting everyone of magic, and concerning Martha (Michael Palaiologos' sister)."[5] The description is inserted here to explain the use of ordeals and torture at the imperial tribunal; it anticipates the commentary on the extraordinary intellectual and literary abilities of Theodore Laskaris in the following chapter, Chapter 13 of the first book. The afflicted emperor is said to have suffered fits or loss of consciousness and to have often fallen to the ground (ἐπείληπτο γὰρ καταπίπτων συχνάκις). A learned digression follows. According to Pachymeres, the reason for Theodore's disease lay in the excessive heat of his heart, which produced a "natural intelligence" (τὸ εὐφυές) above the usual one. Herein is rooted, as we have seen, the influential modern opinion that Theodore Laskaris was a sick genius. Theodore's hot heart is said also to have had an unbeneficial effect, because the heart was the source of one's thoughts. Pachymeres qualified the latter theory by adding that philosophers disagreed on this rather vexed question.[6] As Makris has already detected, Pachymeres borrowed heavily from philosophical and medical literature.[7] According to the medical work of Stephanos the Philosopher (c. AD 600), for example, excess heat in the body caused by a full moon led to epilepsy.[8] According to Aristotle, *Problems*, 30,1 (954a31–34), people who have hot black bile in their bodies are naturally intelligent (εὐφυεῖς) as well as erotically fixated, mad, and predisposed to anger, passion, and loquaciousness.[9] Elsewhere in his *History* Pachymeres lays out an ethnographic climate theory based on the effects of heat and cold on the human body. In a section devoted to the Mamluk state of Egypt, he digresses to point out that people from hot, southern climates closer to the sun are

---

[4] On his connection with Gregory of Mytilene, see Pach. II, 347.26–349.4. On Theophylaktos, see Pach. I, 85.14–20.

[5] Pach. I, 53.11–57.29.   [6] Pach. I, 53.14–21.

[7] Makris 1995:391–92. I agree with Makris' interpretation of τὸ εὐφυές as "sharpness of mind" rather than "air of very good health" in Failler's French translation.

[8] Stephanus the Philosopher, *Commentary on the Prognosticon of Hippocrates*, I, 17 in Duffy 1983:56–57.

[9] *Problemata*, 954a31–38, where emotions like love and anger as well as madness are connected with body heat.

naturally intelligent (εὐφυεῖς), clever, and excel in political organization, skills, and learning, but are otherwise slothful, passive and weak in battle in contrast to the warlike Cumans from the north (that is, the northern Black Sea region).[10]

In contrast to Pachymeres, other Byzantine historians omit any detail about the epilepsy of Theodore Laskaris. George Akropolites and *Synopsis chronike* speak of "a terrible disease" that struck the emperor who, in a very short time, drastically lost weight and was reduced to a skeleton. The doctors were unable to cure him. Gregoras briefly mentions a "grave illness" that consumed him and caused his death.[11] Blemmydes, who witnessed Theodore's disease firsthand and was called upon to help in his capacity as a highly trained physician and spiritual father, gives disappointingly little clinical detail in his autobiography. He writes that "a scourge and a strange disease" fell on Theodore, causing depression and confinement in the palace.[12] Two letters by Theodore Laskaris to Blemmydes (Epp. 45 and 48) during the period of the emperor's terminal illness describe the symptoms and complain about the incompetence of the doctors. This is not the first time that Theodore wrote Blemmydes about his health. We see him in earlier letters (Epp. 9 and 11) expressing his hope that Blemmydes' "holy prayers" would lead to recovery from illness and thanking Blemmydes for his beneficial effect on his health (Epp. 16, 17, and 20). No medical cures are ever mentioned in the correspondence. The emphasis, rather, is on spiritual healing.[13] The beneficial effect attributed to Blemmydes could not be achieved by other physicians, including the head court physician, a man who can be identified with the famous thirteenth-century medical author Nicholas Myrepsos.[14] The first letter (Ep. 45) to Blemmydes dealing with his fatal illness, datable to the autumn of 1257 or 1258, refers briefly to pain

---

[10] Pach. I, 237.1–24.

[11] Akrop. I, §74 (p. 153.4–9: note the powerful word κατασκελετευθείς); *Synopsis chronike*, 533.27–30; Greg. I, 61.19. The fourteenth-century versified chronicle of Ephraim is likewise laconic and refers to a "gravest disease" without providing any detail. See Lampsides 1990:327.9270–74.

[12] Blem., *Autobiographia*, I, 85 (p. 42).

[13] In Ep. 16.19–20 (p. 22), Theodore writes rhetorically that the mental image of the fragrance of Blemmydes' robes, something which the letter carrier evoked, had a salubrious effect on him. A similar statement is found in Ep. 17.5–10 (pp. 22–23), where reading a letter by Blemmydes is said to have alleviated his pain.

[14] In Ep. 20.28–34 (p. 27), Theodore complains that the doctors who were examining him and testing medicines rebelled against "every medical knowledge" and disobeyed Galen. They are contrasted to the effect of the "holy prayers" of Blemmydes. The physician who was their superior is described as "the best human plague" (ἄριστος βροτολοιγός). According to Festa 1909:217, n. 1, he was the court physician (*aktourarios*) Nicholas, described by Akrop. I, §39

in his arm. The second letter (Ep. 48) to Blemmydes, datable to 1258, describes in detail the pain and numbness in his arm. The emperor pins his hope on Blemmydes' prayers and, evidently, his medical knowledge:

> We are afflicted with bodily pain which no one has ever seen or heard. A pain in the arm around the point of the shoulder moves down, as it were, until the elbow, presses the arm, and goes throughout the length of the arm and the forearm. There is no redness or swelling of any size. The aching is so insufferable, and the numbness and paralysis are more painful than the aching. Many times this hand was moved toward inappropriate deeds; now it is receiving punishment, even though one incommensurate with past events (for we are worthy of many terrible things), but a punishment that is painful, grievous, and above human faint-heartedness. A swelling does not show and the pressure is so great. There is no doctor. The ones who are here are stupid. Based on the establishment of the diagnosis and the treatment, one could suppose that they are common peddlers or healers by accident. There is no fever generally. The poor health condition results from the pain or rather from an aggravation due to lack of use of the hand. The hand moves, but not in all directions; in its upward swing it is very much constrained and does not consent to move more.[15]

The symptom described by the patient (radiating pain from his arm and arm numbness) and those mentioned by Akropolites and *Synopsis chronike* (drastic loss of weight) do not support the view that Theodore passed away from epilepsy. What, then, to make of Pachymeres' account? The Nicaea-born historian probably learned from eyewitnesses that the dying emperor suffered from fits and could not maintain his balance, and he overheard, too, that his condition was attributed to epilepsy. Pachymeres himself could not provide any further clinical detail, and his solution was to engage in a learned discussion on the effects of the disease. His diagnosis, therefore, has no historical value beyond its insight into some (but not all) of the symptoms.

(p. 63.12–16) as being particularly close to the imperial family. The court physician Nicholas has been identified with Nicholas Myrepsos, the author of the *Dynameron* (a collection of 2,656 medical recipes), who was highly influential both in Byzantium and the West. See Macrides 2007:212–13, n. 8 (with further bibliography). The letter suggests that the doctors supervised by the court physician ("the best human plague") were trying new pharmaceutical recipes and therefore backs the identification with the medical author. The statement in Ep. 70.22 (p. 97) addressed to Akropolites that "the chief human plague has an Alexandrian inspiration" adds further support, for Nicholas Myrepsos, known in Latin as Alexandrinus, was believed to have spent time in Alexandria in Egypt.

[15] Ep. 48.22–37 (p. 65).

Was Theodore Laskaris a chronically ill man? Here, again, the evidence points in a direction different than chronic epilepsy that could have led to a sudden death during a seizure. The majority of the sources refer to a disease that developed in the last year of his life. Akropolites places the onset of Theodore's fatal medical condition after the change of government in Bulgaria (that is, the accession of Constantine Tikh), which took place sometime in 1257.[16] Nikephoros Gregoras notes that Theodore fell ill when he was in the thirty-sixth year of his life – that is, at the earliest in late 1257 or early 1258.[17] A remarkably precise indication of the beginning of the illness can be found in the polemical letter that Rabbi Jacob ben Elia of Carcassonne wrote around ten years after the emperor's death, in about 1270, in Valencia.[18] Addressed to Pablo Christiani, a famous Jewish convert to Christianity who had entered the Dominican order, the letter provides historical examples, both ancient and relatively recent, of divine wrath against persecutors of the Jews. Thus, the blinding of Theodore Komnenos Doukas when he fell under Bulgarian captivity in 1230 is blamed on his confiscation of Jewish wealth. The death of John Vatatzes from an illness is attributed to an edict on the conversion of the Jews allegedly issued in the last year of his reign. While such legislation is highly doubtful, the proselytization of the Jews in the empire of Nicaea through preaching and economic incentives is well attested.[19] Divine punishment is said to have fallen on Vatatzes' son and grandson. Theodore Laskaris reportedly died after nine months of illness, a duration that agrees with Akropolites' and Gregoras' estimate that the emperor fell ill at the earliest in late 1257. According to Jacob ben Elia's letter, the first signs of his illness would have manifested themselves in November 1257. The close correspondence of this detail with the descriptions by Byzantine historians can be explained by reports that trickled through Mediterranean medical networks, in which Jews traditionally played a prominent role.[20]

The circumstance that Theodore Laskaris contracted a fatal disease during the last year of his life does not mean, of course, that he was continually healthy before this time. Indeed, the theme of illness runs through many of his writings and deserves close attention for any insights

---

[16] Akrop. I, §73 (pp. 152–53).   [17] Greg. I, 61.18–20.

[18] English translation of the section on Byzantium in Bowman 1985:228–30. For the context of composition and a summary of the content of the letter, see Mann 1926.

[19] See 253, n. 106 and the well-founded doubts of Prinzing 1998b (cited in the note) on the existence of such a piece of legislation.

[20] See the twelfth-century example discussed by Goitein (1964) based on a letter from the archive of the Cairo Geniza.

it can give us regarding the state of his health. More than ten letters
(Epp. 9, 10, 11, 13, 14, 16, 17, 20, 70, 98, 118, and 134) written before
November 1254 – most of them addressed to Blemmydes – speak or allude
to medical conditions and thank correspondents for their prayers. Account
needs to be taken of the requirements of the epistolographic genre. Illness
was a common subject in Byzantine epistolography and Theodore Laskaris
is just one letter writer among many to speak both about his own health
and that of his correspondents.[21] In one letter to Blemmydes (Ep. 13),
Theodore responds to the news he has received that his teacher was ill with
a terrible disease and sympathetically describes his own illness. As we have
seen in Appendix 2, more than thirty of Theodore's letters to Mouzalon are
united by the theme of Mouzalon's recovery from illness. In other words,
Theodore Laskaris' epistolary circle displayed the hypochondriac tendencies of other Byzantine letter writers.

The pre-1254 letters sometimes bring up specific medical symptoms, and
so does Theodore's oration in gratitude to Jesus Christ composed after his
recovery from illness, likewise composed before 1254.[22] Ep. 9, addressed to
Blemmydes, refers to a throat and a tongue ache.[23] Ep. 13 (the letter
responding compassionately to the news of Blemmydes' sickness) speaks
of a rash on his head causing pain, sleeplessness, and discomfort.[24] The
complaint of a headache reappears in Ep. 134, addressed to the monk
Akakios.[25] The oration of gratitude to Jesus Christ mentions fever and
nausea.[26] The symptoms are diverse and do not point to one single illness.
In 1909 Nicola Festa attempted to explore the diagnosis behind these
symptoms with the help of a young doctor from Rome and immediately
encountered an obstacle: the chronological uncertainty of the letters that
refer to medical conditions.[27] The chronology of the letters (see Appendix 2)
suggests that some, in fact, were written over a considerable amount of time.

---

[21] Karlsson 1959:138–39; Mullett 1981:78.

[22] Similar words of gratitude to saints and holy figures are found in his encomium on the healing
saints Cosmas and Damian composed in 1252 and in his invocatory hymns composed after
November 1254.

[23] Ep. 9.11–15 (p. 13). According to Festa (1909:216), the references in Ep. 9 to πύκνωσις and
καταπύκνωσις τῶν σωματικῶν πόρων point to a gastric-rheumatic disease. The same term is
found also in Ep. 118.

[24] Ep. 13.21–27 (p. 18).   [25] Ep. 134 (p. 189).

[26] *Oration of Gratitude to Our Lord Jesus Christ Composed upon Recovery from a Terrible Illness,*
A, f. 15r, **P**, f. 27r. The work provides additional information on Theodore's attitudes to doctors
and disease.

[27] Festa 1909:216. Festa made this observation in his review of Pappadopoulos' book, which he
criticized for insufficient attention to the medical information in the letters.

Ep. 9 is among the early letters to Blemmydes, and one can agree with Festa that the disease is the same one to which Ep. 10 alludes at its abrupt end.[28] Ep. 10 (datable to 1243–44) refers to the imminent arrival of the new metropolitan bishop of Ephesos, Nikephoros, at the city to take up his position. However, Ep. 118, addressed to the metropolitan bishop of Phila-delphia, Phokas – a letter in which Theodore complains of disease and expresses his hope for Christ's supernatural intervention – dates to 1252, because it mentions the return of Andronikos of Sardis from an embassy to the papacy.[29] The two letters (Ep. 9 and Ep. 118) are separated by at least eight years and are unlikely to refer to the same disease. This impression is enhanced by the oration to Jesus Christ and by letters (Epp. 16, 17, and 20), in which Theodore speaks about recovering from illness and regaining his health. He appears to have contracted contagious illnesses with flu-like symptoms, but these illnesses proved not to be life-threatening and caused nothing resembling a medical disorder. The prolific evidence for his active lifestyle at times of peace and war, evidence examined above in Chapters 5 and 8, militates strongly against this interpretation.

There are two other things to learn from the medical focus of the letters. The first is that the court physicians were extremely attentive to the health of the only child in the ruling family and designated successor. Physicians were continually in close proximity to the coemperor, even though he expressed to Blemmydes and Akropolites distrust in their expertise and dislike for these "human plagues." Ep. 70 mentions two physicians, Koites and Mauroeides, and as we have seen, alludes to the head physician (*aktouarios*), Nicholas Myrepsos. These doctors belonged to a world of shared medical knowledge in the Mediterranean. Theodore Laskaris com-ments on the "Alexandrian inspiration" of Nicholas Myrepsos.[30] The second thing to learn is that Theodore himself acquired some medical

---

[28] Ep. 10.27 (p. 14) ends enigmatically with the phrase περὶ δὲ τῆς νόσου ἡμῶν followed by a missing text. It is reasonable to assume that the missing text, containing clinical or medical details, was dropped at the time of preparation of the Laurentian epistolary collection, in accordance with the editorial principle of de-concretization noted in Appendix II. Festa (1909:216) suggests that the disease mentioned in Epp. 9 and 10 is the same as the one in Epp. 13 and 14, which is entirely possible. However, it is unlikely that Ep. 118 is a description of the disease, given that the letter dates to 1252.

[29] Ep. 118.29–33 (p. 165). The letter has to be taken into consideration in the editing and analysis of his *Oration of Gratitude to Our Lord Jesus Christ Composed upon Recovery from a Terrible Illness*.

[30] Mauroeides is not necessarily a nickname ("the swarthy one"), because it is attested as a family name. See PLP 17435–36. Festa (Ep., Index, 406) thought that Mauroeides stood for Avicenna, but this seems farfetched. On the puzzling name Koites, see 283, n. 43. On Myrepsos, see 383, n. 14.

knowledge, whether through his studies with Blemmydes, the presence of court physicians or in another way. He mentions the theory of the four humors in philosophical treatises, but also in letters in which he refers to the unnatural flow of the humors during illnesses.[31] He uses the vocabulary of Galenic medicine – terms such as "tightening of the pores" (πύκνωσις) and "confluence of the humors" (σύρροια).[32] He speaks of feeling pain in the union of his soul and body, which accords with the traditional view that illnesses were psychosomatic and affected both one's body and soul.[33] He knew medical recipes and wrote in passing that heated mulled wine alleviated stomachache.[34]

None of the symptoms of Theodore's illnesses before November 1254 corresponds to those of the lethal disease that manifested itself less than one year before his death: pain and numbness of the hand; great loss of weight; fits and inability to maintain balance; and depression. What, then, might have been the cause of Theodore's death? Following Festa's attempt to bring a modern medical perspective to bear on the information found in Theodore's letters, my consultation with psychologists and geneticists has opened some possibilities, even though the information on the clinical picture of our medieval patient is not sufficiently detailed to permit a definitive answer.[35]

The background of consanguinity is a risk for an autosomal recessive disease. His father, John Vatatzes, was blood-related to Theodore's mother, Irene: Vatatzes was the second cousin of Irene's mother. Most autosomal recessive diseases manifest themselves in childhood. The probability of an

---

[31] *Natural Communion*, PG, vol. 140, col. 1313A; KD, I, 106.5–6; Ep. 13.24–25 (p. 18); Sat., 192.923. In light of Theodore's interest in the effects of humors on the body, it is unlikely that the mention of blood flow (Ep. 16:19–20 [p. 22], 17.8 [p. 23]) means that he suffered from hemorrhage, as suggested by Pappadopoulos 1908:22.

[32] On πύκνωσις, see Ep. 9.15 (p. 13), 118.29 (p. 165); Stephanus of Athens, *Commentary on Hippocrates' Aphorisms*, V–VI, in Westerink 1995:84.24, 88.34–35. On σύρροια, see Ep. 118. 29 (p. 165).

[33] *Encomium on the Holy Anargyroi* (the healing saints Cosmas and Damian), in **A**, f. 35r, **P**, f. 56v: ψυχικὰ καὶ σωματικὰ νοσήματα; **A**, f. 39r, **P**, f. 60r: πᾶσαν νόσον ἰᾶται ψυχικὴν ὁμοῦ καὶ σωματικήν; **A**, f. 40v, **P**, f. 61r–v: Ἀλλ᾽ ἐγὼ μὲν ὁ νῦν καὶ σῶμα καὶ νοῦν νοσῶν ἄμφω τε καὶ ψυχὴν τὰς αὐτῶν ποικίλας ἐνεργείας αἰτῶ, ἵνα καὶ τῆς ψυχικῆς ἐκτροπῆς τέλεον λυτρωθῶ καὶ τὴν στοιχειακὴν πῆξιν ἀλλοιωθῶ πρὸς τὸ βέλτιστον; *Oration of Gratitude to Our Lord Jesus Christ Composed upon Recovery from a Terrible Illness*, **A** f. 21v, **P** f. 37r–v ; Ep. 13.18–20 (p. 18), 27.26–28 (p. 37), 98.5 (p. 132): ἀλγοῦντες τὸ σωματικὸν καὶ ψυχικὸν ξυμφυές.

[34] Ep. 54.72–73 (p. 81).

[35] I have benefited from participating in a medical study group at the University of Birmingham (members: Femi Oyebode, professor of psychology, Dr. Lenia Constantine, and Dr. Sandy Robertson) and from discussions with Jordan Smoller, professor of psychiatry at the Harvard Medical School and director of the psychiatric genetics unit.

autosomal genetic disease is diminished, however, because the symptoms of Theodore's fatal illness are different from those reported in texts composed before November 1254.[36] An obstacle to identifying an autosomal or a dominant genetic disease is that the causes of death of his grandparents, parents, and children are not known. On the other hand, the symptoms of Theodore's lethal disease are consistent with an acquired condition and particularly with tumor processes in the brain, the lungs, and the spine. All these tumors can cause, at an initial stage of their progress, arm numbness, which is followed by drastic loss of weight and sometimes seizures. Brain, pulmonary, and spinal cancer can all lead to death within a year of first manifestation of the symptoms, which was the case with the emperor. The possibility that Theodore Laskaris died from cancer – it ought to be stressed – is only a best guess. What can be stated with confidence is that the Nicaean emperor and philosopher was neither a chronically sick man nor a disturbed genius, something for which he acquired a reputation not long after his death.

---

[36] Laskaratos and Zis (1998) preferred to see in the radiating arm pain a neuralgic amyotrophy that may have resulted from a trauma and argued that Theodore Laskaris concealed his epilepsy for a long time. Not only is such a concealment an argument from silence, but it is reasonable to suppose that the emperor's tutor and high official Akropolites would have known about the disease and would have reported it.

Appendix 4 | The Manuscript Portraits

All surviving manuscript portraits of Theodore Laskaris as a crowned emperor go back to the same original image found in a fourteenth-century manuscript of the *History* of George Pachymeres, which is kept today in the Bavarian State Library in Munich, Codex Monacensis gr. 442 (Fig. 1). The manuscript is known to have been in Venice until 1544, when it was sold by Antonios Eparchos from Corfu to the Library of Augsburg. Since 1806 it has been in its current location.[1] The drawing is based on a nonextant official portrait of Theodore Laskaris attached to an imperial grant. The official character of this lost portrait is suggested by the scroll that Theodore holds, namely, the document detailing the grant to the recipient. Another portrait of Theodore Laskaris is known to have been painted on an initial folio of the deluxe manuscript of his *Natural Communion* (BnF, Suppl. gr 460), which was produced in Theodore's lifetime. Unfortunately, the folio was torn off in the nineteenth century and the image, already heavily damaged at the time, has not survived.[2] The portrait in the Munich manuscript has been overpainted and is in a poor state of preservation, but fortunately copies have been made. A fifteenth-century manuscript of the *History* of Pachymeres preserved in Venice's Marciana Library, Codex Marcianus gr. 404, is its apograph and includes a drawing made in Venice based on the portrait of Theodore Laskaris in the Munich manuscript (Fig. 2).[3] Another drawing derived from the portrait in the Munich manuscript, an engraving, was produced for the printed edition of the *History* of Nikephoros Gregoras published in Basel in 1562 by Hieronymus Wolf, the famous Augsburg librarian and pioneer of Byzantine studies (Fig. 3). Thus, as the fourteenth-century manuscript with the portrait of Theodore Laskaris was transported from the Greek East to Venice and from there to Augsburg, copies of the portrait were made in each location.

---

[1] On the Monacensis and its imperial portraits, see Heisenberg 1920:12–25, 132–35; Spatharakis 1976:165–72; Stichel 1996:76–77. For a codicological description of the manuscript itself, see Failler 1979:126–31.

[2] Förstel 2009.   [3] On the Marcianus, see Failler 1979:179–80.

The three images are not without their differences. Theodore looks sideways rather than frontally in the Venice portrait. He has an animated face ready to smile in the drawing printed in 1562, but his expression is more severe in the Venice portrait, with his skinny and youthful face being a common feature. He has a forked beard characteristic of images of his father on coins.[4] Akropolites' words in the burial oration – that he was a living image of his father – thus become more comprehensible. He is dressed in official attire and wears a long black robe (*sakkos*), over which a long and richly bejeweled scarf (*loros*) is wrapped and attached. Traditional for the Byzantine emperor, the same formal clothes appear on his seal (Fig. 17c) and on coins (Fig. 21). There he holds insignia of his authority: a cross and *akakia* on the seal, and a cross and cross-topped globe on the electrum and billon coins. His everyday clothing and headgear must have been different, although these, unfortunately, remain unknown. In the fourteenth century, the daily hats and silk caftans of the emperor were sometimes the same as the clothing worn by leading officials.[5]

[4] Hendy 1969:254. See also Spatharakis 1976:179.
[5] Macrides, Munitiz, and Angelov 2013:345–46.

Appendix 5 | The Burial Sarcophagus

Theodore's burial site at the Sosandra monastery of the Virgin Gorgoepe-koos was long forgotten until the Belgian historian Henri Grégoire repub-lished in 1922 a metrical epitaph from a marble sarcophagus. The tireless French traveler Charles Texier had seen the sarcophagus during a visit to Nif (the Ottoman name of Nymphaion) next to "the house of the agha." The present whereabouts of the monument is not known. In 1844 Texier published a valuable engraving of the sarcophagus, which shows decor-ation with animal reliefs (griffins, peacocks, and birds resembling pigeons) and floral motifs, including fleurs-de-lis (the lilies associated with the cult of St. Tryphon).[1] The metrical epitaph runs as follows: "Now the ornament is sweet, your divine habit is great. Walk now toward God as a crown-wearer!" On the basis of the word "crown-wearer" (στεφηφόρος) and the allusion to the monastic habit of the deceased individual, Grégoire sug-gested that the sarcophagus belonged to Theodore Laskaris.[2] The inscrip-tion, however, does not give any name, and Nymphaion was not the location of the emperor's burial. There were other powerful officials at the thirteenth-century court, such as despots and *sebastokratores*, who wore crowns. It is true that the local Christian population took care to remove the remains of the saintly John Vatatzes from the Sosandra monastery during the Turkish incursions in the early fourteenth century, but they carried the miracle-working relics of the emperor to nearby Magnesia rather than Nymphaion.[3] A rediscovery of the sarcophagus could perhaps shed new light on the character of this monument. For the time being, the hypothesis ought to be considered speculative and questionable.

[1] Texier 1844:323–25, Plate 7.   [2] Grégoire 1922:24–25, no. 83.
[3] Epilogue, p. 222 and n. 29.

Bibliography

ABBREVIATIONS

A	Cod. Ambros. gr. 917 (C. 308 inf.) (13th c.)
Ad Georg. Mouz.	*Response* to George Mouzalon (treatise on politics and friendship): Tartaglia, Op. rhet., 120–40.
Akrop. I and II	*Georgii Acropolitae opera*. 2 vols., eds. A. Heisenberg and P. Wirth. Stuttgart, 1978.
Apol.	*Response to Some Friends Pressing Him to Find a Bride*: Tartaglia, Op. rhet., 110–18.
Apol. Mal.	*Response to Some People Who Trouble Him Malevolently*: Ep., 283–89.
B	*Byzantion*
Blem., *Autobiographia*	*Nicephori Blemmydae autobiographia sive curriculum vitae necnon epistula universalior*, ed. J. Munitiz. Turnhout, 1984.
Blem., Ep.	N. Festa, *Theodori Ducae Lascaris epistulae CCXVII* (Florence, 1898), Appendix III: *Nicephori Epistulae*, 290–329.
Blem., *Imperial Statue*	H. Hunger and I. Ševčenko, *Des Nikephoros Blemmydes* Βασιλικὸς Ἀνδριάς *und dessen Metaphrase von Georgios Galesiotes und Georgios Oinaiotes*. Vienna, 1986.
BF	*Byzantinische Forschungen*
BMGS	*Byzantine and Modern Greek Studies*
BNJ	*Byzantinisch-neugriechische Jahrbücher*
Böhmer, Ficker, and Winkelmann, *Regesten*	Böhmer, J. F., Ficker, J., Winkelmann, E. A. 1881–1901. *Regesta Imperii, V. Die Regesten des Kaiserreichs unter Philipp, Otto IV., Friedrich II., Heinrich (VII.), Conrad IV., Heinrich Raspe, Wilhelm und Richard, 1198–1272*. 3 vols. Innsbruck.
BSl	*Byzantinoslavica*
BZ	*Byzantinische Zeitschrift*
CIG	*Corpus Inscriptionum Graecarum*, 4 vols. Berlin, 1828–77.
Choniates, *Historia*	*Nicetae Choniatae Historia*, ed. J.-L. van Dieten. Berlin, 1975.

Choniates, *Orationes*   *Nicetae Choniatae orationes et epistulae*, ed. J.-L. van Dieten. Berlin, 1972.

Chr. Th.   Θεοδώρου Β΄ Λασκάρεως περὶ χριστιανικῆς θεολογίας λόγοι, ed. Ch. Krikonis. Thessalonica, 1988.

DOC   *Catalogue of the Byzantine Coins in the Dumbarton Oaks Collection and in the Whittemore Collection*, 5 vols. Washington, 1966–99.

Dölger–Wirth, *Regesten*   *Regesten der Kaiserurkunden des oströmischen Reiches von 565–1453*. vol. 3: *Regesten von 1204–1282*, ed. F. Dölger; rev. ed. P. Wirth. Munich, 1977.

DOP   *Dumbarton Oaks Papers*

EEBS   Ἐπετηρὶς Ἑταιρείας Βυζαντινῶν Σπουδῶν

EO   *Échos d'Orient*

Enc. John   *Encomium* on John III Vatatzes: Op. rhet., 24–66.

Enc. Nic.   *Encomium* on Nicaea, in Tartaglia, Op. rhet., 68–84.

Engrapha Patmou   Βυζαντινὰ ἔγγραφα τῆς Μονῆς Πάτμου, 2 vols, eds. E. Vranouse and M. Nystazopoulou-Pelekidou. Athens, 1980.

Ep.   N. Festa, *Theodori Ducae Lascaris epistulae CCXVII*. Florence, 1898.

Greg. I, II, III   *Nicephori Gregorae Byzantina historia*. 3 vols., ed. L. Schopen. CSHB. Bonn, 1829–55.

JÖB   *Jahrbuch der Österreichischen Byzantinistik* (until 1968 published as *Jahrbuch der Österreichischen Byzantinischen Gesellschaft*)

KD, I   N. Festa, "Κοσμικὴ Δήλωσις," *Giornale della Società Asiatica Italiana*, 11 (1897–98), 97–114. (= *Explanation of the World*, I)

KD, II, III, IV   N. Festa, "Κοσμικὴ Δήλωσις," *Giornale della Società Asiatica Italiana* 12 (1899), 1–52. (= *Explanation of the World*, II, III, IV)

Laurent, *Regestes*   V. Laurent, *Les Regestes des actes du Patriarcat de Constantinople*, vol. 1: *Les actes des patriarches*, fasc. 4: *Les Regestes de 1208 à 1309*. Paris, 1971.

Lavra, I   *Actes de Lavra*, I, eds. P. Lemerle, A. Guillou, and N. Svoronos, with D. Papachryssanthou. Archives de l'Athos, 5. Paris, 1970.

LBJ   E. Trapp et al., *Lexikon zur byzantinischen Gräzität besonders des 9.-12. Jahrhunderts*, 8 fascicles, Vienna, 1994–2017.

MM	F. Miklosich and J. Müller, *Acta et diplomata graeca medii aevi sacra et profana.* 6 vols. Vienna, 1860–90; repr. Aalen, 1968.
Mor. P.	D. Angelov, "The *Moral Pieces* by Theodore II Laskaris," *Dumbarton Oaks Papers* 65–66 (2011–12), 237–69.
ODB	*Oxford Dictionary of Byzantium,* ed. A. Kazhdan. Washington, 1991.
Or. Fr.	*Memorial Discourse* for Frederick II Hohenstaufen: Tartaglia, Op. rhet., 86–94.
P	BnF, Cod. gr. 1193 (14th c.).
Pach. I, II, III, IV	George Pachymeres, *Relations historiques*, vols. I and II, ed. A. Failler, trans. V. Laurent. Paris, 1984; vols. III and IV, ed. and tr. Failler. Paris, 1999.
PG	J. P. Migne, *Patrologiae cursus completus, series graeca.* 161 vols. Paris, 1857–66.
PL	J. P. Migne, *Patrologiae cursus completus, series latina.* 221 vols. Paris, 1844–64.
PLP	*Prosopographisches Lexikon der Palaiologenzeit*, 12 vols., eds. E. Trapp et al. Vienna, 1976–96.
REB	*Revue des études byzantines*
Sat.	*Satire of the Tutor (baioulos)*: Tartaglia, Op. rhet., 154–97.
Sathas, MB	K. Sathas, *Μεσαιωνικὴ Βιβλιοθήκη.* 7 vols. Venice, 1872–94.
SK	*Seminarium Kondakovianum*
Synopsis chronike	Theodore Skoutariotes (?), *Synopsis chronike*, in Sathas, MB, vol. 7, 1–556.
Tartaglia, Op. rhet.	*Theodorus II Ducas Lascaris. Opuscula rhetorica,* ed. L. Tartaglia. Munich, 2000.
TM	*Travaux et mémoires*
V	Cod. Vindobonensis Philol. gr. 321 (13th c.).
Vatopedi, I	*Actes de Vatopédi*, I, eds. J. Bompaire, J. Lefort, V. Kravari, and C. Giros. *Archives de l'Athos* 21. Paris, 2001.
Villehardouin	Geoffroi de Villehardouin, *La conquête de Constantinople*, ed. E. Faral. 2 vols. Paris. 1938–39.
VV	*Vizantiiskii Vremennik*
ZRVI	*Zbornik Radova Vizantološkog Instituta*

PRIMARY SOURCES

Greek

Works by Theodore Laskaris

Agapitos, P., Angelov, D. 2018. "Six Essays by Theodore II Laskaris in Vind. Phil. Gr. 321: Edition, Translation, Analysis," *JÖB*, 68:39–75.

Angelov, D. 2011–12. "*The Moral Pieces* by Theodore II Laskaris," *DOP*, 65–66:237–69.

Aubery (Auberius), C. 1571. *Theodori Ducae Lascaris De communicatione naturali libri sex.* Basel.

Bachmann, L. 1847. *Theodori Ducae Lascaris imperatoris in laudem Nicaeae urbis oratio.* Rostock.

Balaschev, G. 1911. "Pismo ot imperatora Teodora II Laskar po skliuchvaneto na mira s tsar Mikhaila Asena (1256 g.)," *Minalo*, 2:60–70.

Dragoumis, S. 1911–12. "Θεοδώρου Δούκα Λασκάρεως ἐπιτάφιος εἰς Φρεδερίκον Β´ βασιλέα τῶν Ἀλαμανῶν," *Byzantis*, 2:404–13.

Festa, N. 1897–98. "Κοσμικὴ Δήλωσις," *Giornale della Società Asiatica Italiana*, 11:97–114.

    1898. *Theodori Ducae Lascaris epistulae CCXVII.* Florence.

    1899. "Κοσμικὴ Δήλωσις," *Giornale della Società Asiatica Italiana*, 12:1–52.

Georgiopoulou, S. 1990. *Theodore II Dukas Laskaris (1222–1258) as an Author and an Intellectual of the XIIIth Century.* PhD Dissertation: Harvard University, Cambridge, MA.

Giannouli, A. 2001. "Eine Rede auf das Akathistos-Fest (BHG³ 1140, CPG 8197) und Theodoros II. Dukas Laskaris," *JÖB*, 51:259–83.

Krikonis, Ch. 1988. *Θεοδώρου Β´ Λασκάρεως περὶ χριστιανικῆς θεολογίας λόγοι.* Thessalonica.

Markopoulos, A. 1968. "Θεοδώρου Β´ Λασκάρεως ἀνέκδοτον ἐγκώμιον πρὸς τὸν Γεώργιον Ἀκροπολίτην," *EEBS*, 36:104–18.

Paléologou, M. 2007. "Deux traités inédits de Théodore II Doucas Lascaris," *Byzantina*, 27:51–90.

Swete, H. B. 1875. *Theodorus Lascaris Junior. De processione Spiritus Sancti oratio apologetica.* London.

Tartaglia, L. 1980–81. "L'opuscolo *De subiectorum in principem officiis* di Teodoro II Lascaris," *Diptycha*, 2:187–222.

    1990. *Teodoro II Duca Lascari. Encomio dell'imperatore Giovanni Duca.* Naples.

    1991. "Una apologia inedita di Teodoro II Duca Lascari," *Bollettino dei classici*, 12:69–82.

    1992. *Teodoro II Duca Lascari. Satira del pedagogo.* Naples.

    2000. *Theodorus II Ducas Lascaris. Opuscula rhetorica.* Munich.

    2008. "Le *Epitomi Etiche* di Teodoro II Duca Lascari," *Atti della Accademia Pontaniana, Napoli*, N.S., 57:145–74.

Historians

Anna Komnene: Reinsch, D., A. Kambylis. 2001. *Annae Comnenae Alexias*. 2 vols. Berlin.

Continuator of John Skylitzes: Tsolakis, E. 1968. Ἡ συνέχεια τῆς χρονογραφίας τοῦ Ἰωάννου Σκυλίτση. Thessalonica.

Doukas: Bekker, I. 1834. *Ducae, Michaelis Ducae nepotis, Historia Byzantina*. Bonn.

Ephraim: Lampsides, O. 1990. *Ephraem Aenii Historia chronica*. Athens.

George Sphrantzes: Grecu, V. 1966. *Georgios Sphrantzes. Memorii, 1401–1477*. Bucharest.

John Kantakouzenos: Schopen, L. 1828–32. *Ioannis Cantacuzeni eximperatoris historiarum libri IV*. 3 vols. Bonn.

John Kinnamos: Meineke, A. 1836. *Ioannis Cinnami epitome rerum ab Ioanne et Alexio Comnenis gestarum*. Bonn.

John Malalas: Thurn, I. 2000. *Ioannis Malalae chronographia*. Berlin.

John Skylitzes: Thurn, I. 1973. *Ioannis Scylitzae synopsis historiarum*. Berlin.

John Zonaras: Pinder, M. 1841. 1844. *Ioannis Zonarae annales*, vol. 1 and 2. Bonn. Büttner-Wobst, T. 1897. *Ioannis Zonarae epitomae historiarum*, vol. 3. Bonn.

Leo the Deacon: Hase, C. 1828. *Leonis diaconi caloënsis historiae libri decem*. Bonn.

Theophanes: De Boor, C. 1883. *Theophanis chronographia*, vol. 1. Leipzig.

Other

Agapitos, P. 2006. Ἀφήγησις Λιβίστρου καὶ Ῥοδάμνης: Κριτικὴ ἔκδοση τῆς διασκευῆς α. Athens.

Allard, A. 1978. "Le premier traité byzantin de calcul indien: classement des manuscrits et édition critique du texte," *Revue d'histoire des textes*, 7:57–107.

Angelou, A. 1991. *Manuel Palaiologos: Dialogue with the Empress-Mother on Marriage*. Vienna.

Arampatzis, Ch. 2004–06. "Ἀνέκδοτη ἐπιστολὴ τοῦ πατριάρχη Κωνσταντινουπόλεως Γερμανοῦ Βʹ πρὸς τοὺς Καρδιναλίους τῆς Ῥώμης," *ΕΕΒΣ*, 52:363–78.

Bartikian, H. 2002. "Hay-Biwzandakan Ekełecʻakan yaraberutʻiwnnerě Pʻastatʻltʻerum," *Ganjasar (Gandzasar)*, 7:50–86. Reprinted in Bartikian, H. 2006. *Studia Armeno-Byzantina*, vol. 3. Yerevan. 27–63.

Beckh, H. 1895. *Geoponica sive Cassiani Bassi scholastici de re rustica eclogae*. Leipzig.

Beihammer, A. 2007. *Griechische Briefe und Urkunden aus dem Zypern der Kreuzfahrerzeit. Die Formularsammlung eines königlichen Sekretärs im Vaticanus Palatinus Graecus 367*. Nicosia.

Berthelot, M., Ruelle, C.-É. 1887–88. *Collection des anciens alchimistes grecs*, 3 vols. Paris.

Burgmann, L., Magdalino, P. 1984. "Michael VIII on Maladministration: An Unpublished Novel of the Early Palaiologan Period," *Fontes Minores*, 6:377–90.

Cappuyns, N. 1935. "Le synodicon de Chypre au XIIe siècle," *B*, 10:489–504.

Chatzipsaltis, K. 1964. "Ἡ ἐκκλησία Κύπρου καὶ τὸ ἐν Νικαίᾳ οἰκουμενικὸν πατρι-αρχεῖον τοῦ ΙΓ΄ μ.Χ. αἰῶνος," *Kypriakai spoudai*, 28:141–68.

Cheynet, J.-C., Theodoridis, D. 2010. *Sceaux byzantins de la collection D. Theodoridis: les sceaux patronymiques*. Paris.

Copenhaver, B. 1995. *Hermetica: the Greek Corpus Hermeticum and the Latin Asclepius in a New English Translation, with Notes and Introduction*. Cambridge.

Couroupou, M. 1981. "Le siège de Philadelphie par Umur pacha d'après le manuscrit de la Bibl. Patriarcale d'Istanbul, Panaghias 58*," in H. Ahrweiler (ed.), *Geographica Byzantina*. Paris. 67–77.

Criscuolo, U. 1982. "Semeioma patriarcale inedito di Manuele Karanteno o Saranteno," *Bollettino della Badia Greca di Grottaferrata Roma*, 36:123–36.

Darrouzès, J. 1965. "Notes sur Euthyme Tornikès, Euthyme Malakès et Georges Tornikès," *REB*, 23:148–67.

  1968. "Les discours d'Euthyme Tornikès (1200–1205)," *REB*, 26:49–121.

  1970a. *Georges et Dèmètrios Tornikès. Lettres et discours*. Paris.

  1970b. *Recherches sur les OFFIKIA de l'Église byzantine*. Paris.

  1981. *Notitiae Episcopatuum Ecclesiae Constantinopolitanae*. Paris.

  1984. "Le traité des transferts: Édition critique et commentaire," *REB*, 42:147–214.

Delehaye, H. 1925. *Acta Sanctorum Novembris IV*. Brussels.

Dennis, G. 1977. *The Letters of Manuel II Palaeologus: Text, Translation, and Notes*. Washington, DC.

Duffy, J. 1983. *Stephanus the Philosopher: Commentary on the Prognosticon of Hippocrates*. Berlin.

Evangelatou-Notara, F. 1989. "Πολεμικὲς ἐπιχειρήσεις στὴ Θράκη τὸ θέρος τοῦ 1247," *BF*, 14:189–97.

Ferrari dalle Spade, G. 1913. "Formulari notarili inediti dell'età bizantina," *Bullettino dell'Istituto Storico Italiano*, 33:41–128.

Fögen, M. Th. 1983. "Ein heißes Eisen," *Rechtshistorisches Journal*, 2:85–96.

Gaisford, T. 1823. *Poetae minores Graeci*, 5 vols. Leipzig.

Gautier, P. 1972. *Michel Italikos: Lettres et discours*. Paris.

  1980. *Théophylacte d'Achrida: Discours, traités, poésies*, vol. 1. Thessalonica.

Gedeon, M. 1911. Ἀρχεῖον ἐκκλησιαστικῆς ἱστορίας, vol. 1. Istanbul.

Giannouli, A. 2007. *Die beiden byzantinischen Kommentare zum Großen Kanon des Andreas von Kreta*. Vienna.

Gill, J. 1974. "An Unpublished Letter of Germanus, Patriarch of Constantinople (1222–1240)," *Byzantion*, 44:138–51.

Grégoire, H. 1922. *Recueil des inscriptions grecques-chrétiennes d'Asie Mineure*. Paris.

  1959–60. "Imperatoris Michaelis Palaeologi de vita sua," *B*, 29–30:447–76.

Haldon, J. 1990. *Constantine Porphyrogenitus: Three Treatises on Imperial Military Expeditions*. Vienna.

Heisenberg, A. 1896. *Nicephori Blemmydae curriculum vitae et carmina*. Leipzig.

1905. "Kaiser Johannes Batatzes der Barmherzige," *BZ*, 14:160–233.

1920. *Aus der Geschichte und Literatur der Palaiologenzeit*. Munich.

1923a. *Neue Quellen zur Geschichte des lateinischen Kaisertums und der Kirchenunion, I: Der Epitaphios des Nikolaos Mesarites auf seinen Bruder Johannes*. Munich.

1923b. *Neue Quellen, II: Die Unionsverhandlungen vom 30. August 1206, Patriarchenwahl und Kaiserkrönung in Nikaia 1208*. Munich.

1923c. *Neue Quellen. III: Der Bericht des Nikolaos Mesarites über die politischen und kirchlichen Ereignisse des Jahres 1214*. Munich.

Hercher, R. 1873. *Epistolographi graeci*. Paris.

Hoeck, J.M., Loenertz, R.-J., 1965. *Nikolaos-Nektarios von Otranto, Abt von Casole: Beiträge zur Geschichte der ost-westlichen Beziehungen unter Innozenz III. und Friedrich II*. Ettal.

Hörandner, W. 1972. "Prodromos-Reminiszenzen bei Dichtern der nikänischen Zeit," *BF*, 4:88–104.

2012. "Pseudo-Gregorios Korinthios, *Über die vier Teile der perfekten Rede*," *Medioevo greco*, 12:87–131.

Horna, K. 1904. "Das Hodoiporikon des Konstantin Manasses," *BZ*, 13:313–55.

1905. "Die Epigramme des Patriarchen Germanos II," *Analekten zur byzantinischen Literatur*. Vienna. 31–35.

Jeffreys, E. 1998. *Digenis Akritis: The Grottaferrata and Escorial Versions*. Cambridge.

Karpozilos, A. 1990. *The Letters of Ioannes Mauropus, Metropolitan of Euchaita: Greek Text, Translation and Commentary*. Thessalonica.

Kiourtzian, G. 2008. "Une nouvelle inscription de Cappadoce du règne de Théodore Ier Lascaris," *Δελτίον τῆς Χριστιανικῆς Ἀρχαιολογικῆς Ἑταιρείας*, 29:131–38.

Kolovou, F. 2001. *Michaelis Choniatae epistulae*. Berlin and New York.

Kourouses, S. 2002–05. "Τὸ ἐπιστολάριον τοῦ κώδικος Vind. Phil. gr. 323 (ιγ′ αἰ.),"*Athena*, 83:533–76.

Kouzis, A. T. 1944. "Τὰ ἰατρικὰ ἔργα τοῦ Νικηφόρου Βλεμμύδου κατὰ τοὺς ὑπάρχοντας κώδικας," *Πρακτικὰ τῆς Ἀκαδημίας Ἀθηνῶν*, 19:56–75.

Lagopates, S. 1913. *Γερμανὸς ὁ Β′ πατριάρχης Κωνσταντινουπόλεως–Νικαίας (1222-1240). Βίος, συγγράμματα καὶ διδασκαλία αὐτοῦ. Ἀνέκδοτοι ὁμιλίαι καὶ ἐπιστολαί*. Tripolis.

Lameere, W. 1937. *La tradition manuscrite de la correspondance de Grégoire de Chypre, Patriarche de Constantinople (1283–1289)*. Brussels and Rome.

Lampros, Sp. 1879–80. *Μιχαὴλ Ἀκομινάτου τοῦ Χωνιάτου τὰ σωζόμενα*, 2 vols. Athens.

Laourdas, V., Westernik, L. 1983–88. *Photii Patriarchae Constantinopolitani epistulae et amphilochia*, 6 vols. Leipzig.

Laurent, V. 1934. "Recherches sur l'histoire et le cartulaire de Notre-Dame de Pitié à Stroumitsa," *Échos d'Orient*, 33:5–27.

1935a. "La correspondance inédite de Georges Babouscomitès," Εἰς μνήμην Σπυρίδωνος Λάμπρου. Athens. 83–100.

1981. *Le corpus des sceaux de l'empire byzantin, II: L'administration centrale.* Paris.

Lauriotes, A. 1901. "Περὶ παραιτήσεως ἐπισκόπου," Ἐκκλησιαστικὴ Ἀλήθεια, 21:53–55.

Leutsch, E., Schneidewin, F. 1839–51. *Corpus paroemiographorum Graecorum,* 2 vols. Göttingen.

Littlewood, A. R. 1985. *Michaelis Pselli Oratoria minora.* Leipzig.

Loenertz, R.-J. 1970. "Lettre de Georges Bardanès, métropolite de Corcyre au patriarche oecuménique Germain II," *Byzantina et Franco-Graeca.* Rome. 467–501.

Loukaki, M. 1996. "Ein unbekanntes Gebet von Georgios Zagarommates an Johannes Prodromos," *JÖB,* 46:243–49.

Macrides, R., Munitiz, J., Angelov, D. 2013. *Pseudo-Kodinos and the Constantino-politan Court: Offices and Ceremonies.* Farnham.

Mango, C. 1994. "Notes d'épigraphie et d'archéologie: Constantinople, Nicée," *TM,* 12:343–57.

Matzukis, C. 2004. Ἡ ἅλωσις τῆς Κωνσταντινουπόλεως: τέταρτη σταυροφορία. The *Fall of Constantinople: Fourth Crusade.* Peristeri.

Mercati, S. 1970. "Iacobi Bulgariae archiepiscopi opuscula," *Collectanea Byzantina,* vol. 1, 66–98.

Merendino, E. 1974–75. "Quattro lettere greche di Federico II," *Atti della Accademia di Scienze, Lettere, e Arti di Palermo* (ser. 4), 34,2:293–343.

Metcalf, D. M. 2004. *Byzantine Lead Seals from Cyprus.* Nicosia.

Mineva, E. 2018. "Izvesten, no ostanal nerazgledan vizantiiski avtor za bŭlgarskata istoriia: Πορνικὴ γὰρ ἡ βασιλεία τῶν Βουλγάρων," in A. Nikolov (ed.), *Bŭlgarsko tsarstvo. Sbornik v chest na 60-godishninata na doc. dr. Georgi N. Nikolov* (*Imperium Bulgariae. Studia in honorem annorum LX Georgii Nikolov*). Sofia. 581–95.

Moravcsik, G. 1967. *Constantine Porphyrogenitus. De Administrando Imperio.* Trans. R. Jenkins. Washington, DC.

Munitiz, J. 1979. *Theognosti Thesaurus.* Turnhout.

1988. *Nikephoros Blemmydes: A Partial Account.* Leuven.

2003. "Blemmydes Revisited: The Letters of Nicephorus Blemmydes to Patriarch Manuel II" in C. Dendrinos, J. Harris, E. Harvalia-Crook, and J. Herrin (eds.), *Porphyrogenita: Essays on the History and Literature of Byzantium and the Latin East in Honour of Julia Chrysostomides.* Aldershot. 369–87.

Nesbitt, J. 2009. *Catalogue of the Byzantine Seals at Dumbarton Oaks and in the Fogg Museum of Art,* vol. 6: *Emperors, Patriarchs of Constantinople, Addenda.* Assisted by C. Morrisson. Washington, DC.

Nesbitt, J., Wassiliou-Seibt, W., Seibt, W. 2009. *Highlights from the Robert Hecht, Jr., Collection of Byzantine Seals.* Thessalonica.

Nicole, J. 1894. "Bref inédit de Germain II, patriarche de Constantinople (année 1230), avec une recension nouvelle du chrysobulle de l'empereur Jean Ducas Vatacès," *Revue des études grecques*, 7:68–80.

Nikolopoulos, P. 1981–82. "Ἀνέκδοτος λόγος εἰς Ἀρσένιον Αὐτωρειανὸν πατριάρχην Κωνσταντινουπόλεως," *EEBS*, 45:406–61.

Nystazopoulou, M. 1964a. "Ὁ Ἀλανικός' τοῦ ἐπισκόπου Ἀλανίας Θεοδώρου καὶ ἡ εἰς τὸν πατριαρχικὸν θρόνον ἀνάρρησις Γερμανοῦ τοῦ Β΄," *EEBS*, 33:270–78.

1966. "Γράμμα τοῦ ἱερέως καὶ νομικοῦ τῶν Παλατίων Νικήτα Καραντηνοῦ πρὸς τὸν ἡγούμενον τῆς ἐν Πάτμῳ μονῆς Ἰωάννου τοῦ Θεολόγου (1256)," *Χαριστήριον εἰς Ἀναστάσιον Κ. Ὀρλάνδον*, 2:286–308.

Odorico, P. 2013. "L'Ekphrasis de la Métropole de Serrès et les Miracles des Saints Théodore par Théodore Pédiasimos," in V. Penna (ed.), *Ναός Περικαλλής. Ψηφίδες ιστορίας και ταυτότητας του Ιερού Ναού των Αγίων Θεοδώρων Σερρών.* Asprovalta. 125–54.

Oikonomides, N. 1964. "Contribution à l'étude de la *pronoia* au XIIIe siècle, une formule d'attribution de parèques à un pronoiaire," *REB*, 22:158–75.

1967. "Cinq actes inédits du Patriarche Michel Autôreianos," *REB*, 25:113–45.

Oudot, I. 1941. *Patriarchatus Constantinopolitani acta selecta*, vol. 1. Vatican City.

Pavlov, A. 1897. "Sinodal'naia gramota 1213 goda o brake grecheskago imperatora s docher'iu armianskago kniazia," *VV*, 4:160–66.

Paramelle, J. 1979. "Πορνικὴ ἡ τῶν Βουλγάρων βασιλεία," *Byzance et les Slaves. Études de civilisation. Mélanges Ivan Dujčev.* Paris. 317–31.

Pieralli, L. 1998. "Una lettera del Patriarca Arsenios Autorianos a Papa Alessandro IV sull'unione delle Chiese," *JÖB*, 48:171–88.

2006. *La corrispondenza diplomatica dell'imperatore bizantino con le potenze estere nel tredicesimo secolo (1204–1282).* Vatican City.

Polemis, D. 1966. "A Manuscript Note of the Year 1247," *BF*, 1:269–76.

1973. "The Speech of Constantine Akropolites on St. John Merciful the Young," *Analecta Bollandiana*, 91:31–54.

Polemis, I. 1995. "Προβλήματα τῆς βυζαντινῆς σχεδογραφίας," *Hellenika*, 45:277–302.

Prinzing, G. 1983. "Die Antigraphe des Patriarchen Germanos II. an Erzbischof Demetrios Chomatenos von Ohrid und die Korrespondenz zum nikäisch-epirotischen Konflikt 1212–1233," *Rivista di studi bizantini e slavi*, 3:21–64.

2002. *Demetrii Chomateni Ponemata diaphora.* Berlin.

Rabe, H. 1913. *Hermogenis opera.* Leipzig.

1926. *Aphthonii progymnasmata.* Leipzig.

1931. *Prolegomenon sylloge.* Leipzig.

Reiske, J. 1829. *De cerimoniis aulae Byzantinae libri duo.* Bonn.

Rhalles, G., Potles, M. 1852–59. *Σύνταγμα τῶν θείων καὶ ἱερῶν κανόνων*, 6 vols. Athens.

Richard, M., Munitiz, J. 2006. *Anastasii Sinaitae Quaestiones et responsiones.* Turnhout.

Riehle, A. 2015. "Epistolographie und Astronomie in der frühen Palaiologenzeit: Ein bislang unedierter Brief des Nikolaos Rhabdas an Andronikos Zarides aus dem Jahr 1321," *JÖB*, 65:243–52.

———. 2016. "Theodoros Xanthopulos, Theodoros Metochites und die spätbyzantinische Gelehrtenkultur," in A. Berger et al. (eds.), *Koinotaton Doron: Das späte Byzanz zwischen Machtlosigkeit und kultureller Blüte (1204–1461)*. Berlin, 161–83.

Riedinger, A. 1995. *Agapetos Diakonos. Der Fürstenspiegel für Kaiser Iustinianos*. Athens.

Roberts, W. R. 1902. *Demetrius On Style. The Greek Text of Demetrius De elocutione*. Cambridge.

Sabatier, J. 1858. "Plombs, bulles et sceaux byzantines," *Revue archéologiques*, 15: 82–100.

Sathas, K. N. 1872–94. *Μεσαιωνικὴ Βιβλιοθήκη*, 7 vols. Venice and Paris.

Scheer, E. 1881–1908. *Lycophronis Alexandra*. 2 vols. Berlin.

Schreiner, P. 1975, 1977, 1979. *Die byzantinischen Kleinchroniken*. 3 vols. Vienna.

———. 1978. "Ein Prostagma Andronikos' III. für die Monembasioten in Pegai (1328) und das gefälschte Chrysobull Andronikos' II. für die Monembasioten im byzantinischen Reich," *JÖB*, 27:203–28.

Shandrovskaia, V. S. 1975. *Vizantiiskie pechati v sobranii Ermitazha*. Leningrad.

Spengel, L. 1853–56. *Rhetores Graeci*. 3 vols. Leipzig.

Solovjev, A., Mošin, V. 1936. *Grčke povelje Srpskih vladara*. Belgrade.

Stavrakos, Ch. 2000. *Die byzantinischen Bleisiegel mit Familiennamen aus der Sammlung des Numismatischen Museums Athen*. Wiesbaden.

Stavrou, M. 2007–13. *Nicéphore Blemmydes. Oeuvres théologiques*. 2 vols. Paris.

Stephanus, R. (Ex officina Roberti Stephani typographi regii) 1545. *Manuelis Moschopuli De ratione examinandae orationis libellus. Ex bibliotheca regia*. Paris.

Treu, M. 1899. *Theodori Pediasimi eiusque amicorum quae extant*. Potsdam.

Vasil'evskii, V. 1896. "Epirotica saeculi XIII," *VV*, 3:233–99.

Verpeaux, J. 1966. *Pseudo-Kodinos: Traité des offices*. Paris.

Vryonis, Sp., Jr. 1957. "The Will of a Provincial Magnate, Eustathius Boilas (1059)," *DOP*, 11:263–77.

Wassiliou, A.-K., Seibt, W. 2004. *Die byzantinischen Bleisiegel in Österreich, 2. Teil: Zentral- und Provinzialverwaltung*. Vienna.

Westerink, L. 1995. *Stephanus of Athens: Commentary on Hippocrates' Aphorisms, Sections V–VI*. Berlin.

Wilson, N., Darrouzès, J. 1968. "Restes du cartulaire de Hiéra-Xérochoraphion," *REB*, 26:5–47.

Xanthopoulos, Nikephoros Kallistos. Διήγησις περὶ τῶν ἐπισκόπων Βυζαντίου καὶ τῶν πατριαρχῶν πάντων Κωνσταντινουπόλεως, *PG*, vol. 147, cols. 449–68.

Xintaras, Z. K. 1999. *Γερμανοῦ Β' Κυριακοδρόμιον*. Athens.

Zacos, G., Veglery, A., 1972–85. *Byzantine Lead Seals*. 2 vols. Basel.

Zepos, P. and I. 1931. *Jus Graecoromanum*, 8 vols. Athens.

Latin and Old French

Historical and other narratives

Alberic of Trois-Fountaines: Scheffer-Boichorst, P. 1874. *Chronica Albrici monachi Trium Fontium,* in *Monumenta Germaniae Historica. Scriptores*, vol. 23. Hannover. 631–950.

Andrea Dandolo: Pastorello, E. 1938. *Andreae Danduli Chronica per extensum descripta,* in *Rerum Italicarum Scriptores*, n.s., vol. 12, 1. Bologna.

Annales Placentini Gibellini: Pertz, G. H. 1863. *Monumenta Germaniae Historica. Scriptores*, vol. 18. Hannover. 457–581.

Annales Urbevetani: Carducci, G., Fiorini, V. 1903. *Rerum Italicarum Scriptores*, n. s. 15, 5. Città di Castello. 125–198.

Francesco Scalamonti: Mitchell, C., Bodnar, E. 1996. *Vita Viri Clarissimi et Famosissimi Kyriaci Anconitani.* Philadelphia.

González de Clavijo, Ruy: López Estrada, F. 1943. *Embajada a Tamorlán.* Madrid. Trans. G. Le Strange. 1928. *Embassy to Tamerlane, 1403–1406.* London.

Joinville: De Wailly, N. 1874. *Histoire de Saint Louis.* Paris.

Marinus Sanuto Torsellus, *Liber secretorum fidelium crucis*: Bongars, H. 1611. *Gesta Dei per Francos*, vol. 2. Hanover.

Martin da Canal: Limentani, A. 1972. *Les Estoires de Venise. Cronaca veneziana in lingua francese dalle origini al 1275.* Florence. Trans. L. Morreale. 2009. Padua.

Matthew Paris: Luard, H.R. 1872–84. *Chronica Majora.* Rolls Series, 57. 7 vols. London.

Niccolò Jamsilla: *Nicolai de Jamsilla Historia antea edita sub inscriptione Anonymi De rebus gestis Friderici II. Imperatoris*: Muratori, L. 1726. *Rerum Italicarum Scriptores*, vol. 8. Milan. 493–584, 585–616.

Richard of San Germano: Garufi, C. 1937–38. *Ryccardi de Sancto Germano Notarii Chronica,* in *Rerum Italicarum Scriptores*, n.s., vol. 7, 2. Bologna.

Robert of Clari: Lauer, Ph. 1924. *La conquête de Constantinople.* Paris. Trans. E. McNeal. 1936. *The Conquest of Constantinople.* New York.

Philippe Mouskes: De Reiffenberg. 1836–38. *Chronique rimée de Philippe Mouskes.* 2 vols. Brussels.

Relatio de Concilio Lugdunensi: Weiland, L. 1896. *Monumenta Germaniae Historica. Leges. Constitutiones et Acta Publica*, vol. 2: *1198–1272.* 513–16.

Salimbene de Adam, *Cronica.* Ed. G. Scalia. 1998–99. 2 vols. Turnhout.

William of Rubruck, *Itinerarium.* Van den Wyngaert, A. 1929. *Sinica franciscana: itinera et relationes Fratrum Minorum saeculi XIII et XIV,* I. Karachi and Florence. 164–332. Trans. P. Jackson. 1990. *The Mission of Friar William of Rubruck: His Journey to the Court of the Great Khan Möngke, 1253–1255.* London.

William of Tyre: Huygens, R.B.C. 1986. *Chronique.* Turnhout.

Other

Andrea, A. 2000. *Contemporary Sources for the Fourth Crusade.* Leiden.

Auvray, L. 1896, 1907, 1907, 1955. *Les registres de Grégoire IX.* 4 vols. Paris.

Balard, M. 1966. "Les Génois en Romanie entre 1204 et 1261. Recherches dans les minutiers notariaux génois," *Mélanges d'archéologie et d'histoire,* 78:467–502.

Belgrano, L. T. 1885. "Cinque documenti genovesi-orientali," *Atti della Società Ligure di Storia Patria,* 17:221–51.

Berger, É. 1884, 1887, 1897, 1920. *Les registres d'Innocent IV.* 4 vols. Paris.

Capasso, B. 1874. *Historia diplomatica regni Siciliae inde ab anno 1250 ad annum 1266.* Naples.

Carile, A. 1965. "Partitio Terrarum Imperii Romanie," *Studi Veneziani,* 7:125–305.

Collenuccio, P. 1929. *Compendio de le istorie del Regno di Napoli.* A. Saviotti (ed.). Bari.

Davidsohn, R. 1896–1919. *Forschungen zur Geschichte von Florenz.* 4 vols. Berlin.

De la Roncière, B., de Loye, J., Coulon, A., and de Cenival, P. 1902, 1917, 1959. *Les registres de Alexandre IV.* 3 vols. Paris.

Golubovich, H. 1919. "Disputatio latinorum et graecorum seu Relatio Apocrisariorum Gregorii IX de gestis Nicaeae in Bithynia et Nymphaeae in Lydia (1234)," *Archivum franciscanum historicum,* 12:418–70.

Górka, O. 1916. *Anonymi descriptio Europae orientalis, "Imperium Constantinopolitanum, Albania, Serbia, Bulgaria, Ruthenia, Ungaria, Polonia, Bohemia," anno MCCCVIII exarata.* Krakow.

Haluščynskyj, Th., Wojnar, M. 1966. *Acta Alexandri PP. IV (1254–1261).* Rome.

Hendrickx, B. 1988. "Régestes des empereurs latins de Constantinople (1204–1261/1272)," *Byzantina,* 14:7–221.

Huillard-Bréholles, J.-L.-A., 1852–61. *Historia diplomatica Friderici secondi.* 6 vols. Paris.

Lorimer, W. L., Minio-Paluello, L. 1965. *De mundo. Translationes Bartholomaei et Nicholai.* Aristoteles Latinus XI 1–2. Bruges and Paris. Rev. edn.

Miret y Sans, J. 1906. "Tres princesas griegas en la corte de Jaime II de Aragón," *Revue hispanique* 15:668–720.

Moscati, A. 1953. "La 'Lamentacio' di Bertoldo di Hohenburg," *Bullettino dell'Istituto storico italiano per il Medio Evo e Archivio Muratoriano,* 65:121–27.

Nicholas of Croton, *Libellus de fide Trinitatis.* H.-F. Dondaine (ed.). *Sancti Thomae de Aquino opera omnia,* vol. 40, part A. Rome, 1967. 109–51.

Pagnotti, F. 1898. "Niccolò da Calvi e la sua Vita d'Innocenzo IV, con una breve introduzione sulla istoriografia pontifica nei secoli XIII e XIV," *Archivio della Società Romana di Storia Patria,* 21:7–120.

Predelli, R. 1872. *Il Liber Communis detto anche Plegiorum.* Venice.

Prinzing, G. 1973. "Der Brief Kaiser Heinrichs von Konstantinopel vom 13. Januar 1212," *B,* 43:395–431.

Riant, P. 1877. *Exuviae Sacrae Constantinopolitanae,* vol. 1. Geneva.

Richard, J. 1965. *Simon de Saint-Quentin. Histoire des Tartares.* Paris.

Schillmann, F. 1908. "Zur byzantinischen Politik Alexanders IV," *Römische Quartalschrift,* 22:108–31.

Tafel, G.L.F., Thomas, G. M., 1856, 1856, 1857. *Urkunden zur älteren Handels- und Staatsgeschichte der Republik Venedig mit besonderer Beziehung auf Byzanz und die Levante.* 3 vols. Vienna.

Theiner, A. 1859. *Vetera monumenta historica Hungariam sacram illustrantia,* vol. 1. Rome.

Thomas, G.M., Predelli, R. 1880–99. *Diplomatarium Veneto-Levantinum,* 2 vols. Venice.

Arabic and Persian

Al-Idrisi: Jaubert, P.-A. 1836–40. *La Géographie d'Édrisi.* 2 vols. Paris.

Cahen, C. 1939. "Quelques textes négligés concernant les Turcomans de Rûm au moment de l'invasion mongole," *B,* 14:131–39.

    1971. "Questions d'histoire de la province de Kastamonu au XIIIe siècle," *Journal of Seljuk Studies,* 3:145–58.

    1974. "Ibn Sa'īd sur l'Asie Mineure Seldjuquide," in *Turcobyzantina et Oriens Christianus.* Study XI. London.

Ibn 'Abd al-Zahir: Sadeque, S.F. 1956. *Baybars I of Egypt.* Dacca.

Ibn Bibi: Duda, H. 1959. *Die Seltschukengeschichte des Ibn Bibi.* Copenhagen.

Ibn Khordadbeh: De Goeje, M. J. 1889. *Liber viarum et regnorum.* Leyden.

Harun ibn Yahya: Vasiliev, A. 1932. "Harun-ibn-Yahya and His Description of Constantinople," *Seminarium Kondakovianum,* 5:149–63.

Makrizi: Quatremère, E. 1837–45. *Histoire des sultans mamlouks, d'Egypte, écrite en arabe.* 2 vols. Paris.

Armenian

Kirakos of Gandzak: Brosset, M. 1870. *Deux historiens arméniens: Kiracos de Gantzac, XIIIe s., Histoire d'Arménie; Oukhtanès d'Ourha, Xe s., Histoire en trois parties,* vol. 1.

St. Petersburg. Khanlarian, L. A. 1976. *Kirakos Gandzaketsi: Istoriia Armenii.* Moscow.

Bedrosian, R. G. 1986. *History of the Armenians.* New York.

Vardan Arewelts'i: Thomson, R. W. 1989. "The Historical Compilation of Vardan Arawelc'i," *DOP,* 43:125–226.

Constable Smbat: Dédéyan, G. 1980. *La Chronique attribuée au Connétable Smbat.* Paris.

Syriac

Bar Hebraeus: Wallis Budge, E. A. 1932. *The Chronography of Gregory Abû'l Faraj, the Son of Aaron, the Hebrew Physician, Commonly Known as Bar Hebraeus,* vol. 1. London.

Hebrew

Benjamin of Tudela: Adler, M. N. 1907. *The Itinerary of Benjamin of Tudela: Critical Text, Translation and Commentary*. London.

Bowman, S. 1985. *The Jews of Byzantium, 1204–1453*. Tuscaloosa, AL.

Mann, J. 1926. "Une *source de l'histoire juive* au XIIIe siècle: la lettre polémique de Jacob b. Elie à Pablo Christiani," *Revue des études juives*, 82:363–77.

Slavic

Bozhilov, I., Totomanova, A., and Biliarski, I. 2010. *Borilov sinodik: izdanie i prevod*. Sofia.

Kałużniacki, E. 1899. *Zur älteren Paraskevalitteratur der Griechen, Slaven und Romänen*. Vienna.

Kozhukharov, S. 1974. "Neizvesten letopisen razkaz ot vremeto na Ivan Asen II," *Literaturna misŭl*, 2:123–35.

Petkov, K. 2008. *The Voices of Medieval Bulgaria, Seventh–Fifteenth Century*. Leiden.

SECONDARY WORKS

Abbott, H. P. 1988. "Autobiography, Autography, Fiction: Groundwork for a Taxonomy of Textual Categories," *New Literary History*, 19:597–615.

Abulafia, D. 1988. *Frederick II: A Medieval Emperor*. Oxford.

Acconcia-Longo, A. 1985–86, "Per la storia di Corfù nel XIII secolo," *Rivista di studi bizantini e neoellenici*, n.s., 22–23:209–43.

Agapitos, P. 1993. "Ἡ χρονολογικὴ ἀκολουθία τῶν μυθιστορημάτων Καλλίμαχος, Βέλθανδρος καὶ Λίβιστρος," in N. M. Panagiotakis (ed.), *Origini della letteratura neogreca*, vol. 2. Venice. 197–234.

    2007. "Blemmydes, Laskaris and Philes," in M. Hinterberger and E. Schiffer (eds.), *Byzantinische Sprachkunst. Studien zur byzantinischen Literatur gewidmet Wolfram Hörandner zum 65. Geburtstag*. Berlin and New York. 1–19.

    2013. "The 'Court of Amorous Dominion' and the 'Gate of Love': Rituals of Empire in a Byzantine Romance of the Thirteenth Century," in Beihammer, Constantinou and Parani 2013:389–416.

    2014. "Grammar, Genre and Patronage in the Twelfth Century: A Scientific Paradigm and Its Implications," *JÖB*, 64:1–22.

    2015. "Karl Krumbacher and the History of Byzantine Literature," *BZ*, 108:1–52.

Ahrweiler, H. 1958. "La politique agraire des empereurs de Nicée," *B*, 28:51–66.

1960. "Les forteresses construites en Asie Mineure face à l'invasion seldjoucide," in F. Dölger and H.-G. Beck (eds.), *Akten des XI. Internationalen Byzantinistenkongresses, Munich 1958*. Munich. 182–89.

1965. "L'histoire et la géographie de la région de Smyrne entre les deux occupations turques (1081–1317), particulièrement au XIIIᵉ siècle," *TM*, 1:1–204.

1966. *Byzance et la mer*. Paris.

1975. "L'expérience nicéenne," *DOP*, 29:21–40.

Alexakis, A. 1996. *Codex Parisinus Graecus 1115 and Its Archetype*. Washington, DC.

Alexander, P. 1985. *The Byzantine Apocalyptic Tradition*, D. Abrahamse (ed.). Berkeley.

Alexiou, M. 1974. *The Ritual Lament in Greek Tradition*. Cambridge.

Allsen, T. 1987. *Mongol Imperialism: The Politics of the Grand Qan Möngke in China, Russia, and the Islamic Lands, 1251–1259*. Berkeley.

Altaner, B. 1934. "Die Kenntnis des Griechischen in den Missionsorden während des 13. und 14. Jahrhunderts," *Zeitschrift für Kirchengeschichte*, 53:436–93.

Amantos, K. 1939. "Ὁ ἅγιος Γεώργιος ὁ Διασορίτης," *Hellenika*, 11:330–31.

1951. "Ἡ οἰκογένεια Βατάτζη," *EEBS*, 21:174–78.

Anderson, J. C., Jeffreys, M. 1994. "The Decoration of the Sevastokratorissa's Tent," *B*, 64:8–18.

Andreeva, M. 1926. "Priem tatarskikh poslov pri Nikeiskom dvore," in *Sbornik statei, posviashchennykh pamiati N. P. Kondakova (Recueil d'études dédiées à la mémoire de N. P. Kondakov)*. Prague, 187–200.

1927. *Ocherki po kul'ture vizantiiskago dvora v XIII veke*. Prague.

1928. "Názory Theodora II. Laskarise na ideálního panovníka," in M. Weingart, J. Dobiás and M. Paulová (eds.), *Z dějin východní Evropy a slovanstva. Sborník věnovaný Jaroslavu Bidlovi profesoru Karlovy University k šedesátým narozeninám*. Prague, 71–76.

1929. "Adresaty i datirovka dvukh pisem Nikifora Vlemmida," in B. Evreinov et al. (eds.). *Sbornik statei, posviashchennykh Pavlu Nikolaevichu Miliukovu (1859–1929)*. Prague, 193–204.

1930. "Polemika Theodora II. Laskaria s Nikiforom Vlemmidom," *Mémoires de la Société royale des sciences de Bohême, classe des lettres, année 1929*. Prague. 1–36.

Angelou, A. 1996. "'Who Am I?' Scholarios' Answers and the Hellenic Identity," in C. Constantinides, N. Panagiotakes, E. Jeffreys and A. Angelou (eds.), *Philhellene: Studies in Honour of Robert Browning*. Venice. 1–19.

Angelov, D. 2005. "Byzantine Ideological Reactions to the Latin Conquest of Constantinople," in Laiou 2005:293–310.

2007. *Imperial Ideology and Political Thought in Byzantium, 1204–1330*. Cambridge.

2011a. "Theodore II Laskaris on the Sultanate of Rum and the Flight of 'Izz al-Dīn Kay Kāwūs II," *Journal of Turkish Studies (=In Memoriam Angeliki Laiou)*, eds. C. Kafadar and N. Necipoğlu, 36:26–43.

2011b. "Prosopography of the Byzantine World (1204–1261) in the Light of Bulgarian Sources," in Herrin and Saint-Guillain 2011:101–20.

2013a. "'Asia and Europe Commonly Called East and West': Constantinople and Geographical Imagination in Byzantium," in S. Bazzaz, Y. Batsaki and D. Angelov (eds.), *Imperial Geographies in Byzantine and Ottoman Space*. Cambridge, MA. 43–68.

2013b. "Theodore II Laskaris, Elena Asenina and Bulgaria," *Srednovekovniiat bŭlgarin i 'drugite' (The Medieval Bulgarian and 'the Other')*. Sofia. 273–97.

Angold, M. 1975a. *A Byzantine Government in Exile: Government and Society under the Laskarids of Nicaea (1204–1261)*. Oxford.

1975b. "Byzantine 'Nationalism' in the Nicaean Empire," *BMGS*, 1:49–70.

1980. "The Interaction of Latins and Byzantines during the Period of the Latin Empire (1204–1261): The Case of the Ordeal," *Actes du XVe Congrès international d'études byzantines*, vol. 4. Athens. 1–10.

1989. "Greeks and Latins after 1204: The Perspective of Exile," *Mediterranean Historical Review*, 4:63–86.

1998. "The Autobiographical Impulse in Byzantium," *DOP*, 52:225–57.

2003a. *The Fourth Crusade: Event and Context*. Harlow.

2003b. "The City of Nicaea ca. 1000–1400," in I. Akbaygil, H. Inalcik and O. Aslanapa (eds.), *Iznik Throughout History*. Istanbul. 27–55.

Antoniadis-Bibicou, H. 1963. *Recherches sur les douanes à Byzance*. Paris.

Aspanovich, O.S. 2007. "K voprosu o dolzhnosti kundastabla u sel'dzhukidov Ruma v XIII v.: Kundastabl Rumi i Mikhail Paleolog," *VV*, 66:171–91.

Astruc, C. 1965. "La tradition manuscrite des oeuvres oratoires profanes de Théodore II Lascaris," *TM*. 1:393–404.

Aylward, W. 2006. "The Byzantine Fortifications at Pegae (Priapus) on the Sea of Marmara," *Studia Troica*, 16:179–203.

Baldwin, B. 1982. "A Talent to Abuse: Some Aspects of Byzantine Satire," *BF*, 8: 19–28.

Bandini, A. M. 1768. *Catalogus codicum manuscriptorum Bibliothecae Mediceae Laurentianae varia continens opera Graecorum patrum*, vol. 2. Florence.

Beck, H.-G. 1955. "Der byzantinische 'Ministerpräsident'," *BZ* 48:309–38.

Bee-Seferli, E. 1971–76. "Ὁ χρόνος στέψεως τοῦ Θεοδώρου Δούκα ὡς προσδιορίζεται ἐξ ἀνεκδότων γραμμάτων Ἰωάννου τοῦ Ἀποκαύκου," *BNJ*, 21:272–79.

Beihammer, A. 2011. "Defection across the Border of Islam and Christianity: Apostasy and Cross-Cultural Interaction in Byzantine-Seljuk Relations," *Speculum*, 86:597–651.

Beihammer, A., Constantinou, S., Parani, M. (eds.) 2013. *Court Ceremonies and Rituals of Power in Byzantium and the Medieval Mediterranean: Comparative Perspectives*. Leiden.

Belke, K. and Mersich, N. 1990. *Phrygien und Pisidien*. Tabula Imperii Byzantini, 7. Vienna.

Berg, B. 1988. "Manfred of Sicily and the Greek East," *Byzantina*, 14:263–89.

Berschin, W. 1988. *Greek Letters and the Latin Middle Ages, from Jerome to Nicholas of Cusa*. Trans. J. C. Frakes. Washington, DC.

Bieg, G., Belke, K. and Tekkök, B. 2009. "Die mittel- bis spätbyzantinische Besiedlung innerhalb des Nationalparks 'Troia und die Troas'," *Studia Troica*, 18:163–97.

Bony, P. 1984–89. "Le gisant en marbre noire de Saint-Denis: les signes symboliques de l'impératrice Marie de Brienne?" *Revue française d'héraldique et de sigillographie*, 54–59:91–110.

Booth, I. 2004. "The Sangarios Frontier: The History and Strategic Role of Paphlagonia in Byzantine Defence in the 13th Century," *BF*, 28:45–86.

Bossier, F. 1989. "Méthode de traduction et problèmes de chronologie," in Brams and Vanhamel 1989:257–94.

Bouras, C. 1997. "Palace of the Despots, Mistra, Greece," in S. Ćurčić and E. Hadjitryphonos (eds.), *Secular Medieval Architecture in the Balkans, 1300–1500, and Its Preservation*. Thessalonica. 242–43.

Bourbou, C. 2010. *Health and Disease in Byzantine Crete (7th–12th Centuries AD)*. Farnham.

Bowersock, G. 1978. *Julian the Apostate*. Cambridge, MA.

Boyle, J. A. 1964. "The Journey of Het'um I, King of Little Armenia, to the Court of the Great Khan Möngke," *Central Asiatic Journal*, 9:175–89.

Bozhilov, I. 1985. *Familiiata na Asenevtsi: genealogiia i prosopografiia*. Sofia.

Brams, J., Vanhamel, W. (eds.) 1989. *Guillaume de Moerbeke: Recueil d'études à l'occasion du 700e anniversaire de sa mort (1286)*. Leuven.

Brams, J. 2006. "Traductions et traducteurs Latins dans l'empire de Nicée et sous les Paléologues," in M. Cacouros and M.-H. Congourdeau (eds.), *Philosophie et sciences à Byzance de 1204 à 1453*. Leuven. 101–12.

Brand, C. 1968. *Byzantium Confronts the West, 1180–1204*. Cambridge, MA.

Bredenkamp, F. 1996. *The Byzantine Empire of Thessaloniki (1224–1242)*. Thessalonica.

Brezeanu, S. 1974. "Notice sur les rapports de Frédéric II de Hohenstaufen avec Jean III Vatatzès," *Revue des études sud-est européennes*, 12:583–85.

1979. "La politique économique des Lascarides à la lumière des relations vénéto -nicéennes," *Etudes byzantines et post-byzantines*, 1:39–54.

Broodbank, C. 2013. *The Making of the Middle Sea: A History of the Mediterranean from the Beginning to the Emergence of the Classical World*. Oxford.

Browning, R. 1975. "Homer in Byzantium," *Viator*, 6:15–33.

Bryer, A. 1994. "The Grand Komnenos and the Great Khan at Karakorum in 1246," in Curiel and Gyselen 1994:257–61.

Buchwald, H. 1979. "Lascarid Architecture," *JÖB*, 28:261–96.

Çağaptay, S. 2010. "How Western is It? The Palace at Nymphaion and Its Architectural Setting," *First International Sevgi Gönül Byzantine Studies Symposium: Change in the Byzantine World in the Twelfth and Thirteenth Centuries.* Istanbul. 357–62.

    2011. "Prousa/Bursa, a City within the City: Chorography, Conversion, and Choreography," *BMGS*, 35:45–69.

Cahen, C. 1940. *La Syrie du Nord à l'époque des Croisades et la principauté franque d'Antioche.* Paris.

    1988. *La Turquie pré-ottomane.* Istanbul.

Cameron, Al. 1976. *Circus Factions: The Blues and the Greens at Rome and in Byzantium.* Oxford.

Cameron, Av. 1978. "The Theotokos in Sixth-Century Constantinople: A City Finds Its Symbol," *Journal of Theological Studies*, n.s. 29:79–108.

    1997. "Sacred and Profane Love: Thoughts on Byzantine Gender," in L. James (ed.), *Women, Men and Eunuchs: Gender in Byzantium.* London. 1–23.

Campagnolo-Pothitou, M. 2009. "Le sceau unique de Constantin Lascaris Comnène, l'empereur non couronné Constantin XI (1204–1205)," *Genava*, 57:209–16.

Cankova-Petkova, G. 1968. "Vosstanovlenie bolgarskogo patriarshestva v 1235 g. i mezhdunarodnoe polozhenie bolgarskogo gosudarstva," *VV*, 28:136–50.

    1969. "Griechisch-bulgarische Bündnisse in den Jahren 1235 und 1246," *Byzantinobulgarica*, 3:49–79.

Caudano, A. 2008. "Un univers sphérique au voûté? Survivance de la cosmologie antiochienne à Byzance (XIe et XIIe s.)," *B*, 78:66–86.

Charanis, P. 1947a. "On the Asiatic Frontiers of Nicaea," *Orientalia Christiana Periodica*, 13:58–62.

    1947b. "The Jews in the Byzantine Empire under the First Palaeologi," *Speculum*, 22:75–77.

    1953. "On the Ethnic Composition of Byzantine Asia Minor in the Thirteenth Century," *Προσφορὰ εἰς Στίλπωνα Π. Κυριακίδην*. Thessalonica. 140–47.

Cheynet, J.-C. 1984. "Philadelphie, un quart de siècle de dissidence, 1182–1206," in H. Ahrweiler (ed.), *Philadelphie et autres études.* Paris. 39–54.

    1987. "Du prénom au patronyme: les étrangers à Byzance (Xe–XIIe siècle)," *Studies in Byzantine Sigillography*, 1:57–66.

    1990. *Pouvoir et contestations à Byzance (963–1210).* Paris.

    2001. "Une famille méconnue: les Kratéroi," *REB*, 59:225–38.

    2008. *La société byzantine: l'apport des sceaux.* 2 vols. Paris.

    2014. "La place de Smyrne dans le thème des Thracésiens," in T. Kolias and K. Pitsakis (eds.), *Aureus: Volume Dedicated to Professor Evangelos K. Chrysos.* Athens. 89–112.

Chrissis, N. 2012. *Crusading in Frankish Greece: A Study of Byzantine–Western Relations and Attitudes, 1204–1282.* Turnhout.

Christophilopoulou, Aik. 1956. Ἐκλογή, ἀναγόρευσις καὶ στέψις τοῦ Βυζαντινοῦ αὐτοκράτορος. Athens.

Končev, D. 1959. "La forteresse Τζέπαινα-Cepina," *BSl,* 20:285–304.

Constable, G. 1975. *Letters and Letter-Collections.* Turnhout.

Constantinides, C. N. 1982. *Higher Education in Byzantium in the Thirteenth and Early Fourteenth Centuries, 1204–ca.1310.* Nicosia.

Cook, J. M. 1999. *The Troad: An Archaeological and Topographical Study.* Oxford. 2nd edn.

Curiel, R., Gyselen, R. (eds.) 1994. *Itinéraires d'Orient. Hommages à Claude Cahen (Res Orientales, 6).* Paris.

Cutler, A 1968. "The *De Signis* of Nicetas Choniates: A Reappraisal," *American Journal of Archaeology,* 72:113–18.

Czebe, G. 1931. "Studien zum Hochverratsprozesse des Michael Paläologos im Jahre 1252," *BNJ,* 8:59–98.

Darrouzès, J. 1978. *REB,* 36:276–77 (review of Schreiner 1975–79).

Dancheva-Vasileva, A. 1985. *Bŭlgariia i latinskata imperiia, 1204–1261.* Sofia, 1985.

Dawkins, R. M. 1947. "The Later History of the Varangian Guard: Some Notes," *Journal of Roman Studies,* 37:39–46.

De Andrés, G. 1968. *Catálogo de los códices griegos desaparecidos de la Real Biblioteca de El Escorial.* El Escorial.

De Leemans, P. 2014. "Bartholomew of Messina, Translator at the Court of Manfred, King of Sicily," in P. De Leemans (ed.), *Translating at the Court: Bartholomew of Messina and Cultural Life at the Court of Manfred, King of Sicily.* Leuven. Xl–XXIX.

Delobette, L. 2006. "Oublier Constantinople? L'*Éloge de Nicée* par Théodore II Lascaris," *Les villes capitales au Moyen Âge.* Paris. 349–72.

Der Nersessian, S. 1969. "The Kingdom of Cilician Armenia," in Wolff and Hazard 1969:630–59.

Devreesse, R. 1939. "Négociations ecclésiastiques arméno-byzantines au XIIIe siècle," *Atti del V Congresso internazionale di studi bizantini,* I. Rome. 146–51.

    1945. *Le patriarcat d'Antioche depuis la paix de l'Eglise jusqu'à la conquête arabe.* Paris.

Diehl, C. 1908. "Constance de Hohenstaufen, impératrice de Nicée," in *Figures byzantines,* vol. 2, Paris, 207–25.

Dimnik, M. 2003. *The Dynasty of Chernigov, 1146–1246.* Cambridge.

Döberl, M. 1894–95. "Berthold von Vohburg-Hohenburg, der letzte Vorkämpfer der deutschen Herrschaft im Königreiche Sicilien. Ein Beitrag zur Geschichte der letzten Staufer," *Deutsche Zeitschrift für Geschichtswissenschaft,* 12:201–78.

Dölger, F. 1927. "Chronologisches und Prosopographisches zur byzantinischen Geschichte des 13. Jahrhunderts," *BZ*, 27:291–320.

1953. "Zur Bedeutung von φιλόσοφος und φιλοσοφία in byzantinischer Zeit," in Dölger, F. *Byzanz und die europäische Staatenwelt*. Ettal. 197–208.

1961. "Zwei byzantinische Reiterheroen erobern die Festung Melnik," *Paraspora*, 1961:299–305.

Dölger, F., Karayannopulos, J. 1968. *Byzantinische Urkundenlehre*. Munich.

Dondaine, A. 1950. "Nicolas de Cotrone et les sources du *Contra errores Graecorum* de Sain Thomas," *Divus Thomas*, 28:313–40.

Dragoumis, S. 1911–12."Ἐπανόρθωσις τοῦ διαγράμματος τῆς πρώτης ἐκ Νικαίας στρατείας τοῦ Ἕλληνος αὐτοκράτορος Θεοδώρου τοῦ Β´," *Byzantis*, 2:201–15.

Drakopoulou, E. 1997. *Ἡ πόλη τῆς Καστορίας τῇ βυζαντινῇ καὶ μεταβυζαντινῇ ἐποχῇ (12ος – 16ος αι.)*. Athens.

Dräseke, J. 1894. "Theodoros Laskaris," *BZ*, 3:498–515.

Drpić, I. 2012. "The Serres Icon of Saints Theodores," *BZ*, 105:645–94.

Duichev, I. 1960. "Un nouveau témoignage de Jacques de Bulgarie," *BSl*, 21:54–61.

Durak, K. 2011. "The Location of Syria in Byzantine Writing: One Question, Many Answers," *Journal of Turkish Studies*, 36:45–55.

Dzielska, M. 1986. *Apollonius of Tyana in Legend and History*. Trans. P. Pieńkowski. Rome.

El-Cheikh, N. M. 2001. "Byzantium through the Islamic Prism from the Twelfth to the Thirteenth Century," in A. Laiou and R. Mottahedeh (eds.), *The Crusades from the Perspective of Byzantium and the Muslim World*. Washington, DC. 53–69.

Elm, S. 2012. *Sons of Hellenism, Fathers of the Church: Emperor Julian, Gregory of Nazianzus, and the Vision of Rome*. Berkeley.

Erdmann, K. 1961–76. *Das anatolische Karavansaray des 13. Jahrhunderts*. 3 vols. Berlin.

Eyice, S. 1960. "Le palais byzantin de Nymphaion près d'Izmir," *Akten des XI. Internationalen Byzantinistenkongresses, Munich 1958*. Munich. 150–3.

Failler, A. 1979. "La tradition manuscrite de l'Histoire de Georges Pachymère (livres I–VI)," *REB*, 37:123–220.

1980. "Chronologie et composition dans l'Histoire de Georges Pachymère," *REB*, 38:5–103.

1981. "Chronologie et composition dans l'Histoire de Georges Pachymère," *REB*, 39:145–249.

1986. "La proclamation impériale de Michel VIII et d'Andronic II," *REB*, 44:237–51.

1996. "Le complot antidynastique de Jean Drimys," *REB*, 54:235–44.

Fassoulakis, S. 1973. *The Byzantine Family of Raoul-Ral(l)es*. Athens.

Feissel, D., Gascou, J. (eds) 2004. *La pétition à Byzance*. Paris.

Felix, W. 1981. *Byzanz und die islamische Welt im früheren 11. Jahrhundert*. Vienna.

Fennell, J. 1983. *The Crisis of Medieval Russia, 1200–1304.* London, 1983.

Fenster, E. 1968. *Laudes Constantinopolitanae.* Munich.

Ferjančić, B. 1960. *Despoti u Vizantiji i Južnoslovenskim zemljama.* Belgrade.

    1979. "Solunski car Manojlo Andjeo (1230–1237)," *Zbornik Filozofskog Fakulteta u Beogradu,* 14:93–101.

Ferro, N. 1992. "Chi fu Bianca Lancia d'Agliano," in R. Bordone (ed.), *Bianca Lancia d'Agliano tra il Piemonte e il Regno di Sicilia. Atti del Convegno (Asti-Agnano, 28–29 aprile 1980).* Alessandria, 55–80.

Festa, N. 1898. "Noterelle alle epistole di Teodoro Duca Lascaris," *Studi italiani di filologia classica,* 6:228, 458.

    1899. "Noterelle alle epistole di Teodoro Duca Lascaris," *Studi italiani di filologia classica,* 7:204.

    1909. *BZ,* 18:213–19 (review of Pappadopoulos 1908).

Ficker, G. 1908. *Die Phundagiagiten.* Leipzig.

Fleming, R. 2009. "Writing Biography at the Edge of History," *American Historical Review,* 114:606–14.

Förstel, C. 2005. "Entre propagande et réalité: la culture dans l'empire de Nicée," in I. Villela-Petit (ed.), *1204, la Quatrième Croisade: de Blois à Constantinople et éclats d'empires. Revue française d'héraldique et de sigillographie,* 73–75:129–34.

    2009. "Auf den Spuren eines verschollenen Bildnisses Kaiser Theodors II," *Nea Rhome, Rivista di ricerche bizantinistiche,* 6:445–9.

Foss, C. 1979a. *Ephesus after Antiquity: A Late Antique, Byzantine and Turkish City.* Cambridge.

    1979b. "Late Byzantine Fortifications in Lydia," *JÖB,* 28:297–320.

    1982. "The Defenses of Asia Minor against the Turks," *Greek Orthodox Theological Review,* 27:145–205.

    1987. "Sites and Strongholds of Northern Lydia," *Anatolian Studies,* 37:81–101.

    1996. *Nicaea: A Byzantine Capital and Its Praises.* With the collaboration of J. Tulchin. Brookline, MA.

    1998. "Byzantine Responses to Turkish Attack: Some Sites of Asia Minor," in I. Ševčenko and I. Hutter (eds.), *Aetos: Studies in Honour of Cyril Mango.* Stuttgart. 154–71.

Foss, C., Winfield, D. 1986. *Byzantine Fortifications: An Introduction.* Pretoria.

Fox, M. 1996. *Roman Historical Myths: The Regal Period in Augustan Literature.* Oxford.

Franchi, A. 1981. *La svolta politico-ecclesiastica tra Roma e Bisanzio (1249–1254). La legazione di Giovanni da Parma. Il ruolo di Federico II.* Rome.

Fryde, E. 2000. *The Early Palaeologan Renaissance (1261–c. 1360).* Leiden.

Gardner, A. 1912. *The Lascarids of Nicaea: The Story of an Empire in Exile.* London.

Gauthier, R. A. 1982. "Notes sure les débuts (1225–1240) du premier Averroïsme," *Revue des sciences philosophiques et théologiques,* 66:321–74.

Geanakoplos, D. 1953a. "The Nicene Revolution of 1258 and the Usurpation of Michael VIII Palaeologus," *Traditio*, 9:420–29.

1953b. "Greco-Latin Relations on the Eve of the Byzantine Restoration: The Battle of Pelagonia – 1259," *DOP*, 7:99–141.

1959. *Emperor Michael Palaeologus and the West, 1258–1282: A Study in Byzantine-Latin Relations*. Cambridge, MA.

1976. "Ordeal by Fire and Judicial Duel at Byzantine Nicaea (1253): Western or Eastern Legal Influence?" in D. Geanakoplos, *Interaction of the "Sibling" Byzantine and Western Cultures in the Middle Ages and the Italian Renaissance (330–1600)*. New Haven and London. 146–55.

Georgieva, S., Nikolova, I., and Angelov, N. 1973. "Arkhitektura na dvoretsa," in K. Miiatev et al. (eds.), *Tsarevgrad Tŭrnovo: Dvorets na bŭlgarskite tsare prez vtorata bŭlgarska dŭrzhava*. Sofia. 39–166.

Giarenis, I. 2008. *Η συγκρότηση και η εδραίωση της αυτοκρατορίας της Νίκαιας: Ο αυτοκράτορας Θεόδωρος Α´ Κομνηνός Λάσκαρις*. Athens.

Gibbon, E. 1788. *The History of the Decline and Fall of the Roman Empire*, vol. 6. London.

Gill, J. 1979. *Byzantium and the Papacy, 1198–1400*. New Brunswick, NJ.

Gjuzelev, V. 1975. "La Bulgarie, Venise et l'Empire latin de Constantinople au milieu du XIIIe siècle," *Bulgarian Historical Review*, 3.4:38–49.

1977. "Bulgarien und das Kaiserreich von Nikaia (1204–1261)," *JÖB*, 26:143–54.

Goitein, S. D. 1964. "A Letter from Seleucia (Cilicia): Dated 21 July 1137," *Speculum*, 39:298–303.

Golden, P. 1997. "Wolves, Dogs, and Qipčaq Religion," *Acta Orientalia Academiae Scientiarum Hungaricae*, 50:87–97.

Gounaridis, P. 1988. "L'exploitation directe de la terre par l'État de Nicée (1204–1261): 'le zeugèlateion'," in P. Doukellis (ed.), *Actes du Congrès franco-hellénique: Le monde rural dans l'aire méditerranéenne*. Athens. 619–26.

Grierson, P., Travaini, L. 1998. *Medieval European Coinage with a Catalogue of the Coins in the Fitzwilliam Museum, Cambridge, 14: Italy (III) (South Italy, Sicily, Sardinia)*. Cambridge.

Grumel, V. 1930. "Un problème littéraire: l'authenticité de la lettre de Jean Vatatzès, empereur de Nicée, au Pape Grégoire IX," *EO*, 29:450–58.

1958. *La chronologie*. Paris.

Güdemann, M. 1884. *Geschichte des Erziehungswesens und der Cultur der Juden in Italien während des Mittelalters*. Vienna.

Guilland, R. 1946–47. "La cérémonie de la προσκύνησις," *Revue des études grecques* 59/60:251–59.

1959. "Recherches sur l'histoire administrative de l'Empire byzantin: Le Despote, δεσπότης," *REB*, 17:52–89.

1967a. "Protovestiarite," *Rivista di studi bizantini e neoellenici*, n.s. 4:3–10.

1967b. "Mémorialiste, apo ton anamneseon, myrtaïte et tatas," *JÖB*, 16:147–52.

Guzman, G. 1971. "Simon of Saint Quentin and the Dominican Mission to the Mongol Baiju: A Reappraisal," *Speculum*, 46:232–49.

Hatlie, P. 1996a. "Redeeming Byzantine Epistolography," *BMGS*, 20:213–48.

1996b. "Life and Artistry in the 'Publication' of Demetrios Kydones' Letter Collection," *Greek, Roman and Byzantine Studies*, 37:75–102.

Hauss, A. R. 1912. *Lebensgeschichte des Kardinals Oktavian Ubaldini bis zum Ausgang seiner ersten lombardischen Legation (1251)*. Heidelberg.

Heisenberg, A. 1900. *BZ*, 9:211–22 (review of *Theodori Ducae Laskaris Epistulae CCXVII*, N. Festa (ed.) (Florence, 1898).

Hendy, M. 1969. *Coinage and Money in the Byzantine Empire*. Washington, DC.

1985. *Studies in the Byzantine Monetary Economy, c. 300–1450*. Cambridge.

1999. *Catalogue of the Byzantine Coins in the Dumbarton Oaks Collection and in the Whittemore Collection*, in A. Bellinger and P. Grierson (eds.), vol. 4: *Alexius I to Michael VIII, 1081–1261*. Washington, DC.

Herrin, J. 1999. "L'enseignement maternel à Byzance," in S. Lebecq et al. (eds.), *Femmes et pouvoirs des femmes à Byzance et en Occident (VIe–XIe siècles)*. Lille. 91–102.

Herrin, J., Saint-Guillain, G. (eds.) 2011. *Identities and Allegiances in the Eastern Mediterranean after 1204*. Aldershot.

Hobsbawm, E. 1992. *Nations and Nationalism since 1780: Programme, Myth, Reality*. Cambridge.

Hoffmann, J. 1974. *Rudimente von Territorialstaaten im byzantinischen Reich (1071–1210)*. Munich.

Holt, P. 1986. *The Age of Crusades: The Near East from the Eleventh Century until 1517*. London.

Hösch, E. 1979. "Russische Fürsten im Donauraum des 13. Jahrhunderts," *Münchner Zeitschrift für Balkankunde*, 2:97–107.

Hinterberger, M. 1999. *Autobiographische Traditionen in Byzanz*. Vienna.

Hunger, H. 1961. *Katalog der griechischen Handschriften der österreichischen Nationalbibliothek, I: Codices historici, Codices philosophici et philologici*. Vienna.

Hutter, I. 1977–97. *Corpus der byzantinischen Miniaturenhandschriften*. 5 vols. Stuttgart.

Ierodiakonou, K., O'Meara, D. 2008. "Philosophies," in E. Jeffreys, J. Haldon and R. Cormack (eds.), *Oxford Handbook of Byzantine Studies*. Oxford. 711–20.

Irmscher, J. 1972. "Nikäa als 'Mittelpunkt' des griechischen Patriotismus," *BF*, 4:114–37.

Jackson, P. 1978. "The Dissolution of the Mongol Empire," *Central Asiatic Journal*, 22:186–244.

1990. "Bāyjū," *Encyclopaedia Iranica*, 4, ed. E. Yarshater. Costa Mesa, CA. 1–2.

1993. "Čormāgūn," *Encyclopaedia Iranica*, 6, ed. E. Yarshater. Costa Mesa, CA. 274.

Jacoby, D. 1961. "La population de Constantinople à l'époque byzantine: un problème de démographie urbaine," *B*, 31:81–109.

1991–92. "Silk in Western Byzantium: Trade before the Fourth Crusade," *BZ*, 84–85:452–500.

1993. "The Venetian Presence in the Latin Empire of Constantinople (1204–1261): The Challenge of Feudalism and the Byzantine Inheritance," *JÖB*, 43:141–201.

1999. "Genoa, Silk Trade and Silk Manufacture in the Mediterranean Region (ca. 1100–1300)," in A. Calderoni Masetti, C. Di Fabio and M. Marcenaro (eds.), *Tessuti, oreficerie, miniature in Liguria XIII–XV secolo*. Bordighera. 11–40.

2001. "The Jews and the Silk Industry of Constantinople," in Jacoby, D., *Byzantium, Latin Romania and the Mediterranean*. Aldershot, no. XI, 1–21.

2002. "Benjamin of Tudela in Byzantium," *Palaeoslavica*, 10:180–85.

2005. "The Economy of Latin Constantinople, 1204–1261," in *Laiou 2005:195–214*.

2009. "Caviar Trading in Byzantium," in R. Shukurov (ed.), *MARE ET LITORA: Essays Presented to Sergei Karpov for his 60th Birthday*. Moscow. 349–64.

2010. "Mediterranean Food and Wine for Constantinople: The Long-Distance Trade, Eleventh to Mid-Fifteenth Century," in E. Kislinger, J. Koder and A. Külzer (eds.), *Handelsgüter und Verkehrswege. Aspekte der Warenversorgung im östlichen Mittelmeerraum*. Vienna. 127–47.

Janin, R. 1950. *Constantinople byzantin: développement urbain et répertoire topographique*. Paris.

1975. *Les églises et les monastères des grands centres byzantins*. Paris.

Jeanselme, E. 1924. "L'épilepsie sur le trône de Byzance," *Bulletin de la société française d'histoire de la médecine*, 18:225–74.

Jenkins, R. 1947. "The Bronze Athena at Byzantium," *Journal of Hellenic Studies*, 67:31–33.

Jeffreys, E. 1979. "The Attitudes of Byzantine Chronicles Towards Ancient History," *Byzantion*, 49:199–238.

Johnson, A. 2012. "Hellenism and Its Discontents," in S. Johnson (ed.), *The Oxford Handbook of Late Antiquity*. Oxford. 437–66.

Jordanov, I. 1981. "Monetosechento na Micho Asen (1256–1263) vŭv Veliki Preslav," *Numizmatika*, 15, 4:21–41.

2001. "Byzantine Lead Seals from the Stronghold near Dorbi Dol, Plovdiv Region," *Revue numismatique*, 157:443–69.

Kaegi, W. 2003. *Heraclius, Emperor of Byzantium*. Cambridge.

Kaldellis, A. 2007. *Hellenism in Byzantium: The Transformations of Greek Identity and the Reception of the Classical Tradition*. Cambridge.

Kalopissi-Verti, S. 1992. *Dedicatory Inscriptions and Donor Portraits in Thirteenth-Century Churches of Greece*. Vienna.

Kalvesmaki, J. 2013. *The Theology of Arithmetic: Number Symbolism in Platonism and Early Christianity*. Washington, DC.

Kanellopoulos, N., Lekea, J. 2007. "The Struggle between the Nicaean Empire and the Bulgarian State (1254–1256): Towards a Revival of Byzantine Military

Tactics under Theodore II Laskaris," *Journal of Medieval Military History*, 5:56–69.

Kantorowicz, E. 1927. *Kaiser Friedrich der Zweite*. Berlin.

1931. *Kaiser Friedrich der Zweite. Ergänzungsband: Quellennachweise und Exkurse*. Berlin.

1963. "Oriens Augusti, Lever du Roi," *DOP*, 17:117–77.

Kaeppeli, Th. 1940. "Kurze Mitteilungen über mittelalterliche Dominikanerschriftsteller," *Archivum Fratrum Praedicatorum*, 10:282–96.

Karlsson, G. 1959. *Idéologie et cérémonial dans l'épistolographie byzantine*. Uppsala.

Karpozilos, A. 1973. *The Ecclesiastical Controversy between the Kingdom of Nicaea and the Principality of Epiros (1217–1233)*. Thessalonica.

1995. "Realia in Byzantine Epistolography XIII–XVc.," *BZ* 88:68–84.

Karpov, S. 2007. *Istoriia Trapezundskoi imperii*. St. Petersburg.

Karst, A. 1897. *Geschichte Manfreds vom Tode Friedrichs II. bis zu seiner Krönung (1250–1258)*. Berlin.

Kazhdan, A. 1982. "Two Notes on Byzantine Demography of the Eleventh and Twelfth Centuries," *BF*, 8:115–22.

Kazhdan, A., Constable, G. 1982. *People and Power in Byzantium: An Introduction to Modern Byzantine Studies*. Washington, DC.

Keaney, J. 1971. "Moschopulea," *BZ*, 64:303–21.

Kiesewetter, A. 1999. "Die Heirat zwischen Konstanze-Anna von Hohenstaufen und Kaiser Johannes III. Batatzes von Nikaia (Ende 1240 oder Anfang 1241) und der Angriff des Johannes Batatzes auf Konstantinopel im Mai oder Juni 1241," *Römische historische Mitteilungen*, 41:239–50.

Koder, J. 2003. "Griechische Identitäten im Mittelalter: Aspekte einer Entwicklung," in A. Avramea, A. Laiou and E. Chrysos (eds.), *Byzantium: State and Society. In Memory of Nikos Oikonomides*. Athens. 297–319.

Konstantinopoulos, V. 1984. "Σεναχηρείμ. Ὑπόμνημα στὸν Ὅμηρο," *Hellenika*, 35:151–56.

Korobeinikov, D. 2003. "Orthodox Communities in Eastern Anatolia in the Thirteenth and Fourteenth Centuries. Part 1: The Two Patriarchates: Constantinople and Antioch," *Al-Masaq*, 15:197–214.

2005. "Mikhail VIII Paleolog v Rumskom sultanate," *VV*, 64:77–98.

2011. "Mikhail VIII Paleolog v Rumskom sultanate: svidetel'stva pozdnikh istochnikov," in M. Bibikov et al. (eds.), *Vizantiiskie ocherki: trudy rossiiskikh uchenykh k XXII Mezhdunarodnomu kongressu vizantinistov*. Moscow. 116–38.

2014. *Byzantium and the Turks in the Thirteenth Century*. Oxford.

Kosztolnyik, Z. 1996. *Hungary in the Thirteenth Century*. Boulder, CO and New York.

Koutouvalas, P. 2014. *Οι επιστολές του Θεόδωρου Β' Δούκα Λάσκαρη. Προσέγγιση της λογοτεχνικής φυσιογνωμίας του αυτοκράτορα*. PhD Dissertation: University of Athens.

Krumbacher, J. 1897. *Geschichte der byzantinischen Litteratur von Justinian bis zum Ende des oströmischen Reiches (527–1453)*. 2nd rev. edn. Munich.

Külzer, A. 2008. *Ostthrakien*. Tabula Imperii Byzantini, 12. Vienna.

Kyriakidis, S. 2014. "Crusaders and Mercenaries: The West-European Soldiers of the Laskarids of Nicaea (1204–1258)," *Mediterranean Historical Review*, 29:139–53.

Kyritses, D. 1999. "The 'Common Chrysobulls' of Cities and the Notion of Property in Late Byzantium," *Symmeikta*, 13:229–45.

Lackner, W. 1972. "Zum Lehrbuch der Physik des Nikephoros Blemmydes," *BF*, 4:157–69.

1981. "Die erste Auflage des Physiklehrbuches des Nikephoros Blemmydes," in F. Patschke (ed.), *Überlieferungsgeschichtliche Untersuchungen*. Berlin. 351–64.

Laiou-Thomadakis, A. 1977. *Peasant Society in the Late Byzantine Empire: A Social and Demographic Study*. Princeton.

Laiou, A. 1984. "Contribution à l'étude de l'institution familiale en Épire au XIIIème siècle," *Fontes Minores*, 6:275–323.

1992. *Mariage, amour et parenté à Byzance aux XIe–XIII siècles*. Paris.

1996. "The Correspondence of Gregorios Kyprios as a Source for the History of Social and Political Behavior in Byzantium or, on Government by Rhetoric." in W. Seibt (ed.), *Geschichte und Kultur der Palaiologenzeit*. Vienna. 91–108.

(ed.) 2002. *The Economic History of Byzantium*. Washington, DC. 3 vols.

(ed.) 2005. *Urbs Capta: The Fourth Crusade and Its Consequences*. Paris.

Lampsidis, O. 1977. "Wunderbare Rettung des Theodoros Laskaris durch den Erzengel Michael," *JÖB*, 26:125–27.

Langdon, J. S. 1978. *John III Ducas Vatatzes' Byzantine Imperium in Anatolian Exile, 1222–1254: The Legacy of His Diplomatic, Military and Internal Program for the Restitutio Orbis*. PhD Dissertation: University of California, Los Angeles.

1985. "The Forgotten Byzantino-Bulgarian Assault and Siege of Constantinople, 1235–1236, and the Breakup of the Entente Cordiale between John III Ducas Vatatzes and John Asen II in 1236 as Background to the Genesis of the Hohenstaufen–Vatatzes Alliance of 1242," *Byzantina kai Metabyzantina* (= *Byzantine Studies in Honor of Milton V. Anastos*, ed. S. Vryonis Jr.), 4:105–35.

1992. *Byzantium's Last Imperial Offensive in Asia Minor: The Documentary Evidence for and Hagiographical Lore about John III Ducas Vatatzes' Crusade against the Turks, 1222 or 1225 to 1231*. New Rochelle, N.Y.

1994. "Byzantium in Anatolian Exile: Imperial Viceregency Reaffirmed during Byzantino–Papal Discussions at Nicaea and Nymphaeum, 1234," *BF*, 20:197–233.

1998. "Byzantium's Initial Encounter with the Chinggisids: An Introduction to the Byzantino–Mongolica," *Viator*, 29:95–140.

2001. "John III Ducas Vatatzes and the Venetians: The Episode of His Anti-Venetian Cretan Campaigns, 1230 and 1234," in C. Sode and S. Takácz (eds.), *Novum Millennium: Studies on Byzantine History and Culture Dedicated to Paul Speck*. Aldershot, 231–49.

2003. "Twilight of the Byzantine Lascarid Basileia in Anatolian Exile, 1254–1258: Continuity and Change in Imperial Geopolitical Strategy," *Viator*, 34:187–207.

Lappa-Zizicas, E. 1950. "Un traité inédit de Théodore II Lascaris," *Actes du VIe Congres international d'études byzantines*, 1. Paris. 119–26.

Lascaratos, J., Zis, P.V. 1998. "The Epilepsy of the Emperor Theodore II Lascaris (1254–1258)," *Journal of Epilepsy*, 11:296–300.

Laurent, V. 1935b. "Le pape Alexandre IV (1254–1261) et l'empire de Nicée," *EO*, 34:26–55.

1953 "Ὁ μέγας βαῖουλος, à l'occasion du parakoimômène Basile Lécapène," *EEBS*, 23:193–205.

1969. "La chronologie des patriarches de Constantinople au XIIIe s. (1208–1309)," *REB*, 27:129–50.

Lemerle, P. 1977. *Cinq études sur le XIe siècle byzantin*. Paris.

1984. "Philadelphie et l'émirat d'Aydin," *Philadelphie et autres etudes*. Paris. 55–67.

1986. *Byzantine Humanism: The First Phase*. Trans. H. Lindsay and A. Moffatt. Canberra.

Lilie, R.-J. 1991. "Twelfth-Century Byzantine and Turkish States," *BF*, 16:35–51.

Lindner, R. P. 1974. "The Challenge of Qılıch Arslan IV," in D. K. Kouymjian (ed.), *Near Eastern Numismatics, Iconography, Epigraphy and History. Studies in Honor of George C. Miles*. Beirut. 411–17.

Lippard, B. 1984. *The Mongols and Byzantium, 1243–1341*. PhD Dissertation, Indiana University, Bloomington, IN.

Littlewood, A. R. 1976. "An 'Icon of the Soul': The Byzantine Letter," *Visible Language*, 10:197–226.

Longnon, J. 1949. *L'Empire latin de Constantinople et la principauté de Morée*. Paris.

1950. "La reprise de Salonique par les Grecs en 1224," *Actes du VIe Congrès international d'études byzantines*, I, Paris, 141–46.

McKee, S. 2000. *Uncommon Dominion: Venetian Crete and the Myth of Ethnic Purity*. Philadelphia.

MacLagan, M. 1975. "A Byzantine Princess in Portugal," in G. Robertson and G. Henderson (eds.), *Studies in Memory of D. T. Rice*. Edinburgh. 284–93.

McNeal, E. H. and Wolff, R. L. 1969. "The Fourth Crusade," in Wolff and Hazard 1969:153–85.

Macrides, R. 1981. "Saints and Sainthood in the Early Palaiologan Period," in S. Hackel (ed.), *The Byzantine Saint*. London. 67–87.

1992. "Bad Historian or Good Lawyer? Demetrios Chomatenos and Novel 131," *DOP*, 46:187–96.

2004. "The Ritual of Petition," in P. Roilos and D. Yatromanolakis (eds.), *Greek Ritual Poetics*. Cambridge, MA. 356–70.

2007. *George Akropolites: The History*. Oxford.

2013. "Trial by Ordeal in Byzantium: On Whose Authority?" in P. Armstrong (ed.), *Authority in Byzantium*. Farnham. 31–46.

Madariaga, E. 2017. "Η βυζαντινή οικογένεια των Αγιοθεοδωριτών (III)," *Byzantina Symmeikta*. 27:53–89.

Madden, T. 1991–92. "The Fires of the Fourth Crusade in Constantinople, 1203–1204: A Damage Assessment," *BZ*, 84–85:72–93.

Magdalino, P. 1977. "A Neglected Authority for the History of the Peloponnese in the Early Thirteenth Century: Demetrios Chomatianos, Archbishop of Bulgaria," *BZ*, 70:316–23.

1991. "Hellenism and Nationalism in Byzantium," *Tradition and Transformation in Medieval Byzantium*. Aldershot. Study XIV.

1993. *The Empire of Manuel I Komnenos, 1143–1180*. Cambridge.

2002. "Medieval Constantinople: Built Environment and Urban Development," in Laiou 2002 II:529–37.

2005a. "Prophecies on the Fall of Constantinople," in Laiou 2005:41–53.

2005b. "Ο οφθαλμός της οικουμένης και ο ομφαλός της γής," in E. Chrysos (ed.), *Byzantium as Oecumene*. Athens. 107–23.

Magdalino, P., Mavroudi, M. 2006. *The Occult Sciences in Byzantium*. Geneva.

Maïer, I. 1965. *Les manuscrits d'Ange Politien. Catalogue descriptif*. Geneva.

Makris, G. 1995. "Zur Epilepsie in Byzanz," *BZ*, 88:363–404.

Maksimović, L., Popović, M. 1990. "Les sceaux byzantins de la région danubienne en Serbie," *Studies in Byzantine Sigillography*, 2:213–34.

Maltezou, Ch. 1989. "L'Impero di Nicea nelle fonti della Creta veneziana," *Symmeikta*, 8:27–32.

Marinesco, C. 1924. "Du nouveau sur Constance de Hohenstaufen, impératrice de Nicée," *B*, 1:451–68.

Métivier, S. 2009. "Les Maurozômai, Byzance et le sultanat de Rūm: Note sur le sceau de Jean Comnène Maurozômès," *REB*, 67:198–207.

2012. "Byzantium in Question in 13th-Century Seljuk Anatolia," in G. Saint-Guillain and D. Stathakopoulos (eds.), *Liquid and Multiple: Individuals and Identities in the Thirteenth-Century Aegean*. Paris. 235–57.

Meyendorff, J. 1981. *Byzantium and the Rise of Russia*. Cambridge.

Miller, W. 1923. "The Empire of Nicaea and the Recovery of Constantinople," in J. R. Tanner, C. W. Previté-Orton, Z. N. Brooke (eds.), *The Cambridge Medieval History, 4: The Eastern Roman Empire (717–1453)*. Cambridge. 478–516.

Minio-Paluello, L. 1950. "Note sull'Aristotele latino medievale," *Rivista di filosofia neo-scolastica*, 42:222–37.

1974. "William of Moerbeke," *Dictionary of Scientific Biography*, 9:434–40.

Minorsky, V. 1953. *Studies in Caucasian History: I. New Light on the Shaddādids of Ganja; II. The Shaddādids of Ani; III. The Prehistory of Saladin*. London.

Mitsiou, E. 2010a. "Versorgungsmodelle im Nikäischen Kaiserreich," in E. Kislinger, J. Koder, A. Külzer (eds.), *Handelsgüter und Verkehrswege. Aspekte der Warenversorgung im östlichen Mittelmeerraum.* Vienna. 223–40.

2010b. "Ideology and Economy in the Politics of John III Vatatzes (1221–1254)," in *First International Sevgi Gönül Byzantine Studies Symposium: Change in the Byzantine World in the Twelfth and Thirteenth Centuries.* Istanbul. 195–205.

2011. "The Monastery of Sosandra: A Contribution to Its History, Dedication and Localisation," *Bulgaria Mediaevalis (Studies in Honour of Professor Vassil Gjuzelev),* 2:665–83.

Mladjov, I. 2012. "The Children of Ivan Asen II and Eirēnē Komnēnē: Contribution to the Prosopography of Medieval Bulgaria," *Bulgaria Mediaevalis,* 3:485–500.

Moravcsik, G. 1927. "Der Verfasser der mittelgriechischen Legende von Johannes dem Barmherzigen," *BZ,* 27:36–39.

Morgan, D. 1986. *The Mongols.* Oxford.

Mullett, M. 1981. "The Classical Tradition in the Byzantine Letter," in M. Mullett and R. Scott (eds.), *Byzantium and the Classical Tradition.* Birmingham. 75–93.

1988. "Byzantium: A Friendly Society?" *Past and Present,* 118:3–24.

2013a. "Experiencing the Byzantine Text, Experiencing the Byzantine Tent," in C. Nesbitt and M. Jackson (eds.), *Experiencing Byzantium.* Farnham. 269–91.

2013b. "Tented Ceremony: Ephemeral Performances under the Komnenoi," in Beihammer, Constantinou and Parani 2013:487–513.

Munitiz, J. 1982. "A 'Wicked Woman' in the 13th Century," *JÖB,* 32.2:529–37.

1992. "Hagiographical Autobiography in the Thirteenth Century," *BSl,* 53:243–49.

1995. "War and Peace Reflected in Some Byzantine 'Mirrors of Princes'," in T. Miller and J. Nesbitt (eds.), *Peace and War in Byzantium: Essays in Honor of George T. Dennis.* Washington, DC. 50–61.

Nasrallah, J. 1968. *Chronologie des patriarches melchites d'Antioche de 1250 à 1500.* Jerusalem.

Neumann, F. 1955–56. "Der Markgraf von Hohenburg," *Zeitschrift für deutsches Altertum und deutsche Literatur,* 86:119–60.

Nicol, D. 1956. "The Date of the Battle of Pelagonia," *BZ* 49:68–71.

1957. *The Despotate of Epiros.* Oxford.

1966. "The Fourth Crusade and the Greek and Latin Empires (1204–61)," in J. Hussey (ed.), *The Cambridge Medieval History, 4. The Byzantine Empire, part I: Byzantium and Its Neighbours.* Cambridge. 275–330.

1968. *The Byzantine Family of Kantakouzenos (Cantacuzenus) ca. 1100–1460.* Washington, DC.

1976. "*Kaisersalbung.* The Unction of Emperors in Late Byzantine Coronation Ritual," *BMGS,* 2:37–52.

1984. *The Despotate of Epiros, 1267–1479: A Contribution to the History of Greece in the Middle Ages.* Cambridge.

1988. *Byzantium and Venice: A Study in Diplomatic and Cultural Relations.* Cambridge.

1996. *The Reluctant Emperor: A Biography of John Cantacuzene, Byzantine Emperor and Monk, c. 1295–1383.* Cambridge.

Nikov, P. 1920. "Bŭlgaro-ungarski otnosheniia ot 1257 do 1277 godina, istoriko-kritichno izsledvane," *Sbornik na Bŭlgarskata Akademiia na Naukite*, 11:1–200.

Nystazopoulou, M. 1964b. "La dernière reconquête de Sinope par les Grecs de Trébizonde (1254–1265)," *REB*, 22:241–49.

Obolensky, D. 1948. *The Bogomils: A Study in Balkan Neo-Manichaeism.* Cambridge.

1988. *Six Byzantine Portraits.* Oxford.

Oikonomides, N. 1976a. "La décomposition de l'empire byzantin à la veille de 1204 et les origines de l'empire de Nicée: à propos de la *Partitio Romaniae*," *Actes du XVe Congrès international d'études byzantines. Rapports et co-rapports*, 1/1. Athens. 3–28. Reprinted in N. Oikonomides, *Byzantium from the Ninth Century to the Fourth Crusade.* Hampshire, 1992. Study XX.

1976b. "L'évolution de l'organisation administrative de l'empire byzantin au XI siècle (1025–1118)," *TM*, 6:125–52.

1978. "The Chancery of the Grand Komnenoi: Imperial Tradition and Political Reality," Ἀρχεῖον Πόντου, 35:299–332.

1985. "La chancellerie impériale de Byzance du 13e au 15e siècle," *REB*, 43:167–95.

Origone, D. 1988. "Oriente e Occidente: Bisanzio e i Lascaris di Ventimiglia," *La storia dei Genovesi: Atti del Convegno di studi sui ceti dirigenti nelle istituzioni della Repubblica di Genova*, 8. Genoa. 427–39.

Ostrogorsky, G. 1951. "Urum-Despotes. Die Anfänge der Despoteswürde in Byzanz," *BZ*, 44:448–60.

1955. "Zur Kaisersalbung und Schilderhebung im spätbyzantinischen Krönungszeremoniell," *Historia*, 4:246–56.

Otto-Dorn, K., Önder, M. 1966. "Bericht über die Grabung in Kobadabad (October 1965)," *Archäologischer Anzeiger*, 81:170–83.

Page, G. 2008. *Being Byzantine: Greek Identity before the Ottomans.* Cambridge.

Palau y Dulcet, A. 1931. *Guia de Montblanch.* Barcelona.

Pano, R. 1958. "Los Láscaris Ribagorza," *Argensola*, 33:49–54.

Papadopoulos-Kerameus, A. 1899. *VV*, 6:548–54 (review of *Theodori Ducae Lascaris Epistulae CCXVII*, ed. N. Festa, Florence, 1898).

Papageorgiu, P. N. 1902a. "Zu den Briefen des Theodoros Laskaris," *BZ*, 11:16–32.

1902b. "Von Saloniki 'nach Europa', von Europa 'nach Griechenland'," *BZ*, 11:109–10.

Papaioannou, S. 2013. *Michael Psellos: Rhetoric and Authorship in Byzantium.* Cambridge.

Pappadopoulos, J. (Papadopoulos, J.) 1908. *Théodore II Lascaris, empereur de Nicée.* Paris.

Pappadopoulos, J. 1929. "La Satire du Précepteur. Oeuvre inédite de Théodore II Lascaris," in D. Anastasijević and Ph. Granić (eds.), *Compte-rendu du deuxième Congrès international d'études byzantines*. Belgrade. 27.

Pargoire, J. 1905. "Les métropolites d'Ephèse au XIIIe siècle," *EO*, 8:286–90.

Patlagean, E. 1998. "L'immunité des Thessaloniciens," *ΕΥΨΥΧΙΑ: Mélanges offerts à Hélène Ahrweiler*, 2. Paris. 591–601.

Peacock, A. 2006. "The Saljūq Campaign against the Crimea and the Expansionist Policy of the Early Reign of 'Alā' al-Dīn Kayqubād," *Journal of the Royal Asiatic Society*, 3rd series, 16:133–49.

  2013. "Court and Nomadic Life in Saljuq Anatolia," in D. Durand-Guedy (ed.), *Turko-Mongol Rulers, Cities and City Life*. Leiden. 191–222.

Pirivatrić, S. 2009. "Jedna pretpostavka o poreklu bugarskog cara Konstantina Asena 'Tiha'," *ZRVI*, 46:313–31.

  2011. "The Boyana Church Portraits: A Contribution to the Prosopography of Sebastokrator Kaloyan," in B. Penkova (ed.), *Boianskata tsŭrkva mezhdu iztoka i zapada v izkustvoto na khristiianska Evropa*. Sofia. 12–35.

Pitamber, N. 2015. *Replacing Byzantium: Laskarid Urban Environments and the Landscape of Loss (1204–1261)*. PhD Dissertation: University of California, Los Angeles.

Pitarakis, B. 2009. "The Material Culture of Childhood in Byzantium," in A. Papaconstantinou and A.-M. Talbot (eds.), *Becoming Byzantine: Children and Childhood in Byzantium*. Washington, DC. 167–251.

Pitsakis, K. 1991. "Ἡ ἔκταση τῆς ἐξουσίας ἑνὸς ὑπερόριου πατριάρχη: ὁ πατριάρχης Ἀντιοχείας στὴν Κωνσταντινούπολη τὸν 12ο αἰῶνα," in N. Oikonomides (ed.), *Byzantium in the Twelfth Century*. Athens. 91–139.

  2000. "Législation et stratégies matrimoniales: parenté et empêchements de mariage dans le droit byzantin," *L'Homme*, 154–55:677–96.

  2005. "*Personae non sunt multiplicandae sine necessitate*. Nouveaux témoignages sur Constantin Kabasilas," in L. Hoffmann (ed.), with A. Monchizadeh, *Zwischen Polis, Provinz und Peripherie. Beiträge zur byzantinischen Geschichte und Kultur*. Wiesbaden. 491–513.

Pizzone, A. (ed.) 2014. *The Author in Middle Byzantine Literature: Modes, Functions, and Identities*. Berlin.

Podskalsky, G. 1972. *Byzantinische Reichseschatologie: Die Periodisierung der Weltgeschichte in den vier Grossreichen (Daniel 2 und 7) und dem tausendjährigen Friedensreiche (Apok. 20)*. Munich.

Polemis, D. 1968. *The Doukai: Contribution to Byzantine Prosopography*. London.

Popović, M. 2007. "Did Dragotas Conquer Melnik in 1255?" *Glasnik na Institutot za natsionalna istoriia*, 51:15–24.

Pralong, A., Grélois, J.-P. 2003. "Les monuments byzantins de la ville haute de Brousse," in B. Geyer and J. Lefort (eds.), *La Bithynie au Moyen Âge. Géographie et habitat*. Paris. 139–49.

Prato, G. 1981. "Un autografo di Teodoro II Lascaris imperatore di Nicea?," *JÖB*, 30:249–58.

Prinzing, G. 1992. "Das byzantinische Kaisertum im Umbruch. Zwischen regionaler Aufspaltung und erneuter Zentrierung in den Jahren 1204–1282," in R. Gundlach and H. Weber (eds.), *Legitimation und Funktion des Herrschers. Vom ägyptischen Pharao zum neuzeitlichen Diktator*. Stuttgart. 129–83.

1998a "Ein Mann τυραννίδος ἄξιος. Zur Darstellung der rebellischen Vergangenheit Michaels VIII. Palaiologos," in I. Vassis, G. Heinrich and D. Reinsch (eds.), *Lesarten. Festschrift für Athanasios Kambylis zum 70. Geburtstag dargebracht von Schülern, Kollegen und Freunden*. Berlin and New York. 180–97.

1998b. "Zu den Minderheiten in der Mäander-Region während der Übergangsepoche von der byzantinischen zur seldschukisch-türkischen Herrschaft (11. Jh. – Anfang 14. Jh)," in P. Herz and J. Kobes (eds.), *Ethnische und religiöse Minderheiten in Kleinasien*. Wiesbaden. 153–77.

Prinzing, G. 2004. "A Quasi Patriarch in the State of Epiros: The Autocephalous Archbishop of 'Boulgaria' (Ohrid) Demetrios Chomatenos," *ZRVI*, 41:165–82.

Pryor, J. 1988. *Geography, Technology, and War: Studies in the Maritime History of the Mediterranean, 649–1571*. Cambridge.

Puech, V. 2011. "The Aristocracy and the Empire of Nicaea," in Herrin and Saint-Guillain 2011:69–79.

Ragia, E. 2008. "The Inscription of Didyma (Hieron) and the Families of Phokas and Karantinos in Western Asia Minor (12th–13th C.)," *BZ*, 100:133–46.

Ramsay, W. M. 1890. *The Historical Geography of Asia Minor*. London.

Rashed, M. 2000. "Sur les deux témoins des oeuvres profanes de Théodore II Lascaris et leur commanditaire (*Parisinus Suppl. Gr. 472; Parisinus Suppl. Gr. 460*)," *Scriptorium*, 54:297–302.

Redford, S. 1993. "Thirteenth-Century Rum Seljuq Palaces and Palace Imagery," *Ars Orientalis*, 23:219–36.

Reh, F. 1933. *Kardinal Peter Capocci. Ein Staatsmann und Feldherr des XIII. Jahrhunderts*. Berlin.

Rey, E. 1896. "Résumé chronologique de l'histoire des princes d'Antioche," *Revue de l'Orient latin*, 4:321–407.

Rheidt, K. 1990. "Byzantinische Wohnhäuser des 11. bis 14. Jahrhunderts in Pergamon," *DOP*, 44:195–204.

1991. *Die Stadtgrabung, 2: Die byzantinische Wohnstadt*. Altertümer von Pergamon, 15/2. Berlin.

2002. "The Urban Economy of Pergamon," in Laiou 2002 II:623–29.

Richter, G. 1989. *Theodoros Dukas Laskaris: Der Natürliche Zusammenhang. Ein Zeugnis vom Stand der byzantinischen Philosophie in der Mitte des 13. Jahrhunderts*. Amsterdam.

Riehle, A. 2011. *Funktionen der byzantinischen Epistolographie: Studien zu den Briefen und Briefsammlungen des Nikephoros Chumnos (ca. 1260–1327)*. PhD Dissertation: University of Munich.

Riley-Smith, J. 2005. "Toward an Understanding of the Fourth Crusade as an Institution," in Laiou 2005:71–87.

Robert, L. 1962. *Villes d'Asie Mineur. Études de géographie ancienne.* 2nd edn. Paris.

Robins, R. 1993. *The Byzantine Grammarians: Their Place in History.* Berlin and New York.

Rostagno, E., Festa, N. 1893. "Indice dei codici greci Laurenziani non compresi nel catalogo del Bandini," *Studi italiani di filologia classica*, 1:129–232.

Roth, F. 1954. *Cardinal Richard Annibaldi: First Protector of the Augustinian Order, 1243–1276.* Louvain.

Runciman, S. 1958. *The Sicilian Vespers: A History of the Mediterranean World in the Later Thirteenth Century.* Cambridge.

Saint-Guillain, G. 2006. "Les conquérants de l'Archipel: l'empire latin de Constantinople, Venise et les premiers seigneurs des Cyclades," in G. Ortalli, G. Ravegnani and P. Schreiner (eds.), *Quarta Crociata: Venezia–Bisanzio–Impero Latino.* Venice. 125–237.

    2010. "Comment les Vénitiens n'ont pas acquis la Crète: note à propos de l'élection impériale de 1204 et du partage projeté de l'Empire byzantin," *TM*, 16:713–58.

    2014. "Les seigneurs de Salona, un lignage picard en Grèce médiévale," *Thesaurismata*, 44:9–50.

    2015. "The Conquest of Monemvasia by the Franks: Date and Context," *Rivista di studi bizantini e neoellenici*, 52:241–94.

Sambin, P. 1954. *Il Vescovo Cotronese Niccolò da Durazzo e un inventario di suoi codici latini e greci (1276).* Rome.

Saunders, J. 1971. *The History of the Mongol Conquests.* London.

Savvides, A. 1987. "Constantine XI Laskaris, Uncrowned and Ephemeral 'Basileus of the Rhomaioi' after the Fall of Constantinople to the Fourth Crusade," *Byzantiaka*, 7:141–74.

Schaller, H. M. 1965. *Politische Propaganda Kaiser Friedrichs II. und seiner Gegner.* Germering.

    1977. "Berthold, Mgf. v. Hohenburg," *Lexikon des Mittelalters*, vol. 1. Stuttgart. col. 2032.

Schmalzbauer, G. 1969. "Die Tornikioi in der Palaiologenzeit," *JÖB*, 18:115–35.

Schmit, Th. 1927. *Die Koimesis-Kirche von Nikaia.* Berlin and Leipzig.

Schneider, A. M., Karnapp, W. 1938. *Die Stadtmauer von Iznik (Nicaea).* Berlin.

    1938. "The City Walls of Nicaea," *Antiquity*, 12 (no. 48):437–43.

    1943. *Die römischen und byzantinischen Denkmäler von Iznik-Nicaea.* Berlin.

Schreiner, P. 1996. "Ritterspiele in Byzanz," *JÖB*, 46:227–41.

Settia, A. 2004a. "Lancia, Bianca." *Dizionario biografico degli italiani*, 63:320–22.

    2004b. "Lancia, Galvano," *Dizionario biografico degli italiani*, 63:330–35.

    2004c. "Lancia, Manfredi," *Dizionario biografico degli italiani*, 63:337–41.

Ševčenko, I. 1978. "A New Manuscript of Nicephorus Blemmydes' 'Imperial Statue,' and of Some Patriarchal Letters," *Byzantine Studies/Études Byzantines* 5:222–32.

Simpson, A. 2006. "Before and After 1204: The Versions of Niketas Choniates' *Historia*," *DOP*, 60:189–221.

  2013. *Niketas Choniates: A Historiographical Study*. Oxford.

Sinogowitz, B. 1952. "Über das byzantinische Kaisertum nach dem Vierten Kreuzzuge (1204–1205)," *BZ*, 45:345–56.

Shawcross, T. 2003. "Re-Inventing the Homeland in the Historiography of Frankish Greece: The Fourth Crusade and the Legend of the Trojan War," *BMGS*, 27:120–52.

  2008. "In the Name of the True Emperor: Politics of Resistance after the Palaiologan Usurpation," *BSl*, 66:203–27.

Shukurov, R. 2008a. "The Byzantine Turks: An Approach to the Study of Late Byzantine Demography," *L'Europa dopo la caduta di Costantinopoli: 29 maggio 1453*. Spoleto, 73–108.

  2008b. "Semeistvo 'Izz al-Dina Kai-Kavusa II v Vizantii," *VV*, 67:89–116.

Soustal, P. 1991. *Thrakien*. Tabula Imperii Byzantini, 6. Vienna.

Spatharakis, I. 1976. *The Portrait in Byzantine Illuminated Manuscripts*. Leiden.

Spearing, A. C. 2012. *Medieval Autographies: The "I" of the Text*. Notre Dame, IN.

Stanojević, S. 1933. "Sv. Sava i proglas bugarske patrijaršije," *Glas Srpske Kral'evske Akademije*, 156:171–88.

Starr, J. 1939. *The Jews in the Byzantine Empire, 641–1204*. Athens.

Stavridou-Zafraka, A. 1988. "Συμβολή στο ζήτημα της αναγόρευσης του Θεόδωρου Δούκα," *Αφιέρωμα στον Εμμανουήλ Κριαρά*. Thessalonica, 37–62.

Stavrou, M. 2009. "De la philosophie à la théologie: l'unité du projet épistémique de Nicéphore Blemmydès (1197-v. 1269)," in A. Rigo and P. Ermilov (eds.), *Byzantine Theologians: The Systematization of Their Own Doctrine and Their Perception of Foreign Doctrine*. Rome. 103–24.

Stichel, R. 1996. "Unbekannte byzantinische Kaiserbilder," *BZ*, 89:74–78.

Stiernon, L. 1965. "Notes de titulature et de prosopographie byzantines. Sébaste et gambros," *REB*, 23:222–43.

Stolte, B. 1990. "Vatatzes versus Baldwin: The Case of the Sovereignty of Constantinople," in K. Ciggaar and A. Van Aalst (eds.), *The Latin Empire: Some Contributions*. Hernen. 127–32.

Stouraitis, I. 2014. "Roman Identity in Byzantium: A Critical Approach," *BZ*, 107:175–220.

Subotić, G. 1998–99. "Portret nepoznate bugarske carice," *Zograf*, 27:93–102.

Talbot, A.-M. 1992. "Empress Theodora Palaiologina, Wife of Michael VIII," *DOP*, 46:295–303.

Texier, C. 1844. "Tombeaux du Moyen Age à Kutayah et à Nymphi (Asie Mineure)," *Revue archéologique*, 1:320–25.

1862. *Asie Mineure: description géographique, historique et archéologique des provinces et des villes de la Chersonnèse d'Asie*. Paris.

Theodoridis, D. 2004. "Die Herkunft des byzantinischen Familiennamens Λάσκαρις," *REB*, 62:269–73.

Thomson, R. 2011. "The Eastern Mediterranean in the Thirteenth Century: Identities and Allegiances. The Peripheries: Armenia," in Herrin and Saint-Guillain 2011:197–214.

Thonemann, P. 2011. *The Maeander Valley: A Historical Geography from Antiquity to Byzantium*. Cambridge.

Tinnefeld, F. 1979. "Das Niveau der abendländischen Wissenschaft aus der Sicht gebildeter Byzantiner im 13. and 14. Jh." *BF*, 6:241–80.

Trapp, E. 1978. "Probleme der Prosopographie der Palaiologenzeit," *JÖB*, 27:181–201.

      1993. "Learned and Vernacular Literature in Byzantium: Dichotomy or Symbiosis?" *DOP*, 47:115–29.

      2003. "The Role of Vocabulary in Byzantine Rhetoric as a Stylistic Device," in E. Jeffreys (ed.), *Rhetoric in Byzantium*. Aldershot. 137–49.

Troianos, S. 1990. "Zauberei und Giftmischerei in mittelbyzantinischer Zeit," in G. Prinzing and D. Simon (eds.), *Fest und Alltag in Byzanz*. Munich. 37–51.

Tsvetkov, B. 1985. "Arkheologicheski razkopki v Melnik i vŭstanieto na Dragota ot 1255 g.," *Istoricheski Pregled*, 11:47–53.

Turan, O. 1953. "Les souverains seldjoukides et leurs sujets non-musulmans," *Studia Islamica*, 1:65–100.

Uspenskii, Th. 1879. *Obrazovaniie vtorago Bolgarskago tsarstva*. Odessa.

Vacalopoulos, A. 1970. *Origins of the Greek Nation: The Byzantine Period, 1204-1461*. New Brunswick, NJ.

Valdenberg, V. 1929–30. "Notes sur l'oraison funèbre de G. Acropolite," *BZ*, 30:91–95.

Van Cleve, T. 1972. *The Emperor Frederick II of Hohenstaufen, Immutator Mundi*. Oxford.

Van Dieten, J.-L. 1970. *Zur Überlieferung und Veröffentlichung der Panoplia dogmatike des Niketas Choniates*. Amsterdam.

Vannier, J.-F. 1986. "Les premiers Paléologues. Étude généalogique et prosopographique," in J.-C. Cheynet and J.-F. Vannier (eds.), *Études prosopographiques*. Paris. 123–87.

Van Tricht, F. 2013. "Robert of Courtenay (1221–1227): An Idiot on the Throne of Constantinople?" *Speculum*, 88:996–1034.

Varzos, K. 1984. Ἡ Γενεαλογία τῶν Κομνηνῶν, 2 vols. Thessalonica.

Vásáry, I. 2005. *Cumans and Tatars: Oriental Military in the Pre-Ottoman Balkans, 1185-1365*. Cambridge.

Vasiliev, A. 1936. "The Foundation of the Empire of Trebizond (1204–1222)," *Speculum*, 11:3–37.

Vassis, I. 2002. "Τῶν νέων φιλολόγων παλαίσματα: Ἡ συλλογὴ σχεδῶν τοῦ κώδικα Vaticanus Palatinus gr. 92," *Hellenika*, 52:37–68.

Vogel, M., Gardthausen, V. 1909. *Die griechischen Schreiber des Mittelalters und der Renaissance*. Leipzig.

Volk, O. 1955. *Die byzantinischen Klosterbibliotheken von Konstantinopel, Thessalonike und Kleinasien*. PhD Dissertation: University of Munich.

Vryonis, S., Jr., 1971. *The Decline of Medieval Hellenism in Asia Minor and the Process of Islamization from the Eleventh through the Fifteenth Century*. Berkeley.

Vuillemin-Diem, G. 1987. "La traduction de la Métaphysique d'Aristote par Guillaume de Moerbeke et son exemplaire grec: Vind. phil. gr. 100," in J. Wiesner (ed.), *Aristoteles, Werk und Wirkung: Paul Moraux gewidmet*, vol. 2. Berlin. 434–86.

    1989. "La liste des oeuvres d'Hippocrate dans le *Vindobonensis phil. gr.* 100: un autographe de Guillaume de Moerbeke," in Brams and Vanhamel 1989:135–83.

    1995. *Metaphysica, Lib. I–XIV. Recensio et Translatio Guillelmi de Moerbeka*. Praefatio. Aristoteles Latinus XXV 3.1. Leiden.

Wallace-Hadrill, A. 1998. "To Be Roman, Go Greek: Thoughts on Hellenization at Rome," in M. Austin, J. Harries and C. Smith (eds.), *Modus Operandi: Essays in Honour of Geoffrey Rickman*. London. 79–91.

Walter, B. 1967. "Bertoldo di Hohenburg," *Dizionario biografico degli italiani*, 6:582–87.

Warren, W. 1982. "Biography and the Medieval Historian," in D. Morgan (ed.), *Medieval Historical Writing in the Christian and Islamic Worlds*. London. 5–18.

Wassiliou, A.-K. 1997. "Ὁ ἅγιος Γεώργιος ὁ Διασορίτης auf Siegeln: Ein Beitrag zur Frühgeschichte der Laskariden," *BZ*, 90:416–24.

Wellas, M. B. 1983. *Griechisches aus dem Umkreis Kaiser Friedrichs II*. Munich.

Wilson, N. G. 1996. *Scholars of Byzantium*. London. Rev. edn.

Wirth, P. 1961. "Die Begründung der Kaisermacht Michaels VIII. Palaiologos," *JÖBG*, 10:85–91.

    1962. "Kaiser Manuel I. Komnenos und die Ostgrenze. Rückeroberung und Wiederaufbau der Festung Dorylaion," *BZ*, 55:21–29.

Wolff, R. L. 1944. "The Latin Empire of Constantinople and the Franciscans," *Traditio*, 2:213–37.

    1954. "Mortgage and Redemption of an Emperor's Son: Castile and the Latin Empire of Constantinople," *Speculum*, 29:45–84.

    1969. "The Latin Empire of Constantinople, 1204–1261," in Wolff and Hazard 1969:186–233.

Wolff, R. L., Hazard, H. (eds.), 1969. *The Later Crusades, 1189–1311. (A History of the Crusades*, ed. K. Setton, vol. 2). Madison, WI. 2nd edn.

Wood, M. 1985. *In Search of the Trojan War*. Berkeley.

Woolf, G. 1994. "Becoming Roman, Staying Greek: Culture, Identity and the Civilizing Process in the Roman East," *Proceedings of the Cambridge Philological Society*, 40:116–43.

Yıldız, S. N. 2011. "Manuel Komnenos Mavrozomes and His Descendents at the Seljuk Court: The Formation of a Christian Seljuk-Komnenian Elite," in S. Leder (ed.), *Crossroads between Latin Europe and the Near East: Corollaries of the Frankish Presence in the Eastern Mediterranean (12th–14th Centuries)*. Würzburg. 55–77.

Zachariadou, E. 1994. "The Oğuz Tribes: The Silence of the Byzantine Sources," in Curiel and Gyselen 1994:285–89.

Zafeiris, K. 2011. "The Issue of the Authorship of the Synopsis Chronike and Theodore Skoutariotes," *REB*, 69:253–63.

Zakythenos, D. 1941. "Μελεταὶ περὶ τῆς διοικητικῆς καὶ τῆς ἐπαρχιακῆς διοικήσεως ἐν τῷ Βυζαντινῷ κράτει, I," *EEBS*, 17:208–74.

Zhavoronkov, P. 1978. "Nikeiskaia imperiia i vostok," *VV*, 39:93–101.

1982. "Nikeiskaia imperiia i kniazhestva drevnei Rusi," *VV*, 43:81–89.

2001. "Pervyi pokhod Ioanna III Vatatza na Fessaloniku (1243 g.) i smert' Ioanna II Asenya (1242 g.): problemy datirovki," *VV*, 60:69–74.

2006. "Byl li Feodor II Laskar' soimperatorom?" in G. Litavrin et al. (eds.), *Vizantiiskie ocherki: Trudy rossiiskikh uchenykh k XXI Mezhdunarodnomu kongressu vizantinistov*. St. Petersburg. 76–80.

Zlatarski, V. 1940. *Istoriia na bŭlgarskata dŭrzhava prez srednite vekove*, vol. 3. Sofia.

Index

430